Mozambique

the Bradt Travel Guide

Philip Briggs

Updated by Sandra Turay

edition
7

www.

Bradt Travel
The Globe Pe

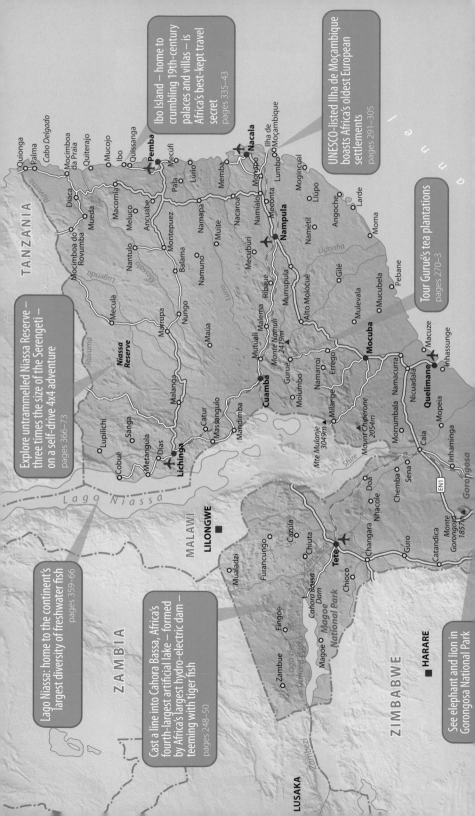

Ibo Island – home to crumbling 19th-century palaces and villas – is Africa's best-kept travel secret
pages 335–43

UNESCO-listed Ilha de Moçambique boasts Africa's oldest European settlements
pages 291–305

Explore untrammelled Niassa Reserve – three times the size of the Serengeti – on a self-drive 4x4 adventure
pages 366–73

Tour Gurué's tea plantations
pages 270–3

Lago Niassa: home to the continent's largest diversity of freshwater fish
pages 359–66

Cast a line into Cahora Bassa, Africa's fourth-largest artificial lake – formed by Africa's largest hydro-electric dam – teeming with tiger fish
pages 248–50

See elephant and lion in Gorongosa National Park

TANZANIA

ZAMBIA

MALAWI
LILONGWE

ZIMBABWE
HARARE

LUSAKA

Lago Niassa

Niassa Reserve

Ruvuma
Rovuma

Lugenda

Messalo

Lúrio

Ligonha

Zambezi

Shire

Cahora Bassa Dam

Lago de Cahora Bassa

Magoe National Park

Gorongosa

Quionga
Palma
Cabo Delgado
Mocímboa da Praia
Quiterajo
Diaca
Mucojo
Ibo
Quissanga
Pemba
Mecúfi
Mueda
Mocímboa do Rovuma
Macomia
Ancuabe
Pala
Memba
Nacala
Ilha de Moçambique
Lumbo
Macuco
Montepuez
Namapa
Nacaroa
Namialo
Monapo
Mossuril
Nantulo
Balama
Muite
Mecubúri
Mecula
Marrupa
Namuno
Maúa
Namapa
Nungo
Ribáuè
Murrupula
Nampula
Naméti
Angoche
Liupo
Larde
Moma
Mutuali
Malema
Monte Namuli 2419m
Gurué
Alto Molócuè
Gilé
Mulevala
Mucubela
Pebane
Lupilichi
Sanga
Catur
Massangulo
Mandimba
Cobué
Metangula
Dias
Lichinga
Malanga
Molumbo
Namarroi
Errego
Milange
Mte Mulanje 3049m
Mount Chiperone 2054m
Mocuba
Namacurra
Nicuadala
Quelimane
Macuze
Whassunge
Morrumbala
Mopeia
Caia
Mualadzi
Furancungo
Cazula
Chiuta
Chiúta
Zambue
Fingoe
Magoe
Zumbue
Catandica
Monte Gorongosa 1857m
Doa
Nhacole
Chemba
Sena
Inhaminga
Changara
Guro
Chioco
Tete
EN1
Cuamba

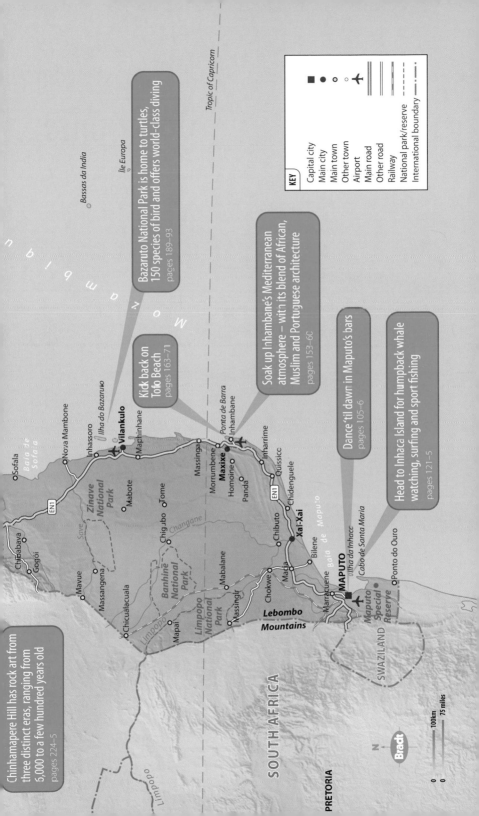

Chinhamapere Hill has rock art from three distinct eras, ranging from 5,000 to a few hundred years old
pages 224–5

Bazaruto National Park is home to turtles, 150 species of bird and offers world-class diving
pages 189–93

Kick back on Tofo Beach
pages 163–71

Soak up Inhambane's Mediterranean atmosphere – with its blend of African, Muslim and Portuguese architecture
pages 153–6C

Dance 'til dawn in Maputo's bars
pages 105–6

Head to Inhaca Island for humpback whale watching, surfing and sport fishing
pages 121–5

KEY

■ Capital city
● Main city
● Main town
○ Other town
✈ Airport
Main road
Other road
Railway
National park/reserve
International boundary

Tropic of Capricorn

Ile Europa

Bassas da India

M o z a m b i q u e

Sofala
Baia de Sofa·a
Chibabava
Gogoi
Mavue
Massangena
Chicualacuala
Mapai
Massingir
Chokwe
Madja
Marracuene
MAPUTO
Ilha da Inhaca
Ponto do Ouro
Cabo de Santa Maria
Maputo Special Reserve
Bilene
Chibuto
Xai-Xai
Chidenguele
Quissico
Inharrime
Panda
Homoine
Maxixe
Morrumbene
Massinga
Inhambane
Ponta de Barra
Maphinhane
Vilankulo
Ilha do Bazaruto
Inhassoro
Nova Mambone
Inhassoro
Zinave National Park
Mabote
Tome
Chig.bo
Changane
Banhine National Park
Mabalane
Limpopo National Park
Limpopo
Save
EN1
EN1
Baia de Maputo
Lebombo Mountains
SWAZILAND
SOUTH AFRICA
PRETORIA

N

Bract

0   100km
0   75 miles

Mozambique
Don't miss...

Sailing on a handmade dhow
In more remote parts of the country, such as
Benguerra Island, private fishing dhows are a
common way of getting around
(AVZ) page 193

Art Deco architecture
Inhambane's striking Ciné-Teatro Tofo hosts an
African film festival every year
(EL) page 159

Deserted beaches

In a country that boasts miles of exquisite coastline and truly untouched beaches, Bazaruto Archipelago has some of the best (ST) pages 189–93

World class snorkelling and diving

Whale sharks (*Rhincodon typus*) are especially common in the waters around Tofo and Inhambane (c/S) page 165

Maputo

Mozambique's capital, where centuries of architecture provide captivating backdrops for the port city's distinctive Afro-Mediterranean atmosphere (AVZ) pages 87–117

Mozambique in colour

above Songo is home to two remarkable mosaic monuments, each 2ha in size, crafted by Tete-born artist **Naguib Elias** (SC) page 250

below left Inhambane has a strikingly Mediterranean feel, with leafy avenues and pastel-coloured colonial **buildings** (EL) pages 153–60

below right Beira's beach market: a sunny counterpart to Beira's central market in the city's old fort and jail (AVZ) pages 208–9

above   Chinhamapere Hill is the site of one of
Mozambique's most important rock art
shelters, with friezes created by hunter-
gatherer peoples up to 6,000 years ago
(AVZ) pages 224–5

right   Macua women often paint their faces with
musiro, a bark paste, in order to soften the
skin and protect it from the sun
(AL/S) page 316

below   Fishing is a mainstay of the local economy
on old-world Ilha de Moçambique (EL)
pages 291–300

above   Maputo boasts eight markets — some of the most vibrant in Africa — including one dedicated to drink, one to fish, and a few traditional-style markets selling fresh produce and local crafts (FS/S and AVZ) page 109

below   Maputo is home to a range of diverse architectural gems, including the Casa de Ferro designed by Gustave Eiffel, who also had a hand in the railway station, and the 19th-century mosque Masquita da Baixa, or Jumma Masjid (IB/FLPA and AVZ) pages 114–17

bottom   Boats for commerce, transport and recreation keep Maputo harbour bustling from dawn til dusk (SS) page 115

AUTHOR

Philip Briggs is a travel writer specialising in Africa. Raised in South Africa, where he still lives, Philip first visited East Africa in 1986 and has since spent an average of six months annually exploring the highways and back roads of the continent. His first Bradt Travel Guide, to South Africa, was published in 1991, and he has subsequently written Bradt guides to Tanzania, Uganda, Ethiopia, Malawi, Mozambique, Ghana, Rwanda, Somaliland and East African wildlife. Philip has contributed to more than  a dozen other books about Africa, and his work regularly appears in magazines such as *Africa Geographic, Travel Africa* and *Wanderlust*. He also acts as an advisor to specialist tour operator Expert Africa, helping to develop their programmes.

UPDATER

Sandra Turay is a full-time drifter – whether that's down a river or across a country depends on the season. When she isn't writing or travelling, she bases herself in Utah, USA and finds work as a white-water river guide, ski patroller or some other type of fresh-air, adventure-laced job. Raised and educated in Michigan, Sandra is a graduate in Ethnic Studies and Journalism. Her curiosity for the world's peoples and places have led her to study, work, teach, volunteer  (Peace Corps Ethiopia) and travel throughout Africa and hideaways across the globe. Sandra also updated the seventh edition of Bradt's guide to Malawi.

CONTRIBUTORS

Sean Connolly, who updated the sixth edition of Bradt's *Mozambique* and contributed plenty of new material in the process, has been an English teacher in Somaliland, a student in Ghana, a writer in Malawi and a backpacker across much of the African continent. He is the author of Bradt's guide to Senegal and has also updated recent editions of Bradt's *Malawi, Rwanda* and *Ghana*.

Hannah Fagerbakke is from Topanga, California and attended the University of Puget Sound in Tacoma, Washington. She recently finished her Peace Corps service in Mozambique, where she was an English teacher in the small community of Vanduzi in Manica province.

Sterling Jarrett served as an education volunteer for the Peace Corps in Cateme, Tete Province, Mozambique from 2014 to 2016. She worked primarily as a computer teacher at the local secondary school but was also involved in programmes dedicated to improving local literacy, girls' empowerment and health education. Originally from South Carolina, USA, Sterling is a graduate of psychology and business from Wofford College.

PUBLISHER'S FOREWORD   *Adrian Phillips, Managing Director*

Now into its seventh edition, Bradt's *Mozambique* has been an essential travellers' resource for many years. Philip Briggs is our most prolific author, and knows much of Africa inside out. This book allows visitors to explore not only the sandy beaches of the south but also the little-visited north of the country. Philip's thorough research and honest reviews – supplemented by information from trusted updater Sandra Turay – do the Bradt name proud. You have a treat ahead of you, both in reading about and travelling around this lovely country.

Seventh edition published August 2017   First published 1997

Bradt Travel Guides Ltd, IDC House, The Vale, Chalfont St Peter, Bucks SL9 9RZ, England
www.bradtguides.com
Print edition published in the USA by The Globe Pequot Press Inc,
PO Box 480, Guilford, Connecticut 06437-0480

Text copyright © 2017 Philip Briggs
Map content copyright © 2017 Philip Briggs
Illustrations copyright © 2017 Individual photographers and artists (see below)
Project Manager: Susannah Lord
Cover Research: Joe Collins

ISBN-13: 978 1 78477 055 6 (print)
e-ISBN: 978 1 78477 516 2 (e-pub)
e-ISBN: 978 1 78477 417 2 (mobi)

British Library Cataloguing in Publication Data
A catalogue record for this book is available from the British Library

Photographs Alamy Stock Photo: Africa Media Online (AMO/A); Sean Connolly (SC); www.flpa.com: ImageBroker (IB/FLPA), Michael Krabs, Imag/Imagebroker (MK/IB/FLPA), Gerard Soury/Biosphoto (GS/B/FLPA), Martin B Withers (MBW/FLPA); Eric Lafforgue (EL); Shutterstock.com: BarryTuck (BT/S), cdclacy (c/S), Andrzej Grzegorczyk (AG/S), James Harrison (JH/S), Katiekk (K/S), Alberto Loyo (AL/S), nicolasdecorte (nd/S), Fedor Selivanov (FS/S); SuperStock (SS); Sandra Turay (ST); Ariadne Van Zandbergen (www.africaimagelibrary.com) (AVZ)

Front cover Musician on the beach (AMO/A)
Back cover Woman from Limpopo National Park (ST), Fishermen working on their boat at low tide, Ibo Island (K/S)
Title page Sunset over Gorongosa National Park (nd/S), Macua women wearing *musira* (AL/S), Detail of mosaic in Songo, by Naguib Elias (SC)
Part openers Fishermen in the shallows, Inhambane Beach (page 83; JH/S), Common waterbuck, Gorongosa National Park (page 195; AG/S), Boats on Pangane Beach (page 253; AL/S)

Maps David McCutcheon, FBCart.S
Illustrations Annabel Milne

Typeset by Dataworks and Ian Spick, Bradt Travel Guides
Production managed by Jellyfish Print Solutions; printed in India
Digital conversion by www.dataworks.co.in

Acknowledgements

SANDRA TURAY An immense amount of gratitude goes out to Philip Briggs, Sean Connolly and the Bradt team for all their efforts towards making the new edition a success. Your guidance on this fantastically challenging project has been invaluable.
Thank you to all of the lodges and their welcoming staff for hosting me along the way. Your generosity and infectious pride of Mozambique made updating a true pleasure. Thank you to Pumbas Backpackers (South Africa), Fátima's Place Backpackers, Casa Jules/Zombie Cucumber, Bahia Mar, Fátima's Nest, Break Away Chalets, White Pearl Resort, Nkwichi Lodge, SIM's Guesthouse, Pemba Magic Lodge, Cinco Portas, Libélula, Casa Paula, Ruby Backpackers Nampula, Machangulo Beach Lodge, Tan 'n Biki, Bulbul Backpackers, Dunes de Dovela Eco-Lodge, Travessia Beach Lodge, Turtle Cove, Villa Cool, Tsamisseka Xai–Xai Guesthouse, Covane Community Lodge, Elite Guesthouse and Anantara Bazaruto. Again, thank you for contributing to the success of the new edition.
I convey a special thank you to all of the Peace Corps volunteers in Mozambique for hosting me, helping me gather information, translating, networking across the country and for sharing with me the Mozambique you are proud to have called home. Thank you to Kevin Hale, Eric Wilburn, Jamie Backhaus, Tommy Lee, Dillon Tindall, Anneke Claypool, Taylor Marshall, Matt Derrico, Julian Pawliekewicz, Janis Luna, Callie Koller, Evan Briscoe, Raven Smith, Lee Gerston, Hannah Fagerbakke, Nicky Linder, James Bennett, Diana Fernanda Rojas, Isabel Elliott, Eileen Enright and Sterling Jarrett.
To all of the wonderful people who helped me in various ways throughout the updating process, whether that was giving me a lift, providing crucial travel advice or some other kind act of assistance, I'm extremely grateful for your willingness to help, along with the encouraging smiles! Thank you to Stuart MacDonald (and Lilly), Jenny Flint, Crisaldo Azarias and Celso Manuel of the Upstairs Café, Jill Pohle, Jeff Moises of Sunset Dhow Safaris, Harvey Gawie Roets, Paul Roach, Michael Meyer, Monique Coetsee, Philip Baker, Shawn Reichard, Brendon Bekker, Dino Ferreira, Peter Leitner of Limpopo National Park, Russell of Pemba Magic Lodge, Diversity Scuba, Kaskazini Travel, Brodie of Tofo Scuba, and Pete and Gail of Ilha Blue.
And to all of those folks I met in passing along the way, thank you for the help, laughs and many moments that have become the stories I tell when I speak of my time in Mozambique – which was nothing short of epic! Thank you.

Contents

	Introduction	ix
PART ONE	**GENERAL INFORMATION**	**1**
Chapter 1	**Background Information**	**3**
	Geography 3, Climate 4, History 4, Government and politics 20, Economy 20, People 23, Language 24, Religion 25, Culture 25	
Chapter 2	**Natural History**	**29**
	Vegetation 29, Mammals 30, Birds 34, Reptiles 36, Marine life 38	
Chapter 3	**Practical Information**	**41**
	When to visit 41, Highlights 41, Tourist information 42, Tour operators 42, Red tape 44, Getting there and away 45, Crime and safety 49, Women travellers 50, Gay travellers 51, Travellers with a disability 51, Travelling with children 51, What to take 51, Money 54, Budgeting 54, Getting around 55, Accommodation 59, Eating and drinking 61, Public holidays 63, Shopping 63, Photography 64, Media and communications 65, Responsible tourism 66, Getting involved 67	
Chapter 4	**Health**	**69**
	Preparations 69, Medical problems 70, Other safety concerns 74	
Chapter 5	**Diving and Snorkelling**	**75**
	Choosing an operator 75, Preparations before diving 75, During the dive 78, Snorkelling 81	
PART TWO	**SOUTHERN MOZAMBIQUE**	**83**
Chapter 6	**Maputo**	**87**
	History 88, Getting there and away 92, Getting around 93, Where to stay 94, Where to eat and drink 101, Nightlife 105, Safety and hassles 106, Entertainment 107, Shopping 109, Other practicalities 110, What to see and do 113, City walks 114, Day trips from Maputo 117	

| Chapter 7 | **Maputaland** | **121** |
| | Inhaca Island 121, Catembe 125, Bela Vista and Salamanga 126, Maputo Special Reserve 127, Ponta Mamoli and Malongane 129, Ponta do Ouro 130 | |

| Chapter 8 | **The Limpopo Valley and Coast South of Inhambane** | **137** |
| | Marracuene and surrounds 137, Bilene 138, Limpopo National Park 140, Xai-Xai 144, Beaches around Xai-Xai 148, Northeast of Xai-Xai 149 | |

| Chapter 9 | **Inhambane and Surrounds** | **153** |
| | Inhambane 153, Maxixe 160, Beaches around Inhambane 162, North of Inhambane 174 | |

| Chapter 10 | **Vilankulo, Inhassoro and Bazaruto National Park** | **177** |
| | Vilankulo 177, Inhassoro 185, Bazaruto National Park 189 | |

| **PART THREE** | **CENTRAL MOZAMBIQUE** | **195** |

| Chapter 11 | **Beira** | **199** |
| | History 199, Getting there and away 200, Orientation and getting around 202, Where to stay 202, Where to eat and drink 206, Other practicalities 207, What to see and do 209 | |

| Chapter 12 | **Chimoio and the Manica Highlands** | **213** |
| | Chimoio 215, Lake Chicamba 220, Manica 221, Penhalonga 225, Chimanimani National Reserve 226 | |

| Chapter 13 | **Gorongosa and the Caia Road** | **229** |
| | Gorongosa National Park 229, Mount Gorongosa 235, The EN1 from Inchope to Caia 237 | |

| Chapter 14 | **Tete** | **241** |
| | Tete 242, Around Tete 248 | |

| **PART FOUR** | **NORTHERN MOZAMBIQUE** | **253** |

| Chapter 15 | **Zambézia** | **257** |
| | Quelimane 257, The Quelimane–Nampula Road 265, The Western Highlands 270 | |

| Chapter 16 | **Nampula** | **279** |
| | Getting there and away 279, Where to stay 280, Where to eat and drink 283, Other practicalities 284, What to see and do 285, Around Nampula 285 | |

| Chapter 17 | **Ilha de Moçambique and Surrounds** | **291** |
| | History 292, Getting there and away 294, Where to stay 294, Where to eat and drink 298, Shopping 299, Other practicalities 299, Exploring Ilha de Moçambique 300, Mossuril Bay 305, Nacala 309 | |

| Chapter 18 | **Pemba and the Northeast** | 315 |
| | Pemba 315, Montepuez 324, Towards Tanzania 325 | |

| Chapter 19 | **The Quirimbas** | 333 |
| | History 334, Ibo 335, Other islands of the Quirimbas 343, The Quirimbas mainland 348, Pangane 350 | |

| Chapter 20 | **Niassa Province** | 351 |
| | Cuamba 351, Mandimba and Massangulo 353, Lichinga 354, Lago Niassa (Lake Malawi) 359, Niassa Reserve 366 | |

| Appendix 1 | **Language** | 374 |

| Appendix 2 | **Further Information** | 378 |

| Index | | 382 |

| Index of Advertisers | | 386 |

FEEDBACK REQUEST AND UPDATES WEBSITE

Administered by author Philip Briggs, Bradt's *Mozambique* update website (w *bradtupdates.com/mozambique*) is an online forum where travellers can post and read the latest travel news, trip reports and factual updates from Mozambique. The website is a free service to readers, or to anybody else who cares to drop by, and travellers to Mozambique and people in the tourist industry are encouraged to use it to share their comments, grumbles, insights, news or other feedback. These can be posted directly on the website, or emailed to Philip (e *philip.briggs@bradtguides.com*).

It's easy to keep up to date with the latest posts by following Philip on Twitter (🐦 *@philipbriggs*) and/or liking his Facebook page (ﬀ *pb.travel. updates*). You can also add a review of the book to w bradtguides.com or Amazon.

SEND US YOUR SNAPS!

We'd love to follow your adventures using our *Mozambique* guide – why not send us your photos and stories via Twitter (*@BradtGuides*) and Instagram (*@bradtguides*) using the hashtag #Mozambique. Alternatively, you can upload your photos directly to the gallery on the Mozambique destination page via our website (w *bradtguides.com/mozambique*).

LIST OF MAPS

Alto Molócuè	268	Maputo: The Baixa	98
Angoche	286	Maputo: orientation	90–1
Bazaruto Archipelago	190	Maputo: Polana District	95
Beira: centre	204–5	Maxixe	161
Beira: orientation	201	Metangula	362
Bilene	139	Milange	277
Chimoio	217	Mocuba	266
Chimoio and the		Montepuez	324
Manica Highlands	214	Mossuril Bay	307
Cóbuè	365	Mozambique 1st colour section	
Cuamba	353	Mozambique, central	196–7
Gorongosa National Park	230	Mozambique, northern	254–5
Gurué	271	Mozambique, southern	84–5
Ibo	338	Mueda	327
Ilha de Moçambique	290	Nacala	311
Ilha de Moçambique:		Namialo	289
Stone Town	296	Nampula	282
Inhaca Island and Santa Maria		Pemba: centre	318
Peninsula	122	Pemba and Wimbe	
Inhambane	157	Beach: orientation	314
Inhambane and surrounds	155	Ponta do Ouro	131
Inhassoro	187	Quelimane	259
Lichinga	356	Quirimbas, south	332
Macomia	326	Tete	244
Mandimba	354	Tofo and Tofinho	164
Manica	222	Vilankulo	176
Maputaland and		Xai-Xai	146
Maputo Special Reserve	120		

Updating the Mozambique guide has been one of the most rewarding travel experiences of all of my wanderings thus far. Offering such a diverse blend of adventure potential alongside a fusion of cultural flare, each destination I found myself in had a vibrancy all its own. Whether I was along the coast kayaking, scuba diving or watching the waves break against the miles of palm-fringed beaches, or making my way through the lush, inselberg-dotted hinterland via dusty lorry, each day I was greeted by authentic and captivating experiences that positively ruined my best efforts at maintaining an itinerary.

The rhythm of the country is such that one can't help but become enchanted by the gradual progress of modernity balanced by its distinct meld of historical and natural splendour. The size of the country seemed daunting at times but, even after hours in crowded *chapas*, I'd find myself smiling at the reciprocal curiosity and the subsequent interactions derived from being a stranger welcomed by cheery locals. Such genuine experiences made any leg cramp a small price to pay for such wonderful memories. I was invited into homes for home-cooked meals, invited for coffee and conversation, given lifts to difficult-to-reach places, and I shared in countless laughing moments that often arise from experiencing a new land.

At the 'end' of my trip, I even delayed my ticket home in order to watch a few more whales play offshore, take in several more majestic Indian Ocean sunrises, munch a few more piri-piri infused prawns and soak in the contagious vibe of paradise that is part landscape, part community and part coconut water (and perhaps a 2M or splash of Tipo Tinto).

I hope this new edition helps you craft an itinerary for the exploration and relaxation you seek in your travels, as well as make a few marvellous memories of the Mozambique I've come to cherish.

Introduction

Visit Mozambique today, and you'll find it difficult to imagine that it once attracted a larger number of tourists than South Africa and Rhodesia. Equally incredible, for that matter, is the realisation that, over the 15 years prior to 1992, this beguiling country was embroiled in an all-consuming civil war that claimed the lives of almost a million people, and caused the displacement of five times more.

Fortunately, the war is long over, and Mozambique is celebrating over 20 years of political stability, economic growth and progressive governance. Indeed, one of the most notable things when talking to Mozambicans about their recent history is how much more interested they are in making the most of the future rather than sliding back into the arguments of the past.

Recent figures suggest that, of all the countries in the world, Mozambique is a front runner as far as developing tourism is concerned. True, this statistic is to some extent reflective of the tiny base from which tourism has grown since the early 1990s. Equally, during South African and Zimbabwean school vacations, the resorts that line the coast between Maputo and Beira are bursting with cross-border holidaymakers, to the extent that in some resorts you'll hear more English and Afrikaans spoken than Portuguese or any indigenous language.

So far as tourists are concerned, Mozambique might just as well be two countries. Linked only by a solitary new bridge that spans the mighty Zambezi River at Caia, and divided by the more than 1,000km of road connecting Beira and Nampula, southern Mozambique and northern Mozambique offer entirely different experiences to visitors. The two parts of the country have in common the widespread use of Portuguese and a quite startlingly beautiful coastline. The difference is that the south coast of Mozambique is already established as a tourist destination, with rapidly improving facilities and a ready-made market in the form of its eastern neighbours. The north, by contrast, has few facilities for tourists, and getting to those that do exist takes determination and either time or money, although once you reach them they are the equal of anything in the region, and in some cases the world.

The majority of people who buy this guide will probably confine their travels to southern Mozambique. Not only does this part of the country offer good roads, reasonable public transport, some exceptional restaurants and any number of beach resorts suitable for all tastes and budgets, it is also within a day's drive of Johannesburg, the subcontinent's largest city and major international transport hub. The south coast of Mozambique is exceptionally beautiful – truly the archetype of palm-lined tropical-beach nirvana – as well as boasting snorkelling, diving and game fishing to rank with the very best in the world. Add to this Maputo, one of Africa's most attractive cities, plus the old-world gem that is Inhambane town, and you are looking at a stretch of coast as varied and attractive as any in Africa.

Any honest description of travel conditions on Mozambique's northern mainland – serious linguistic barriers to non-Portuguese speakers, humidity levels that reach intolerable proportions in summer, relatively high costs and a public transport system that in places defies rational comprehension – is bound to ring alarm bells with anybody seeking comfort, predictability or packaged entertainment. Equally, it is likely to whet the appetite of travellers looking for an adventurous trip through one of southern Africa's least-explored regions. The northern provinces of Zambézia, Niassa, Nampula and Cabo Delgado have a remote, isolated and self-contained feel – not surprising when you consider that they are collectively bordered by the undeveloped southeast quarter of Tanzania to the north, and by the vast watery expanses of the Indian Ocean and Lago Niassa to the east and west.

That said, northern Mozambique now boasts a number of upmarket resorts – mostly on the Quirimbas and the mainland around Pemba – that meet world-class standards, making the area highly attractive to fly-in visitors who are able to foot the rather hefty bills associated with these idyllic examples of 'barefoot luxury'. And while backpackers will find that much of northern Mozambique feels like travel for its own sake (a great deal of bumpy motion with relatively few highlights), the area does boast two historical attractions of quite compelling singularity, namely the former Portuguese capital of Ilha de Moçambique and the ancient island town of Ibo.

A recent development in Mozambique is the upgrading and opening up of several national parks and other potential safari destinations that suffered heavy losses to poaching during the years of civil war. Foremost among these is the refurbished Gorongosa National Park, which is showing the potential to become as important an attraction in the future as it was in the colonial era, when it was known as the Serengeti of southern Africa. Other important reserves with newly improved facilities include Limpopo National Park (which combines with South Africa's Kruger National Park and Zimbabwe's Gonarezhou National Park to form the Great Limpopo Transfrontier Park), the Maputo Special Reserve (home to several hundred elephant) and the inconceivably vast Niassa Reserve in the far north.

Mozambique may not be the easiest country in which to travel; in the northeast it can be downright frustrating. But this will change. And as this stands, it is not the least of Mozambique's attractions that it still offers ample scope for genuinely exploratory travel, offering adventurous travellers the opportunity to experience it entirely for themselves, without the distorting medium of a developed tourist industry.

HOW TO USE THIS GUIDE

LISTINGS Unless stated otherwise in the text, hotels and restaurants with entries in the *Where to stay* and *Where to eat and drink* sections in each chapter are listed alphabetically, or where applicable by price bracket, then alphabetically within each bracket. For accommodation and restaurant price codes, see pages 60 and 61 respectively (see also inside front cover).

MAPS
Keys and symbols Maps include alphabetical keys covering the locations of those places to stay, eat or drink that are featured in the book. Note that regional maps may not show all hotels and restaurants in the area: other establishments may be located in towns shown on the map.

On occasion, hotels or restaurants that are not listed in the guide (but which might serve as alternative options if required or serve as useful landmarks to aid navigation) are also included on the maps; these are marked with accommodation (⌂) or restaurant (✗) symbols.

Grids and grid references Several maps use grid lines to allow easy location of sites. Map grid references are listed in square brackets after the name of the place or sight of interest in the text, with page number followed by grid number, eg: [103 C3].

ATTENTION WILDLIFE ENTHUSIASTS

For more on wildlife in Mozambique, why not check out Bradt's *Southern African Wildlife*? Go to **w** bradtguides.com and key in MOZAMBIQUE20 at the checkout for your 20% discount (while stocks last).

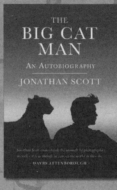

Part One

GENERAL INFORMATION

MOZAMBIQUE AT A GLANCE

Location Mozambique extends for 2,500km along the east coast of Africa, between latitudes 11° and 26°S and longitudes 30° and 40°E

Neighbouring countries Tanzania, Malawi, Zambia, Zimbabwe, South Africa, Swaziland

Area 799,380km^2, of which 13,000km^2 is water. It is the 16th-largest country in Africa, roughly two-thirds the size of the neighbouring Republic of South Africa, about three times the size of Great Britain and slightly larger than the state of Texas.

Climate Almost all the country is below 2,000m, and covered in a mixture of subtropical scrub. The south tends to be cooler and drier than the north.

Status Multi-party republic

Population 28 million (2016 estimate)

Life expectancy 55

Capital Maputo (population around 2.2 million including Matola)

Other main towns Nampula (638,000); Beira (462,000); Chimoio (325,000); Nacala (244,000); Quelimane (245,000)

Economy Predominantly subsistence agriculture, although this is changing as exploitation of mineral resources increases

GDP US$116 per capita PPP (2015); annual growth (2015) 6.6%

Languages The official language, Portuguese, is mother tongue to only 11% of the population. Some 40 indigenous languages are all classified in the Bantu linguistic group, the most widely spoken being Macua (25% of the population), Sena (11%) and Tsonga (11%). English and Swahili are widely understood in some border areas.

Religion About 52% of the population is Christian, with Catholicism dominating, and 18% is Muslim. The remainder hold traditional beliefs or profess no religion.

Currency Metical (Mt, plural meticais)

Exchange rates US$1=Mt61; £1=Mt79; €1=Mt68 (May 2017)

National airline Linhas Aéreas de Moçambique (LAM). Airports with scheduled direct international connections are in Maputo, Inhambane, Vilankulo, Quelimane, Beira, Tete, Nampula and Pemba.

International telephone code +258

Time GMT +2

Electrical voltage 220V, 50Hz

Weights and measures Metric

Flag Three horizontal bands: from top, green, white-edged black and yellow. There is a red triangle on the hoist side, centred on a yellow star bearing an open white book on which are depicted a crossed AK47 and a hoe in black.

National sports Football, basketball

Public holidays Mozambique has 12 national public holidays (see page 63).

National anthem *Pátria Amada* ('Beloved Fatherland')

1

Background Information

GEOGRAPHY

The topography of eastern Mozambique is dominated by a low-lying coastal belt that widens from north to south to account for almost half of the country's surface area. The coastal plain rises gradually towards the west to meet a high plateau of 500–1,000m. Mozambique is generally characterised by relatively flat terrain, though much of the northwest is mountainous and several areas of the western plateaux are dotted with isolated granite inselbergs known in southern Africa as *koppies*.

In the areas bordering Malawi and Zimbabwe, there are a few mountains that rise to an altitude of more than 1,800m. Mount Binga in the Chimanimani Range on the Zimbabwean border is Mozambique's highest peak at 2,436m. Other notable mountains include the massive inselberg of Gorongosa (1,862m) in Sofala Province, Mount Domue (2,095m) near Bragança in Tete Province, Mount Chiperone (2,054m) near Milange and Mount Namuli (2,419m) near Gurué in Zambézia, and Mount Txitonga (1,848m) and Mount Jeci (1,836m) on the Rift Valley escarpment north of Lichinga in Niassa Province.

Mozambique is traversed by several major river systems, all of which flow eastward into the Indian Ocean. The mouths of these rivers have played a significant role in Mozambican history: many of the country's older towns are situated on large river mouths, and the rivers themselves often formed important trade routes into the interior. The Zambezi is Africa's fourth-largest river and the Limpopo its tenth largest. The Zambezi Basin, at 1,330,000km², is the third-largest drainage system

MOZAMBIQUE: PROVINCE BY PROVINCE

Province	Capital	Area (km²)	Population (2016 estimate)
Cabo Delgado	Pemba	82,625	1,923,300
Gaza	Xai-Xai	75,709	1,442,100
Inhambane	Inhambane	68,615	1,523,600
Manica	Chimoio	61,661	2,001,900
Maputo	Matola	26,058	1,782,400
Maputo City	Maputo	300	1,257,500
Nampula	Nampula	81,606	5,130,000
Niassa	Lichinga	129,056	1,722,100
Sofala	Beira	68,018	2,099,200
Tete	Tete	100,724	2,618,900
Zambézia	Quelimane	105,008	4,922,700

		Temp	Rainfall	Humidity
January	Maputo	21–30°C	130mm	73%
	Beira	24–32°C	270mm	75%
July	Maputo	13–25°C	15mm	73%
	Beira	16–25°C	30mm	79%

in Africa (after the Zaïre and the Nile) and the 13th largest in the world. Of the 820km-long Mozambican section of the Zambezi, 460km are navigable.

Other main river systems are the Ruvuma on the Tanzanian border, the Lúrio on the border of Cabo Delgado and Nampula provinces, the Save on the border of Sofala and Inhambane provinces, and the Limpopo in the south of the country.

Roughly 200km of the eastern shore of Africa's third-largest freshwater body, Lake Malawi, lies in Mozambique, where it is known as Lago Niassa. Further south, the lake formed by the Cahora Bassa Dam is one of the 15 largest in Africa, its exact ranking depending on the effects of rainy seasons and swamp flooding at three other lakes.

Mozambique is divided into ten provinces. Each province is divided into districts, further subdivided into administrative areas and civil parishes. Zambézia and Nampula provinces in the northern half of the country contain the richest agricultural land and 40% of the population, whereas the three southern provinces of Gaza, Inhambane and Maputo are mostly arid and previously served as labour reserves for Mozambique's industries and for mines and farms in South Africa.

CLIMATE

The climate in most of Mozambique is tropical and warm with a dry cooler season from April until September and a wet hot season with temperatures of around 28°C at the coast from October until April. In winter the weather at the coast is sunny and pleasantly warm (the average temperature in Maputo in June and July is 19°C). The dry and relatively cool winter months between April and September offer the most comfortable and easy travel conditions.

Temperatures and rainfall figures vary widely across the country. Hottest and most humid are the northeastern coast and the upper Zambezi Valley, while the coolest areas are those at higher altitudes, such as the highlands of Niassa and Nampula provinces. Most of northeastern and central Mozambique has an annual average rainfall in excess of 1,000mm, with the wettest part of the country being the highlands east of Malawi, where several areas experience almost 2,000mm of rain annually. The south is generally much drier, with coastal regions south of Beira generally receiving around 900mm of rain and some parts of the interior of Gaza Province dropping to an average of below 500mm annually. The rainy season in the south runs from October to March, while north of the Zambezi it tends to start and end a month or two later.

HISTORY

EARLY HISTORY
The interior It is widely agreed that humans evolved in East Africa. Mozambique itself has yielded few notable hominid fossils, but it is nevertheless reasonable to

assume that it has supported human life for millions of years. Southeast Africa has incurred two major **population influxes from West Africa** in the last few millennia. The first occurred roughly 3,000 years ago, when the lightly built Batwa hunter-gatherers – similar in appearance and culture to the modern Bushmen of Namibia – spread throughout the region. Roughly a thousand years later, the Bantu-speakers who still occupy most of the region started to expand into eastern Africa, reaching the Indian Ocean coast in about AD400, an influx which broadly coincided with the spread of Iron Age culture in the region. Although there is little concrete evidence of the mechanisms of this so-called Bantu migration, the records of early Portuguese adventurers leave us with a good idea of the main Bantu-speaking groupings of the southeast African interior in around 1500.

The low-lying, dry and disease-prone Mozambican lowveld was then, as it is now, relatively thinly populated, with the dominant ethnolinguistic groupings being the Macua north of the Zambezi River, the Tonga between the Zambezi and the Inhambane area, and the Nguni south of Inhambane into modern-day South Africa. The three main ethnolinguistic groups of the lowveld had discrete social and economic systems: the Macua had a matrilineal social structure as opposed to the patrilineal system favoured further south, while the Nguni had a cattle-based economy and the Tonga a mixed farming economy supplemented by revenue from the trade routes passing through their territory.

What the people of the lowveld had in common was a decentralised political structure, based around fragmented local chieftaincies. In direct contrast, the Karanga (or Shona) who occupied the highveld of what is now Zimbabwe had a highly centralised political structure with an ancient tradition of stone building that evidently dates to around AD1000. At the centre of this region stood the extensive and magnificent city of **Great Zimbabwe**, which is thought to have had a population of more than 10,000 at its peak. The economy of Karangaland was probably based around cattle ownership, but its external relations were shaped by the coastal trade in gold, which has been mined in the Zimbabwean highlands since around AD900.

Karangaland appears to have gone through a major political upheaval in the second half of the 15th century. Great Zimbabwe was abandoned in roughly 1450, for reasons that remain a matter of speculation but which are probably linked to local environmental degradation or a secession struggle. Whatever the cause, the abandonment of Great Zimbabwe coincided with a northerly reorientation of the highland kingdoms and a corresponding shift in the main trade routes. During the 15th century, the trade routes fanning from the Zambezi assumed greater importance, while the established route inland of Sofala along the Buzi River appears to have diminished in use. It is highly probable that the Karanga kingdoms known to the earliest Portuguese explorers were relatively new creations resulting from the upheavals of the late 15th century.

By 1500, the three main kingdoms of the highveld were **Butua**, in what is now the Bulawayo area of Zimbabwe; **Monomotapa**, in what is now central Zimbabwe; and **Manica**, in the highlands of what is now the Zimbabwean–Mozambican border area. The upheavals also resulted in two Karanga chieftaincies being established in what had formerly been Tonga territory: Barue in the lowveld south of the Zambezi and west of Sena, and Kiteve in the lowveld between the Pungué and Buzi rivers. Of these five main kingdoms, Butua was the only one to retain the stone building tradition, while Monomotapa established itself as the paramount dynasty in the region.

The coast The East African coast has long been a centre of international trade. Starting in around 2500BC, the ancient Egyptians evidently entered into spasmodic

1

trade with an East African port they knew as **Punt**. From about 600BC, the Phoenicians and Romans are known to have traded with an East African port called **Rhapta**. The location of Punt remains a matter of pure speculation, but detailed references to Rhapta in Ptolemy's 4th-century *Geography* and in an older Phoenician document, *Periplus of the Ancient Sea*, point to a location somewhere in present-day Tanzania, possibly near the mouth of the Pangani River.

The **collapse of the Roman Empire** signalled a temporary end to maritime trade with the East African coast, and it presumably forced the closure of any contemporary trade routes into the African interior. Ptolemy claims that a Greek explorer called Diogenes saw two snow-capped mountains 25 days upriver from Rhapta and that he was told by other traders of vast lakes further inland, which indicates that 4th-century trade routes must have penetrated the interior as far as Mounts Kenya and Kilimanjaro, and possibly also Lakes Victoria and Tanganyika.

The **rise of Islam** in the 7th century AD revived the maritime trade with East Africa. The writings of Ali Masudi in AD947 make it clear that Arab mariners had by this time entered into regular trade with Madagascar and that they were aware that the main source of Africa's gold was Sofala, near the mouth of the Buzi River in what is now central Mozambique. The presence of 9th-century Islamic ruins on Manda Island off the Kenyan coast indicates that Arabic traders started settling in East Africa at a very early point in this era of trade. The 12th-century geographer Al Idrisi refers to Sofala as an important source of iron, gold and animal skins, and he indicates that by this time China and India were both trading with East Africa. By the 13th century, the coast between Somalia and central Mozambique was dotted with some 30 or 40 Swahili city-states, among the most important of which were Mogadishu, Malindi, Mombasa, Pangani, Zanzibar, Kilwa and Sofala.

Although many of these ancient Swahili cities have survived into the modern era, our best idea of what they must have looked like comes from the extensive ruins of those that haven't – notably Kilwa in southern Tanzania and Gedi in Kenya. The impressive rag coral architecture and overwhelming Muslim influence of such places has led many popular accounts to treat them as little more than Arabic implants. However, most modern historians are agreed that this is an outdated interpretation, and that there was a high level of integration between Arabic settlers and the indigenous peoples of the coast. It is true that the Islamic religion was adopted all along the coast, but then so was the Swahili language, which is self-evidently Bantu in origin, and which adopted elements of Arabic vocabulary only after the arrival of the Omani Arabs in the 18th century.

Several modern Mozambican ports have been built over medieval Swahili trade settlements – most notably Ilha de Moçambique, but also Angoche, Ibo and possibly Inhambane. However, the most important port south of Kilwa in medieval times, Sofala, is no longer in existence. The port of **Sofala** is thought to have been founded as a trading post in the 9th century, as a result of an Arabic ship being blown off course to hit land south of the Zambezi. Sofala is said to have had a population of around 10,000 by the 15th century. The absence of suitable building material meant that the medieval cities of Mozambique were never built as durably as those located further north, so little physical evidence of Sofala remains. Even if Sofala had been a stone city, it would now be submerged off the ever-mutating sandy shoreline south of the Buzi River.

Despite the absence of tangible ruins at Sofala, one should not underestimate its importance in medieval times, when it formed the pivotal link between the gold mines of Karangaland and Manica and the port of Kilwa. Sofala was best known to Arabs as the source of Kilwa's gold, but it was also an important trade centre in its own right, with direct maritime links to Madagascar and indirect links via Madagascar to India and Indonesia. Sofala's main exports, apart from gold, were worked iron, copper, ivory and cotton – the last grown as far south as Inhambane by the 15th century.

There is strong evidence to suggest that Arabic vessels explored the Zambezi as far inland as Cahora Bassa. It also seems highly probable that Muslim traders settled along the Zambezi long before the arrival of the Portuguese. Despite the oft-repeated assertion that Portugal founded the river ports at Sena and Tete in 1531, the greater probability is that Portuguese traders occupied existing Muslim settlements at these locations. Particularly compelling evidence of this comes from a 12th-century Arab document that refers to a town called Seyouna located near the confluence of two large rivers and a large mountain – the similarity in name and the geographical details would point to Seyouna and Sena being one and the same place. It has also been suggested that a town referred to as Dendema in a 14th-century document was in the same locality as present-day Tete.

PORTUGUESE OCCUPATION OF EAST AFRICA 1488–1530 The well-established trade links that bonded East Africa to the Gulf and to Asia were to alter dramatically in the 16th century following the arrival of the Portuguese on the Indian Ocean. Throughout the 15th century, Portugal attempted to find a route around Africa, with the main impetus of establishing direct control over the eastern spice trade. After Portugal captured the Moroccan port of Ceuta in 1415, it also became conscious of the fact that somewhere in Africa lay the source of the gold traded in that city. Furthermore, the Portuguese Crown was eager to establish the whereabouts of the legendary kingdom of **Prester John** (the name by which they knew present-day Ethiopia) and to forge links with this isolated Christian empire.

It took Portugal almost a century to circumnavigate Africa, quite simply because they underestimated the continent's size. Nevertheless, Portuguese explorers had sailed as far south as Senegal by 1444; they reached the Gambia River in 1446; Sierra Leone in 1460; and São Tomé in 1474. In 1485, under King João II, an expedition led by **Diogo Cão** sailed up the Congo River as far as it was navigable, then continued south as far as Cape Cross in present-day Namibia. Cão died near Cape Cross, but when the survivors of his journey returned to Portugal, King João ordered **Bartolomeu Dias** to continue where he had left off. Dias set sail in August 1487, and in early 1488 he unwittingly rounded the Cape of Good Hope into the Indian Ocean, eventually sailing to roughly 50km past the point where the city of Port Elizabeth stands today. While Dias was exploring the route via West Africa, another Portuguese explorer, Pêro da Covilhã, made his way overland and along the East African coastline to Kilwa and Sofala. The two routes of exploration finally connected in 1498, when Vasco da Gama sailed around Africa, stopping at Mozambique Island before continuing as far north as Malindi and, with the help of a Swahili navigator, crossing the Indian Ocean to India.

In 1505, the Portuguese decided to occupy the East African coast. In July, Kilwa was captured and a friendly sheikh installed on its throne. Two months after that, a Portuguese boat landed at Sofala and was given permission by the local sheikh to erect a **fort and trading factory** – however, the sheikh and his allies attacked the Portuguese stockade within a year of its foundation, resulting in the sheikh being killed and replaced by a Portuguese puppet. In 1507, a **permanent Portuguese settlement** was established on Mozambique Island, which so rapidly became the centre of Portuguese operations that Kilwa was abandoned by its colonisers in 1513.

Portugal also set about attacking rival Muslim centres of commerce: Oja, Bravo and Socatra on the north coast were sacked in 1507, and the islands of Mafia, Pemba and Zanzibar followed in 1509. Several Muslims from Mozambique Island and Sofala were forced to relocate to Angoche and Querimba Island, where they started a clandestine trade which was temporarily halted when Portugal razed Angoche in 1511 and Querimba in 1522. By 1530, practically the whole East African coast north of Sofala was under Portuguese control.

THE EAST AFRICAN COAST 1530–1600 The boundaries of modern Mozambique were in many instances shaped by events during the first four centuries of the Portuguese occupation of the coast, but Mozambique as we know it is in essence a 20th-century entity. The expansions and contractions of Portuguese influence between 1500 and 1890 don't really reflect a considered policy, but rather a haphazard sequence of largely unsuccessful attempts at formal expansion from a few coastal strongholds.

The Portuguese presence in East Africa was characterised by a high level of disunity. The interests of the Crown and the appointed Captain of Mozambique (who prior to 1670 ran the 'colony' as a private trade enterprise) were often in conflict, as were those of the many Portuguese deserters who fled from the few formal Portuguese settlements to intermarry with locals and form a distinct group of mixed-race *mazungos*. Contrary to popular perception, Mozambique prior to 1890 was not so much a Portuguese territory as a patchwork of endlessly mutating and fragmenting fiefdoms, some of which were under the nominal or real rule of the Portuguese Crown, but the greater number of which were lorded over by self-appointed despots, be they renegade mazungos, indigenous chiefs or Muslim sheikhs.

In the early years of the Portuguese occupation, the **kingdom of Monomotapa** (more accurately transcribed as Mwene Mutapa, ie: the state of the Mutapa dynasty) took on legendary proportions in the mind of its would-be conquerors. For centuries, it has been assumed that Monomotapa was a vast and all-powerful homogeneous empire covering most of modern-day Zimbabwe as well as parts of Botswana and Mozambique. Modern academics, however, believe that the kingdom's size and importance were exaggerated by Portugal, and that the Mutapa dynasty ruled over what was merely one of many loosely defined Karanga kingdoms. Quite how Monomotapa's mythical status arose is an open question, but it is fairly certain that it would have suited Portuguese interests to perpetuate the myth that the whole interior was one vast centralised kingdom – especially after 1607, when Portugal signed a treaty with the Mutapa empire, giving it full access to all gold, copper and silver mines in the kingdom.

The earliest sanctioned exploration of the Mozambican interior was made by **António Fernandes**, who reported on the main gold trade routes over three journeys between 1511 and 1513, and who was probably the first Portuguese to visit the capital of Monomotapa in the Cahora Bassa Region. However, Fernandes's findings did not result in the official occupation of the interior – on the contrary, the Portuguese Crown appears to have been content to trade with local chiefs from its coastal fortresses. The disruption caused to the gold trade by the upheavals in Karangaland and the clandestine approach of the Muslim gold traders at places like Angoche forced the Portuguese to turn their attention to ivory, which by 1530 had replaced gold as the main item of export. The Portuguese fortresses on the coast also required large amounts of food, which created a secondary trade network between the representatives of the Crown and established chiefs. Despite initial tensions, the market for food and ivory eventually created a mutual dependence and stable relations.

Once Portugal realised that it would be unable to wrest control of the elusive gold trade from the Muslim traders by force, it attempted to take control of the routes to the interior by occupying the existing Muslim settlements at Tete, Sena and Quelimane in 1531.

The only concerted effort made by the Crown to conquer Monomotapa in the 16th century was an expedition of a thousand men led by **Francisco Barreto**, which arrived at Sena in December 1571. Hundreds of Barreto's men had died of fever along the way and – ignorant of tsetse fly and mosquito-borne diseases – Barreto blamed his losses on the black magic of the Muslims at Sena. The Portuguese troops attacked Sena, killing most of its Muslim population and capturing the 19 men they identified as its leaders, who were then tortured to death at the rate of two a day. In July 1572, Barreto marched towards Tete with 650 men but, before he could reach his destination, his troops were attacked by a force of 16,000 Africans led by a Maravi king known as **Mambo**. Barreto's men were forced to turn back after killing some 4,000 of their attackers. Only 180 of the men who left Sena returned there alive, and Barreto himself died of fever on the way. Two years later, another group of soldiers marched 450km inland, defeating the Kiteve capital but achieving little else before they returned to the coast with their numbers reduced to a third by malaria.

The Portuguese occupation of Mozambique should not be seen as colonisation in the way we understand it today. Most of the infiltration of the interior and the coast away from the fortress towns was the work of **Afro-Portuguese mazungos**, many of whom were refugees from the Crown. Armed with muskets, many of these refugees married into local communities and assumed the role of surrogate chiefs, building up their own private armies and trade empires. During the 16th century, not only did various mazungos establish themselves at practically every port and island along the coast, but they also settled along the southern bank of the Zambezi as far as Tete, setting up what were in effect minor chieftaincies over the local Tonga.

Ironically, it could be argued that the most successful expansionists in 16th-century Mozambique were not of European but of African origin. Probably as a result of a drought, cannibalistic **Zimba warbands** from the Maravi Kingdom of the Shire Highlands (in Malawi) swept into Mozambique in the late 1560s. The Zimba attacked Tete in the 1560s, halted Barreto's progress in 1572, and then continued northward, razing Kilwa and Mombasa and eating many of their occupants. The Zimba were eventually defeated near Malindi in 1587, but the survivors returned southward to settle in the area between the Rovuma and Zambezi rivers, practically all of which was ruled over by one or other Maravi chieftaincy at the beginning of the 17th century.

Towards the end of the century, Portugal's dominance in the region was threatened by Turks, for which reason the fortifications of Mozambique Island and Mombasa were vastly improved and the coast was divided into two administrative regions with Cabo Delgado as the boundary. This border has remained significant ever since and now separates Tanzania from Mozambique.

THE EAST AFRICAN COAST 1600–1800 In the early 17th century, Portugal experienced the first serious rivalry to its status as the dominant European power in the Indian Ocean. In 1602, barely a decade after the first Dutch and British ships had rounded the Cape of Good Hope, the **Dutch East India Company** (VOC) was formed with the intent of taking over Portugal's Indian Ocean trade. In 1607, the Dutch made a concerted effort to capture the Portuguese capital on Mozambique Island, a six-week siege which failed only because the invaders were unable to take the Portuguese fortress. After a second attempt at ousting Portugal in 1608, the Dutch fleets left Mozambique Island alone, but in alliance with English ships they captured several other Portuguese territories in the Indian Ocean. This period of instability ended in the late 1630s, when treaties were signed between the three countries.

The beginning of the 17th century also saw Karangaland fall into an extended period of instability following the death of the Monomotapa in 1597. The succeeding Monomotapa, Gatse Lucere, became dependent on the protection of the mazungo Diego Madeira's armies to retain control over his kingdom, which Madeira saw as more or less an invitation to take over Karangaland following the signing of a mineral rights treaty in 1607. Gatse Lucere died in 1623, to be succeeded by **Inhamba**, who in 1628 murdered the Portuguese envoy to his capital, prompting a full-scale war with Portugal. Inhamba was driven from his capital, and a baptised Mutapa was installed in his place. However, this puppet ruler had little support, and in 1631 Inhamba led an uprising in which he recaptured the Crown and killed several hundreds of Portuguese and their supporters. Meanwhile, the Maravi took advantage of the chaos in Monomotapa to capture Quelimane.

In 1632, Portugal had one of its few successful military forays in the Mozambican interior. Under the leadership of **Sousa de Meneses**, 2,000 troops landed at Quelimane, where they booted out the Maravi, then marched to Karangaland, destroyed Inhamba's army and installed a vassal Monomotapa. So began a 60-year period in which Portugal was to have its only sustained control of Karangaland. During this time, major Portuguese settlements grew up around the various gold fairs of the interior, notably Dambarare (near modern-day Harare) and Masekesa (on the site of Manica town).

The Crown's tenuous supremacy in Karangaland ended in 1693, when a Changamire chief called Dombo attacked Dambarare and killed all its Portuguese inhabitants. Other Portuguese settlements in Karangaland were evacuated and the Changamire proceeded to attack all the gold fairs in Manica. As things settled down, the Changamire took effective control of the highlands to found the **Rozvi Kingdom**, while the Portuguese kept control of the lowveld. This boundary is reflected in the modern one between Mozambique and Zimbabwe.

Events on the coast in the late 17th century reinforced what was eventually to become the northern border of modern Mozambique. In 1650, Muscat was captured by Omani Arabs and used as a base from which to launch an attack on the East African coast. Omani ships attacked Zanzibar in 1652 and Mombasa in 1661. Ten years later, Mozambique Island was looted by **Omani sailors**, and once again it was only the fortress of São Sebastião that prevented Portugal being ousted from their East African capital. The Omani never again attempted to attack Portuguese settlements in what is now Mozambique, but in 1698 they captured Mombasa. The coast north of Cabo Delgado was lost to Portugal for ever.

The period between 1650 and 1800 saw the informal mazungo chieftaincies of the Zambezi Valley formalised into a network of *prazo* **estates** – large tracts of land granted to settlers and wealthy traders by the Portuguese Crown. The prazo leases were good for three generations, and they were inherited by females, presumably as a way of encouraging wealthy Portuguese to settle in the Zambezi Valley. In theory, no person was allowed to own more than one prazo, but in reality large blocks of prazos were linked by marriage. The holders of the leases, known as *prazeros*, ruled over their estates with absolute authority. In effect, the prazos were run as small feudal empires, and the prazeros derived most of their income by forcing tributes from people living on their estate rather than by developing the estate for agriculture.

MOZAMBIQUE IN THE 19TH CENTURY The early part of the 19th century was a time of great hardship in southeastern Africa, as the region was gripped by **severe droughts** between 1794 and 1802 and again between 1817 and 1832. These droughts were to have far-reaching effects on Mozambique and many other parts of southeast

Africa, most significantly among the Nguni people of southern Mozambique and the east coast of South Africa. During the first years of the drought, the Nguni became increasingly dependent on **cattle raids** to support themselves, which led to a high degree of militarisation and eventually to the centralisation of the Nguni into three main kingdoms: the Zulu, Swazi and Ndandwe. The Zulus, who emerged as the most powerful of these kingdoms under the leadership of Shaka, raided and looted surrounding territories, causing vast tracts of the South African highveld to become depopulated and forcing many people to migrate to other areas.

In 1819, the Zulus conquered the **Ndandwe Kingdom**, causing the survivors to emigrate from the area in a number of large warbands which grew in size as they raided and plundered the villages that they passed through. The warband that was to have the greatest effect on Mozambique was that led by **Nxaba**, who attacked Inhambane in 1824 and conquered many of the chieftaincies of Manica in 1827. In the early 1830s, with the drought at its peak, Nxaba was based around the Gorongosa area, and in 1836 he plundered Sofala. Following a Nguni leadership battle in 1837, Nxaba and his followers were forced to flee Mozambique, while the victor, Shoshangane, founded the Gaza Kingdom, which covered most of Mozambique south of the Zambezi between 1840 and its conquest by Portugal in 1895.

Elsewhere, the Rozvi Empire of the Zimbabwean highlands was destroyed and the Changamire killed by a Nguni warband, and eastern Zimbabwe was eventually settled by the Matabele, another Nguni offshoot. Within Mozambique, a Nguni leader called Maseko established a kingdom north of Tete, while another called Gwangwara established himself along what is now the Tanzanian border. The Nguni invasion made travel in the interior unsafe, and Nguni warbands destroyed many of the gold fairs, practically forcing the closure of the gold trade.

Another significant feature of the first half of the 19th century, one that was not entirely unrelated to the drop in the gold trade, was a rapid increase in **slave trading** along the East African coast. Prior to the mid 18th century, slaves formed only a small part of the Indian Ocean trade network, but this started to change after the 1770s with the emergence of clandestine trade between the Muslims of Ibo and the French sugar plantations of the Indian Ocean islands. In the 1770s, the number of slaves being exported from Mozambique was still relatively low – fewer than 2,000 annually – but as increasing restrictions were imposed on the trade out of West Africa, prices rose and so did the number of slaves being exported from the ports of East Africa. Between 1825 and 1830, around 20,000 slaves were shipped out of Mozambique annually, to destinations as far afield as the USA and Brazil. It has been estimated that more than a million Africans were shipped out of the ports of Mozambique in the 19th century.

Britain persuaded Portugal to abolish the slave trade in 1836, in effect driving it underground – the number of slaves shipped out in the 1850s probably exceeded that in the 1830s. Public attention was drawn to this clandestine trade when the Scottish missionary David Livingstone published reports of his Zambezi expedition of 1858–64. Following Livingstone's death in 1875, several Scottish missions were established in the Shire Highlands (a part of modern-day Malawi that would otherwise almost certainly have been incorporated in Mozambique later in the century).

The great droughts undermined the agricultural base of the Zambezi Valley, forcing many prazeros to abandon their estates. By the mid 19th century, power in this important area had become consolidated under five large feudal fiefdoms ruled over by powerful mazungo families or other settlers. The Zambezi Valley became a lawless zone, characterised by interfamily feuds and mini wars, starting in 1840 with an unsuccessful attack on the Pereira family by the Portuguese authorities, and reaching a peak in 1867–69 with four abortive and bloody attempts to capture the Da Cruz family stockade at Massangano. The Zambezi Valley was only fully brought under government control in 1887, when Massangano was captured by the Governor of Manica.

An important feature of 19th-century Mozambique was the strong British influence on the East African coast following its successful takeover of the Cape Colony in 1806 and Mauritius in 1810. In 1820, the British flag was raised on the southern part of Delagoa Bay, initiating a protracted period of disputes between Britain, Portugal and the Boer Republic of the Transvaal over the control of this strategic possession. This dispute was only resolved in 1875, when French arbitrators gave the whole bay to Mozambique. Meanwhile, as the so-called **Scramble for Africa** approached its climax, the Beira Corridor area became something of a battleground between the British imperialist and founder of Rhodesia, Cecil Rhodes, and his Portuguese counterpart Paiva de Andrade.

After a couple of years of haggling over boundaries and disputed territories, Britain and Portugal signed a treaty in May 1891 and Mozambique took its modern shape. The northern boundary with German East Africa (Tanzania) simply followed the border established centuries before between the administrative regions of Mombasa and Mozambique Island. The northwestern borders were more keenly contested, but they were basically settled in favour of the power that had the higher presence in each area – hence northern Mozambique was bisected by the Scottish-settled area that is now southern Malawi. The southwestern borders followed well-established divides: the border with Zimbabwe was similar to the one that separated the Rozvi and Portuguese spheres of influence between around 1700 and 1840; the western borders with the Transvaal followed the one agreed to in the Boer–Portuguese treaty of 1869; and the southern border with the British colony of Natal had been determined by French arbitration in 1875.

THE COLONIAL PERIOD 1890–1975 Mozambique is less arbitrarily delineated than many other countries in Africa. Nevertheless, it was anything but a cohesive entity at the time its boundaries were defined, and parts of the country remained entirely independent of Portugal as late as 1914. As an indication of the weakness of Portuguese colonial rule during the closing decade of the 19th century, it is interesting to note that Britain and Germany signed a **secret treaty** determining how Mozambique and Angola should be divided in the event of their being abandoned by Portugal.

Only four of Mozambique's ten modern-day provinces were directly administered by the colonial authorities. The area south of the Save River – basically the modern provinces of Maputo, Inhambane and Gaza – was given a reasonable degree of political coherence by the Gaza monarchy, who were conquered by Portugal between 1895 and 1897. The other part of the country that fell under direct colonial rule was the area around Mozambique Island (modern-day Nampula Province), but the Portuguese presence in much of this area was rather tenuous until around the time of the outbreak of World War I. In 1904, the Portuguese in this area were attacked by a collection of Muslim and African chiefs, and forced to take refuge on Mozambique Island.

The rest of the country fell under indirect rule. The present-day provinces of Niassa and Cabo Delgado were leased to the **Niassa Company** between 1894 and 1929. The Niassa Company was almost totally ineffective until 1908, when it was taken over by a South African company and started to make its presence felt in the northern interior. The Yao capital at Mwende was captured by the Niassa Company in 1912, but the Makonde Plateau remained independent until after World War I. Meanwhile, most of what are now Tete and Zambézia provinces were controlled by prazeros, while the area now incorporated into the provinces of Sofala and Manica was leased to the Mozambique Company from 1891 to 1941.

A significant trend in the first decade of formal colonialism was the rising economic importance of southern Mozambique. This was directly due to the proximity of Lourenço Marques to the gold mines of the Witwatersrand in South Africa. Following the completion of the **rail link to the Witwatersrand** in 1894, the port at Lourenço Marques exported roughly a third of this wealthy area's minerals.

No less significant was the volume of migrant labour from southern Mozambique to the mines of Witwatersrand. The Witwatersrand Native Labour Association employed between 50,000 and 100,000 Mozambicans annually between the end of the Boer War and the start of World War II. In some years, the tax contributed by the migrant workers of southern Mozambique amounted to more than half of the total revenue raised by the colonial government.

At around the turn of the 20th century, Lourenço Marques was made the official capital of Mozambique, replacing the former capital of Mozambique Island after almost four centuries (strangely, various sources give an array of different dates for when the capital was transferred, the main contenders being 1886, 1897, 1898, 1902 or 1907 – though the year 1898, as quoted by the official Lourenço Marques city guide published in 1964, seems most plausible).

Migrant labour had been an important factor in the Mozambican economy even before 1890, but the volume of workers increased dramatically following the **Colonial Labour Law** of 1899. Not only did this decree divide Mozambicans into two classes, indigenous and non-indigenous, but it also required that all indigenous males and females aged between 14 and 60 had to work and had to pay hut tax. It can be argued that the Labour Law rescued Mozambique from the bleak economic future that many had predicted at the time of its formal colonisation, but it is equally true that by imposing the obligation to work on the indigenous population it allowed them to be exploited in a manner that was little better than slavery. Paradoxically, it was the people who lived in the prazos and company concessions who were most ruthlessly exploited – until the 1930s, people in these areas were regularly press-ganged into 'employment'. The migrant labour of southern Mozambique was socially disruptive, but it also meant better wages and a lower cost of living, so that even as late as 1967, roughly half a million Mozambicans (out of a total population of eight million) were working in South Africa or Rhodesia.

In 1926, Portugal's Republican government was overthrown in a military coup, leading to the so-called '**New State**', a dictatorship dominated by António Salazar, prime minister from 1932 to 1968. Salazar envisaged a future wherein Portugal and its colonies would form a self-sufficient closed economy with the mother country serving as the industrial core and the dependencies providing the agricultural produce and raw materials. He outlawed the company concessions and prazos which had until then practically ruled two-thirds of Mozambique, and was largely successful in his efforts to create a more unitary administration. Forced labour was replaced by forced agricultural schemes, leading to a tenfold increase in Mozambique's cotton and rice production between 1930 and 1950. As a result, Mozambique enjoyed something of an economic boom, particularly during **World War II** when Portugal's neutral stance allowed Mozambique to concentrate on food production and benefit from a 500% increase in the value of its exports. However, the war also meant a decrease in the activity of the mines of South Africa and Rhodesia, and the return of large numbers of migrant labourers, one result of which was the introduction of population control rulings that mimicked the South African Pass Laws.

The post-war period saw greater economic diversification in Mozambique, with the development of secondary industries, particularly in Lourenço Marques and Beira, and a boom in incoming tourism from South Africa and Rhodesia. The outcome of the war encouraged Salazar to drop his more fascist policies and to enter NATO in 1949, one result of which was the admittedly rather semantic change in Mozambique's status from a colony to an overseas province.

After World War II, almost all of Europe's African colonies experienced a vociferous and sometimes violent campaign for independence. Generally, these calls for liberation were initiated by African soldiers who had fought for democracy in Europe and then returned home to find that they remained second-class citizens in the country of their birth. That no significant liberation movement existed in Mozambique prior to 1960 can probably be attributed to Portugal's neutrality during the war. Nevertheless, following a violent uprising in Angola in February 1961, the ever-astute Salazar decided to try to forestall the inevitable, first by allowing Portugal's overseas provinces to be represented in the Lisbon government, and secondly by bestowing full citizenship on the indigenous population. In December of that year, Portugal's three colonial enclaves in Asia were reclaimed by India, and Salazar decided to oppose similar calls from his African colonies with force.

Mozambique's first broad-based **liberation movement** was formed in exile in 1963, when President Nyerere of Tanzania persuaded a number of small-time liberation groups to amalgamate into an organisation called the **Front for the Liberation of Mozambique (Frelimo)**, held together by the powerful leadership of Eduardo Mondlane, a Mozambican academic living in the USA. In 1964, Frelimo decided on a militant policy, and by the end of 1965 it had captured much of Cabo Delgado and Niassa provinces. Portugal responded by arresting 1,500 Frelimo agents in southern Mozambique, effectively destroying the organisation in this part of the country. Meanwhile, Frelimo started to factionalise in the north, with the educated leadership on the one side and the traditionalist chiefs on the other. In 1968, the Frelimo offices in Dar es Salaam were raided by traditionalists, and rioting in the Frelimo-run school there forced its closure. In February 1969, Mondlane was assassinated using a letter bomb. The ensuing power struggle forced out the traditionalists and saw the military commander, **Samora Machel**, take over the party presidency in May 1970.

Machel faced an immediate challenge in the form of 35,000 troops sent by the government to clear Frelimo out of northern Mozambique and attack its bases in Tanzania. Instead of fighting, Frelimo evacuated the north, slipped through Malawi, and relocated its centre of internal operations to the area north of Tete. With the support of the local Chewa people, Frelimo attempted to destabilise the Tete and Beira corridors and to disrupt the construction of the Cahora Bassa Dam, a policy that culminated in the derailing of trains to Beira in 1974.

The extent to which Frelimo's limited attacks influenced Mozambique's eventual independence is debatable. At least as significant were the concurrent political changes in Portugal. Upon entering the European Common Market in 1970, Portugal was forced to dismantle its rigid trade agreements with Mozambique. The result was an almost immediate realignment of the Mozambican economy towards South Africa – by 1974, South Africa had already become the main investor in Mozambique, as well as its principal trading partner. Even more critical to Mozambique's future was the left-wing coup that took place in Lisbon in April 1974. Within two months, the new government of Portugal had entered into negotiations with Frelimo. In September 1974, the two sides signed the **Lusaka Accord**: Mozambique would be granted independence after a mere nine months of interim government, and power would transfer to Frelimo without even the pretence of a referendum or election.

INDEPENDENT MOZAMBIQUE Three factors were to prove critical in shaping Mozambique during the first two decades of independence: the mess left behind by the colonisers; the leadership of Frelimo; and the destabilising policies of South Africa's nationalist government.

It would be easy enough to see the first 15 years of Frelimo government as typical of the sort of Marxist dictatorship that has characterised post-independence Africa. It would also be rather simplistic. Frelimo assumed a dictatorial role through circumstance as much as intent – there simply *was* no viable opposition in the decade following independence – and its progressive, humanitarian ideals were a far cry from the self-serving, repressive policies enacted by many of its peers. Frelimo's undeniable failures can be attributed partly to unfortunate circumstance, but most of all to its intellectual and interventionist policies – idealistic grand schemes which failed to take into account the importance of ethnicity, tradition and religion in rural African societies, and which ultimately alienated the peasantry.

The party's most notable successes were on the social front. In the first few years of independence, **primary school attendance** doubled and enrolment at secondary schools increased sevenfold. The new government attempted to combat the appalling literacy rate of less than 5% at the time of independence by initiating an **adult literacy scheme** that benefited hundreds of thousands of Mozambicans, and sought to undermine the problem of ethnicity by spreading the use of Portuguese as a common language. Despite there being fewer than a hundred trained doctors in the country in 1975, Frelimo launched an ambitious programme of immunisations, praised by the World Health Organization (WHO) as one of the most successful ever initiated in Africa. The scheme reached 90% of the population in the first five years of Frelimo rule, resulting in a 20% drop in infant mortality. Frelimo's emphasis on sexual equality was underscored by the fact that 28% of the people elected to popular assemblies in 1977 were women – a higher figure than almost anywhere else in the world.

Frelimo's critical failing was on the economic front which, while caused partly by its own policies, was undoubtedly exacerbated by the situation in which the newly independent country found itself. Mozambique's economy, never the most developed in southern Africa, was further damaged by emerging in the middle of the global depression following the 1973 oil crisis. The crisis not only damaged Mozambican businesses but also led to the South African gold mines laying off two-thirds of their Mozambican workers in 1976, with a resultant loss of significant foreign earnings.

Portuguese settlers, faced with a choice between immediate repatriation or enforced Mozambican citizenship, chose **mass exodus**, stripping assets as they went. The loss of capital and expertise caused the collapse of many of the country's secondary industries, most of which remain moribund. Frelimo attempted to abate this outflow by nationalising a number of industries, but at a pace that only caused the situation to spiral, and which gave many Portuguese settlers a pretext for destroying anything that they couldn't take out of the country. Meanwhile Frelimo's ambitious agricultural schemes were obstructed by climatic factors: disastrous floods hit the main agricultural areas in the summer of 1977/78, followed by four years of nationwide drought.

Lastly, Mozambique was surrounded by hostile countries. South Africa and Zimbabwe (then Rhodesia) were still white-ruled and feared independence movements that had proved so effective in neighbouring countries springing up in their own backyards. Malawi, while nominally independent, adopted a heavily pro-Western approach and actively supported the activities of the white minority governments.

Shortly after Mozambique became independent, the Rhodesian Special Branch – aided by former members of the Portuguese Security Police – set up a guerrilla organisation called the **Mozambican National Resistance (Renamo)**. At that time, the Frelimo government was allowing Zimbabwean liberation movements to operate out of Manica, and Renamo was conceived as a fifth column to attack strategic bases in Mozambique. After Zimbabwe achieved independence in 1980, the South African Defence Force (SADF) took over the organisation and retrained its soldiers at Phalaborwa in northern Transvaal. With SADF backing, Renamo enjoyed considerable success – most notably by blowing up the Zambezi rail bridge in 1983 – and boosted its ranks by kidnapping young boys in rural areas. Assisted by various anti-Marxist American groups, South Africa managed to give its sponsored outlaws some sort of credibility by establishing Renamo offices in several capital cities, most of them manned by non-Africans. However, it has to be emphasised that Renamo did not have a coherent political philosophy until after the 1994 peace accord – it existed solely as South Africa's destabilisation arm.

On 16 March 1984, Mozambique and South Africa signed the **Nkomati Accord**, an agreement that neither country would support elements hostile to the other. Mozambique abided by the accord, but the SADF continued to give clandestine and possibly unofficial support to Renamo, helped by Malawi's President Banda, who allowed the organisation to operate out of his country. In September 1986, President Samora Machel of Mozambique, along with the presidents of Zimbabwe and Zambia, held a summit with Banda in Malawi and persuaded him to boot out Renamo. On the return flight to Maputo, Machel's plane was diverted by a South African radio signal and crashed in South African territory, killing everybody on board. Conspiracy theories abound, the most likely being that of South African sabotage. Indeed, after an inquiry launched in May 1998, South Africa's Truth and Reconciliation Committee decided that the incident raised questions that merited further investigation by an appropriate body.

In December 1986, Malawi signed a **mutual security agreement** with Mozambique's newly installed President Joaquim Chissano. Left with nowhere else to run, Renamo was forced to base itself permanently in Mozambique, where it took on a life of its own. Formerly, Renamo had limited its activities to occasional raids on strategic targets. From 1987 onwards, Renamo warbands roamed through the Mozambican countryside, supporting themselves with random raids on rural villages in what an official of the US State Department described as 'one of the most brutal holocausts against ordinary human beings since World War II'. By 1990, Frelimo's control barely extended beyond the main towns. It has been estimated that Renamo killed 100,000 Mozambicans during this period, and that as many as one-third of Mozambique's human population was displaced or forced into exile by the raiding warbands. The country's economic infrastructure, already crippled by the post-independence withdrawal of skills and funds, then by years of misplaced Marxist policies, was practically destroyed. Frelimo's social achievements were reduced to cinders along with roughly 2,500 primary schools and 800 clinics and hospitals. Teachers, doctors and educated administrative staff who hadn't managed to flee the country in time were systematically executed by Renamo.

In November 1990, pressured by overseas aid donors, Frelimo unveiled a new constitution denouncing its former Marxist policies and allowing for multi-party elections. However, the civil war continued into 1992, when the **Rome Conference** in October resulted in a ceasefire being signed by President Chissano and the Renamo leader Afonso Dhlakama. Mozambique's first democratic elections, which achieved an 85% turnout, were held in October 1994, with Chissano obtaining 53% of the presidential vote and Dhlakama 34%. Neither party achieved an absolute majority in the parliamentary elections, with Frelimo picking up 44% of the vote to Renamo's 38%. The strongest Renamo support came from the central provinces of Nampula, Zambézia, Sofala, Manica and Tete, where it attained a majority of parliamentary seats, while the northern and southern provinces went to Frelimo. Renamo's relative success in the election came as a surprise to many, considering its history and the fact that it had no real policies other than being anti-Frelimo. The good showing was probably due to Frelimo's low-key campaigning and failure to connect with the populace at grass-roots level rather than any inherent virtues seen to be attached to Renamo.

The remainder of the 1990s was characterised by an uneasy peace and the **jostling for political power** that invariably follows a protracted civil war. After the 1994 parliamentary election, Renamo asserted the right to the governorships in the provinces where it had won majorities, a claim that was swiftly rejected by Chissano. Frelimo further bolstered its authority in the May 1998 local elections – boycotted by Renamo and 16 other opposition parties – in which it won almost everything up for grabs. It came as little surprise, then, that in general elections held in December 1999, Chissano was re-elected president for a further five-year term, Frelimo won an outright majority of parliamentary seats, and Renamo contested the result on the basis that the voting had been fraudulent. Although international monitors declared that the election had been free and fair, Renamo threatened unilaterally to establish a parallel government in the central and northern regions unless the vote was recounted or new elections held. As Mozambique moved into the new century, however, it continued to be governed by a single authority which, although by no means perfect, could at least claim to exercise effective and legitimate control in a country where such a feat has never been easy to achieve.

THE 21ST CENTURY In February 2000, attention was detracted from the Frelimo/Renamo soap opera by the worst flooding in Mozambique for nearly 50 years. After weeks of heavy rains and a wet and windy **cyclone**, rivers in southern and central parts of the country burst their banks. In the resulting floods, hundreds lost their lives and thousands more their homes and livelihoods. Television sets the world over broadcast the unforgettably tragic images of families hanging from treetops, their homes submerged under muddy waters, as helicopters tried to save what was left of their broken lives. The rainy season the following year caused similar damage, although on a slightly lesser scale. The main areas of flooding were in the valleys of the Zambezi and Limpopo rivers, which had burst their banks after the combined effects of weeks of torrential rain and the 260km/h winds of Cyclone Eline. Floodplains along these two rivers were, at some points, 5km wide, and the water level was 7m higher than usual. The waters began to recede in the beginning of March, leaving the country to count the cost. Some 700 people had died and 500,000 more had been made homeless. Roads, bridges and railway lines had been destroyed, an estimated quarter of the country's agriculture had been damaged, and 80% of the livestock in Mozambique had perished. The floodwaters had also dislodged landmines laid during the civil war, repositioning them elsewhere.

Meanwhile President Chissano remained in power. In September 2004, having declared that he would not stand for a third term, he made a farewell tour of all the country's ten provinces, by which time over nine million people had registered to vote in the forthcoming election. In the national elections of December 2004, the Frelimo candidate Armando Guebuza was elected president with 64% of the vote, exactly twice as many as his Renamo rival Afonso Dhlakama. Guebuza was inaugurated as president in February 2005 and three months later his predecessor Chissano was named the UN's top official for Guinea Bissau. Renamo lost further ground in the 2009 presidential elections, in which Guebuza garnered 75% of the vote and 8.6% went to the Mozambique Democratic Movement (MDM), which splintered from Renamo in March 2009 under the leadership of the relatively young Mayor of Beira, Daviz Simango, leaving Dhlakama with a mere 16.4% of electoral support.

Municipal elections marked by violence in Sofala and other central provinces were held in November 2013. Officially boycotted by Renamo over disputes on the composition of certain electoral and supervisory bodies, armed elements loyal to Dhlakama bombastically declared the Rome ceasefire signed in 1992 to be null and void, returned to the bush in the lead-up to the vote, and began to ambush vehicles travelling on the EN1 through Sofala province. Over the course of several months, these unpredictable attacks claimed dozens of lives, both military and civilian, and seriously impacted north–south trade and transport within the country. The vote went ahead as planned and, suddenly finding themselves the only opposition party on the ballot, the elections were a strong showing for MDM, and they either took or held several significant mayorships including Beira, Nampula, Quelimane and Gurué.

While the attacks on road traffic in Sofala province continued despite a mandatory military escort for all vehicles, Renamo and government negotiators in Maputo reached a compromise, and attacks largely stopped by January 2014, when Renamo seemingly returned to the political process in order to contest the presidential election in October 2014 with perennial candidate and leader Afonso Dhlakama at the helm. Public opinion in Mozambique turned even more sharply against Renamo during the 2013 crisis, however, and the violence was largely seen as a desperate move from a greatly diminished party facing political irrelevance. Thus, it was expected that the ascendant MDM led by Daviz Simango presented the most credible challenge to Frelimo in the 2014 elections, but the ballots declared otherwise. When the results were totalled, Frelimo's candidate, defence minister Filipe Nysusi, collected 57% of the vote, while Renamo's Afonso Dhlakama gathered 36.6% and MDM's Daviz Simango came in with a mere 6.4%, – solidifying the continued, genuine popular support for Frelimo; the party has won every presidential vote since 1994.

Despite the national popular vote favouring Frelimo, such was not the case at the provincial level, where Renamo draws support from the economically disenfranchised public. Renamo quickly latched on to the disparity of the provincial polls to contest the election, claiming fraud, and subsequently proceeded to reignite localised attacks in Sofala, Tete and Zambézia. Renamo, refusing to acknowledge the results of the 2014 election, sought the governance of Manica, Sofala, Tete, Zambézia, Nampula and Niassa provinces – where Renamo outperformed Frelimo – not as an attempt to divide the country, but rather to shift the political power to the provincial level and break Frelimo's hold on political appointments.

By mid 2015, tensions were steeply rising, forcing around 12,000 Mozambicans to flee to Malawi to avoid the escalating violence. The prospect of a national unity government was suggested and declined by Dhlakama, reiterating the overall goal of a decentralised government versus the integration of Renamo officials into a Frelimo government. Renamo proposed a constitutional amendment that would restructure economics to the provincial level, granting 50% of the mining, gas and oil revenues to the provincial authorities. However, with the two parties refusing to make necessary concessions, the conflict continued, and by early 2016 a second mandatory, military escort convoy was instated for a 300km stretch in Manica province, from Vanduzi to the Luenha River, bordering Tete Province.

Finally, by mid 2016, international mediators were brought in to facilitate the negotiation process. The isolated armed conflict continued up to the end of December 2016, as negotiations reached their fifth and final round, with minimal progress being made towards an affable solution for both the opposing political parties. At that time, the international mediators were called off and a one-week truce was instituted as an act of good faith towards both parties reaching an agreeable solution. The truce, which involved the removal of convoys (box, page 216), was extended and remained active as of April 2017. A 'working group' consisting of international ambassadors was assembled to help resolve the military deadlock and to draft the necessary constitutional amendments that would facilitate the decentralisation of political power by the pressing deadline of municipal elections in 2018 and the general elections in 2019.

Encouragingly, on the whole, while travelling in the unaffected areas during the summer of 2016, essentially south of the Save River and north of the Zambezi, it was difficult to tell such a conflict persisted in the central region of the country. Overall, both parties are being pushed towards negotiating a peaceful solution, one that will address the economic stress the country is currently experiencing, bridging the gap between the village and national agenda.

Adding fuel to the political tensions and distrust of the government, in April 2016 a national secret debt of US$2.2 billion was discovered, forcing the IMF and other international donors to withdraw funding. By December 2016, the full picture was only beginning to emerge, indicating the debt was incurred illegally under the previous administration, under President Armando Guebuza, and involved the use of three state-owned companies fronting as fishing-related businesses in order secretly to finance 'strategic military' spending.

Although Mozambique has enjoyed a high level of stability since the civil war ended, the peace has been punctuated by episodes of localised violence, such as the aforementioned Renamo attacks in 2013. Prior to that, in September 2010, Maputo experienced a two-day standstill after police opened fire on a mass protest against an official rise in bread prices, leading to widespread vandalism and looting, and at least 14 deaths. The riot did encourage the government to announce a subsidy on bread prices, and Maputo had all but returned to normal within 48 hours of the riots starting. Nevertheless, growing **public dissatisfaction** at rising living costs (30% inflation expected) seems inevitable in a country ranking 180 out of 188 for human development, where 66% of the population is under 25 years of age, the unemployment rate hovers around 40%, food production has yet to reach subsistence levels since the agricultural sector collapsed in the civil war and recent years of drought, and the currency has depreciated against that of its major trading partner (South Africa) to the order of more than 50% in 12 months. The currency is expected to devalue by at least 100%.

Overall, the impending wealth of the country's extractive industry has the potential to boost Mozambique's stability. However, as long as Mozambique carries an unsustainable amount of debt and the general public continues to be marginalised by governmental mismanagement, general economic and political stability remains a goal for the future, with no indication of significant relief until post-2020.

GOVERNMENT AND POLITICS

Mozambique is a multi-party democracy led by an elected president. In practice, it has been a two-party state for most of the post-civil-war period, dominated by the struggle between Frelimo and Renamo. The former, which has held power since independence in 1975, has increased its stranglehold on power over the course of the four elections since 1994, squeezing through with slightly more than 50% of the vote in 1994 and 1999, but gaining 64% of the vote in 2004, 75% in 2009 and dropping in 2014 to 57%. Frelimo's dominance will continue as Renamo's influence wanes, but the MDM has grown exponentially since its establishment in 2009 and it is now Frelimo's most significant electoral challenger, looking likely to replace the fading Renamo as Mozambique's official opposition in the coming years.

A political force that shouldn't be ignored is that of the traditional chiefs, many of whom still wield considerable clout. Indeed in rural areas it's not unknown for the traditional chief to be the de facto power of his area, with the local political appointees being largely ignored.

ECONOMY

Mozambique is a country with tremendous economic potential. There is no shortage of arable land, water resources or woodland. Extensive tracts of tropical hardwoods still exist in many places which, if managed responsibly, offer economic possibilities. The country has considerable mineral reserves, and modern ports linked to a rail network constructed for the transportation of goods to and from the states of southern central Africa. The sea has plentiful supplies of fish, and the islands and coastline are ideally suited to tourism. This economic potential has never been developed to the full, either in Portuguese colonial times or since.

During the civil war, Mozambique's economic development was predictably sluggish, and a shortage of skilled labour combined with Frelimo's rigid, centrally planned economic policies didn't exactly help the situation. Since the ceasefire in 1992, however, **agricultural production** has been increasing gradually, and Frelimo has instigated market-orientated reforms, including privatisation in several important industrial sectors. In June 1999, the International Monetary Fund (IMF) and World Bank agreed to reduce Mozambique's public debt by two-thirds, which, along with other debt-relief programmes, augured well for the country's continued economic improvement. Then came the floods in February 2000 (page 17), which washed away over 100,000ha of crops, killed more than 40,000 cattle and caused considerable infrastructural damage. The extent to which the country's economic recovery will continue following this setback is dependent on the foreign assistance made available to repair the damage.

The Mozambican economy in 2016 was dominated by commerce and services, accounting for 54.9%. Next was agriculture, with 25.3%, followed by industry at 19.8%. In practice, however, agriculture is the main preoccupation of most Mozambicans. An estimated 81% of Mozambique's population relies on subsistence agriculture and fishing to survive, although the enduring effects of the war, droughts and floods continue to hinder the country's efforts to regain self-sufficiency in food production. The **main export crops** are prawns, cotton, cashew nuts, sugarcane, citrus and copra, while the principal subsistence crops are cassava, corn, beans and wet rice grown in the floodplains of the country's many rivers.

The third major contributor to the economy is **industry**, primarily food processing, beverages, tobacco, textiles, edible oils, soaps, cement, aluminium, bulk electricity and other consumer goods. During Portuguese times, Mozambique was the fourth industrial power in Africa although, considering the relatively low rate of industrialisation of the continent, this is no great claim. In the first ten years after independence the country's industrial sector slowed at an alarming pace, primarily because most whites had fled the country in fear of Frelimo and the uncertainty of its policies during the transitional phase to independence. Companies were deserted by their owners, machinery often destroyed.

The **exodus of the settler population** meant the loss of management expertise, skilled workers and capital, and by the end of the 1980s industry had ground to an almost complete halt. Frelimo embarked on a policy of privatisation after the end of the civil war in an attempt to kick-start the industrial sector, and during the 1990s hundreds of enterprises were bought by private investors. Past problems have doomed some of these privatisations to failure; others – particularly those backed by foreign investment – have been more successful.

A particular growth area at the moment is **mining and heavy industry**. Mozambique lays claim to the world's largest ruby, titanium, high-grade graphite, and natural gas deposits. Several billion-dollar projects have been set up in recent years – the Mozal aluminium smelter project in Maputo, the Heavy Sands ore extraction project in Nampula Province, the Rovuma Basin gas field in offshore Cabo Delgado, the graphite and ruby mines in nearby Montepuez (Cabo Delgado Province) and the coal mines in Tete are all major projects with significant levels of foreign investment, predominantly from South Africa, Brazil, China, Australia and the USA. Mozambique also has the only bauxite mine in southern Africa. This influx of foreign capital has led to a building boom across the country, most visibly in cities such as Tete, Pemba and Maputo. Another sector showing considerable growth is the **provision of electricity to neighbouring countries** from the generators of Cahora Bassa (also in Tete). There is some debate about the long-term value of such projects to the economy as a whole, and it has been suggested that they may stifle the development of other sectors by pushing up the exchange rate and sucking up huge amounts of the country's limited resources.

FOREIGN INVESTMENT The Mozambican economy is dependent on foreign investment, and the government is trying hard to improve conditions and attract foreign money once again. In Maputo there is a chamber of commerce.

Câmara de Comércio de Moçambique [95 B5] (*452 Rua Mateus Sansão Muthemba, CP 1836, Maputo;* m *82 877 8410;* e *info@ccmoz.org.mz;* f *CamaraDeComercioDeMocambique*). Private banks, both local and foreign, are now permitted to operate in the country, and private farmland that was brought under state control during the revolutionary years is now being returned to its Portuguese and South African owners. There are 'industrial free zones' in Maputo, Beira, Mocuba and Nacala intended to encourage investors to come to the country. In these zones, certain taxes and duties are waived in favour of a small royalty on sales.

Certain businesses, previously state-owned, have been offered for sale by tender. In 1994, for instance, a short list of about a dozen enterprises covered a range of industries from plastics to pasta, from transport to tea – over US$60 million of sales turnover. Arguably the largest carrots for foreign investors are the transportation 'corridors' linking the landlocked countries of southern Africa to the Mozambican ports of Maputo, Beira and Nacala (box, page 58). In January 2000, for example, a consortium led by South African, Portuguese and US companies was granted a concession to manage the port of Nacala and the Malawi–Nacala railway, and negotiations for similar concessions for the Maputo and Beira corridors were also under way. In 2013, a concession was granted to Italian–Thai Development Mozambique, of which CFM is part owner, to build a new, standard-gauge railway line between Tete and Macuse, in Zambézia province (35km north of Quelimane), in addition to a deep-water offshore port, but falling coal prices and obscure funding have delayed construction. Inevitably, fears have been expressed in the country of a sell-out of Mozambican resources to foreign countries. But without foreign investment Mozambique will have very little chance of ever getting back on its feet economically.

Without doubt, the most influential of all Mozambique's trading partners is South Africa, whose businesspeople seem to be buying up everything – factories, mines, breweries, hotels, transport concerns and so on.

FOREIGN EXCHANGE During Portuguese colonial times the main sources of foreign exchange were the export of agricultural produce; rail transport and provision of ports for South Africa, Northern Rhodesia (Zambia), Southern Rhodesia (Zimbabwe), Nyasaland (Malawi) and Swaziland; income from the supply of manpower to South African and Rhodesian mines and plantations; and tourism from South Africa and Rhodesia.

Except for agricultural exports, these sources of income have since more or less disappeared, although tourism is slowly beginning to re-emerge, particularly south of Beira. Rail transportation to neighbouring countries is now only possible on a small scale as a result of the civil war. After the government's severing of trade links with South Africa at the beginning of the 1980s, South Africa terminated the existing agreement on the employment of Mozambican workers by the South African mines. This agreement between Portugal and South Africa, dating from 1928, had been particularly lucrative for Mozambique since it meant that 60% of the salaries were paid at a fixed gold price.

Nowadays, since the rehabilitation of the Cahora Bassa hydro-electric plant in 1997 and the beginning of construction of two new coal-powered plants near Tete, some 70km downstream of Cahora Bassa, as well as a floating power plant in Nacala harbour, Mozambique is beginning to earn a considerable amount of its foreign exchange from the export of electricity to neighbouring countries.

NATURAL RESOURCES During colonial times there was almost no exploitation of the country's large mineral deposits; it is estimated that more geological investigations were conducted in Mozambique between 1977 and 1983 than during the entire colonial period. In the course of these investigations, rich deposits of coal, salt, iron ore and phosphate, as well as gold, tantalum, chromium, copper, bauxite, nickel and many other minerals, were discovered. At present, coal, salt, graphite and rubies are mined in significant quantities, although bauxite is starting to be exploited at commercially viable levels. Other resources with potential include titanium, the world's largest reserve of which was discovered in Gaza Province in 1999, and gas, found principally in Inhambane Province. Once again, the exploitation of these natural resources is dependent on large amounts of foreign investment.

FACIM TRADE FAIR Mozambique's window on the world, economically speaking, is the Feira Internacional de Maputo, or FACIM. It is the only real trade fair in Mozambique and attracts considerable international participation. It is held just outside Maputo annually towards the end of August. For further information, contact **FACIM/Maputo Trade Fair** [91 F7] (*1008 Av 25 de Setembro, Maputo;* \ *21 307257/8;* e *info@facim.org.mz;* w *facim.org.mz*).

TOURISM Prior to independence, Mozambique was one of the most popular tourist destinations in southern Africa. In those days, thousands of Rhodesians and South Africans flocked to the beaches and offshore islands in the south, and Gorongosa National Park was one of the region's major attractions. The bottom fell out of the tourism industry after independence, and the outbreak of civil war hardly helped to bring the tourists back. The statistics speak for themselves: in 1972, 292,000 people visited Mozambique; by 1981, this number had fallen to just 1,000. It was never in much doubt, however, that once a semblance of stability had returned to the country, tourism would again play an important economic role. Sure enough, by the end of the 1990s, tourism was the fastest-growing sector of the Mozambican economy, and it is still growing rapidly today.

As an indication of the importance attached to encouraging this industry, the post of Minister for Tourism was created following the 1999 election. Then came the National Policy of Tourism, outlining the way in which the government would like to see tourism develop in the near future. The areas prioritised for immediate 'exploration' were, predictably, the beach resorts near Maputo and Beira.

The national parks are gradually being developed, with most activity at the time of writing being based around Limpopo and Bazaruto in the south, Gorongosa in the middle of the country, and Niassa and the Quirimba in the north.

PEOPLE

Over 99% of the people in Mozambique are African, which stands to reason. The remainder of the population is made up of Europeans (mainly Portuguese), Indians, east Asians and *mestiços* (people of mixed African-European ancestry). As in most of Africa, the tribes living in Mozambique share cultural and linguistic similarities with their counterparts in neighbouring states.

The basic **tribal pattern** in Mozambique is a result of pre-19th-century migrations from the north and west, and the fleeing of people in the early 19th century from the violent Zulu Kingdom in South Africa. This has left a north–south split, with the Zambezi River as the dividing line. The tribes north of the Zambezi are predominantly agriculturists and have matrilineal societies. The two largest tribes, the Macua and the Lomwe, who are concentrated in Zambézia, Nampula, Niassa and Cabo Delgado provinces, together make up about 35% of the total Mozambican population. Another northern tribe worth knowing is the Makonde, famous for its art and its wooden statues and masks, who live on both the Mozambican and Tanzanian sides of the Rovuma River. The tribes south of the Zambezi River are mainly cattle-rearing and have patrilineal societies. The most important is the Thonga, the country's second-largest ethnic group, who are concentrated in the area south of the Save River and make up around 23% of the population. The majority of Africans in Maputo are Thonga. Meanwhile, most of Sofala and Manica provinces are inhabited by Shona, a tribe whose numbers have grown due to migrations into Mozambique of Shona from Zimbabwe and South Africa. In addition to the tribal differences north and south of the Zambezi River, a third distinct region is formed by the Zambezi Valley itself, which has historically been influenced by the Portuguese and Arabs who used the river to access the interior.

The **population of Mozambique** was estimated at 28 million in 2016, and is expected to exceed 30 million by 2020. The average life expectancy is around 55 years. Approximately 67% of the population live in rural areas, but there is an ongoing trend of gravitation to the cities.

Mozambique has one of the lowest population densities in southern and eastern Africa, currently standing at roughly 35 inhabitants per km². Excluding the desert countries of Namibia and Botswana, Zambia is the only country in the region more thinly populated than Mozambique. It has been suggested that the low population density was due to the protracted civil war. In fact, the interior of Mozambique has always been sparsely populated, and the population has increased more than 2½ times in the 40-plus years since independence. The most densely populated provinces are Zambézia, Nampula and Maputo.

Minority population groups include Indians and Pakistanis, particularly around Nampula, and Portuguese, who are concentrated in the cities of Maputo and Beira.

LANGUAGE

Portuguese is the official language of Mozambique, but it is generally only spoken by the 45% or thereabouts of the population who have been to school. This creates serious problems: the economic, business and legal language is Portuguese; tuition in high schools, colleges and universities is exclusively in Portuguese and thus debars the many who have had no chance to learn it in primary education; many of the younger people grew up in refugee camps and have had little formal education, let alone in what is essentially a foreign tongue, and about 40% of the population are illiterate, despite considerable efforts by themselves and by the government. The problems with education, both in languages and in general, have become so acute that some schools have started to work a shift system: children of one age group go to school every day for a few hours in the morning, children of another in the afternoon.

All of Mozambique's **indigenous languages** belong to the Bantu family. The root Bantu language is thought to have spread through eastern and southern Africa during the first half of the first millennium AD, since when it has diversified into many linguistic subfamilies and several hundred languages and closely related dialects. Roughly 40 distinct languages and dialects are spoken in Mozambique. The various dialects of Macua-Lomwe are spoken only north of the Zambezi, but they nevertheless account for the home language of around 25% of the total population of Mozambique. In the south, the majority of people speak dialects of Tsonga, a language also spoken in South Africa. Various Tsonga and Shona dialects are spoken in central Mozambique.

In northern coastal regions, some people speak **KiSwahili**, a variant Bantu language with some Arabic influences that became the lingua franca of coastal trading centres between Mogadishu and Sofala in medieval times.

Visitors who are unfamiliar with Portuguese and Bantu languages will find that most Mozambicans are extremely helpful and will do what they can to overcome your language barrier. The mixing of the people during the war has made them adept at getting along and making themselves understood in a variety of communication forms: a bit of gesturing and drawing in the dirt with a stick can overcome many barriers. Often, people will simply lead you to where you want to go. For practical information on speaking Portuguese, see pages 374–7.

Concern has recently been expressed in Lisbon that the end of apartheid and the democratisation of South Africa will lead to the **anglicisation** of Mozambique. Since Portuguese is not an indigenous language and all of Mozambique's neighbours and SADC partners (Angola excepted) use English as an official language, as do most donor countries, there would be a certain logic to replacing Portuguese with English as the main language of education and government. In recognition of the importance of English to furthering international trade, English is now being taught a few years earlier at school than it has been in the past, but all official government business is still conducted in Portuguese.

RELIGION

About 52% of Mozambicans are Christian, with Catholicism being followed by 28% of the population and various Protestant denominations by 12%; 18% of the population is Muslim. Christianity is more common in urban areas, while the Muslim faith is predominantly confined to the north. Many Mozambicans either adhere to traditional beliefs or have a dualistic faith that integrates Christian/Muslim beliefs with traditional animism or pantheism. Traditional faiths and medicines were suppressed as backward and unscientific during the communist era, but are now enjoying something of a resurgence, encouraged by the resumption of authority of many local chiefs in the absence of any other effective management. Traditional healers are also enjoying a comeback as part of this cultural renaissance.

CULTURE

ART Maputo was a hotbed of artistic creativity in the decade following independence, a scene centred upon the Centro de Estudos Culturais. Artistic activity was stifled during the long years of war that followed, and it has never picked up in quite the same way again, though the best of the Makonde-influenced artworks sold at craft markets throughout the country are of a far higher standard than the tourist tat available in most African countries. There are also many quality murals in the country's larger towns and cities, often depicting events from the liberation or civil wars. It seems Mozambique is on the verge of an artistic resurgence once again, especially with the opening of the Chinese-financed National School of Visual Arts (ENAV) in 2010. Many contemporary artists are working to express a modern sense what it means to be Mozambican, in particular painter Noel Langa and sculptor Gonçalo Mabunda. Langa's latest work is aimed at honouring Mozambique's vibrant, cultural roots; whereas Mabunda's striking sculptures encapsulate the country's tumultuous yet tenacious existence through repurposed weapons of Mozambique's war for independence and civil war.

Visitors interested in the visual arts should visit the Museu Nacional das Artes, the Cultural Franco-Mozambicain and Núcleo de Arte in Maputo, as well as the house of the late Alberto Chissano in nearby Matola. Born in 1934, Alberto Chissano is arguably the finest sculptor to have worked in Mozambique, a former soldier and miner who first exhibited at the Núcleo de Arte in 1964 and won several awards for his wood and stone sculptures prior to his death in 1994. His contemporary Malangatana Ngwenya, a politicised painter and poet who mostly exhibited under his first name only, was born in the far south of the country in 1964 and studied art in Lisbon in 1971 following 18 months' imprisonment by the colonial secret police for his involvement in Frelimo. Malangatana painted several of the war murals that adorn Mozambique's cities, and in more recent years he was the founder of the

Mozambican Peace Movement and several cultural institutions prior to his death in Portugal in January 2011.

FICTION Naturally the bulk of Mozambican fiction has been written in Portuguese, and until recently comparatively little has been available in English. This is now starting to change.

The Mozambican writer Mia Couto is an international literary star whose books have been published in more than 20 countries. Several of his novels, including *Under the Frangipani*, *A River Called Time*, *The Last Flight of the Flamingo* and *Sleepwalking Land*, are available in excellent English translations by David Brookshaw from Serpent's Tail in London. In 2013, Couto won the Neustadt International Prize for Literature, the first Mozambican author to do so, and as such his novels are essential reading for anyone planning to visit Mozambique. *Neighbours: The Story of a Murder*, by the highly regarded – if less famous – Lilia Momplé, is also available in English from Penguin Classics.

Paulina Chiziane was the first Mozambican woman to publish a novel. She has been translated into numerous languages and is well known in both Europe and parts of Asia. Her comic novel *Niketche: A Story of Polygamy* was finally published in an English translation in 2010.

Several of Luis Bernado Honwana's stories have been translated and included in anthologies, and another name to look out for is Nelson Saute, translations of whose work can't be far off.

Mozambican **poets** José Craveirinha and Rui Knopfli have an international reputation, and their anthologies shouldn't be hard to track down.

The Swedish novelist, Henning Mankell, spent a great deal of time in Mozambique prior to his death in 2015. His novel about Maputo street children, *Chronicler of the Winds*, is easily obtainable in English. His two novels *Secrets in the Fire* and *Playing with Fire* are based on the true story of a young girl growing up during the war who is disabled by a landmine.

There are also foreign writers who live in Mozambique, including the Nigerian Nobel Laureate Wole Soyinka who wrote the poem 'Ogun Abibiman', based on Samora Machel's 1976 declaration putting Mozambique on a war footing with white Rhodesia.

Meet Me in Mozambique by Montserrat author E A Markham is partially set in the idealism of pre-revolutionary Mozambique.

British author Lisa St Aubin de Terán lives in rural Nampula Province running an NGO. Her book *Mozambique Mysteries*, a memoir of the culture of that region, was published in September 2007 by Virago.

You should be able to get most of the above from any good bookshop, but an excellent source is the **Africa Book Centre**, which (as the name suggests) covers the whole continent. A browse of their website (w *africabookcentre.com*) is recommended.

MUSIC Mozambique has long suffered from a lack of professional recordings of its music, but this is thankfully beginning to change. Long a crossroads of culture, trade and customs, traditional Mozambican music is as diverse as the country itself, with the Swahili-influenced north, Shona central regions and Tonga south all deeply connected to their neighbours by culture and kin. Thus, as is often the case in Africa, Mozambique's musical styles don't correspond neatly with its national borders, and many of Mozambique's favourite musicians have deep ties to other countries in the region (ie: South Africa), or throughout the Lusophone world, such as Brazil and Angola. For aspiring ethnomusicologists and fans of traditional styles, pioneering field recorder **Hugh Tracy** visited Mozambique in the course of his African travels where he collected countless hours of folk and traditional music, some of which is now available on CD. *Southern Mozambique* showcases indigenous styles typical of the region, including the magnificent xylophone orchestras of the Chopi, an ethnic group native to Inhambane province. *Forgotten Guitars from Mozambique* chronicles the acoustic stylings of itinerant miners returning from South Africa in the 1950s with a new instrument under their arms, and a new beat in their hearts – one that would soon conquer Mozambique's airwaves and dance floors.

That style was *marrabenta*, and it quickly became Mozambique's most beloved popular music, its guitar-based groove somewhere between Congolese *soukous*, Zimbabwean *sungura* and the Tonga roots of its practitioners. Marrabenta traces its origins to early/mid-20th-century Lourenço Marques (now Maputo), and though the style has changed a great deal since then, it's still popular in urban centres throughout the country. Commercially available marrabenta recordings are sadly few and far between, though, and the early years of the style are largely unavailable, save on locally released 7″ records that occasionally pop up as collectors' items on eBay. Perhaps the most striking example of this paucity of recordings is Dilon Djindji, one of the 'grand old men' of marrabenta, who, despite performing since the age of 15, released his first studio album, *Dilon*, in 2002, at the tender age of 75! *The Rough Guide to Marrabenta Mozambique* is an excellent introduction to the style, containing classics as well as new songs recorded for the collection. Other artists to look out for include Orchestra Marrabenta Star de Moçambique, Wazimbo and Fany Pfumo.

What you're really likely to hear on the streets of Mozambique today, though, is a **variety of styles** from southern Africa, namely South Africa and Angola. From across the border in South Africa, you'll encounter *kwaito* and house, interrelated genres of pulsating electronic music popular with DJs throughout Mozambique for their soulful vocals, floor-shaking beats and danceable tempos. Pushing the beats per minute even higher is *kuduro*, a massively frenetic dance craze out of Angola known for its blistering tempos, acrobatic dance moves and rowdy chanted lyrics. *Kizomba* is another popular genre in Lusophone Africa, but considerably more smooth and sensual than its *kuduro* cousin, taking its cues from Latin styles such as *bachata* and *zouk*. Finally, *pandza* is perhaps Mozambique's newest style, incorporating elements of marrabenta, dancehall reggae, *kuduro* and more into an eminently danceable melange that's been keeping butts shaking across Mozambique for the past several years. Keep your ears open for MC Roger, Mr Cizer Boss, Ziqo, Gabriela, Lizha James, Anita Macuacua or Mr Bow, or simply ask any of Maputo's countless CD vendors which tracks you should be checking for this month.

2

Natural History

Unlike most other countries in subequatorial Africa, Mozambique is not primarily or even secondarily a safari destination. Although more than 10% of the country has been designated as some form of protected area, little of this land is readily accessible to visitors, and the once-abundant wildlife was severely depleted during the long years of civil war and associated poaching (the elephant population, for instance, dropped from around 65,000 to 15,000 between 1970 and 1995, though it has increased steadily in subsequent years).

Today, the country has seven national parks, of which Quirimba and Bazaruto are primarily marine reserves, while Zinave and Banhine have very limited facilities and support little wildlife. There are also eight national or special reserves, but most of these are remote and poorly developed. However, facilities in certain reserves and parks have improved greatly in the past few years, and Mozambique does now offer a few decent wildlife-viewing opportunities, most notably at the rehabilitated and relatively accessible Gorongosa National Park. Also worth considering are the vast Niassa Reserve (for self-drivers), the much more accessible Limpopo National Park (a Mozambican extension of South Africa's famous Kruger Park), the Maputo Special Reserve south of the capital, and (especially for backpackers) the Chimanimani National Reserve.

VEGETATION

Most of Mozambique is covered in savannah, a loosely applied term that can be used to cover practically any wooded habitat that doesn't have a closed canopy. Characteristically, the Mozambican savannah is much more densely wooded than similar habitats in Zimbabwe and South Africa, and the trees are much taller. Brachystegia woodland, named after the most common tree, is the main savannah type throughout northern Mozambique, in the Zimbabwean and Zambian border areas, and along the coastal belt north of the Limpopo. In total, it covers about 70% of the country, but is replaced by mopane woodland in drier areas such as Tete Province south of the Zambezi and the interior of Gaza Province, and by acacia woodland in parts of the south and along the main watercourses of the north.

The coastal beaches are typically covered in dense, scrubby thickets and palm groves, the latter particularly impressive around Inhambane and Quelimane. The floodplains of major rivers such as the Limpopo, Zambezi and Pungué, and the area near Lake Chilwa on the Malawian border, are covered in alluvial grasslands

MOZAMBIQUE WILDLIFE

For more on wildlife in Mozambique, check out Bradt's *Southern African Wildlife*. See page xi for a special discount offer.

and marshes. The largest alluvial plain in Mozambique is the Zambezi Delta, a vast marshy area of thick grassland and borassus palms that stretches for 120km along the coast and covers an area of roughly 8,000km^2.

Only a tiny portion of Mozambique is covered in true forest. There are rainforests on the upper slopes of a few mountains, notably Mount Gorongosa in Sofala, the Chimanimani and Inyanga highlands on the Zimbabwean border, and mounts Murrumbala, Namuli, Mabu and Chiperone in western Zambézia. Dry lowland forest occurs in patches in some coastal areas, notably in northern Cabo Delgado and around Dondo near Beira, while several rivers support thin belts of riparian forest.

MAMMALS

Several useful field guides to African mammals are available for the purpose of identification. What most such guides lack is detailed distribution details for individual countries, so the following notes should be seen as a Mozambique-specific supplement to a regional or continental field guide.

Leopard

PREDATORS A firm safari favourite, the **lion**, Africa's largest cat, is a sociable animal that lives in family prides of up to 15 animals and tends to hunt by night, favouring large and medium-sized antelopes. Though widespread in Mozambique (a recent survey suggests a national population in excess of 2,000), it is likely to be seen by visitors only in Gorongosa National Park and, to a lesser extent, the Niassa Reserve. The smaller, solitary and more secretive **leopard**, with its distinctive black-on-gold rosetted coat, is also still widespread in Mozambique, and far more numerous than the lion, but sightings are very uncommon. As far as we are aware, the more streamlined **cheetah**, a plains dweller with distinctive black 'tear marks' running down its face, is more or less extinct in Mozambique. Several smaller species of cat, such as **caracal**, **serval** and **African wild cat**, occur in Mozambique, but they are rarely seen on account of their nocturnal habits.

Cheetah

Caracal

The largest indigenous canine species, the **African hunting dog**, is unmistakable on account of its blotchy black, brown and cream coat. Hunting dogs live and hunt in packs, normally about ten animals strong. The introduction to Africa of canine diseases such as rabies has caused a severe decline in hunting dog numbers in recent years, and this endangered species has been on the IUCN Red List of Threatened Animals since 1984. Mozambique is one of the most important strongholds for this rare creature, which is still quite numerous in the northerly Niassa Reserve and Quirimbas National Park. The more lightly built **side-striped** and **black-backed jackals**, mostly nocturnal in habit and generally seen either singly or in pairs, are widespread in brachystegia and acacia habitats respectively.

African hunting dog

Spotted hyena

The **spotted hyena** is a large, bulky, widespread predator with a sloping back, black-on-brown lightly spotted coat and doglike face. Contrary to popular myth, it is not a type of dog, nor is it exclusively a scavenger or hermaphroditic. The Viverridae family comprises a group of small predators that includes **mongooses** and the catlike **civets** and **genets**. At least ten mongoose species have been recorded in Mozambique, most of which can be readily observed in the right habitat. The African civet, tree civet and large-spotted genet are all present too, but they are rarely seen except on night drives in Gorongosa National Park or the Niassa Reserve. Four representatives of the Mustelidae family occur: the **honey-badger**, **Cape clawless otter**, **spotted necked otter** and **striped polecat**.

PRIMATES The most common primate in Mozambique is probably the **vervet monkey**, a small, grey animal with a black face and, in the male, blue genitals.

Vervet monkeys live in large troops in most habitats except desert and evergreen forest. The closely related **samango** or **blue monkey** is a less common and more cryptically marked species associated with evergreen and riverine forests, as well

Vervet monkey

Samango monkey

Bushbaby

as coastal thicket. The **yellow baboon** is common in northern Mozambique, while the greyer **chacma baboon** occurs in the south, with the population in Gorongosa possibly representing an intermediate form. The wide-eyed bushbaby, a small nocturnal primate that is heard more often than seen, can often be located at night by tracing its distinctive, piercing call to a tree and then using a flashlight to pick up its eyes.

ANTELOPE A number of large antelope species occur in Mozambique, with the greatest variety in Gorongosa, Niassa and Maputo Special Reserve. These include the **eland**, Africa's largest antelope, and the handsomely marked **greater kudu**, immediately recognisable by the male's immense spiralling horns. Gorongosa is one of the best places in Africa to see the striking **sable antelope**, the male of which has large, backward-curving horns and a glossy black coat. Easily seen near water in several reserves, the **common waterbuck** has a shaggy coat and a distinctive white horseshoe on its rump. Other large antelope associated mainly with the northern reserves are the closely related and

Eland

Greater kudu

DANGEROUS ANIMALS

Contrary to popular belief, most wild animals fear us more than we fear them, and their normal response to human contact is to flee. That said, a number of fatalities have been caused by such incidents.

The need for caution is greatest near water. Hippos are responsible for more human fatalities than any other large mammal, not because they are aggressive but because they panic when something comes between them and the safety of the water. Never walk between a hippo and water, and never walk along riverbanks or through reed beds, especially in overcast weather or at dusk or dawn, when hippos are grazing.

Watch out, too, for crocodiles. Only a very large crocodile is likely to attack a person, and then only in the water or right on the shore. Near settlements, you can be fairly sure any such beast will have been consigned to its maker, so the risk is greatest away from human habitation. It is also near water that you might unwittingly come upon a bushbuck; though normally placid, it has a reputation as the most dangerous African antelope when cornered.

There are areas where hikers may still stumble across an elephant or a buffalo, the most dangerous of Africa's terrestrial herbivores. Elephants almost invariably mock charge and indulge in some trumpeting before attacking in earnest. Provided you back off at the first sign, they are unlikely to take further notice of you. If you see them before they see you, give them a wide berth.

If an animal charges you, the safest course of action is to climb the nearest tree. Black rhinos can charge without provocation, but they're too rare in Mozambique to be of great concern. Elephants are the only animals to pose a danger to a vehicle – if an elephant doesn't want you to pass, back off and wait until it has moved away before you try again. Leave your engine running when close to an elephant, and don't get boxed in between an elephant and another vehicle.

Common reedbuck

equally doleful-looking **Niassa wildebeest** and paler and more lightly built **Lichtenstein's hartebeest**.

The most widespread medium-sized antelope is the thicket- and forest-associated **bushbuck**. The male has a dark chestnut coat marked with white stripes and spots, while the female is lighter with similar markings, giving it an appearance much like a European deer. The closely related **nyala** is a southern African species that might be seen in well-wooded habitats as far north as Gorongosa. The **impala**, a gregarious, gazelle-like antelope that is numerous in savannah, has a bright chestnut coat, distinctive white-and-black stripes on its rump, and (male only) large lyre-shaped horns. The **southern reedbuck**, a lightly coloured, somewhat nondescript antelope almost always associated with water, is particularly common in Maputo Special Reserve.

Impala

Smaller antelope include the **klipspringer**, which has a grey, bristly coat and lives exclusively on rocky outcrops where it displays a goat-like ability to jump and climb up almost vertical rock faces. The grassland-dwelling **oribi** is a tan-coloured antelope with a white belly, black tail and a diagnostic black patch beneath its ears. **Livingstone's**

Vervet monkeys and baboons have become pests at some campsites. Feeding them is highly irresponsible, since it encourages them to scavenge and may lead to their being shot. Vervet monkeys are too small to be more than a nuisance, but baboons have killed children and maimed adults with their teeth. Do not tease or underestimate them. If primates are hanging around a campsite and you wander off leaving fruit in your tent, don't expect the tent to be standing when you return.

Most large predators stay clear of humans and are only likely to kill accidentally or in self-defence. Lions are arguably the exception. Should you encounter one on foot, don't run, since this is likely to trigger the instinct to give chase. Of the other cats, cheetahs represent no threat and leopards only really attack when cornered. Hyenas are potentially dangerous, but in practice are more likely to slink off into the shadows when disturbed.

A slight but real danger when sleeping in the bush without a tent is that a passing hyena or lion might investigate a hairy object sticking out of a sleeping bag, and decapitate you out of predatorial curiosity. In areas where large predators are common, a sealed tent practically guarantees your safety – but don't sleep with your head sticking out and don't put meat in the tent.

All manner of venomous snakes occur in Mozambique, but they generally slither away when they sense the vibrations of a person walking. For more details, see pages 36–7.

When all is said and done, the most dangerous animal in Africa, exponentially a greater threat than everything mentioned above, is the *anopheles* mosquito, which carries the malaria parasite. Humans – particularly behind a steering wheel – run them a close second!

suni is a tiny grey antelope that lives in coastal scrub. The **grey** or **common duiker**, a greyish antelope with a white belly and a tuft between its small horns, is widespread, while the smaller and more beautiful **Natal red duiker** and **blue duiker** are confined almost exclusively to forest interiors.

Klipspringer

OTHER UNGULATES Despite the heavy poaching of the war years, the **African elephant** is still reasonably common in the Gorongosa and Quirimba national parks as well as the Niassa and Maputo Special Reserve. **Black** and **white rhinos** are officially extinct, but as fences between the Limpopo and Kruger national parks fall into disrepair (they will eventually drop altogether) it seems likely that some individuals will cross into the Mozambican part of this transfrontier park. **Hippos** have also suffered from poaching, but they are easily seen in the Niassa and Maputo Special Reserve, as well as in Gorongosa. **African buffalo**, **Burchell's zebra** and **southern giraffe** are also present in some reserves. Two swine species are common: the diurnal and

Natal red duiker

Black rhino

easily seen **warthog**, which has a uniform bristly grey coat and the distinctive habit of holding its tail erect when it runs, and the more secretive and nocturnal **bushpig**.

BIRDS *With Vincent Parker, Keith Barnes and Josh Engel*

The exact number of birds recorded in Mozambique is open to debate, with various sources listing between 750 and 800 species, a discrepancy attributable to various controversial taxonomic splits as well as one's acceptance of vagrant and uncorroborated records. A useful checklist can be found online at w birdlist.org/mozambique.htm and a good field guide will help identify most of the birds you see. This list includes one full endemic, the *Namuli apalis*, along with the olive-headed weaver, which of all the bird species resident in southern Africa has possibly been seen by the fewest birdwatchers (a patch of tall brachystegia woodland just south of the town of Panda, 60km inland of Inharrime in Inhambane Province, is the only locality in the region where the birder has a chance of seeing it).

Mozambique is an important destination for southern African birders. Of the 850-odd bird species that are resident in or regular migrants to Africa south of the Zambezi, roughly 30 have been recorded only in Mozambique or else have their main concentration there. Some of the birds fitting into one of these categories are the Madagascar squacco heron, eastern saw-wing swallow, Böhm's bee-eater, palm-nut vulture, silvery-cheeked hornbill, green tinkerbird, green-backed woodpecker, green-headed oriole, tiny greenbul, stripe-cheeked greenbul, white-chested alethe, Swynnerton's robin, East Coast akalat (Gunning's robin), Chirinda apalis, black-headed apalis, moustached grass warbler, Robert's warbler, mashona hyliota, yellow-breasted hyliota, black-and-white flycatcher, Woodward's batis, pale batis, Livingstone's flycatcher, Achieta's tchagra, chestnut-fronted helmet-shrike, red-headed quelea, cardinal quelea, olive-headed weaver, lesser seedcracker, yellow-bellied waxbill and lemon-breasted canary.

Visitors to southern Mozambique seldom stray far inland. Among the exciting birds to be found along the coast are crab plovers, which are seen regularly in and around the Bazaruto Archipelago in summer, and occasionally as far south as Inhaca Island near Maputo. One of the rarest raptors in the world, Eleanora's falcon, has been seen at Vilankulo and Pomene. Vast flocks of migrant waders include bar-tailed godwit, terek sandpiper and greater sandplover. The rarely seen gull-billed tern has recently been spotted at freshwater lakes in three localities. Indigenous woodland is scarce along the coast, having been largely replaced by exotic coconut palms and cashew trees. However, the red-throated twinspot, Livingstone's turaco and brown scrub-robin can still be found near Xai-Xai and in Maputaland.

Other exciting birds to be seen in the brachystegia woodlands of the Mozambican interior south of the Save River include chestnut-fronted helmet-shrike, racket-tailed roller, mottled spinetail, Rudd's apalis, Livingstone's flycatcher, plain-backed sunbird, Neergaard's sunbird and pink-throated twinspot. In central Mozambique, two localities of great interest to birders are Gorongosa Mountain (near Gorongosa National Park) and the forests north of Dondo. Species that cannot be seen elsewhere in southern Africa include green-headed oriole and East Coast akalat.

Northern Mozambique is particularly alluring to birders, since many areas have yet to be thoroughly explored and birdwatchers are likely to find species new to the Mozambique list – and possibly even new to science. Birders in northern Mozambique will certainly encounter species that are not included in southern African field guides, so they will need to refer to a second field guide (page 379). Some of the birds that are known to occur in northern Mozambique but not in

BIRDING EQUIPMENT

OPTICAL EQUIPMENT A sealed and waterproof pair of binoculars is the most essential piece of equipment. Someone who has been thrifty on binoculars will soon realise that they have wasted their time and money, because once your bins fill with water or mist, they become useless. In the rainforest, 8x32 magnification is normally the safest bet as this tends to gather more light and pinning down the bird in your viewfinder is easier. In open areas such as savannah, 10x40s are more useful as the image is larger. Telescopes can be useful, particularly in the savannahs or when watching waterbirds on an open lake. In the forest a telescope is of limited use and cumbersome to carry.

RAINGEAR The only thing worse than your binoculars being filled with water is being soaking wet yourself. Be sure to get sturdy waterproof boots, ponchos and rainproof trousers. Boots also double as protection from ant swarms, and ponchos make excellent makeshift hides. Peak or broad-brimmed hats keep rainwater out of your eyes and binoculars.

SOUND GEAR Much forest birding depends on your ability to recognise, follow, locate and reproduce bird sounds. These days, mp3 players with an attached amplified speaker are the norm. Southern Africa has a superb set of bird sounds in the form of Guy Gibbons's *Southern African Bird Sounds* CDs available from Wildsounds (w *sabirding.co.za*)

GPS These units are extremely useful both for finding your way and for marking locations for future birders. Their compass and altitude features are also very helpful, but be warned that signals may not be available under forest canopy. Also be sure to seek local advice before wandering off the beaten track, as landmines are a serious issue.

FLASHLIGHT A powerful flashlight will help you find night birds. As much birding in Mozambique requires camping, this will be particularly rewarding.

BOOKS A good field guide is essential; see page 379 for recommendations.

southern Africa are pale-billed hornbill; brown-breasted barbet; mountain, little, grey-olive, Fischer's and Cabanis's greenbuls; Thyolo alethe; central bearded scrub-robin; evergreen and red-capped forest warblers; Kretchmar's longbill; white-winged apalis; long-billed tailorbird; white-tailed blue flycatcher; mountain babbler; red-and-blue and eastern double-collared sunbirds; Bertram's weaver; Zanzibar red bishop; African citril; and stripe-breasted canary.

For further information on birding expeditions and conservation in Mozambique, it would be worth checking out the Maputo-based **Associação Ambiente, Conservação e Educação Moçambique** (AACEM; m *82 565 9897*; e *chirruma@yahoo.co.uk*; w *mozambiquebirds.com*), or their associated Facebook group (f *groups/420903014675631*).

IBAS   *Keith Barnes and Josh Engel*

What are IBAs? Put simply, IBAs (Important Bird Areas) are sites, either protected or unprotected, that are vital for bird conservation. Because IBAs target specific categories of birds, normally threatened, rare or range-restricted, they often double as some of the finest birding destinations, particularly for those birders seeking more elusive species. Mount Gorongosa and Gorongosa National Park, Maputo Special Reserve, Mount Namuli and the Zambezi River Delta are all IBAs.

What makes them IBAs is that they are well-defined sites with boundaries – making it possible to demarcate and conserve them – and that they each hold one or more of a particular set of special birds worthy of conservation attention. Also, because IBAs are selected using identical and standardised criteria, an IBA in Mozambique is the same as an IBA in South Africa, Malawi, Thailand or England; as a result they form a global conservation currency. Mozambique holds 16 IBAs that support an excellent cross section of the country's threatened and unique avifauna. Often these sites double as key birdwatching areas, with ecotourism-based initiatives alongside them.

How are IBAs protected? Selecting IBAs according to the criteria is probably the easiest part of the process. The publication of the directories documenting the sites is only a beginning. The directories serve to highlight certain areas requiring additional conservation attention, as an alarming proportion of the sites fall outside the official protected area network. The most difficult job is to get people to sit up and listen. Unfortunately, Mozambique lacks a BirdLife partnership. These partnerships have been most influential in this regard, liaising with government officials, international conservation bodies and key global decision makers to further the ends of the programme.

Mozambique's national IBA programme stands to benefit from concerned individuals taking an interest in their local IBAs, as volunteers or custodians. If you would like to become involved, please contact the **BirdLife International Secretariat** (〜 *01223 277318 (UK);* e *birdlife@birdlife.org;* w *birdlife.org*).

REPTILES

NILE CROCODILE The order Crocodilia dates back at least 150 million years, and fossil forms that lived contemporaneously with dinosaurs are remarkably similar to their modern counterparts. The Nile crocodile is the largest living reptile, regularly growing to lengths of up to 6m. Widespread throughout Africa, it was once common in most large rivers and lakes, but it has been exterminated in many areas over the past century – hunted professionally for its skin as well as by vengeful local villagers. Contrary to popular legend, Nile crocodiles feed mostly on fish, at least where densities are sufficient. They will also prey on drinking or swimming mammals when the opportunity presents itself, dragging their victim underwater until it drowns, then storing it under a submerged log or tree until it has decomposed sufficiently for them to eat. A large crocodile is capable of killing a lion or wildebeest, or an adult human for that matter. Today, large specimens are mostly confined to protected areas, and are especially common along the rivers through the Niassa Reserve.

SNAKES A wide variety of snakes occurs in Mozambique, though – fortunately, most would agree – they are typically shy and unlikely to be seen unless actively sought. One of the snakes most likely to be seen on safari is Africa's largest, the **rock python**, which has a gold-on-black mottled skin and regularly grows to lengths exceeding 5m. Non-venomous, pythons kill their prey by strangulation, wrapping their muscular bodies around it until it cannot breathe, then swallowing it whole and dozing off for a couple of months while it is digested. Pythons feed mainly on small antelopes, large rodents and similar. They are harmless to adult humans, but could conceivably kill a small child.

Of the venomous snakes, one of the most commonly encountered is the **puff adder**, a large, thick resident of savannah and rocky habitats. Several **cobra** species are present, most with characteristic hoods that they raise when about to strike, though they are seldom seen. Another widespread family is the mambas, of which the **black mamba** – which will only attack when cornered, despite an unfounded reputation for unprovoked aggression – is the largest venomous snake in Africa, measuring up to 3.5m long. Theoretically, the most toxic of Africa's snakes is the **boomslang**, a variably coloured and largely arboreal snake, but it is back-fanged and very passive, and the only human fatalities recorded involve snake handlers.

Most snakes are non-venomous and harmless to any living creature much bigger than a rat. One common species is the **green tree snake** (sometimes mistaken for a boomslang, though the latter is never as green and more often brown), which feeds mostly on amphibians. The **mole snake** is a common grey-brown savannah resident that grows up to 2m long and feeds on moles and other rodents. The remarkable **egg-eating snake** lives exclusively on bird eggs, dislocating its jaws to swallow the egg whole, then eventually regurgitating the crushed shell in a neat little package. Many snakes will take eggs opportunistically, for which reason large-scale agitation among birds in a tree is often a good indication that a snake (or small bird of prey) is around.

LIZARDS All African lizards are harmless to humans, with the arguable exception of the giant **monitor lizards**, which could in theory inflict a nasty bite if cornered. Two species occur in Mozambique: the **water** and the **savannah monitor**, the latter growing up to 2.2m long and occasionally seen in the vicinity of termite mounds, the former slightly smaller but far more regularly observed by tourists. Their size alone might make it possible to fleetingly mistake a monitor for a small crocodile, but their more colourful yellow-dappled skin precludes sustained confusion. Both species are predatorial, feeding on anything from bird eggs to smaller reptiles and mammals, but will also eat carrion opportunistically.

The common **house gecko** is an endearing bug-eyed, translucent white lizard that inhabits most houses as well as lodge rooms, scampering up walls and upside down across the ceiling in pursuit of pesky insects attracted to the lights. Also very common in some areas are various **agama** species, distinguished from other common lizards by their relatively large size of around 20–25cm, basking habits, and almost plastic-looking scaling – depending on the species, a combination of blue, purple, orange or red, with the flattened head generally a different colour from the torso. Another common family is the **skinks** – small, long-tailed lizards, most of which are quite dark and have a few thin black stripes running from head to tail. The most charismatic of all lizard groups, the swivel-eyed, colour-changing **chameleons**, are also well represented in Mozambique.

TORTOISES AND TERRAPINS These peculiar reptiles are unique in being protected by a prototypical suit of armour formed by their heavy exoskeleton. The most common of the region's terrestrial tortoises is the **leopard tortoise**, which is named after its gold-and-black mottled shell, can weigh up to 30kg, and has been known to live for more than 50 years in captivity. It is often seen motoring along in the slow lane of game reserve roads. Three species of terrapin – essentially the freshwater equivalent of turtles – are resident in Mozambique, all somewhat flatter in shape than the tortoises, and generally with a plainer brown shell. They might be seen sunning themselves on rocks close to water or peering out from roadside puddles.

MARINE LIFE

Uniquely in southern and eastern Africa, Mozambique is better known and more often visited for its wealth of marine wildlife than for the terrestrial creatures that roam its relatively under-utilised game reserves. For much of its 2,470km length, Mozambique's Indian Ocean coastline is protected by a succession of offshore coral reefs that offer sublime conditions for snorkelling and diving, along with dozens of small islands such as those that make up the Bazaruto and Quirimbas archipelagos, both of which are protected within national parks.

There are dozens of established dive and snorkel sites along the coast, and many more that remain undeveloped for tourism, but the main centres for viewing marine life are Ponta do Ouro (known for reef fish and ragged-tooth sharks), the coast around Inhambane, Tofo and Závora (where ocean safaris offer snorkellers and divers the opportunity to swim with marine giants such as whale shark, manta ray and dolphins), Vilankulo and the nearby Bazaruto Archipelago (a huge diversity of reef fish and the one place where snorkellers regularly encounter turtles, also with very occasional dugong sightings) and the Quirimbas (superb for reef fish but less good for larger marine creatures). A brief overview of some of the marine wildlife likely to be seen along the Mozambican coast follows below.

MARINE MAMMALS At least ten species of cetacean (whales and dolphins) are resident along, or seasonal visitors to, the Mozambican coast. These remarkable mammals have a similar body temperature to humans, and are as dependent on atmospheric oxygen as any terrestrial creature, yet they lead a totally aquatic existence, often in water so cold it would induce fatal hypothermia in most other mammals. Some species can spend up to an hour below water without surfacing, thanks to their large lungs, capacity to replenish 90% of their air supply in one breath, and the ability to store oxygen in their muscles, while a dense subcutaneous layer of insulating blubber protects them from the cold. Unfortunately, the commercial value of this blubber has also led to their persecution by the lucrative whaling industry – the global population of the blue whale, for instance, is estimated to be around 10,000–25,000 (3–11% of their 1911 population) after at least 300,000 individuals were harpooned in the 20th century.

Cetaceans are divided into two distinct groups, based on their feeding anatomy. **Baleen whales** are named for the comb-like baleen upper-jaw plates that are used to sieve plankton, other tiny invertebrates and small pelagic fish from the water as they swim. Surprisingly perhaps, the largest creature ever to inhabit our planet, the **blue whale** – at upwards of 200 tonnes, some 20–30 times heavier than an African elephant – feeds on near-microscopic organisms in this somewhat passive manner. Blue whales are extremely rare off the coast of Mozambique, but the 30–50-tonne **humpback whale** is seasonally very common, and it is often seen on ocean safaris out of Tofo from June to December. The slightly bulkier **southern right whale** is often seen in the far south of Mozambique at the same time of year, while the **southern minke whale**, the smallest of the baleen whales, is resident throughout the year, often feeding in small groups in bays.

The other main group, comprising **dolphins**, **porpoises** and **toothed whales**, are the **odontocetic cetaceans**: active hunters whose dental structure resembles that of the terrestrial carnivores. Eight families are recognised, all of which feed mainly on large invertebrates and fish. Quite commonly seen from boats off Mozambique, the spinner dolphin is named for its occasional habit of pirouetting longitudinally when it leaps out of the water. Also present are the false killer whale, Blainville's whale, spotted dolphin, common dolphin and humpback dolphin.

Commonest in Mozambique's warm to temperate waters, however, is the bottlenose dolphin, which is the most globally abundant and widespread cetacean. Named for the elongated upper and lower jaws that create its characteristic smiling expression, it is dark grey above and paler below, grows to a length of up to 4m, weighs up to 650kg, and typically lives in pods of 3–12 individuals. Known for its friendly character and curiosity about humans, the bottlenose is often seen playing in the surf or swimming in the wake of a boat. It sometimes places a marine sponge on its beak as protection when it forages in the sandy sea bottom, the only known instance of tool use in a marine mammal.

The Bazaruto Archipelago is one of the last few strongholds for the **dugong**, a bulky (up to 1,000kg) marine mammal that feeds mainly on sea-grass and is placed alongside the manatee of the Atlantic Ocean in the family Sirinia, whose closest terrestrial relatives are elephants and hyraxes. The name 'Sirinia', a reference to the Sirens of Greek legend, has been given to this family of marine animals because they are considered the most likely source of the mermaid myth. Dugongs used to be abundant throughout the Indo-Pacific region, and as recently as the early 1970s groups of four to five were commonly seen in places such as Inhambane, Angoche and even near Maputo. Unfortunately, they have suffered a drastic population decrease in the past few decades, probably because so many are trapped in fish nets. IUCN-listed as Vulnerable, the dugong is now threatened with extinction except in the seas around northern Australia and the Arabian Gulf.

TURTLES The Mozambican coastline is one of the most prolific regions globally for marine turtles, representatives of conservative reptilian lineage that first appeared in the fossil record more than 100 million years ago and had evidently evolved into distinctive modern genera some 60 million years back. Five marine turtle species are either resident or regular visitors to the Mozambican coast, including the **soft-shelled leatherback**, which is the world's bulkiest marine reptile, the largest on record having measured about 3m long and weighed 916kg. More common, however, are the breeding **green** and **loggerhead turtles**, while other species that visit with varying degrees of regularity are the **olive ridley** and **hawksbill**.

Marine turtles remained common to abundant throughout their natural range until the late 19th century, since when the combination of hunting (for food, skin and tortoiseshell), accidental trapping, habitat destruction and pollution has resulted in a serious decline in numbers. Indeed, of the seven recognised species, all but one is listed on the IUCN Red List, with eventual extinction being a distinct possibility for three species listed as Critically Endangered (Kemp's ridley, hawksbill and leatherback).

The life cycle of marine turtles is unusual. Their full lifespan remains a matter of speculation, but most species reach sexual maturity in their 20s or later, and many individuals probably live for longer than a century. The main breeding season in Mozambique is between October and February, when male and female turtles converge offshore to mate. Once the eggs are ripe – usually on a moonlit night – the female crawls on to the beach to dig a 50cm-deep hole, lays up to 120 eggs, and covers them with sand, leaving them to hatch about two months later. Oddly, water temperature affects the sex of the hatchlings – a balance between male and female is to be expected at 28°C, but males will predominate in cooler waters and females in warmer water.

FISH Although exact figures are unavailable, it is estimated that more than 2,000 species of marine fish, including 17 endemics, occur along the Mozambican coastline (a national tally boosted by around 350 freshwater species, including another 11 endemics, most of which are associated exclusively with Lago Niassa). For visitors, the most interesting marine fish fall into three broad categories. Most prolific among these is a kaleidoscopic miscellany of hundreds of colourful **reef**

fish, several dozen of which might be encountered on a single snorkelling or diving session. Less numerous but arguably more exciting are cartilaginous marine giants such as **sharks and rays**, which are something of a speciality off the coast around Tofo and Inhambane. Finally, there are the **game fish** – marlins, sailfish, barracuda and such – that attract dedicated fishermen (box, page 184).

Among the cartilaginous fish most eagerly sought by divers are the whale shark, the world's largest fish, and the equally impressive manta ray, both of which employ similar filter-feeding methods to the baleen whales (box, page 165). Many more actively predatory shark species occur off the Mozambican coast, among them the legendarily aggressive great white shark, which can grow up to 8m long, and the more docile ragged-toothed shark, the latter often seen by divers in the far south of the country. The region is also a stronghold for the Zambezi bull shark, a 300kg marine species that can live for long periods in fresh water, where it frequently attacks unsuspecting villagers as they bathe or do their laundry. Snorkellers and divers may also encounter several of the region's species of stingray, most of which have a 'wingspan' of around 75cm to 1.5m and tend to swim close to the sandy ocean floor.

Some of the world's finest and best-preserved coral reefs lie off the shore of Mozambique, all the way from Ponta do Ouro on the South African border to the Quirimbas Archipelago in the far north. These spectacular multihued natural aquaria form the focal point of most diving and snorkelling excursions in Mozambique, and support a total of about 800 reef fish species, with biodiversity increasing as you head further north. When exploring these reefs, one visual sweep of your surrounds might reveal a selection of a dozen or more species, whose memorable names reflect an extraordinary range of shapes and colours. There are the closely related devil's firefish and red lionfish, whose gaudy pattern and poisonous spines have the appearance of psychedelic marine porcupines. Other memorable genera and species include the brilliantly colourful sweet-lips, angelfishes, butterfly fishes and wrasses, the predatory honeycomb eel and scalloped hammerhead, and the elongated needlefish and outsized rock cods.

The oceanic waters off Mozambique are also home to the coelacanth, a peculiar 2m-long fish that was known only from fossils – and thought to have been extinct for more than 60 million years – prior to the discovery of the first living specimen off the southeast coast of South Africa in 1938. Now regarded as the world's oldest surviving vertebrate species, the coelacanth is known to inhabit the underwater canyons carved into the continental shelf offshore the Mozambican–South African border area, where the first documentary footage of these extraordinary 'living fossils' was captured in the year 2000.

OTHER MARINE CREATURES The oceanic waters off Mozambique support a diversity of invertebrate species more remarkable even than its fish. For instance, coral, contrary to its rocklike appearance, is an organic entity comprising the limestone exoskeleton of colonial polyps that are related to sea anemones and feed mainly on photosynthetic algae, which thrive at a depth of up to 15m in warm, aerated water along the continental shelf. One single reef might be composed of more than 50 different coral species and, as you examine the reefs closely, you will see it is studded with sea anemones, spiky predatory polyps that often possess a nasty sting. There are also thousands of sea molluscs, crustaceans and other creatures with shells or exoskeletons, among them crabs and crayfish, and rock-loving invertebrates such as mussels, oysters, barnacles and periwinkles, which are often associated with intertidal rock pools. Several islands off the north of Mozambique are home to the giant coconut crab, which can weigh up to 5kg, making it the world's largest terrestrial crustacean (box, page 347).

3

Practical Information

WHEN TO VISIT

The coastal regions of Mozambique are best visited in the dry winter months of May through to October, when daytime temperatures are generally around 20–25°C. There is no major obstacle to visiting Mozambique during the summer months of November to April, except that climatic conditions are oppressively hot and humid at this time of year, especially along the north coast. Because most of the country's rain falls during the summer months, there is also an increased risk of contracting malaria and of dirt roads being washed out.

Unless you are a South African with children at school, it is emphatically worth avoiding the south coast of Mozambique during South African school holidays, when campsites as far north as Vilankulo tend to be very crowded and hotels are often fully booked. The exact dates of South African school holidays vary slightly on a provincial basis, but the main ones to avoid are those for Gauteng (the province that includes Johannesburg, South Africa's most populous city and only a day's drive from Maputo). To give a rough idea of the periods to avoid, there are four annual school holidays in Gauteng: a three-week holiday that starts in the last week of March and ends in the middle of April, a month-long holiday running from late June to late July, a two-week holiday starting in late September, and a six-week holiday from early December to mid-January (for exact dates, check w schoolguide.co.za/school-holidays.html or contact a South African embassy). If you do visit southern Mozambique during school holidays, then you should make reservations for all the hotels and campsites at which you plan to stay.

School holidays in landlocked Zimbabwe see a substantial influx of Zimbabwean tourists into southern Mozambique, so that most resorts between Beira and Xai-Xai are more crowded than usual. Provided you have a tent, you shouldn't get stuck at these times. Few South Africans or Zimbabweans currently venture north of the Beira Corridor (the road and railway line linking Beira to the Zimbabwean border town of Mutare), so school holidays have no notable effect on tourist patterns in northern Mozambique.

HIGHLIGHTS

DESERTED BEACHES Most people who visit Mozambique, whether they're from South Africa, Zimbabwe or further afield, do so for the country's coastal attractions. Indeed, there are few other countries in the world with such an extensive, beautiful and largely undeveloped coastline. This means that travellers will find truly deserted beaches, many of which stretch for kilometres on end, even at the more built-up resorts. The top upmarket beach destinations in Mozambique are the Bazaruto and Quirimba archipelagos, while more affordable mainland options include Ponta do Ouro, Tofo (near Inhambane) and Vilankulo.

DIVING AND FISHING Once you have made the effort to get to these beaches, the opportunities for diving and fishing are among the best in southern Africa. Once again, the infrastructure underpinning these activities is still in its infancy, which means that dive sites are uncrowded and the fish varied and plentiful.

WHALES Another attraction of the southern Mozambican coastline is the very high probability of seeing humpback whales between July and October as they head north with their newly born calves, and Tofo has a reputation as being one of the best places in the world to see manta rays.

BIRDWATCHING Nature lovers, especially birdwatchers, will find plenty to see on dry land provided that they are prepared to make the effort to get to the country's national parks and reserves. The most accessible of these are Limpopo and Gorongosa national parks, both of which have seen considerable development in recent years. Animals are less numerous here than in the well-stocked parks of neighbouring countries, but the atmosphere is 100% wild.

HISTORIC TOWNS And then there are the towns. Sleepy, historic **Inhambane** would be a highlight on any African itinerary, and should not be missed by travellers to Mozambique. **Ilha de Moçambique** and **Ibo Island** are no less historic and even more compelling, although it will take slightly more effort to get to them. **Maputo**, meanwhile, is as clean and safe a city as you'll find in Africa; and with an increasing number of quality hotels, restaurants and other facilities, it's the perfect base for a trip around Mozambique.

THE PEOPLE The main highlight of a trip to Mozambique is the people. Generally unassuming, helpful, funny and honest, the Mozambicans are what really makes Mozambique one of the greatest travel destinations in Africa.

TOURIST INFORMATION

Resources are limited. Most tourist-orientated hotels will have a certain amount of tourist information available, although it's not always particularly up to date, and (certainly in the backpackers' hostels in Maputo) may well cover South Africa rather than Mozambique. There are also a couple of privately run tourist information offices, notably the tourist office in Vilankulo and Kaskazini in Pemba. The Pink Papaya in Chimoio and Ruby Backpackers on Ilha de Moçambique are both run by well-informed and helpful owner-managers. Online, Mike Slater's estimable w mozguide.com ought to be anyone's first stop for practical information. A special mention must also go to the Maputo-based w clubofmozambique.com (**f** *club. mozambique*) as perhaps the best online portal for Mozambican current events in English; they also publish a monthly newsletter known as *The Mozambican Traveller*. Useful sources of non-travel information include w verdade.co.mz, home of the *Verdade* newspaper available in English, and w poptel.org.uk/mozambique-news (the English version of the Mozambican news agency).

TOUR OPERATORS

UK
Aardvark Safaris \\+44 (0) 1980 849160 or +44 (0) 1578 760222; e mail@aardvarksafaris.

com; w aardvarksafaris.co.uk. Offers tailor-made safaris using small, owner-run camps. ATOL protected.

Africa Explorer ↘+44 (0) 20 8987 8742;
e john@africa-explorer.co.uk; w africa-explorer.co.uk.
Specialist in tailor-made safaris across southern Africa.
Africa Odyssey ↘+44 (0) 20 8704 1216;
e info@africaodyssey.com; w africaodyssey.com.
Tailor-made itineraries in Mozambique including
the island archipelagos of Quirimba & Bazaruto.
Africa Travel ↘+44 (0)20 7843 3500; e info@
africatravel.com; w africatravel.com. Tailor-made
specialist with 25 years' experience; offers beach
resorts, island retreats, city hotels & flights.
Audley Travel ↘+44 (0) 1993 838000;
w audleytravel.com. Award-winning UK operator
with a top-notch selection of Mozambican itineraries.
Baobab Travel Ltd ↘+44 (0) 121 314 6011;
e info@baobabtravel.com; w baobabtravel.com.
UK-based tour operator specialising in tailor-made
African holidays promoting a form of responsible
tourism.
Bridge & Wickers ↘+44 (0)203 811 3491;
e sales@bridgeandwickers.com; w bridgeandwickers.
co.uk. A knowledgeable team of Mozambique
specialists (they've all visited several times) &
particular expertise in the best places to dive.
Expert Africa ↘+44 (0) 20 8232 9777;
e info@expertafrica.com; w expertafrica.com.
Knowledgeable African safari company offering an
unusually wide choice of options on Mozambique's
islands.
Imagine Africa ↘+44 (0)20 3603 8595; e info@
imaginetravel.com; w imaginetravel.com. Has
more than 25 years' travel experience of luxury
safari & beach holidays to Africa & the Indian
Ocean, including Mozambique.
J & C Voyageurs Ltd ↘+44 (0) 1373 832111;
e mail@jandcvoyageurs.com; w jandcvoyageurs.
com. Individually tailored holidays, specialising in
small exclusive beach & safari properties.
Okavango Tours & Safaris ↘+44 (0) 7721
387738; e info@okavango.com; w okavango.
com. Individually tailored safaris combined with
barefoot luxury on beaches.
Original Travel ↘+44 (0) 20 7978 7333;
e ask@originaltravel.co.uk; w originaltravel.com.
Specialises in tailor-made safaris, family holidays
& honeymoons.
Rainbow Tours ↘+44 (0) 20 3131 5300;
e info@rainbowtours.co.uk; w rainbowtours.
co.uk. Award-winning UK-based tour operator
offering tailor-made beach & safari holidays,
especially to Bazaruto & the Quirimbas.

Steppes Travel ↘+44 (0) 1285 601495;
e enquiry@steppestravel.co.uk; w steppestravel.
co.uk. Steppes Travel offers luxury tailor-made
holidays to both southern & northern Mozambique.
Time for Travel ↘+44 (0) 1798 867750; e sales@
timefortravel.co.uk; w timefortravel.co.uk. Tailor-
made holidays to Africa & the Indian Ocean islands.
Trailfinders ↘+44 (0) 20 7368 1200; w trailfinders.
com. More than 20 offices around the UK. Includes
Mozambique among the 10 African countries it visits.
World Odyssey ↘+44 (0) 1905 731373;
e info@world-odyssey.com; w world-odyssey.
com. Arranges tailor-made holidays to the
Bazaruto & Quirimba archipelagos in Mozambique.
Zambezi Safari & Travel Co Ltd ↘+44 (0) 1752
878858; e info@zambezi.com; w zambezi.com.
UK- & Africa-based safari specialists operating
through East & southern Africa. ATOL protected.

USA
African Safari Co 2835 31st Av, W. Seattle,
WA 98199; ↘+1 800 414 3090 (toll-free USA &
Canada); e info@africansafarico.com;
w africansafarico.com. Offers luxury honeymoon
& beach extensions to their safari packages.
Ker & Downey 6703 Highway Bd, Katy, TX
77494; ↘+1 800 423 4236 (toll-free USA &
Canada); e info@kerdowney.com; w kerdowney.
com. Upmarket southern African safaris with beach
extensions to Bazaruto & the Quirimbas.

AFRICA
Dana Tours Lda ↘+258 214 95514; m +258 84
404 0710; e info@danatours.com; w danatours.
com; see ad, page 86. Small, efficient Maputo-
based company offering tailor-made itineraries.
Kaskazini m +258 82 309 6990; e info@
kaskazini.com; w kaskazini.com. Based in Pemba,
these helpful folk are the acknowledged on-the-
ground experts in travel in the northern provinces
of Niassa, Nampula & Cabo Delgado.
Mabeco Tours ↘+258 21 307579; m +258
84 885 9992; e mabeco@mabecotours.com or
bookings@mabecotours.com; w mabecotours.
com; [f] mabecotoursmaputo. Based in Maputo,
this new tour company offers luxury safaris in
Mozambique & neighbouring countries. They offer
city tours, road & 4x4 transfers, cultural tours, bush
& beach packages, & corporate team building.
Mozaic Travel ↘+258 21 451379; m +258 84 333
2111/301 5167; e maputo@mozaictravel.com;

3

w mozaictravel.com. Excellent Maputo-based company specialising in safaris & beach holidays countrywide.

Mozambique Connection   PO Box 2861, Rivonia 212; +27 11 465 3427; e bookings@mozcon. com; w mozcon.com

Mozambique Travel   +27 21 785 5498; e admin@mozambiquetravel.com; w mozambiquetravel.com. Based in Cape Town, this specialist operator has hands-on managers who know Mozambique backwards & can put together everything from honeymoon & beach holidays to

birding trips & safaris. It also operates a special offers website (w *mozambiquespecials.com*).

Pulse Africa Johannesburg   +27 11 325 2290; e info@pulseafrica.com; w pulseafrica.com. Booking agent for flights & beach packages to Mozambique.

GLOBAL

Flight Centre   w flightcentre.com. Offices in Australia, Canada, New Zealand, South Africa, the UK & the USA.

STA Travel   w statravel.com. Operates in more than 20 countries.

RED TAPE

A valid passport is required to enter Mozambique. The date of expiry should be at least six months after you intend to end your travels; if it is likely to expire before that, get a new passport.

VISAS

South Africans If you are travelling on a South African passport (or one from another neighbouring country), you no longer need a visa to enter Mozambique: when you arrive at the border, you will be given a free entry permit valid for up to 30 days. However, these permits cannot be extended in Mozambique itself. If you intend on staying longer, then either you will need to get a single-entry visa valid for the required period in advance, or you must leave and re-enter Mozambique before that month expires.

All other nationalities Visas are required by everyone else and individual visitors are allotted a maximum of 90 days per year on a tourist visa. As of February 2017, it is now possible to purchase a 30-day, single-entry tourist visa upon arrival at 44 border crossings (the remaining 14 borders are the least crossed and are expected to have the capability to issue visas upon arrival in the near future), including international airports. The cost per visa is Mt2,000 (approx US$40), but, if you lack local currency, you could be charged as much as US$80. The visa can be extended in-country up to two times for an additional 30 days (making 90 days in total) at any of the immigration offices that are located in all provincial capitals. By contrast, purchasing a 90-day multi-entry visa in advance may require you to cross a border in and out of the country every 30 days. Although each office tends to have its own flow rate, extensions typically require at least a week for processing, so be sure to submit your passport for extensions two to three business days prior to the visa's expiration and plan on picking it up a week from submission. This can be something of a nuisance for travellers on the go, so be sure to plan accordingly.

CUSTOMS Vigorous steps have been taken recently to eradicate corruption in the Mozambique customs service. New staff have been recruited and trained, and there is even a special authority to deal with officials who attempt to solicit bribes during the course of their duties. Those who have a legitimate complaint should contact the Internal Irregularities Unit in Maputo (21 308584), taking note of the fact that offering or paying a bribe is also a criminal offence.

Import limits

Groceries Mt5,000 per person (approx US$100, for which you may need to provide receipts)

Alcohol 2.25 litres of wine and 1 litre of spirits

Tobacco 400 cigarettes or 100 small cigars or 50 big cigars or 250g loose tobacco

Perfume 50ml

Medication Reasonable quantities for personal use

Firearms Only permitted with a special licence

Narcotics and **pornography** are prohibited.

Currency controls You are not permitted to enter or exit the country with more than Mt500 (less than US$10).

EMBASSIES, CONSULATES AND HIGH COMMISSIONS A full list of Mozambican embassies and consulates outside the country can be found at w embassiesabroad. com/embassies-of/Mozambique. A selection of those most likely to be useful to readers is as follows:

Belgium 97 Bd Saint Michel, B-1040 Brussels; +32 2 736 0096/2564; e mozambiqueembassy@yahoo.com

France 82 Rue Laugier, 75017 Paris; +33 1 47 64 91 32; e embaocparis@compuserve.com

Germany Strom Strasse 47, 10551 Berlin; +49 30 398 76500/1/2; e emoza@aol.com

Malawi Lilongwe +265 1784100; e mozambique@malawi.net; Blantyre +265 1643189; e mozamcons@malawi.net

Portugal Av de Berna 71050, Lisbon; +351 21 797 1994; e embaoc.portugal@minec.gov.mz

South Africa Pretoria +27 12 401 0300; e albertinamabuiangue@yahoo.com; Johannesburg +27 11 325 5704; e cgeral@intekom.co.za; Cape Town +27 21 426 2944/5; e mozambiqueconsulatecpt@telkomsa.co.za; Durban +27 31 304 0200; e mozamcom@mweb.co.za; Nelspruit +27 13 752 7396; e mozamcom@mweb.co.za; w embamoc.co.za

Swaziland Highlands View, Princess Drive Rd, Mbabane; +268 404 1296/7; e moz.high-swd@africaonline.co.sz

Tanzania 25 Garden Av, PO Box 9370, Dar es Salaam; +255 22 211 6502; e embamoc@africaonline.co.tz

UK 21 Fitzroy Sq, London W1T 6EL; 020 7383 3800; e sectorconsular@mozambiquehc.co.uk; w mozambiquehighcommission.org.uk

USA 1990 M St, NW Suite 570, Washington, DC 20036; +1 202 293 7146/9; e embamoc@aol.com

Zambia 9592 Kacha Rd, Northmead, Lusaka; +260 1 239 135; e mozhclsk@zamnet.zm

Zimbabwe 152 Herbert Chitepo Av, Harare; +263 4 253 871/3; e embamoc@embamoc.org.zw

GETTING THERE AND AWAY

BY AIR The only airline with direct flights to/from Europe is **TAP Air Portugal** (w *flytap.com*), which will involve routing through Lisbon (unless that is where you are flying from anyway). Another reasonably direct option from certain European cities, including London, is **Ethiopian Airlines** (w *ethiopianairlines.com*), routing through Addis Ababa, or **Kenya Airways** (w *kenya-airways.com*), routing through Nairobi. It is more common for European and other intercontinental visitors to fly to Johannesburg (South Africa) and transfer to Mozambique from there, and **Qatar Airways** (w *qatarairways.com*) now flies from Doha to Maputo (some flights have a technical stop in Johannesburg). The national carrier **LAM** (w *lam.co.mz*) and **South African Airways** (w *flysaa.com*) operate plenty of flights daily between

Johannesburg and Maputo, and the former also flies from Maputo to all provincial capitals in Mozambique. SAA also flies direct to Maputo from Durban, as well as directly from Johannesburg to Vilankulo, Beira, Tete, Nampula and Pemba in partnership with **Airlink** (w *flyairlink.com*). The Nacala airport could start receiving international flights – as was initially intended but, since opening in 2014, has yet to do – during the lifespan of this edition as well.

Provided that you have a valid passport and visa, and a return ticket, you should whizz through the entrance formalities at Mozambique's international airports with a minimum of fuss, though do note that the direct TAP flight from Lisbon is sometimes more thoroughly scrutinised owing to the growing number of Portuguese jobseekers arriving in Mozambique.

BY LAND Provided you arrive at the border with a visa, you should have no problem entering Mozambique overland, nor is there a serious likelihood of being asked about onward tickets, funds or vaccination certificates. About the worst you can expect at customs is a cursory search of your luggage (page 44).

If you have a car... Things are a little more complex, although not outrageously so. You'll need a 'temporary export document' (signed by immigration authorities) from whichever country you are coming from before you can pass through the exit gate at the border post. This will need to be taken to the customs officials on the Mozambican side who'll stamp them and charge you a nominal fee, payable in meticais. Before you leave them check the expiry date of the export documents – they may not be the same as the expiry date on your visa. You will also need to buy third-party insurance, which will cost around US$15 for a car and an additional US$10 if you have a trailer as well. If you do have a trailer then you have to have a little triangular blue-and-orange sign on the front of your car and the back of your trailer. Once you have your stamped export document and insurance papers, take them to a third official who will sign off your gate pass and check your vehicle.

CHANGING MONEY AT BORDERS

At most land borders there is nowhere to change money legally, which means that you may have to change money with a private individual. Although this is not always strictly legal, the trade is conducted perfectly openly at most borders – though obviously it is wise to be discreet in the presence of officialdom. Generally, the rates you get at borders are lower than they would be elsewhere. At some borders, there's a lot of hustle attached to changing money privately, and especially along the Beira Corridor there is a real risk of being conned.

One solution would be to arrange in advance to be carrying money for the country you are entering – ask travellers coming in the opposite direction if they have any leftover cash to swap. If you can't do this, try to carry a small surplus of the currency from the country you are leaving (say around US$20) and to change this at the border rather than using up your hard currency. Whatever else you do, try to establish the rough exchange rate in advance and avoid changing significantly more than you will need until you can get to a bank. It is a good idea to keep the money you intend to change separate from the rest of your hard currency and/or travellers' cheques.

Don't forget to get your passport stamped too! For more advice on driving in Mozambique, see pages 56–8.

Overland routes into Mozambique
Mozambique has land borders with an unusually large number of other countries: South Africa, Swaziland, Zimbabwe, Zambia, Malawi and Tanzania.

South Africa
Ponta do Ouro: Kosi Bay (⊕ 08.00–16.00) This border on the southern coast is normally used to get to and from Ponta do Ouro and the other resorts in the deep south of the country. Road links to Maputo (and hence the rest of the country) are poor, and you'll need a 4x4. A newly surfaced road is expected to be complete by the end of 2017.

Ressano Garcia: Komatipoort (⊕ 06.00–midnight, although apparently it's open 24hrs during the busy Dec holiday period & Easter) The most-used border between South Africa and Mozambique; the road links to Maputo and further north are good quality tarmac. If you're travelling by public transport, there is a daily train to Maputo from Ressano Garcia and plenty of buses on both sides.

Giriyondo (⊕ Oct–Mar 08.00–16.00; 08.00–15.00 at other times. Visas are issued in 10mins) The main crossing within the Great Limpopo Transfrontier Park is 95km from Phalaborwa via Letaba Rest Camp, and about 450km from Maputo. A vehicle with good ground clearance is recommended, but a 4x4 is not essential. Note that when using this border, one night must be spent within the parks on either side (or Covane Community Lodge; page 143) so plan accordingly and make a reservation prior to travel with receipt of booking to show at the border. Park fees also apply.

Pafuri: Pafuri (⊕ 08.00–16.00) This little-used crossing is way up at the northern end of the Great Limpopo Transfrontier Park. A 4x4 is essential. The requirement of an overnight stay within either Kruger National Park or Great Limpopo Transfrontier Park did not apply to this border post as of 2016.

Swaziland
Namaacha: Lomahasha (⊕ 08.00–17.00) This busy crossing is up in the Swazi Mountains.

Goba: Mhlumeni (⊕ 24hrs) A quieter alternative to the Namaacha crossing a short distance further north, but with longer hours. Many *chapa* (page 58) drivers also seem to prefer this route.

Zimbabwe
Espungabera: Mount Selina (⊕ 06.00–18.00) Little known and little used in the Chimanimani Mountains, this is probably only for those with their own transport and a hankering for roughing it.

Machipanda: Mutare (⊕ 06.00–18.00) The western end of the Beira Corridor and a major route both for trade goods and Zimbabwean holidaymakers. The road is good quality tarmac all the way to the Indian Ocean.

Cuchamano: Nyamapanda (⊕ 06.00–18.00) The western end of the Tete Corridor between Zimbabwe and Malawi and a well-trodden route for both tourists and freight. The road is good quality tarmac all the way to Malawi.

Chicualacuala (Vila Eduardo Mondlane): Sango (🕐 *06.00–18.00*) The weekly train from Maputo connects with its Zimbabwean counterpart here for the journey to Bulawayo.

Zumbo: Kanyemba (🕐 *06.00–18.00*) At the tri-point between Zambia, Zimbabwe and Mozambique, this crossing is passable only by boat, normally a dugout canoe.

Mucumbura: Mukumbura (🕐 *06.00–18.00*) In a remote area of western Tete Province on the south side of Lake Cahora Bassa.

Zambia
Zumbo: Luangwa (🕐 *08.00–15.00*) One of the most intriguing crossings but also one of the most remote. The border is reputedly crossable only by dugout canoe.

Cassacatiza: Chanida (🕐 *06.00–18.00*) The major trade route between Zambia and Mozambique, though still pretty minor by other standards.

Malawi
Calómuè: Dedza (🕐 *08.00–16.00*) Less used than the Zóbuè crossing further south, this is the most direct route to Lilongwe. It is about 125km further on from Zóbuè though, so if you're transiting from Zimbabwe to Malawi you'd probably end up spending a night in Mozambique if you try to use this border.

Zóbuè: Mwanza (🕐 *06.00–18.00*) The eastern end of the Tete Corridor and the most common route for travellers.

Milange: Muloza (🕐 *08.00–16.00*) A busy trade border, but little used by travellers.

Entre Lagos: Nayuchi (🕐 *06.00–18.00*) Formerly one of the more popular routes for tourists, but not since trains stopped running through here.

Mandimba: Chiponde (🕐 *06.00–18.00*) The road from Mandimba runs down to Mangochi at the bottom end of Lake Malawi and is really rather attractive. This crossing links in with the passenger train service from Cuamba to Nampula (for Ilha de Moçambique or Pemba).

Cóbuè: Likoma The Likoma Islands are in Mozambican waters but are Malawian territory, and this is a good place to get a Mozambican visa on arrival. See page 365 for further details on this crossing.

Tanzania
Namuiranga: Mwambo (🕐 *08.00–16.00*) The Ruvuma River is one of the tougher crossings, not so much for the river itself but because of the effort it takes to get there in the first place.

Negomane: Masuguru This is the new crossing at the Unity Bridge, but it remains difficult to access because of poor road links to the bridge itself. See box, page 328 for more details.

Matchedje (Segundo Congresso): Mitomoni One of the most remote crossings in the country and the second bridge to span the Rovuma, this short one-lane bridge is known as Unity II.

CRIME AND SAFETY

THEFT AND VIOLENCE Bearing in mind that no country in the world is totally free of crime, and that tourists to so-called developing nations are always conspicuously wealthy targets, Mozambique is a relatively low-risk country so far as crime is concerned. Compared with parts of Kenya and South Africa, mugging is rare and the sort of con tricks that abound in Nairobi and Dar es Salaam even rarer. Petty theft such as pickpocketing and bag-snatching is a risk in markets and other crowded places, but on a scale that should prompt caution rather than paranoia. Walking around large towns at night feels safe enough, though it would be tempting fate to wander alone along unlit streets or to carry large sums of money or valuables. On the basis that it is preferable to err on the side of caution, here are a few tips that apply to travelling anywhere in Africa:

- Most casual thieves operate in busy markets and bus stations. Keep a close watch on your possessions in such places, and avoid having valuables or large amounts of money loose in your daypack or pocket.
- Keep all your valuables and the bulk of your money in a hidden money belt. Never show this money belt in public. Keep any spare cash you need elsewhere on your person.
- A buttoned-up pocket on the front of the shirt is one of the most secure places as money cannot be snatched from it without the thief coming into your view. It is also advisable to keep a small amount of hard currency (ideally cash) hidden away in your luggage so that, should you lose your money belt, you have something to fall back on.
- Where the choice exists between carrying valuables on your person or leaving them in a locked room, the latter option is generally safer, though obviously you should use your judgement and be sure the room is absolutely secure. Some travellers' cheque companies will not refund cheques stolen from a room, or might reject the claim on a technicality, for instance if the door wasn't damaged during the robbery.
- Leave any jewellery of financial or sentimental value at home.

BANDITRY Mozambique has a long history of banditry. During the civil war, a significant risk of being held up at gunpoint was attached to driving practically anywhere in the country. This risk has abated in the past few years, but it still exists, though it is probably only of concern to people driving themselves through Mozambique, and seems to be confined to the south coast. Incidents are probably fairly random, and they appear to be related to the car-hijacking syndicates that are rife in South Africa, which means that new minibuses, pick-up trucks and 4x4s are probably at greater risk of being hijacked than are older vehicles and saloon cars. For South Africans, the risk of armed hijacking is probably less than it would be in Johannesburg.

There are certainly a few precautions you can take against hijacking. The first and most obvious is never to drive at night, and to set off travelling as early as possible so that you have the maximum available time to deal with unexpected car problems during daylight hours. In Johannesburg, most people now drive around with doors permanently locked and windows raised high enough so that nobody can reach in and open the lock – an obvious precaution in an urban context, perhaps less so in rural Mozambique, but one that can do no harm.

3

BRIBERY, FINES AND BUREAUCRACY Corruption is widespread, though as a tourist you are most likely to see it at roadblocks, when the driver of your *chapa* will slip the traffic policeman something to ease the journey. If you are driving your own vehicle, then you are a little more vulnerable (pages 56–8). If you are fined for any reason, then you should be given a receipt for the payment – this will usually entail going to a police station. If the officer seems reluctant to go to a police station, there is a good chance that he is trying to bump up his income.

One thing that has to be stated is that offering or paying a bribe is a criminal offence in Mozambique, and there is an established anti-corruption programme, though it is not clear whether any local pays it a blind bit of notice (page 44).

If you do happen to get caught in an attempt to extract a bribe, taking out your mobile phone and saying you're going to ring your embassy can make a difference (although obviously it only works in an area where you have reception). The British embassy maintains a record of bribe attempts that it passes to the Mozambican government on a regular basis, and other embassies may also do this. If you are forced to go to this extreme, get the officer's name and number – all police officers are required to carry ID papers while on duty and produce them when requested.

There is a tendency to portray African bureaucrats as difficult and inefficient in their dealings with tourists. As a rule, this reputation says more about Western prejudices than it does about Mozambique. Sure, you come across the odd unhelpful official, but that's the nature of the beast everywhere in the world and the vast majority of officials encountered in Africa are courteous and helpful in their dealings with tourists, often to a degree that is almost embarrassing. The most frustrating aspect of Mozambican officialdom is the length of time that it seems to take to do anything. Once you accept that, it is usually quite straightforward to deal with them.

The biggest factor in determining the response you receive from African officials will be your own attitude. If you walk into every official encounter with an aggressive, paranoid approach, you are quite likely to kindle the feeling held by many Africans that Europeans are arrogant and offhand in their dealings with other races. Instead, try to be friendly and patient, and to accept that the person to whom you are talking probably doesn't speak English. Treat people with respect rather than disdain, and they'll tend to treat you in the same way.

LANDMINES In 2015, Mozambique was declared officially landmine-free. At the end of the civil war, there were estimates of over two million landmines in the country, many in poorly marked locations, and de-mining operations were given a high priority. HALO Trust, a humanitarian organisation dedicated to mine clearance, led the government in removal and cleared 171,000 landmines, over 80% of the total removed, declaring a total of 17 million square metres landmine-free. For more information visit w halotrust.org/where-we-work/africa/mozambique.

WOMEN TRAVELLERS

Women travellers generally regard subequatorial Africa as one of the safest places to travel alone anywhere in the world. Mozambique in particular poses few if any risks specific to female travellers. It is reasonable to expect a fair bit of flirting and the odd direct proposition, especially if you mingle in local bars, but a firm 'no' should be enough to defuse any potential situation. To be fair to Mozambican men, you can expect the same sort of thing in any country, and – probably with a far greater degree of persistence – from many male travellers.

Presumably as a result of Frelimo's feminist leanings, Mozambican women tend to dress and behave far less conservatively than their counterparts in neighbouring countries. You will often see evidently 'respectable' women drinking in bars and smoking on the street, behaviour that is seen as the preserve of males and prostitutes in many other parts of East and southern Africa. As for dress codes, Muslims in Mozambique seem far less orthodox than in some other African countries, but overly revealing clothes will undoubtedly attract the attention of males.

Tampons are not readily available in smaller towns, though you should be able to locate them in Beira and Maputo. If you're travelling in out-of-the-way places, it's advisable to carry enough to see you through to the next time you'll be in a large city, bearing in mind that travelling in the tropics can sometimes cause women to have heavier or more regular periods than they would at home.

GAY TRAVELLERS

Unlike some of its neighbouring African countries, homosexuality is now legal in Mozambique. As of June 2015, Mozambique became the 12th African country to decriminalise homosexuality. As such, while it is legal, that isn't to say that the overall attitude towards homosexuality has changed, but travellers are unlikely to encounter any problems. The Mozambique Association for Sexual Minority Rights (LAMBDA; w *lambdamoz.org*; f *LambdaMoz*) has been active in the country (albeit unregistered) since 2006. For more information and details of social events, visit their website or Facebook page.

TRAVELLERS WITH A DISABILITY

Mozambique's idyllic coastal resorts and stunning colonial architecture are, by their very nature, relatively inaccessible. Soft sand, pot-holed pavements and steep stone stairways are certain wheelchair stoppers, and will challenge even those with fewer mobility problems. However, if you are well organised, prepared to compromise, and can put up with some hardship, then a rewarding visit is quite possible.

The UK's **gov.uk** website (w *gov.uk/guidance/foreign-travel-for-disabled-people*) provides general advice and practical information for travellers with a disability (and their companions) preparing for overseas travel.

TRAVELLING WITH CHILDREN

The south coast has several resort areas – Bilene, Ponta do Ouro, Xai-Xai, Tofo and Vilankulo among them – whose main high-season clientele comprises South African families containing children of all ages. However, while there is no obstacle to visiting these places with children, it should be noted that most South African visitors focus strongly on fishing and other marine activities, usually bringing all their own gear, and there are few public facilities aimed at youngsters. The rest of Mozambique offers quite challenging travel conditions, and lacks child-specific facilities, so it should only be attempted with children who have experienced (and enjoyed) travel in more mainstream destinations.

WHAT TO TAKE

LUGGAGE If you intend using public transport or doing much hiking, it's best to carry your luggage on your back. There are three ways of doing this: with a purpose-made backpack, with a suitcase that converts to a rucksack, or with a large daypack. The choice between a convertible suitcase or a purpose-built backpack rests mainly on your style of travel. If you intend doing a lot of hiking, you're definitely best off with a proper backpack. However, if you carry everything in a smaller 35–45-litre daypack, the advantages are manifold on public transport and in terms of overall mobility.

CAMPING GEAR Accommodation in Mozambique isn't as cheap as it used to be, so you can make a significant saving by carrying camping gear – a lightweight tent, a bedroll and a sleeping bag. For most purposes, a light sheet sleeping bag is as useful as the real thing, performing the important role of enclosing and insulating your body, and your tent should be as light as possible. Camping gear probably won't squeeze into a daypack, in which case a sensible compromise is to carry a large daypack in your rucksack. That way, you can carry a tent and other camping equipment when you need it, but at other times you can reduce your luggage to fit into a daypack and leave what you're not using in storage.

MONEY BELT It is advisable to carry all your hard currency and credit cards, as well as your passport and other important documentation, in a money belt. The ideal money belt for Africa can be hidden beneath your clothing, as externally worn money belts are as good as telling thieves that all your valuables are there for the taking. Use a money belt made of cotton or another natural fabric, though bearing in mind that such fabrics tend to soak up a lot of sweat, you will need to wrap plastic around everything inside the money belt.

CLOTHING If you're carrying your luggage on your back, restrict your clothes to the minimum, ie: one or two pairs of trousers and/or skirts, one pair of shorts, three shirts or T-shirts, at least one sweater (or similar) depending on when and where you are visiting, enough socks and underwear to last a week, one pair of solid shoes and one of flip-flops or sandals.

Ideally, bring light cotton or microfibre trousers. Jeans are also great for durability, but they can be uncomfortable in hot weather and slow to dry after washing. Skirts, like trousers, are best made of a light fabric, and should reach below the knee (short skirts will cause needless offence to some Muslim Mozambicans and may be perceived as provocative). Any fast-drying, lightweight shirts are good, but pack at least one with long sleeves for sun protection. For general purposes, one warm sweater or fleece should be adequate. During the rainy season, it's worth carrying a light waterproof jacket or an umbrella.

Socks and underwear must be made from natural fabrics, and bear in mind that re-using them when sweaty will encourage fungal infections such as athlete's foot, as well as prickly heat in the groin. Socks and underpants are light and compact enough to make it worth bringing a week's supply. As for shoes, bulky hiking boots are probably over the top for most people, but a good pair of walking shoes, preferably with some ankle support, is recommended. It's also useful to carry sandals, flip-flops or other light shoes.

OTHER USEFUL ITEMS A mobile phone (unlocked or get it unlocked in any city) will be useful. You can buy a local SIM card for next to nothing and top-up cards are readily available and inexpensive. This also doubles as your alarm clock for any early starts.

Binoculars are essential for close-up views of wildlife, especially birds. Compact binoculars are more backpack-friendly, but their restricted field of vision compared with that of traditional binoculars can make it difficult to pick up animals in thick bush. For most purposes, 7x magnification is fine, but birdwatchers might find a 10x magnification more useful.

If you stay in local hotels, carry a padlock, as many places don't supply them. You should also carry a towel, soap, shampoo, toilet paper and any other toiletries you need (all of which are now available in Shoprite and some other supermarkets, including tampons). A torch is essential as electricity is never guaranteed. Another perennial favourite is a Swiss Army knife or multi-purpose tool.

Secondhand English-language novels can often be exchanged at beach resorts or hostels, but you won't find them on sale in many places, so it's a good idea to bring a few with you.

If travelling in your own vehicle, make sure you have a good set of tools, a selection of wire, string and rope, your driving licence and the vehicle's registration papers (and a letter of permission to use the vehicle if it is not registered in your name). Depending on how far, where and when you're driving, you might also consider spare engine oil, a jerrycan for fuel, a fan belt, spare fuses and an LED light that plugs into the cigarette lighter.

Medical kits and health-related subjects are discussed on pages 69–74, but do note that contact-lens solutions may not be available, so bring enough to last the whole trip – and bring glasses in case the intense sun and dry climate irritate your eyes.

ELECTRICAL Electricity is 220V AC at 50Hz cycles and available in most towns and cities across the country. You're less likely to find it in rural areas or the remoter towns in the north. European-style two-pin plugs are in use and there is no earthing wire, but it's worth noting that many resorts in the south will *only* have three-prong South African outlets, so it could be useful to bring an adaptor for these. Stabilisers are required for sensitive devices and adaptors for appliances using 110V. AA and D batteries sold on the street are made in China and mostly of very poor quality. You can get higher-quality Western batteries in Maputo, Beira and Nampula, but expect to pay a premium. If you need any other type of battery, you're strongly advised to bring them with you. With rechargeable batteries, your charger should work perfectly well all over the country.

MAPS Backpackers and other travellers who need a good map of Mozambique for hitching or driving purposes have a few choices. Arguably the most useful is the German *Reise Know How Mosambik & Malawi* (w *reise-know-how.de*), which is up to date and accurate, and contains a wealth of information without being cluttered. It's also waterproof and claims to be tear-proof, something you ideally won't need to put to the test. Also recommended is the Map Studio's *Mozambique Road Atlas* (w *mapstudio.com*), which has lots of town plans and regional maps, but tends to be less accurate. There is always the option to download a map application on a smartphone or tablet; free versions are available (eg: w *maps.me*).

DOCUMENTATION You are legally required to carry identification papers with you at all times, which in practice means your passport. If this gives you the willies, then a notarised copy is acceptable. There are photocopy shops in all the provincial capitals and any good hotel should be able to direct you to the nearest *notário*. If you have submitted your passport to an immigration office for a visa extension (page 44), the receipt provided acts as your identification until you retrieve your passport; a photocopy backup or a photo on a smartphone would be advisable.

MONEY

The Mozambican unit of currency is the metical (Mt, plural meticais). In some places you may find it easier to use foreign currency than meticais. South African rand (ZAR) can be used at many South African-owned resorts in the south of the country, many of which price themselves in ZAR rather than Mt. Up on the shores of Lake Malawi, Malawian kwacha are easier to use than meticais, mainly because of the greater availability of change for kwacha.

TRAVELLERS' CHEQUES Travellers' cheques are not as useful as they used to be, and an exorbitant commission is charged at the few outlets that accept them. These days, the ATM network is so good that it has to be the preferred method of accessing currency.

CASH You won't have any problems changing foreign currency in banks or *câmbios* anywhere in Mozambique, although at a bank you may have to queue (an experience in itself). There doesn't seem to be a huge variation in rates, so it's up to you how much time you're willing to spend hunting for the best deal. It is worth having a rough idea of the current rate before you change money – ask around or visit the website **w** xe.com, which has a currency converter that covers every world currency.

Changing money on the streets is possible, and it may be necessary at some border crossings or if you arrive from another country after banking hours, but otherwise it carries more risks than benefits.

CREDIT CARDS It is staggering quite how good the ATM (Auto Teller Machine) network is. All the provincial capitals have several different ATMs available, and most of the smaller towns will have at least one. However, most ATMs accept Visa cards only, though Millennium BIM and Standard Bank also accept MasterCard. There doesn't appear to be anywhere that takes American Express. Most ATMs have a daily withdrawal limit of Mt3,000 (about US$60) but Barclays and Standard Bank have a more useful daily limit of Mt10,000. That being said, it is wise to carry one or two backup cards in case your primary card fails to work or a certain branch ATM machine is out of money. Also note that it is not uncommon for ATM queues to be quite lengthy.

CHANGE Most visitors to Africa will have had problems getting change for large banknotes every now and again, one of those slightly charming little quirks that can just be laughed off as local colour. But it is noticeably worse (and significantly more annoying) in Mozambique, particularly once you get north of the Zambezi and out into rural areas. It is worth stocking up on change when you are in any town, and resolutely holding on to any change that does happen to come your way.

BUDGETING

Day-to-day expenses tend to be quite high and often poor value for money – what might be described as African standards at Western prices. The cheap-and-cheerful, few-dollars-a-night African-style lodges that exist in neighbouring countries (especially Malawi) are few and far between in Mozambique. As elsewhere, any budget will depend greatly on how and where you travel, but the following guidelines may be useful to people trying to keep costs to a minimum.

A NOTE ON PRICES

All prices in this edition were collected in late 2016 and are quoted in US dollars, but might originally have been in meticais (Mt), US dollars (US$) or South African rand (ZAR). They are based on a rough exchange rate of Mt50/ZAR13 to the US dollar. Given the current volatility of the dollar, these rates will almost certainly have changed by the time you read this. The biggest increases tend to be with the cost of accommodation – as a very rough estimate you might expect to pay 10% more than the quoted price for each calendar year after they were collected.

If you travel widely in Mozambique, it will be difficult to keep your basic travel expenses (food, transport, accommodation and drink) to much below US$50 per day for one person or US$70 per day for a couple. Your main expense will probably be accommodation: in many towns, you'll be lucky to find a double room for less than US$30, and there are plenty of places where camping costs around US$10 per person. A meal in a restaurant will typically cost US$6–10 per head, though you can save considerably by putting together your own food or eating at market stalls. Transport costs will probably work out at around US$5 daily, assuming that you're on the move every other day or thereabouts. It is possible to travel more cheaply if you carry a tent, are selective about where you visit, and stay put in cheaper places for a few days.

GETTING AROUND

BY AIR Given Mozambique's size, and the variable conditions of some of the roads, internal flights can be an attractive option. The provincial capitals all have their own airports and most have regular scheduled flights. Prices tend to be high, however, a situation that dates back to when the national airline, LAM, had a monopoly on internal flights. This is beginning to change, and you can often pick up (relatively) competitive flight prices on their website (w *lam.co.mz/en*). Alternatively, pop into the airline office or a travel agency to make a booking. Airports tend to be somewhat chaotic, and the usual rules about not leaving baggage lying around apply.

BY BOAT There are regular ferries between Maputo, Catembe and Inhaca, as well as between Maxixe and Inhambane. Boats must also be used to get between Vilankulo or Inhassoro and the islands of the Bazaruto Archipelago, to Ibo Island in northern Mozambique, and to cross some of the country's main rivers and inland waterways (the Zambezi River, Ruvuma River and Lago Niassa, for instance). If travelling by sea is your thing, you may be able to find the odd trawler plying the coast between Beira and Quelimane, or the occasional supply boat to coastal villages south of Beira; in the far north near the Tanzanian border, private fishing dhows are a legitimate alternative to travelling by road.

BY RAIL There are only four passenger routes that would interest travellers: between Maputo and the South African border at Ressano Garcia; between Nampula and Cuamba; between Cuamba and Lichinga; and to/from Maputo and the Zimbabwean border at Chicualacuala (Vila Eduardo Mondlane). The rest of the network, though marked on the maps, is either out of action or only used for freight trains and, while you may be able to hitch a lift on one, travelling by road will be quicker and easier.

BY ROAD The road network in Mozambique has historically suffered from underinvestment. In the days of the Portuguese, the railways were the dominant means of getting around the country, and little investment was available for the roads during the civil war. Since the end of the war there has been an increase in civil projects (often funded by foreign aid packages) aimed at improving the major roads, and this is gradually bearing fruit despite setbacks caused by flooding during the rainy season.

As a general rule, roads in Mozambique fall into three main categories: tarmac, graded dirt and ungraded dirt, and (as you'd expect) are somewhat variable in quality. Details of the major roads in each province are included in the relevant chapters. However, it does need to be stressed that the combination of the weather and the road-repair programme will change things. Good maps are hard to come by in the country, so best buy one before you travel (page 53).

Driving in Mozambique Mozambique (like neighbouring countries) drives on the left-hand side of the road, at least where pot-holes permit it. As a general rule you won't have any problems travelling in a saloon car on major roads as far north as Palma, with the exception of the road between Nampula and Cuamba. The main hazard to your vehicle on Mozambican roads comes from pot-holes. You are advised to keep your eyes glued to the road ahead and to slow down for oncoming traffic, since a vehicle passing in the opposite direction will impede your ability to manoeuvre around an unexpected pot-hole. If you're travelling off the major roads then you'd be strongly recommended to use a high-clearance 4x4. Livestock and pedestrians frequently wander into the middle of the road, and motorists tend to be more reckless, not to mention inebriated, than in Europe, so drive more defensively than you would at home. Driving at night is inadvisable, partly for security reasons, but also because the general chaos on the road is exacerbated by vehicles lacking headlights.

Another source of chaos and possible damage is the lack of warning triangles. While there is a legal requirement for all vehicles to carry one, this is more honoured in the breach than the observance (and lack thereof is dealt with by bribing the relevant officer). The alternative used is to pop into the bush, hack off some branches and lay them behind the broken-down vehicle, so if you do see a series of branches lying on one side of the road, slow down and be prepared. This method also seems to be used for roadworks.

Finally, be aware of cyclists – bicycles are a common form of local transport. They won't necessarily be aware of your presence so you'll have to be aware of theirs.

At the moment petrol in Mozambique costs around US$1.00 per litre, but the current fluctuations in petrol prices mean that the odds on it staying there for long are slim.

Traffic police Police in Mozambique come in two flavours: civic police (who dress in grey uniforms) and traffic police (who dress in white uniforms). Traffic police are the only ones who can officially stop vehicles and there should be one at every roadblock. They will want to see your vehicle documents, whereas civic police should only ask to see your personal ID. In our experience (about 10,000km driving in Mozambique), traffic police will only create problems if you break the law, or are perceived to, in which case they can occasionally become extremely difficult and unpleasant in the hope of levering you into paying a bribe.

Documents You should always have the following with you:

- Personal ID (your passport or a notarised copy thereof)
- Driving licence (an international one)
- Vehicle registration and ownership documents
- Third-party insurance (the one you bought at the border)
- Temporary import certificate (again, the one you got at the border).

Indicating If you are stopped, then always indicate as you pull into the side of the road, and put your hazards on while stopped.

Speed limits Usually 50km/h in towns, 100km/h outside, although if you see a different limit on a sign make sure you stick to that. There are at least two mobile speed traps operating on the EN1, there may be others elsewhere, and officers favour setting up the traps on the outskirts of villages where an incongruously low speed limit is often indicated on a sign. Speeding fines start at Mt1,000 for driving 1–20km/h above the limit within towns (add 10km/h to the range for outside of towns) and progress to Mt2,000 for violations of 20–40km/h above the speed limit, Mt4,000 for violations of 40–60km/h above the speed limit and Mt8,000 for any violation of more than 60km/h above the speed limit; it's up to you whether you take advantage of the negotiable clemency offered to motorists who don't require a receipt.

Reflective jackets and warning breakdown triangles You are legally obliged to have a warning triangle in your vehicle, although you may be better off having two – the lack of a second is frequently used as leverage for a bribe by traffic police. It is also required to carry an orange reflective jacket slung on the back of the driver's seat. Both are available at the border coming from Komatipoort in South Africa.

Trailer signs If you are towing a trailer, you should display blue-and-orange triangular signs on the front of your vehicle and the rear of the trailer.

Seat belts Must be worn at all times.

Sunglasses While there doesn't seem to be any legal basis, you hear occasional reports of traffic police stopping and trying to fine people who wear sunglasses while driving, usually on the grounds that their driving licence doesn't state they need correction to their vision. This appears to be a scam – the threat of contacting the anti-corruption campaign or your embassy should see you on your way.

If you suspect that you're being scammed The first thing to do is ask the official for his name and number and note it down. If he refuses to give them and he's on a motorbike or in a car, take the registration number of that. If the fine is genuine he is legally obliged to give you a receipt. If he is reluctant to do this then it could be an indication of a scam.

Parking It is illegal to park on the side of the road that faces oncoming traffic – in other words, except on one-way streets, you must always park on the left side of the road in relation to the direction you are driving, never on the right.

Hiring a vehicle Having a 4x4 vehicle at your disposal is a definite luxury, permitting you to forget the hassles of public transport and navigate the more difficult tracks to out-of-the-way places. This luxury, however, comes at a hefty

3

price. A 4x4, for example, rarely costs much less than US$100 per day, and quite often considerably more. The larger hotels and most travel agents can arrange car hire. Alternatively, go directly to the car-rental agencies, most of which are based at the country's larger airports (ie: Maputo, Beira and Nampula). If using one of the smaller car-hire firms, be warned that we've had iffy reports of some of them: one or two people have had their hire cars impounded by the police. Owner-operated **Rent Maputo** (**w** *rentmaputo.com*) is a thoroughly reputable local agency based in Maputo, with saloon cars starting at US$50/day and 4x4s at US$110. International rental agencies operating in Mozambique include **Avis** (**w** *avis.com*), **Europcar** (**w** *europcar.com*), **Hertz** (**w** *hertz.com*) and **Sixt** (**w** sixt.com).

Buses If you're planning on using public transport, there are two words that you'll need to become very familiar with: *machimbombo* and *chapa*. Both are forms of buses, but machimbombo refers only to coaches. Chapa has much wider application and can pretty much apply to any other form of public transport, up to and including lorries. You should be aware that, regardless of what form of vehicle you end up in, it is very unlikely that it would pass a European safety test. Most chapas are in better condition, but it's still not comfortable being crammed into the back seat of one with three other people bouncing along a rough track. The most common form of chapa is the minibus. These are the workhorses of the Mozambican public transport system and you'll see them everywhere. They are, almost without exception, packed, and if you have a long journey they can make for a very uncomfortable ride, particularly if you get stuck at the back. The best seats in a minibus are the two at the front, next to the driver.

Small lorries are almost as common as minibuses in the north of the country. While lorry rides often entail sitting on your rucksack or a bag of dried fish and hanging on for dear life, an advantage over minibuses is that you do at least have the sun on your back and the wind in your hair. It is unusual for lorries to offer any shade (although a few have a tarpaulin cover), and with journey times of up to 6 hours there's a strong risk

CORRIDORS OF POWER

While misfortune has hit Mozambique hard in recent years (civil war, droughts, floods, etc), the country can claim one big advantage over its neighbours: its location. For Mozambique is the southern African middleman, providing a vital outlet for landlocked countries such as Swaziland, Zimbabwe, Malawi, Zambia and even the Democratic Republic of Congo, while South Africa, although it boasts the continent's longest coastline, also relies heavily on Mozambican ports. To facilitate the movement of goods from these countries to the Indian Ocean, several transportation corridors exist in Mozambique. The Maputo Corridor serves mainly South Africa and Swaziland; the Beira Corridor links Zimbabwe and Zambia to the port of Beira; the Limpopo Corridor links Zimbabwe to the port of Maputo; and the Nacala Corridor is for Malawi. All of these corridors have railway lines, and the ports of Maputo, Beira and Nacala are the country's three most important. Middlemen always make money, and Mozambique has earned some vital hard currency by selling concessions to foreign investors to manage the railway lines along these corridors, as well as the ports at the end of them. Another vital transportation route, and a popular one with travellers, is the Tete Corridor, which links Zimbabwe to Malawi via the Mozambican town of Tete.

of sunburn, so you'd be well advised to have a hat with a chinstrap to hold it on. Hats without chinstraps have a tendency to disappear over the side early in the journey, and the likelihood of the driver noticing and stopping is slim to none. Suntan lotion is a must.

Chapas obey the usual African laws of leaving when they are full – there is no schedule, and a good chance that the chapa you are travelling in will be hanging around for some time after you get into it while the crew (driver and conductor) get more passengers together. Machimbombos may leave at a set time, although this is really limited to the big transport groups such as Nagi Nagi, Maning Nice or PostBus. Tickets should be purchased on the machimbombo itself or from the ticket office the day before you intend to depart. And be aware that, on many routes, most or all transport leaves very early in the morning – typically around 05.00 or earlier – so when in doubt, if you absolutely need to get somewhere on any given day, an early start is always recommended.

Costs of chapas are not (in comparison with accommodation) expensive in Mozambique. As a very general rule of thumb, expect to pay around US$1–1.50 per hour of travel (typically Mt1/km on main routes). Costs are listed at relevant points in this guide, but there's no substitute for going down to the chapa terminal and asking the other passengers. Doing this also means that you can work out how much time you need to allow for the walk from your hotel to the chapa terminal, which may grant you an extra half-hour in bed. It's not unknown for you to be charged for baggage that goes in the hold or on the roof. The latter cost may be in the region of US$1 and seems to be charged across the board, rather than just to foreigners. It seems to be more common in the south of the country than it is north of the Zambezi.

Hitching Hitching is a viable option south of Vilankulo, where there is a fair amount of private transport, and on the roads between Tete, Chimoio and Beira. It is generally slower in northern Mozambique, and the line between hitching and public transport is rather blurred here as elsewhere in Africa: most truck drivers will informally carry passengers for the same fee charged by buses and chapas, so expect to pay for any lift offered by a Mozambican.

ACCOMMODATION

As a rule, accommodation at the budget end of the scale is overpriced for what you get by almost any standards, but smarter rooms can be better value. Tourism in Mozambique is still a developing industry and the network of Western-orientated hotels is smaller than that elsewhere, so you may occasionally need to bite the bullet and take a room somewhere that is less comfortable than you would normally accept – needless to say the further you travel from the established tourist destinations, the more likely this is. There is a variety of different types of accommodation, some of which require a little explanation:

PENSÃO This is the Portuguese word for a guesthouse and is widely used throughout the country. It can be anything from a room in a family house to a fully fledged hotel. Generally speaking, they won't be organised for travellers, but can be very good value.

POUSADA Literally means 'inn' but is interchangeable with pensão.

COMPLEXO TURÍSTICO Normally a compound with a restaurant, bar, parking and rooms for hire. May also have a disco on-site.

ACCOMMODATION PRICE CODES

Price of a double room with breakfast, including tax.

Exclusive/luxury	$$$$$	US$300+
Upmarket	$$$$	US$100–300
Mid range	$$$	US$50–100
Budget	$$	US$30–50
Shoestring	$	up to US$30

BOMA Camping-specific, this refers to a pitch surrounded by a fence of wood or reeds to provide some privacy from the rest of the campsite.

BARRACA Also camping-specific, this is a large bivouac beneath which you can pitch tents. (Barraca also refers to small shops or bars, ie: Barracas do Museu in Maputo.)

Detailed accommodation listings for specific places are given in the regional part of the guide and graded into five categories: exclusive/luxury, upmarket, mid range, budget and shoestring. The purpose of this categorisation is twofold: to break up long hotel listings that span a wide price range, and to help readers isolate the range of hotels that will best suit their budget and taste. The application of categories is not rigid. Aside from an inevitable element of subjectivity, it is based as much on the feel of a hotel as its rates (which are quoted anyway) and placement may also be influenced by the standard of other accommodation in the same place. Room rates in this guide are in accordance with the normal way the specific establishment charges, ie: B&B for bed and breakfast, DB&B for dinner, bed and breakfast, FB for full board (all meals included) or all inclusive (which usually means activities are included along with all meals). Where none of the above is indicated, the rate is bed only.

EXCLUSIVE/LUXURY This category embraces a handful of international four- and five-star luxury hotels, as well as a few select smaller lodges and resorts notable less for their luxury than for offering a genuinely exclusive experience. Rates are typically upwards of US$300 for a double. This is the category to look at if you want the best and/or most characterful accommodation and have few financial restrictions.

UPMARKET This category includes most Western-style hotels, lodges and resorts that cater mainly to international tourists or business travellers but lack the special something that might elevate them into the luxury or exclusive category. Hotels in this range would typically be accorded a two- or three-star ranking elsewhere, and they offer smart en-suite accommodation with a good selection of facilities. Rates are typically around US$100–300 for a double, dependent on quality and location. Most package tours and privately booked safaris use accommodation in this range.

MID RANGE This is the most nebulous category, essentially consisting of hotels which couldn't really be classified as upmarket, but are a notch or two above the budget category in terms of price and/or quality. In cities, expect unpretentious en-suite accommodation with hot water and possibly television, a decent restaurant and efficient English-speaking staff. In more resort-like areas, a lot of the accommodation in this category comprises the self-catering units favoured by South Africans. Prices are generally in the US$50–100 range. This is the category to look at if you are travelling privately on a limited or low budget and expect a reasonably high but not luxurious standard of accommodation.

BUDGET Accommodation in this category falls into two broad types. There are hotels aimed largely at the local market that don't approach international standards, but are still reasonably clean and comfortable with a decent restaurant attached and en-suite rooms with running cold or possibly hot water. Then there are the more Westernised but equally affordable backpacker hostels and beach resorts that form the accommodation mainstay for many independent travellers to Mozambique. Expect to pay around US$30–50 for a double, depending on the location, or less to pitch a tent or stay in a dorm. This is the category to look at if you are on a limited budget, but want to avoid total squalor.

SHOESTRING This is the very bottom end of the market, usually small local guesthouses with simple rooms and common showers and toilets. Running the gamut from pleasantly clean to decidedly squalid, hotels in this category typically cost around US$15–30 for a room. It is the category for those to whom keeping down costs is the main imperative.

CAMPING Any backpacker hostels and beach resorts allow camping, typically at a cost of around US$6–10 per person. Campsites are split across the accommodation categories but would most often be associated with the budget range.

EATING AND DRINKING

FOOD Mozambique's lack of infrastructure and general easy-going attitude mean that restaurants tend to adopt a rather laissez-faire attitude towards both menus and opening hours. The further you are from the city centres, the more flexible you'll need to be. As a very general guideline, the more Westernised restaurants in the biggest cities (Maputo, Beira and to a lesser extent Nampula) will be open from around 10.00 to 20.00/21.00 and will have most of their menus available. As you go into the hinterland it becomes more important that you check with the establishment in question whether they will be open that evening and what they'll have on the menu. It may well be worth placing an order in advance and agreeing a time when you'll arrive.

In remote rural areas, food will by and large be limited to *ncima* and meat, chicken, fish, beans or similar. Meat (if you're offered it) will be goat – beef is very

RESTAURANT PRICE CODES		
Price of an average main course dish. Drinks and service charge are extra.		
Expensive	$$$$$	US$15+
Above average	$$$$	US$12-15
Mid range	$$$	US$9–12
Cheap and cheerful	$$	US$6–9
Rock bottom	$	up to US$6

cheese	*queijo*
chips	*batatas fritas*
crab	*caranguejo*
egg	*ovo*
fish	*peixe*
lobster	*langosta*
meat	*carne* (note that this may be either beef or goat)
octopus	*polvo*
Portuguese spicy sausage	*chouriço*
potato	*batata*
prawn	*camarão*
rice	*arroz*
sandwiches/snacks	*petiscos*
squid	*lula*

rarely available outside the major towns, unless you are (for whatever reason) an honoured guest. Ncima (which is also known as *ugi, ugali, sadza* or *pap*) is a form of porridge made by mixing ground maize with water and boiling it until it forms a starchy paste. It can then either be eaten as a hot porridge or left to set and eaten cold in chunks. Many foreigners are indifferent to the stodgy result, but Africans by and large love it – so much so that if offered a choice between ncima and a more Western staple such as potatoes or rice, they will choose the ncima.

In the bigger towns, menus tend to be either chips or rice with a side salad (usually heavy on tomatoes and onions) and fish (or some other form of seafood), chicken or beef. Chicken and fish will tend to be grilled or fried, while beef will almost always be a variant on a Portuguese dish called a *prego*. A prego is essentially a minute steak, usually boiled with a sauce that tastes a little like a toned-down Worcestershire sauce. The classic *prego no prato* (literally 'prego on a plate') will be served with a portion of rice, a portion of chips, the side salad and a fried egg on top. A common snack is the *prego no pão*, a prego in a bread roll. Many of the dishes that you'll see in the swankier restaurants will be variants on the prego no prato, sometimes with added ingredients (*chouriço* sausage, for instance).

Given the length of the coastline, it would be surprising if the Mozambican seafood wasn't outstanding, and Mozambican prawns do indeed have a global reputation, but the crab, lobster, crayfish and octopus are equally good.

These are some other dishes that you might come across:

Matapa or *mu-kwame*	A paste made of shredded cassava leaves, ground peanuts and coconut
Lomino	Coconut milk-based curry
Caldeirada	A stew with a mixture of different fish/seafood in a potato, onion and tomato sauce
Kitole	Rice and beans with fish and a tomato and onion sauce
Xicontombuilo	A mixture of cassava and beans
Makuchoho	Crushed maize and coconut milk
Piri-piri	Chilli sauce which can vary from merely piquant to mouth-roaringly hot. There are a few other flavours (garlic and lemon is very nice).

DRINKS Coca-Cola is the undisputed champion of the cola wars in Mozambique, being available virtually everywhere across the country, along with various flavours of Fanta (its stablemate). Sparletta, another range of soft drinks, is also universally available – the lemon-twist flavour is quite refreshing. They will almost always be brought to you sealed and opened in front of you. You can buy fruit juices in the Shoprite supermarkets, and you should be able to get the mixed fruit juice called Santal in most of the larger towns. Bottled water is ubiquitous but again make sure it's sealed.

The most widespread beers are 2M (named after a Frenchman called Mac-Mahon – you can read more about him in the introduction to Tete Province, see page 241), Laurentina (which comes in three styles: two Continental-style lagers and a stout), and Manica. You can also get South African brands such as Castle and Savanna cider.

Wine is imported, mostly from South Africa but also from Portugal. You can get it in bottles as normal, or (if you're willing to risk it) in five-litre containers with a plastic raffia-style handle. The wine in the latter is undoubtedly an acquired taste.

The locally made Tipo Tinto rum (with the rather incongruous parasol-wielding geisha on the label) is something of a cult favourite in the southern beachside towns, particularly when mixed with raspberry Sparletta to make an R&R (rum and raspberry).

PUBLIC HOLIDAYS

In addition to the fixed public holidays listed below, Good Friday and Easter Monday are recognised as public holidays in Mozambique. Other Muslim and Christian religious holidays are widely observed as well. Many of these days will be marked by heavily orchestrated public demonstrations and marches. There are also marked commemorative days and, in addition, most larger cities have their own public holiday; Maputo's is on 10 November.

FIXED PUBLIC HOLIDAYS
1 January	New Year's Day
3 February	Heroes' Day
7 April	Women's Day
1 May	Labour Day
25 June	National Day (Independence Day)
7 September	Lusaka Accord Day
25 September	Armed Forces Day
25 December	Family Day

MARKED COMMEMORATIVE DAYS
25 May	Day of African Unity
1 June	International Children's Day
16 June	Resistance Day
20 September	Assumption of Power by Transitional Government

SHOPPING

The north of the country has a craft industry, primarily making wooden furniture of simple but handsome appearance. Other crafts include the well-known Makonde carvings. The Makonde are centred on Mueda in the northeast, and here you can get representative items of their work very cheaply. Other places where you might find selections are Nampula, Nacala and Pemba.

Apart from in Maputo, where there are galleries and shops specialising in arts and crafts, most of the souvenirs that you'll find on your travels will be sold on the street outside hotels, restaurants and other places frequented by tourists. Even this is a relatively recent development; a few years ago it was difficult to find souvenirs of any description sold anywhere. As elsewhere in Africa, bargaining for souvenirs is expected, although you should conduct such negotiations in a respectful and responsible manner (see below for further details).

If you are in Nampula or Cabo Delgado, keep an eye open for cashew nuts being sold on the street.

BARGAINING AND OVERCHARGING The emphasis that some tourists (both package and independent) place on bargaining can be a little over the top. Bargaining has its place but the common assumption that every individual you come across will quote inflated prices to tourists is nonsensical. Hotels, pensões, restaurants and supermarkets will display prices for their wares, so bargaining is of no value. In the off-season, some of the more expensive hotels may have special rates that will be worth asking about, but that's not a bargaining situation as such.

Buses and taxis also tend to operate standard rates, but it is harder to find out what these are. The best way is just to ask a few people what a fair price is from X to Y – the consensus will give you a good guide. There may be some flexibility with taxis but it's highly unlikely with buses.

Fruit and vegetable markets and stalls are a different proposition. Hang about any market for a short while and you will see bargaining going on between locals, so this is a situation where bargaining is acceptable. As ever the better informed you are at the start of the process, the more likely you are to be able to come to a mutually satisfying agreement, so it's worth asking at a few stalls to see what the norm is before starting your bargaining. In addition you'll find that stallholders will be far more amenable if you are buying a range of produce rather than just one or two items. The longer you spend in a town, the easier you will find it to gauge what is a fair price for the items you are buying there.

Similarly arts and crafts have scope for a degree of bargaining, and in fact the vendors would probably be hugely surprised if you didn't haggle to some extent. Again it will be easier to gain a reduction if you are buying a range of items rather than just the one. In some places (notably the Makonde carving collectives in Nampula and Pemba) the carvings are all individually priced using sticky labels; haggling is not expected here.

The key thing when bargaining is to be relaxed about the whole business. Adopting an aggressive posture is only likely to irritate the other party and lowers the likelihood of a successful conclusion to the whole business.

Above all it's crucial to retain a sense of proportion. Regardless of how poor you are in Western terms, you will have far more money than the person you're dealing with. Temper your desire for a bargain with some generosity and you will find that you get a better deal as a result.

PHOTOGRAPHY

Taking photographs is part and parcel of travelling, but it needs to be done with sensitivity. Taking wildlife photographs and scenic views is fine, but you do need to be a little more circumspect when taking photographs of buildings and people. It is illegal to take photographs of any public buildings in Maputo, and there is a danger of being fined if you are caught doing so. Similarly, if you are caught taking photographs of military or government buildings anywhere in the country you may be in for a bumpy ride.

When taking photographs of specific individuals it is vital that you ask their permission first. Like many African countries, Mozambique is socially a little more conservative than the West, and pointing a camera at someone without asking can cause offence. One of the most common reactions of people who do not want to be photographed is to turn their face away from the camera or hide behind their hand – if you see this reaction then point your camera in a different direction. It may seem silly to us, but appearing to continue photographing them will cause grave offence. At best it will just reinforce the stereotype of tourists being rude, at worst it may lead to a public altercation. Although it's impossible to ask everyone in a street scene, you should watch for similar reactions there. If it's clear that a significant number of people are disturbed by your camera, put it away.

The above does make it sound as though people in Mozambique are generally averse to having their photographs taken, but this isn't the case – the majority will be more than happy to have you snap them, providing you ask first. With children it's not unknown for a scrum to develop as everyone tries to get themselves in shot. If you are shooting digital, it's well worth showing them the resultant photographs – the overwhelming reaction is paroxysms of delight.

MEDIA AND COMMUNICATIONS

NEWSPAPERS The main daily newspapers are *Noticias* (Maputo), which supports the government, and *Diario* (Beira). The main weeklies are *Savana*, *Domingo* (coming out on Sundays), the newer *Verdade* and the magazine *Tempo*. If you are craving an English-language news fix, South African newspapers are also available in a very few places in Maputo, normally a day or two old and at a very high price.

TELEVISION AND RADIO Radio Mozambique broadcasts on three channels in Portuguese as well as several local languages. Since 1981 there has been experimental television, TV Mozambique, which broadcasts imported Portuguese and Brazilian programmes alongside Mozambican programmes. There is also an independent station, RTK Television, with an English-language bias. Many upmarket hotels pick up DSTV, a South African service offering a varied bouquet of international satellite sports, news, movie and other channels.

TELEPHONE The international telephone code for Mozambique is +258, and the internal telephone system is surprisingly efficient. The national backbone is reasonably extensive and stable; if you're dialling in-country, just knock the +258 off the front. Mobile phones have really taken off in Mozambique, and the coverage is extensive. The three major networks are the home-grown mCel (numbers beginning with 82), the South African Vodacom (numbers beginning with 84) and Movitel (numbers beginning with 86 or 87), also from Mozambique; the prefix 88 is shared by various networks. For all mobile-phone networks, phone numbers have nine digits, and you'll have no problems buying SIM cards or top-up vouchers in places where there is coverage. All networks have coverage in all the provincial capitals, and along most of the major roads south of the Zambezi. North of the river, things are patchier and in the very far north you won't have coverage outside the larger towns, though this is changing incredibly fast as the networks expand. As a rule, Movitel has the widest service in rural areas. On the shores of Lake Malawi, you may find it easier to connect to a Malawian network than a

Mozambican one. All landline and mobile numbers in Mozambique used to have a leading 0, but this was ditched a few years ago, reputedly only as a temporary measure, although no-one seems in a rush to reinstate it.

POST Post from Mozambique is reasonably reliable, but it is often very slow and can be expensive, costing around US$4 to send a postcard. Postcards are difficult to find in Mozambique anyway, and they are often very expensive as well.

EMAIL AND INTERNET The network of internet cafés is not as wide, or as cheap or as fast, as in the rest of the world, but it does at least exist in the larger towns, most of the time. You will find privately run internet cafés, which vary in quality and cost, listed at relevant points in this guide. It is increasingly common for restaurants and hotels to offer Wi-Fi, and these are indicated as well. If you need regular internet access, the easiest solution is to buy a mobile phone with internet functionality, and get somebody at mCel, Vodacom or Movitel to rig it up to browse – this takes 5 minutes to set up, and gives you inexpensive internet access wherever there is mobile reception. USB dongles are available from all three service providers, allowing you to browse the internet from your computer in the same way (if you have a smartphone, you can create a hot spot and save the expense of another gadget).

RESPONSIBLE TOURISM

BEFORE YOU LEAVE If you want to swot up beforehand on what it means to be a responsible tourist, a UK-based source of information is **Tourism Concern** (↘ 020 8263 6007; e info@tourismconcern.org.uk; w tourismconcern.org.uk). It's also good to do some research about the country you're about to visit – not just its weather and its costs and its hotels, but also what makes it tick: its history, culture, achievements, failures, and so on. It can help to break the ice with local people if you know something (anything!) about their country and way of life.

CARBON EMISSIONS If you'd like to offset the carbon footprint of your flight, try w carbonneutral.com, run by a UK organisation. The website has an easy-to-use emissions calculator and a range of offset programmes.

IN MOZAMBIQUE Fancy terms such as 'cultural sensitivity' and 'low-impact tourism' just boil down to good old-fashioned respect and common sense. As a visitor, you should be willing to adapt to and respect local customs and traditions. For example, learn a bit of the local language, seek the permission of the community leader before roaming through villages, and ask before you take photographs. In conservative rural areas, note how the local people dress and don't expose parts of yourself that they keep hidden. Of course pick up your litter or don't drop it in the first place – and don't uproot plants and flowers. Also be careful to use energy resources such as water and electricity efficiently, not to wash in lakes or rivers (regardless of local practices, because of pollution) or get too close to the wildlife.

Shop locally and use the services of local people whenever possible. Buy souvenirs from the craftspeople who made them rather than via middlemen who will siphon off profits, and patronise small street vendors rather than big supermarkets. Don't bargain unreasonably; the difference may be the cost of a drink to you but a whole family meal to the vendor. Use the services of a local guide, or a child who wants to help, and pay a fair rate.

If you have spent time in a village and become friendly with its inhabitants, why not consider donating pens, crayons and notebooks to the local primary school? It's easy to buy stationery in local markets. Ask to meet the schoolteacher, so that he/she can receive and officially distribute the gift. Offer to spend some time in the school, being questioned by the children about your home country.

A warning: travellers often collect up pens/biros at home beforehand and bring them over to donate – but, in this case, *please* check that they work and have plenty of ink before handing them over. To an impoverished rural child, a new pen is a huge and thrilling gift. He/she is so proud and happy – and then so bitterly disappointed when it stops working after only a few hours. And do bear in mind the damage you can do by giving little gifts (coins, sweets, pens, cookies or whatever) to a child or youngster who comes up and begs, however cutely. If the begging bears fruit (and if the gift isn't immediately grabbed by a bigger child), he/she will start to pester all visitors. Or begging may appear more profitable than going to school.

GETTING INVOLVED *With Janice Booth*

Don't lose sight of the fact that you contribute to a country's economy simply by being there. Every time you travel by public transport, eat in a restaurant, buy a paper from a street vendor or give a few coins to a local guide you are providing a very real benefit to them and their families. But there are ways in which you can help more. Some of the lodges have established development programmes – with the best of these the programmes would have been a major part of the original plan and will have evolved as the lodge developed. Particularly good examples are mentioned in the text. If this is something you'd like to encourage, then ask your lodge in advance about community programmes it is involved with. If you like what you hear then stay there, and if you don't then try one of the other places listed.

After you've returned home, try to be an ambassador. Share your experiences, and keep in touch with the people you've met on your travels. Mozambique's international image can be rather negative, and simply by talking about the country's beauty and many other positive aspects you can help to dispel misconceptions.

If you've enjoyed Mozambique and feel that you'd like to stay in touch with the country or to put something back into it, here are a few suggestions. If you ask around on the spot, you'll certainly find others.

If you'd like to return as a **volunteer** and have some relevant skills, check out **Voluntary Service Overseas** (w *vso.org.uk*). They also welcome donations, from small amounts up to the cost of maintaining a volunteer in a developing country. Also worth checking out is **Travel People and Places** (w *travel-peopleandplaces. co.uk*) and **International Voluntary Service** (w *ivsgb.org*).

A way to volunteer without leaving home is via the **Online Volunteering Service** (w *onlinevolunteering.org*); it's managed by the United Nations Volunteers Programme (UNV), which is the volunteer arm of the UN. Volunteers need reliable access to a computer and the internet, and some relevant skill or experience.

It's sometimes hard to remember that the work of the massive international **charities** reaches down to benefit the poorest, and that they need our small donations. But it does, and they do. For making a general donation you could do far worse. Check which come closest to your interests. If it's wildlife that appeals to you, then you'll already know about the **Worldwide Fund for Nature** (w *wwf.org*), which has a big presence in Mozambique and particularly in the Quirimbas National Park (page 333). Overleaf are some others.

PRACTICAL ACTION (w *practicalaction.org*) Formerly the Independent Technology Group (w *itdg.org*), founded in 1966 by the radical economist Dr E F Schumacher, Practical Action works to show that correctly chosen technologies can help people to find lasting, appropriate solutions to poverty, and that a small-scale approach can bring results that benefit whole communities long into the future. It enables poor communities to discover how new technologies, adapted in the right way, can improve their lives.

BOOK AID INTERNATIONAL (w *bookaid.org*) This is another organisation well worth supporting. A UK-based charity established in the 1950s, it works in 17 sub-Saharan African countries. The majority of its partners are urban and rural libraries that are free for use by all, but it also works with schools throughout the region. Book Aid prides itself on ensuring that the books it sends out are of genuine educational value and covering as wide a range of subjects as possible.

SAVE THE CHILDREN (w *savethechildren.org.uk*) It started work in Mozambique in 1984. Its aim is to improve the lives of children and young people and to ensure that they have access to good quality basic services. It works in partnership with the government, donors, local and international NGOs and local communities.

SOS CHILDREN'S VILLAGES (w *soschildrensvillages.org.uk*) This organisation constructed its first community in Mozambique in 1987, in Tete, for children who had lost their parents in the war. Since then it has opened villages and/or centres in Maputo and Pemba. These include schools, medical centres and vocational training. Contact details for SOS Children's Villages in Mozambique are on the website.

WATERAID (w *wateraid.org.uk*) This much-praised charity is dedicated to the provision of safe domestic water, sanitation and hygiene education to the world's poorest people. In Mozambique, it has already helped more than 270,000 people to access clean water. WaterAid's partner in Mozambique, ESTAMOS, has won the Mozambique Development Prize for its work in ecological sanitation.

A highly commendable local organisation with volunteer placements worth checking out is the **Manda Wilderness Community Trust** at Nkwichi Lodge (w *mandawilderness.org*).

MOZAMBIQUE ONLINE

For additional online content, articles, photos and more on Mozambique, why not visit w bradtguides.com/mozambique.

4

Health

with Dr Felicity Nicholson

People new to exotic travel often worry about tropical diseases, but it is accidents that are most likely to carry you off. Road accidents are very common in many parts of Mozambique so be aware and do what you can to reduce risks (pages 56–8). Listen to local advice about areas where violent crime is rife, too.

In Mozambique there are private clinics, hospitals and pharmacies in most large towns, but unless you speak Portuguese you may have difficulty communicating your needs beyond relatively straightforward requests such as a malaria test – try to find somebody bilingual to visit the hospital with you. Consultation fees and laboratory tests are remarkably inexpensive when compared with those in Western countries so, if you do fall ill, it would be absurd to let financial considerations dissuade you from seeking medical help. You should be able to buy such commonly required medicines as broad-spectrum antibiotics and metronidazole (Flagyl) in any sizeable town. If you are wandering off the beaten track, it might be worth carrying the obvious with you. As for malaria tablets, whether for prophylaxis or treatment, you would be wise to get them before you go as not all tablets are available readily.

PREPARATIONS

Sensible preparation will go a long way to ensuring your trip goes smoothly. Particularly for first-time visitors to Africa, this includes a visit to a travel clinic at least eight weeks in advance of your trip to discuss matters such as vaccinations and malaria prevention. A full list of travel clinic websites worldwide is available at w itsm.org, and other useful websites for prospective travellers include w travelhealthpro.org.uk (formerly Nathnac) and w netdoctor.co.uk/travel. All advice found online should be used in conjunction with expert advice received prior to or during travel.

The Bradt website now carries a health section online (w *bradtguides.com/ africahealth*) to help travellers prepare for their African trip, elaborating on most issues raised below, but the following summary points are worth emphasising:

- Don't travel without good quality, comprehensive **medical travel insurance** that covers the activities you intend to pursue, is adequate for your health needs and will fly you home in an emergency. You would be advised to read the small print on your travel insurance documents to ensure that you are covered for vaccine-preventable diseases if you decide not to take the vaccines.
- Make sure all your immunisations are up to date. Proof of vaccination against **yellow fever** is needed for entry into Mozambique if you are coming from a yellow fever endemic area. Please discuss with a travel health expert. If the vaccine is not suitable for you, then obtain an exemption certificate from your GP or a travel clinic, although there is no guarantee that the Mozambique

border guards will accept this. It is also wise to be up to date on **tetanus**, **polio** and **diphtheria** (now given as an all-in-one vaccine, Revaxis, which lasts for ten years), **typhoid** and **hepatitis A**. Vaccination against **hepatitis B and rabies** may be recommended. Cholera vaccine is usually only recommended during outbreaks and if there is little or no guarantee of clean water.

- The biggest health threat is **malaria**. There is no vaccine against this mosquito-borne disease, but a variety of preventative drugs is available, including mefloquine, atovaquone/progunail (Malarone) and the antibiotic doxycycline. The most suitable choice of drug varies depending on the individual and the country they are visiting, so visit your GP or a travel clinic for medical advice. If you will be spending a long time in Africa, and expect to visit remote areas, be aware that no preventative drug is 100% effective, so carry a cure too. It is also worth noting that no homeopathic prophylactic for malaria exists, nor can any traveller acquire effective resistance to malaria. Those who don't make use of preventative drugs risk their life in a manner that is both foolish and unnecessary.

- Though advised for everyone, a pre-exposure **rabies** vaccination, involving three doses taken over a minimum of 21 days, is particularly important if you intend to have contact with animals, or are likely to be 24 hours away from medical help. It is very difficult to get treatment for rabies in Mozambique if you have not had the pre-exposure vaccine.

- Anybody travelling away from major centres should carry a **personal first-aid kit**. Contents might include a good drying antiseptic (eg: iodine or potassium permanganate), Band-Aids, suncream, insect repellent, aspirin or paracetamol, antifungal cream (eg: Canesten), ciprofloxacin or norfloxacin (for severe diarrhoea), antibiotic eye drops, tweezers, condoms or femidoms, a digital thermometer and a needle-and-syringe kit with accompanying letter from a healthcare professional.

- Bring any drugs or devices relating to **known medical conditions** with you. That applies both to those who are on medication prior to departure, and those who are, for instance, allergic to bee stings, or are prone to attacks of asthma.

- Prolonged immobility on long-haul flights can result in **deep-vein thrombosis** (DVT), which can be dangerous if the clot travels to the lungs to cause pulmonary embolus. The risk increases with age, and is higher in obese or pregnant travellers, heavy smokers, those taller than 6ft/1.8m or shorter than 5ft/1.5m, and anybody with a history of clots, recent major operation or varicose veins surgery, cancer, a stroke or heart disease. If any of these criteria apply, consult a doctor before you travel.

MEDICAL PROBLEMS

MALARIA Along with road accidents, malaria poses the single biggest serious threat to the health of travellers in most parts of tropical Africa, Mozambique included: the *Anopheles* mosquito that transmits the parasite is found throughout the country all year round and should be assumed to be present at all altitudes below 1,800m (the risk of malaria above 1,800m above sea level is low). It is unwise to travel in malarial parts of Africa while pregnant or with children: the risk of malaria in many parts is considerable and these travellers are likely to succumb rapidly to the disease.

Since no malaria prophylactic is 100% effective, it makes sense to take all reasonable precautions against being bitten by the nocturnal *Anopheles* mosquitoes that transmit the disease (box, page 74). Malaria usually manifests within two weeks of transmission (though it can be as short as seven days), but it can take months, which means that short-stay visitors are most likely to experience symptoms after they return home. These typically include a rapid rise in temperature (over 38°C), and any combination of a headache, flu-like aches and pains, a general sense of disorientation, and possibly even nausea and diarrhoea. The earlier malaria is detected, the better it usually responds to treatment. So if you display possible symptoms, get to a doctor or clinic immediately. A simple test, available at even the most rural clinic in Africa, is usually adequate to determine whether you have malaria. However, if the test is returned negative, be sure to stay nearby so the test can be repeated up to three days in a row to ensure it is a true result. And while experts differ on the question of self-diagnosis and self-treatment, the reality is that, if you think you have malaria and are not within easy reach of a doctor, it would be wisest to start treatment. Travellers to remote parts of Mozambique would be advised to carry with them a course of treatment.

OTHER INSECT-BORNE DISEASES Although malaria is the insect-borne disease that attracts the most attention in Africa, and rightly so, there are others, most too uncommon to be a significant concern to short-stay travellers. These include dengue fever and other arboviruses (spread by diurnal mosquitoes), sleeping sickness (tsetse flies), and river blindness (blackflies). Bearing this in mind, however, it is clearly sensible, and makes for a more pleasant trip, to avoid insect bites as far as possible (box, page 74). Two nasty (though ultimately relatively harmless) flesh-eating insects associated with tropical Africa are mango flies (also called *tumbu* or *putsi* flies), which lay eggs, often on drying laundry, that hatch and bury themselves under the skin when they come into contact with humans; and jiggers, which latch on to bare feet and set up home, usually at the side of a toenail, where they cause a painful boil-like swelling. Drying laundry indoors and wearing shoes are the best ways to deter this pair of flesh-eaters. Symptoms and treatment of all these afflictions are described in greater detail on Bradt's website (w *bradtguides.com/africahealth*).

TRAVELLERS' DIARRHOEA Travelling in Mozambique carries a fairly high risk of getting a dose of travellers' diarrhoea; perhaps half of all visitors will suffer and the newer you are to exotic travel, the more likely you will be to suffer. By taking precautions against travellers' diarrhoea you will also avoid typhoid, paratyphoid, cholera, hepatitis, dysentery, worms, etc. This most often results from cooks not washing their hands after a trip to the toilet, but even if the restaurant cook does not understand basic hygiene you will be safe if your food has been properly cooked and arrives piping hot. The most important prevention strategy is to wash your hands before eating anything. You can pick up salmonella and shigella from toilet door handles and possibly banknotes. The maxim to remind you what you can safely eat is:

PEEL IT, BOIL IT, COOK IT OR FORGET IT

This means that fruit you have washed and peeled yourself, and hot foods, should be safe but raw foods, cold cooked foods, salads, fruit salads that have been prepared by others, ice cream and ice are all risky, and foods kept lukewarm in hotel buffets are often dangerous. That said, plenty of travellers and expatriates enjoy fruit and vegetables, so do keep a sense of perspective: food served in a fairly decent hotel in a large town or a place regularly frequented by expatriates is likely to be safe.

If you suffer a bout of diarrhoea, it is dehydration that makes you feel awful, so drink lots of water and other clear fluids. These can be infused with sachets of oral

You can fall ill from drinking contaminated water so try to drink from safe sources, eg: bottled water where available. If you are away from shops and your bottled water runs out, make tea, pour the remaining boiled water into a clean container and use it for drinking. Alternatively, water should be passed through a good bacteriological filter or purified with iodine or the less-effective chlorine tablets (eg: Puritabs).

rehydration salts, though any dilute mixture of sugar and salt in water will do you good, for instance a bottled soda with a pinch of salt. If diarrhoea persists beyond a couple of days, it is possible it is a symptom of a more serious sanitation-related illness (typhoid, cholera, hepatitis, dysentery, worms, etc), so get to a doctor. If the diarrhoea is greasy and bulky, and is accompanied by sulphurous (eggy) burps, one likely cause is **giardia**, which is best treated with tinidazole (four x 500mg in one dose, repeated seven days later if symptoms persist).

EYE PROBLEMS Bacterial conjunctivitis (pink eye) is a common infection in Africa; people who wear contact lenses are most open to this irritating problem. The eyes feel sore and gritty and they will often be stuck together in the mornings. They will need treatment with antibiotic drops or ointment. Lesser eye irritation should settle with bathing in salt water and keeping the eyes shaded. If an insect flies into your eye, extract it with great care, ensuring you do not crush or damage it, otherwise you may get a nastily inflamed eye from toxins secreted by the creature. Small elongated red-and-black blister beetles have warning coloration to tell you not to crush them anywhere against your skin.

PRICKLY HEAT A fine pimply rash on the trunk is likely to be heat rash; taking cool showers, dabbing dry and applying talc will help. Treat the problem by slowing down to a relaxed schedule, wearing only loose, baggy, 100% cotton clothes and sleeping naked under a fan; if it's bad you may need to check into an air-conditioned hotel room for a while.

SKIN INFECTIONS Any mosquito bite or small nick in the skin gives an opportunity for bacteria to foil the body's usually excellent defences; it will surprise many travellers how quickly skin infections start in warm, humid climates and it is essential to clean and cover even the slightest wound. Creams are not as effective as a good drying antiseptic, eg: Savlon dry spray or an equivalent. It is worth carrying this in your medical kit. If the wound starts to throb, or becomes red and the redness starts to spread, or the wound oozes, and especially if you develop a fever, antibiotics will probably be needed.

Fungal infections also get a hold easily in hot, moist climates so wear 100% cotton socks and underwear, and shower frequently, drying thoroughly. An itchy rash in the groin or flaking between the toes is likely to be a fungal infection. This needs treatment with an antifungal cream such as Canesten (clotrimazole); if this is not available try Whitfield's ointment (compound benzoic acid ointment) or crystal violet (although this will turn you purple!).

SUNSTROKE AND DEHYDRATION Overexposure to the sun can lead to short-term sunburn or sunstroke, and increases the long-term risk of skin cancer. Keep out of the sun during the middle of the day and, if you must expose yourself to the sun, build up gradually from 20 minutes per day. Be especially careful of exposure in the middle of the day and of sun reflected off water, and wear a T-shirt and lots of waterproof suncream (at least SPF25) when swimming. When visiting outdoor sites, cover up with long, loose clothes, wear a hat and use sunscreen. The glare and the dust can be hard on the eyes too, so bring UV-protecting sunglasses and, perhaps, a soothing eyebath. A less direct effect of the tropical heat is dehydration, so drink more fluids than you would at home.

BILHARZIA Also known as schistosomiasis, bilharzia is an unpleasant parasitic disease transmitted by freshwater snails most often associated with reedy shores where there is lots of water weed. This parasite is common in almost all water sources in Mozambique, even places advertised as 'bilharzia free'. The most risky shores will be close to places where infected people use water, wash clothes, etc. Ideally, however, you should avoid swimming in any fresh water other than an artificial pool. If you do swim, you'll reduce the risk by applying DEET insect repellent first, staying in the water for under 10 minutes, and drying off vigorously with a towel. Bilharzia is often asymptomatic in its early stages, but some people experience an intense immune reaction, including fever, cough, abdominal pain and an itching rash, around four to six weeks after infection. Later symptoms vary but often include a general feeling of tiredness and lethargy. Bilharzia is difficult to diagnose, but it can be tested for at specialist travel clinics, ideally at least six weeks after likely exposure. Fortunately, it is easy to treat at present.

HIV/AIDS The risks of sexually transmitted infection are extremely high in Mozambique, whether you sleep with fellow travellers or locals. About 40% of HIV infections in British heterosexuals are acquired abroad (most of which come from Africa). If you must indulge, use condoms or femidoms, which help reduce the risk of transmission. If you notice any genital ulcers or discharge, get treatment promptly since these increase the risk of acquiring HIV. If you do have unprotected sex, visit a clinic as soon as possible; this should be within 24 hours, or no later than 72 hours, for post-exposure prophylaxis.

RABIES This deadly disease can be carried by any mammal and is usually transmitted to humans via a bite or deep scratch. Beware village dogs and habituated monkeys, but assume that any mammal that bites or scratches you (or even licks your skin) might be rabid. First, scrub the wound or area contaminated with saliva with soap under a running tap, or while pouring water from a jug, then pour on a strong iodine or alcohol solution, which will guard against infections and might reduce the risk of the rabies virus entering the body. Whether or not you underwent pre-exposure vaccination, it is vital to obtain post-exposure prophylaxis as soon as possible after the incident. However, if you have had the vaccine before exposure, treatment is very much easier. It removes the need for a human blood product (Rabies Immunoglobulin; RIG) which is not pleasant to have, expensive and often hard to find. Death from rabies is probably one of the worst ways to go, and once you show symptoms it is too late to do anything – the mortality rate is 100%.

TICK BITES Ticks in Africa are not the rampant disease transmitters that they are in the Americas, but they may spread tickbite fever along with a few dangerous rarities in Mozambique. Ticks should ideally be removed complete, and as soon as possible, to reduce the chance of infection. The best way to do this is to grasp the

The *Anopheles* mosquitoes that spread malaria are active at dusk and after dark. Most bites can thus be avoided by covering up at night. This means donning a long-sleeved shirt, trousers and socks from around 30 minutes before dusk until you retire to bed, and applying a DEET-based insect repellent to any exposed flesh. It is best to sleep under a net, or in an air-conditioned room, though burning a mosquito coil and/or sleeping under a fan will also reduce (though not entirely eliminate) bites. Travel clinics usually sell a good range of nets and repellents, as well as Permethrin treatment kits, which will render even the tattiest net a lot more protective, and helps prevent mosquitoes from biting through a net when you roll against it. These measures will also do much to reduce exposure to other nocturnal biters. Bear in mind, too, that most flying insects are attracted to light: leaving a lamp standing near a tent opening or a light on in a poorly screened hotel room will greatly increase the insect presence in your sleeping quarters.

It is also advisable to think about avoiding bites when walking in the countryside by day, especially in wetland habitats, which often teem with diurnal mosquitoes. Wear a long loose shirt and trousers, preferably 100% cotton, as well as proper walking or hiking shoes with heavy socks (the ankle is particularly vulnerable to bites), and apply a DEET-based insect repellent to any exposed skin.

tick with your finger nails as close to your body as possible, and pull it away steadily and firmly at right angles to your skin (do not jerk or twist it). If possible douse the wound with alcohol (any spirit will do) or iodine. If you are travelling with small children, remember to check their heads, and particularly behind the ears, for ticks. Spreading redness around the bite and/or fever and/or aching joints after a tick bite imply that you have an infection that requires antibiotic treatment, so seek advice.

SNAKE BITES Snakes rarely attack unless provoked, and bites in travellers are unusual. You are less likely to get bitten if you wear stout shoes and long trousers when in the bush. Most snakes are harmless and even venomous species will dispense venom in only about half of their bites. If bitten, then, you are unlikely to have received venom; keeping this fact in mind may help you to stay calm. Many so-called first-aid techniques do more harm than good: cutting into the wound is harmful; tourniquets are dangerous; suction and electrical inactivation devices do not work. It is important to keep the victim calm and inactive, and to seek urgent medical attention. At the time of writing, antivenom was known to be available in Maputo.

OTHER SAFETY CONCERNS

CAR ACCIDENTS Dangerous driving is probably the biggest threat to life and limb in most parts of Africa. On a self-drive visit, drive defensively, being especially wary of stray livestock, gaping pot-holes, and imbecilic or bullying overtaking manoeuvres. Many vehicles lack headlights and most local drivers are reluctant headlight-users, so avoid driving at night and pull over in heavy storms. On a chauffeured tour, don't be afraid to tell the driver to slow or calm down if you think he is too fast or reckless. Always wear a seat belt and refuse to be driven by anyone who has been drinking.

5

Diving and Snorkelling

Danny Edmunds

The diving in Mozambique is as good as you'll find anywhere along the East African coastline south of the Equator, but the remoteness of the location and comparative lack of diving-specific medical facilities mean that you need to be savvy. Most of the following applies to divers, so a separate section on snorkelling is included at the end.

CHOOSING AN OPERATOR

Dive operators are opening up all the way along the coastline, and the vast majority are affiliated to PADI (Professional Association of Diving Instructors) or another internationally recognised training and certification organisation. In addition there are a few operators who don't have affiliation to any of the dive associations. It would be unfair to label the latter as bad a priori, but they don't operate to the same level of inspection as an affiliated operator. If you can't see the logo for your preferred association, then ask – if affiliated they should be able to produce the relevant certificate. However, certification is only one indicator you should look for – the section below also gives some pointers. It's also worth asking other divers and locals their opinions.

PREPARATIONS BEFORE DIVING

QUALIFICATIONS Any reputable operator should check both your qualification level (as shown on your C-card) and your recent dive history. They should then tailor the dive to the ability level of the least-qualified diver or, if this isn't feasible, split the group.

KIT In remote places, kit will almost certainly be serviced on-site. It may look worn and faded but providing it's been well maintained it will be reliable. Personally I always put together any kit that I am going to use myself, and I check the following:

Regulators
- Does it have an octopus? Do both sets of regulators breathe easily on the surface, with no evidence of juddering?
- Is the contents gauge showing zero before the regulators are connected to the tank? Does it show the correct pressure once the regulators are pressurised? Turn the tank off again and breathe through the regulator – the needle should move down smoothly.
- When the regulators are pressurised, can you detect any leakages from the hoses? If possible, dunk the pressurised set in the water before you get on the boat – can you see any obvious leakages? If you can't dunk it while still on the shore, do a check once you are in the water, but make sure you do it *before* leaving the surface.

- Check the hoses connecting the first stage to the second stage for cracking or other damage.
- If there is a depth gauge on the unit, check that the marker needle is moved back to zero before you get in the water. Keep an eye on it as you descend through the first few metres – it should clearly indicate the depth change.

Stab/BC
- Does it fit properly? If it's too big or too small, get another one.
- What is the condition of the clips that hold it together? They should fit securely enough to hold during normal use and yet still be breakable should you need to dump the kit in a hurry.
- Does the inflator valve connect properly to the hose? Always test the inflator before leaving the shore to make sure that you can fully inflate the stab. It should not deflate when dunked in water. In particular check the seams of the stab for leaks.
- Do all the dump valves work properly? Make sure you are familiar with their location on the kit and that you can work them easily while wearing the kit.

Tank
- Check the condition of the tank for signs of rust and external damage, and also check the condition of the pillar valve – it should take a little effort to open and close (thus ensuring that it's not going to close accidentally during the dive). If there is any visible damage to the pillar valve or it appears to stick, get a replacement tank.
- Is there enough air in the tank for the dive you are intending to do? Does it taste clean and dry when you test the regulators?
- Look for evidence of testing on the cylinders. This can be tricky in Mozambique, but the standard in the UK is for each tank to have the date and type of its last test stamped into it. If you're unsure then ask for clarification on precisely when, where and how the tanks were last tested.

Fins and booties You will probably be offered a choice between separate booties with rear-entry fins (where you put the booties on like shoes and then slip into the fins) or slipper fins (where the booties and fins are combined into one unit). I'd only recommend the latter if you know for sure that you'll be able to walk across clean sand to the boat. If you have any doubt or are going to have to wade to the boat or the dive site, take separate booties and fins.

Check the fit of the booties and fins before you leave the shop – too loose and you risk losing them during your dive; too tight and you'll get cramp and blisters and may find yourself unable to fin.

Weight belt
- Weight is carried to compensate for the air lost during the dive, so the ideal amount of weight to carry is enough to enable you to hover comfortably at 5m with only 50 bar remaining for a few minutes. You should know how much weight you need from the details in your logbook.
- Check the weight belt fabric – it should be strong with little fraying or cuts.
- Check the buckle – it should hold in any position but still be undoable in an emergency. Bear in mind that during the dive it will become looser as your wetsuit compresses, so you may need to readjust it occasionally. The belt should be tight enough to stay in position without restricting your breathing.

- Check the fixing of the weights. They should be secured so that they don't move around during the dive. Needless to say they should not be capable of falling off during the dive.

Clothing

- The surface temperature of the seas in Mozambique is likely to be in the region of 23–28°C depending on the time of year. You may feel that this is warm enough to dive wearing only a T-shirt and shorts but bear in mind that thermoclines can occur where you'll lose up to 5°C, so a wetsuit covering at least your torso is highly recommended.
- Wetsuits will also protect you from jellies, hydroids and other stinging things.

Masks

- It is crucial that the mask fits your face, and the best way of checking this is to put the mask on your face so that it seals around your eyes and nose. Breathe in through your nose and hold your breath – the mask should stay attached to your face with no leakages. If it loosens or drops off then try another mask.
- Check the skirt (the latex seal) around the mask – it should be reasonably flexible with no damage or tears.
- Check the side clips holding the mask-strap on to the mask – they should be sound and secure.
- Check the strap – it should be in good condition with some slack in it when you are wearing it. It's important that you don't have the strap too tight.
- If you need prescription lenses, then I'd strongly recommend that you take your own mask with you.

Computers/dive watches It's highly unlikely that you'll be given a computer or dive watch as part of the basic kit. However, it is crucial that you have a means of measuring both the length of time you have been underwater and the depth you're at (pages 78–81). Personally, I carry my dive computer with me when I travel somewhere I might be diving.

DIVE BRIEFING This should be accurate and reasonably concise. At the very minimum I would expect the following to be adequately covered:

- Site orientation, including a map giving the general lie of the site, clear waypoints, tidal direction and likely strength, entry and exit points (if a shore dive), boat position (if a boat dive) and danger points (downward rip currents, disorientating holes, areas of entanglement).
- Emergency and problem procedures, which should include clear instructions on signals to be used. It should also give clear indications of what is expected by the boat crew and the help that they will be able to give you in the event of an emergency.
- Depth and time plans, including any decompression stops. You should have some method of checking and recording this for reference during the dive. Check the tables before getting on the boat to see how much leeway there is in the plan, bearing in mind that the closer you are to 'no stop' limits the higher the risk of running short of air and ending up with excessive nitrogen in your bloodstream. If you feel that the dive is too long or too deep, then ask for the plan to be revised. Make a note of the plan and the fall-back if you go slightly deeper or stay slightly longer than intended.

5

- If you have any questions, make sure that you ask them – if you aren't happy with the answers then ask again. Remember that you are paying for the dive and the operator has a duty to keep you safe and satisfied.

THE DIVE BOAT As a bare minimum the boat should have oxygen, a radio, life jackets, a first-aid kit, an engine and alternate means of propulsion. However, this is where the very nature of Mozambique requires a degree of compromise. A radio is only of any use if there is going to be someone listening out for a call. In addition, not all of the dive operators I saw carried oxygen – they should do, but it wasn't common practice while I was there (for more on this, see *Decompression illness*, below).

Drivers should be trained and competent in diver pick-up, and if you are diving from a hard boat or one with high sides, a solid (ie: not rope) ladder should be provided for climbing aboard.

DURING THE DIVE

- Watch where you are in relation to your buddy and the rest of the group. You should under no circumstances stray more than a few metres from any other diver – remember that if your air fails without warning then you have to cover that distance, almost certainly without any air in your lungs. Don't rely on your buddy (or nearest diver) realising what's going on.
- Keep an eye on the divers around you. If everyone is keeping an eye on everyone else then problems should be spotted early and resolved before they become dangerous.
- Keep an eye on your depth gauge and watch or your computer and air contents gauge. You should be checking these once a minute at the very minimum. Inform the dive leader when you reach the predetermined quantity of air left and make sure that the message is received and understood.
- If you are separated from the rest of the group, *do not* continue the dive alone. Look around for between 30 seconds and 1 minute (certainly no longer) and then ascend to 6m. Unless there is some other major problem (for instance you're out of air), carry out the planned decompression (if any) between 5m and 6m and then take 1 minute to continue to the surface. Always try to add a 3-minute safety stop on top of any planned decompression. It's possible that on surfacing you'll work out where the group are – *under no circumstances should you attempt to rejoin them under the water*.
- Try to avoid touching the reef. Not only is this likely to harm the coral and other animals living there, but the reef contains organisms that will sting or bite you. Do not pick anything up – again, it's damaging to the reef, and there are one or two animals that are quite capable of killing you (page 81).

DECOMPRESSION ILLNESS There isn't space here for an in-depth section on decompression, so I will give an overview and concentrate on avoidance and treatment. Any decent dive course book will give a good basic understanding of the physical and biological actions that lead to decompression illness (DCI), colloquially known as 'the bends'.

During any dive nitrogen from the compressed air we breathe is absorbed into our tissues at rates higher than we experience on the surface, and the amount of nitrogen absorbed is directly related to the length of time we spend underwater and the depths we have visited. As we rise from the deepest part of our dive, the absorbed nitrogen starts to come out of solution and form bubbles within the body. Providing these bubbles are small enough they are carried to the bloodstream and thence to the lungs to be exhaled. If we rise too fast the bubbles get too big to be transported in this manner, and there is a risk that they will get stuck somewhere in the body. This is what causes DCI.

There is no way to avoid nitrogen uptake and release during a dive, so the key is to ensure that the nitrogen is released slowly enough to pass to the lungs safely. Algorithms have been developed over the decades to help measure this, and these algorithms form the basis of all dive tables and dive computers, which is why it is so important that we dive within the limits prescribed by them.

However, diving within the limits set by tables or your computer is not going to eliminate the risk of a bend developing – it will merely reduce the risk to acceptable levels. It is perfectly possible for an individual to dive well within their tables and perfectly sensibly and still end up with a bend. It also needs to be stated that neither tables nor dive computers are intended to bring you back to the surface completely decompressed – the process of nitrogen release will continue for some hours after the end of any dive. This becomes important when considering flights.

One major factor in many bends is dehydration, often (if not exclusively) linked to excessive drinking. There is a clear linkage between the two, so if you are intending to dive, it's best to limit yourself to one or two the night before.

The only cure for a serious bend is recompression in a hyperbaric chamber to push the bubbles back into solution in a controlled manner. The decompression process can then be carried out under controlled circumstances with proper medical supervision. The closest chambers to Mozambique are in Durban or Johannesburg in South Africa, so any evacuation for a major bend will involve a flight.

For minor bends administration of 100% oxygen can prove useful, but this is not a cure and is entirely inappropriate with a bend affecting any of the major organs or the central nervous system. However, I came across few dive operators that had oxygen available during my travels around Mozambique – those considering diving off the coast will need to bear this in mind.

Flying involves a degree of depressurisation and it should be obvious that this presents further danger of DCI in those who have recently dived. The various diving associations give different times that should be observed between the end of the last dive and take-off, but the consensus seems to be in the region of 16 hours. Personally, I always allow 24 hours between the end of my last dive and my flight home. The only time this rule should be broken is with medical evacuations. If you have to be medically evacuated after a dive (regardless of the reason) then it must be emphasised to the pilot that under no circumstances should the flight be higher than 500m above sea level. The same is true of land evacuations – in the event of a major DCI, the diver must be kept below 500m above sea level and got to a chamber as soon as possible.

Medical evacuation and chamber treatment is fearsomely expensive (the bill can come to tens of thousands of US dollars) so it is important to check the terms of your medical insurance and not stray outside those. The freephone helplines that are so often touted may be of limited use in cases of DCI, so it may help to speak to someone with specialist knowledge of diving. The Divers Alert Network (w *dan.org*) isn't bad, but their knowledge of facilities outside the USA is limited. Personally, I'd contact the London Diving Chamber (w *londondivingchamber.co.uk*) – officially they deal only with members (as do DAN), but they will never turn away someone in trouble and have done a lot of pro bono work back in the UK. Lastly, be aware that some chambers may well be reluctant to provide treatment (I've heard a few horror stories of divers with major bends being told to treat themselves with vitamin B12 or that 'it's too late to treat'): if this should happen to you, ring the London Diving Chamber's emergency line and get them to talk to the chamber in question.

Hopefully you can see why it is important to dive extremely conservatively in Mozambique – the medical facilities are far below those available in many dive locations so you have to dive defensively. The golden rule with DCI is that any abnormal symptoms that exist after a dive should be regarded as DCI until proven otherwise.

NASTIES In all my time diving in tropical waters, the worst injuries I've had have been coral cuts and sea urchin spines. There are numerous things that might bite or sting you out of fear, curiosity or just plain accident, but only around 2% of diving incidents are caused by marine wildlife – you're much more at risk from your fellow divers.

Jellyfish There are plenty of jellyfish in Mozambican waters but none of them is regarded as life-threatening to a healthy adult (which doesn't rule out the risk of severe allergic reaction). Portuguese men-of-war (*Physalia physalia*) are fairly common at certain times of year, as are purple stingers (*Pelagia noctiluca*), and both of these can give nasty stings, which are on very rare occasions fatal.

If you are stung by a jellyfish, pour vinegar (or in the absence of vinegar, urine) over the affected area – the venom from the vast majority of jellyfish is alkaline and will be neutralised by the acid. Try to remove any remaining stinging cells from the skin with a stick (not your fingers). If this fails, dust the area with flour and scrape the resulting gloop off with a blunt knife. Treat any swelling with a mild steroid cream (such as hydrocortisone). In the event of allergic reaction it's vital to get to medical aid as soon as possible.

Coral stings There are thousands of different coral species, the identification of most of which involves microscopic examination of the polyps, so generally corals are referred to by the forms their colonies grow into. The only coral form you need to be actively aware of is the fire coral, which classically has a bright yellow margin running along its crown. The sting is in itself not fatal but may hurt. As with the jellyfish there is the possibility of allergic reaction. Treatment is the same as for jellyfish stings, but if the skin is broken you'll need to treat for cuts and scrapes (below).

Cuts and scrapes The coastal islands of Mozambique are all based on a hard core of coral rag overlaid with sand. Coral rag is a concrete mixture of coral skeleton, sand and shell, cemented and hardened by the actions of the wind and waves. It's surprisingly brittle but can cut very deeply so, if you are ever walking on coral rag, you must wear some form of foot protection. The biggest risk with a coral cut is that minute particles of the rag break off inside the cut. These particles will be laden with bacteria, algae and coral polyps that will merrily begin to grow inside the cut. It's vital that you thoroughly wash out any cut as soon as possible, then treat it with antiseptic and cover. Check it on a regular basis – one of the peculiarities of tiny cuts in marine tropical environments is that they very quickly form abscesses which can take a surprisingly long time to heal.

Animals that can cause cuts and scrapes range from members of the shark family (obviously the teeth can inflict cuts, but the skin also presents a risk, being covered in tiny scales called denticles that act as a form of sandpaper), surgeonfish (which have tiny blades at the base of their tails), lobsters, crabs and other crustaceans, moray eels, barracuda and titan triggerfish.

The best way to avoid getting bitten is not to irritate the animal in question – the vast majority of fish would rather steer well clear of you and will only attack when cornered. However, the titan triggerfish (*Balistoides viridescens*) is highly territorial and there are many recorded incidents of attacks on divers who have accidentally or deliberately strayed into a nesting zone.

Sharks have, in my opinion, been given a bad rap over the years, but it's undeniable that some species, including several regularly found in Mozambican waters, will attack humans. Reading shark behaviour is complex and best left to the experts, so ask your dive guides what sharks are likely to be present, whether they are dangerous and what the warning signs are.

Venom Many of the animals in the coastal waters of Mozambique have venom, either as protection from hunters or to help hunt for food. This venom can give an extremely painful sting but is only in itself fatal in a very few species. The treatment for the venom from virtually all of these animals is to immerse the sting site in water as hot as possible – the heat breaks the toxins down. This basic treatment will cover the vast majority of stinging animals from sea urchins and fire worms through to sea snakes and striped catfish (*Plotosus lineatus*) and the various members of the scorpionfish family (including lionfish, devilfish and stonefish). Of this last group the worst is unquestionably the stonefish, the sting of which has been implicated in several deaths, although it's unclear whether the venom was directly fatal or whether the victim died of some other problem brought on by the pain caused by that venom. At any rate, all of them have venom that can be broken down by heat.

The most important exception to the hot water treatment is the cone shell. Two species of cone shell – the textile cone (*Conus textile*) and the geographic cone (*Conus geographus*) – are found on the Mozambican coastline and both have been responsible for fatalities. There is antivenom but it is absolutely crucial that the affected area be immobilised and the victim transported to medical care immediately. It has to be restated that it is highly unlikely that a normal medical centre on the coast of Mozambique will carry the antivenom as a matter of course, and the more sensible approach is not to get stung in the first place – in other words, don't touch anything.

Spines The coastal area of Mozambique is littered with various species of black spiny sea urchins, the spines of which are often coated with a venomous mucus. Puncture wounds from these often contain the tips of spines and will readily abscess. Removal of tips trapped in the skin should only be done by qualified medics. There are several species of spiny starfish that have similar spines and should be treated in the same manner, and there have also been occasions where the stinging spines of scorpionfish and catfish have broken off in the wound.

SNORKELLING

Much of the diving section also applies to snorkelling – while you don't need to worry about DCI, the nasties won't make the distinction between divers and snorkellers (or indeed those just splashing around in the surf).

ADDITIONAL KIT Mask and fin fitting are as important for snorkellers as for divers. The snorkel should fit comfortably in your mouth and be easily replaceable if it happens to come out. Some snorkels have clearance valves on them and these can be useful if you can't muster the puff to clear the tube in the traditional manner. A less helpful tweak is a flexible tube between the main body of the snorkel and the mouthpiece – the theory behind them is that they provide a more comfortable fit, but I've found that they tend to fall away from your mouth at the wrong moment. You may also want to ask for a buoyancy device – this is a little like a waistcoat filled with buoyant material that will prevent you from sinking to the bottom of the ocean.

BRIEFINGS These are as crucial to snorkellers as they are to divers and should contain much the same sort of information, particularly with regard to surface currents. You also need to know where the lookout is going to be sited – they may be your only means of communication with the shore. Check to see whether there will be a cover boat to pick you up if you do get out of your depth.

SAFETY TIPS
Beware sunburn You're far more susceptible to sunburn while snorkelling than while diving or just sitting on the beach. Avoidance tactics include wearing a T-shirt to protect your back, and a hat to protect the top of your head (make sure it has a chinstrap). You may want to invest in one of the Lycra bodysuits which will keep you warm and protect you from sunburn and jellyfish stings. Any bits that aren't covered need to be liberally coated in a good high-factor sunblock – as a guide I'd suggest a minimum of SPF 40 – which must be waterproof. From personal experience I'd suggest applying a thick layer to the backs of the ears.

Beware cold It may seem stupid but you can lose sufficient core body temperature during a long snorkel session (particularly when there's a bit of wind) to bring you into danger of shock. Lycra bodysuits can protect against this, or just pop out every now and again to warm up a bit.

Don't go out of sight Always bear in mind that if you can't see the lookout, they can't see you, and if you've wandered off from the main group searching for peace and quiet, remember that it's the group they will be watching.

Keep an ear open for the warning signal While there aren't any formal beach lifeguards in Mozambique, it's likely that any snorkel operator will have an established system of signalling (usually blasts on a whistle) for the lookout to communicate with the snorkellers. It's vital that you keep an ear open for this and that you make a clear response when you hear it.

Part Two

SOUTHERN MOZAMBIQUE

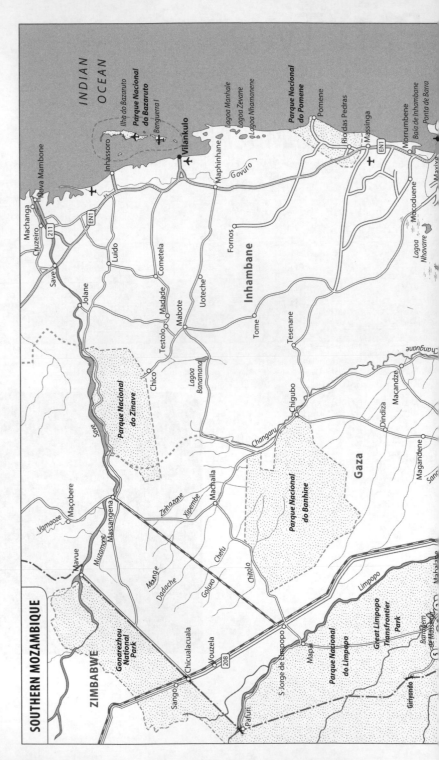

SOUTHERN MOZAMBIQUE

INDIAN OCEAN

Ilha do Bazaruto

Parque Nacional do Bazaruto

Benguerra I

Inhassoro

Vilankulo

Lagoa Manhale

Lagoa Zevane

Lagoa Nhamanene

Maphinhane

Govuro

Parque Nacional do Pomene

Pomene

Rio das Pedras

Massinga

Morrumbene

Baía de Inhambane

Ponta da Barra

Machanga

Cruzeiro

Save

Nova Mambone

EN1

211

Luido

Jolane

Cometela

Fornos

EN1

Lagoa Nhavare

Mocoduene

Maxixe

Testolo

Madade

Mabote

Uoteche

Inhambane

Tome

Tesenane

Chico

Lagoa Banamana

Chigubo

Dindiza

Macandze

Parque Nacional do Zinave

Save

Changaru

Parque Nacional do Banhine

Gaza

Sanc

Magandene

Macobere

Massangena

Machaila

Zinhazone

Xipembe

Vamaoze

Muzomone

Mange

Chefu

Chitolo

Goluvo

Dadache

Navue

Limpopo

Mahalao

Gonarezhou National Park

ZIMBABWE

Chicualacuala

Vouzela

Sango

S. Jorge de Limpopo

Mapai

208

Parque Nacional do Limpopo

Great Limpopo Transfrontier Park

Barragem de Massingir

Pafuri

Giriyondo

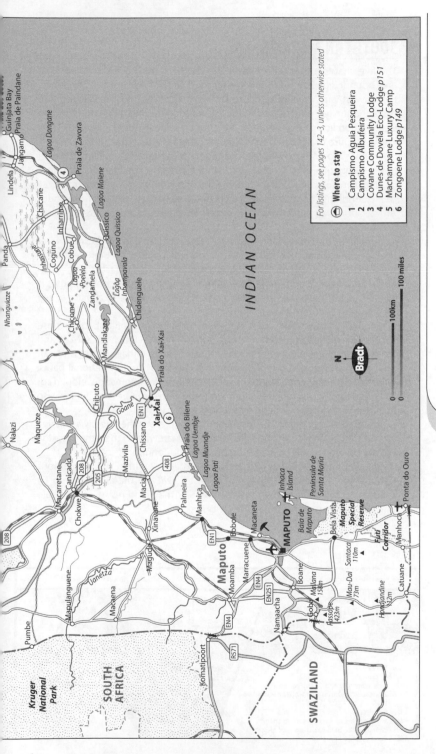

For listings, see pages 142–3, unless otherwise stated

Where to stay

1 Campismo Aguia Pesqueira
2 Campismo Albufeira
3 Covane Community Lodge
4 Dunes de Dovela Eco-Lodge *p151*
5 Machampane Luxury Camp
6 Zongoene Lodge *p149*

INDIAN OCEAN

0 100km
0 100 miles

SOUTH AFRICA

Kruger National Park

SWAZILAND

SOUTHERN MOZAMBIQUE

The five chapters that follow cover the southern third of Mozambique, an area bounded by South Africa in the far southwest, Swaziland and Zimbabwe to the west, and the Save River to the north. It is the most developed and heavily touristed part of Mozambique, boasting around 1,000km of Indian Ocean shoreline and several of the country's most popular resorts, from Ponta do Ouro in the south to Vilankulo and Inhassoro in the north.

Chapter 6 focuses on Maputo, the country's capital and largest city, which has a distinctive and likeable Afro-Mediterranean character but is rather lacking in major tourist attractions. Maputo is the main international gateway to Mozambique for business travellers and backpackers coming from South Africa, but is frequently bypassed by self-drive visitors and leisure travellers arriving by air.

Chapter 7 covers the wildly attractive mosaic of forested dunes, freshwater lakes and idyllic beaches that lies to the south of Maputo, a region frequently referred to as Maputaland. Its best-known attractions are Inhaca Island, which lies in Maputo Bay, and Ponta do Ouro on the South African border, but it is also the site of the underrated Maputo Special Reserve, the best place to see elephants in southern Mozambique.

Chapter 8 covers the coast between Maputo and Inhambane, whose succession of beach resorts – most notably Bilene, Praia do Xai-Xai and Závora – cater mainly to the South African family-holiday market and can feel rather abandoned out of season. It also covers a trio of national parks: Limpopo, Banhine and Zinave, of which the first is the most developed for tourists, forming part of the Great Limpopo Transfrontier Park, which also includes South Africa's legendary Kruger Park.

Heading further north, the focal point of *Chapter 9* is the sleepily attractive town of Inhambane, which is also the main gateway to the other seaside resorts covered in this chapter, notably Tofo and Tofinho.

The offshore Bazaruto Archipelago, protected within an eponymous national park, is the centrepiece of tourist activity in the area covered by *Chapter 10*, which also describes the popular mainland resort of Vilankulo and the rapidly growing Inhassoro to its north.

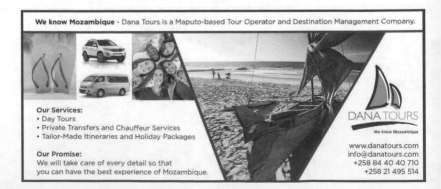

6

Maputo

The largest urban centre in Mozambique, Maputo is a bustling and attractive port city that has served as the national capital since 1898, when it was known as Lourenço Marques (LM for short). It lies on the Gulf of Maputo (formerly Delagoa Bay) in the far south of Mozambique, within 100km of the South African and Swaziland borders. As such, it often feels more strongly connected to South Africa than to the rest of Mozambique, a circumstance reflected in a popular saying that likens Mozambique to a funnel – all the money flows down south!

Maputo was formerly the administrative capital of a province of the same name, which extended all the way south to the borders with South Africa and Swaziland. In 1998, the city became a separate administrative entity called Maputo Cidade, which is by far the smallest and most densely populated of Mozambique's 11 provinces, while the satellite city of Matola was made capital of the more rural Maputo Province. The current population of Maputo stands at around 1.2 million, and is further boosted by the estimated 962,000 residents of Matola, which is technically the second-largest city in Mozambique but more sensibly treated as part of a greater urban conglomeration centred on Maputo.

Outside images of post-civil-war Maputo, like those of Mozambique itself, have been dominated by stereotypes relating to its intense poverty, flagrant corruption and run-down architecture. There is a small – and ever-decreasing – element of truth to these stereotypes, but overall Maputo comes across as an intensely agreeable city, whose charms tend to grow on visitors the longer they stay. No longer severely pot-holed, the *avenidas* of the city centre are wide and tree-lined, sloping down towards an attractive seafront and harbour, and for every faded architectural gem there are two others that are well maintained and smart. The streets and markets are busy and energetic, and drivers tend to be courteous and somewhat less manic than in many other parts of Africa. Furthermore, while it would be disingenuous to claim Maputo is entirely bereft of poverty, its more shanty-like suburbs are no slummier than their counterparts in, say, Nairobi, Lilongwe or (dare it be said) Johannesburg.

Arrive in Maputo without prejudice and it is, quite simply, a most likeable city – as safe as any in Africa, and with a good deal more character than most. The avenidas, lined with jacaranda, flame and palm trees and numerous street cafés, have a relaxed, hassle-free, Afro-Mediterranean atmosphere that is distinctively Mozambican. And they are flanked by any number of attractive old colonial buildings in various states of renovation and disrepair, ranging in style from pre-World War I Classical to later Art Deco, all dwarfed in places by various incongruous high-rise relics of the 1950s and 1960s, when the city was something of a laboratory for devotees of the Bauhaus architectural style. Add to these a new crop of office buildings, shopping complexes, hotels and condominiums – with more under construction – and you get the impression that this is a city with not only a memorable past but also a bright future.

Maputo has a beautiful location at the mouth of the Matola, Umbeluzi and Tembe rivers on the Indian Ocean, and is a great base for day trips to places such as sleepy Catembe on the opposite side of the harbour mouth, or the more remote Maputo Special Reserve with its resident elephants. The city is an absolute culinary delight, especially for seafood and/or spice enthusiasts, and it also boasts a lively nightlife and some of the most vibrant markets in Africa. Maputo, in short, is a compulsive and endlessly rewarding city, with a vibe that strongly recalls Lourenço Marques in the 'good old days' so often alluded to by sentimental white South Africans – except that today Mozambicans are as free as anybody else to enjoy their vibrant capital city.

HISTORY

Maputo (Delagoa) Bay lay to the south of the medieval trade routes used by the Swahili, and there is no particular reason to suppose that the area was ever visited by Muslim sailors prior to the Portuguese era. Nevertheless, the evidence suggests that the bay supported a substantial ocean-going fishing community prior to the 16th century, and also that it was the apex of a local trade network running along the five navigable rivers that flow into it.

In 1502, the Portuguese captain Luis Fernandes sailed a short distance upriver from what was almost certainly Maputo Bay, at first thinking he was at the entrance to Sofala. He recorded visiting a sizeable African river port, which impressed him mostly for its numerous cattle – large plump beasts that sold for two copper coins apiece. Once he realised that he was not at Sofala, Fernandes gave the bay the name Baía da Lagoa, in the belief that its rivers all originated in an inland lagoon.

The first European to explore Maputo Bay was the Portuguese navigator **Lourenço Marques**, who visited it in 1544 on the instruction of the Captain of Moçambique and Sofala. Marques noted large numbers of elephants in the area, and he found that the natives of the bay were prepared to trade ivory for a few cheap beads. Shortly after this, King João III renamed the bay after Marques. Over the course of the next century, the bay was visited by a Portuguese ship almost every year. Typically, the ship would spend about four months encamped on Inhaca Island, from where it traded for ivory with the local chiefs on the mainland.

During the second half of the 17th century, the **Portuguese ivory trade** became increasingly centred on the more northerly ports of Kilwa and Quelimane, which meant that Maputo Bay often went for years without seeing a Portuguese trading vessel. Portugal's partial abandonment of the southern trade opened the way for English and Dutch traders to such an extent that five British ships were recorded in the bay at one time in 1685.

The earliest attempt to establish a **permanent European settlement** on Maputo Bay was not initiated by Portugal, as might be supposed, but rather by the Netherlands. In 1721, the Dutch East India Company established a trading factory and fort on the site of present-day Maputo, but this was abandoned as unprofitable in 1730. Another trading factory was established on Inhaca Island in 1778 by one William Bolts, a British adventurer in Austrian employ. The Austrian settlement was expelled in 1781 when Portugal finally decided to establish a permanent trading post and fort at Delagoa Bay.

In 1781, the Portuguese placed a small garrison on Inhaca Island and set about building a fort on the site of present-day Maputo but, as it turned out, the future capital of Mozambique was to have a less than auspicious start. In May 1782, barely a month after the fort had been completed, the entire settlement burned to the ground. It was quickly rebuilt, but an argument between the newly appointed

Governor of Lourenço Marques and local chiefs forced Portugal to evacuate it in 1783. The settlement was reoccupied under a new governor in 1784, and a stronger fortress was built on the site of the modern one, but the garrison of 80 men was plagued by fever and so, when three French gunboats arrived in the harbour in October 1796, the Portuguese settlers fled inland. The fortress was reoccupied in 1800, after which time Portugal retained a permanent presence on the bay.

In the early 19th century, Lourenço Marques was a modest and unremarkable trading outpost; in 1825, the only permanent building apart from the fort was a solitary corrugated-iron homestead. Nevertheless, the settlement stood at the centre of a vast trading network that spread along the rivers into the present-day South African provinces of Mpumalanga and KwaZulu-Natal. These inland trade routes to Maputo Bay were fiercely contested by various local chieftaincies, especially after the great drought of the 1790s initiated an unprecedented and highly militant phase of empire building among the Nguni peoples of the lowveld. In 1833, Lourenço Marques was razed and its governor killed by Dingane's Zulu army. After 1838, when the Boers defeated the Zulu army at Blood River, the trade routes to Lourenço Marques became the focus of an ongoing battle between the Swazi and Gaza kingdoms.

In terms of the development of southern Mozambique in general and Lourenço Marques in particular, the most portentous event of 1838 was the arrival at Delagoa Bay of the Boer leader **Louis Trichardt**. The Boers of the Transvaal were eager to open an export route to Delagoa Bay, not only because it was the closest port to the Boer Republic, but also because it would put an end to their dependence on British ports such as Cape Town and Durban. Trichardt died of malaria in Delagoa Bay, but his visit there signalled the beginning of a protracted three-way dispute over the control of what is arguably southeast Africa's finest natural harbour.

The competition for control of Maputo Bay increased after the **discovery of diamonds** at Kimberley in 1867 and gold at Lydenberg in 1869. In 1868, the government of the Transvaal claimed that its frontier extended to the coast, a claim that was immediately contested by Britain and Portugal. As a result, the Transvaal and Portugal signed a treaty that not only delineated the modern border between Mozambique and South Africa north of Swaziland, but also, and no less significantly, provided for the joint construction of a road between the Transvaal and Lourenço Marques.

Unwilling to see the Transvaal establish links with a Portuguese port, Britain immediately and unilaterally annexed the southern part of Delagoa Bay and Inhaca Island to their **Natal Colony**. Portugal called on France to arbitrate over the territorial dispute, and in 1875 it was awarded the entire bay. This was a major blow to the British policy of keeping indirect economic control over the Boer Republic – so much so that Britain annexed the Transvaal to its Cape Colony between 1877 and 1881, thereby stalling the development of transport links to Lourenço Marques.

Following the **discovery of gold** on the Witwatersrand in 1886, Portugal and the Transvaal decided to build a railway line between Pretoria and Lourenço Marques. It was the completion of this line in 1894 that prompted the modern growth of the city. In 1870, Lourenço Marques was a tiny, stagnant trading centre protected by an unimpressive fort. By the turn of the century, the city centre had taken on its modern shape, the port handled roughly one-third of exports and imports from the Transvaal, and the railway line carried over 80,000 passengers annually. On 12 November 1898, Lourenço Marques formally replaced Ilha de Moçambique as the capital of Portugal's East African colony. After independence, the city was renamed after the Rio Maputo.

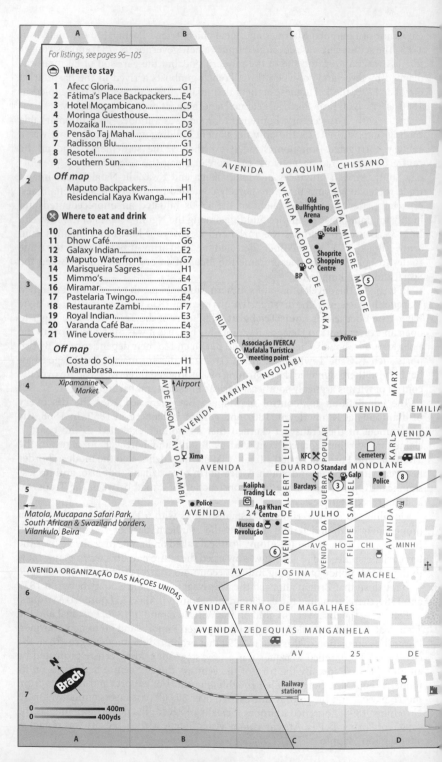

For listings, see pages 96–105

Where to stay
1 Afecc Gloria.................................G1
2 Fátima's Place Backpackers.....E4
3 Hotel Moçambicano....................C5
4 Moringa Guesthouse..................D4
5 Mozaika II.....................................D3
6 Pensão Taj Mahal........................C6
7 Radisson Blu................................G1
8 Resotel..D5
9 Southern Sun..............................H1

Off map
Maputo Backpackers..................H1
Residencial Kaya Kwanga..........H1

Where to eat and drink
10 Cantinha do Brasil.....................E5
11 Dhow Café....................................G6
12 Galaxy Indian..............................E2
13 Maputo Waterfront...................G7
14 Marisqueira Sagres....................H1
15 Mimmo's..E4
16 Miramar..G1
17 Pastelaria Twingo......................E4
18 Restaurante Zambi.....................F7
19 Royal Indian.................................E3
20 Varanda Café Bar........................E4
21 Wine Lovers.................................E3

Off map
Costa do Sol..................................H1
Marnabrasa....................................H1

AVENIDA JOAQUIM CHISSANO

AVENIDA ACORDOS DE LUSAKA

AVENIDA JOAQUIM

AVENIDA MILAGRE MABOTE

Old Bullfighting Arena

Total

Shoprite Shopping Centre

BP

Police

RUA DE GOA

Associação IVERCA/ Mafalala Turística meeting point

AVENIDA MARIAN NGOUABI

Xipamanine Market

Airport

AV DE ANGOLA

AV DA ZAMBIA

Xima

MARX

AVENIDA EMILIA

AVENIDA

AVENIDA KARL

LTM

Cemetery

KFC Standard MONDLANE

AVENIDA EDUARDO

AVENIDA ALBERT LUTHULI

AVENIDA POPULAR

AVENIDA DA GUERRA

Kalipha Trading Ldc

Barclays

Galp

Police

Aga Khan Centre

24

Matola, Mucapana Safari Park, South African & Swaziland borders, Vilankulo, Beira

Police

AVENIDA

DE JULHO

Museu da Revolução

AVENIDA FILIPE SAMUEL

AV HO CHI MINH

AVENIDA

AV JOSINA

MACHEL

AVENIDA ORGANIZAÇÃO DAS NAÇÕES UNIDAS

AVENIDA FERNÃO DE MAGALHÃES

AVENIDA ZEDEQUIAS MANGANHELA

AV 25 DE

Railway station

N

Bradt

0 ———— 400m
0 ———— 400yds

A   B   C   D

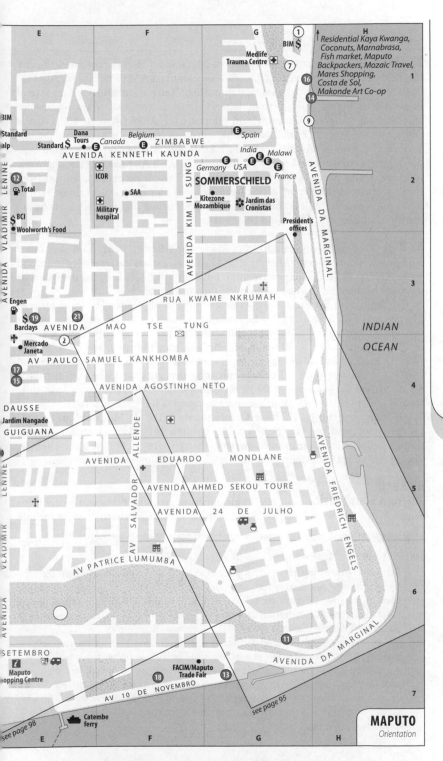

BIM $

Medlife
Trauma Centre ✚

Residential Kaya Kwanga,
Coconuts, Marnabrasa,
Fish market, Maputo
Backpackers, Mozaic Travel,
Mares Shopping,
Costa de Sol,
Makonde Art Co-op

BIM

Standard
alp   Standard $

Dana
Tours � Canada ⊕ Belgium
⊕   ⊕   ZIMBABWE

⊕ Spain

AVENIDA KENNETH KAUNDA

India ⊕ ⊕ Malawi
⊕ ⊕
Germany USA ⊕ France

✚
ICOR

SOMMERSCHIELD

AVENIDA KIM IL SUNG

AVENIDA DA MARGINAL

Total

SAA

Kitezone
Mozambique Jardim das
Cronistas

✚
Military
hospital

President's
offices

BCI

Woolworth's Food

INDIAN

OCEAN

Engen

✝
RUA KWAME NKRUMAH

$ ⑲ AVENIDA ㉑   MAO TSE TUNG
Barclays
② ✉

✝
Mercado
Janeta

AV PAULO SAMUEL KANKHOMBA

⑰
⑮

AVENIDA AGOSTINHO NETO

DAUSSE

Jardim Nangade

GUIGUANA

AVENIDA ALLENDE

AVENIDA FRIEDRICH ENGELS

✚

AVENIDA   EDUARDO   MONDLANE

AVENIDA SALVADOR

✚

AVENIDA AHMED SEKOU TOURÉ

✝

AVENIDA 24 DE JULHO

AVENIDA VLADIMIR LENINE

AV PATRICE LUMUMBA

AVENIDA

SETEMBRO

ℹ
Maputo
opping Centre

⑪

AV 10 DE NOVEMBRO

⑱ FACIM/Maputo
Trade Fair ⑬

AVENIDA DA MARGINAL

see page 98

see page 95

Catembe
ferry

MAPUTO
Orientation

BY AIR Maputo International Airport [90 B4] is about 5km northwest of the city centre, up at the end of Avenida Accordos de Zambia. **LAM** (w *lam.co.mz*) flies to/from Maputo from all provincial capitals north of Xai-Xai and also operates several international flights daily to/from Johannesburg and several times weekly to/from Luanda (Angola), Dar es Salaam (Tanzania), Nairobi (Kenya), Addis Ababa (Ethiopia) and Harare (Zimbabwe). Other international carriers to Maputo include **TAP** (w *flytap.com*), **SAA** (w *flysaa.com*), **Ethiopian Airlines** (w *ethiopianairlines.com*), **Kenya Airways** (w *kenya-airways.com*), **Turkish Airlines** (w *turkishairlines.com*) and **Qatar Airways** (w *qatarairways.com*). There is no public transport from the city centre to the airport, though some *chapas* do run to within about 1km of it. It's not walkable (unless you're really into your urban hiking), though taxis are readily available and cost around US$10–16.

BY RAIL There is a daily train to/from Maputo and Ressano Garcia on the border with South Africa. It leaves Maputo at 07.45 daily and starts the return leg at around noon. Tickets are very inexpensive but it takes up to 4 hours in either direction, as opposed to about an hour by car to cover the same route.

For those with a taste for the difficult, there is also a weekly train to/from Maputo and Chicualacuala (Vila Eduardo Mondlane) on the Zimbabwean border in Gaza Province. Trains depart Maputo around 13.00 on Wednesdays, arriving in Chicualacuala close to 20 hours later on Thursday morning, and head back to Maputo at 13.00 the following Sunday. From here, you can cross the border and connect to Bulawayo on a Zimbabwean train departing at 15.20 on Thursdays, which arrives in Bulawayo at 09.10 on Fridays. On the Mozambican side, only second and third class are available, so it's as cheap as it is uncomfortable.

All trains are run by **Portos e Caminhos de Ferro de Moçambique** (CFM) (w *cfm.co.mz*) and you may be able to dig up more information on their website, though it is oriented more towards investors than passengers. For the train schedule, visit w cfm.co.mz/index.php/pt/documentos-e-media/horario-de-comboios.

BY ROAD
To/from South Africa See page 47 for details of arriving in Maputo by car from South Africa and Swaziland. Reliable South African-based coach services include

---

YOUR FIRST HALF-HOUR: ARRIVING AT MAPUTO AIRPORT

Maputo is one of the easier international airports. Immigration and customs are simple and reasonably fast, and you won't be hassled by taxi drivers as soon as you step through the doors. There are the usual facilities – a bank, a câmbio, a snack bar, car-rental agencies and an ATM that takes Visa. These can all be found in the departures terminal, a few yards from arrivals.

Taxis are clearly marked and will cost you about US$10–16 for the ride to the city. If you are staying at one of the more upmarket hotels there will be a courtesy bus waiting for you, and the three backpacker hostels will also pick you up if you let them know when you are arriving. As a last resort, chapas leave from the roundabout at the end of Avenida dos Accordos de Lusaka heading towards the Baixa – but unless you're travelling with minimal luggage a taxi is preferable.

Intercape (*Av 25 de Setembro;* m *82 308 1334;* w *intercape.co.za*), **Translux** (w *translux.co.za*) and **Greyhound** (w *greyhound.co.za*), which operate affordable daily services between Pretoria and Maputo stopping at Midrand, Johannesburg, Nelspruit and Komatipoort. Tickets from Johannesburg to Maputo cost around US$30, credit-card bookings can be made online or by phone, and the websites contain full details of pick-up and drop-off points. Alternatively, a handful of anonymous coach companies have ticket offices on Avenida Zedequias Manganhela behind the central post office, including **Weng Express/África Bus** (m *82 082 0820 or 84 084 0840*) or **Luciano Luxury Coach** (☏ *+27 82 390 3870 (South Africa);* ⧉ *LucianoLuxuryCoaches*), which runs directly to Durban via Swaziland several times a week for around US$24, or chapa-style minibuses for Johannesburg which leave from Avenida Albert Luthuli next to the stadium and cost in the region of US$20. It is very unlikely that your large rucksack will be put inside the minibus with you unless you are willing to pay a carriage charge. Like all chapas, they leave when they are full enough to make it worthwhile.

In Mozambique If your first stop out of Maputo is Inhambane, Tofo or any place along the EN1 south of that, then there's a lot to be said for using the daily **shuttle service** linking Maputo to Tofo. This leaves Maputo at 05.00 daily, stopping right outside Fátima's Place [91 E4] and Base Backpackers [98 F3]. Tickets, which cost around US$16, can be booked at the reception desk of either hostel. The two most reliable air-conditioned coach services for places north of Inhambane are **Linhas Terrestres de Moçambique** (LTM; m *82 558 8995 or 84 418 1421;* w *ltmmocambique. com/contact*), which runs to Beira (*US$30*) four times a week, departing from their office on Avenida Eduardo Mondlane [90 D5] at 03.00, and the highly regarded **Postbus** (☏ *21 430061/2;* m *82 305 7378 or 84 312 3102/3/4;* w *correios.co.mz*) runs buses to Beira on Wednesday and Sunday, returning on Wednesday and Saturday, for US$30; Quelimane on Thursday and Sunday, returning on Wednesday and Sunday, for US$40; and Tete on Wednesday, returning on Saturday, for US$34. All buses depart at 03.00 from the Postbus office on Avenida 25 de Setembro [98 C3]. Both services take about 16 hours to Beira, with stops at Vilankulo and Maxixe (for Inhambane and Tofo). LTM charges the full fare wherever you disembark, whereas Postbus charges pro rata. Both companies also have onward connections to Tete from Beira.

All other long-distance buses start from a place outside the city centre called Junta, which is the closest Maputo has to a bus terminal. Getting there isn't difficult as many internal chapa routes run through there (if in doubt, ask the people on the bus). Once you're there, simply wander around until you find a bus heading in the direction you're going. You'll definitely get buses to Beira and Chimoio, and will probably find them going as far as Tete if you are there on the right day. The chapa fare from the town centre to Junta will be less than US$1, while a taxi will cost around US$8.

GETTING AROUND

BY TAXI Taxis are more numerous than they used to be, and you can usually rely on there being some at the airport taxi rank, outside the central market [98 B2], anywhere along Avenida Julius Nyerere, and outside upmarket hotels such as the Cardoso [95 A5] and Polana Serena [95 D2]. Taxi fares are negotiable, but you can expect to pay around US$5 for a ride within the city centre and up to US$15 between the city centre and the airport. Tuk-tuks, known locally as *tchopelas*, ply the city as well, and are slightly cheaper than conventional taxis. The two radio-dispatched taxis in Maputo belong to **Taxi Marcelo** (m *82/84/86 505 0050;* w *taximarcelo.com*) and **EasyTaxiMZ**

(m *82 319 7158 or 84 332 1028;* 🅵 *easytaximz*). Taxi Marcelo operates day or night, while EasyTaxiMZ operates between 07.00 and 18.00, and both will even give you a price beforehand over the phone.

BY CHAPA Minibus chapas travel the length and breadth of the city, with major bus stands in front of the Natural History Museum [95 A5] (described simply as 'museu' on the front of buses) and the large markets. You will probably have absolutely no idea where most of these buses are going at first, so the best advice is to stay on the main thoroughfares and be prepared to take more than one to get to your final destination. Fares are typically around US$0.20.

CAR HIRE Owner-operated **Rent Maputo** (w *rentmaputo.com*) is a thoroughly reputable local agency based in Maputo, with saloon cars starting at US$50/day and 4x4s at US$110/day. International agencies include **Avis** (w *avis.com*), **Europcar** (w *europcar.com*), **Hertz** (w *hertz.com*) and **Sixt** (w *sixt.com*).

TOURS British expat **Jane Flood** (m *82 419 0574;* e *jane.flood@gmail.com;* 🅵 *Maputo.a.Pe*) lives and breathes all things art and architecture, and she sets up and guides highly customisable walking tours in and around Maputo.

   Mozaic Travel [91 H1] (☏ *21 451376;* m *84 333 2111/301 5167;* e *maputo@ mozaictravel.com;* w *mozaictravel.com*) and **Dana Tours** [91 E2] (☏ *21 495514;* e *info@danatours.com;* w *danatours.com; see ad, page 86*) also run half-day motorised city tours.

   For those looking to dive in and explore beyond Maputo's glossy exterior, the locally owned **Associação IVERCA/Mafalala Turística** [90 C4] (m *82 418 0314/415 1580;* e *associacao.iverca@gmail.com;* w *iverca.org*) runs walking tours in Mafalala, the 'township' where Africans were permitted to reside during Portuguese rule. It's a workaday slice of the capital few tourists see, and the excellent guided tours cover everything from a trip to the *curandeira* (traditional healer) to Samora Machel's former home. Tours leave at 10.00 on Friday, Saturday and Sunday, but it's best to call ahead and confirm when you'll meet.

🏠 **WHERE TO STAY**

Nowhere is Maputo's current prosperity more evident than in the number of high-quality hotels that can now be found here. Generally speaking, the upper-range hotels are the best value for money you'll find in Mozambique, and if you feel like

MAPUTO Polana District
For listings, see pages 96–105

🛏 **Where to stay**

1	Duqueza de Connaught	C5
2	Hotel Avenida	C4
3	Hotel Cardoso	A5
4	Hotel Terminus	B4
5	Hotel Villa das Mangas	B4
6	Hoyo Hoyo Residencial	B3
7	Mozaika Guesthouse 1	A1
8	Polana Serena	D2
9	Villa Das Arabias	A4

❌ **Where to eat and drink**

10	A Esquina	B5
11	A Nossa Tasca	C5
12	Acacia Café	A5
13	Bairro Alto	B5
14	Bairro Bistro	C4
15	Bar Lounge 1908	A2
16	Bel Piatto	C5
17	Dolce Vita	C3
18	Horoscopo	B5
19	Il Gelato	A3
20	Mimmo's Pronto	C4
21	Moksha Indian	C3
22	Mundo's	C4
23	New Galaxy Indian	B5
24	Peace Love Pizza	B2
25	Pekai's Thai Pub & Restaurant	B5
26	Pirata	C5
27	PiriPiri	C4
28	Pizza House	B1
29	Restaurante Cristal	B4
30	Restaurante Spicy Thai	C4
31	Shamwari	B5
32	Tacos Café	B3
	Taverna Dolce 1	(see 33)
33	Taverna Portuguesa	D2
34	Treehouse	B4
35	Txhapo Txhapo	C4

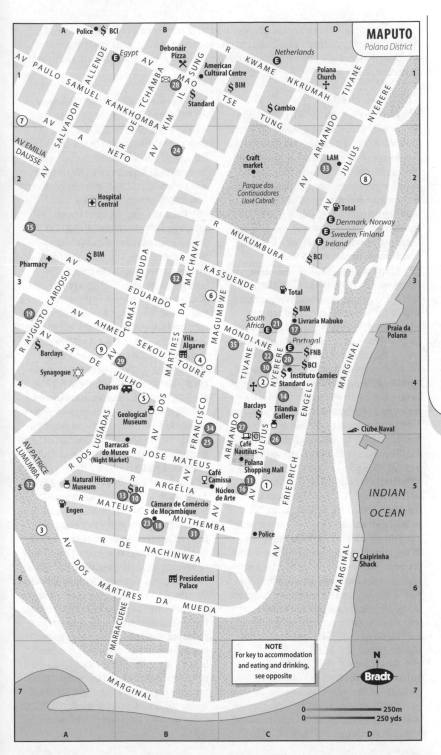

MAPUTO
Polana District

A Police ● $ BCI

AV PAULO SAMUEL KANKHOMBA

E Egypt

Debonair Pizza

American Cultural Centre

Netherlands **E**

Polana Church ✝

R KWAME NKRUMAH

28 ✉

$ BIM

$ Standard

$ Cambio

24

LAM **33**

8

AV SALVADOR ALLENDE DE A NETO

AV EMILIA DAUSSE

7

15

Craft market

Parque dos Continuadores (José Cabral)

Hospital Central ✚

AV ARMANDO JULIUS TIVANE

☐ Total

E Denmark, Norway

E Sweden, Finland

E Ireland

$ BCI

Pharmacy ✚

$ BIM

AV AJGUSTO CARDOSO

AV AHMED SEKOU TOURÉ

EDUARDO DA MACHAVA

32

R KASSUENDE

R MUKUMBURA

☐ Total

$ BIM

6

Livraria Mabuko

21

South Africa **E**

17

Portugal **E**

Praia da Polana

19

Vila Algarve

35

$ FNB

20

$ BCI

$ Barclays

9

29

4

22

30

Instituto Camões

$ Standard

Synagogue ✡

R 24 DE JULHO

Chapas 🚐

5

Geological Museum

Barracas do Museu (Night Market)

2

✝

14

Barclays $

Tilandia Gallery

34

27

25

Café Nautilus ☕

26

Clube Naval ⛵

Natural History Museum

12

R JOSÉ MATEUS

R ARGÉLIA

Café Camissa 🍷

Núcleo de Arte

Polana Shopping Mall

11

16

1

INDIAN

OCEAN

$ BCI

13

10

Câmara de Comércio de Moçambique

23 **18**

R MUTHEMBA

31

● Police

Engen ⛽

R MATEUS

AV PATRICE LUMUMBA

3

R DE NACHINWEA

Presidential Palace

Caipirinha Shack 🍷

AV DOS MARTIRES DA MUEDA

R MARRACUENE

MARGINAL

MARGINAL

NOTE
For key to accommodation and eating and drinking, see opposite

N

Bradt

0 ———— 250m
0 ———— 250 yds

A   B   C   D

spoiling yourself, these are the places to do it. If these are a trifle above your budget there are plenty of three-star hotels to choose from, and if your budget is lower still a range of places offer cheap, safe and clean accommodation, although only three of these are really geared to backpackers.

EXCLUSIVE/LUXURY

🏠 **Afecc Gloria Hotel** [91 G1] (258 rooms) Av da Marginal; ☎ 21 266666; e info@maputo-grand. gloriahotels.com; w maputo-grand.gloriahotels. com. Glorious in all its 5-star luxury, this stunning new US$300 million hotel boasts fantastic sea views & a grand contemporary design. Amenities inc swimming pool, gym, tennis court, snooker room, squash court & 6 restaurants & bars (among them a speciality international & Chinese restaurant, tearoom, grill room, wine & cigar bar). Introductory rates of *US$333*. **$$$$$**

🏠 **Afrin Prestige** [98 D4] (88 rooms) Rua Ngungunyana; ☎ 21 358900; m 82 358 0001 or 84 358 0001; e prestige.reservas@afrinhotels.co.mz; w afrin-hotels.com. Warmly praised by people who've stayed here, this hotel is next to the Maputo Shopping Centre, near the Catembe ferry & within walking distance of most places in the city centre. Less staid than its more established competitors, it combines comfortable furnishings & all the expected facilities with an airy ambience enhanced by the contemporary African artwork in the reception areas. There's a restaurant, bar, swimming pool, gym & business centre, & all rooms have DSTV, Wi-Fi, & AC. *US$191/212 sgl/dbl; US$219/247 exec sgl/dbl; suites from US$348.* **$$$$**

🏠 **Hotel Avenida** [95 C4] (159 rooms) 627 Av Julius Nyerere; ☎ 21 484400; e bookings. avenida@tdhotels.com; w tdhotels.com. This well-established hotel a few blocks further south along the same road as the Polana Serena lacks its neighbour's intimacy, Edwardian grace & direct sea views, but otherwise the comfortable & well-equipped rooms are much on a par, with DTSV, AC, Wi-Fi & minibar. There is a rooftop swimming pool, sauna, gym, piano bar & good restaurant, & it is well placed for eating out in the heart of Maputo. *US$215/250 sgl/dbl; US$415 exec dbl; suites from US$280; all rates B&B.* **$$$$**

🏠 **Hotel Cardoso** [95 A5] (130 rooms) 707 Av Mártires de Mueda; ☎ 21 491071/5; m 82 311 8070; e info@hotelcardoso.co.mz; w cardoso-hotel.com. Part of the highly regarded international Lonrho group, the Cardoso is another Maputo institution, situated in a quiet corner of

town opposite the Natural History Museum on a cliff offering a view over the city centre to the harbour & Catembe. The large tiled rooms are decorated with sedate good taste & come with flat-screen TV, AC & Wi-Fi. There's a pool, gym, business centre & gardens. *US$290/320 sgl/dbl with city view; US$315/345 with sea view; suites from US$505; all rates B&B.* **$$$$**

🏠 **Polana Serena** [95 D2] (142 rooms) Av Julius Nyerere; ☎ 21 241700/800; m 82 320 1450; e reservations@serenahotels.co.mz; w serenahotels.com. Sited on a low cliff overlooking the Indian Ocean, Maputo's most prestigious hotel since it opened in 1922 has only gained in stature following a takeover by the highly regarded Kenya-based Serena chain & extensive renovations completed in late 2010. Although it fell into a state of neglect during the civil war, it has since reclaimed its status as one of the most elegant & well-run hotels in Africa, combining Edwardian grace with modern luxuries such as DSTV, free Wi-Fi & AC in all rooms, internet access, tennis court, business centre, gymnasium, spa, casino, gift shop, 3 gourmet restaurants & 1 of the most attractive swimming pools on the continent. *US$360/395 courtyard-/sea-facing dbl; US$540/575 exec city-/sea-facing dbl; all rates B&B.* **$$$$$**

🏠 **Radisson Blu** [91 G1] (154 rooms) Av da Marginal; ☎ 21 242400; e info.maputo@ radissonblu.com; w radissonblu.com/hotel-maputo. Perhaps the most visible example of Maputo's recent economic good fortune, this towering hotel is a stunner, offering international-calibre accommodation overlooking the Costa do Sol. Rooms are über-modern & decked out with all the expected amenities inc many with balconies, & the hotel itself boasts no fewer than 3 separate bars, an Italian-inspired terrace restaurant, swimming pool, tanning area, fitness centre, 3hr laundry service, & unlimited Wi-Fi. It obviously lacks the long history of the Polana Serena, but for contemporary business accommodation, it's the top of the pile. Rates fluctuate daily, but expect around *US$225/265 standard sgl/dbl; US$245/285 sea-view sgl/dbl; suites from US$585; all rates B&B.* **$$$$**

🏠 **Southern Sun** [91 H1] (269 rooms) 4016 Av da Marginal; 🔲 21 495050; e ssmaputo.reservation@ tsogosun.com; w tsogosun.com. Formerly the Holiday Inn, this hotel was renovated & a new wing with more than 100 rooms added in 2014. It lacks the colonial character of the Polana Serena (page 96) but compensates with its understated Afro-chic resort-like beachfront setting less than 1km from the city centre. The comfortable & modern rooms are artfully decorated & have similar facilities to the Polana, inc gift shop, infinity pool, business centre & good restaurant. It is also well placed to eat at the cluster of restaurants running along the Av da Marginal just 200m further north. It also has jazz on Sun. *US$295–326 dbl; US$315–345 sea-facing dbl; suites from US$455; all rates B&B.* **$$$$$**

UPMARKET

🏠 **Hotel Villa das Mangas** [95 B4] (21 rooms) 401 Av 24 de Julho; 🔲 21 497078; e res@ villadasmangas.com; w villadasmangas.com. One of the few Maputo hotels to which the adjective 'boutique' could be added, this characterful place stands in an old house beside the Geological Museum in Polana. The compact en-suite rooms & suites, clustered around a pretty little garden with a swimming pool, all have TVCabo & AC, & are decorated in funky African style. A decent restaurant is attached. Just up the road, its sister boutique hotel with Arabic décor, Villa das Aràbias [94 A4], offers similar amenities (inc pool) & pricing. *US$107 standard dbl; US$129 superior or cabana dbl; US$149 luxury suite; all rates B&B.* **$$$$**

🏠 **Montebelo Girassol** [98 F3] (45 rooms, 30 under construction) 737 Av Patrice Lumumba; 🔲 21 480505; e reservasmontebelo@ montebelohotels.com; w montebelohotels.com. Following new ownership in 2016, this hotel has had a contemporary makeover & its facilities improved with the addition of a restaurant, balcony, swimming pool & gym. It is set in a quiet part of the city centre & offers a commanding view of the bay across to Catembe from the bar/restaurant area, as well as from the sea-facing rooms at the back. The spacious rooms come with Wi-Fi, TVCabo & AC, & the hotel is within walking distance of a good selection of shops & restaurants. *US$153/167 sgl/dbl; suites from US$199; all rates B&B.* **$$$$**

🏠 **Pestana Rovuma** [98 D2] (117 rooms) 114 Rua da Sé; 🔲 21 305000; m 82 130 5000; e reservas.africa@pestana.com or trade@ pestana.com; w pestana.com. One of the finest hotels in the Baixa area – along with the cathedral it dominates the eastern edge of the Praça Independência. Its main selling point is its location right in the heart of Maputo, a 5min walk to the shops, restaurants & bars on & around the Av 25 de Setembro & only about 15mins by foot from the Polana district. Rooms have Wi-Fi, DSTV, AC & other facilities inc swimming pool, gym, sauna & business centre. At the time of our visit, half of the rooms were closed for renovation. Good value at *US$183/198 sgl/dbl; US$210/225 exec sgl/dbl; suites from US$240; all rates B&B.* **$$$$**

MID RANGE

🏠 **Duqueza de Connaught** [95 C5] (8 rooms) 290 Av Julius Nyerere; 🔲 21 302155/492190; e info@duquezadeconnaught. com; w duquezadeconnaught.com. As central as can be in the Polana, this fabulously restored old house is some of the best-value accommodation in Maputo. The immaculate rooms are light & airy with flat-screen DSTV, fridge, kettle, writing desk, safe, AC, & some with large balconies. Décor is understated, with linen, wood & wrought-iron trimmings, there's a swimming pool in the gardens out back, & it's spitting distance from just about everything. *US$77/99 sgl/dbl B&B.* **$$$**

🏠 **Hotel Moçambicano** [90 C5] (63 rooms) 961 Av Filipe Samuel Magaia; 🔲 21 310600; m 82 305 2890 or 84 305 2890; e reservas@ hotelmocambicano.com; w hotelmocambicano. com. The contemporary décor, though a little bombastic for some tastes, sets this comfortable, central hotel apart, & it is centred on a green courtyard with a swimming pool. There's free 24hr internet & a 24hr lobby bar, restaurant & clean en-suite rooms with DTSV & AC. *US$67/78 sgl/dbl, US$101 dbl executive, B&B.* **$$$**

🏠 **Hotel Terminus** [95 B4] (45 rooms) 587 Av Francisco Orlando Magumbwe; 🔲 21 491333; m 82 303 4630/4790; e info@terminus.co.mz; w terminus.co.mz. Set on a quiet street in the Polana district, the Terminus advertises itself as a '5-star hotel at 3-star prices', which is a bit of a stretch, but it does boast most of the facilities of the bigger fish above, an extremely friendly staff & good-value rack rates. *US$123 dbl; suites from US$160; all rates B&B.* **$$$**

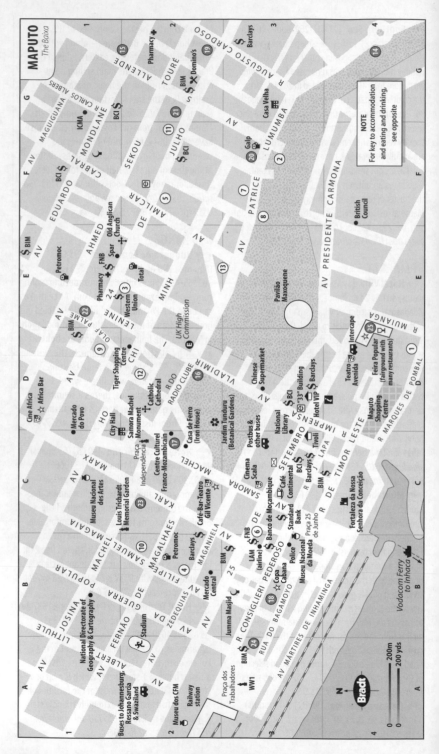

MAPUTO
The Baixa

NOTE
For key to accommodation
and eating and drinking,
see opposite

98

MAPUTO *The Baixa*
For listings, see pages 96–102

◉ **Where to stay**
1	Afrin Prestige	D4
2	The Base Backpackers	F3
3	Hotel Atlantis	E2
4	Hotel Continental	B2
5	Hotel Santa Cruz	F2
6	Hotel Turismo	C3
7	Monte Carlo	F3
8	Montebelo Girassol	F3
9	Pensão Central	D1
10	Pensão da Baixa	B2
11	Pensão Martins	F2
12	Pestana Rovuma	D2
13	Residencial Palmeiras	E3

✖ **Where to eat and drink**
14	Acacia Café	G4
15	Bar Lounge 1908	G2
16	Café-Bar Radio Mozambique	D2
17	Centre Cultural Franco-Mozambicain	C2
18	Gypsy's Bar	B3
19	Il Gelato	G2
20	Khana Khazana	F3
21	Mimmo's	G2
22	Restaurante Coculucho	E1
23	Restaurante Impala	C2
24	Rui's Bar	A3

25	*Feira Popular:*	
	Lua	D4
	Restaurante Bamboo	D4
	Restaurante Escorpião	D4
	Restaurante O Coqueiro	D4
	Snack Bar Pakit-Ket	D4

🏠 **Hotel Turismo** [98 C3] (165 rooms) Av 25 de Setembro; ☎21 352200; m 82 317 8040 or 84 399 8504; e reservas@hturismo.com. This impeccably central multi-storey hotel might be a little short on character, but the en-suite rooms are very comfortable, brightly decorated & come with DTSV, AC & Wi-Fi. Great value at *US$69/77 sgl/dbl B&B or US$92 suite.* **$$$**

🏠 **Monte Carlo** [98 F3] (58 rooms) 620 Av Patrice Lumumba; ☎21 304048; e reservas@ montecarlo.co.mz; ⦿ HotelMonteCarloMaputo. This sister hotel to the Terminus (page 97) shares its older & slightly pricier sibling's slogan, & offers much the same ambience (or lack thereof) & value for money. Wi-Fi, TVCabo & kettle in en-suite rooms. *US$90/110 sgl/dbl, B&B.* **$$$**

🏠 **Moringa Guesthouse** [90 D4] (9 rooms) 798 Av Emilia Dausse; ☎21 303965; m 82 321 9210; e moringamoz@gmail.com. Located in a pleasant compound with a garden & pool, this guesthouse offers en-suite accommodation with AC, net, kettle, Wi-Fi & DSTV. Rooms are clean & comfortable. *US$75/80 sgl/dbl, B&B.* **$$$**

🏠 **Mozaika Guesthouse 1** [95 A1] (9 rooms) 769 Av Agostinho Neto; ☎21 303939/65; m 84 577 0627/367 4650; e mozaika.guesthouse1@ tdm.co.mz. Full last time we checked in, en-suite rooms here open up on to a riotously colourful central courtyard, with a swimming pool set under an enormous mango tree. There's AC, TV, free Wi-Fi & a café attached, & it comes highly recommended. They've also got an equally pleasant annex at Av Milagre Mabote [90 D3], so be sure to know which one you're booked at if calling ahead. *US$135 standard sgl; US$164 exec dbl or twin; all rates B&B.* **$$$**

🏠 **Residencial Kaya Kwanga** [91 H1] (44 rooms) Rua D J João de Castro 321; ☎21 492706/7; e reservas@kayakwanga.co.mz; w kayakwanga. co.mz. The least urbanised hotel in Maputo, this sprawling chalet complex lies about 1km north of the Southern Sun along the beachfront road to the Costa do Sol. There are two swimming pools, pretty green gardens scattered with indigenous trees, a salon & nursery, as well as a good restaurant within the complex. Rooms have AC, DTSV, barbecue facilities & private parking. *US$80/90 sgl/ dbl B&B.* **$$$**

🏠 **Residencial Palmeiras** [98 E3] (6 rooms) Av Patrice Lumumba; ☎21 300199; m 82 306 9200; e carlos.pereira@tvcabo.co.mz; w palmeiras-guesthouse.com. This pleasant small guesthouse, set in an old, funkily decorated, double-storey building along the same road as the Cardoso (page 96), provides an agreeable & characterful alternative to the more institutional large hotels that dominate its price range. *US$81/99 sgl/dbl B&B.* **$$$**

🏠 **Resotel** [90 D5] (68 rooms) Av Karl Marx; ☎21 320929; m 82 224 7643 or 84 560 4476; e reservas@resotelmoz.com; w resotelmoz.com. This new hotel has a great, central location near the LTM bus ticket office. The en-suite sgl, dbl & twin rooms are a bit small & characterless, but otherwise clean & comfortable with AC & Wi-Fi. Family rooms are a bit more spacious. There are 2 restaurants & parking as well. *US$95 sgl, twin or dbl, US$111 family room, all rates B&B.* **$$$**

BUDGET
🏠 **Fátima's Place Backpackers** [91 E4] (13 rooms, 5 dorms) 1321 Av Mao Tse Tung; ☎21 302994; m 82 185 1577; e fatimasbackpackersmozambique@gmail.com;

w mozambiquebackpackers.com; reception ⊕ 07.00–22.00; see ad, page 119. Under the same owner-manager since it opened its doors in 1992, Fátima's is the most established backpackers in Maputo. Assets inc clued-up English-speaking staff, Wi-Fi, lively décor, a chilled sociable atmosphere, kitchen, plenty of outdoor seating, safe parking, laundry, baggage storage, mosquito netting on all beds & free pick-up from the airport (or elsewhere in Maputo) during daylight hrs. The staff & noticeboard are useful sources of information about Maputo & elsewhere in Mozambique, as – usually – are the other travellers you will meet there. Limited camping space. Advance booking is strongly recommended. *US$50/80/100/120 sgl/dbl/trpl/quad en suite; US$45/60/80/100 sgl/dbl/trpl/quad with shared bathroom; US$16 dorm; US$16 camping.* **$$$**

🏠 **Hotel Atlantis** [98 E2] (28 rooms) Av 24 de Julho; ☎ 21 420397; **e** info@atlantismz.com; **w** atlantismz.com. Opened in 2014, this hotel offers plain en-suite rooms with AC, DSTV, Wi-Fi, kettle & minibar. The rooms are a bit small. *US$69/80/102 sgl/twin/dbl, B&B.* **$$$**

🏠 **Hotel Continental** [98 B2] (40 rooms) 177 Av Filipe Samuel Magaia; ☎ 21 080349; **m** 84 644 1251; **e** maputocontinentalinfo@gmail. com or info@hotelcontinentalmaputo.com; **w** hotelcontinentalmaputo.com; 🟦 MaputoHotelContinental. This multi-storey hotel has new owners & is just around the corner from the central market with simple but very clean tiled en-suite rooms, with flat-screen TV, Wi-Fi & AC. It could be convenient for catching a morning chapa, & is good value overall. There's a restaurant on-site serving all the usuals. *US$40/50/54/70 sgl/twin/dbl/ trpl, B&B.* **$$**

🏠 **Hotel Santa Cruz** [98 F2] (84 rooms) Av 24 de Julho; ☎ 21 303004; **m** 84 166 4111; **e** hsantacruz@teledata.mz. A clean, comfortable option with simple appointments. All rooms en suite with AC, writing desk, fridge & Wi-Fi in the works. *US$48 sgl or dbl, B&B.* **$$**

🏠 **Hoyo Hoyo Residencial** [95 B3] (37 rooms) 837 Av Francisco Orlando Magumbwe; ☎ 21 490701/494297/491500; **m** 82 300 9950; **e** reservas@residencialhoyohoyo.com; **w** residencialhoyohoyo.co.mz. One of the best-value hotels in Maputo, offering accommodation in comfortable en-suite rooms with AC, DSTV & paid Wi-Fi, usefully located within walking distance of numerous restaurants. *US$59/74 sgl/dbl; US$89 suite, all rates B&B.* **$$$**

🏠 **Pensão Martins** [98 F2] (26 rooms) 1098 Av 24 de Julho; ☎ 21 301429; **m** 84 563 8602; **e** pensaomartins@gmail.com. This small but nicely laid-out & quite quaintly decorated hotel offers good-value en-suite accommodation in bright but small rooms with parquet floor, DSTV & AC, & it lies close to the heart of Maputo's main dining-out area. *US$50/60 sgl/dbl or twin, US$90 suite.* **$$$**

SHOESTRING

🏠 **The Base Backpackers** [98 F3] (2 rooms, 3 dorms) 545 Av Patrice Lumumba; ☎ 21 302723; **m** 82 820 7673 or 84 844 7579; **e** thebasebackpackers@gmail.com. Cheaper, quieter & slightly more downmarket than Fátima's, this small central backpackers overlooking the bay has a self-catering kitchen, laundry service, Wi-Fi, TVCabo in sitting area & a great location for exploring the city centre. Mosquito nets not supplied. The shuttle for Fátima's Nest (page 167) in Tofo also stops here before departing. *US$10 pp dorm or US$30 dbl using shared ablutions.* **$**

🏠 **Maputo Backpackers** [91 H1] (9 rooms & dorms) Rua das Palmeiras; ☎ 21 451213; **m** 82 467 2230 or 84 657 6414; **e** maputobp@gmail.com. Situated off the Av da Marginal about 5km north of the city centre, a couple of mins' walk from the beach, this place has a variety of dorms & smaller rooms spread over 3 storeys of a residential property. Facilities inc lounge with TVCabo, a self-catering kitchen, a nice garden, free pick-up from the city centre & a nightly drop-off at any restaurant in town. Chapas between Costa do Sol & central Maputo pass within 100m of the hostel & cost around US$0.20. *US$42/50 sgl/dbl or twin; US$15 pp dorm.* **$$**

🏠 **Pensão Central** [98 D1] (24 rooms) 1957 Av 24 de Julho; ☎ 21 324476; **m** 84 443 2673. This basic, reasonably priced pensão is clean & has staff who are eager to please. The perfectly acceptable en-suite rooms have ceiling fans but don't inc mosquito nets. *US$13/17/26 sgl/dbl/ trpl.* **$**

🏠 **Pensão da Baixa** [98 B2] (14 rooms) Av Filipe Samuel Magaia; ☎ 21 308190; **m** 82 757 0617 or 84 714 4821. Decent central option with clean rooms & fans but shared bathrooms & no nets. A little overpriced at *US$28/32 twin or dbl/en-suite dbl.* **$$**

🏠 **Pensão Taj Mahal** [90 C6] (28 rooms) Av Ho Chi Min; ☎ 21 402350. An extremely popular option, well run & worth a look, particularly if you need to be near the buses, but vacant rooms are often in short supply. *US$12/17 sgl/dbl without AC,* *US$28/30 dbl/trpl with AC, US$36 en-suite dbl with AC & TV.* **$**

❮ WHERE TO EAT AND DRINK

One thing you'll never have to worry about in Maputo is finding a decent meal – there are restaurants everywhere catering to all tastes and budgets. The emphasis is on seafood and Portuguese dishes such as the ubiquitous chicken piri-piri, but there are also a good number of specialised places ranging from pizzerias and steakhouses to Indian and oriental restaurants.

FEIRA POPULAR

(*Av 25 de Setembro; entrance fee US$0.40*) If you aren't sure what you feel like, or just want to browse a bit without stretching the legs too much, then this is an excellent place to start. In addition to the fairground rides, the Feira hosts more than a dozen eateries serving a far greater variety of food than the burger 'n' chips combos that might be expected, & you can wander between them clutching a beer until you find something that takes your fancy.

✖ **Lua** [98 D4] Cryptically named but excellent Chinese restaurant close to the main entrance. **$$**

✖ **Restaurante Bamboo** [98 D4] Inexpensive but good Vietnamese dishes, with Korean BBQ-style grills at each table. **$$**

✖ **Restaurante Escorpião** [98 D4] Lays claim to being the most popular eating place in Maputo & does mainly Portuguese dishes, reasonably priced & more than generous. **$$**

✖ **Restaurante O Coqueiro** [98 D4] Specialises in food from the Mozambican province of Zambézia. **$$**

✖ **Snack Bar Pakit-Ket** [98 D4] Right at the entrance of the Feira, this place does excellent *matapa*. **$$**

BAIXA

✖ **Bar Lounge 1908** [98 G2] Cnr avs Eduardo Mondlane & Salvador Allende; ☏ 21 321908; 🅵 BarLounge1908; ⏰ 11.00–midnight Tue–Sun, later at w/ends. Set in a beautiful colonial house complete with period furnishing, this is one of the most outstanding purveyors of Mozambican cuisine in Maputo, with the choice of eating formally indoors or in the shady gardens, & it stays open late, transformed into one of the classiest nightspots in town. Free Wi-Fi. *Most mains around US$15, tapas US$4–6.* **$$$$**

✖ **Café-Bar Radio Mozambique** [98 D2] Rua do Radio Clube; ⏰ 07.00–23.30 daily. At the northern end of the botanical gardens, this has a nice terrace but feels a little run-down indoors. Still, the Mozambican fare is pretty good & well priced. This could change with the ongoing renovations at the botanical gardens, though. *Petiscos for around US$5, mains at US$5–11.* **$$$**

✖ **Centre Cultural Franco-Mozambicain** [98 C2] Av Samora Machel; ☏ 21 314590; 📱 82 301 8000 or 84 626 7752; 🌐 ccfmoz.com; ⏰ noon–19.00 Mon, 10.00–19.00 Tue–Sat. The café at this trendy arts centre serves a selection of filled focaccia & other light meals. Service can be slow but, if you are not in a hurry, the ambience compensates. *Around US$8.* **$$**

✖ **Gypsy's Bar** [98 B3] Rua do Bagamoyo; ☏ 21 312668; 📱 82 427 8540; ⏰ 07.30–late Fri, 07.30–17.00 Sat/Sun. This popular sports bar has flat-screen TVs for sporting events & is a favourite among local businessmen. The bullfighting memorabilia on the walls is particularly interesting. Pizza, seafood, & Portuguese food are served for *around US$6–10.* **$$**

✖ **Il Gelato** [98 G2] Av 24 de Julho; 📱 84 530 3033; ⏰ 06.30–22.30 daily. Stupendous Italian gelato with a few locations around town. Light meals, b/fast, burgers, pizza & pastries are served as well, but the sorbet is the star of the show. *US$1–7.* **$**

✖ **Khana Khazana** [98 F3] Av Patrice Lumumba; ☏ 21 313872; 📱 82 318 6840 or 84 715 3784; ⏰ 11.30–15.00 & 19.00–23.00 daily. Directly opposite the Base Backpackers (page 100), this quality Indian restaurant offers a wide range of tandoori dishes & curries, incl extensive vegetarian selection, with a few Chinese dishes to keep things interesting. Alcohol is served. Free Wi-Fi. *Mains are typically around US$6–11.* **$$**

✗ Maputo Waterfront [91 G7] Av 10 de Novembro; ☎21 301408; m 84 305 3209; w maputowaterfront.com; ⏱ 11.30–22.30 Mon–Thu, 11.30–23.30 Sat/Sun, 11.00–16.00 Sun. Arguably the best location in all Maputo, overlooking the harbour & Catembe, this highly rated & often very busy sports-bar-cum-restaurant is a great spot for sundowners. It also boasts a swimming pool & live jazz on Wed, Fri & Sat with a US$10 cover. *The menu offers chicken, meat & a huge variety of seafood dishes & combos (US$8–16).* **$$$**

✗ Mimmo's [98 G2] Cnr avs 24 de Julho & Salvador Allende; ☎21 309491; m 82 948 7420; w mimmos.co.za; opening hrs & prices as for the branch on Av Vladimir Lenine (page 104).

✗ Restaurante Coculucho [98 E1] 1044 Av Eduardo Mondlane; m 84 249 5096/475 5808; ⏱ 07.00–late daily. This popular restaurant with indoor & outdoor seating serves a Portuguese menu & daily specials. *US$7–13.* **$$$**

✗ Restaurante Impala [98 C2] Cnr avs Karl Marx & Josina Machel; ☎21 305636; m 84 555 5444; ⏱ 10.00–22.00 daily. This long-serving central eatery serves a fine range of Pakistani, Indian & Portuguese meals. One portion of rice & a main dish is more than enough for all but the hungriest eaters. Alcohol isn't served. *Mains US$5–9.* **$$**

✗ Restaurante Zambi [91 F7] Av 10 de Novembro; m 84 339 2624; 🇫 RestauranteZambi; ⏱ noon–22.00 Mon–Thu, noon–23.00 Fri/Sat, noon–16.30 Sun. Facing the waterfront looking across to Catembe, this has a large breezy terrace & formal indoor seating. *Highly rated menu of seafood, sushi, steaks & salads mostly in the US$8–24 range; some seafood as much as US$40.* **$$$$$**

✗ Rui's Bar [98 A3] 378 Rua do Bagamoyo; ☎21 333088; m 82 769 6170; ⏱ 07.00–21.00 Mon–Fri, 07.00–23.00 Fri/Sat. With the hole-in-the-wall vibe of a true insider's joint & pictures of old Maputo on the walls, this colourful sanctuary is a great place to duck off the street for a drink or a meal. There's beer on tap, & a selection of food ranging from pregos to prawns. *US$6–12.* **$$$$**

POLANA

✗ A Esquina [95 B5] Cnr avs dos Mártires da Machava & Mateus S Muthemba; m 84 310 2735; ⏱ 17.00–23.00 Mon–Sat. This corner tapas bar serves 60 different types of wine with a selection available by the glass. *Tapas US$6–11, wine US$10–50.* **$$$**

✗ A Nossa Tasca [95 C5] 245 Av Julius Nyerere; m 82 107 1539 or 84 450 6174; ⏱ noon–23.00 Thu–Sat, noon–22.00 Mon–Tue. A swanky new tapas bar with a great wine selection. *Tapas US$4–10; mains US$10–20; wine US$16–60.* **$$$**

✗ Acacia Café [95 A5] Jardim dos Professores; ☎21 300640; ⏱ 08.00–20.00 daily. Affiliated with the neighbouring Hotel Cardoso (page 96), this sleek café has one of the best locations in town, anchoring a lively green park with spectacular views over the Baixa. The menu covers a variety of Italian-inspired café favourites such as paninis, along with a range of wines & coffee-based drinks perfect for a languid afternoon on the terrace. *US$5–8.* **$$**

✗ Bairro Alto Restaurante [95 B5] 264 Rua Mateus S Muthemba; m 84 345 7570; ⏱ noon–midnight Tue–Sun. With indoor & outdoor seating, this is another new Portuguese restaurant serving a tasty menu of seafood, meat, soups & salads. *US$7–14.* **$$$$**

✗ Bairro Bistro [95 C4] 562 Av Julius Nyerere; m 82 788 2548 or 84 687 5054; w bairroaltomaputo.com; ⏱ 10.00–19.00 Mon–Thu & Sat, 10.00–late Fri. This restaurant & bar serves quiche, salads, sandwiches, soups, meat, seafood & natural juices, located alongside an art gallery & boutique shop with Afro-chique style clothing & jewellery. There's swing dancing on Fri night. **$$$**

✗ Bel Piatto [95 C5] Cnr avs Julius Nyerere & Argélia; ☎21 491130; m 84 457 3747; ⏱ noon–14.30 & 19.00–22.30 Mon–Fri, 19.00–22.30 Sat. At the formal end of things, this stylishly swanky Italian restaurant serves pastas & grills. *US$13–20.* **$$$$**

✗ Dhow Café [91 G6] 4 Rua de Marracuene; ☎21 492115; m 82 024 7340/149 2491; w dhow.co.mz; ⏱ 10.00–19.00 Mon–Wed, 10.00–17.30 Fri/Sat. Tucked away on a quiet street & smack dab on the edge of the escarpment leading to the Baixa, this cultivated café is half import store, with a dazzling variety of art & home goods from around the world. It's undeniably taken its place among Maputo's most fashionable locales, & the brilliant view across to Catembe certainly adds to its cachet. The menu takes its cue from the Greek proprietress, & on any given day you're likely to be choosing from sandwiches, phyllo wraps, spanakopita or small plates known as *meze*. There are desserts & wine aplenty, & even a small swimming pool should the mood strike you. *US$6–15.* **$$$$**

✗ Dolce Vita [95 C3] Av Julius Nyerere; **m** 82 892 7697; **f** dolcevita.maputo; ⊕ 08.00–midnight Mon–Wed & Sun, 08.00–02.00 Thu–Sat. Good for b/fast, lunch, a last late round or sundowners from the extensive cocktail menu, this trendy café serves salads, brochettes, pizza & pasta, & tiramisu for dessert. There is live music on Thu & Sun. *US$7–12.* **$$$**

✗ Moksha Indian [95 C3] 933 Av Julius Nyerere; ☎21 498333; ⊕ 09.00–23.00 Mon–Fri, 10.00–late Sat/Sun. A good Indian restaurant a bit more upscale than Galaxy Indian (page 104). Mains around *US$6–14.* **$$$$**

✗ Mundo's [95 C4] Cnr avs Julius Nyerere & Eduardo Mondlane; ☎21 494080; **m** 84 468 6367; **w** mundosmaputo.com; ⊕ 08.00–late daily. The business card describes it as a 'restaurant, pub & everything', & it's difficult to quibble with that when it's divided into 4 indoor & outdoor areas of varying informality. It's also a popular drinking hole with expats, with a selection of beers on tap, a private dining area for hire & large screens that draw crowds for major sporting events. A cover of US$10 is charged on busy sporting nights. *Light meals for US$5–7, pizzas for around US$9, & seafood & meat grills for US$10–16.* **$$$**

✗ New Galaxy Indian Restaurant [95 B5] Av dos Mártires da Machava; ☎21 497852; **m** 82 291 3047, 84 522 1202 or 86 209 0156; ⊕ 10.00–23.00 daily. With a freshly repainted dining area, this Indian & Pakistani restaurant offers a selection of meat & vegetarian noodle & rice dishes, as well as a more Western menu with burgers & pizza. Dine-in, take-away or delivery available. Halal. *Most mains US$4–7.* **$$**

✗ Peace Love Pizza [95 B2] 159 Rua Paulo Samuel Kankhomba; **m** 84 528 0907. Serving heart-shaped pizza, salads, natural juices & ice cream – hard not to feel the love here! *US$6–10* **$$$**

✗ Pekai's Thai Pub & Restaurant [95 B5] Av Francisco O Magumbwe; **m** 82 045 5220; ⊕ 10.00–23.00 Mon–Sat. This new Thai restaurant is the best in town & offers a full menu of curries & hotpots, plus coconut cocktails. *US$4–12.* **$$$**

✗ Pirata [95 C5] Cnr avs Julius Nyerere & 24 de Julho; **m** 84 433 7984; ⊕ 10.00–22.30 daily. One of the better-value eateries along Av Julius Nyerere, this informal Italian & seafood restaurant, set on an enclosed patio, serves tasty pastas, grills, burgers, salads & filled pitas, alongside a long list of signature pizzas. There's MTV & football on the big screen. *US$7–11.* **$$$**

✗ PiriPiri Restaurant [95 C4] Cnr avs 24 de Julho & Julius Nyerere; ☎21 492379; **m** 84 672 4350; **e** rest.piripiri@tvcabo.co.mz; ⊕ 11.00–midnight daily. Best known for its curries but also strong on chicken piri-piri & seafood, this is a popular place to hang out while recuperating from those Sunday-afternoon hangovers. *Most mains around US$10–16.* **$$$$**

✗ Pizza House [95 B1] Av Mao Tse Tung; ☎21 485257; **m** 82 056 9690 or 84 555 5557; ⊕ 06.30–22.30 daily. This place is always busy, & deservedly so, with a wide assortment of pastries, sandwiches & pizzas, & a good plate of the day. The outdoor terrace is excellent for people-watching. No alcohol served, but there's good coffee. *Sandwiches & snacks US$2–4, mains US$6–9.* **$$**

✗ Restaurante Cristal [95 B4] Av 24 de Julho; **m** 82 281 5180 or 84 302 3560; **f** restaurantepastelariacristal; ⊕ 06.30–22.30 daily. Open continuously since the colonial era & with the retro décor to prove it, this place is highly rated for its tasty but reasonably priced seafood & traditional Mozambican dishes. With indoor & outdoor seating, it's a great spot for b/fast or a drink at the fantastically long bar. *Sandwiches & snacks US$4–8, mains mostly US$11–15.* **$$$$**

✗ Restaurante Spicy Thai [95 C4] Av Julius Nyerere; ☎21 497644; **m** 84 209 9993; ⊕ 09.00–22.00 daily. A refreshing change from the Continental & Mozambican fare that dominates in Maputo, this serves a varied selection & there's a reasonably priced lunch buffet. *Meat, vegetarian green & red curries, stir-fries & salads in the US$10 range; seafood dishes are mostly around US$15; lunch buffet US$10.* **$$$**

✗ Tacos Café [95 B3] 190 Rua do Telégrafo; **m** 84 215 4198/016 9593; ⊕ 09.00–18.00 Mon–Fri, 10.00–19.00 Sat. Claiming to serve the best Mexican food in Africa, this new restaurant is the stationary version of a popular food truck in Maputo & offers a range of burritos, nachos, tacos, empanadas, salads, burgers & cocktails. *US$5–8.* **$$**

✘ **Taverna Portuguesa** [95 D2]
Av Mao Tse Tung; m 82 199 8514; f grupo.
restaurante.e.pastelaria.taverna; ◷ noon–15.00 &
18.00–22.00 Mon–Sat, noon–16.00 Sun. This smart
Portuguese restaurant has an extensive menu, with
an impressive selection of Portuguese & Cape wines.
They also have an Italian restaurant on Av Julius
Nyerere, as well as several pastelarias. *Meat, chicken
& seafood dishes in the US$13–26 range.* $$$$$

✘ **Treehouse** [95 B4] Av Francisco O
Magumbwe; m 82 109 9358; ◷ noon–22.00
daily. A Brazilian-style barbecue restaurant with
indoor & outdoor seating, serving seafood & meat
skewers with a selection of sides. *US$8–18.* $$$$

✘ **Txhapo Txhapo** [95 C4] 173 Av Eduardo
Mondlane; m 84 541 9820; ◷ noon–14.30 Mon–Fri,
18.00–22.00 Mon, Wed–Fri, noon–22.00 Sat. This
new restaurant serves mixed cuisine with a chalkboard
menu offering Portuguese, Arabian, Mozambican
& internationally inspired cuisine, & a daily special.
Happy hr 18.00–21.00. *US$6–11.* $$$

⌷ **Horoscopo** [95 B5] Av Mateus S Muthemba;
m 82 759 2533; ◷ 07.00–22.00 Mon–Sat.
Choose from deli-style light meals & salads or more
substantial meat & seafood grills at this popular
café. Paid Wi-Fi. *Most dishes clock in at US$5–8, with
a plate of the day for US$10.* $$

⌷ **Shamwari** [95 B5] Av Mateus S Muthemba;
☎ 21 081719; ◷ 06.00–23.00 Mon–Fri, 09.00–
23.00 Sat. This popular café at the south end of the
Polana district with indoor & outdoor seating serves
delicious pastries, inexpensive filled rolls & salads
& invigorating espressos. *A few meals of the day &
sandwiches in the US$8–10 range.* $$$

⌷ **Taverna Dolce 1** [95 D2] Av Mao Tse Tung;
m 82 199 7514; f grupo.restaurante.e.pastelaria.
taverna; ◷ 07.00–20.00 Mon–Sat, 07.00–16.00
Sun. An extension of Taverna Portuguesa next door,
this café offers an impressive selection of fresh
pastries & sandwiches. There's ice cream & a small
shop selling fresh breads, meats & cheeses. Very
smart café. *US$2–10 range.* $$$

NORTH OF THE CITY CENTRE

✘ **Cantinho do Brasil** [91 E5] Av Vladimir
Lenine; m 82 785 0627 or 84 510 8660;
◷ 06.00–22.00 Mon–Sat, 08.00–20.00 Sun.
Offering a menu of Brazilian specialities, snacks &
sandwiches. *US$2–4.* $

✘ **Costa do Sol** [91 H1] Av da Marginal;
☎ 21 450115; e rcs@teledata.mz; ◷ 08.00–23.00

Tue–Sun. Reopened in 2014 after major
renovations, the grande dame of Maputo eateries
lies about 7km out of town just off the beach also
known as Costa do Sol & has a long reputation for
its seafood. *Mains are around US$12–18.* $$$$

✘ **Galaxy Indian** [91 E2] Av Vladimir Lenine;
☎ 21 415668; m 82 314 0270/254 1940 or 84 471
0600; ◷ 10.30–23.30 daily. Located just east of
Av Vladimir Lenine near the Total gas station, this
restaurant is a relative to New Galaxy Indian (page
103) & offers the same menu. $$$

✘ **Marisqueira Sagres** [91 H1] Av da Marginal;
☎ 21 495201; ◷ 11.00–midnight Tue–Sun. This
highly regarded eatery combines a great seafront
location (near the Southern Sun Hotel) with a
tasty & sensibly priced menu dominated by but
not restricted to seafood – the seafood rice dishes
are recommended. There's a TV for sports as well.
Mains are in the US$12–26 range. $$$$$

✘ **Marnabrasa** [91 H1] Av da Marginal;
☎ 21 489080; m 82 300 0792 or 84 300 0792;
f marnabrasa; ◷ noon–23.30 daily. Serving
up Brazilian-style meat & seafood mains in the
US$12–18 range. Live music Thu (jazz), Fri (local),
Sat (Brazilian). $$$$

✘ **Mimmo's** [91 E4] Av Vladimir Lenine;
☎ 21 313492; m 82 307 0420; ◷ 11.00–23.00
Sun–Thu; 11.00–midnight Fri/Sat; w mimmos.
co.za. This popular South African franchise, a 5min
walk from Fátima's Place (page 99), is best known
for its pizzas & pastas, but also has an extensive
selection of more expensive steaks & seafood grills &
a good selection of everyday Cape wines for around
US$12 per bottle. There is large-screen DSTV for
major sporting events. There's also a Mimmo's Pronto
(take-away) on Av Julius Nyerere [95 C4] (m *84 999
9966)* & a location at Mare's Shopping Centre [91 H1]
(m *84 378 95190). US$7–14.* $$$$

✘ **Miramar** [91 G1] Av da Marginal; m 82
649 5335/6; ◷ 09.00–midnight daily. A Maputo
institution, this seafront bar-restaurant near the
Southern Sun Hotel is all about seafood, which is
usually excellent. *US$9 upwards for a main.* $$$

✘ **Royal Indian** [91 E3] Av Mao Tse Tung;
m 82 301 7625; ◷ 10.30–22.30 daily. Catering
mainly to the local market, the closest eatery to
Fátima's Place (page 99) serves a selection of meat
& vegetarian Indian, Chinese & Western fare with
Indian sweets for dessert. *US$4–6.* $

✘ **Varanda Café Bar** [91 E4] Av Vladimir
Lenine; ☎ 21 420600; m 82 740 7927; ◷ 07.30–

21.30 Mon–Thu, 7.30–late Fri/Sat. This pleasant, new café offers Portuguese & Mozambican food. *Daily specials US$3–9, most mains US$5–11.* **$$$**

✕ **Wine Lovers** [91 E3] 1258 Av Mao Tse Tung; m 84 261 9214/334 4466; f WineLovers.Maputo; ⊕ 10.00–22.00 Mon–Sat, later at w/ends. The city's only wine bar, this place in a converted house is cosy & slick, with a seriously well-dressed clientele. As would be expected, the wine selection here is fantastic, & they do tasting courses & live music on Sat. Tapas, chouriço, cheese platters & homemade jams round off the food selection, & there's a breezy terrace out back. Great for a classy night out, & surprisingly easy on the wallet. *US$7–12 cheese platters & tapas, US$16 avg bottle of wine.* **$$$$**

⧉ **Pastelaria Twingo** [91 E4] Av Vladimir Lenine; ☎ 21 333463; m 82 675 0597; ⊕ 06.30–22.30 daily. This excellent pastelaria, situated on the same block as Mimmo's (page 104), serves sandwiches, burgers, pizzas & Mozambican dishes, & a selection of pastries, as well as espresso. There's Wi-Fi as well. *US$2–6.* **$**

JUNK FOOD If you're desperate for good old-fashioned junk food then next to the Hotel VIP [98 D3] on Av 25 de Setembro is a block of South African fast-food joints, inc Steers, Debonair Pizza, Nando's & Kentucky Fried Chicken. A similar & even more varied selection of snack bars & fast-food outlets can be found in the courtyard of the Maputo Shopping Centre [98 D4] near the Catembe ferry pier. In addition there is a Pizza Hut on Av Mao Tse Tung opposite the Parque dos Continuadores [95 C2]. Strangest of all is a Domino's Pizza [98 G2] (☎ 21 313702) on Av 24 de Julho just down from Mimmo's. To all intents and purposes it is a corner shop selling all the usual things, but it also has what appears to be a legitimate Domino's take-away licence. You can even phone your order in – apparently they'll deliver it.

PASTELARIAS Cafés where you can sit & enjoy a slice of cake along with your tea; Maputo is so littered with these that there are too many to list. Many are linked to an espresso machine franchise called Delta – look for a red triangle on a green background. It is quite possible to spend days eating your body weight in cake should you so desire. Many also serve savoury dishes & full meals that are far cheaper than the same thing at proper restaurants.

NIGHTLIFE

Maputo has largely reclaimed the reputation for lively nightlife that it held back in the late colonial era, and is one of the better places in the region for an extended bar crawl. The usual caveats over security apply, and taxis are strongly recommended: 'in-town' journeys should cost in the region of US$5, while more remote journeys will be around US$8. Be aware that in Maputo, as in many African capitals, nightclubs and live venues tend to peak in the small hours, so places that seem dead when you arrive after dinner might start gathering momentum at around 23.00 and be in full swing by 01.00.

In addition to the venues listed below and on the following pages, several of the restaurants covered on the previous pages also have popular bars, most notably **Mundo's** (page 103) and **Maputo Waterfront** (page 102), both of which are popular rendezvous for expats, and the trio of beachfront seafood restaurants on the Avenida da Marginal north of the Southern Sun, while **Dolce Vita** (page 103) and **Bar Lounge 1908** (page 101) both stay open late. An option for a cheap boozy night out is the **Barracas do Museu**, also known as the **Night Market** (page 109), where the more hardcore stalls will stay open until the wee hours.

☆ **Africa Bar** [98 D1] Cnr avs 24 de Julho & Karl Marx; m 84 829 8494; f africabar. Situated alongside the Cine Africa, this is popular on Thu nights, when there is usually live jazz or Mozambican music. It has a reputation as a pick-up joint & single travellers both male & female can expect a lot of hassle unless they come in a group.

☆ **Café-Bar-Teatro Gil Vincente** [98 C2] 43 Av Samora Machel; m 84 586 4582; f GilVicenteCafeBar; ⊕ 18.00–02.00 Tue–Sat.

Situated opposite the botanical gardens, this intimate venue feels a little like a transplant from a trendy European capital, though the emphasis is strongly on live African music & jazz, almost always at w/ends & often on weeknights too. Check the posters outside or the website for what's playing here & at the next-door theatre. Entrance on live music nights is around US$6.

☆ **Coconuts** [91 H1] Av da Marginal; ✆21 322217; m 84 802 9285. Opposite the beach about 1km north of the Southern Sun, Maputo's best-known upmarket nightspot is actually 3 separate venues. The swish Ice Lounge (*entrance US$8 pp*) is a chilled dancing spot with a DJ, while The Lounge is similar but cheaper & generally busier. Coconuts itself often hosts live music at w/ends (*cover charge of US$10–20, depending on who's playing*). The club is safe & usually hassle-free, but walking across to the beach or going home on foot is inadvisable as you might be followed – take a taxi.

☆ **Copa Cabana** [98 B3] Rua do Bagamoyo. The best known of the half-dozen or so strip & other clubs that line Maputo's seedy 'Street of Trouble', an area best avoided after dark unless you're with a group or prepared for a lot of hassle.

☆ **Feira Popular** [98 D4] Av 25 de Setembro. A conglomeration of dozens of bars & restaurants (page 101), also with a variety of fairground rides, this is one of the liveliest places for a night out in Maputo, though it has no pretensions to being hip or happening in any way. If you do hit problems, then there is a police stand in the middle of the area.

♀ **Café Camissa** [95 B5] 194 Rua da Argélia; m 84 749 4505; ◷ 09.00–20.00 daily. Situated next to the Núcleo de Arte, this trendy café attracts a cosmopolitan arty crowd & often hosts live music, usually on Sun. It's more of an early-evening venue than a real nightspot, but it often stays open long past the official closing time.

♀ **Centenario Caipirinha Shack** [95 D6] Av Marginal; ◷ daily. A great local spot for a sundowner caipirinha.

♀ **Xima** [90 B5] Av Eduardo Mondlane. At the west end of the city centre near the statue of Eduardo Mondlane, this popular venue caters more to locals than to expats or tourists, but there is often live music, & entrance fees are nominal.

SAFETY AND HASSLES

Maputo is no more dangerous than any other large city; indeed, crime levels are very low compared with Nairobi, Lagos and Johannesburg, and violent crime against tourists is highly unusual. It's certainly very safe to walk around the city by day – pickpockets, con artists and the like are few and far between, and the occasional hawker tends to be far less persistent than is the case in many other cities in the continent. Crowded places, particularly the markets, should be approached with mild caution – stash valuables out of reach of wandering hands, and don't display flashy jewellery, bulging wallets or expensive cameras. It's also a good idea to carry some ready cash (a few low-value notes and some coinage, which makes a distracting noise when shaken) in a small accessible wallet or pocket, and to use that throughout the day, keeping your main stash of cash tucked out of sight.

There's no great risk associated with walking along the main streets in the early evening – they are reasonably lit and there are plenty of other pedestrians around – but the alleys and back ways should be avoided. Later in the evening it's probably advisable to use taxis for all your journeys. Two places which have seen several muggings by day and night, and should be steered clear of at all times, are the winding roads connecting Avenida Friedrich Engels and Avenida da Marginal, and the overgrown escarpment between the Baixa and Polana districts.

There does appear to be a fair amount of property crime in Maputo, particularly against motor vehicles – car parts aren't readily available and so they are subject to a growing shady market. If you are carrying stuff in the back of a pick-up truck, be careful in traffic jams or at traffic lights, as you may be distracted in some way by a couple of people while their friends help themselves to anything that's not secured. You also hear stories, possibly apocryphal, of people grabbing accessories like hubcaps and indicator light covers off cars while they're stalled at traffic lights. It is definitely unsafe to leave a car parked on the street overnight; don't stay at a hotel unless it can offer you somewhere safe to park.

Drugs are not tolerated – if you do get caught carrying them then prepare either to pay a hefty bribe or to spend longer than you expected in the country in distinctly less salubrious surroundings than you paid for. Knives are also not tolerated – if you are stopped carrying them they will be confiscated and the very least you will get is a stiff talking to in Portuguese.

ENTERTAINMENT

Nowadays, there are enough facilities in Maputo to make it possible to indulge most pastimes.

TENNIS CLUB [98 D2] (m *84 559 3569;* e *tennismaputo@gmail.com;* ⊕ *06.00–20.00 Mon–Sat, 06.00–19.00 Sun*) In the botanical garden, with six courts and changing rooms. Non-members can play for around US$7 per hour during the day and US$10 per hour in the evening.

SWIMMING POOLS Found at all of the capital's major hotels and some of the lesser ones, most can be used by non-residents on payment of a fee, though the Polana now restricts use to hotel residents. One of the best pools – Olympic-size and right on the seafront – is at the Clube Naval [95 D4], which charges around US$3 per person and lies on Avenida da Marginal south of the Southern Sun.

KITESURFING Kitezone Mozambique [91 G2] (*257 Rua Lucas Elias Kumato;* m *84 411 8318;* e *stephane@kitezonemoz.com;* w *kitezonemoz.com*) offers lessons at all skill levels in the waters just off the Costa do Sol and sells all the required kit.

FOOTBALL MATCHES Stadiums are at Costa do Sol, Desportivo, Machava and Maxaquene.

CINEMAS AND THEATRES There are a few dotted around the city centre, mostly showing a mix of dubbed or subtitled Hollywood films. You may find more arty stuff at some of the arts foundations. Theatrical productions are mostly in Portuguese.

Centre Cultural Franco-Mozambicain [98 C2] Av Samora Machel; ☎ 21 314590; m 82 301 8000; w ccfmoz.com. This arty venue, set in an 1898 building abutting the botanical garden, has a busy programme of live performances, ranging from contemporary music to theatre. The website contains full details of up-&-coming events (in Portuguese & French only).
Cinema Gil Vincente [98 C2] 45 Av Samora Machel; ☎ 21 308768; m 84 586 4582; part of the café-bar of the same name (page 105), with occasional live performances.

Cinemas Lusomundo [98 D4] Maputo Shopping Centre; ☎ 21 320073; m 84 687 5910; ⨍ LusomundoMocambique. This theatre in the mall has popcorn & 4 screens, & shows the latest Hollywood productions – some even in 3D.
Teatro Avenida [98 D4] m 82 430 8230. On Av 25 de Setembro just down from the Hotel Tivoli, this has occasional theatrical & operatic performances, most often at w/ends – check the posters outside for forthcoming attractions.

CULTURAL CENTRES In addition to the Franco-Mozambican centre listed above, there are some other centres offering art, music and other cultural programmes.

POLICE AND PASSPORTS

The biggest hassle most travellers face in Maputo comes not from lawbreakers but law enforcers. Mozambican law requires that people carry valid identification on them at all times, which in the case of foreign travellers means their passport. And there are plenty of police in Maputo who take great delight in enforcing this law – or, more accurately, in using it as a pretext to stop travellers in the street in the hope of extracting a bribe.

If this happens, and you are not carrying your passport, the normal drill is for the police to threaten to take you to a police station to pay a fine, and if that doesn't leave you looking suitably intimidated, they might also threaten to detain you overnight on some logistical pretext (for instance, the guy who makes out the invoices has knocked off for the day). And even if you are carrying a passport, they may decide you have committed some other offence, for instance not stopping in time, and either way the conversation will lead to your paying them a bribe in exchange for your freedom.

However the scenario builds up, the one thing that needs to be stressed is that the police in Maputo are generally as unenthusiastic as you when it comes to laying a formal charge of this sort. All they want is a bribe, and the moment they sense that this won't be forthcoming, they will lose interest. So just play it cool, be friendly, smile a lot, and generally convey the impression that a visit to the police station, or even an overnight stay there, is absolutely good with you, and it is almost certain they will let you go after 10 minutes or so.

That said, the whole thing can be an irritating waste of time, so if you will be staying in Maputo a while and are disinclined to expose your passport to pickpockets *et al.*, a notarised copy of the document costs next to nothing to make, and it will do just as well. There is a good notary around the corner from Fátima's Place on Avenida Vladimir Lenine, but there are several others dotted around the city and any hotel will be able to point you to one nearby.

American Cultural Centre [95 B1] 542 Av Mao Tse Tung; ✆ 21 491916; e maputoirc@state.gov; ◼ U.S.EmbassyMozambique or pages/Centro-Cultural-Americano-Maputo; ⊕ 09.00–17.00 Mon, Tue & Thu to the general public, by appointment only. Facilities inc library, video library, computers & a range of events from information sessions on studying in the USA to music performances, American dancing lessons & English-language clubs.

Instituto Camões [95 C4] 720 Av Julius Nyerere; ✆ 21 493892; e ic-ccpmaputo@tvcabo.co.mz. Next to the Portuguese embassy, there's usually an art exhibition of some sort going on here, as well as occasional book launches & film screenings, & a library.

Instituto Cultural Moçambique-Alemanha (ICMA) [98 G1] 89 Rua Carlos Albers; ✆ 21 308594; e cultura@icma.org.mz; w goethe. de/Maputo. In an unassuming compound just off Av Eduardo Mondlane, this German cultural centre puts on a bunch of programmes, from poetry readings & live music to Shangaan-language classes. Even better, there's a cheery restaurant-bar on-site with an eclectic menu & German beers.

AZGO FESTIVAL Held annually in Maputo since 2011, the AZGO Festival (✆ 21 320142; m 82 704 2526; e *info@azgofestival.com*; w *azgofestival.com*; ◼ *azgofestival. official*) brings together dozens of top Mozambican and international artists every May for a non-stop weekend of music, art, dance and film.

MARKETS

Barracas do Museu [95 B5] Rua dos Lusiados. The so-called Night Market does open at night, but sells nothing but drink. A warren-like conglomeration of perhaps a hundred bars, this is one of the most extraordinary places to drink in Africa, & is highly recommended provided that you don't carry vast sums of money or valuables on your person.

Fish market [91 H1] Av da Marginal, opposite the Club Maritimo, along the road to the Costa do Sol about 1.5km north of the Southern Sun. Modernised with the financial help of the Japanese government in 2015, the fish market is the cheapest place to buy fresh fish. It is also a place of interest to amateur ichthyologists for the variety of tropical ocean fish that can be seen (even if they are out of their natural habitat). It's one of Maputo's most distinctive eateries: pick a fish, pay for it, then pick one of the many barracas waiting to grill it up for you with a side of your choice. Recommended.

Makonde Art Co-op [91 H1] Av da Marginal. About 1.5km north of the Southern Sun, shortly after the junction for the fish market, this is the best place in Maputo to buy intricate Makonde carvings & paintings from northern Mozambique.

Mercado Artesanato (FEIMA) [95 C2] Parque dos Continuadores. Open daily, this is without doubt the best craft shopping in the country. T-shirts, flags, a singular variety of woodcarvings, leather goods, basketry, batiks & items crafted from semi-precious stones such as malachite are all available here, & the shopping is low-pressure & very pleasantly arranged in the park. There are 2 good outdoor cafés here: Mamma Mia (m 82 616 4320) & Restaurante Greciana (m 84 818 0318), so it's very easy to spend a pleasant morning strolling around the market & break for lunch at either restaurant. It's also home to a food festival on the last w/end of every month.

Mercado Central [98 B2] Av 25 de Setembro. Housed in an impressive building dating from 1901, this is a good place to buy a variety of fresh & frozen fish, as well as other fresh produce. It's the prettiest market in Maputo: lively, African & colourful. In addition to vegetables, fruit & everyday household goods, carvings, baskets & other souvenirs are available at the back right-hand side.

Mercado do Povo [98 C1] Cnr avs Karl Marx & Ho Chi Min. It reputedly sells a variety of groceries & vegetables & large numbers of chickens, which are tucked away at night when the market becomes one of the liveliest places for a cheap, informal beer in the city centre.

Mercado Janeta [91 E4] Behind the church near the intersection of avs Vladimir Lenine & Mao Tse Tung. A good place for fruit & vegetables & for a cheap meal of chicken or fish with rice, & conveniently close for those staying at Fátima's Place. Get there early-ish in the morning & take your pick from the finest selections of produce you'll see in the country.

Xipamanine Market [90 A4] This huge warren of tiny shops & alleyways is known for its traditional medicines & associated items. It's located outside the city centre in the Alte Mae district, so you'll need to take a bus to get there. Look for anything heading towards Xipamanine – they all stop right outside the market. The journey should cost around US$0.20. You may share your return journey with chickens.

SUPERMARKETS AND MALLS There are dozens of supermarkets in the city, some more tucked away than others. The **Spar** [98 E1] on Avenida 24 de Julho is a solid bet, and **Woolworths Food** [91 E2] at the north end of Avenida Vladimir Lenine is also good. In terms of size, the biggest Western-style supermarket is **Shoprite** [90 C3], which lies in the Shoprite Shopping Centre on Avenida Accordos de Lusaka about 1km north of the city centre, along with a collection of banks and ATMs, a CNA news agency, large clothing shops and a Woolworths. If you visit this mall, check out the monumental Praça do Taurus (Bullfighting Arena) [90 C2] immediately north of it; if it looks familiar that's probably because it is the setting of a scene in the film *The Interpreter* starring Sean Penn and Nicole Kidman. North of town on the Costa do Sol road is **Mares Shopping** [91 H1], which opened in 2012 and plays host to Shoprite and Game, among other international chains.

Maputo SHOPPING

6

Two large malls can be found in the city centre. The **Polana Shopping Mall** [95 C5] on Avenida Julius Nyerere has several banks and ATMs, a superb deli, and a selection of stylish upmarket boutiques, salons and outlets for upmarket brands (Lacoste, Swatch) familiar even to this fashion-illiterate writer. The **Maputo Shopping Centre** [98 D4] on Avenida Ngungunyana, near the Catembe ferry jetty, is a four-storey building containing more than a hundred different shops, ranging from a dedicated tobacconist and gaming shop to cosmetics and baby clothing shops, shoe shops and a cinema. There is also a large hypermarket, a vast outlet of the South African clothes chain Mr Price, and a food courtyard with at least a dozen pastelarias, fast-food outlets and other affordable eateries.

HANDICRAFTS Look no further than Parque dos Continuadores [95 C2], at the intersection of avenidas Mao Tse Tung and Armando Tivane. There are well over a hundred stalls here, selling everything from batiks and Makonde paintings to woodcarvings and cheap jewellery. Friendly bargaining is the order of the day here, and it is worth looking at a few stalls to get a feel for prices and quality before you actually part with any cash.

OTHER PRACTICALITIES

AIRLINES The main **LAM** office [98 B3] is on Avenida Karl Marx, just off Avenida 25 de Setembro in the heart of downtown Maputo with a subsidiary office near the Polana Serena Hotel on the corner of avenidas Mao Tse Tung and Julius Nyerere [95 D2] (✆ *21 326001;* w *lam.co.mz*). Other airlines represented in Maputo include **SAA** [91 F2] (*Av do Zimbabwe;* ✆ *21 488970;* w *flysaa.com*) and **TAP Air Portugal** [98 D2] (*Pestana Rovuma Hotel;* ✆ *21 303927;* w *flytap.com*).

COMMUNICATIONS AND MEDIA
Books Only a small selection of English-language newspapers (mostly from South Africa) and magazines is available at the kiosks at the tourist-class hotels. English-language books and novels are even more difficult to come by. There is a very small selection of English-language books (predominantly coffee-table photo books) at **Livraria Mabuko** [95 C3] on Avenida Julius Nyerere opposite the South African High Commission; you may find some more if you hike around the other *livrarias*.

Internet At first glance internet cafés are not easy to find, as they are either tucked away in corners of shopping centres or disguised as the front rooms of private houses, but they are there. Reasonable (if not fast) connection speeds and decent-quality PCs to run them with are the norm. **Kalipha Trading Ldc** (*Av Romão Fernandes Farinha;* ⊕ *08.00–20.00 Mon–Sat*) has a dozen or so computers, plus Wi-Fi, and costs less than US$1 per hour. The folks at childhood literacy programme **Livro Aberto** (m *82 161 7231;* w *livroaberto.org*) are currently repurposing some old shipping containers into an admirable library with internet access at the Jardim dos Professores. Other places to browse are the **Café Nautilus** [95 C4] (next to PiriPiri Restaurant) and **Dolce Vita** [95 C3]. Most upmarket and luxury hotels also have internet, though it tends to be costly for non-residents, and **Fátima's Place** [91 E4] also has paid Wi-Fi. For anybody spending time in Maputo, a better option than using internet cafés would be to buy a local SIM card direct from a Vodacom, mCel or Movitel shop and ask the staff to set up your phone to get 4G internet access (which is so cheap it's as good as free) or, if you have a laptop, to buy a USB modem for it or create a hot spot from a smartphone and do the same.

Maps All in all it's best to get your maps before you arrive. For detailed 1:50,000 maps, there is a helpful map sales office in the **National Directorate of Geography and Cartography** [98 B1] (DINAGECA; ✆ *21 300486;* ⊕ *07.00–15.30 Mon–Fri*) on Avenida Josina Machel, a block west of Avenida Guerra Popular. Individual sheets cost US$1–2.

Phone You can make telephone calls (local, national and international) at the post office or from any one of a number of telephone bureaux dotted around the city. SIM cards for your mobile can be bought and topped up from dozens of places, and text messages are very cheap to send all around the globe.

Post The main post office [98 C3] occupies an impressive colonial building on Avenida 25 de Setembro complete with decorative mosaics at the front. (Its sister building, the National Library just down the street, has been spruced up and is also worth a look.)

FOREIGN EMBASSIES Office hours are usually 07.30–12.30 and 14.00–17.30 Monday–Thursday, 07.30–12.30 and 14.00–17.00 Friday. It's not unknown for embassies to change their phone numbers, so it may be worth checking when you arrive in the country. Be aware that your embassy may charge you for their time if you need to call on them for trivial matters.

☻ **Belgium** [91 G2] 470 Av Kenneth Kaunda; ✆ 21 492009; e mariajoao.regocosta@diplobel.be

☻ **Canada** [91 F2] 1374 Av do Zimbabwé; ✆ 21 492623; e mputo@international.gc.ca; w canadainternational.gc.ca/mozambique

☻ **France** [91 G2] 2361 Av Julius Nyerere; ✆ 21 484600; e contact@ambafrance-mz.org; w ambafrance-mz.org

☻ **Germany** [91 G2] 506 Rua Damião Góis; ✆ 21 482700; e info@maputo.diplo.de; w maputo. diplo.de

☻ **India** [91 G2] 167 Av Kenneth Kaunda; ✆ 21 492437; e hc.maputo@mea.gov.in; w hicomind-maputo.org

☻ **Ireland** [95 D3] 3630 Av Julius Nyerere; ✆ 21 491440; e maputoembassy@dfa.ie; w dfa.ie/ irish-embassy/mozambique

☻ **Malawi** [91 G2] 75 Av Kenneth Kaunda; ✆ 21 492676; e malawmoz@virconn.com

☻ **Netherlands** [95 C1] 324 Rua Kwame Nkrumah; ✆ 21 484200; e map@minbuza.nl; w mozambique.nlembassy.org

☻ **Norway** [95 D2] 1162 Av Julius Nyerere; ✆ 21 480100; e emb.maputo@mfa.no; w norway. org.mz

☻ **Poland** 39 Rua Clarim de Chaves; ✆ 21 329111; e consulado_rp@wp.pl

☻ **Portugal** [95 C4] 720 Av Julius Nyerere; ✆ 21 490316; e Maputo@mne.pt; w maputo. embaixadaportugal.mne.pt

☻ **South Africa** [95 C3] 41 Av Eduardo Mondlane; ✆ 21 243000; e SAHCMaputoenquiries@dirco.gov. za; w dirco.gov.za/maputo

☻ **Spain** [91 G2] 347 Rua Damião Góis; ✆ 21 492025; e emb.maputo@maec.es; w exteriores.gob.es/embajadas/maputo

☻ **Swaziland** 1271 Rua Luis Pasteur; ✆ 21 491601

☻ **Sweden** [95 D3] 1128 Av Julius Nyerere; ✆ 21 480300; e ambassaden.maputo@gov.se; w swedenabroad.com/maputo

☻ **Switzerland** 637 Av Ahmed Sékou Touré; ✆ 21 321337/8; e southernafrica@eda.admin.ch or Maputo@eda.admin.ch; w eda.admin.ch/maputo

☻ **Tanzania** 852 Av dos Mártires da Machava; ✆ 21 490110; e tanzrep-maputo@tvcabo.co.mz

☻ **UK** [98 D2] 310 Av Vladimir Lenine; ✆ 21 356000; e maputo.consularenquiries@fco. gov.uk

☻ **USA** [91 G2] 193 Av Kenneth Kaunda; ✆ 21 492797; e consularmaputo@state.gov; w maputo.usembassy.gov

☻ **Zambia** 1286 Av Kenneth Kaunda; ✆ 21 492452; e zhcmap@tvcabo.co.mz

☻ **Zimbabwe** 1657 Av dos Mártires da Machava; ✆ 21 494680; e zimmaputo@tdm.co.mz

MEDICAL

Hospitals There are six major hospitals in Maputo, but the most central hospital lies on the corner of avenidas Eduardo Mondlane and Agostinho Neto [95 A2] (↘ *21 325002/320828*). Medlife Trauma Centre on Avenida Julius Nyerere [91 G1] (*Av Julius Nyerere;* ↘ *21 485052/3;* m *84 302 0999;* w *medlife.co.mz;* f *medlifemz*) is the newest private hospital, having opened in 2013. There are others on Avenida das Forças Populares de Libertação de Moçambique, Avenida da Organização da Unidade Africana, and Rua do Jardim.

Medical centres There are a number of these dotted around the city and it's probably best to ask your hotel/hostel for the nearest, or failing that head straight for the hospital. Recommended is the **Instituto do Coração (ICOR)** [91 F2] (*1111 Av Kenneth Kaunda;* ↘ *21 411000;* m *82/84 327 4800;* w *icor.co.mz*).

Pharmacy There is a 24-hour pharmacy [98 E1] on Avenida 24 de Julho just down from the corner with Avenida Amilcar Cabral. Next to it is an ATM that takes Visa. Medlife Trauma Centre (above) also has a 24-hour pharmacy.

MONEY

Cash The streets of Maputo are lined with *câmbios* willing to take your hard currency in exchange for meticais. You could spend years going from one to the next trying to find the best rate. There doesn't seem to be a huge difference in the rate offered by banks as opposed to câmbios. Beware of the rate offered by the hotels and pensões – in the more expensive ones you will probably get a reasonable rate, but the cheaper ones (and this includes the backpacker hostels) seem to be somewhat lax in updating their rates so if you're not careful you may end up out of pocket.

You can change money on the black market if you choose, but you won't get a significantly better rate. If you do decide to do this, the place where the minibuses leave for Johannesburg [98 A2] would be a good place to start. The Mercado Central [98 B2] has also been suggested as a possible location, but it's a little too crowded and busy for comfort. The police seem to take a relaxed view of black-market deals, but that cuts both ways – they may not be all that proactive if you do get ripped off.

Credit cards ATMs taking credit cards can be found all over central Maputo (indeed it is unusual to walk more than two blocks without encountering one), and this is by far the best option for accessing your currency (page 54). Visa is far and away the most useful brand of card in Maputo (as elsewhere in Mozambique), and it is accepted at practically all ATMs. MasterCard and Maestro are very poor seconds, accepted at some ATMs, and American Express and other more obscure brands are as good as useless. If you decide to pay for goods and accommodation using a card, it will almost certainly have to be a Visa card, and you may have a small percentage added to your bill (in which case you might prefer to pop round the corner to draw cash from an ATM before paying your bill).

Travellers' cheques The only place that will now take travellers' cheques is the Polana Serena Hotel (page 96). You may get lucky and find a câmbio somewhere that will change them, but expect to pay an exorbitant commission.

POLICE
The police can be contacted on ↘ 21 325031/422002. Police stations can be found at the locations listed on page 113. In addition, there are also police stands

in the Feira Popular [98 E4], in the Mercado Central [98 B2], and one next to the Museu Nacional da Moeda [98 B3].

Av Amilcar Cabral [95 A1] Between Av Mao Tse Tung & Rua Kwame Nkrumah
Av Eduardo Mondlane [90 D5] Between Av Karl Marx & Rua de Redondo
Av Julius Nyerere [95 C5] At the junction with Rua Mateus S Muthemba

Av Marian Ngoudai [90 C4] Cnr with Av Acordos de Lusaka
Av de Zambia [90 B5] Between Av Ahmed Sékou Touré & Av Eduardo Mondlane

WHAT TO SEE AND DO

MUSEUMS AND GALLERIES
Natural History Museum [95 A5] (*104 Praça da Travessia do Zambeze, opposite the Hotel Cardoso;* ⤷ *21 485401;* ⊕ *08.30–15.30 Tue–Fri, 10.00–17.00 Sat/Sun; entrance US$1*) Housed in one of the finest buildings in Maputo, a palace built in the Manueline style (a sort of Portuguese Gothic) and decorated with wonderfully ornamental plasterwork. The collections are somewhat dusty and dilapidated, but there has been some attempt to keep them scientifically up to date – one of the more bizarre exhibits is a display on genetics and heredity, including the ideas of dominance and recession, although there is no text accompanying the diagrams. Also on display is a series showing the development during gestation of elephant embryos, proudly announced as the only such display in the world.

Geological Museum [95 B4] (*Cnr avs 24 de Julho & dos Mártires da Machava;* ⤷ *21 313508;* ⊕ *09.00–17.00 Tue–Fri, 09.00–14.00 Sat, 14.00–17.00 Sun; entrance US$1*) This rather unlikely museum is housed in an ornate old building and has an interesting collection of geological exhibits from around the country.

Museu dos CFM [98 B3] (*Av 25 de Setembro;* ⤷ *21 307385;* e *museu@cfm.co.mz;* w *cfm.co.mz;* ⊕ *10.00–17.00 Tue–Fri, 10.00–16.00 Sat/Sun; entrance US$1*) One of the better-quality museums in Maputo, this new museum hosts a series of maps, photos and railway memorabilia that tell the story of the port and railway industry in Mozambique.

Museu Nacional da Moeda [98 B3] (*Praça 25 de Junho;* ⤷ *21 320290;* ⊕ *09.00– 17.00 Tue–Fri, 09.00–15.30 Sat, 14.00–17.00 Sun; entrance US$0.40*) The potentially dry 'money museum' is actually surprisingly worthwhile, displaying currency from across the world, with the most interesting items dating back to before the arrival of the Portuguese. It is housed in one of the oldest buildings in Maputo, the Casa Amarela ('Yellow House'), which dates from the 1860s.

Museu da Revolução [91 C5] (*Av 24 de Julho;* ⊕ *formerly 09.00–noon & 14.00– 18.00 w/days (exc Wed), 14.00–18.00 Sat, 09.00–noon & 15.00–18.00 Sun; entrance US$0.40*) For those interested in the history of Mozambique's revolution, this is also surprisingly interesting, with many of the accompanying texts having a distinct whiff of Cold War rhetoric. It was closed for renovations in late 2010 and has yet to reopen.

Museu Nacional das Artes [98 C1] (*Av Ho Chi Min;* ⊕ *11.00–18.00 Tue–Fri, 14.00–16.00 Sat/Sun; entrance US$0.40*) Dedicated to paintings and sculptures by some of Mozambique's better-known artists, it also holds other exhibitions which are listed on posters at the entrance.

Núcleo de Arte [95 B5] (*Rua da Argélia, off Av Julius Nyerere;* \ *21 492523;* m *82 754 4438 or 84 486 5820;* e *nucleodarte@gmail.com;* f *nucleodarte;* ⊕ *10.00–20.00 daily*) A collective where artists can work and display their pieces, this also has a rather good café, internet access and occasional exhibitions. It was involved in a rather famous project to make sculptures from old AK47 guns, landmines and other weapons associated with the civil war, and several of the results of this experiment are on display. There's live music here on Sunday evenings as well.

Fortaleza da Nossa Senhora da Conceição [98 C4] (*Praça 25 de Junho;* ⊕ *09.00–17.00 daily; entrance free*) This burnished waterfront fortress encloses an area of 3,000m² and was constructed between 1851 and 1867 on the site of a smaller fort built in 1791 (see the plaque above the main entrance). Architecturally, it is a classic Portuguese fort of its era, built of red sandstone in a rough square topped with battlements. Inside there is a display of old cannons in the courtyard and on the battlements. Owned by Eduardo Mondlane University, the whole structure is in remarkably good condition, and the courtyard contains some interesting artworks, including some larger-than-life cast-iron statues of Portuguese colonial bigwigs on horseback, and murals depicting the 19th-century battles between the Portuguese settlers at Maputo and the local Gaza Kingdom.

CITY WALKS

Maputo lends itself to casual exploration on foot, with several interesting colonial buildings and a buzzing street life. Walking around the Polana district is particularly pleasant on a Sunday when the streets are quiet and most of the hawkers are sleeping off the previous night's revelries. In addition to the two walks described below, it's very pleasant to walk along the seafront along the Avenida da Marginal which is usually pretty quiet, with just a few anglers and other promenaders, and a nice breeze through the palms. Don't be tempted to cut off the road, though – there have been several muggings in the bush area around there. Keep your eyes peeled for the information signs in the Baixa with maps and historical titbits as well.

POLANA Start from the **Polana Serena** (page 96; formerly the Hotel Polana), for decades the showpiece of Maputo's hotels, situated on a rise high above the Bay of Maputo in the quarter of the same name, east of the city centre on Avenida Julius Nyerere. Built in 1922, it was designed by the celebrated architect Sir Herbert Baker, who also created Cape Town's iconic Mount Nelson Hotel and the Union Buildings in Pretoria, where Nelson Mandela was inaugurated as President of South Africa in 1994. The Polana survived the revolution in a somewhat run-down condition, but was refurbished by a South African hotel chain in the early 1990s and is now restored to its former glory.

Heading south from the Polana, turn off Avenida Julius Nyerere into the first street to the left and walk along Avenida Friedrich Engels, which runs high above the coast. This shady road is lined with trees, bougainvillea-draped lookout points and well-maintained benches, and the view extends over the Clube Naval beyond the Bay of Maputo to the island of Inhaca. One can walk along Avenida Friedrich Engels almost as far as the Presidential Palace [95 B6] (don't approach the security gates) and then turn right into Rua Mateus Muthemba, perhaps enjoying a coffee in the Acacia Café [95 A5] with its fine views of the wide river estuary and the harbour.

Near the Hotel Cardoso, on the Praça da Travessia do Zambeze, lies the Natural History Museum [95 A5]. One block further, on the Avenida Tomás Nduda, is the old Maputo **synagogue** [95 A4], built in 1926 and restored in 2013. There are no formal visits, but you might be able to get the caretaker to show you around. On the Avenida Patrice Lumumba, the Casa Velha, with adjoining amphitheatre for open-air performances, is well worth seeing.

If you like tumbledown buildings then there's a gorgeous old colonial house called Vila Algarve [95 B4] on the corner of Avenida Ahmed Sékou Touré and Avenida dos Mártires da Machava (next door to the Hotel Terminus; page 97). Covered in intricate mosaics, it's a beautiful building, though your admiration may be tempered by the realisation that it was the centre for the security police in latter colonial times, and a byword for torture and murder. Today there's still ample reason to admire from a safe distance, as we've had several reports of tourists who were robbed while exploring the building.

THE BAIXA The best place to begin a walking tour of the city centre is at the intersection of Avenida 25 de Setembro and Avenida Samora Machel, with the **Café Continental** [98 C3] on one corner and the Cinema Scala, built in 1931, on the other. Start by walking down Avenida 25 de Setembro in a westerly direction (away from the Feira Popular).

After the next street to the right (Avenida Karl Marx) you reach the Mercado Central [98 B2]. The surrounding streets have several Asian-owned shops with a decent selection of imported hardware items (flashlights, lanterns, tools, etc). Continue along Avenida 25 de Setembro and walk down Avenida Guerra Popular, which brings you to the Praça dos Trabalhadores [98 A3], at the centre of which lies a large, rather ugly memorial to the Portuguese soldiers killed in World War I.

On the western side of the square is the palatial green-and-white **railway station** [98 A2], built in 1910 following a design by the architect Gustave Eiffel (of Eiffel Tower fame) and notable for its plethora of marble pillars and wrought-iron detail. Once the terminus of the most important railway line in southern Africa, the shortest coastal connection from the industrial areas and gold mines of the Witwatersrand and Johannesburg and the mines of southern Zimbabwe, the opulent, Victorian-style station is little used these days, which gives it a rather sad appearance but does not detract from its importance as an architectural monument. *Newsweek* magazine once named it as one of the world's ten most impressive railway stations, the only African selection on the list.

Close to the railway station lies the entrance to the harbour [98 C4]. During colonial times, Maputo harbour was more important to southern Africa than even Durban, a status it seems unlikely to reclaim in the foreseeable future. From the quay, with its huge cranes, there is a view of the ships anchored in the Bay of Maputo.

Between the station forecourt and Avenida Samora Machel is the **Old Town**. Most of the buildings constructed in the late 19th century are quite run-down but they still have a certain charm. Many are still graced by wood or iron filigree and covered balconies, reminiscent of the Creole style of Mauritius and Réunion, and a few have been restored in recent years. It's worth poking around these streets, taking in the variety of buildings, and in particular having a look at the Jumma Masjid [98 B3], a large, well-kept and much-frequented mosque. As usual with religious buildings, be respectful – the mosque doesn't seem to allow visitors and it's probably best not to push the point. (Though the attached take-away is a good place for a snack and very welcoming.)

East of the station, **Rua do Bagamoyo** – formerly known as the 'Street of Trouble' by sailors who frequented its many bars – is still not the most peaceful or salubrious of places. Indeed, it pretty much serves as Maputo's red light district, with its numerous down-at-heel bars and strip clubs, though there is little evidence of this in daylight hours. Rua do Bagamoyo terminates at the Praça dos 25 de Junho [98 C3], where you'll find the Fortaleza Nossa Senhora da Conceição and Museu Nacional da Moeda (page 113) keeping each other company on either side of the square.

Immediately opposite the fort is the Ministério da Indústria e Comércio, a strong contender for the title of 'ugliest building in Maputo'. It's a large Stalinesque concrete slab with an utterly bizarre tower that seems to have been based on a German alpine castle. The overall effect is to make it look like a nightmarish experiment. Some of the cannons in the fort are pointing directly at it, and it's tempting to think that the only reason it's still standing is that they are waiting for the right calibre ammunition to arrive.

Next to the money museum is a police station and next to that is the Banco de Moçambique with a stylish glass-and-steel frontage. Take the street heading north opposite the bank to Avenida 25 de Setembro and walk back towards the crossroads with Avenida Samora Machel, then turn north towards the **Jardim Tunduru (Botanical Gardens)** [98 D2], a public park with many large shady trees, currently being rehabilitated by CFM. It's particularly pleasant towards the end of the day as the lowering sun casts yellowing stripes on the grass. You'll have to share the park with many courting couples.

To the left of the main entrance gate, on the Praça de Independência, is a **statue of Samora Machel** [98 C2], the country's first president. Donated by Kim Il-Sung of North Korea, the statue of Machel bears a strange and inaccurate resemblance to Chairman Mao. Just up from there is the **Casa de Ferro** (Iron House) [98 C2], a construction of prefabricated metal parts designed by the French engineer Eiffel. Opposite, on the east side of the Tunduru gardens, is the palace in which Paul Kruger, President of the South African Republic, resided after fleeing from British troops at the end of the 19th century. This old building now houses the **Centre Cultural Franco-Mozambicain** [98 C2] (page 101), which has a pleasant semi-outdoor café, regular art exhibitions and a funky little shop selling locally made handicrafts and clothing.

Continuing up Avenida Samora Machel brings you to the imposing town hall and yet another statue of Samora Machel; this one is the largest in the country. On its right

LOUIS TRICHARDT MEMORIAL GARDEN

Situated on the alleged spot where the famous great trek leader Louis Trichardt died of malaria in October 1838, this large memorial garden [98 C2] consists of a stone frieze reminiscent of Pretoria's Voortrekker Monument and a circular pond, at the base of which is a ceramic map depicting Trichardt's route from the Cape to Maputo, complete with stylised mosaics of African chiefs in headdress and Bushmen bearing bows and arrows. Alongside the frieze, under the inscription 'They Harnessed the Wilds', the story of Trichardt's trek is told in the sort of messianic tones you might expect of a monument opened in 1968 by the South African Nationalist Party's Minister of Education, one J De Klerk. Odd enough to find this anachronistic and rather culture-bound slice of apartheid chic still exists in 21st-century Maputo; odder still that it has been maintained with meticulous care throughout the last 35 years of civil war, socialism and democracy.

is the glistening white **Catholic cathedral** [98 D2], a boldly unattractive structure that was completed in 1944. From the cathedral, cross the Praça de Independência and walk along Avenida Josina Machel for a block and a half. On the southern side of the road is perhaps the most surprising monument in the Baixa, the **Louis Trichardt Memorial Garden** (box, page 116), which lies on Avenida Josina Machel immediately west of Avenida Karl Marx, and is worth seeing if only because it is so incongruous. Finish off your walk by going back along Avenida Josina Machel to the Praça de Independência, and put your feet up at the Centre Cultural Franco-Mozambicain with a cold beer and a perfect spot to watch passers-by in the twilight.

DAY TRIPS FROM MAPUTO

The opportunities for exploring around Maputo are limited and, if you are dependent on public transport, the most intriguing possibility is a day trip across the harbour to Catembe, which can easily be twinned with a walking tour of the main sights in the Baixa. Further afield, the private Mucapana Park north of town is a pleasant enough goal for a day of low-key game viewing, birdwatching and stylish dining. For business travellers with a day or two to spare, more serious day and overnight game-viewing excursions to Maputo Special Reserve and across the border to the Kruger National Park are a possibility, or you could arrange to take a day or overnight trip to Inhaca Island. Note that Catembe, Inhaca and Maputo Special Reserve are covered in the next chapter.

Recommended operators for day trips out of Maputo include **Mozaic Travel** [91 H1] (\ *21 451379;* m *84 333 2111/301 5167;* e *maputo@mozaictravel.com;* w *mozaictravel.com*) and **Dana Tours** [91 E2] (\ *21 495514;* m *84 404 0710;* e *info@ danatours.com;* w *danatours.com; see ad, page 86*).

ILHA DA XEFINA This island, slightly to the north of Maputo, was once a leper colony and still has the remains of one of the old Portuguese forts on it, complete with disused cannon. There is no accommodation on the island but it is possible to do it as a day trip from Maputo. **Maputo Yachting** (m *84 900 9899;* e *info@ maputoyachting.com;* w *maputoyachting.com*) has a boat that can be chartered for the day.

COSTA DO SOL The best way to enjoy the sea close to the city is to take a trip up to the Costa do Sol Restaurant (page 104). It's too far to walk, so head for the upper end of Avenida Julius Nyerere and look for buses heading to Costa do Sol – the ride will cost US$0.20. From Maputo onwards, one casuarina tree-lined beach after the other lines the coastline. The seabed is very flat, however, and one must wade out a long way to be able to swim. The water is also often cloudy and brown as a result of the river mouth nearby. In the Costa do Sol Restaurant at the end of the street, you can eat well and at a reasonable price. The road is lined with little drinks booths, some of which also serve food. One or two of them even have tables and chairs on the beach where you can enjoy your drink while the chickens that feature on the menu peck the sand at your feet.

MATOLA It has to be said that Matola is most definitely not a tourist destination, but it will give you a taste of the 'real Mozambique' that seems to be so popular. Situated a little way to the southwest of Maputo, Matola is a pleasant, quiet, tree-lined town – if you are still labouring under the illusion that Mozambique is a land of run-down buildings handicapped by intense poverty then Matola will set you

The Crocodile Bridge entrance gate to South Africa's legendary Kruger National Park is little more than an hour's drive west of Maputo, ideally with the earliest possible start, via the Komatipoort/Ressano Garcia border post, and it makes for a superb day or overnight excursion from the capital for anybody stuck there on business over a weekend. No less so because the part of Kruger closest to Maputo is among the finest for game viewing, with white rhino especially common along the road connecting Crocodile Bridge to Lower Sabie Rest Camp, which lies in an area famed for its concentrations of lion, elephant and buffalo. As with any large African game reserve, the Kruger offers no guarantees about what might be seen where on any given day, but day trippers from Maputo might reasonably hope to see three of the Big Five in the course of a day, and an overnight stay would greatly boost your chances of a full house. Either way, the scenery along the Sabie River in particular is riveting, and the birdlife can be utterly spectacular. A recommended operator for Kruger day and overnight trips (or longer trips embracing the Mozambican sector of the Great Limpopo Transfrontier Park; page 140) is Mozaic Travel (page 43).

straight: it's as close as you'll get to suburban Mozambique, clearly well off and well kept with a quiet but discernible civic pride in itself and its country.

Technically this is the industrial zone of Maputo. At the end of the Portuguese colonial period, Mozambique was the fourth most industrialised country in Africa. Most of the industries did not withstand the first years of the socialist People's Republic, and few still function properly. The policy of economic reconstruction begun in the late 1980s is intended to change this. You can experience something of the scenery and atmosphere of southern Mozambique if you cross the Matola River from the town. Matola lay outside the army's protective cordon during the war and consequently suffered significant damage, so that much of the land is now turned over to agriculture.

Matola is the site of the home and burial place of the sculptor Alberto Chissano, one of Mozambique's leading artists (page 25), who committed suicide in 1994. His home on Rua Torre de Vale now functions as the Galleria Chissano (⊕ *09.00–noon & 15.00–17.00 daily (exc Mon); free admission*) and displays a selection of his work alongside that of other Mozambican artists.

To get to Matola, catch a chapa marked 'C Matola-Museu'. It'll cost you around US$0.20.

MUCAPANA SAFARI PARK This private park 35km north of Maputo hosts a variety of introduced game, including giraffe, ostrich, zebra and various antelopes, and is also home to a rich birdlife. It opens at weekends only and can be visited as an organised day trip including a large buffet lunch of traditional African cuisine and seafood overlooking a waterhole where animals come to drink. It lacks the authenticity of the larger parks further north, but nevertheless it makes for an enjoyable day out in the bush for anybody stuck in the city over a weekend. Tours run on Saturday and Sunday, departing Maputo at around 09.00, returning at 18.00, and cost US$100 for one person, US$70 per person for two or more people. Bookings can be made through the park (m *82 304 6990 or 84 304 6990*) or any tour operator in Maputo, as well as through most upmarket hotels and at the reception of Fátima's Place (page 99).

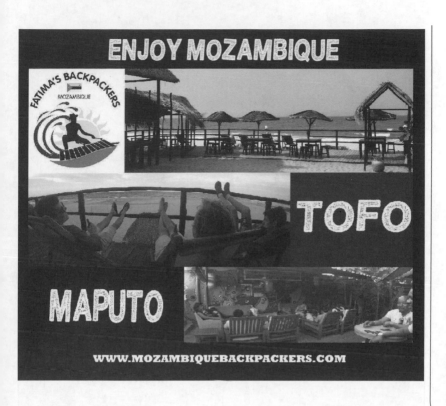

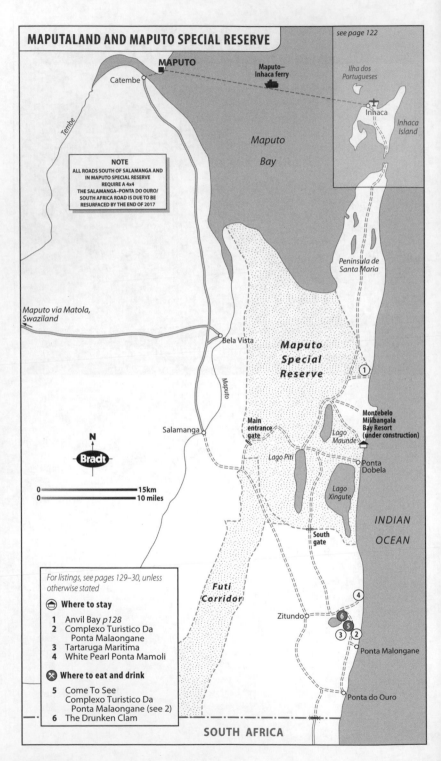

MAPUTALAND AND MAPUTO SPECIAL RESERVE

see page 122

MAPUTO

Catembe

Maputo–Inhaca ferry

Ilha dos Portugueses

Inhaca

Inhaca Island

Maputo Bay

Tembe

NOTE
ALL ROADS SOUTH OF SALAMANGA AND IN MAPUTO SPECIAL RESERVE REQUIRE A 4x4
THE SALAMANGA–PONTA DO OURO/SOUTH AFRICA ROAD IS DUE TO BE RESURFACED BY THE END OF 2017

Peninsula de Santa Maria

Maputo via Matola, Swaziland

Bela Vista

Maputo

Maputo Special Reserve

N

Bradt

Salamanga

Main entrance gate

Lago Maunde

Montebelo Milibangala Bay Resort (under construction)

0 —————— 15km
0 —————— 10 miles

Lago Piti

Ponta Dobela

Lago Xingute

INDIAN OCEAN

South gate

For listings, see pages 129–30, unless otherwise stated

🛏 **Where to stay**
1 Anvil Bay *p128*
2 Complexo Turistico Da Ponta Malaongane
3 Tartaruga Maritima
4 White Pearl Ponta Mamoli

Futi Corridor

Zitundo

4

6

5

3 2

Ponta Malongane

❌ **Where to eat and drink**
5 Come To See Complexo Turistico Da Ponta Malaongane (see 2)
6 The Drunken Clam

Ponta do Ouro

SOUTH AFRICA

120

7

Maputaland

The small block of Mozambican territory that lies to the south of Maputo has a very different feel from the rest of the country, and much of it is more accessible – or at least more commonly visited – from South Africa than from the capital, the notable exception being Inhaca Island. Often referred to as Maputaland, it is a wild and thinly populated region, whose utterly beautiful coastline hems in a hinterland of tall vegetated dunes, shallow lakes, dense coastal forests and grassy slopes inhabited by what is surely the most southerly free-ranging elephant population in Africa. The more popular beaches retain a pristine quality often lacking in their counterparts further north. No higher tribute can be paid to this fascinating area than to say that it is so very reminiscent of South Africa's bordering iSimangaliso (formerly Greater St Lucia) Wetland Park, a UNESCO World Heritage Site.

The main beach resorts in this area are Inhaca Island, which lies in Maputo Bay and is easily visited from the capital, as well as Ponta do Ouro and Ponta Malongane, close to the South African border and renowned for their diving and snorkelling. The other potential tourist attraction is the Maputo Special Reserve, home to several hundred elephants and a variety of other wildlife. It has been the subject of some big plans for development over the years, and plans that are finally starting to come to fruition with the milestone opening of the reserve headquarters in 2014, the opening of the upmarket Anvil Bay within the reserve, and continued wildlife restocking efforts. Birdwatching is superb throughout the region, and several archaeological sites, currently closed to the public, have potential for development. Much of the region requires a 4x4 to explore properly, but this looks like it's finally set to change, as long-delayed plans to surface the main road between Catembe and the border are beginning to sound credible.

INHACA ISLAND

Situated about 35km from central Maputo, Inhaca is a dislocated extension of the narrow peninsula that runs northward from Maputo Special Reserve to Cabo Santa Maria, from which it is separated by a shallow channel just 500m wide. Effectively forming the shore of Maputo Bay, Inhaca is among the most accessible of Mozambique's many offshore islands, and ideally situated for a short break from the capital. It luxuriates in an archetypal tropical island atmosphere, with a couple of good beaches, a mangrove-lined north coast and brightly coloured reefs off the west coast. The main tourist focus is Inhaca village, a tiny settlement dominated by a centre crammed with bars. The beach directly in front of the lodges is an interesting place to sit and watch the boats as the sun goes down. Away from the village, the beaches on both the western side of the island (facing Maputo) and its eastern side (facing the Indian Ocean) are utterly deserted, and offer mile after mile of sun-kissed, wave-swept sand. The reefs of Inhaca are among the most southerly in Africa and, as the water in the gulf is 5°C warmer than elsewhere at this latitude, the island has been a centre of scientific research for over 50 years. The island is host to more than 300 species of birds, and more than 150 types of coral live in the surrounding waters. If you're looking for diving the outer reefs are well worth visiting, and a large number of the region's diveable wrecks are scattered among the islands. There's good humpback whale watching between September and November, while back on terra firma, butterflies and dragonflies seem to swarm from every bush in summer.

There is also a nascent surfing scene, with the reef crest between the north end of Inhaca and Ilha Portuguesa becoming increasingly well known in the community. If you are interested in sport fishing, Inhaca has some of the finest opportunities south of Beira. Every May, the Inhaca Challenge brings fishermen from all over the region to compete against one another. Two international sailing challenges start from here – the Inhaca Race (to Richards Bay) at Easter and the Vasco da Gama Race in July. Add to the mix the marine reserves, the deserted beaches, the relaxed feel of the island and the fact that it's within 3 hours of Maputo Airport, and it's surprising that Inhaca hasn't become a much more popular destination. A park entrance fee equivalent to around US$4 is charged to all visitors to Inhaca.

HISTORY The island is named for the Inhaca chieftaincy, the dominant power on the southern mainland of the Gulf of Maputo in the 16th century. Chief Inhaca offered a hospitable welcome to the Portuguese trader Lourenço Marques, and frequently came to the assistance of shipwrecked Portuguese sailors. From about 1550 onwards, a Portuguese ship would set up camp on Inhaca Island for a few months annually to trade ivory with the chief's town on the mainland. In 1593, one Portuguese navigator settled on the island for a year before he was murdered and his ship looted by a rival chieftaincy. After 1621, Inhaca fell out of favour with the Portuguese: the ships relocated their annual encampment to Xefina Island and obtained their ivory from the Tembe chieftaincy on the northern part of the bay.

INHACA ISLAND AND SANTA MARIA PENINSULA

N

Bradt

Ilha dos Portugueses

0 — 2km
0 — 2 miles

Monte Inhaca ▲ 104m

Inhaca

Maputo–Inhaca ferry

Airport

Inhaca Island

Reserve da Inhaca

Marine Research Station

Ponta Ponduine

Ponta Torres

Maputo Bay

Ponta Torres

Peninsula de Santa Maria

For listings, see pages 123–4 & 128

🛏 **Where to stay**

1 Bemugi's Place
2 Camp Carlos
3 Machangulo Beach Lodge
4 Manico Camp
5 Marine Research Station
6 Nayheeni Lodge
7 Nhonguane Lodge
8 Nhoxani Villas
9 Ross Ramos Camp

GETTING THERE AND AWAY

By boat/ferry There is only one regular **boat service** between Maputo and Inhaca: a government-run slow ferry, known as the *Nyelete*. The government has promised a new ferry to service Inhaca Island, but in the meantime the *Nyelete* will continue to make its rounds every Monday, Wednesday, Friday, Saturday and Sunday. It leaves from the end of the jetty on Avenida 10 de Novembro (where the Catembe ferry docks) at around 07.00, but you're strongly recommended to get there early as this can depend on the tide. It returns later the same day from the jetty at Inhaca at around 15.00, again tide-dependent. The journey takes around 3 hours, weather permitting. If you're returning to Maputo on the Sunday afternoon, be warned that you may be accompanied by a number of individuals who have over-indulged – it can be an unpleasantly messy trip. One-way tickets cost under US$10 and can be bought from the ticket office at the entrance to the jetty for the outbound journey and on the ferry itself for the return leg.

Additionally, **Maputo Yachting** (m *84 900 9899*; e *order@maputoyachting.com*; w *maputoyachting.com*) offers luxury day trips to Inhaca for US$150 per person with a minimum of six passengers.

By air Alternatively, **CR Aviation** (w *craviation.co.mz*) can be hired for a 15-minute charter flight from Maputo to Inhaca Island.

WHERE TO STAY, EAT AND DRINK *Map, page 122*

It should be pointed out that at certain times of year – notably the Christmas period and during the Inhaca Challenge and the two yacht races – Inhaca becomes very busy. The costs listed below will rise and you may have trouble finding accommodation. In the village there are several bars and small local restaurants, all serving much the same fare.

⌂ **Inhaca Lodge** (40 rooms) Formerly operated by Pestana, this lodge is currently closed. Perhaps during the lifespan of this edition a new operator will take over.

⌂ **Inhacazul Lodge** ☎ +27 78 701 6510 (South Africa); e andyaccrue@gmail.com; w inhacazullodge.itgo.com. Closed at the time of research. This hidden treasure historically consisted of a mixture of well-equipped chalets & cabins, beach bar, restaurant & small shop. Likely to reopen during the lifespan of this edition.

⌂ **Manico Camp** ☎21 498778; e manico@mozambicanaccommodation.com; w manicocampinhaca.com. Located at the northern end of the island with views of Ilha Portuguesa, the camp has 10 chalets with twin beds, an ablution block with hot water, self-catering kitchen, restaurant & complimentary transfers from the Inhaca Pier. *US$27 pp.* **$$**

⌂ **Marine Research Station** ☎21 760009/13. Located to the south of Inhaca village, the research station may take visitors if there is space, although priority is given to researchers rather than the public, so ring ahead. Rooms cost around US$20 pp. **$$**

⌂ **Nayheeni Lodge** m +27 83 541 0391 (South Africa) or 84 281 8560/307 1940; e info@ nahyeenilodge.com or nahyeenilodge@intra.co.mz; w nayhennilodge.com. Prided with having had former President Nyusis as a guest, this lodge is situated on a hilltop overlooking the Bay of Maputo, with views of Ilha das Portugueses. Offering both self-catering & FB options in private chalets or en-suite rooms, the facilities include a pool, full bar, library, flatscreen TVs with DSTV, full modern kitchen, tea-/coffee-making facilities & mini-fridge. Nayheeni provides hammocks – in the indigenous gardens that surround the lodge – direct access to the beach, snorkelling, whale watching, fishing & other tours. Boat transfers available. *US$99 pp self-catering, US$155 pp FB; rates higher in peak season.* **$$$$**

⌂ **Rita's Place** m 82 054 2770/784 7736; e ritasplaceinhaca@gmail.com; ⨍ ritasplace. inhaca. With a clutch of brightly painted chalets built around a sunny compound, this locally owned place is a good choice for budget travellers & campers. The dbl rooms, some en suite, come with fans & nets, & they can arrange rides around the island as well. There's a kitchen for guests, & meals available on request. Cool Runnings (m *82 616 4084*) is run by Rita's brother, & offers a similar range of accommodation just 200m down the road. *US$30–40 dbl.* **$$**

🏠 **Ross Ramos Camp** m +27 71 641 0861 (South Africa); e info@rossramoscamp.co.za; w rossramoscamp.co.za. Sited next to the airport, the camp is a tightly packed but well-maintained collection of chalets & tents. *US$50 for a log cabin* or rondavel (sleeping 2); US$34 standing tent (sleeping 2).* **$$**

✖ **Restaurant Lucas** m 82 616 2835 or 87 611 3006; f restaurantelucasinhaca; ⏱ 08.00–22.00 daily, later at w/ends. Right in the heart of the village, this local institution has been open since 1989 & is easily the best on the island, specialising in seafood, but not cheap (though they do accept Visa). The crayfish is quite superb. At busy times let them know you'll be eating there. *Mains US$8–15.* **$$$$**

WHAT TO SEE AND DO

Marine station Inhaca has been a centre of scientific research since 1951. An interesting marine research station lies to the south of Inhaca village, along with a well-kept **museum of natural history**. In 2016, with renewed investment, the station built a new residential building for graduate and resident researchers, and received a new research vessel as well as equipment required for its continued work in the Indian Ocean. For those with a strong interest in the island's ecology, it's worth trying to get hold of a copy of *The Natural History of Inhaca Island* (edited by Margaret Kalk, Wits University Press, Johannesburg, 1958), a 395-page book that includes comprehensive species descriptions of the fauna and flora as well as line drawings depicting the more common species. The station can be reached by walking either along the road or along the western beaches.

Activities The only charter company currently running near the island is **Gozo Azul** (m *84 339 2910;* e *info@gozoazul.com;* w *gozoazul.com*). Located on the mainland, on Santa Maria Peninsula, they offer a variety of excursions including snorkelling (*US$23 pp, min 4 people to Inhaca Island*), diving, fishing (*full-day charter starting at US$615 for 6 people*), sunset cruises and whale watching in season (*US$26–46 pp, min 6 people*).

The northern lighthouse Another good walk (around 3 hours each way), through grassland, local fields, salt flats and mangroves. Take the road south of the airport and keep checking with the people you meet – asking '*O caminho para farol?*' and pointing should do the trick. You must take water. If you're interested in riding the surf, you'll need to head here, but given the distance you might prefer to organise a lift. Maurice (m *82 766 4770*) in the village will take you there for around US$15. Arrange to be collected again.

The west beaches You can walk all the way around the island should you wish, but a good alternative is to take the west side from the jetty down to the marine station – mile after mile of perfect deserted beach. It's worth stopping every now and again just to listen to the waves on the shore and the wind in the palm trees. It's almost impossible to believe that you're only a short distance from Maputo, until you look to the horizon where you can see the buildings gleaming in the sunlight. The walk takes 1½–2 hours each way, and check the state of the tide – it may not be passable at high spring tides, and there are one or two places where you'll need to scramble over rocks, so sandals are a good idea.

Birdwatching With more than 300 species recorded in an area of only 40km², Inhaca offers some very good birding, with a variety of marine species alongside those more associated with coastal thickets and scrub. Among the most striking or beautiful species associated with vegetated habitats are the African fish eagle, trumpeter hornbill, green pigeon, Narina trogon, African hoopoe and green twinspot, while the sandy shores of the island often host large mixed groups of migrant and resident waders, ranging from the localised crab plover and bulky curlew to diminutive sandpipers and stints. Pelicans and cormorants are common around the bay, while offshore birds, most likely to be seen in flight, include half a dozen species of tern (including the localised black-naped tern), three types of skua, Cape gannet and Pintado petrel.

Ilha Portuguesa A small island to the north of Inhaca itself, this island is now a nature reserve. In Portuguese colonial times it was a leper colony, and there are supposedly some ruins from those days, although they haven't been found again since the 1960s. The beaches tend to be very flat with large sandbanks at low tide. If the tide is particularly low, you can cross the channel between the two islands on foot, although you must take a guide and be aware that the tide may rise faster than you think. It's safer to take a boat from Inhaca – ask at the lodges for help arranging this. The best swimming beach is the one facing Inhaca, but it is dangerous to swim out too far as the current is very strong. You can walk round Ilha Portuguesa in approximately 1½ hours.

CATEMBE

Situated on the southern bank of Maputo Bay, directly opposite Maputo city centre, the little fishing village of Catembe is both a popular goal for a day trip out of the capital and the main domestic gateway to all destinations further south in Maputaland, including Maputo Special Reserve and Ponta do Ouro. There is no direct road link between Maputo and Catembe, only a ferry service, so that the village retains a very different and distinctly more rustic vibe from its vast, sprawling neighbour. Indeed, were it not for the high-rise skyline to the north, Catembe would have little to distinguish it from hundreds of other small fishing villages along the Mozambican coastline. That said, Catembe is poised for radical change when the long-promised bridge from Maputo is complete, scheduled by the end of 2017. The bridge will be the longest suspension bridge in Africa and will cut about 4 hours from the current commute for vehicle traffic between Catembe and Maputo.

As you walk along the landing quay (where there are a couple of basic restaurants), check out the dilapidated jetty to the right, and its gradually disintegrating old ferry. A little way along the beach, fishing vessels land their catch at the end of the day. The fish are sold at the small market lining the left-hand side of the jetty – but be aware that untreated sewage is pumped into Maputo Bay, so you may think twice before buying any. The village and surrounding beaches are well worth exploring, and the many bars that line the waterfront are pleasant places to sit and people-watch. Large banknotes may not be appreciated here.

GETTING THERE AND AWAY The ferry to Catembe, when not in for mechanical repairs, usually runs from dawn to dusk daily, with boats typically leaving in either direction every 15–30 minutes. The terminal is located at the west end of Avenida 10 de Novembro. The journey itself takes around 10 minutes, but loading the ferries (particularly the car ferry) takes significantly longer, and can cause huge amusement. Tickets can be bought at the little hut next to the jetty and cost next to nothing for foot passengers. Cars must pay US$3 on weekdays and US$5 at weekends – more for trucks. When the ferry isn't in service, foot passengers can still cross via the smaller *mapapai* boats that cross in either direction from the same docks as the ferry. Regular chapas to Bela Vista and more occasional ones to Ponta do Ouro leave from the end of the Catembe pier. Also worth noting, this is the last place with an ATM until Ponta do Ouro.

🏠 WHERE TO STAY, EAT AND DRINK

🏠 **Catembe Beach Lodge & Garden Guesthouse** (13 rooms) m 82 939 9132 or 84 578 9356; e catembebeachlodge@gmail.com. Set in a restored colonial house 400m up the coastal road from the Gallery Hotel, this recently renovated lodge has a variety of tiled rooms all with AC & some rooms are en suite. There's safe parking in its grassy compound & it has a pool. It's right on the beach & the views of Maputo are stunning, though it could be better value. *US$30/40 sgl/dbl with shared ablutions, US$60 dbl en suite, US$160/200 queen/presidential dbl suite.* **$$$**

🏠 **Catembe Gallery Hotel** (15 rooms) 📞 21 900225/6; m 84 228 3623 or 86 556 4950; e reservations@galleryhotel.co.mz; w galleryhotel.co.mz. The view over the water to Maputo is very pretty, & the en-suite rooms are comfortable & warmly decorated, with TV, AC, walk-in nets & Wi-Fi, & some have sea-view balconies. Penthouse suites are available for larger groups, & it's got 2 restaurants serving seafood & tapas, one of them at the end of a fantastically scenic pier. *US$124/157/189 standard/luxury/chalet dbl, penthouses starting at US$330 dbl, all rooms B&B.* **$$$$**

✖ **Restaurante Diogo** m 82 390 8600 or 84 362 1659. About 500m from the ferry jetty, this place is legendary for its 3rd-generation, good but inexpensive seafood, in particular prawns. There's a new beachfront deck with views of Maputo across the bay. *Mains are in the US$6–16 range.* **$$$$**

BELA VISTA AND SALAMANGA

The largest town in Maputaland, Bela Vista stands on the west bank of the Rio Maputo some 42km south of the Catembe ferry. It has an isolated and rather spaced-out feel, more like an unfinished plan than an actual town, centred on a misproportioned praça that could embrace several football fields. The only real attraction in the town itself is the river views from the jetty at the end of the main road, but there is also a large market. Bela Vista would be a useful base for early-ish game drives in nearby Maputo Special Reserve. About 15km past the town, the road south crosses the Rio Maputo at Salamanga, where there is a rather officious police roadblock and, right alongside it, the elaborate Shree Ram Hindu Temple. Constructed in 1908, this is one of the largest such shrines anywhere in Mozambique despite its remote location, and arguably the most beautiful. Visitors are welcomed.

GETTING THERE AND AWAY Coming from Maputo, you must first cross the Catembe ferry, from where it is 42km south to Bela Vista and another 15km to Salamanga along a well-maintained murram (and in places tar) road, on which you should be able to maintain a speed of around 60–70km/h, though it can be slippery in parts when wet. Bela Vista itself lies a couple of kilometres east of the main road along a tarred feeder road. There are plenty of chapas between Catembe and Bela Vista, which continue to Salamanga along the road to Ponto do Ouro and the South African border. There are two other possible approaches to Bela Vista: the 80km **EN202** (EN3/R407/N200) from the quiet Goba border post with Swaziland, and the 90km EN3 from Maputo via Matola and Boane (which joins the EN202 30km before Bela Vista). At the time of writing, both are in fair condition and can be travelled in a sturdy saloon car, but the latter route between Matola and Boane is scheduled to be completely resurfaced by the end of 2017, following the construction of the bridge between Maputo and Catembe.

WHERE TO STAY, EAT AND DRINK

Complexo Quinta Mila (16 rooms)
\21 620027; m 82 320 4500; e quinta.mila@
gmail.com. This unexpectedly pleasant little hotel,
set in green grounds overlooking the riverbank in

Bela Vista, has a decent restaurant serving typical
Mozambican mains for around US$8. All rooms
are en suite. *US$35 twin, US$55 dbl suite with TV
& AC.* **$$$**

MAPUTO SPECIAL RESERVE

This little-known 890km² reserve extends over a lushly scenic, lake-studded tract of coastal bush and grassland running for about 50km south from the Bay of Maputo to within 10km of Ponta Mamoli. It is one of the oldest conservation areas in Mozambique, established in 1932 as the Maputo Elephant Reserve (not, incidentally, after the city then known as Lourenço Marques, but after the Rio Maputo, which runs along part of its western boundary), and now forms a part of the Ndumo-Tembe-Futi Transfrontier Conservation Area, which otherwise lies mainly within South Africa and is connected to it by an ancient elephant migration route along the newly protected Futi Corridor. Although the reserve supports a few farming and fishing communities, fewer than a thousand people in total, their activities are monitored by the authorities and most of it remains ecologically pristine.

The special reserve has had a chequered history in terms of conservation and tourist development. As with most other Mozambican reserves, it was heavily poached during the war years: the 65 white rhinos that were introduced from South Africa in the 1960s were killed, many other large mammal species including cheetah and buffalo became locally extinct, and the elephant population plummeted from 350 in 1970 to fewer than 60 in 1994. Since 2006, the reserve has been co-managed by the Mozambican government and the Peace Parks Foundation (w *peaceparks. org*) and is slowly being developed as a tourist destination, beginning with intensive restocking of zebra, warthog, wildebeest, giraffe and antelope since 2010 and the reserve's expansion to include the 240km² Futi Corridor in 2011. The construction of upmarket accommodation has finally come to fruition with the opening of Anvil Bay (page 128) in 2016. Thus, although the reserve is officially open to visitors, facilities remain fairly limited at the time of writing, though it is hoped that this will change during the lifespan of this edition.

Today, the special reserve is well worth a slight diversion for the opportunity to see elephants (probably about 50/50 on a day trip), and highly recommended as a scenic destination and for its superb birdwatching. However, the majority of visitors are there for the lovely swimming beaches, the superb fishing and challenging 4x4-only roads, which means that the campsites tend to be quite busy over long weekends and South African school holidays. At other times, you would most likely have the reserve practically to yourself.

An entrance fee equivalent to around US$8 per person and US$8 per vehicle must be paid at the entrance gate and permits a stay of 48 hours.

GETTING THERE AND AWAY The main entrance gate is about 1 hour's drive from Catembe, a couple of kilometres north of the main road towards Ponta do Ouro, along a turn-off that is clearly signposted about 5km past Salamanga. A saloon car could easily make it as far as the entrance gate in dry conditions, but the roads within the reserve are strictly 4x4 only. Mozaic Travel (page 43) runs regular day trips to the special reserve from Maputo city centre, and longer trips can be arranged. Mabeco Tours (page 43) operates overnight camping safaris in the park as well.

7

🏠 **WHERE TO STAY** There are no longer any established campsites within the reserve. The former campsite at Ponta Milibangalala (about 25km from the entrance gate) is currently being developed by Montebelo Hotels to become Montebelo Milibangalala Bay Resort.

Anvil Bay [map, page 120] (m *84 247 6322;* e *info@anvilbay.com;* w *anvilbay. com*), the long-awaited upmarket resort, is now open at Ponta Chemucane and is the only accommodation within the reserve at the time of writing. Comprising nine forest *casinhas* set among pristine coastal wilderness, Anvil Bay offers barefoot luxury with miles of secluded beach to explore on foot, by bike or by kayak. Also available are snorkelling, fishing, whale watching and ocean safaris. Opening rates are US$390/520 (single/double), full board.

The reserve can still easily be visited as a day trip from Bela Vista, about 25km from the entrance gate, as well as from Maputo (ideally catching the first ferry to Catembe, around 05.00) or Ponta do Ouro. On the Santa Maria Peninsula immediately north of the reserve, accessible only by 4x4 or boat, are a handful of remote lodges and self-catering options [map, page 122]: the highly regarded **Machangulo Beach Lodge** (✆ *+27 13 744 0422 (South Africa);* m *84 722 7699;* e *res@machangulobeachlodge.com;* w *machangulobeachlodge.com*) with full-board accommodation in 14 luxury chalets for US$563/750 (single/double), **Nhonguane Lodge** (✆ *+27 82 880 5628 (South Africa);* m *84 426 4801/385 6863;* e *trynie6@gmail.com;* w *nhonguanelodge.co.za*), which offers self-catering houses and standing tents starting at US$60 per tent, and **Bemugi's Place** (m *84 248 0047/385 6863;* e *bemugis@gmail.com;* w *bemugis.com*) offering budget en-suite accommodation with air-conditioning, hot water, fan, kitchen, camping facilities, and one of the best restaurants in the area. Other notable self-catering options include **Nhoxani Villas** (m *+27 83 419 9874 (South Africa);* e *mbraby@global.co.za;* w *nhoxani. com*) and **Camp Carlos** (m *+27 81 024 6235 (South Africa);* e *info@campcarlos. co.za;* w *campcarlos.co.za;* 🟥 *CampCarlosMoz*). Machangulo Beach Lodge has a dive centre that opens to the public, once the diving needs of its overnight guests have been accommodated. Bemugi's can also arrange boat excursions, and groceries from Maputo, with advanced notice and for a slight fee, for those looking to self-cater. In addition, the upmarket **Barra Resorts** (w *barraresorts.com*) chain holds a concession at Ponta Dobela in the south of the reserve, though it has yet to be developed.

GAME VIEWING The reserve today offers a mixed bag when it comes to the large stuff. Elephants, the only confirmed member of the so-called Big Five, have largely recovered from the poaching of the 1980s, and the population is now thought to stand at around 400. They remain shy and aggressive following years of persecution, however, so sightings tend to be sporadic and fleeting, and the matriarchs in particular should be treated with respect. As of September 2016, the reserve supports an estimated population of around 2,600 common reedbuck, which is the most visible antelope, usually seen singly or in small parties in relatively open habitats. Grey duiker, red duiker and nyala are all quite common too, and greater kudu, common waterbuck, impala, bushbuck, suni and steenbok occur in small numbers. It is unclear whether leopards survive, but side-striped jackal and various smaller predators are present. The lakes support an estimated 750 hippos, and small pods are almost guaranteed where the road to Ponta Milibangalala passes the northern end of Lagoa Xingute and the northwest shore of Lagoa Maunda. Turtles nest on some of the beaches and might be observed in the breeding season, and whales also come past seasonally.

Though relatively small in area, Maputo Special Reserve supports a wide diversity of habitats, including mangroves, freshwater wetlands, dune and riparian forest, open grassland and thick acacia and albizia woodland. Thanks to this, it has an astonishingly varied avifauna, with some 350 species recorded to date. An excellent spot for freshwater birds is the northern floodplain of Lagoa Xingute, which supports large numbers of waders and shorebirds, with Caspian tern, pied avocet, African spoonbill and various sandpipers, storks, herons and egrets all likely, while African fish eagles are resident in the forested floodplain edge. Elsewhere, ponds with lily pads often have African pygmy-goose and lesser jacana among more common waterbirds.

The various wooded habitats support several birds with restricted ranges, and some that are eagerly sought by birders, among them palm-nut vulture, grey crowned crane, green coucal, spotted ground thrush, brown robin, Rudd's apalis, Woodward's batis, Neergaard's sunbird and pink-throated twinspot. The grasslands around the reserve have a number of uncommon species, including Denham's bustard, Senegal lapwing, black coucal (seasonal) and the localised rosy-breasted longclaw. Overall, this is probably the single most exciting birding destination in southern Mozambique, and it is well worth devoting a few days to it if you want to see all the local specialities. See also the detailed booklet *Birds of the Maputo Special Reserve, Mozambique*, which can be bought online at w nhbs.com (if they've managed to source the out-of-print book).

PONTA MAMOLI AND MALONGANE

Less well known than the more southerly Ponta do Ouro, these two isolated resorts retain a genuine bush feel, dominated by coastal scrub and forested dune inhabited by a rich array of birds and plentiful vervet and blue monkeys. The diving and snorkelling are comparable to Ponto do Ouro, though the choice of operators is more limited, but the reward is one of the most wildly beautiful beach destinations anywhere in the country. Ponta Mamoli is the more isolated and undeveloped of the two, though it's now home to the superlative White Pearl Resort, while Ponta Malongane has better facilities for budget and mid-range travellers and campers, and its one upmarket lodge, Tartaruga Maritima, is a forest-swathed delight.

GETTING THERE AND AWAY Both resorts are ideally accessed by 4x4 only, though a powerful 2x4 pick-up with diff-lock and heavily deflated tyres should also get through. Coming from South Africa, as most visitors do, follow the same directions as for Ponta do Ouro, from where a signposted track that more or less demands 4x4 leads north through the coastal scrub, arriving at Ponta Mamoli after about 20km and passing through Ponta Malongane roughly halfway. Coming from Maputo, follow the main road south from Catembe towards the South African border as far as Zitundo, which lies 36km past Salamanga. As of March 2017, large stretches of the road were tarred, and the rest graded.

At Zitundo, instead of following the road signposted for the border, turn left on to an adequate tar road that leads to Ponta Mamoli after 11km. If you are heading to Ponta Malongane, follow this road for about 7km out of Zitundo until you see a papyrus-fringed lake to your right; immediately after passing it, turn right on to a sandy track that leads through a follow-your-nose network of other criss-crossing tracks that bring you where you need to be after about 20 minutes (it may help you orientate to know that the hillside aerials you see in the distance behind the lake are at Ponta Malongane).

WHERE TO STAY *Map, page 120*
Exclusive/luxury
🏠 **White Pearl Ponta Mamoli** (21 units)
📞+27 11 026 2674 (South Africa); m 84 605 8112; e reservations@whitepearlresorts.com;

w whitepearlresorts.com; see ad, 2nd colour section. Opened in Nov 2011 & set on a tall forested dune about 20km up the coast from Ponta do Ouro, this isolated luxury resort has a stunning location overlooking a fine beach. It offers 'barefoot luxury' opulence of the type more often found in the Bazaruto & Quirimbas archipelagos further north, & indulgence is certainly the operative word here, with each chalet boasting its own plunge pool on a private veranda overlooking the ocean, outdoor showers, lounge space, minibar, AC, flat-screen with DSTV, Wi-Fi & a king-size bed. Beach pool suites are plonked right next to the sand, while pool suites are further up the dune. Facilities at the lodge area inc swish open-air seafood restaurant & pool with swim-up bar, & the on-site activities centre arranges fishing, diving, horseriding, whale watching & other excursions. *US$938–1,103/1,250–1,470 sgl/dbl pool suites; US$1,020–1,200/1,360–1,600 sgl/dbl beach pool suites depending on season; all rooms FB, HB also available.* **$$$$$**

Mid range and camping

⌂ **Complexo Turístico Da Ponta Malongane** (about 80 units) \ +27 76 418 2523 (South Africa); e reservations@malongane.com; w malongane.com. Next door to Tartaruga Maritimia (opposite) &, like its more upmarket neighbour, carved attractively into the thick coastal scrub, though with far more vegetation cleared, this resort caters mainly to the South African fishing market, so

occupation is highly seasonal. It has its own activities centre offering a variety of diving, snorkelling, dolphin-watching & marine excursions. Occasionally there are music festivals as well. There's a decent restaurant with indoor & outdoor seating, & seafood & other dishes in the US$5–8 range. *US$90–150 for 4–6-bed huts & chalets; US$33–43 dbl hut; US$20–25 twin standing tent; US$7–9 pp camping.* **$$**

⌂ **Tartaruga Maritima** (8 units) \ +27 35 340 7013 (South Africa); m +27 83 301 2958 (South Africa) or 84 373 0067; e tartaruga@mweb.co.za; w tartaruga.co.za. Named after the turtles that sometimes nest on the beach below, this nature-lover's paradise is carved into a patch of dense coastal dune forest alive with birds & monkeys, & leads to a quiet and idyllic swimming beach. The bush-meets-beach feel is typified by rustic but well-equipped standing tents on tall stilted timber bases, with private balconies, ceiling fans, mosquito netting & en-suite shower. Instead of a restaurant, there is a large common lounge with loads of fridge space & well-equipped self-catering facilities; alternatively you can eat at Parque de Malongane or one of the nearby local places. There is also a swimming pool & TV lounge with DSTV. For activities, visit the dive centre at Parque de Malongane. *US$38 pp during low season, US$51 during high season.* **$$**

✗ **WHERE TO EAT AND DRINK** *Map, page 120*
Aside from the restaurant at Complexo Turístico Da Ponta Malongane, you could try the locally run **Come To See Restaurant** (🕐 *08.00–22.00 daily;* **$$**), in the village outside the entrance to Tartaruga Maritima, which serves a range of seafood and other dishes, mostly in the US$6–10 range, though prawns are a lot pricier. Also check out **The Drunken Clam** (m *84 851 6255;* ❋ *drunkenclammalongane;* **$$$**), a new bar and restaurant that opened in October 2016.

PONTA DO OURO

Situated in the far south of the country, just a few kilometres north of the South African village of Kosi Bay, small, isolated Ponta do Ouro (literally 'Cape of Gold') is something of an anomaly in Mozambique, operating almost as an annex of South Africa, with rands more freely accepted than meticais, and English and Afrikaans heard as much as Portuguese. The main reasons for this, aside from the obvious one of border proximity, are that road links between Ponta do Ouro and the rest of Mozambique are very poor indeed, and that its waters offer perhaps the finest fishing and diving opportunities anywhere along the African coastline south of Maputo. Until the road from Catembe is surfaced (due by the end of 2017), Ponta do Ouro remains difficult to access without a 4x4. Once there, however, facilities are quite good, and include several resorts and restaurants, a few basic shops and even an ATM.

Diving is the main thing here and, in addition to some excellent reef fish, lucky visitors stand a chance of seeing, among other things, Zambezi and hammerhead

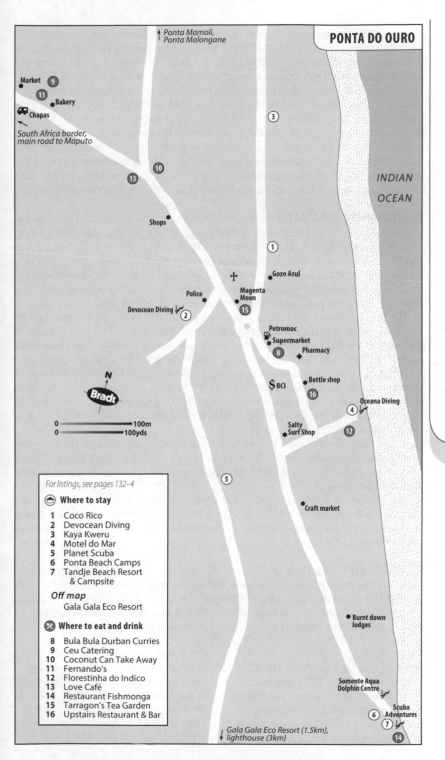

PONTA DO OURO

↑ Ponta Mamoli,
Ponta Malongane

Market ⑨

⑪ ●Bakery

🚌 Chapas

South Africa border,
main road to Maputo

③

INDIAN

OCEAN

⑩

⑬

Shops ●

①

✝   ●Gozo Azul

Police ●   Magenta
              Moon
Devocean Diving ⑮
②

          Petromoc
          🚌
          ●Supermarket
          ⑧   ✚ Pharmacy

          $ BCI   ●Bottle shop
                  ⑯
                        Oceana Diving
                        ④
                  Salty   ⑫
                  ● Surf Shop

⑤

          ● Craft market

          ● Burnt down
            lodges

For listings, see pages 132–4

🛏 Where to stay

1 Coco Rico
2 Devocean Diving
3 Kaya Kweru
4 Motel do Mar
5 Planet Scuba
6 Ponta Beach Camps
7 Tandje Beach Resort
   & Campsite

Off map
   Gala Gala Eco Resort

✖ Where to eat and drink

8   Bula Bula Durban Curries
9   Ceu Catering
10 Coconut Can Take Away
11 Fernando's
12 Florestinha do Indico
13 Love Café
14 Restaurant Fishmonga
15 Tarragon's Tea Garden
16 Upstairs Restaurant & Bar

          Somente Aqua
          Dolphin Centre
                        Scuba
                        Adventures
                  ⑥ ⑦

Gala Gala Eco Resort (1.5km),
↓ lighthouse (3km)

                  ⑭

0 ━━━━━━━ 100m
0 ━━━━━━━ 100yds

N

Bradt

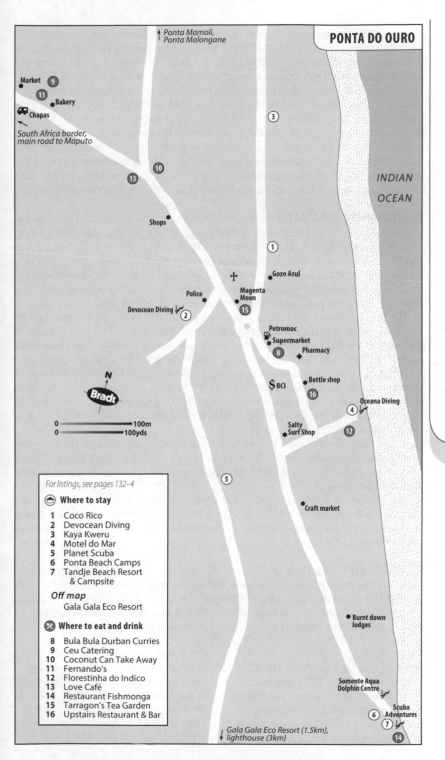

shark, kingfish, barracuda and potato bass. The waters offshore have been protected since 2009 as part of the Ponta do Ouro Partial Marine Reserve (w *peaceparks.org*), which stretches all the way north to Inhaca Island. The beaches around here are also strikingly beautiful, hemmed in by tall and largely untouched forested dunes, whose lush indigenous vegetation stands in contrast to most other Mozambican resorts, whose natural ecology has been degraded by the planting of casuarinas, palms and various invasive species. The birdlife is excellent too, with the dune forests sheltering a host of colourful and eagerly sought species, including green coucal, Livingstone's turaco, yellow-rumped tinkerbird, square-tailed drongo, fan-tailed flycatcher, olive bush-shrike, starred robin and forest weaver. The walking trail at Praia do Ouro Sol is an excellent place to seek out these forest birds, while another popular walk leads to the lighthouse about 3km south of the town centre.

GETTING THERE AND AWAY Most visitors come from the South African side, crossing the border at Kosi Bay (which is accessible on a good tar road) and then driving along the 10km track to Ponta do Ouro. This is a very sandy track, crossing thick dunes, and is ideally tackled in a 4x4, though the odds of getting through are pretty good in a strong 2x4 pick-up, provided that the tyres are heavily deflated for traction. Alternatively, for those with less powerful vehicles, there is safe parking at the border and any of the resorts in Ponta do Ouro can arrange a transfer from there for a small fee.

The poor quality of the road between the border and Ponto do Ouro has given rise to the myth that the road north to Maputo is even worse. This isn't the case at all – indeed the dirt road from Maputo is very good as far as Salamanga (page 126), an hour's drive from the Catembe ferry, and pretty good for another 25km or so after that, deteriorating only as you approach Zitundo (page 129). From Zitundo to Ponta do Ouro, the coastal route via Ponta Malongane is usually a better bet than following the main road towards the border and taking the last junction to Ponta do Ouro, but this will change when the long-promised surfaced road from Catembe to the border is completed by the end of 2017.

A few daily chapas to Ponta do Ouro leave from the entrance to the Catembe pier. The journey takes around 4 hours (although it can be longer if there's been heavy rain) and costs around US$4. It is also possible to hop down in stages via Bela Vista and Salamanga.

Most lodges will arrange private transfers from Maputo for a price, and Laki at **1-Way Adventures** (m *84 475 2656* or *+27 82 447 5488 (South Africa);* e *laki.star@gmail.com or laki.papadakis@1-wayadventures.com;* w *1-wayadventures.com*) regularly makes the trip as well.

WHERE TO STAY *Map, page 131*
Note that a cluster of reed-hut resorts and dive camps situated between the craft market and Ponto do Ouro campsite burned down in mid 2010. Nobody was hurt, but the general consensus, at least in hindsight, is that they had been a firetrap. As of July 2016, it is still unclear what, if anything, will replace them.

Upmarket

Coco Rico (20 chalets) ☎+27 34 413 2515 (South Africa); m 84 875 8029; e info@cocorico.co.mz; w cocorico.co.mz. Modern & well equipped, but comparatively soulless, this central complex is aimed mainly at families & other large parties, with all accommodation being in 8-bed chalets with AC, fully equipped kitchen, DSTV, safe & barbecue. There is also a communal swimming pool, restaurant, gym & games room. *US$170–300 per unit, depending on season.* **$$$$**

Gala Gala Eco Resort m 84 545 8494 (South Africa); e manday@gala-gala.co.za; w gala-gala.co.za. This delightful eco-lodge lies on a forested dune about 3km south of the town centre, where it overlooks the spectacular undeveloped beach running towards Kosi Bay. The cabanas are set in a wonderful patch of unspoilt dune forest, & the connecting roads & paths offer superlative birdwatching. A short hiking trail, leading through the dunes to the beach, can be walked in 45mins & offers a good chance of spotting samango monkey & red duiker. 2 types of dbl or twin accommodation are offered: reed cabanas with nets, fans & common bathrooms, kitchen, braai, dining area & splash pool, or de luxe en-suite cabanas with hammock, net, fan & kitchen. There are also private campsites with bathroom, wash area & electricity available. There's a bar, café & dive centre, Blowing Bubbles. *US$56/108 dbl/4-sleeper reed cabana; US$99/145 dbl/4-sleeper de luxe cabana; US$13 pp camping. Room rates slightly lower in low season, camping in high season is per campsite for US$90 with 6 person max occupancy.* $$$

Mid range

🏠 **Devocean Diving** ☎+27 76 718 7761 (South Africa); m 84 418 2252; e info@ devoceandiving.com; w devoceandiving.com. This diving operation in the town centre offers accommodation in standing tents, & self-catering chalets that sleep up to 5. Looks a bit disorganised. *Tents from US$20 pp sharing; chalets US$60–110, depending on season, with discounts for divers.* $$$

🏠 **Kaya Kweru** (24 rooms) m 82 527 6378 or 84 527 6378; e bookings@kaya-kweru.com or bookings@visitmozambique.co.mz; w kaya-kweru.com. This popular beachfront complex, centred on a large swimming pool at the north end of town, has attractive tiled en-suite rooms, self-catering 6-sleeper units, free Wi-Fi & a good restaurant with sea views. *US$45–54 pp DB&B, US$115–230 self-catering unit.* $$$

🏠 **Motel do Mar** (60 rooms) ☎21 650000; m 82 764 0380 or 84 507 9552; e moteldomar@

gmail.com; w pontadoouro.co.za. The large central complex has an outmoded 1960s-motel feel, & fails to capitalise on its seaside location, but it offers pleasant enough self-catering accommodation in small mini suites with tiled floor, twin beds, fan, fridge, barbecue area & kitchenette. A restaurant is attached, Oceana Diving (f Oceana.Diving.Ponta) has a its base here & the so-called museum houses a hydro-electric generator from the 1960s. *US$65–125 4-sleeper depending on season & location.* $$

🏠 **Planet Scuba** (18 rooms) m 84 718 8773; e info@scubaaddicts.com; w planetscuba.co.za. This friendly private house, set on a dune overlooking the town centre, has a shared kitchen, DSTV lounge, plunge pool, Wi-Fi & a variety of rooms, all with their own bathroom but not always en suite. Bookings are for lodge/diving packages only. A 10-day package is available. *US$1,290 pp sharing.* $$$

Budget and camping

⚕ **Ponta Beach Camps** ☎+27 11 648 9648 (South Africa); m 84 230 6379 or 87 902 3044; e res@moz.co.mz or info@moz.travel; w pontabeachcamps.co.za. Beachfront location offering en-suite safari-style tents, reed barracas & private camping area with ablution blocks, kitchens, restaurant & communal area. *US$83–143 dbl beachfront en suite, US$28–45 dbl barraca; US$42–82 per 4-person campsite.* $$$

⚕ **Tandje Beach Resort & Campsite** (24 chalets) ☎21 900430 or +27 11 465 3427 (South Africa); m 84 230 6379 or 87 902 3044; e reservations@tandjebeachresort.com; w tandjebeachresort.com. With a perfect beachfront location at the southern end of the beach & town centre, this campsite doubles as a dive camp for Scuba Adventures, & offers rustic accommodation. *US$42/75–99/130 2/4/6-bed chalets; US$6–12 pp camping depending on location & electricity.* $$$

WHERE TO EAT AND DRINK *Map, page 131*

✖ **Bula Bula Durban Curries** m 82 962 3874; ⏰ 08.00–20.00 daily exc Wed. This central restaurant has breezy balcony seating & a varied menu with grills, curries, pizzas, local cuisine & coffee. *Mains from US$8.* $$

✖ **Ceu Catering** m 84 754 7259; ⏰ 07.00–late daily. For cheap & cheerful local food served up

with a smile, go no further. Spitting distance from Fernando's, they've got stews, grills & a catch of the day, & it's a good spot for a beer. *US$2–6.* $

✖ **Coconut Can Take Away** m 84 036 8803; ⏰ 08.00–20.00 daily. This brightly coloured food truck offers up burgers & ice cream. $

✘ **Florestinha do Indico** m 84 528 3841/215 3844; ☺ 10.00–22.00 daily, later at w/ends. The speciality at this Portuguese eatery near the Motel do Mar is chicken piri-piri, but it also has a good seafood menu & pizza. *Most mains in the US$6–12 range.* $$$

✘ **Love Café** m 84 230 6333; ☺ 08.00–21.00 Thu–Sat & Mon/Tue, 08.00–17.00 Sun. In a compound along the main road along with a surf shop & boutique, you won't miss this funky new restaurant with its bright, eclectic mosaics, indoor/outdoor seating & Alice-in-Wonderland vibe. The menu's got pizza, pasta, sandwiches & good coffee, & there's live Afro-jazz on Fri nights. *Mains US$9–12.* $$$

✘ **Restaurant Fishmonga** m 84 398 8366; ☺ 10.00–23.00 daily. Recently relocated to Ponta Beach Bar at Ponta do Ouro Campsite, this restaurant is reckoned to serve the best seafood & fish in town & is clearly modelled on the South African Fishmonger chain, with a good wine list & likeable ambience. *Steeply priced, with mains in the US$10–20 range.* $$$$$

✘ **Tarragon's Tea Garden** m 84 440 2273; ☺ 09.00–17.00 Mon & Wed–Sat, 09.00–16.00 Sun. In a lush patch of green at the main roundabout next to Magenta Moon, this café has a noteworthy menu of Mediterranean-inspired dishes inc hummus, salads, pesto & homemade desserts, & a full variety of tea & coffee. You can sit at the bar & check out the open kitchen, or pull up a chair in the eponymous garden. *US$6–8.* $$

✘ **Upstairs Restaurant & Bar** m 82 495 2034 or 84 619 5105; ☺ 07.30–late daily. Situated on the top floor of the town's small shopping mall, this has indoor & outdoor seating & serves a range of seafood, burgers, pizza, b/fasts, sandwiches & other light meals. There's a big-screen TV for sports enthusiasts, full bar & espresso coffee. Paid Wi-Fi. *US$5–10.* $$$

♀ **Fernando's** ☺ 07.00–late daily. This popular drinking hole next to the market has a relaxed ambience, beer on tap &, at the time of writing, a limited (& temporarily suspended) selection of typical Mozambican dishes – grilled prawns, chicken piri-piri. *Around US$12–15 per plate.* $$$$

OTHER PRACTICALITIES

Banks It should be stressed that this part of Mozambique is so economically tied to its neighbour that the South African rand is accepted everywhere, and some places might actually refuse meticais. So if you are coming from South Africa, you are unlikely to need any local currency. However, there is now a BCI Bank with two ATMs in the main mall.

Diving, snorkelling and fishing There are several dive operations scattered around town, and their websites provide detailed breakdowns of the strengths of each of the area's main dive sites, which include a full 21 offshore reefs, some of which also provide great snorkelling opportunities while others are better suited for seeking large fish such as sharks and rays. Also on offer are 'swim with dolphins' excursions and various fishing trips. Recommended operators include **Devocean Diving** (☏ +27 76 718 7761 (South Africa); m 84 418 2252; e info@devoceandiving. com; w devoceandiving.com), **Somente Aqua Dolphin Centre** (☏ 21 901189; m 84 242 9864; e info@somenteaqua.com; w dolphincenter.org), and the mercifully pun-free **Gozo Azul-Ponta do Ouro** (m 84 451 6110/942 0031; e natalie@gozo-azul.co.za; w gozoazul.co.za). Most offer the choice of single dives, courses or full packages including accommodation at a dive camp.

Internet So far as we could ascertain, there is no public internet facility in Ponta do Ouro, but Upstairs Restaurant, Bula Bula Durban Curries and Love Café offer paid Wi-Fi with your own device.

Shopping The main market, at the north end of the town centre alongside the road to the border, is reasonably well stocked with vegetables and other fresh fare. There is an acceptably stocked **supermarket** next to Petromoc, but you'd be better off getting your fruit and veg at the market. In the main shopping mall, there's a liquor store and another small grocery. There are also several surf and fishing shops in the same complex. If it is handicrafts and gifts you are after, there is a good craft market along the main road between the shopping mall and Tandje Beach Resort. Also worth a look is **Magenta Moon** (⊕ *09.00–17.00 Mon–Sat, 09.00–16.00 Sun*), which has the vaguely hippyish feel its name projects, and sells a miscellany of soaps, beads, jewellery and other items. In the Petromoc filling station, a small shop called **Ponki** (**w** *ponki.weebly.com*) sells hand-woven kikois made on the premises (you can watch the weaver at work on a wooden loom).

SEND US YOUR SNAPS!

We'd love to follow your adventures using our *Mozambique* guide – why not send us your photos and stories via Twitter (*@BradtGuides*) and Instagram (*@bradtguides*) using the hashtag #Mozambique. Alternatively, you can upload your photos directly to the gallery on the Mozambique destination page via our website (**w** *bradtguides.com/mozambique*).

FOLLOW BRADT

For the latest news, special offers and competitions, subscribe to the Bradt newsletter via the website (**w** *bradtguides.com*) and follow Bradt on:

◻ BradtTravelGuides
🐦 @BradtGuides
◻ @bradtguides
◻ bradtguides

8

The Limpopo Valley and Coast South of Inhambane

The long and heavily populated coastline between the cities of Maputo and Inhambane is one of the most developed parts of Mozambique in touristic terms, and is lined with a series of resorts that collectively offer a full range of beach and marine activities. Some resorts, for instance Marracuene and Praia do Xai-Xai, are oriented mainly towards the fishing fraternity, while others such as Závora and Bilene are more suited to snorkelling and diving. As the closest stretch of coastline to South Africa's densely populated province of Gauteng, the region looks squarely across the border for its main source of tourist custom, and facilities tend to reflect the sensibilities and requirements of self-catering South African family parties rather than those of international tourists or backpackers.

In comparison with the coastal belt, the interior of Gaza (the province that divides Maputo and Inhambane provinces) is thinly populated and visited by relatively few tourists. Its rather monotonous landscape of dry acacia and mopane woodland is run through by Kipling's 'great grey-green, greasy Limpopo', the second-largest African river (after the Zambezi) to drain into the Indian Ocean. The Limpopo reaches the ocean a short distance south of Xai-Xai, the provincial capital of Gaza, but before doing so it flows for about 200km along the northeastern border of Mozambique's largest national park, to which it also lends its name. This is the 1,000km² Limpopo National Park, a former hunting concession which – after long decades of only nominal protection – is currently enjoying a welcome renaissance, both as the site of several new tourist developments and as the Mozambican component in the Great Limpopo Transfrontier Park (which also includes South Africa's world-famous Kruger).

The emphasis on the South African market means that the coast between Maputo and Inhambane displays high seasonal duality dictated by the timing of school holidays across the border (page 41). During the holidays, resorts and campsites throughout the region charge inflated prices and are often booked solid and unpleasantly crowded. At other times of the year, the same resorts can feel a little *too* abandoned for comfort (the Morrissey line about 'the coastal town that they forgot to close down' springs to mind). In all honesty, unless you are visiting Mozambique from South Africa and have strict time limitations, our firm recommendation would be to bypass this stretch of coast entirely, and head further north to the likes of Inhambane, Tofo or Vilankulo, or else to veer inland to Limpopo National Park.

MARRACUENE AND SURROUNDS

Straddling the EN1 about 35km past Maputo, Marracuene is where northbound travellers can start to relax and take a deep breath of fresh coastal air, and southbound travellers must brace themselves for the traffic bottlenecks and exhaust fumes of the capital. Situated near the Incomati River mouth, it is also the junction town for Macaneta, the closest beach resort to Maputo and a popular weekend outing with people working in the capital. Travellers with their own transport can also now reach Marracuene by continuing north from Maputo along the Costa do Sol road, which was upgraded in 2014 as part of the Maputo ring road project. The major attractions here are excellent game fishing and an attractive clean beach, but the sea isn't particularly suitable for snorkelling, diving or swimming. For those arriving late in the day from South Africa, it's also worth knowing that a couple of very pleasant lodges provide affordable overnight accommodation on the west side of the EN1 near Bobole, about 20km north of Marracuene.

GETTING THERE AND AWAY Once accessible only by ferry, Macaneta can now be reached by road, thanks to the completion of a bridge between Marracuene and Macaneta in 2016. To access it, follow an unsignposted turn on the east side of the EN1 just outside Marracuene, passing a mosque to the left and taking the left turn at the bottom of the road towards the bridge. The dock is still nearby, down a small sand road, and ferries still run in the event of bridge maintenance. The wait for the ferry should be no more than 20 minutes, but allow longer on Sundays and holidays. A taxi or *chopela* from Maputo will cost US$20–30.

WHERE TO STAY
Macaneta
🏠 **El Paso** m 84 483 3048; e elpasomoz@ gmail.com; 📘 ElPASOMozambique. Offering a slice of the Wild West, this cowboy-themed lodge has 2 4-person self-catering chalets & a restaurant. It also offers horseback riding & line dancing. *US$24 pp self-catering chalet, US$30 pp B&B chalet.* **$$**

🏠 **Jay's Beach Lodge** m 84 863 0714; e reservations@jaysbeachlodge.co.za; w jaysbeachlodge.co.za. This relaxed lodge offers inexpensive en-suite self-catering accommodation with fridges, & it also has a restaurant & campsite. *US$19 pp chalet; US$8 pp camping.* **$**

🏠 **Macaneta Holiday Resort** m 82 715 2813/307 0190; e macanetalodge@gmail.com; w macanetaresort.org. This popular resort has 2- & 4-bed chalets for rent & is known for good seafood. *US$75/140 for 2-/4-bed chalet.* **$$$**

🏠 **Tan 'n Biki** 📞 +27 82 852 8389 (South Africa); m 84 629 0446; e tanbiki@tanbiki. co.za; w tanbiki.co.za. This lodge complex offers camping, en-suite dbl rooms & 4- to 12-bed chalets. Fishing, whale watching & Inhaca day trips can be arranged. There is a pool, restaurant & bar. *From US$66 4-bed chalets; US$112 dbl suite with AC, DSTV, B&B; US$12 pp camping. Discounts in low season.* **$$$**

Bobole
🏠 **Blue Anchor Inn** 📞 219 00559; m 82 325 3050; e blueanchorinn@teledata. mz; w blueanchorinn.com. This is actually a landlocked bush lodge, offering AC & en-suite accommodation, situated about 3km north of Bobole. *US$48/74 sgl/dbl.* **$$$**

BILENE

The first major resort along the coast northeast of Maputo, this quiet town of around 5,000 inhabitants overlooks the pretty Uembje Lagoon, which is separated from the Indian Ocean by a large tidal sandbar. Historically, Bilene is of significance as the headquarters and burial place of the Nguni general Soshangane, who fled northward from present-day KwaZulu-Natal with his followers c1819 following a defeat by Shaka Zulu, then went on to overrun the Portuguese settlements at Maputo and Inhambane, and to found and give (most of) his name to the Shangaan nation, prior to his death in 1856. In colonial times, Bilene was called São Martinho, a

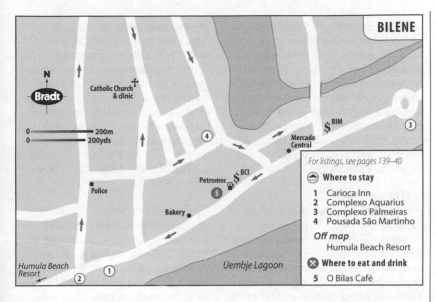

BILENE

Catholic Church & clinic

N

Bradt

0 ——— 200m
0 ——— 200yds

Police

Bakery

Petromoc $ BCI

5

Mercado Central

$ BIM

3

Humula Beach Resort

2 1

Uembje Lagoon

For listings, see pages 139–40

🏠 **Where to stay**
1 Carioca Inn
2 Complexo Aquarius
3 Complexo Palmeiras
4 Pousada São Martinho
Off map
   Humula Beach Resort

❌ **Where to eat and drink**
5 O Bilas Café

name that is still much in evidence here today, and whose feast day of 11 November is still celebrated with some vigour by locals.

Today, Bilene is known less for its tempestuous past than for the calm waters of its lagoon, which is popular with watersports enthusiasts and offers safe swimming from idyllic white beaches, but lacks the game-fishing opportunities that exist further north. The lagoon is also ideal for snorkelling, canoeing, windsurfing and, when the open sea is too rough, diving (you can see seahorses in the lagoon). Otherwise, there is 22km of reef beyond the lagoon for more serious dives. Whale watching is also possible from roughly September to the middle of November.

Bilene is the closest Mozambican resort to Johannesburg, and particularly suitable for family holidays, so it tends to be very crowded during South African school holidays, while at weekends the wealthy of Maputo descend on the resort to race their cars along its main drag. The rest of the time it's practically deserted.

GETTING THERE AND AWAY The signposted turn-off to Bilene is at the village of Macia, about 150km from Maputo along a well-maintained surfaced stretch of the **EN1**. From Macia, a good 30km surfaced road leads to the main roundabout, about 1km from the beach. Using public transport, *chapas* between Maputo and Macia cost US$4 and take about 4 hours, while chapas from Macia to Bilene cost less than US$1 and take up to 45 minutes.

WHERE TO STAY *Map, above*
Bilene boasts one of the highest concentrations of tourist facilities in Mozambique, though the vast majority are self-catering establishments aimed squarely at South African families and anglers. The following are a few of the places more likely to appeal to international visitors, but be warned that everywhere tends to be very busy (and prices rocket) during South African school holidays.

Upmarket
🏠 **Humula Beach Resort** (59 rooms)
📞 282 59111; m 82 328 3106 or 84 310 1874;

e reservas.resort@humula.co.mz; w humula. co.mz. Unquestionably the nicest place to stay around Bilene, this small bush-style resort is carved into an isolated patch of dense coastal woodland about 2km west of town along a sandy track. Spacious chalets are woven into the woodland & come with queen- or king-size bed, walk-in net, tea/coffee, fan, AC, TV, en-suite shower, private veranda & plenty of birdsong floating in through the windows. Other facilities inc beautiful restaurant with views over the lagoon & meals in the US$8–18 range, & a plunge pool. *US$203/252 standard sgl/dbl; US$283/356 sgl/dbl executive suite; B&B.* **$$$$**

Mid range

🏠 **Complexo Aquarius** (36 rooms) ☎282 59000; m 82 301 9000; e styleaquarius@ hotmail.com; 🅵 aquariusbilene. The pick of the tourist complexes lining the main lagoonside road, this has comfortable rooms with dbl or twin bed, fridge, DSTV, AC & a small en-suite bathroom, clustered in circular groups of 4 along a beach with the whitest sand imaginable (room numbers ending in 4 have the best sea view). There is a large swimming pool, a beachfront restaurant serving meals for around US$8–10 & an 'art gallery' (basically just a craft shop). The casas are nice, & right on the beach. *US$60 dbl.* **$$$**

🏠 **Complexo Palmeiras** (10 units) ☎282 59019; m 82 304 3720/138 8658; e palmeirasbilene@gmail.com; w complexopalmeiras.blogspot.com. Situated on a pretty beach a short walk northeast of the town centre, this is the best place to pitch a tent in Bilene, & also has nice huts with roof fan & outside barbecue (but no kitchen). The restaurant has a TV, beachfront veranda & seafood meals from US$8–18 as well as cheaper snacks. *US$65/77 2-/4-sleeper hut; US$5 pp camping.* **$$$**

Budget/shoestring

🏠 **Carioca Inn** m 82 514 7571/582 5439; e cariocainn@gmail.com; w cariocainn.info. A favourite among local Peace Corps volunteers, this is Bilene's cheapest option, offering simple en-suite self-catering rooms with net & fan. The owners can arrange marine & terrestrial excursions. *US$16 dbl.* **$**

🏠 **Pousada São Martinho** m 82 576 6106. Set back from the beach, this rather uninspiring complex has in its favour a swimming pool & some of the cheapest rooms in town, as well as larger chalets aimed at families. *US$30 dbl using common ablutions; from US$70 chalets.* **$$$**

✖ **WHERE TO EAT AND DRINK** *Map, page 139*

Of the places listed above, Humula Beach Resort, Complexo Aquarius and Complexo Palmeiras all have good restaurants with seafront terraces and outdoor seating. The other place that stands out is **O Bilas Café** (🕐 *07.00–21.00 daily except Tue;* **$$**), which serves a selection of sandwiches, burgers and other snacks for US$4–6, as well as fresh coffee and bread, and a selection of imported packaged goods.

OTHER PRACTICALITIES There is a BCI **ATM** located at the petrol station and a BIM bank along the main road, just before coming into town.

LIMPOPO NATIONAL PARK

The Limpopo National Park (or more properly Parque Nacional do Limpopo) is the Mozambican counterpart to South Africa's legendary Kruger National Park, with which it shares the full length of its 200km eastern border. Something of a work in progress, it is the main Mozambican component in the proposed Great Limpopo Transfrontier Park (GLTF), and there is every reason to hope it will emerge as one of the country's most popular tourist destinations over the next decade or so. As things stand, however, wildlife densities are very low by comparison with its western neighbour, the internal road system is negligible, and overnight facilities are limited to one luxury tented camp and a trio of more basic camps and campsites, all concentrated in the far southwest close to Massingir Dam. But while it hardly qualifies as a populist safari destination, Limpopo National Park does now offer a range of adventure activities – overnight hikes, canoeing and 4x4 trails – that make it highly alluring to active safari-goers looking for a genuinely participatory wilderness experience in Big Five terrain. A daily entrance fee equivalent to around US$8 per person and US$8 per vehicle is levied.

HISTORY AND CONSERVATION In November 2000, the environmental ministers of Mozambique, South Africa and Zimbabwe signed a Memorandum of Understanding to initiate the creation of the Great Limpopo Transfrontier Park, the first phase of which involves linking South Africa's Kruger National Park to Gonarezhou National Park in Zimbabwe and what was then a poorly managed Mozambican hunting concession called Coutade 16, to form a contiguous unfenced 35,000km^2 cross-border conservation unit. A year later, Coutade 16 was regazetted as the 10,000km^2 Limpopo National Park, and subsequent years have seen the formal translocation there of substantial elephant and antelope herds from Kruger, along with an increased amount of natural migration between the two parks as damaged fences are left unrepaired, with a long-term view to dropping them entirely. Other developments have been the gradual resettlement of about one-third of the 20,000 people who were resident in the park at the time of its creation, and the opening of the Giriyondo border post, allowing tourists to travel directly between Limpopo and Kruger, in August 2006. The establishment of the GLTP is perceived as the first phase in creating a 100,000km^2 transfrontier park whose Mozambican component will stretch northwest to Banhine and Zinave national parks. Conservation considerations aside, the economic implications for Mozambique could be enormous, bearing in mind that the Kruger National Park now attracts more than a million visitors annually.

GEOGRAPHY AND VEGETATION The terrain of Limpopo National Park is mostly flat and dry, with the main relief feature being the Lebombo Mountains, which rise to about 500m above sea level along the border with South Africa. The entire park falls within the drainage basin of the Limpopo River, which runs along its northeast border for around 200km. Other important perennial waterways that flow across from South Africa include the Olifants (or Elefantes), whose confluence with the Limpopo forms the park's southeastern extremity, and the Shingwedzi, a tributary of the Olifants. The Olifants is dammed at Massingir, near the park's main entrance gate, to form a pretty reservoir that extends over 120km^2. The main vegetation types are mopane woodland, which dominates in the poorly drained sandy-clay soils of the north, giving way to mixed acacia–combretum woodland in the south. The rivers and waterways also support ribbons of lush riparian forest.

WILDLIFE Limpopo National Park has been poorly studied relative to the Kruger, and it probably supports a more limited habitat diversity. Furthermore, wildlife populations have been compromised by decades of hunting and encroachment, though this is improving, a trend that will most likely gather pace as fences between the two parks deteriorate further or are removed altogether. In essence, most large mammals associated with the Kruger might be seen in Limpopo, and a quick overview of this diversity makes for tantalising reading indeed. In total, 147 mammal species have been recorded in Kruger, more than any other African national park, with some of the more abundant species being African elephant (estimated 2009 population 11,600), Cape buffalo (27,000), plains zebra

8

(18,000), giraffe (5,000), greater kudu (6,000), hippopotamus (3,000), waterbuck (5,000), blue wildebeest (10,000) and impala (90,000). The park also harbours high predator densities, including an estimated 2,000 spotted hyena, 1,500 lion, 1,000 leopard and 200 cheetah. The Kruger population of African wild dogs, estimated at 350, is probably the largest outside the Selous-Niassa ecosystem, the black rhinoceros population of 300–400 is the second highest in the world, and the estimated 7,000–10,000 white rhinoceros represent about half the global total. In addition, around 510 bird, 115 reptile and 30 amphibian species have been recorded.

GETTING THERE AND AWAY Coming from elsewhere in Mozambique, the only **entrance gate** is at Massingir, about 400km from Maputo along a surfaced road that is in pretty good condition, having been repaired after the 2013 floods. The drive takes about 5 hours. As with Bilene, the junction for Massingir is about 150km northeast of Maputo, at Macia, where the park is signposted to the left. Once in Massingir (where BCI has an ATM), the road continues 5km along the top of the dam to the park gate. The limited unsurfaced road network within the park will require high clearance, or better still 4x4, and a speed limit of 40km/h is imposed. Estimated driving times from Massingir are 45 minutes to Campismo Aguia Pesqueira, 1½ hours to Machampane Luxury Camp and 2 hours to the Giriyondo border post.

Coming **from South Africa**, as many visitors currently do, the main point of entry is Giriyondo, which lies on the eastern border of the Kruger Park about 95km from the town of Phalaborwa (which is serviced by regular flights from Johannesburg) and 40km from Letaba Rest Camp. This road is surfaced for all but the last 25km, which are decent gravel, but allow at least 3 hours as game viewing can be excellent, particularly in the vicinity of Letaba. The border post at Giriyondo is open from 08.00 to 16.00 in summer and 08.00 to 15.00 in winter, and visas take a few minutes to be issued. The drive from the Giriyondo border post to the Elephant Release Boma (starting point of the Palarangala Wilderness Trail, Lebombo Hiking Trail and Olifants Gorge Backpacking and Fishing Trail) or Machampane Tented Camp takes about an hour, and a high-clearance vehicle is advised. The management of Machampane can also arrange transfers from Letaba or Phalaborwa to the camp or trail heads.

It is also possible to enter Limpopo National Park at the **Pafuri border post** in the far north of the park, but this is only viable with a sturdy 4x4 and should ideally be done in convoy. The Shingwedzi 4x4 Eco-trail uses this route, first meeting at the Pafuri Picnic Site in the Kruger Park.

You can get to Massingir on chapas from Macia, but to get into the park itself you'd have to arrange transport with a lodge or try to hitch.

 WHERE TO STAY, EAT AND DRINK *Map, pages 84–5*
Exclusive/luxury

 Machampane Luxury Camp (5 rooms)
☎ +27 217 01 7860 (South Africa); m 84 254 5604; e enquiry@dolimpopo.com or reservations@ tfpd.co.za; w dolimpopo.com. Set on the forested banks of the Machampane River, a tributary of the Olifants, this is the only upmarket tented camp on the Mozambican side of the GLTP. It lies in the south of the national park, about halfway between Massingir Dam & the Giriyondo border post, and 2–3hrs' drive from the Kruger's Letaba Rest Camp. Accommodation is in comfortable twin tents with en-suite hot showers & private balconies facing the river. There are no roads in the area, so the main activity is guided bush walks, & the emphasis is less on the Big Five (all of which are present, but cannot be considered common) than on general ecological awareness encompassing insects, plants,

birds & smaller mammals. The bush atmosphere is complemented by the cuisine, which incorporates elements of Mozambican cooking & is eaten at a communal table, whenever possible under the stars. *US$270/415 sgl/dbl inc meals & activities.* **$$$$$**

Mid range and camping

🏠 **Campismo Aguia Pesqueira** (4 chalets) m 84 301 1719; e pnlimpopo@gmail.com; w limpopopn.gov.mz. One of 2 basic campsites operated by the national park authorities, this stands on a plateau about halfway between the Giriyondo & Massingir gates, & is named after the handsome fish eagles that are common along the shores of Massingir Dam, which it overlooks. Recently built chalets are en suite with kitchen & veranda. *US$60 dbl; US$4 pp camping.* **$$$**

🏠 **Campismo Albufeira** (10 chalets) m 84 301 1719; e pnlimpopo@gmail.com; w limpopopn.gov.mz. Situated immediately

inside the Massingir entrance gate, this offers accommodation in well-equipped self-catering chalets, as well as space for camping. *US$48 dbl; US$4 pp camping.* **$$**

🏠 **Covane Community Lodge** (7 units) 📞 289 51055; m 86 958 7864/357 9954; e info@covanecommunitylodge.com; w covanecommunitylodge.com. Perched on an escarpment overlooking Massingir Dam, this rustic community-run lodge lies outside the park about 13km from Massingir township & the eponymous entrance gate. Accommodation is in recently remodelled twin chalets overlooking the lake or 3-bed huts, & there is also a campsite. There are full self-catering facilities for campers & simple meals can be arranged with notice. Other activities inc traditional Shangaan dances, guided game walks, cultural visits & boat trips on the lake. *US$48/96 dbl lake-view chalet; US$56 3-bed bush hut; US$6.50 pp camping; add US$4.50 pp to all rates for community bed levy.* **$$$**

ACTIVITIES Limpopo National Park has a very limited road system and as things stand game drives are effectively limited to the main road between Massingir and Giriyondo as well as a smattering of short side roads leading out from it. For this reason, Machampane Luxury Camp concentrates mainly on game walks rather than drives, and guided walks and boat trips on Massingir Dam are also offered at Covane Community Lodge. The management of Machampane has also established a range of multi-day wilderness trails suited to reasonably fit and adventurous travellers (all described in further detail at w dolimpopo.com) as follows.

Rio Elefantes Canoeing Trail
This catered three-night/four-day canoe trail starts at Campismo Albufeira, from where it's a 40km drive to the trail head at the confluence of the Shingwedzi and Olifants rivers. From there you paddle a total of 50km downstream to the Limpopo confluence, sleeping in three different rustic bush camps on the forested riverbanks. Trailists are bound to see hippos, crocs and an abundance of birds, with the chance of larger terrestrial wildlife too, and tiger fishing is possible. Group size four to ten; around US$600 per person. Call ahead as the Olifants River has been affected by recent droughts and may not be flowing.

4x4 Self-Drive Eco-Trails
Offers a range of excursions to destinations within the park, aimed at those seeking a guided yet uncatered wilderness experience. It is emphatically more about the wilderness experience and 4x4 challenge than ticking off the Big Five, but there is a fair amount of wildlife around and previous trailists have encountered species previously thought to be extinct in the park, such as wild dog, cheetah and black rhino. Three–six vehicles; around US$600 per vehicle.

Hiking trails
There are three options: the portered and catered three-night/four-day Lebombo Trail through the Lebombo foothills, the unportered but catered

Remote and little visited even by the standards of Mozambique's national parks, Banhine extends over some 7,000km² of mixed woodland and open grassland to the northwest of Limpopo National Park, and is likely to be eventually co-opted into the Great Limpopo Transfrontier Park. Gazetted as a restricted hunting area in 1969 and upgraded to national park status three years later, it was reputedly dubbed the 'Serengeti of Mozambique' in its heyday, thanks to the large herds of zebra and eland that grazed on its open plains. It is also known for the extensive seasonal pans and wetlands in the north, which are fed by the Changane and associated tributaries and host an important population of the endangered wattled crane, but cannot easily be visited in the wet season when birdlife is most prolific. Recent reports suggest that, while the birdlife can be spectacular, other wildlife populations are less than impressive. Elephant, giraffe, antelope, eland and zebra are all thought to be locally extinct, though an aerial survey undertaken by the African Wildlife Foundation (AWF) in 2004 reported healthy populations of ostrich, greater kudu, impala, reedbuck, duiker, oribi, steenbok, porcupine and warthog. The scenery is impressive, however, and guided walks can be undertaken with the rangers.

The only accommodation in Banhine is the **AWF Camp** (w *awf.org/projects/ banhine-national-park-revitalization*), which comprises six standing twin tents and a fully equipped communal self-catering kitchen, and costs US$50 per person. It is seldom full, so small parties should be safe just pitching up on the day, but bookings can be made through Mozaic Travel (page 43). Access is by 4x4 only, and even then it is only a realistic prospect in the dry winter months, ideally travelling in expedition mode and frame of mind, with two or more vehicles in convoy. One possible approach road is from Pafuri in the northern Kruger Park, from where you

three-night/four-day Palarangala Trail operating out of a rustic unfenced bush camp set in the riverine forest along the Palarangala River, and the fully self-sufficient four-night/five-day Olifants Gorge Backpacking and Fishing Trail in the gorge of the same name. Prices start at around US$540 per person.

XAI-XAI

The capital of Gaza Province, Xai-Xai (pronounced *Shy-Shy*) is the largest town in the southern Mozambican interior, with a population of 130,000 and a convenient location along the EN1 immediately after it crosses the Limpopo 215km northeast of Maputo. Coming from the north, the South African influence here is tangible, but otherwise this is a fairly nondescript and functional town, and the majority of motorised travellers will probably take one look around before heading on to somewhere more inspiring. For backpackers, it is of interest as a potential stopover along the EN1 or to pick up public transport to the nearby beach. It is worth noting that, contrary to expectations, the local orientation of the EN1 means that people heading from Maputo and other places further south along the coast will actually enter Xai-Xai at the north end of town, and vice versa.

Should you overnight in Xai-Xai, the bustling **Limpopo Market** on the outskirts of town is definitely worth a visit, and you might also want to take a peek at the colonial **cathedral** *en route*. That the town lies on the west bank of the mighty Limpopo is not immediately obvious, but there is actually a good viewpoint over the river opposite the central Praça Municipalia, and a stroll along the lush, marshy can follow the southwest bank of the Limpopo through Limpopo National Park to Mapai. This is the best place to cross the Limpopo in the dry season, over a rickety log crossing maintained by locals, who charge around US$2 to use it. Northeast of Mapai, the well-maintained road to Machaila skirts the northern border of Banhine. Another approach is from Macia on the EN1 via Chokwe and Dindiza to Chigubo, on the southeastern boundary of the park. Either way, a usable dry-season track connects Chigubo to Domase on the road between Mapai and Machaila.

Even more remote than Banhine, but also mooted as a future element in the Great Limpopo Transfrontier Park, the more northerly Zinave National Park protects a 4,000km² tract of mixed brachystegia, mopane and acacia–combretum woodland. Although not exactly prolific, the wildlife here is considerably more visible than in Banhine, with significant populations of greater kudu, sable antelope, hippo, impala, leopard and lion thought to survive. The main centre of activity here is the national park headquarters at Cavane, which has a superb location alongside a section of the Save River where hippos and crocs are resident. As things stand, self-sufficient campers can pitch a tent here, but a more upmarket concession with chalets is planned (contact Mozaic Travel, page 43, for developments). Coming from Banhine, it is possible to continue eastward from Machaila to Mabote, passing within about 20km of the main access road to Zinave. Mabote can also be approached from Mapinhane, on the EN1 south of Vilankulo, following an excellent unsurfaced road. Allow at least two days to drive from either Pafuri or Chigubo to Vilankulo in 'getting from A to B' mode, several days if you want to explore the region properly.

riverbank further north might prove rewarding to birders. Of greater tourist interest than the town itself, however, are the nearby beaches of **Praia do Xai-Xai** and **Zongoene** (pages 148–9).

HISTORY Xai-Xai was founded on the southwest bank of the Limpopo in the early 20th century as a satellite port to Lourenço Marques (Maputo) and to service local towns. Known as João Belo prior to independence, it was the terminus of a narrow-gauge railway that stretched 100km inland and was constructed during 1909–12. Of all the large towns in Mozambique, it was the hardest hit by the 2000 floods, thanks to its proximity to the Limpopo. Locals talk of the lower parts of town being submerged under 3m of water, and landmarks such as the BCM Building only just peeking above the rising waters. Miraculously, however, once the waters had receded and the buildings dried out, most businesses reopened and continued trading as before, and today there is no indication of the flooding.

GETTING THERE AND AWAY
By car Xai-Xai town straddles the **EN1** roughly 215km north of Maputo – your arrival is heralded by the crossing of a large bridge over the impressive Limpopo River on to Avenida Samora Machel, as the EN1 is known within the town. The road between Maputo and Xai-Xai is surfaced in its entirety and there are practically no serious pot-holes to worry about, but traffic can be very heavy for the first 30km or so out of Maputo, so allow 3 hours for the drive.

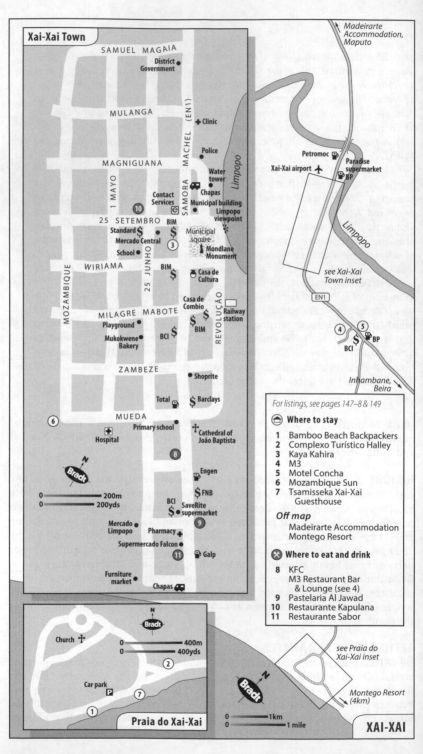

Xai-Xai Town

SAMUEL MAGAIA

District Government

MULANGA

Clinic

Police

MAGNIGUANA

Water tower

Chapas

SAMORA MACHEL (EN1)

1 MAYO

Contact Services

Municipal building

Limpopo viewpoint

25 SETEMBRO

BIM

Standard

Mercado Central

School

Municipal square

Mondlane Monument

WIRIAMA

25 JUNHO

BIM

Casa de Cultura

Casa de Combio

Railway station

MILAGRE MABOTE

Playground

BCI

BIM

REVOLUÇÃO

Mukokwene Bakery

MOZAMBIQUE

ZAMBEZE

Shoprite

Total

Barclays

MUEDA

Primary school

Cathedral of João Baptista

Hospital

Engen

FNB

BCI

SaveRite supermarket

Mercado Limpopo

Pharmacy

Supermercado Falcon

Galp

Furniture market

Chapas

Madeirarte Accommodation, Maputo

Petromoc

Xai-Xai airport

Paradise supermarket

BP

Limpopo

see Xai-Xai Town inset

EN1

BCI

BP

Inhambane, Beira

0 ——— 200m
0 ——— 200yds

Bradt N

Praia do Xai-Xai

Church

Car park

Bradt N

0 ——— 400m
0 ——— 400yds

Bradt N

0 ——— 1km
0 ——— 1 mile

Montego Resort (4km)

see Praia do Xai-Xai inset

For listings, see pages 147–8 & 149

⌂ **Where to stay**

1 Bamboo Beach Backpackers
2 Complexo Turístico Halley
3 Kaya Kahira
4 M3
5 Motel Concha
6 Mozambique Sun
7 Tsamisseka Xai-Xai Guesthouse

Off map

Madeirarte Accommodation
Montego Resort

✕ **Where to eat and drink**

8 KFC
M3 Restaurant Bar & Lounge (see 4)
9 Pastelaria Al Jawad
10 Restaurante Kapulana
11 Restaurante Sabor

XAI-XAI

146

By bus/chapa Regular buses and chapas do the 4-hour run from Maputo to Xai-Xai, costing around US$5. Transport north to Inhambane and Maxixe runs throughout the day; the fare is US$8. Transport to destinations south leaves from the depot on the same block as the municipal building and to destinations north from the depot near Limpopo Market.

WHERE TO STAY *Map, opposite*

Mid range

🏠 **Madeirarte Accommodation** (18 units) \+27 79 887 3037 (South Africa); m 84 500 3687; e madeirarte.accommodation@gmail.com; w madeirarte-accommodation.co.za. Situated 15km out of town alongside the EN1 towards Maputo, this friendly owner-managed complex (formerly the Honey Pot) is aimed squarely at self-drivers looking for somewhere to overnight *en route* to/from resorts further north. It is a far more attractive option than anything in Xai-Xai itself. Accommodation is in a variety of rustic wooden huts scattered in a patch of indigenous woodland, & facilities inc restaurant-bar serving meals in the US$6–10 range, a swimming pool & barbecue areas. *US$34 small dbl huts using common showers; US$38/77 per unit for larger en-suite self-catering 2–4 sleepers; US$163 per unit AC 8-sleeper chalets with enclosed barbecue areas; US$9 pp camping, US$5 for scholars/students.* **$$$**

🏠 **Mozambique Sun** (38 rooms) Rua Mueda; m 84 406 0001; e reservas@ mozambiquesun.co.mz. Aimed squarely at the conference market, this new hotel is nonetheless a good option for self-drivers looking to break up their journey. Simple & characterless en-suite rooms come with AC & DSTV. There's secure parking, pool, gym & restaurant. *US$60/70/70 sgl/dbl/twin B&B.* **$$$**

Budget

🏠 **Kaya Kahira** (22 rooms) 1st Floor, 34 Av Samora Machel; \282 22391; m 84 894 4244. This hotel facing the central Praça Municipalia is the smartest in town, offering a selection of reasonably priced rooms that vary in dimensions & facilities, but are uniformly clean & airy. There is also a pleasant ground-floor restaurant serving seafood & meat dishes in the US$9–14 range. *US$22/30 sgl/dbl using common ablutions; US$44 en-suite twin or dbl; US$60 large en-suite dbl with AC & TV.* **$$**

🏠 **M3** (2 rooms) Rua do M3, Bairro 11 no. 1010; m 84 619 2578; e m3restaurant. barlounge@gmail.com. Located at the back of the popular M3 Restaurant Bar & Lounge, these en-suite dbl rooms with AC & DSTV are easily the smartest in town. Good value. *US$50 dbl.* **$$**

🏠 **Motel Concha** (25 rooms) \282 25099; m 82 560 5505 or 86 925 7759. Set in large gardens on the EN1 about 3km east of the town centre (near the turn-off to Praia do Xai-Xai), this adequate but slightly run-down motel comes complete with an OK restaurant & empty swimming pool. *US$50 large en-suite twin with AC.* **$$**

WHERE TO EAT AND DRINK *Map, opposite*

✖ **KFC** \282 22277; ⏰ 09.00–22.00 daily. The American chicken behemoth isn't much worth mentioning, only if you're headed north, it'll be the last one until Maxixe. Self-drivers can take advantage of the drive-thru. *US$3–8.* **$$**

✖ **M3 Restaurant Bar & Lounge** \282 26992; m 84 619 2578; ⏰ 11.00–01.00 daily. Situated about 100m off the EN1 near the Motel Concha, this slick restaurant with AC, TV & terrace seating serves good pizzas for around US$9, & seafood & meat dishes. *US$7–10, with cheap daily specials.* **$$$**

✖ **Pastelaria Al Jawad** m 82/84 033 0200; ⏰ 07.00–23.00 daily. A pleasant café with a varied menu offering pastries, sandwiches, pizza, meat & seafood for a reasonable price. *US$4–10.* **$$**

✖ **Restaurante Kapulana** m 84 309 1660; ⏰ 07.00–23.00 Mon–Sat. Probably the nicest sit-down establishment in town, this has a cool – air-conditioned – classic atmosphere about it & serves the usual range of sandwiches, pizzas, meat & seafood. *US$1.50–10.* **$$$**

✕ **Restaurante Sabor** m 82 418 1414; ⏱ 10.00–23.00 daily. This eclectic eatery offers Indian, Italian & local Mozambican dishes alongside seafood, pizza & burgers. There is a special, private room just behind the main dining area for those wishing to dine *sans* the presence of alcohol or animal products. *US$4–9.* $$

OTHER PRACTICALITIES

Banks and ATMs The main banks all have branches with ATMs. Barclays, BCI, FNB and BIM Millennium are along Avenida Samora Machel, and the Standard Bank is a block east on Avenida 25 de Junho. There's a private forex bureau just off the main strip on Rua Milagre Mabote. There is also a BCI with an ATM near the junction for Praia do Xai-Xai, more or less opposite the Motel Concha.

Entertainment Brightly decorated in ethnic African style, the **Casa da Cultura** (*Av Samora Machel*) hosts occasional live music performances and expositions, usually on Friday evenings. Check the flyers out front for upcoming events.

Hospital At the south end of Avenida 1 de Maio. There is a 24-hour pharmacy next to Supermercado Falcon on Avenida Samora Machel.

Internet There are a handful of computers with internet access at **Contact Services** (⏱ *08.00–17.30 Mon–Fri, 08.00–noon Sat*) on Rua 25 de Setembro.

Police On Avenida Samora Machel next to the bus depot for destinations south.

Shopping Cheap meals and fruit and vegetables are available at both the **Central Market** (*Rua 25 Setembro*) and the Limpopo Market. There are several good supermarkets on or near Avenida Samora Machel, including SaveRite, Shoprite and Supermercado Falcon, as well as the Paradise Supermarket on the road out to the Limpopo Bridge. If you are staying at Praia do Xai-Xai and intend to cater for yourself, then you would be advised to bring what you need from Xai-Xai itself.

BEACHES AROUND XAI-XAI

PRAIA DO XAI-XAI Situated 12km southeast of the town centre, Praia do Xai-Xai is the sort of idyllic stretch of white sand so characteristic of Mozambique, in this case with the addition of a reef about 30m out from the shore. The sea here is renowned for its excellent game fishing, and for the snorkelling and diving possibilities in the many coral reefs lying within 6km of the shore. However, it must be stressed that there are dangerous undercurrents in the area; signs on the beach indicate non-swimming places and you are highly recommended to take notice of them. There are points of interest on the shore: the ruined Motel Chonguene just next to the Golfinho Azul and the equally ruined hotel between them and the campsite. Neither motel nor hotel has been open since independence.

About 2km to the west of the main road that loops past the beach lies the Wenela tide-pool. It is linked to the sea by an underwater tunnel blow-hole, which you should not even think about trying to swim through. Lined by thick coastal scrub as opposed to the palm trees that characterise beaches further north, Praia do Xai-Xai is surprisingly rich in birdlife, with the beautiful green-and-red Livingstone's loerie being a common resident.

The range of entertainment on offer at Xai-Xai is far from vast – if you are expecting the diving schools, surfing shops and other attractions available elsewhere, you will be disappointed. Indeed, outside the South African school holidays, when it is overrun with anglers from across the border, the resort has a rather moribund boarded-up air, one that might appeal if you're after somewhere quiet to spend a few days birdwatching or fishing.

Getting there and away The turn-off to Praia do Xai-Xai is clearly signposted on the Maxixe side of town about 200m after the BP garage in front of the Motel Concha. A good surfaced 10km road leads to the main roundabout above the beach. Here, you should take the road to your left down to the beach. After a couple of hundred metres, an unsignposted dirt track to your left leads to the hotel and caravan park. Regular minibuses from Xai-Xai cost around US$0.15.

Where to stay, eat and drink *Map, page 146*

Mid range

🏠 **Complexo Turístico Halley** (24 rooms) \282 35003; m 82 312 5900 or 84 947 7050; e complexohalley1@yahoo.com.br. This long-serving complex doesn't have much character, but the comfortable rooms seem fair value & come with AC & TV. The restaurant serves a selection of seafood dishes for around US$15 plus cheaper sandwiches & chicken dishes. *US$50–60 en-suite dbl.* **$$$**

🏠 **Tsamisseka Xai-Xai Guesthouse** (6 rooms) m 84 637 6866 or 82 684 0866; e lynnxaixai@gmail.com; w xaixaiguesthouse.com. Central beachfront house with clean en-suite rooms with twin beds, DSTV, fridge, AC & nets. It seems a likeable set-up, with private gardens & self-catering facilities. *US$46/54 sgl/dbl B&B; US$60 dbl self-catering.* **$$$**

Budget

🏠 **Bamboo Beach Backpackers** m 82 677 8429 or 84 227 3957; e bamboobeach.moz@gmail.

com; w bamboobeachbackpackers.com. This place, formerly Golfina, has simple & clean private rooms & dorms with fan, linen & towels. The seafront eatery serves good fish dishes, as well as chicken & ribs for around US$5. *US$10/15 pp dorm/private room.* **$**

🏠 **Montego Resort** (13 units) \+27 82 653 8197 (South Africa); m 84 207 1650; w montegomoz.co.za. Located 4km east along the main beach road, this pleasant beachfront resort is very spacious & surrounded by dense coastal scrub. It has adequate en-suite 2- to 12-sleeper chalets with fans & nets. There is a self-catering kitchen for campers. The restaurant has great ocean views & serves mains in the US$6–11 range (the half-chicken piri-piri is recommended). The owner-managers are very helpful & can arrange pick-up from either the praia or town, as well as whale watching, fishing, 4x4 excursions & cultural tours. Free Wi-Fi. *US$18 pp chalet; US$6 pp camping.* **$$**

ZONGOENE BEACH Beautifully located at the mouth of the Limpopo, some 20km southwest of Xai-Xai as the crow flies (but a lot further by road), Zongoene is one of the more secluded and unspoilt beaches on this part of the Mozambican coast. The most likely reason you'd be coming here is to stay at **Zongoene Lodge** (\282 42003; m 82 402 6791 or 84 205 4657; e info@zongoene.com; w zongoene.com; **$$**), a highly regarded set-up that offers B&B chalets for US$65/91 single/double and self-catering accommodation for US$78/188/250 for houses sleeping four, six or eight, as well as camping for US$7 per person. The turn-off is signposted about 15km from Xai-Xai along the EN1 to Maputo, and it is another 35km from there to the lodge on a sandy track that may require a 4x4.

NORTHEAST OF XAI-XAI

About 60km northeast of Xai-Xai, just before leaving Gaza Province, the EN1 passes within 5km of the coast at sleepy **Chidenguele**, which means 'High Place' in the local Chope language, a reference to the striking colonial church built on a hill above the town. Church aside, there is little to detain the tourist in the town itself, but the surrounding lakes are very pretty and host a varied birdlife. About 5km out of town, the **Paraíso de Chidenguele** (m *84 390 9999;* e *res@thereservationsgroup.com;* w *chidbeachresort.com*) is a lovely low-key resort built on a sand dune overlooking the ocean. Best known for its fishing, the resort also offers good snorkelling, walking and birding opportunities. Accommodation is in chalets sleeping two to eight people and prices vary from US$60 for a double (throughout the year) to US$200 for an eight-bed chalet in season. About 15km from Chidenguele along a 4x4-only track lies the luxurious **Naara Eco Lodge** (m *84 321 2209;* e *reservations@ naaraecolodge.com;* w *naaraecolodge.com*), uniquely positioned not on the ocean, but on the shore of the freshwater Lake Nhambavale, just inland. Accommodation is in ten luxury safari tents with verandas overlooking the lake, which are excellent value at US$150/190 double low/high season. All the usual marine activities are offered, and there's a spa as well.

Follow the EN1 northeast for another 65km and you'll arrive at the compact town of **Quissico**, set in an area notable for its deep blue freshwater lakes. One of the larger lakes lies immediately southeast of Quissico; there is a good view of it from the EN1 as you leave Quissico for Maxixe, and from the municipal building about 200m off the main road. The lake can be reached along a 10km dirt road that leaves the EN1 just outside town. You could probably get there more directly by foot – the shore can't be more than 3km from town as the crow flies, but ask for local advice regarding footpaths, as you may encounter landmines away from the established tracks. Signposted from town, the remote **LaGoa Eco Village** (☎ *+268 766 60600 (Swaziland);* m *82 381 3636 or 84 577 2946/84;* e *infolagoaquissico@gmail.com;* f *LaGoaEcoVillageBackpackers*) is a low-key, sustainability-minded set-up, offering lagoonside accommodation built exclusively from local materials, with camping at US$6 per person, dorms at US$10, and rondavels starting at US$35. Also just outside Quissico is **BulBul Backpackers** (m *84 801 4141;* e *dmazzeld@yahoo.co.uk;* w *bulbulbackpackers. com*), offers camping with ablution block and dorm-style accommodation with two luxury chalets in the works.

Roughly 45km past Quissico, the EN1 crosses the startlingly beautiful **Lake Poelela**, reputed to be where Vasco da Gama first landed in Mozambique in January 1498. You'll get a fair view of the lake from the road, but since there are no facilities in the area and no roads leading to the rest of the lake, the risk of treading on a landmine, however slight, should be viewed as a persuasive deterrent to off-the-beaten-track exploration.

The main resort in this area, **Praia do Závora** is an outstanding spot for snorkelling and game fishing, reached along a 15km dirt road signposted a few kilometres northeast of the bridge across Lake Poelela. The wide arcing beach here is inherently very beautiful, set below tall vegetated dunes, but it suffers from a degree of unnecessary uglification in the form of the abundant concrete structures perched on the dune's rim. As compensation, a long reef 500m from the beach offers superb offshore snorkelling, and it is one of several excellent dive sites visited by the local dive company **Mozdivers** (m *84 216 4077;* e *jon@mozdivers.com;* w *mozdivers.com*).

The main hub of activity at Závora is **Závora Lodge** (☎ *+27 83 268 5396 (South Africa);* m *84 702 2660;* e *reservations@zavoralodge.com;* w *zavoralodge.com*), an unpretentious dune-top set-up that traditionally caters to the South African fishing market, but which also now doubles as a low-key backpackers and offers transfers from the nearby towns of Inhambane or Inharrime. The lodge has a varied selection of accommodation in barracas, bungalows and houses sleeping two to eight people, ranging from US$10 per person for a backpackers' room throughout the year to US$170 for a four-bedroom house in high season. Camping costs US$8 per person.

About 20km north of Inharrime, turn right off the EN1 for **Dunes de Dovela Eco-Lodge** [map, pages 84–5] (❧ *293 56055;* m *87 262 9164 or 82 700 0743;* e *contact@dunesdedovela.com;* w *dunesdedovela.com; see ad, 2nd colour section*), a luxurious owner-managed getaway that opened in 2012. From the turning, it's 12km down a 4x4 track – free transfers are available for guests – until you reach the lodge, where there are three magnificently positioned thatch bungalows on the dunes above the ocean for US$195/450 single/double and four luxury platform tents in the coastal forest for US$117/180 single/double. All guests are hosted on a full-board basis (non-motorised activities included) and dine in the French-inspired restaurant, which also, naturally, has a spectacular view.

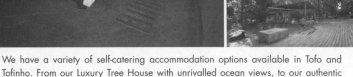
152

9

Inhambane and Surrounds

Noted for its fine beaches, seemingly endless stands of tall coconut palms and superb marine activities, the coast around Inhambane is one of the country's most important tourist hubs, studded with dozens upon dozens of homely self-catering resorts, smarter beach lodges, busy backpackers and rustic campsites, yet facilities are sufficiently spread out that it seldom feels crowded. The most popular resort in the region is Tofo, whose lovely beach is overlooked by a small village packed with lodges, restaurants, dive centres and other amenities catering to travellers. More remote and unspoilt, but difficult of access without a private 4x4, are the relatively undeveloped Barra Beach and Guinjata Bay. Whichever beach you head for, however, the diving and snorkelling around Inhambane are legendary, and there is no better place anywhere for submarine encounters with manta rays and whale sharks.

The twin gateways to the region are the towns of Maxixe and Inhambane, which lie a few kilometres apart on opposite sides of Inhambane Bay, and are linked by a regular ferry service but otherwise have little in common. Where Maxixe, straddling the EN1 some 470km north of Maputo, is large, modern, functional and unmemorable, the sleepier and smaller Inhambane is undoubtedly the most architecturally characterful town in southern Mozambique, and worth more than the fleeting visit most travellers accord it *en route* to Tofo or the other beaches.

INHAMBANE

The eponymous capital of Inhambane Province lies on the eastern shore of Inhambane Bay, an attractive natural harbour formed by a deep inlet at the mouth of the small Matumba River. It is the oldest extant settlement between Maputo and Beira, and one of the more substantial, with a population estimated at 80,000 and a distinctly

CYCLONE DINEO

In February 2017, Cyclone Dineo hit Mozambique, primarily in the Inhambane Province. A category 1 hurricane, with windspeeds of around 130km/h, Cyclone Dineo caused serious damage to an estimated 49 hospitals, 105 schools and public buildings and 22,000 homes, leaving at least 130,000 people displaced. Many of the tourist facilities in the area also suffered damage: as such, it is best to call ahead to your intended lodging as rebuilding will, no doubt, be an on-going process for quite some time.

Mediterranean character, thanks to its spacious layout of leafy avenues lined with eye-pleasing colonial buildings. It is also refreshingly clean and orderly, with few of the run-down buildings that exist elsewhere in Mozambique – an anomaly that may be explained by the abundance of NGOs operating out of town – and a good selection of eateries and other tourist amenities. This, in short, is an unusually pleasant town, and while most travellers treat Inhambane as nothing more than a passing stop *en route* to the nearby beaches at Tofo and Barra, it is worth an overnight stay, possibly before crossing the bay to Maxixe to catch an early morning bus north or south.

HISTORY Little is known of Inhambane's history prior to the 18th century, although it has been suggested that there was a town here by the 10th century. Vasco da Gama arrived in 1498 to resupply and liked the place so much he named it Terra de Boa Gente ('Land of the Good People'), and it was subsequently visited by several Portuguese traders in the early 16th century. In 1560, Inhambane was selected as the site of a short-lived **Jesuit mission**, the first in East Africa, and when the leader of the mission arrived he noted that several Portuguese traders had settled there. By the end of the 16th century it had been incorporated into the Portuguese East African monopoly and had become a regular port of call for Portuguese ivory-trading ships. During the 17th and early 18th centuries, Inhambane was, along with Delagoa Bay (Maputo), the most important trade terminus between the coast and interior of what is now southern Mozambique.

In 1727, the Portuguese commander **Bernardo Soares** discovered a Dutch vessel trading with the local chiefs of Inhambane. Following this, a punitive expedition led by Domingos Rebello arrived at Inhambane from Sofala, destroying several villages and killing at least two local chiefs as a punishment for trading with another European power. Commander Soares stayed on at Inhambane, where he built a fort large enough to house a garrison of 50 men. Soares's fort was hardly the most impressive defensive structure (a compatriot remarked that 'it would have been enough for [the Dutch] to have laid eyes on it to capture it'), but its presence evidently discouraged further Dutch trade, and it laid the foundation for a permanent Portuguese settlement.

Although Inhambane was officially recognised as a Portuguese town in 1763, the local ivory trade was in reality dominated by Indians rather than Portuguese. This situation dated to the early 18th century, when the port had briefly been leased to an Indian trader called Calcanagi Velabo. At the end of the 18th century, Inhambane's Christian population numbered only 200, and – remarkably – several parish priests appointed at around this time were of Indian extraction.

The town grew rapidly in prosperity during its early years (in 1770, the customs revenue raised at Inhambane was almost equal to that raised at Quelimane), not least because it was the first Mozambican

INHAMBANE
and surrounds

🛏 **Where to stay**

1 Barra Beach Club *p172*
2 Blue Footprints Eco Lodge *p172*
3 Blue Moon Resort *p173*
4 Break Away Chalets *p173*
5 Castelo do Mar *p174*
6 Coconut Bay Beach Resort *p173*
7 Cumbini Resort *p173*
8 Daghatane Estate *p173*
9 Esperanza Lodge *p173*
10 Flamingo Bay Water Lodge *p172*
11 Funky Monkeys *p174*
12 Jeff's Resort *p173*
13 Mango Beach *p167*
14 Neptune's Lodge & Beach Bar *p172*
15 Paindane Beach Resort *p173*
16 Seabound Charters Bed & Breakfast *p174*
17 White Sands *p172*

Off map

Massinga Beach Lodge *p175*
Pomene Lodge *p175*
Ponta Morrungulo Beach Resort *p175*
Travessia Beach Lodge *p174*

✖ **Where to eat and drink**

18 Chill Bar *p172*
19 Green Turtle *p172*

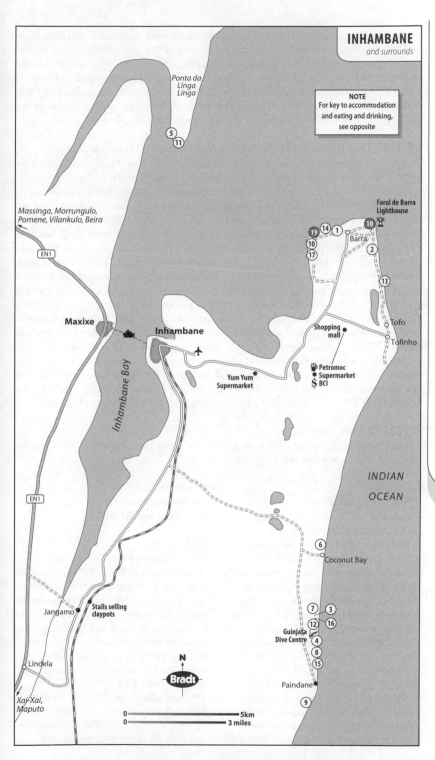

INHAMBANE
and surrounds

NOTE
For key to accommodation
and eating and drinking,
see opposite

Ponta da
Linga
Linga

⑤
⑪

Massinga, Morrungulo,
Pomene, Vilankulo, Beira

EN1

Farol de Barra
Lighthouse

⑲ ⑭ ① ⑱
Barra
⑩
⑰ ②

⑬

Maxixe Inhambane

Tofo
Tofinho

Shopping
mall

Inhambane Bay

Yum Yum
Supermarket

Petromoc
Supermarket
$ BCI

INDIAN
OCEAN

EN1

⑥
Coconut Bay

Jangamo Stalls selling
claypots

⑦ ③
⑫ ⑯
Guinjata
Dive Centre ④
⑧
⑮

Lindela

N

Bradt

Xai-Xai,
Maputo

Paindane

⑨

0   5km
0   3 miles

port to establish a trade in slaves. Roughly 400 slaves were exported from Inhambane in 1762, a number that had quadrupled by the end of that decade while ivory export figures steadily sank. In 1834, Inhambane was practically razed by Soshangane's **Gaza warriors**, and most of its traders were killed, but the town soon recovered and by 1858 it had a population of roughly 4,000 (of which 75% were slaves). As recently as 1928, Inhambane was the third-largest centre of population in Mozambique, after the capital city and Beira, but today it scrapes in at the bottom of the top 20.

GETTING THERE AND AWAY Situated 470km north of Maputo and 260km past Xai-Xai, Inhambane is isolated from the rest of the Mozambican mainland by Inhambane Bay – indeed, while the town is less than 3km from Maxixe (on the opposite side of the bay) as the gull soars, the road distance between the two towns is around 60km. The only **land access** to Inhambane is via a well-maintained surfaced 30km feeder road that branches northeast from the EN1 at Lindela, about 30km south of Maxixe, and carries on through the town to Tofo and Barra beaches.

For this reason, public transport to/from all destinations further north leaves and arrives from Maxixe, which is connected to Inhambane by regular **ferries**. These run from around 05.30 to 22.30, the crossing takes an extremely pleasant 20 minutes or so, and tickets (*around US$0.15 one-way*) are bought at a ticket window at the base of the pier. By contrast, direct public transport connections link Inhambane to more southerly towns such as Xai-Xai and Maputo in the form of the plentiful minibuses that bustle around the chapa station next to the Mercado Central. There are also plenty of chapas from Inhambane to Tofo and Barra.

There are no longer rail services to Inhambane and the old station now serves as the tourism department of Eduardo Mondlane University. Inhambane Airport lies off the Tofo road about 5km east of the town centre and is serviced by daily LAM **flights** from Maputo, Beira and Johannesburg, and twice-weekly flights from Vilankulo.

 WHERE TO STAY *Map, opposite*
Inhambane is lacking in choice of accommodation in comparison with nearby Tofo, but there are a few good options.

Upmarket

🏠 **Hotel Casa do Capitão** (25 rooms) Rua Maguiguana; ✆ 293 21408/9; e reservations@ hotelcasadocapitao.co.mz; w hotelcasadocapitao. co.mz. Opened in Jun 2010, this modern hotel stands on the site of the old Captain's House on the northwest end of the town centre overlooking the bay. The architecture & décor combine clean modernistic lines with uncluttered contemporary furniture to stunning effect, while the spacious airy rooms all come with king-size bed, large flat-screen DSTV, AC, Wi-Fi, minibar, private balcony with sea view, & en-suite bathroom with tub & shower. The stylish restaurant serves seafood & other mains in the US$10–17 range, & leads out to a large palm-lined swimming pool that juts into the harbour to dramatic effect. The existence of a hotel of this calibre & price range in sleepy Inhambane might prove a misjudgement of monumental proportions,

but there is no questioning its class. *US$200/235 low/high season standard dbl; US$235/270 low/high season dbl; all rates B&B.* **$$$$**

Mid range

🏠 **Casa Jensen & Casa Jensen Annex** (11 rooms) ✆ 293 20886; m 82 859 6150 or 84 595 7642; e contact@casajensen.com; w casajensen. com. Situated about 500m east of the town centre near Gilo Market, this small owner-managed lodge is understandably popular with businessmen. The smart tiled rooms have a king-size bed, en-suite hot shower, DSTV, tea/coffee-making, fridge, writing desk & bright ethnic décor. *Good value at US$73/97 sgl/dbl.* **$$$**

🏠 **Hotel Inhambane** (27 rooms) Cnr avs da Vigilância & Independência; ✆ 293 21225; m 84 389 3839 or 82 276 4340; e hotelinhambane@sirmotors. com. Set on the 1st floor of a restored colonial

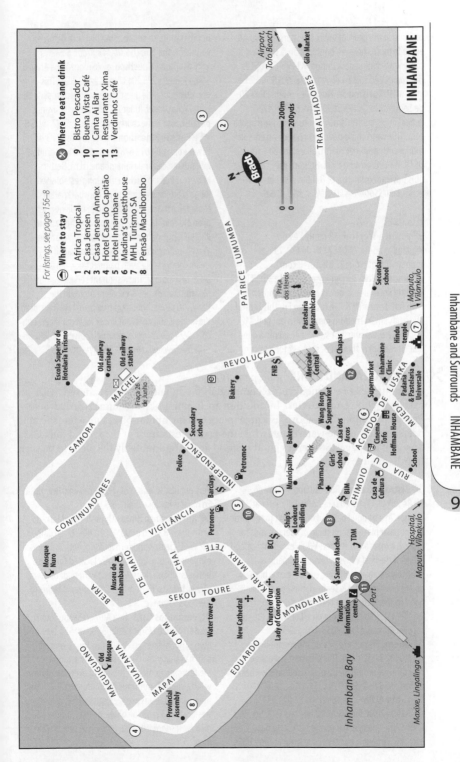

9

INHAMBANE

For listings, see pages 156–8

Where to stay
1 Africa Tropical
2 Casa Jensen
3 Casa Jensen Annex
4 Hotel Casa do Capitão
5 Hotel Inhambane
6 Madina's Guesthouse
7 MHL Turismo SA
8 Pensão Machimbombo

Where to eat and drink
9   Bistro Pescador
10 Buena Vista Café
11 Canta Ai Bar
12 Restaurante Xima
13 Verdinhos Café

Airport,
Tofo Beach

Gilo Market

TRABALHADORES

PATRICE LUMUMBA

Praça
dos Heróis

Pastelaria
Mozambicano

Secondary
school

Maputo,
Vilankulo

Hindu
temple

REVOLUÇÃO

FNB

Mercado
Central

Chapas

Inhambane
Clinic

Supermarket

Padaria
& Pastelaria
Universale

MUEDA DE LUSAKA

Bakery

Wang Rong
Supermarket

ACORDOS

Casa dos
Arcos

Cinema
Tofo

Hoffman House

School

RUA OUA

Escola Superior de
Hotelaria Turismo

Old railway
carriage

Old railway
station

MACHEL

Praça 26
de Junho

SAMORA

Secondary
school

Bakery

INDEPENDÊNCIA

Police

Petromoc

Municipality

Bakery

Park

Pharmacy

Girls'
school

CHIMOIO

BIM

Casa de
Cultura

CONTINUADORES

VIGILÂNCIA

Petromoc

Bardlays

10

5

1

Ship's
Lookout
Building

13

BCI

TDM

Mosque
Nuro

BEIRA

Museu de
Inhambane

CHAI

KARL MARX TETE

1 DE MAIO

SEKOU TOURE

Maritime
Admin

Samora Machel

MONDLANE

9

11

Port

Tourism
information
centre

MAGUIGUANO

NUAZANIA

Old
Mosque

Mosque

Water tower

New Cathedral

Church of Our
Lady of Conception

EDUARDO

MAPAI

Provincial
Assembly

8

4

Inhambane Bay

Maxixe, Lingalinga

Hospital;
Maputo, Vilankulo

N

Bradt

0   200m
0   200yds

building in the heart of town, the sparsely decorated en-suite rooms here are bright, clean & spacious, & come with writing desk, fridge, Wi-Fi, AC & DSTV. *Fair value at US$68/83 dbl/trpl B&B.* **$$$**

🏠 **MHL Turismo SA Hotel** (5 rooms) Rua 20 de Septembro; ✆ 293 20999; m 84 246 4236; e bookings@mhlturismosa.com; w mhlturismosa. com. This welcoming new hotel has clean en-suite rooms with minimal charm, all equipped with AC, DSTV, Wi-Fi & writing desk. Sgls are very small but dbls have adequate space & 1 has a street-view veranda. *US$60/70–80 sgl/dbl, B&B.* **$$$**

Budget

🏠 **Africa Tropical** (8 rooms) Av da Vigilância; m 82 777 4871 or 84 641 7312; e pedroalbuquerque82@hotmail.com; f africatropical. Tucked away behind a small but brightly decorated & newly renovated garden bar with flat-screen TV & live music on Fri, this central place has smart modern rooms with dbl bed, TV, AC, fridge & en-suite hot shower. It seems a good deal at the price, though best to ask for a lower-number room to create some distance between yourself & the bar. *US$30/34 sgl/dbl.* **$$**

🏠 **Madina's Guesthouse** (6 rooms) Rua Ahmed Sékou Touré; ✆ 293 20431; m 82 489 2020. This unpretentious little guesthouse has clean en-suite dbls with TV, hot water, fridge, AC & kettle set in a small private house & the courtyard behind. *US$47 dbl.* **$$**

🏠 **Pensão Machibombo** (7 rooms) Av 3 de Fevereiro; m 84 012 6787 or 82 569 8111; e info@ inhambane.co.za; w inhambane.co.za. Better known as Pensão Pachiça, this long-established lodge is effectively the town's only backpackers, though it attracts a broader range of clients. Set in an old colonial house overlooking the harbour, it has a range of brightly decorated private rooms, as well as dormitory accommodation, all of it clean, comfortable, with parquet floor, fan & nets (AC is coming…). The restaurant serves seafood, Mozambican dishes & excellent pizzas in the US$7–10 range. Though the website says it is closed, the lodge is still open but under local management. *US$20/24 sgl/dbl using common showers; US$50 en-suite room sleeping up to 4; US$8 pp dorm.* **$**

✗ WHERE TO EAT AND DRINK *Map, page 157*

Given its relative paucity of accommodation, Inhambane is scattered with an excellent choice of eateries. In addition to the bespoke restaurants listed below, Pensão Machibombo (above) is a great place to hang out for pizza and a few sociable beers in view of the waterfront, while the pricey restaurant at the swish Hotel Casa do Capitão (page 156) serves good seafood and is undoubtedly *the* place to be seen in Inhambane.

✗ **Bistro Pescador** Rua Eduardo Mondlane; m 84 251 0911; ◷ 08.00–22.00 daily, later at w/ends. In a tranquil patch of green next to the jetty, this popular place is something of a rendezvous for locals & expats alike. It offers Wi-Fi, excellent seafood & one of the best views in town. The menu is relatively extensive, offering curries, pizza, burgers, grilled chicken, meat & seafood, there's a full bar & good coffee, & they do a plate of the day too. It's an excellent spot to check your email or watch the sun set over Maxixe. *Mains US$5–10.* **$$$**

✗ **Buena Vista Café** Av da Independência; ◷ 07.30–21.30 daily. This pleasant streetside café offers a simple menu of toasted sandwiches & coffees. *US$4–8.* **$$**

✗ **Canta Ai Bar** Port Bldg; m 84 023 9513; ◷ 10.00–20.00 Sun–Thu, 10.00–late Fri & Sat. This bright little eatery & bar on the ferry jetty has a view over the harbour & bar-style snacks for around US$4.

Very popular w/end spot with occasional live music. Fri night is karaoke night. **$$**

✗ **Restaurante Xima** Opposite the Mercado Central; m 82 066 6006; ◷ 10.00–21.00 daily exc Wed. Clean & modern looking, with indoor & outdoor seating. Conveniently located for a bite between chapa rides. Serves a variety of burgers, pizzas, b/fasts, light meals & ice cream. *Mains in the US$5–9 range.* **$$**

✗ **Verdinhos Café** Rua Ahmed Sékou Touré; m 84 145 9201/563 1260; ◷ 08.00–23.00 Mon–Thu, til later Fri & Sat. This funky central café has shady courtyard seating & a varied Mediterranean menu embracing everything from salads, soups & hummus to panini, pizzas & light meals. Vegetarians are well catered for, & it serves fresh coffee & most alcoholic drinks. *Around US$3 for a light snack; US$4–6 for a more substantial meal.* **$$**

OTHER PRACTICALITIES

Banks The main banks are all represented and most have branches on the west end of Avenida da Independência or within a block either side of it. There are ATMs at Barclays, BIM Millennium and BCI.

Cinema and entertainment The striking Art Deco **Ciné-Teatro Tofo** (*Av de OAU;* m 84 610 3040; 🇫 *Cine-Teatro-Tofo-281197632090786*) is once again offering weekly showings in addition to its annual African film festival held in May. Enquire at the Casa de Cultura opposite about any one-off cultural events that might be worth attending.

Hospital (☎ *293 20345/21112*) About 1km out of town along the feeder road back to the EN1. The Inhambane Clinic (☎ *293 21003*) is more central and reasonably efficient.

Internet Inhambane has one internet café on Rua da Revolução, 100m from the university.

Police The police (☎ *293 20830*) are based at the entrance to the town itself but there are always a few hanging around on Avenida da Independência.

Shopping The **Mercado Central** is an excellent place for craft shopping, with a good selection of basketry, woodcarvings and paintings, and tends to be cheaper than Tofo. Also on sale is an unusually varied selection of fresh and tinned produce, bootleg DVDs and music CDs, clothing and hardware. **Gilo Market** on the Tofo road is also very busy though less geared to touristic interests. The Chinese-owned **Wang Rong Supermarket** on Rua da OUA is probably the best in town, but the **supermarket** on Rua Ahmed Sékou Touré opposite Hoffman House is also good. Further down the same road, the **Padaria & Pastelaria Universale** has fresh bread and pastries as well as imported confectionery on sale, while a more limited selection is available at **Pastelaria Mozambicano** opposite the Mercado Central.

Tours A company called **Terra Agua Céu** (☎ *293 21551;* m *82 021 6250;* e *info@ travel2mozambique.com;* w *travel2mozambique.com*) can arrange guided historical tours of the old town, as well as providing the usual tour operator services such as transfers and hotel bookings. There is also a tourism information centre at the end of the jetty to Maxixe.

WHAT TO SEE AND DO Inhambane today is anything but the bustling trade centre that it once was – it is difficult to think of a more sedate town anywhere on the East African coast – but neither has it fallen into the state of disrepair that is often synonymous with the term 'historical coastal town'. The seafront itself is very pretty, particularly at sunset, though swimming might not be such a great idea. Most of the older buildings are clustered around an open square at the jetty end of Avenida da Independência, and can be visited on foot within an hour or so. It's a pleasant walk just for the sake of the architecture, a peculiar mix of classic Portuguese with African and Muslim influences. The following buildings are of special note.

Church of Our Lady of Conception (*Rua Karl Marx*) Probably the most distinctive building in Inhambane, this Catholic edifice stands on the site of an earlier wooden church shown on the original 17th-century Portuguese plan of the town. The present building was constructed between 1854 and 1870, and its striking clocktower dates to the 1930s, when the clock was donated by a wealthy local family. The church fell into disuse in the late 20th century, but has recently been restored and sometimes serves as a library. It is the only building on one side of the street (which was surely named with deliberate irony), while the uglier new cathedral is the only building on the other.

Museu de Inhambane (*Cnr avs 1 de Maio & da Vigilância;* \ *293 20756;* m *82 425 5180;* ⊕ *08.00–15.00 Mon–Fri, 08.00–14.00 Sat, closed Sun; entrance free but donation expected*) Though not exactly a 'must see', this moderately diverting museum, established in 1988, probably deserves 15 minutes of your time. It houses a seemingly arbitrary selection of African musical instruments and household items, imported oddities (such as vintage radios and trunks) and displays relating to the history of the railway, as well as some photographs of the town taken in the 1920s. Most explanations are in English, as well as Portuguese.

Old Mosque (*Rua Maguiguana*) Situated near the corner with Rua da Mapai, this attractive small building, originally built between 1840 and 1860 using French brick and stone quarried near Maxixe, was restored in 1928 and again in 1985. Visitors are welcome provided they are dressed appropriately.

Ship's Lookout Building (*Av da Independência*) Situated a block up from the jetty, this was built between 1940 and 1950 in a style known as Streamline Moderne, a development from Art Deco. Its lines supposedly resemble those of a ship's prow, and it is now a general store. The Ciné-Teatro Tofo (page 159) dates from the same period and is in the same style.

Hoffman House (*Rua Ahmed Sékou Touré*) With its ornate façade and railings, this two-storey building is one of the most ostentatious in Inhambane. Built in the late 19th century using stones quarried near Ilha de Moçambique, it was originally the home and shop of the merchant Oswald Hoffman and later served as a hotel, while today it's home to a printing press.

Escola 7 de Abril (*Av da Vigilância*) Built as a school in the late 19th century (a function is still serves today), this building is notable for its classical lines and extended front archway. The municipal office on Avenida da Independência is similar in style and vintage, as is the waterfront TDM office diagonally opposite the port.

Casa dos Arcos (*Av Acordos de Lusaka*) Built in the late 19th century, possibly as a church or hotel, the enigmatic 'House of Arches' was extended to a second floor, reached via an internal spiral staircase, in the early 20th century and boasts several interesting classical features, including arched doors and windows, crescent-shaped nooks and stone columns.

Mercado Central (*Av da Revolução*) Not as touristy as you might expect, the bustling central market sprawls around a handsome building that dates to the late 1950s when the market relocated here from the park in front of the municipal office.

MAXIXE

Situated on the western shore of Inhambane Bay, Maxixe (pronounced '*Masheesh*') represents the only point where the EN1 between Maputo and Beria actually skims the coast. It is also the largest town in Inhambane Province, with a population estimated at 110,000, but it remains politically subservient to the eponymous provincial capital a mere 3km across the bay. People driving from Maputo to places further north might find it convenient to break the journey here, while for southbound travellers using public transport, Maxixe represents the gateway to Inhambane – a 20-minute ferry trip across Inhambane Bay as opposed to a circuitous 60km by road – and thus to nearby Tofo and Barra Beach.

For all its logistical significance, Maxixe is not the most inherently interesting of places. Indeed, the stark grid layout and bustling African market-town atmosphere couldn't offer a greater contrast to the seductive old-world sleepiness that envelops Inhambane. In its favour, Maxixe lies on a pretty palm-lined stretch of coast that offers a lovely view across the water to Inhambane at dusk, and it has a fair selection of lodges and eateries, along with other urban amenities such as filling stations and ATMs. Be warned, however, that the town centre has a somewhat seedy reputation at night – best to be off the streets or to walk in groups after dark, and for single women the streets are a definite no-no. It also has a reputation for car crime, so off-street parking should be considered: even if you aren't staying there, you can usually park in Campismo de Maxixe for a fee, space permitting.

GETTING THERE AND AWAY Maxixe straddles the surfaced **EN1** about 470km north of Maputo, 260km from Xai-Xai and 600km south of the Inchope junction with the **EN6** connecting Beira to Chimoio. It is an easy drive in all directions. Chapas to most destinations between Maputo and Beira leave the same praça as

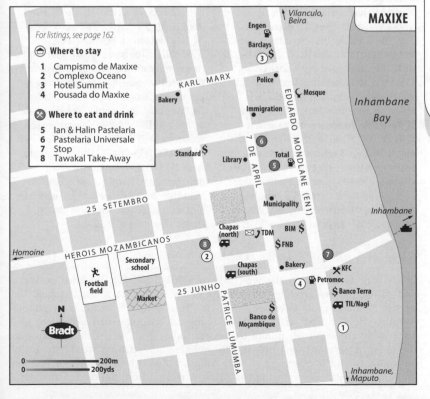

MAXIXE

↑ Vilanculo, Beira

Engen
Barclays
(3)

For listings, see page 162

Where to stay
1 Campismo de Maxixe
2 Complexo Oceano
3 Hotel Summit
4 Pousada do Maxixe

Where to eat and drink
5 Ian & Halin Pastelaria
6 Pastelaria Universale
7 Stop
8 Tawakal Take-Away

KARL MARX

Bakery

Police
Mosque
Immigration

Inhambane Bay

EDUARDO MONDLANE (EN1)

7 DE ABRIL

Standard
Library
Total
(6)
(5)

Municipality

Inhambane

25 SETEMBRO

Homoine

HEROIS MOZAMBICANOS

(8)
(2)

Chapas (north)
TDM
BIM
$ FNB

Chapas (south)
Bakery
(7)
KFC
Petromoc
(4)
$ Banco Terra
TIL/Nagi
(1)

Secondary school

Football field

Market

25 JUNHO

PATRICE LUMUMBA

Banco de Moçambique

N

Bradt

0   200m
0   200yds

↓ Inhambane, Maputo

the post office and TDM, two blocks west of the ferry jetty. Chapas to Maputo cost US$11 and to Vilankulo US$5. Coming from further afield – Maputo, Beira or Chimoio – it is worth paying extra to catch the TIL (Leo) or Nagi bus, which is far more comfortable than a chapa. Boats between Inhambane and Maxixe run regularly from 05.30 to 22.30, a 20-minute crossing that costs US$0.15.

WHERE TO STAY Map, page 161

Campismo de Maxixe (7 rooms) 293 30351; m 84 201 0056. This is probably the best place to stay in Maxixe, set in large leafy grounds that occupy an attractive spot on the bay, though the proximity to the EN1 might make the evenings noisy. In addition to camping, wooden huts are available & there are also a couple of caravans for hire. *US$16 en-suite dbl; US$13 twin/caravan using shared showers; US$3 pp camping.* **$**

Complexo Oceano 293 30096; m 82 307 2600 or 84 256 6782. This run-down place opposite the bus station has affordability on its side, but is otherwise worth considering only if the alternatives are full. *US$8/12 sgl/dbl; US$16 en-suite dbl; US$22 en-suite dbl with AC.* **$**

Hotel Summit (15 rooms) m 84 499 9307. In the same building as the very much defunct Hotel Tania; if you can get past the intimidatingly derelict stairwell, the 2nd-floor rooms here are actually rather neat, with AC & en-suite hot showers. *US$30 twin or dbl.* **$**

Pousada do Maxixe (15 rooms) 293 30199; m 84 853 0670/030 8740. Situated right opposite the jetty, this is the pick of the town's limited guesthouse-style accommodation. The clean & pleasant en-suite dbls have hot water, AC & TV, & there are also more basic rooms using shared showers. The ground-floor restaurant serves the usual Mozambican staples. *US$28 en-suite dbl; US$20 twin with common showers.* **$**

WHERE TO EAT AND DRINK Map, page 161

Ian & Halin Pastelaria Av 25 de Septembro; 229 39977; m 84 953 6428 or 87 665 3262; ☺ 07.00–22.30 daily. This new pastelaria serves the typical fare for a Mozambican café with toasted sandwiches, salads, hamburgers, pizza, chicken & local food, alongside pastries & coffee. A lunch buffet is available on w/days for around US$4 while other menu items ring in at US$2–7. **$$**

Pastelaria Universale Av 7 de Abril; m 84 295 6047; ☺ 06.30–22.00 daily, later at w/ends. This clean & versatile pastelaria is the best eatery in town, serving everything from fresh pastries & sandwiches to curries & seafood. Coffee & alcoholic beverages are served, & it also sells pastries & imported confectionery. *Most items are in the range US$4–9 & pizzas are around US$8. The*

plate of the day is great value at US$6 & it arrives nice & quickly. **$$**

Stop Restaurant Right next to the jetty; 293 30025; ☺ 06.00–22.00 daily, which could be convenient if you're waiting for a bus. Overlooking the bay to Inhambane, this garden restaurant is probably the most scenic place to eat in Maxixe. The food is good, especially the fish & chicken, the waiters speak English & there's a swimming pool you can use for US$2. *Mains US$2–8.* **$$**

Tawakal Take-Away Av Patrice Lumumba; m 84 286 3333; ☺ b/fast, lunch & dinner daily. Right across from the chapa station, this Somali hangout is the place to go for a quick bite in between buses, with sandwiches, chicken, chapattis & pastries. *US$1.50–6.* **$**

BEACHES AROUND INHAMBANE

Inhambane town lies on the west side of a 25km peninsula whose northern and eastern shores are fringed by some of Mozambique's finest beaches. The best known and most developed of these, **Tofo** and its immediate neighbour **Tofinho**, lie due east of Inhambane along an adequate surfaced road, and are readily accessible on public transport. Today, Tofo vies with Vilankulo as the most important travel hub in Mozambique, attracting a steady stream of backpackers and overlanders all year round, boosted by an influx of families and angling enthusiasts during the South African school holidays. Other less-developed beaches, most relatively inaccessible without private transport (and in many cases 4x4), are **Barra**, to the north of Tofo, and the more southerly cluster of **Coconut Bay**, **Guinjata Bay** and **Paindane**. In addition to some lovely beaches, this stretch of coastline is known for its fine reefs and excellent diving opportunities, particularly at **Manta Reef**, which is often described as a 'manta ray cleaning centre' and regularly features in the 'Top 5' lists of African dive sites. Of special note, the ocean safaris run by most operators in Tofo offer a rare opportunity for non-divers to encounter and snorkel with such outsized marine creatures as manta rays, whale sharks, turtles and dolphins. Between July and the middle of November, divers and snorkellers might also see humpback whales, or hear their plaintive moans.

TOFO AND TOFINHO Probably the most developed resort in Mozambique, Tofo (often pronounced more like 'Tofu') Beach sprawls for several kilometres along the sliver of land that separates the Indian Ocean and the freshwater Lake Pembane. The hub of activity here is the small village of Tofo, a 500m triangle of sandy roads lined with an assortment of shops, lodges and eateries, leading down to a central market that overlooks the tantalising wide sandy beach known as Praia do Tofo. The south side of this beach is hemmed in by the elevated black coral rock peninsula on which lies Tofinho, a suburb of holiday homes and self-catering resorts that lies 20 minutes' walk from central Tofo by road but can be reached in a couple of minutes along the beach. By contrast, the sandy road that heads northward from the village towards Mango Beach Lodge (page 167) is flanked by the lake to the west and by tall vegetated dunes to the east, the latter forming an elongated crest above a fine white beach that is effectively an extension of Praia do Tofo.

The main attraction of Tofo is its **beach**, which is the sort of place people dream about, and the fishing, diving and surfing are as good as they get in the area. The small town centre boasts arguably the densest concentration of tourist facilities in Mozambique, ranging from dive and surf shops to budget lodges and seafood eateries, and the lively easy-going mood recalls such backpacker-friendly haunts as Nkhata Bay and Cape Maclear in neighbouring Malawi, frequently tantalising travellers (and updaters) into staying for far longer than they had planned. There is plenty of nightlife too, and this can be as raucous or as sedate as you wish – it's all a matter of picking the right place to hang out. Note, however, that Tofo can become uncomfortably busy, and undergoes a distinct change in atmosphere, during South African school holidays.

TOFO AND TOFINHO
For listings, see pages 166–9

⬭ **Where to stay**
1 A Streetcar Named Desire
2 Albatroz Lodge
3 Annastasea
4 Aquatico Beachside Casitas
5 Baia Sonâmbula
6 Casa Barry
7 Casa do Mar
8 Casa na Praia & Casa Azul
9 CFM Tofo Lodge
10 Fátima's Nest
11 Hotel Tofo Mar
12 Mozambeat Motel
13 Nordin's Lodge
14 Tofo Beach Cottages
15 Tofo Beach Cottage #7
16 Turtle Cove
17 Wuyani Pariango Beach Motel

Off map
   Mango Beach

✪ **Where to eat and drink**
   A Streetcar Named Desire (see 1)
18 Beach Barraca
19 Black & White
20 Branko's
   Casa Barry (see 6)
21 Casa de Comer
22 Dino's Beach Bar
23 Oyster Bar
24 The Time Will Tell Bar
25 Tofo Online
26 Tofo Tofo
   Turtle Cove (see 16)
27 What U Want

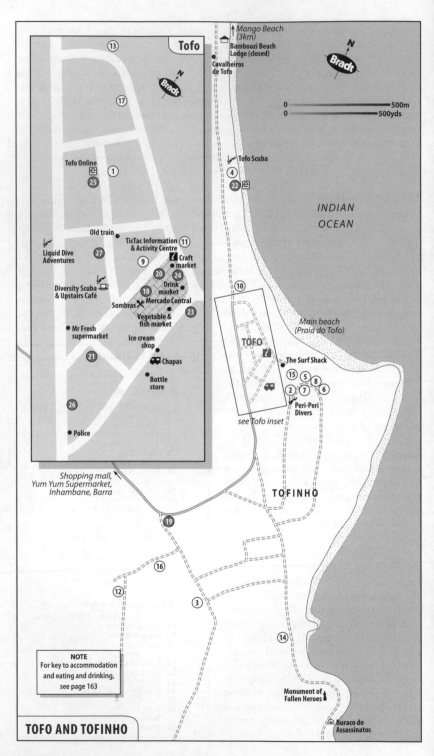

TOFO AND TOFINHO

Tofo

Mango Beach
(3km)
Bamboozi Beach
Lodge (closed)
Cavalheiros
de Tofo

Tofo Scuba

INDIAN
OCEAN

Tofo Online
25 1

Old train
Liquid Dive
Adventures
27
TicTac Information
& Activity Centre
11
9
Craft
market
20 24
Drink
market
Diversity Scuba
& Upstairs Café
18
Sombras
Mercado Central
23
Vegetable &
fish market
Mr Fresh
supermarket
Ice cream
shop
21
Chapas
Bottle
store
26
Police

Main beach
(Praia do Tofo)

TOFO
10
The Surf Shack
15 5
8
2 7 6
Peri-Peri
Divers

see Tofo inset

Shopping mall,
Yum Yum Supermarket,
Inhambane, Barra

TOFINHO

19

16
12
3

14

NOTE
For key to accommodation
and eating and drinking,
see page 163

Monument of
Fallen Heroes

Buraco do
Assassinatos

0   500m
0   500yds

164

GIANTS OF TOFO

The whale shark *Rhincodon typus* is the bulkiest living fish species, typically reaching a length of 12m (though the largest ever measured was 18.8m) and weighing up to 35 tonnes, with a lifespan comparable to a human or elephant. As one of only three filter-feeding shark species, this passive, slow-swimming giant is essentially harmless to humans (or anything else much larger than a goldfish), though there is a slight danger of snorkellers or divers being swiped by its powerful tail fins. In common with whales, this gigantic shark feeds mainly on plankton and other microscopic organisms, which are imbibed together with water through its wide mouth and trapped in a specially adapted gill apparatus when the water is expelled, though it will also occasionally eat small fish. Found throughout the tropics, the whale shark is listed as Endangered by the IUCN as of 2016, following a review by Dr Simon Pierce, Principal Scientist of the Tofo-based Marine Megafauna Foundation (MMF), which indicated a global decline of greater than 55% over the past ten years. The main threat to its survival is direct fishing (including by-catch). Easily distinguished by the combination of immense bulk, wide mouth and striped and spotted skin pattern, it is common in the waters around Tofo and Inhambane throughout the year.

Commoner still, and present in large numbers all year through, the manta is the world's largest ray, with some specimens weighing more than two tonnes and boasting a 'diskwidth' of 7.5m. The manta ray has been the subject of some taxonomic controversy, but recent research undertaken by the MMF's Dr Andrea Marshall recognises at least two species, with *Manta birostris* being larger and migratory, while *M. alfredi* is slightly smaller and non-migratory. A third species has recently been proposed. Although mantas have a flattened shape and long tails similar to stingrays, they cannot sting and are totally harmless to divers. Indeed, like so many other marine giants, they are filter feeders whose main diet is plankton and other tiny suspended organisms. An intriguing aspect of manta behaviour is the regular gathering of several individuals at cleaning stations (such as the one at Manta Reef), where wrasse and other reef fish feed on the parasites and dead tissue accumulated in their gills. They are also capable of breaching the surface and launching into the air, a rare but spectacular sight.

Tofo is home to the Marine Megafauna Foundation (MMF), which was created in 2009 to research and conserve Mozambique's sharks, rays, turtles, whales and dolphins. MMF biologists work with the marine tourism industry, conservation organisations, local communities and the Mozambican government to identify and solve problems faced by manta rays and whale sharks. Based at Casa Barry, it gives talks there at 18.00 every Monday, Wednesday and Friday (*cover charge US$2*). Visit w marinemegafauna.org for further details.

Getting there and away Tofo lies 22km east of Inhambane along a surfaced road that can be traversed in any vehicle, though some caution is advised with low clearance, and a couple of the roads within Tofinho might be tricky without a 4x4. Turn right when you reach the roundabout about 17km out of Inhambane.

As far as public transport is concerned, there are regular chapas to Tofo from Inhambane, leaving from the station in front of the Mercado Central. Coming from Maputo, there's a lot to be said for using the daily shuttle service from Fátima's Place and Base Backpackers to Tofo, which costs US$16 and leaves Maputo at about 05.00. The return trip to Maputo departs Tofo at 04.00 daily and can be booked at Fátima's Nest. It is also possible to get a direct chapa to Tofo, but these leave less frequently and, since they have to pass through Inhambane anyway, there is no real point in waiting around for one. Coming from the north, you'll need to get a chapa or bus to Maxixe, cross to Inhambane by ferry, and then pick up a chapa to Tofo. Some travellers coming from Maputo may also prefer to bus to Maxixe with PostBus or Nagi, which is more comfortable and faster than a chapa, and then cross to Inhambane by ferry.

Where to stay *Map, page 164, unless otherwise stated*

Upmarket

Baia Sonâmbula (6 rooms) m 82 309 7250 or 84 855 2739; e reservation@baiasonambula.com; w baiasonambula.com. Terraced into the hillside a few steps from the main beach, this superb guesthouse has whitewashed en-suite rooms, 3 of which have their own private verandas overlooking the ocean. The décor is warm & inviting, there's Wi-Fi, an honesty bar & indoor/outdoor lounge areas. Recommended. *US$70/87 garden sgl/dbl; US$113–190/160–234 sea-view sgl/dbl; all rates B&B.* **$$$$**

Casa Barry (25 units) ☎293 29007, +27 31 767 0111 (South Africa); e cbreceptiontofo@gmail.com; w casabarry.com. Situated in Tofinho right above Praia do Tofo, & only 2mins' walk from the village centre, Casa Barry has maintained an excellent reputation for several years now, & it is also the base for the Manta Ray & Whale Shark Research Centre, which gives 3 weekly talks here & occasionally takes on volunteers. Accommodation is in rustically attractive chalets with various sleeping capacities, but all have fan, nets & tiled en-suite hot shower. An excellent beachfront restaurant is attached. *US$72 reed & thatch dbl; US$87 brick dbl; US$250 4-bed chalet; US$296 6-bed chalet. Slight low-season discounts are offered.* **$$$**

Casa do Mar (9 rooms) ☎+27 82 455 7481/325 7729 (South Africa); m 84 662 1169/027 9048; e info@casadomar-gh.com; w casadomar-gh.com. Conspicuously lurking on the hill above Praia do Tofo, this South African-style lodge leaves much to be desired architecturally, but the en-suite rooms are spotless, with décor reminiscent of coastal New England. Views from here are fantastic, & there's a swimming pool as well. *US$120/140 dbl in low/high season.* **$$$$**

Casa na Praia & Casa Azul (8 rooms) m 82 821 5921/84; e reservas@casanapraiatofo.com; w casanapraiatofo.com. It would be tough to find a better location than these adjoining casas, perched front & centre on Praia do Tofo. Rooms in Casa Azul were renovated in 2016 & are casual & en suite, while Casa na Praia is considerably more upmarket, with flowing concrete rooms & shady private terraces & a new tree-house suite. *US$70–80 dbl in Casa Azul; US$120–130 dbl in Casa na Praia B&B.* **$$$$**

Hotel Tofo Mar (13 rooms) m 82 393 2545; e htofomar@gmail.com; w hoteltofomar.com. Renovated from the ground up & reopened in 2012, this beachfront Art Deco stalwart is once again among Tofo's smartest hotels. Done up in an angular, minimalist style, rooms are bright white & modern, though perhaps a bit under-appointed. Sea-facing rooms have either a balcony or floor-to-ceiling windows, de luxe rooms have flat-screen DSTV, & all have AC, but the standard rooms are rather spartan. The restaurant, known for sushi, has beautiful indoor/outdoor seating & is surprisingly affordable. Every Fri night Tofo starts the party here with weekly live music. *From US$85 standard dbl out of season to US$255 suite in season.* **$$$$**

Mid range

Annastasea (4 units) ☎+27 11 803 4185 (South Africa); m 82 719 4848 or 84 731 2027; e info@turtlecovetofo.com; w turtlecovetofo.com. This attractive property in Tofinho, about 10mins' walk from the beach, consists of 4 thatched dbl chalets & a common self-catering lapa offering a view to a nearby dune. Other self-catering properties available are the Beach House & Tree House, located on the Casa Barry road. *Aimed mainly at groups, it is rented out in its entirety for* around US$230 per night in high season, but the chalets may be rented out individually for around US$15 pp at other times of year. **$$$**

🏠 **Aquatico Beachside Casitas** (5 rooms) m 84 373 2533; e aquatico.lodge@outlook.com; w aquaticolodge.com. Sandwiched between Tofu Diving & Dino's Bar (page 169) about 1km north of Tofo village, these beachfront rooms each sleep 3 & have a kitchenette at the rear & a bathroom at the side. The location is superb & the accommodation very comfortable. *US$50 per unit.* **$$**

🏠 **Mango Beach** [map, page 155] m 84 262 3704; e bookings@mangobeachtofo. co.za; w mangobeachtofo.co.za. Located just over 3km north of Tofo on the beach road, this lodge has secluded beach access & comprises a dune-top restaurant & cabana-style accommodation with a bush setting behind the dune as opposed to the usual sea view. A self-catering kitchen is available & the ablution block has hot water. *US$70–100 cabana using shared ablutions, US$77–115 en-suite cabana, low- to high-season rates.* **$$$**

🏠 **CFM Tofo Lodge** (10 rooms) m 82 791 9259. Situated opposite Hotel Tofo Mar just 50m from the beach, this central lodge has pleasant tiled rooms with AC, nets & en-suite hot shower. *US$40 dbl.* **$$**

🏠 **Tofo Beach Cottages** (7 units) ☎+27 72 413 9698 (South Africa); m 84 026 2038/243 2096; e bookings@tofo.co.za; w tofo.co.za. This collection of 7 individualised cottages, sleeping up to 7 people each, is scattered all around Tofo & Tofinho. The cottages are very well equipped & cover some prime spots: Casa #7, for instance, enjoys a superb location right on Praia do Tofo, while several other units stand on the slopes leading down to sleepy Tofinho Beach (for photos & details of individual cottages, check their website). *Different cottages are rented out at US$46–62 per unit in low season, & up to US$150 in peak season, which makes them very attractive to small groups.* **$$$**

🏠 **Turtle Cove** (20 units) ☎+27 11 465 3427 (South Africa); m 82 719 4848 or 84 731 2027; e info@turtlecovetofo.com; w turtlecovetofo. com; see ad, page 152. This pleasant, reasonably priced, owner-managed lodge in Tofinho offers comfortable bungalow accommodation in leafy gardens about 15mins' walk from the beach. Combining West African architectural influences

with earthy décor, it is one of the few lodges in the area with any discernible character, & facilities inc swimming pool, a good restaurant & daily yoga classes in a special yoga room. All rooms are en suite with dbl or twin beds, net & fan, & family units & dorms are available. *US$40/50 sgl/dbl with a low-season discount of around 30%; from US$15 pp family rooms; US$10 pp dorm; US$7 pp camping.* **$$**

Budget

🏠 **Albatroz Lodge** ☎293 29005; m 82 255 8450; e restalbatroz@teledata.mz; w albatrozlodge.com. Situated in Tofinho near Casa Barry, this clifftop lodge overlooking Tofo Beach is one of the best-value set-ups in the area, offering accommodation in comfortable thatched & whitewashed chalets with kitchen, fan, nets & private balconies. There's also a restaurant & swimming pool attached. *US$70–135 for a 4–8 sleeper, depending on number of people & season.* **$$**

🏠 **Fátima's Nest** m 82 185 1575; e fatimasbackpackersmozambique@gmail.com; w mozambiquebackpackers.com; see ad, page 119. One of Tofo's longest-standing backpackers, this younger sister of Fátima's in Maputo (page 99) has an all-day party atmosphere, with music playing from early morning til late evening. It also has an attractive beachfront setting on the edge of the village centre, 500m from the chapa station. It offers a range of semi-tired-looking accommodation, from camping to en-suite chalets, & a restaurant serves decent meals, inc daily special at around US$5 & good vegetarian fare. *US$40/56/72/88 sgl/dbl/trpl/quad en suite; US$24/45/60/80 sgl/dbl/trpl/quad with shared bathroom; US$12 dorm; US$10 camping.* **$$$**

🏠 **Mozambeat Motel** (9 rooms, 1 dorm) m 84 422 3515/500 0383; e info@ mozambeatmotel.com; w mozambeatmotel. com. Opened in 2012, this backpackers in Tofinho has grabbed the backpacker zeitgeist by the horns & refocused it squarely on Tofinho. Funky & energetic, there's something going on most nights of the week, inc BBQs, film screenings, live music & fitness/dance classes. The music selection at the restaurant-bar is unrivalled, & the food is damn good too. Rooms are done up in a colourful favela-chic style, & all are kitted out with fans, nets & indoor/outdoor

BARRACO DOS ASSASSINATOS

Situated on the Tofinho headland about 2km south of Praia do Tofo, the Barraco dos Assassinatos (House of Murders) was the site of some of the most callous atrocities committed by the notorious Portuguese security police during the war for independence. The police would chain suspected dissidents and Frelimo members to the wall of this coral sea cave at low tide, and leave them to drown as the water rose or to be battered to death by waves. Today, the site is commemorated by the Tofinho Monument, or Monument of Fallen Heroes, a large unadorned obelisk topped by a small statue of a shackled arm. The base of the monument reputedly holds several human bones recovered from the cave, which is signposted a few metres further along the coast.

bathroom. The grounds are green & spacious, with a swimming pool & 2nd-floor terrace with views. Exactly what a backpackers should be. *US$33/38/45/51 sgl/dbl/trpl/quad cabin, add US$7 per night for optional AC; US$28/35/43/47 sgl/dbl/trpl/quad suite; US$11 dorm bed; US$11/16 sgl/dbl pre-pitched tent, US$6.50 own tent. Rates increase during high & peak season.* **$$**

🏠 **Nordin's Lodge** (6 rooms) m 82 312 4770/520 4777; e binos50@hotmail.com. This has a perfect location in a beachfront casuarina grove around the corner from Fátima's, but the accommodation – a row of rather gloomy chalets with fan, fridge, en-suite shower & balcony – doesn't quite match up, but is still decent value. *US$40–50 twin or dbl chalet depending on season; US$10 dorm.* **$$**

🏠 **Wuyani Pariango Beach Motel** (12 rooms, 5 dorms) m 84 712 8963; e pariangobeach@gmail.com; w pariangobeach.com. Opposite the beach &

just north of the central market, this newly renovated budget backpackers is a great low-key option with thatched A-frames, dorms & rondavels in a sandy compound. There are full kitchen facilities, lots of hammocks, lots of music, & couches for lounging near the bar. It's a friendly set-up & among the cheapest in town, & quickly becoming the go-to in-town backpacker spot. *US$40 en-suite dbl chalet; US$30 dbl tipi; US$24 twin casita; US$8 dorm bed; US$6 pp camping.* **$$**

Shoestring

🏠 **A Streetcar Named Desire** (6 rooms) m 84 107 3364; e johnintofo@gmail.com. Often referred to as John's place, the rooms are simple but clean with fan, & on the same central property as the eponymous rockstar-themed restaurant. The rooms are as good value as you'll get in Tofo, & there is also a 4-bed dorm. *US$12 dbl.* **$**

✗ Where to eat and drink *Map, page 164*

In addition to the places listed below, the restaurants at Fátima's Nest and Mozambeat's (page 167) are both worth a try – the former for its affordable plate of the day, and the latter for its weekly events list. Tofo Scuba, Diversity Scuba and Liquid Dive Adventures each has its own café serving up a range of breakfast and lunch items with coffee and teas. Diversity Scuba's **Upstairs Café** has the best cakes, pies and brownies in town. The restaurants in the market offer some of the best local eats, with **Sombras** being the current standout, though most seem to change ownership every couple of years.

✗ **A Streetcar Named Desire** m 84 107 3364; ⏱ 16.00–22.00 daily. The option of sitting outdoors or in the cosy bar, the best steaks in

town, a good vegetarian selection, tasty curries & reasonable prices make this place well worth a visit. *US$9–12 for meat dishes; US$6 for curries.* **$$$**

✕ Beach Barraca m 84 244 8919; ⏰ 06.30–20.00 daily exc Tue. This local favourite b/fast & lunch spot does fresh sandwiches, wraps, smoothies & juices. *US$2–7.* **$$**

✕ Black & White m 84 555 1415; ⏰ 10.00–23.00 daily, later at w/ends. This thatched bar on the main road in Tofinho does good local meals all day, & the party goes on till late at w/ends. They've got a couple of flat-screen TVs, pool table, & a good sound system too. *Around US$5.* **$**

✕ Branko's m 84 296 4305; ⏰ noon–late daily. A hot spot – quite literally – & a favourite among tourists & locals, offering up pizza or hot-rock-style beef, prawns, scallops, squid or tuna in a chill restaurant. *US$5–7 for pizza, US$3–8 hot rock.* **$$**

✕ Casa Barry (page 166) ⏰ b/fast, lunch & dinner daily. The restaurant at this lodge overlooking Praia do Tofo certainly has a great location, especially for catching sunsets, & many residents rate it the best in town. *The seafood & meat dishes are relatively pricey at around US$7–13 for a main course.* **$$$**

✕ Casa de Comer m 84 355 2163; ⏰ 08.30–23.00 daily. In the midst of a makeover during research, this restaurant has a contemporary feel, outdoor seating under a thatched roof, & an imaginative seafood-dominated menu that fuses French & Mozambican influences. *Most mains are in the US$6–10 range.* **$$$**

✕ Dino's Beach Bar m 84 719 0699; ⏰ 10.00–late daily, except Wed out of season. Situated between Fátima's & Tofo Scuba, Dino's is a long-standing favourite for sundowners, not least for its superb beachfront location. It's a reliable party spot too, with live music & DJs at w/ends. There's also paid Wi-Fi. *Seafood, meat dishes & pizzas are in the US$4–10 range.* **$$$**

✕ Oyster Bar m 84 261 1706; ⏰ 10.30–22.30 daily. Directly opposite the market & main praia, this is a popular spot for sundowners, with outdoor seating positioned to catch the sea breeze, & it serves a varied selection of local food, seafood & meat, as well as cheaper snacks. *US$4–9 range.* **$$**

✕ The Time Will Tell Bar m 84 505 1214; ⏰ 15.00–late daily. Pumping out the music nightly, this local bar inside the market offers piri-piri infused tipo-tinto to prime patrons before hitting the dance floor. *Bar snacks & braai beef, chicken & fish are available for US$2–5.* **$**

🖵 Tofo Online m 84 719 0702; ⏰ 09.00–18.00 daily exc Tue. This internet café with computers & paid Wi-Fi offers a range of snacks, sandwiches, smoothies & milkshakes for US$2–4. **$**

✕ Tofo Tofo m 84 467 0367; ⏰ 11.00–22.00 daily except Mon. On the main road into town, this half-restaurant, half-shop is a good place to try local specialities such as matapa, & they also do a nice variety of grills & seafood curries. *US$4–8.* **$$**

✕ Turtle Cove (page 167; see also ad, page 152) ⏰ b/fast, lunch & dinner daily. Owned by a qualified chef, this lodge offers the usual Mozambican seafood dishes, along with a more innovative menu of daily specials, often with Thai or other Asian influences. Vegetarians are catered for, & it hosts regular sushi evenings. *US$6–10.* **$$$**

✕ What U Want m 84 929 6936; ⏰ noon–22.30 Tue–Sun; 🇫 whatuwant22. This relaxed outdoor café is the place to go for pizza, with nearly 20 varieties available. It also serves Italian-inspired salads, pasta & good coffee. There's occasional live music & a good selection of wine as well. *US$5–8.* **$$**

Shopping

Mercado Central Opposite Praia do Tofo, this is one of the best places for craft shopping in the country, with numerous stalls selling all manner of paintings, wood & stone carvings, batiks & other handicrafts. There is also a good booze section (huge choice of wine & spirits) & plenty of fresh produce in the market right next door, where local fishermen gather to sell fresh fish, calamari, prawns & other seafood to self-caterers.

Mr. Fresh Located across from Liquid Dive Adventures, this has a limited stock of dry & frozen goods but covers the basics.

Shopping mall The mall on the south side of the Inhambane road 4km out of Tofo has a couple of shops of interest. The anonymous supermarket here stocks a more varied selection of goods, many imported from South Africa, than anywhere else in town. There is also a boutique here called Mozkito, specialising in ethnic-style clothes.

Yum Yum Supermarket Located 8km from Tofo, this is the best-stocked grocer in the area, selling dry goods, meats, cheeses, fresh produce & products from its on-site bakery.

Other practicalities

Banks There is no bank in Tofo itself, but there is a BCI ATM that accepts Visa and MasterCard at the shopping mall 4km from town, and of course plenty of banks and ATMs in Inhambane itself.

Fuel The only filling station this side of Inhambane is the Petromoc in the same mall as BCI.

Internet There are two internet cafés in the village, both run by **Tofo Online**. Their primary location (⊕ *09.00–18.00 daily exc Tue*) is opposite A Streetcar Named Desire (page 168), and they also have a branch (⊕ *10.00–18.00 daily exc Wed*) up the road at Dino's Beach Bar (page 169).

Marine talks The researchers based at Casa Barry hold talks in the Big Screen Room there three times a week, starting at 18.00, with a cover charge of US$2. The talks cover manta rays (Monday), whale sharks (Wednesday) and general marine life (Friday).

What to see and do It wouldn't be difficult to spend a few days at Tofo and do very little that qualified as an organised activity. The beaches that run north and south from Praia do Tofo are little short of idyllic, whether you fancy swimming, sunbathing, surfing or a long seaside walk, and the village itself is a very relaxed place to hang out. For more active travellers with a bit of spare cash, however, Tofo is renowned for its diving opportunities and 'ocean safaris', while other activities include horseback trips along the beach, kayak safaris, surfing and big-game fishing. You can also visit the TicTac Information and Activity Centre in the market (w *tofoactivitycentre.com*).

Marine activities Compared with most other diving and snorkelling sites in Mozambique, Tofo isn't so much about masses of colourful reef-dwellers as a pair of gargantuan plankton-eaters, namely the manta ray and whale shark (box, page 165). These two immense but harmless fish are especially common in the waters off Tofo, and are likely to be seen on most **dives**, though whale sharks are mostly summer visitors and commonest from November to April. The top diving site in the vicinity, Manta Reef (24–28m) lies a short distance offshore some 15km south of Tofo and, though reliably good for mantas, it also usually yields sightings of smaller rays and sharks, moray eels and barracudas, along with myriad smaller reef fish. Other excellent diving sites include Oasis Reef, which lies to the north of Tofo about 10km out at sea, and the relatively shallow Crocodile Rock (named for the crocodile fish, not the reptile) and Praia do Rocha (seasonally very good for whale sharks). Single dives start at around US$40 per person, with further dives getting progressively cheaper, and courses are also offered by most operators.

For non-divers, the most alluring activity at Tofo, offered by at least three operators, is one of the **ocean safaris** that leave daily at around 10.30. These safaris run on semi-inflatable boats that launch from Praia do Tofo and scour the surrounding waters for about 2 hours in search of large marine creatures such as manta rays, whale sharks, dolphins and turtles. The odds of seeing at least one or two of these marine giants are excellent, and all participants are issued with snorkelling masks and fins so they can jump in alongside them – an utterly thrilling experience. From June until late October, humpback whales visit the area in large numbers, and they are frequently seen on ocean safaris, though it isn't permitted to snorkel alongside them. Most companies charge around US$40 per person for ocean safaris.

The following operators all offer ocean safaris, and most can also offer dives, game-fishing excursions and other activities:

Diversity Scuba 293 29002; m 84 968 2169; e info@diversityscuba.com; w diversityscuba.com. Based in the heart of Tofo, next to What U Want. Offering a range of dive options, scuba courses, ocean safaris as well as local tours, fat-bike & surfboard rentals.

Liquid Dive Adventures m 84 613 0316/827 6026; e info@liquiddiveadventures.com; w liquiddiveadventures.com. Based on the main road into town, this offers the usual range of diving courses, as well as sea-kayaking trips to a nearby island, & whale watching (in season). They have surf & body boards for hire.

Peri-Peri Divers m 84 026 3373 or 82 550 5661; e nick@peri-peridivers.com or steve@peri-peridivers.com; w peri-peridivers.com. Situated in Tofinho next to Albatroz Lodge.

Tofo Scuba 293 29030; m 82 826 0140 or 84 752 5141; e info@tofoscuba.co.za; w tofoscuba.com. Based a few steps up the road from Dino's Bar. They are also planning to offer accommodation at Tilak Lodge during the lifespan of this edition.

Horseriding Ninety-minute horseback safaris through the coconut groves and beaches are offered by **Cavalheiros do Tofo** (m *82 308 0300*; e *gvhorst@gmx. net*) for around US$24 per person. The stables are about 1.5km from central Tofo opposite Bamboozi Beach Lodge (closed), but they will pick up clients in the village by arrangement.

Surfing and windsurfing Located on the main beach, **The Surf Shack** (m *84 364 9517*; e *info@thesurfshacktofo.com*; w *thesurfshacktofo.com*) offers lessons, rentals, clothing and repairs. **Tofo Watersports** (m *84 433 9531*; e *surfwatersports@yahoo.co.uk*), located at Tofo Scuba, offers kitesurfing and surfing lessons, as well as rental gear.

BARRA BEACH To the north of Tofo, Barra lies at the northern tip of the peninsula, where it is guarded by the prominent Farol de Barra (Barra Lighthouse). Though rather remote, the site is flanked by attractive beaches in both directions, and the area also protects some extensive areas of mangroves. Few independent travellers make it up here, however, as most of the accommodation is strongly geared towards South African self-caterers, though there are a few exceptions, notably Blue Footprints Eco Lodge and Flamingo Bay (both page 172), which rank among the most alluring upmarket retreats in this part of Mozambique, while the campsite at White Sands is popular among overlanders. Marine activities on offer here are very similar to Tofo, with Barra Reef Dive at Neptune's Lodge (page 172) being the main operator in the area. Deep-sea fishing charters can be arranged through **Barra Ocean Adventures** (m *82 197 6651*; e *blurain000@gmail.com*; *barraoceanadventures*).

Getting there and away Coming from Inhambane, you need to follow the road to Tofo for 17km, but instead of turning right at the roundabout, just keep going straight. This road was once passable by 4x4 only, but today you can easily get as far

9

as Barra Lodge or Flamingo Bay in a sturdy saloon car. Note, however, that the 2km turn-off to Farol de Barra is very sandy and a 4x4 is essential.

Where to stay   *Map, page 155*
Exclusive/luxury

Flamingo Bay Water Lodge
(20 rooms) m 82 320 6070 or 84 244 1691;
e flamingoreception@barraresorts.com or info@
barraresorts.com; w barraresorts.com. Set on the
northwest of the peninsula, this unique stilted
lodge is a popular honeymoon destination, and
though it temporarily closed due to fire damage,
it should reopen within the lifespan of this
edition. The design gets full marks for originality.
It is reached via a long boardwalk through the
mangroves, & a similar construction links the main
building to the rooms, which stand in a stilted arc
in a calm, clear, turquoise lagoon which usually
fills with flamingos over Apr/May. The comfortable
rooms all have king-size or twin beds, minibar,
tea/coffee, AC, en-suite hot shower & private
balcony facing the open sea. The main building
inc swimming pool, dining room, well-stocked
gift shop & spa. Dives & other activities can be
arranged. The stuff of desert-island fantasies.
*Expect prices to be around US$180/321 sgl/dbl
DB&B, rising to US$217/362 in the high season,
though it's worth checking the website for specials
upon reopening.* **$$$$**

Blue Footprints Eco Lodge   (5 rooms)
m 84 890 0507; e info@bluefootprints.com;
w bluefootprints.com. Nestled among the dunes, the
en-suite villas at this luxurious off-the-grid hideaway
all have a stunning sea view & come with indoor &
outdoor showers, twin or king-size beds with net,
& deck with hammock & loungers. The main lodge
has a pool & the restaurant offers seasonally crafted
3-course dinners & a light lunch menu. Activities
& excursions to Barra or Tofo can be arranged, or
guests can take a 7km stroll along the beach to Tofo.
US$188/208 pp low/high season, DB&B. **$$$$**

Upmarket

Barra Beach Club   (12 units) ☎293 56076;
e gm@barrabeachclub.co.za; w barrabeachclub.
co.za. A sister to Casa do Capitão in Inhambane,
this offers smart & comfortable en-suite
accommodation with AC, DSTV & Wi-Fi. Although
none of the rooms has a beach view, the green
gardens, pool, restaurant & artfully appointed
lodge compensate. *Starting at US$230/330 sgl/dbl
lodge suite, US$250/350 sgl/dbl villa, US$ 430 dbl,
DB&B.* **$$$$$**

Mid range

Neptune's Lodge & Beach Bar   (7 units)
m 84 054 9311; e neptuneslodge@yahoo.com;
w neptunes-lodge.com. Home to Barra Reef
Divers, this beachside lodge has 4 AC family casitas
with king or twin beds with nets, kitchen & rooftop
braai area, as well as 2 en-suite beach suites & a
honeymoon chalet. Surfing, kayaking, quad bike,
snorkelling & boat trips can be arranged, & the
restaurant serves up seafood, burgers, pizza & local
mains for around US$8. *Starting at US$92 2- to
5-sleeper casita, US$30/60 sgl/dbl beach suite, B&B,
US$80 dbl honeymoon suite, B&B.* **$$$**

Camping

White Sands   m 84 409 2174;
e whitesandsmoz@gmail.com; w whitesands-
mozambique.co.za. Located on the west end of the
peninsula at the opening of Inhambane Bay & the
sea, this campsite offers open or sheltered camping
under barracas & self-catering accommodation
in 6- to 8-sleeper chalets/houses. There is a pool,
restaurant & bar, & boat activities can be arranged.
*Starting at US$8 pp camping (use of barraca extra
US$9), US$65–115 6- to 8-sleeper chalet/houses in
low season.* **$$**

Where to eat and drink   *Map, page 155*
Chill Bar   m 84 283 6933; ⏱ 10.00–20.00
Tue–Sun out of season, 09.00–late daily in season.
A popular place to toss a few back & socialise, this
bar-restaurant offers burgers, wraps, chicken, pizza
& seafood. *US$5–9.* **$$**

Green Turtle   m 82 026 0580; ⏱ 08.00–
20.00 Mon–Sat, 09.00–20.00 Sun. Owned by a
French couple, this is easily one of the finest dining
experiences around.The daily menu of expertly
crafted Afro-Euro fusion cuisine uses fresh local
ingredients. Reservations highly recommended.
Mains US$8–14. **$$$**

COCONUT BAY, GUINJATA AND PAINDANE Strung along the east shore of the peninsula 15–25km south of Tofo, this trio of beaches is much more quiet and secluded out of season than Tofo or Barra, making it the place to head for if you really want to get away from it all but don't want to make the arduous slog up to the coastal areas of northern Mozambique. However, since most of the resorts here cater almost exclusively to the South African market, it can be pretty hectic during school holidays across the border, and prices rocket as a result. Activities and attractions are similar to those in Barra and Tofo (indeed, these are the closest mainland resorts to the legendary Manta Reef; page 163), but access is difficult if you don't have private transport (ideally 4x4) and there is no equivalent to Tofo village's cluster of amenities when it comes to eating, drinking or chilling out. For those who do make it, **Taurus Supermarket** offers a decent selection of items to self-caterers. Those looking to dive should contact **Guinjata Dive Centre** (w *guinjata.co.za*), which also has accommodation.

Getting there and away These resorts all lie southeast of Inhambane and the junction to them is signposted about 10km south of the town centre along the feeder road back to the **EN1**. The road is unsurfaced and sandy in patches, but it should be possible to drive the 15km from the junction to Coconut Bay in a saloon car. The 12km road south of here to Guinjata and Paindane is best tackled in a 4x4. There is infrequent public transport along this road, but most resorts can provide a transfer from Inhambane by prior arrangement.

Where to stay, eat and drink *Map, page 155*
Aside from the options listed below, there is a large selection of self-catering accommodation ranging from the luxurious **Daghatane Estate** (w *daghatane. com*) to the mom-'n'-pop style **Break Away Chalets** (m *84 923 8181*; e *johncon@ vodacom.co.za*). Other popular picks near Paindane are **Blue Moon Resort** (m *84 746 9757*; e *bluemoonmoz@gmail.com*) and **Esperanza Lodge** (w *esperanzalodge. co.za*). A bit further north there is **Coconut Bay Beach Resort** (m *84 461 6905*; e *coconutbaymx@gmail.com*). All of the aforementioned lodges can arrange meals or have a restaurant for guests.

🏠 **Cumbini Resort** ☎+27 83 226 0932 (South Africa); m 84 292 3390/803 0658; e cumbinimoz@yahoo.com; w cumbiniresort. com. Tucked into the dunes above Guinjata Bay, this resort has a variety of thatched beachfront chalets with 2–4 bedrooms & comes equipped with deep freeze, fridge, stove, bedding, hot water & fully equipped kitchen. There is a sports bar with satellite TV, a beach restaurant serving good seafood dishes & pizzas, & they can arrange the usual aquatic activities. *From US$46 for a 2-bedroom, 4-person chalet out of season to US$203 for a 4-bedroom chalet in season. Sheltered barracas for camping cost US$21 plus US$9 pp in season.* **$$**
🏠 **Jeff's Resort** ☎+27 13 932 1263 (South Africa); m +27 83 254 4862 (South Africa) or 84 735 3117; e jeffsmoz@mweb.co.za; w jeffsmoz. com. Sited on a palm-lined dune about 30km

south of Inhambane, Jeff's offers a range of accommodation from barracas to an 8-bed villa. Fishing, diving, snorkelling & swimming are all available, plus day trips to Inhambane. *From US$72 for a 4-bed unit out of season to US$280 for an 8-bed villa in season.* **$$**
🏠 **Paindane Beach Resort** (25 units) ☎293 56310; m +27 82 569 3436 (South Africa); e paindane.sa@mweb.co.za; w paindane. com. Sited about 20km south of Inhambane, Paindane stands on a magnificent vegetated dune overlooking an 800m-long reef that not only provides shelter for swimmers, but also offers superb offshore snorkelling. Aiming mainly at self-caterers, accommodation is in well-equipped chalets with 1–4 bedrooms. There is also a campsite & an on-site dive centre offering the usual activities. *From US$92 1-bedroom, 4-sleeper;*

US$149 for a 2-bedroom, 6-sleeper chalet to US$297 for a 4-bedroom 12-sleeper chalet in season; from US$11 pp camping. **$$**

🏠 **Seabound Charters Bed & Breakfast**
(7 rooms) **m** 84 244 2916/493 2099; **e** info@ seabound.co.za; **w** seabound.co.za. Located on the beach, this guesthouse offers a pool, bar,

restaurant & views of Guinjata Bay. The tastefully & individually decorated en-suite rooms come with net & fan. There is a self-catering kitchen, as well as a large communal space. The hosts offer dinner on request & fishing charters. *Prices range from US$62–100 pp depending on season.* **$$$**

NORTH OF INHAMBANE

A sprinkling of small, low-key resorts runs along the coast between Inhambane and Vilankulo, all of them offering a similar range of activities and attractions to Tofo, but with a more isolated location and a less sociable vibe. First up is the isolated peninsula of **Ponta da Linga Linga**, site of a village that more or less faces Inhambane but lies on the northern side of the same bay. Further north, 65km from Maxixe near the town of **Massinga**, is the site of the highly regarded Massinga Beach Lodge. About 100km north of Maxixe, **Morrungulo** is renowned for the diving and snorkelling at Zambia Reef, with its outstanding soft and hard corals. Another 50km north of this is **Pomene**, site of the latest and most remote of the three lodges operated by Barra Resorts.

GETTING THERE AND AROUND Linga Linga is accessible by road via the EN1 with a 4x4 only, but occasional ferries make the short crossing there from Inhambane, and it is also possible to catch a dhow from Morrumbene on the **EN1** 30km north of Maxixe. To get to Morrungulo in a private vehicle, you must follow the EN1 70km north of Maxixe to Massinga, then stick on the EN1 north for another 7km until you reach the signposted junction, from where it is 13km along a very sandy road that sometimes necessitates a 4x4. The turn-off for Pomene is another 5km or so past the one for Morrungulo, and from there it is a 50km drive along a sandy track that requires a 4x4.

 WHERE TO STAY *Map, page 155*
The accommodation options below are listed in geographical order, running from south to north.

🏠 **Castelo do Mar** (21 rooms) Ponta da Linga Linga; **📞** +27 31 563 1016 (South Africa); **m** 84 586 3579; **e** gm@castelodomar.co.za; **w** castelodomar.co.za. This upmarket all-inclusive villa comprises 6 en-suite bedrooms in the main building, 14 beachfront suites, & 1 honeymoon suite with private jacuzzi. All rooms come with AC, library, pool table, free non-motorised sports (exc fishing gear rentals), & blissfully isolated location. Activities & tours such as ocean safaris, mangrove tours, deep-sea fishing, waterskiing & Pansy Island tours can be arranged. There's also a spa. *Starting at US$140–200 pp low–high season, FB.* **$$$$**

⋏ **Funky Monkeys** Ponta da Linga Linga. This back-to-basics campsite can provide food. **$**

🏠 **Travessia Beach Lodge** (4 rooms) District de Morrumbene; **m** 84 049 2942; **e** julie@ travessialodge.com; **w** travessialodge.com. Located about 44km north of Maxixe on the EN1 & another 6km down a sandy track, this remote & exclusive lodge offers the pleasures of paradise alongside simple creature comforts (minus the TV!). The en-suite solar-powered rooms have queen, king or twin beds, nets, outdoor showers & large decks with hammock & sea view. Aquatic activities & day trips to Inhambane can be arranged – assuming you can peel yourself away from the miles of secluded beach! *US$165/250 sgl/dbl chalet, US$325 4-person family chalet, low season, US$215/330 sgl/dbl chalet, US$495 4-person family chalet, high season, all rates FB.* **$$$$**

⌂ Massinga Beach Lodge (32 units)
☏+27 11 796 5029 (South Africa); m 84 789 5444; e reservations@massingabeach.co.za; w massingabeach.co.za. With the area's only 'barefoot luxury' accommodation, this isolated honeymoon-ready retreat is located on a 4x4-only road, 14km off the EN1. The free-standing cottages slung along the beach have all the fineries & amenities, & de luxe rooms feature wide balconies with plunge pools overlooking the ocean. *Starting at US$300/460 suite; US$360/560 sgl/dbl de luxe; all rates FB.* **$$$$**

⌂ Ponta Morrungulo Beach Resort
(15 units) Morrungulo; ☏293 70101; m 84 246 7533; e morrungulo.resort@gmail.com; w morrungulo.com. Camping facilities, a few smart self-catering chalets, private villa & self-catering casitas. Facilities inc organised scuba diving & deep-sea fishing excursions, & you can also rent snorkelling equipment. *From US$154 4-sleeper villa; US$100 4-sleeper self-catering beachfront chalets; US$85 4-sleeper casita; US$10 pp camping. Rates higher in season.* **$$**

⌂ Pomene Lodge Pomene; m 84 027 9506; e pomene@barraresorts.com; w barraresorts.com. Part of the Barra Group, this isolated lodge is renowned for its lovely setting, & its choice of DB&B accommodation in chalets or self-catering in fishermen's cottages. Diving & other marine activities are offered in-house. *US$92/155 sgl/dbl chalet low season; from US$115 for a 4-bed unit out of season to US$262 for an 8-bed unit in season; US$10/14 pp camping low/high season.* **$$$$**

Inhambane and Surrounds   NORTH OF INHAMBANE

9

UPDATES WEBSITE

Go to w bradtupdates.com/mozambique for the latest on-the-ground travel news, trip reports and factual updates. Keep up to date with the latest posts by following Philip on Twitter (*@philipbriggs*) and via Facebook (**f** *pb.travel.updates*). And, if you have any comments, queries, grumbles, insights, news or other feedback, you're invited to post them directly on the website, or to email them to Philip (e *philip.briggs@bradtguides.com*) for inclusion.

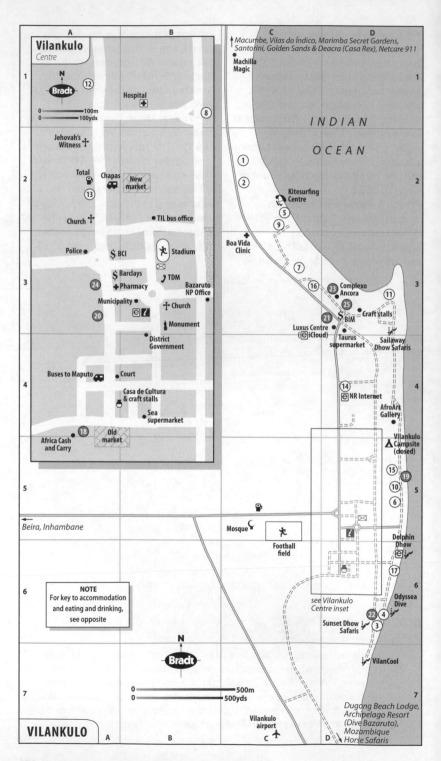

Vilankulo
Centre

A

N
Bradt ⑫

0 ———— 100m
0 ———— 100yds

Jehovah's
Witness ✝

Total ⛽
Chapas 🚐
⑬

Church ✝

Police ●
$ BCI
$ Barclays
⊕ Pharmacy
②④
Municipality ●
⑳ ℮ 🛈
District
Government ●

Buses to Maputo 🚐 ● Court

Casa de Cultura
& craft stalls 🏛
Sea
supermarket ●

⑱
Africa Cash
and Carry ● Old
market

B

Hospital ⊞

⑧

New market

● TIL bus office

🏃 Stadium

✉ TDM
♪
Bazaruto
NP Office ●

✝ Church

🚹 Monument

Beira, Inhambane ←

Mosque ☪

🏃
Football
field

NOTE
For key to accommodation
and eating and drinking,
see opposite

N
Bradt

0 ———— 500m
0 ———— 500yds

VILANKULO

Vilankulo
airport ✈

C **D**

↑ *Macumbe, Vilas do Índico, Marimba Secret Gardens,*
Santorini, Golden Sands & Deacra (Casa Rex), Netcare 911

● Machilla
Magic

INDIAN

OCEAN

①
②
🏄 Kitesurfing
Centre
⑤
⑨

Boa Vida ✝
Clinic

⑦

⑯ ㉓ Complexo
Ancora
㉕
● Craft stalls
⑪
$ BIM
②①
Luxus Centre ● Taurus
℮ iCloud supermarket
🚤
Sailaway
Dhow Safaris

⑭
℮ NR Internet

AfroArt
Gallery ●
● Vilankulo
⚑ Campsite
(closed)
⑮
⑩ ⑲
⑥

✉
🛈
Dolphin ●
Dhow
℮ 🚤
⑰

see Vilankulo
Centre inset

Odyssea ●
Dive
㉒ ④
Sunset Dhow 🚤 ③
Safaris

🚤 VilanCool

Dugong Beach Lodge,
Archipelago Resort
(Dive Bazaruto),
Mozambique
Horse Safaris

A **B** **C** **D**

10

Vilankulo, Inhassoro and Bazaruto National Park

Vying with the Inhambane area as the most important centre of coastal tourism in Mozambique, the twin mainland towns of Vilankulo and Inhassoro are also gateways to the spectacular Bazaruto National Park. The country's only dedicated marine park, gazetted back in 1971, it protects the offshore Bazaruto Archipelago, whose unspoilt reefs rank among the most exciting diving and snorkelling sites on Africa's Indian Ocean coastline.

The three main tourist bases in the area offer access to similar sights and activities, but each targets a very different market. Within Bazaruto National Park there are only three fully functioning beach lodges (one is closed for renovation and another is in the works), which range from the expensive and luxurious to the even-more-expensive and even-more-luxurious, and essentially attract an international fly-in safari clientele. By contrast, low-key Inhassoro is an increasingly popular base for family holidays (in particular with Zimbabweans), whereas cosmopolitan Vilankulo has pretty much cornered the backpacker and independent travel market, though it too has some genuinely upmarket options and several more family-oriented resorts. Wherever you base yourself, however, the area offers some of the best facilities anywhere in Mozambique, and the diving and snorkelling are truly unforgettable.

VILANKULO

The small but sprawling and fast-growing town of Vilankulo, supporting a population of around 50,000 and site of an increasingly important international airport, vies with the more southerly resort of Tofo as the most important tourist focal point in Mozambique. It is also one of the few Mozambican coastal

VILANKULO
For listings, see pages 179–83

Where to stay

1 Aguia Negra...C2
2 Bahia Mar Club.......................................C2
3 Baobab Beach Backpackers.............D6
4 Casa Babi...D6
5 Casa Cabana Beach..............................C2
6 Casa Jules & Zombie Cucumber.....D5
7 Casa Rex..C3
8 Complexo Alemanha/
   Vilankulo Backpackers....................B1
9 Complexo Samara...............................C2
10 Complexo Turístico Josef é Tina.....D5
11 Dona Ana..D3
12 Hotel Bernna...A1
13 Hotel Central...A2
14 Motel Dércia..D4
15 Palmeiras Lodge...................................D5
16 Pescador...C3
17 Varanda...D6

Off map
    Archipelago Resort..............................D7
    Dugong Beach Lodge.........................D7
    Marimba Secret Gardens...................C1
    Santorini...C1
    Vilas do Índico......................................C1

Where to eat and drink

18 Afro Bar.. A4
19 Bar Tropical...D5
20 Café Mozambicano.............................A3
    Casa Rex...(see 7)
    The Casbah.....................................(see 5)
21 Kilimanjaro Café...................................D3
22 Leopoldina's Food...............................D6
23 New York Pizza......................................D3
    Restaurant Em Cima...................(see 8)
24 Restaurante Ti-Zé................................ A3
    Samara...(see 9)
25 Upper Deck Pub & Grill.....................D3
    Varanda...(see 17)

resorts to cater to the full spectrum of tourists, from backpackers and overlanders to fly-in holidaymakers and parties of anglers and diving enthusiasts from across the border, with the latter dominating the scene during South African school holidays. Consequently, the town has as diverse a range of accommodation, restaurants and other tourist facilities as you'll find in the country, many of which were flattened by Hurricane Favio in 2007, though you'd scarcely notice it today.

Vilankulo is a pleasant place simply to hang out for a few days to enjoy the sunshine and beaches. Of particular interest is the beach running east of the town centre, south past Baobab Beach Backpackers, a hive of activity when the fishing boats come ashore in the early morning or late afternoon. There are lots of shorebirds here, too, particularly along the mangroves, which often harbour plentiful little egrets along with various gulls, terns, plovers and other waders. There shouldn't be a problem with theft here so long as you carry your possessions with you, but don't leave valuables on the beach while you swim.

The main local attraction, however, is the nearby Bazaruto Archipelago, whose reefs offer some of the finest snorkelling and diving anywhere in southern Mozambique, and can be visited as a day trip out of Vilankulo by those who cannot afford the ultra-expensive lodges that stud the actual islands.

The town is named after the late chief Gamala Vilankulo Mukoke, whose surname is still borne by many people living in the area. During colonial times the town was known as Vilanculos – as the district of which its capital is still called – but the traditional spelling of Vilankulo was restored shortly after independence.

GETTING THERE AND AWAY

By air LAM (w *flylam.co.za*) flies daily from Maputo and Inhambane to Vilankulo International Airport, about 5km from the town centre, and **Airlink** (w *flyairlink. com*) flies to Johannesburg daily. In addition, **CR Aviation** (w *craviation.co.mz*) operates at least one daily flight connecting Vilankulo to the various islands of the Bazaruto Archipelago.

By car Coming by road from the south, as most people do, Vilankulo lies 20km east of the **EN1** along a good surfaced road. The signposted turn-off at Pambora junction is roughly 220km north of Maxixe, but watch for a BP garage to your left – shortly afterwards you'll reach a large intersection around which lies a cluster of small shops. The drive from Maxixe usually takes up to 3 hours, while those heading north to Beira should expect it to take around 7–8 hours.

By bus/chapa Most buses and chapas leave in the early morning (check the afternoon before for current departure times) from near the new market [176 A2]. These include at least one daily bus to/from Maputo with **TIL (Leo) Bus** (m *84 792 3894*), leaving at around 03.00, costing around US$19 and taking up to 10 hours, and a bus to Beira leaving at around 04.30 and costing US$12. You can buy tickets for the TIL (Leo) Bus the previous afternoon at their office [176 B2] near the *correios*. Regular chapas to Maxixe (from where you can catch a ferry to Inhambane) cost around US$5, take 4 hours, and run throughout the day, as do chapas to Inhassoro (*US$2; 1hr*). The walk between the chapa station and virtually all of the town's accommodation options is long, and dark in the early morning, so you might want to enquire about the taxi services listed in the following section.

CAR HIRE Internationally accredited **Europcar** (m *84 300 2410*; w *europcar.com*) has a branch at the airport and rents sedans and 4x4s for US$70–115 per day.

PERSONAL SAFETY Although Vilankulo is as safe as anywhere in Africa in the daytime, it does have a reputation for occasional assaults on tourists walking between the market and one of the lodges at night. Generally, it would be unwise to walk along the unlit roads or the Avenida Marginal after dark, particularly if you are alone. Some of the restaurants will arrange free transport back to your lodging if you ask. Failing that, try the reliable 24-hour taxi services operated by **Junior** (m *82 462 4700*) or **Eusebio** (m *82 681 3383*). If you're staying at one of the upmarket hotels to the north, then ask at reception – they may have a bus running in your direction.

WHERE TO STAY
Exclusive/luxury
🏠 **Bahia Mar Club** [176 C2] (5 units)
📞293 82391; m 84 275 4389; e bookings@ bahiamarclub.com; w bahiamarclub.com. Opened in 2013, Bahia Mar quickly became the talk of the town thanks to its smart & luxurious accommodation in sea-view & self-catering beach suites. Facilities inc gym, spa, business centre, pool, restaurant & bar. Sea-view suites have AC, bed, net & private varanda, while beach suites have a kitchenette, sitting area with TV, plunge pool, braal & veranda. *US$155/230 sgl/dbl sea-view B&B; US$265/385 sgl/dbl self-catering beach suite; US$750 family suite sleeping 3–6.* **$$$$**
🏠 **Casa Rex** [176 C3] (15 rooms) 📞293 82048; m 82 917 7720 or 84 890 4628; e reservations@ casmaratrading.com; w solresortsonline.com/ casa-rex. Shady well-tended gardens set around a swimming pool & a clifftop location offering a lovely view over the bay are features of this slick, spacious & stylish small lodge about 1km northwest of the town centre. There's also an appealing combination of contemporary & vintage colonial furniture, a footpath leading directly to the beach, an excellent seafood restaurant & good amenities inc Wi-Fi. This lodge aims for the same market as its counterparts on the islands, with a comparable standard of accommodation & range of activities, but is cheaper & has the advantage (or disadvantage, depending on your point of view) of being closer to town. The premier courtyard suites come with king-size beds, walk-in nets, sofa, great sea views, en-suite bathroom with tub, AC & plenty of wood and muted pastel colours. Other rooms are similar but smaller, with twin or dbl bed. For a more remote self-catering experience with all of the Casa Rex charm, ask about Golden Sands apartments or Deacra villas & bungalows, both located about 5km north of Casa Rex. *US$150/240 standard sgl/dbl; US$190/320 in*

Acacia Wing; US$225/390 Courtyard Suite; all rates B&B. **$$$$**
🏠 **Dugong Beach Lodge** [176 D7] (12 rooms) 📞+27 12 000 0595/443 6700 (South Africa); e reservations@legendlodges.co.za; w dugonglodge.co.za. This highly exclusive lodge on the Ponta de São Sebastião south of Vilankulo is accessible only by boat or light aircraft charter from the airport. *US$630/900 sgl/dbl low season, rising to US$745/1060 high season, inc all meals & non-motorised activities, but exc boat or air transfer.* **$$$$$**
🏠 **Santorini** [176 C1] (9 units) 📞+27 76 941 4951 (South Africa); e reservations@santorinimozambique.com; w santorinimozambique.com. A new & fantastic addition to Vilankulo's luxury options, Santorini is a magnificent Greek-style villa complex overlooking the bay a few kilometres north of town. Main villa comprises 5 en-suite suites with private verandas, while Chapel Villa is a romantic & private 1-bedroom unit & Villa de Praia has 3 bedrooms. All accommodation uses facilities at the main villa, which inc swimming pool, courtyard, two dining areas, martini deck, TV & pool room, library, private chef & access to a secluded beach. Activities & spa treatments can be arranged. *US$550–780 dbl suite, US$1,530–1,890 Chapel, US$2,350–3,150 Villa de Praia; low to high season; all rates FB.* **$$$$$**

Upmarket
🏠 **Aguia Negra** [176 C2] (24 rooms) 📞293 82387; e aguianegra@tdm.co.mz; w aguianegrahotel.com. This offers accommodation in stilted & thatched A-frame chalets, all of which have 1 large main bedroom with dbl bed, a loft with twin beds, AC & private balcony. There are spectacular sea views from the restaurant, which serves seafood in the US$9–12 range, & 2 swimming pools set within lush gardens which run

10

down to an adequate swimming beach. *US$64/115 sgl/dbl B&B; US$85/138 luxury rooms.* **$$$$**

🏠 **Archipelago Resort** [176 D7] (18 rooms) 📞293 84022; m 84 712 8180/775 8433; e accounts@archipelago-resort.com or archipelago.resort@gmail.com; w archipelago-resort.com. Situated about 10mins' drive south of the airport, this attractively rustic isolated resort effectively has its own private beach, overlooked by the excellent stilted Vista do Mar Restaurant, & is also the home of Dive Bazaruto, which offers the full range of marine activities. Accommodation is in large stilted thatch cottages, all of which have an en-suite master bedroom with king-size bed, walk-in nets & fan, room for 4 more people to sleep, & full self-catering facilities inc fridge & freezer for those who prefer not to use the restaurant (🕐 *early–20.00). Rates are affected by group size, seasonality, & whether you take a beachfront chalet, but expect to pay around US$120 for up to 4 people except over the Christmas & Easter holidays, when prices increase.* **$$$**

🏠 **Casa Babi** [176 D6] (5 units) m 84 412 6478 or 82 781 7130; e info@casababi.com; w casababi.com. Part of Odyssea Dive (page 185), this boutique lodge has airy rooms, subtly decorated with local materials & with walk-in nets, reading lights, rainfall showers & private balconies facing the ocean. There's a small swimming pool, excellent French-inspired food, Wi-Fi & a troop of friendly dogs rounding out the welcoming committee. Guests get discounts on dive programmes, & there's a self-catering unit that can sleep up to 5. *US$130/180 sgl/dbl B&B; US$145–250 self-catering unit sleeping 2–5.* **$$$$**

🏠 **Dona Ana** [176 D3] (50 rooms) 📞293 83200; e res@keychainhospitality.co.za; w thehoteldonaana.com. Originally built in 1967 & reopened at the tail end of 2013 after years of dereliction, this Art Deco gem is poised to take up its mantle once again as the place to see & be seen in Vilankulo. Done up in new pastels & perched at the end of its own peninsula, it's got 2 swimming pools, an Afro-Portuguese-inspired restaurant, lounge & poolside bar, as well as an activities centre where most aquatic pursuits can be arranged. Rooms are bright & pleasant, & all have AC, balcony, flat-screen TV, safe & minibar. *Classic rooms starting at US$145/240 sgl/dbl; US$180/296 exec sgl/dbl; suites starting at US$210/350 sgl/dbl; all rates B&B.* **$$$$**

🏠 **Pescador Hotel** [176 C3] (14 rooms) 📞293 82312; m 84 891 0003; e pescadorbooking@hotmail.com; w pescadorhotel.com. Opened in 2007, this smart modern hotel is well equipped with a saltwater swimming pool, DSTV in the lounge, good seafood restaurant, internet access & spacious, attractively decorated rooms with tiled floor, AC, fan & en-suite bathroom with tub. It's not on the sea but has good beach access & seems like excellent value if you can live with that one drawback. *US$90 for a smaller downstairs dbl or twin; US$120 for an upstairs dbl; all rates B&B.* **$$$$**

🏠 **Vilas do Índico** [176 C1] (12 rooms) m 84 713 2018 or 86 774 4006; e reservations@villasdoindico.com; w villasdoindico.com. Situated on an isolated beach about 10km north of town along a 4x4-only road, this intimate lodge offers accommodation in en-suite thatched chalets with private seafront verandas offering a panoramic view of the Bazaruto Islands. The seafood has a great reputation & the usual range of activities is offered. *US$115/190 en-suite sgl/dbl B&B; US$60/110 sgl/dbl with shared ablutions B&B; US$15 pp camping.* **$$$$**

Mid range

🏠 **Casa Cabana Beach** [176 C2] m 84 707 3693; e casacabana@icon.co.za; w casacabanabeach.com. On the beach next to Complexo Samara, this place is a solid choice for self-caterers, though it is also home to the gorgeous 'Casbah' restaurant with seafood specialities & a breezy North African vibe. Rooms are well equipped, the grounds are idyllic, & it's also the place to go for kitesurfing. *US$70 pp chalet B&B; US$85 pp self-catering house.* **$$$**

🏠 **Casa Jules & Zombie Cucumber** [176 D5] (12 rooms, 1 dorm) m 82 804 9410 or 84 686 9870; e info@casajules.com; w casajules.com or w zombiecucumber.com. Under new management since 2012, this venerable backpackers has undergone something of a change in focus with the opening of its more upmarket sister hotel, Casa Jules. It's still got the friendly atmosphere & laid-back feel it always did, but the backpacker party vibe has been traded in for a healthy dose of tranquillity. Rooms at Zombie are simple but clean with dbl bed, walk-in netting & a macuti thatch roof, while the en-suite rooms at Casa Jules are invitingly modern & comfortably appointed, each with their own private veranda. The Wi-Fi-equipped restaurant-bar spills across the shaded patio to the small swimming pool, & does an appetising variety of meals & snacks, inc some really fantastic pizza. It's likely the dorms will be phased out in time, but for now it's excellent value for travellers seeking an upmarket experience at a backpacker price. *US$50 dbl, US$10 pp dorm at Zombie; US$60/80 dbl/trpl at Casa Jules.* **$$**

🏠 **Complexo Samara** [176 C2] (11 rooms) m 82 380 6865 or 84 417 1814; e samara@ tdm.co.mz. Set in busy gardens overlooking the beach, this place is known as one of the best-value seafood eateries in town, but also has a variety of clean en-suite rooms, some with self-catering kitchenettes. *From US$56/64 sgl/dbl B&B (negotiable for larger groups).* **$$$**

🏠 **Palmeiras Lodge** [176 D5] (7 rooms) ↘ 293 82050; m 84 380 2842; e palmeiraslodge@ gmail.com; w palmeiras-lodge.net. Set in pretty flowering beachfront grounds with a small swimming pool, this smart lodge has recently upgraded en-suite chalets with AC & nets all connected by a series of paths through the remarkably lush gardens. There's Wi-Fi, & the thatch restaurant & lounge has books to read & meals on request. *US$54/108 sgl/dbl B&B with discount in low season.* **$$$**

🏠 **Varanda** [176 D6] (6 rooms) ↘ 293 82412; m 82 861 2540; e varanda.barko@yahoo.com; f varanda.vilanculos. Set into a hillside overlooking the beach, the sea-view rooms here are each individually decorated, but all are whitewashed & have AC, with high thatched ceilings & lovely sand-floored balconies facing the ocean. There is a restaurant as well. *US$60 dbl; B&B.* **$$$**

Budget

🏠 **Baobab Beach Backpackers** [176 D6] (18 rooms, 2 dorms) m 82 731 5420 or 84 413 3057; e info@baobabbeach.net or baobabmoz@ yahoo.com; w baobabbeach.net. This has a pleasantly shaded location, but is quite a walk from the town centre, which may be a factor if you have an early bus to catch, although there are signs indicating that the guard will accompany you to the market if you ask or you can arrange a lift for around US$4. It's got a range of accommodation – camping, dorms, huts & some lovely chalets overlooking the beach – as well as a varied menu with most meals under US$9. The staff are generally very pleasant & helpful,

speaking good English. With the shift in focus at Zombie Cucumber, this is in fact Vilankulo's go-to backpacker hub. Accommodation prices vary according to location, occupancy & season, but expect *US$47 en-suite dbl beach chalet; US$33 dbl hut; US$10 dorm bed; US$9 pp camping in high season.* **$$**

🏠 **Complexo Alemanha/Vilankulo Backpackers** [176 B1] (6 rooms, 1 dorms) m 84 261 0487; e bernddehoag@gmail.com; f vilanculosbackpackershostel. 2 names for the same operation, owned & run by an energetic German, this has pleasant chalet accommodation with private balcony & fan, as well as a 10-bed dorm. It's very close to the chapa station, sited on a rise overlooking the bay with great views. There is also the inexpensive rooftop Restaurant Em Cima, occasional disco nights, some self-catering facilities, safe parking & a hot shower block. There are 2 dbl beds in the dorms for couples tired of being separated on bunk-beds. *US$14 dbl; US$5 pp dorm.* **$**

🏠 **Hotel Bernna** [176 A1] (10 rooms) m 84 651 2431/465 1536; e hotelbernna@tdm.co.mz. This pleasant new budget lodge has clean no-frills en-suite twin or dbl rooms with AC, TV, fridge, nets & writing desk. The restaurant serves local meals for US$5–12 & cheaper snacks. *US$60 twin or dbl.* **$$**

🏠 **Hotel Central** [176 A2] (42 rooms) ↘ 293 82024; m 84 071 1166/454 6761. Conveniently situated right opposite the chapa station, this totally non-resort-like establishment is unexceptional & unmemorable but adequate value, with a variety of clean rooms with nets, & a decent restaurant attached. *US$64 dbl with DSTV, walk-in net & AC; US$45 dbl with AC; US$24 dbl.* **$$**

🏠 **Marimba Secret Gardens** [176 C1] (6 rooms) m 84 048 9098 or 82 005 3015; e info@ marimba.ch; w marimba.ch. True to its name, this superb Swiss-run resort is hidden away on a 4x4 track 20km north of Vilanculo, but it remains easy to access for backpackers thanks to regular transfers from town. Perched high on stilts, the octagonal reed-&-thatch rooms are arranged in a wide circle around the evening firepit, each with their own private veranda. Snorkelling, kitesurfing & walks into the bush & nearby communities can all be easily arranged, & the restaurant-bar does a daily dinner of fresh-caught seafood & produce from their organic garden. *US$52/55 dbl/twin; US$26/18 pp 3/6-bed family room.* **$$$**

Shoestring

Complexo Turístico Josef é Tina [176 D5] **m** 82 311 4200 or 84 259 5754. One of the more established options, this unpretentious place offers accommodation in simple reed huts using common showers, & trim en-suite rooms. It is probably not as good value as the other places listed in this price range, nor so convenient for catching chapas, but does have the advantage of being in a large green compound right on the beachfront Av Marginal. *US$20 en-suite dbl; US$16 dbl.* **$**

Motel Dércia [176 D4] (30 rooms) **m** 84 297 8572. This quiet little place off the main road is quite close to the bus station & well placed for eating out, if less so for the beach. Rooms are nothing to write home about, but pleasant enough & sensibly priced, though it is worth looking at a few rooms as the quality of rooms varies a lot more than prices. *US$14 en-suite dbl with net & fan; US$10 twin without shower.* **$**

✖ WHERE TO EAT AND DRINK The upmarket hotels all have their own restaurants, which are as good as you would expect them to be, but there are also several other options in town.

Town centre

✖ Kilimanjaro Café [176 D3] **m** 84 256 3932; ⊕ 08.00–17.00 daily. This South African-style indoor/outdoor café in the Luxus Centre does an appetising range of toasted sandwiches, salads, burgers & pastries, & perhaps most importantly, they've got Wi-Fi for diners. *Mains US$5–10, cheaper sandwiches & snacks.* **$$**

✖ Leopoldina's Food [176 D6] **m** 84 595 1462; ⊕ lunch & dinner daily. This diminutive diner around the corner from Baobab Beach boasts all of 1 table, but the welcome is warm & so is the food. It's a good place to try *matapa. Around US$5.* **$**

✖ Restaurant Em Cima [176 B1] **m** 84 261 0487. This worthwhile budget eatery, part of Vilankulo Backpackers, combines a breezy rooftop setting, ocean views, a pleasant semi-outdoor ambience & an affordable menu of seafood, burgers, pasta & local vegetarian dishes. In keeping with the German theme, they've even got schnitzel. *Mostly less than US$5 per main.* **$**

✖ Restaurante Ti-Zé [176 A3] ⊕ 07.00–23.00 daily. Situated on the main road, just outside the market, Ti-Zé does all the usuals, & they've got a pool table. *Mains around US$6.* **$**

▭ Café Mozambicano [176 A3] ⊕ 07.00–19.00 Mon–Sat. Fresh espresso, pastries, filled rolls & a selection of imported confectionery are sold at this small pastelaria near the old market. **$**

♀ Afro Bar [176 A4] Around the corner from the market, this is a likeable, no-nonsense place, popular with locals & expats alike. It's got live music at w/ends, & the party really gets cracking after midnight. Walking back to your hotel from here at night is not recommended; catch a taxi. **$**

Seafront

✖ Bar Tropical [176 D5] **m** 84 380 6816; ⊕ 08.30–late Mon–Sat, 11.30–late Sun. On the Av Marginal near Zombie Cucumber, this is a good place to have sundowners overlooking the sea. Also serves a few local dishes for under *US$5.* **$**

✖ Casa Rex [176 C3] ✆ 293 82048; **m** 84 033 5446; ⊕ b/fast, lunch & dinner daily. This attractive, refined hotel overlooking the sea has possibly the most highly regarded restaurant in town, with seafood the main speciality alongside a varied selection of curries & salads. *Mains in the US$8–20 range.* **$$$**

✖ The Casbah [176 C2] **m** 84 707 3693; ⊕ lunch & dinner daily. Part of Casa Cabana & a favourite among locals, this restaurant & bar is located directly on the beach & serves up piri-piri chicken, burgers, fish & a range of snacks & starters. *Most mains around US$8.* **$$**

✖ New York Pizza [176 D3] **m** 82 389 9999; ⊕ lunch & dinner daily. Part of Complexo Ancora, this place has long served the best pizzas in town, but also has a good selection of pasta & seafood, & a great view over the bay. Orders can be phoned in and/or collected as take-away. No alcohol. *Most mains & medium pizzas are around US$9.* **$$**

✖ Samara Restaurant [176 C2] **m** 82 380 6865; ⊕ b/fast, lunch & dinner daily. A short walk past Casa Rex, this good-value restaurant has nice sea views from the upper deck & serves a good selection of seafood, chicken & other grills, cooked to perfection on hot coals. *Mains in the US$7–11 range.* **$$$**

✖ Upper Deck Pub & Grill [176 D3] **m** 84 419 4295; ⊕ 08.00–late daily. Overlooking the harbour, this pleasant spot offers free Wi-Fi, DSTV & serves grills of all sorts, salads, wraps & sandwiches. There's even a trampoline for kids. *Mains in the US$6–10 range.* $$

✗ Varanda [176 D6] ✆293 82412; m 82 861 2540; e varanda.barko@yahoo.com; ◷ 08.00–21.00 Tue–Sun. Situated on the dunes overlooking the beach where the fishing dhows come to land their catches, this long-standing favourite serves great Mozambican-style seafood & superb chicken piri-piri. The only downside is that the street immediately outside is unlit, so you might want to go in a group. *Mains are in the US$7–11 range.* $$$

OTHER PRACTICALITIES

Banks Standard, Barclays, BCI and BIM Millennium all have branches in the town centre, and ATMs taking international Visa cards. BIM Millennium also takes MasterCard.

Hospital For emergencies contact the hospital [176 B1] (✆ 293 30622) or the private Boa Vida Clinic [176 C3] (m 82 256 0474 or 84 513 1490), opened in 2013 and recommended. A Netcare 911 clinic [176 C1] (w netcare.co.za) has also opened just north of town. There's a pharmacy next to Barclays at the roundabout in the centre of town [176 A3].

Internet The best place is **iCloud** (◷ 09.00–17.00 daily) at the Luxus Centre [176 D3] but **Dolphin Dhow** [176 D6]and **NR Internet** [176 D4] near the Motel Dércia are both options as well. Kilimanjaro Café, also in the Luxus Centre, has Wi-Fi for customers.

Police The Machiquechique police station [176 A3] is on the main road leading into town.

Shopping Vilankulo has two excellent markets, the old one being situated at the southern end of the town centre [176 A4] and the new one behind the chapa station opposite the Hotel Central [176 B2]. The former is good for crafts and both are good for fresh groceries. The Taurus Supermarket [176 D3] at the north end of the town centre is outstanding, selling fresh fruit, frozen meat and a huge selection of imported goods, but the Africa Cash & Carry [176 A4] near the old market is also good. For craft shopping, there are a few stalls on the Avenida Marginal, as well as at the north end of the town centre near Complexo Ancora [176 D3], and at the south end of town in front of the Casa de Cultura. Also worth a mention is the Afro Art Gallery [176 D4] next to Vilankulo Camping (closed), and the upmarket Papagayo Craft Shop in the Luxus Centre [176 D3].

A special mention goes to **Machilla Magic** [176 C1] (m 82 393 3428; e info@machillamagic.com; w machillamagic.com), which sells a huge variety of crafts made by more than 60 local families at the village of Macumbe, 25km north of town, for distribution throughout southern Africa. The quality crafts are made using overwhelmingly recycled materials and are very varied in style, and their gallery next to the Vilanculos Beach Lodge (closed) is definitely worth a visit. They can also arrange personalised art tours to area villages, where you can meet the artisans themselves. The helpful **tourist office** [176 B3] (m 82 525 0457; e ndembeka@gmail.com; ◷ 08.30–12.30 & 13.30–18.30 Mon–Fri, 08.30–noon Sat) is set in the central municipal building and can arrange accommodation and provide you with a useful range of brochures and booklets, as well as advice on dhow trips. It is run as a community project, and an internet café is attached.

WHAT TO SEE AND DO

Manyikeni Ruins Some 50km inland of Vilankulo, the overgrown ruins of Manyikeni are probably the best surviving example of a Zimbabwean-style stone enclosure in Mozambique. Occupied from the 12th to the 17th centuries, this was the site of an important outpost of the Karanga Kingdom, and the main enclosure, typical of such sites, was situated on the top of a small hill, a location believed to be symbolic of royal power. A wealth of glass beads has been unearthed at the site, along with loose globules of gold and a single iron gong, suggesting strong cultural links with what is now the Zimbabwe interior as well as trade links with the coast, probably through the abandoned port of Chibuene. Although it is not developed for tourism, Manyikeni (together with Chibuene) was placed on the tentative list of UNESCO World Heritage Sites in 1997. To get there from Vilankulo, follow the EN1 south from Pambora junction for about 30km as far as Mapinhane, then turn right on to a good dirt road and follow it inland for about 10km until you reach an unsignposted dirt road heading north. The ruins are about 5km along this road and may be difficult to locate without a guide.

Diving and snorkelling The prime reason for visiting Vilankulo is to go snorkelling or diving in the Bazaruto Archipelago, a subject dealt with in detail on page 192. Boats to the islands are readily available through a number of diving operations scattered around town. Many first-timers are persuaded to join an excursion to **Magaruque**, which is the closest island to Vilankulo, and thus the cheapest to visit, but offers significantly inferior snorkelling to other reefs in the area. A far better option, emphatically worth the additional cost, is a day trip to **Two Mile Reef**, which offers the best snorkelling and diving in the archipelago, and can easily be combined with a visit to the spectacular dunes at the southern end of **Bazaruto Island**.

The operators listed below are all recommended for diving, snorkelling and other activities.

Dive Bazaruto [176 D7] ✆ 293 84252; m 84 850 6507/060 9309; e info@divebazaruto. com; w divebazaruto.com. Based at Archipelago Resort. Prices vary according to number of people & dive/snorkel location. A double-dive trip to Magaruque/Two Mile Reef runs for US$130 pp.
Dolphin Dhow [176 D6] ✆ 293 82466; m 82 462 4700 or 84 462 4700; e dolphindhowvlk@yahoo.com. Sited on

---

GAME FISHING AND DIVING FROM BENGUERRA   *Bob de Lacy Smith*

The Bazaruto area offers some of the most challenging game fishing in southern Africa. Large black and striped marlins are regularly taken between October and December. Prior to the civil war, specimens weighing in the region of 500kg were caught off the islands, and the recent record is more than 400kg. Sailfish can be caught throughout the year, with July and August being the best months for these fine fighters. The largest specimen so far is 55kg. Other game fish to be taken include tuna, all types of bonito, wahoo, king and queen mackerel, dorado, rainbow runner, prodigal son, giant barracuda and several species of kingfish including the mighty giant trevall (*Caranx ignoblis*).

Saltwater fly-fishing has also taken off in the area and regular clinics are held where experts pass on their knowledge to novices. The sport has a growing following and conditions on the islands are ideal. The much-sought-after bonefish occurs in the area, and specimens of up to 8.2kg have been caught by local fishermen.

Av Marginal & run by Junior who also has a taxi service, car rental & accommodation, this does full-day trips to Magaruque for US$55 pp & Benguerra for US$65. Ask about backpacker discounts.

Odyssea Dive [176 D6] m 82 781 7130 or 84 412 6478; e info@odysseadive.com; w odysseadive. com. This well-established company, situated in the grounds of their own guesthouse Casa Babi, offers a range of good-value activities in & around the water, starting with a full-day island safari, taking in Bazaruto & Benguerra Island, as well as snorkelling on Two Mile Reef, for US$63 pp. 2-dive day packages go for US$128, and PADI Open Water certification for US$457. Discounts are available for Casa Babi guests.

Sailaway Dhow Safaris [176 D3] m 82 387 6350 or 84 708 9627; e david@sailaway. co.za; w sailaway.co.za. Sailaway runs dhow trips to the various islands, with 1-, 2- or 3-day excursions, costing US$85, US$220 and US$340 pp respectively, inc food, soft drinks, snorkelling kit & park fees – in fact everything except alcohol.

Sunset Dhow Safaris [176 D6] m 82 912 0658 or 84 720 6223; e info@sunsetdhowsafari. com or sunsetdhowsafari@gmail.com; w sunsetdhowsafari.com. Locally owned & managed, Sunset offers dhow trips, snorkelling & whale watching, & sunset cruises in the US$25–95pp range, depending on the destination.

Other tours Very popular are the horseback trips around Vilankulo and on the islands run by **Mozambique Horse Safaris** (☎ 293 84247; m 84 251 2910; e mozmandy2@gmail.com; w mozambiquehorsesafari.com), which charges from US$50 per person for a ride and is based south of town near the Archipelago Resort. For a glimpse into local village life, contact Faquir Nhamué of **Vilankulo Village Tours** (m 84 711 2948); tours cost US$20 per person. Camelback excursions on the beach are offered by the **Complexo Ancora** [176 D3] at the north end of town. The **Kitesurfing Centre** [176 C2] (m 84 449 2263; e kitesurfcentre@gmail.com; w kitesurfingcentre. com) does everything its name implies, with lessons, rentals and kitesurfing excursions all on offer. **VilanCool** [176 D7] (m 84 786 2170/720 6223; e hello@vilancool.com; w vilancool.com) offers watersports of all kinds including kitesurfing, stand-up paddle boarding, snorkelling and dhow safaris. It also offers a 2-floor, self-catering villa fit for 2 or 4 people. The **Vilanculos Activity Centre** (m 84 602 8692; w southeastafricasafaris.com), located in the Luxus Centre [176 D3], is famed for its evening canoe safaris through the Govuro wetlands, but can arrange almost any activity a tourist might want – including excursions to the Manyikeni Ruins (page 184).

INHASSORO

Heading north along the EN1, Inhassoro is the final mainland coastal resort before the road veers inland for the 330km trip via the Save River to Inchope junction (on the EN6 between Beira and Chimoio). Much smaller than Vilankulo, but with a similarly sprawling layout, Inhassoro hasn't traditionally attracted much in the way of international tourism. However, as the closest beach resort to Zimbabwe it has become a popular retreat with tourists from across the border, so that high seasons tally more or less exactly with Zimbabwean school holidays. At the time of writing, there is something of a work-in-progress feel about the small town centre: banking facilities arrived in 2009 in the form of two different outlets with ATMs, as did the first filling station and a spanking new supermarket, and there is an unusually high proportion of half-constructed buildings, creating the overall impression of a small village inching its way towards becoming a fledgling resort town.

The main attraction at Inhassoro is the near-perfect beach, which stretches for several kilometres either side of the town centre. The beach here is far cleaner and quieter than its counterpart at Vilankulo, and considerably better suited to swimming and beach-oriented holidays. The resort lies opposite the northern end of the Bazaruto Archipelago, and is the closest place to pick up boats to Santa

Carolina Island and the northern end of Bazaruto Island, though in practice it is probably less often used for that purpose than Vilankulo. In theory, Inhassoro offers similar snorkelling and diving opportunities to Vilankulo, centred on the islands rather than the town itself, but there has been no dive operation here for several years, and what boat excursions there are typically involve hooks and bait rather than fins and masks. This, of course, could change in the near future.

GETTING THERE AND AWAY

By car Inhassoro lies 13km along a surfaced feeder road that's clearly signposted on the east side of the **EN1**, some 50km north of the turn-off to Vilankulo, and about 330km south of Inchope on the **EN6** between Beira and Chimoio. The drive from Vilankulo should take an hour at most, but you are looking at around 5 hours to or from Beira or Chimoio.

By chapa Using public transport, there are regular chapas to and from Vilankulo, a 1-hour ride that costs around US$2. Chapas mostly leave from in front of the market, but they can usually also be picked up on the main road into town. There's a daily bus to Maputo for US$24 with **Transportes Nhancale**, departing at midnight from the bright green petrol station.

WHERE TO STAY *Map, opposite*
Note that most of the lodges and resorts in Inhassoro have pages on **w** inhassoro. org, but they're woefully out of date at the moment.

Upmarket

Billfish Lodge/Rio Azul Lodge
(10 units) Billfish: **m** 84 060 1572/298 5472; **e** billfishlodge@gmail.com; **f** billfishlodge; Rio Azul: **m** 84 387 5719; **e** info@rioazul-lodge. com; **w** rioazul-lodge.com. Rather awkwardly, this lodge has now become two separately run establishments due to a dispute between the owners. Nevertheless, assuming you can get past the tension of the shared entrance & communal space, it – whichever side you choose to stay – is still probably the smartest lodge around Inhassoro. Situated on the low cliffs north of the town centre, out past Canta Libre, accommodation is in warm, earthy thatched houses, each of which sleeps up to 10 & has full self-catering facilities. There is also an excellent on-site restaurant (*closed Sun evenings*) & bar, & facilities inc swimming pool. *US$50 pp B&B at Billfish, US$250 pp FB with limited activities inc at Rio Azul. Good luck.* **$$$–$$$$**

Casa Luna Lodge (16 rooms) ☎ 293 84259; **m** 82 065 0055 or 84 045 5025; **e** casalunalodge@ hotmail.com. Set on a slight rise overlooking the beach north of the town centre, this attractive bush-meets-beach lodge lies in compact green gardens, whose indigenous scrub is offset by a network of wooden walkways, decks & a swimming pool. There

is the choice of stilted safari-style standing tents with fan & private veranda, or more conventional chalets with AC, en-suite bathroom with tub & outdoor shower. A highly rated restaurant serves seafood & other dishes in the US$6–12 range along with a selection of cheaper snacks. *US$84 dbl room; US$64 dbl tent; all rates B&B.* **$$$**

Dream Catcher Lodge (15 units) **m** 82 343 6235 or 84 839 4966; **e** stay@ mozamdreamlodge.com; **w** mozamdreamlodge. com. This well-maintained complex of en-suite 2- to 5-bed chalets is set among beautifully manicured grounds with direct access to the beach. Each chalet has nets, AC, fridge & kettle, & self-catering chalets also have a full kitchen. Amenities inc fantastic restaurant-bar, a pool & Wi-Fi. *US$50–70 pp depending on season.* **$$$**

Dugong Lodge (10 units) **m** 84 389 1471 or 82 456 7170; **e** info@dugongmoz.com; **w** dugongmozambique.com. Situated in idyllic indigenous gardens running down to a postcard-perfect swimming beach about 2km south of town, this bush-style lodge comprises a cluster of immaculate 5- to 10-bed beach lodges, plus a few smaller dbl chalets at the back. The lodges are fully equipped for self-catering & have large private balconies, while other facilities inc beachfront

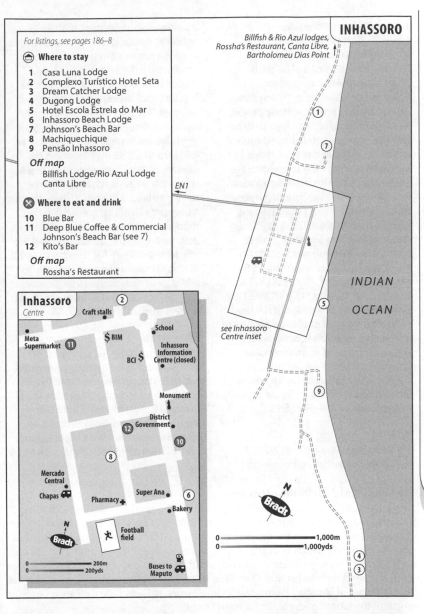

Billfish & Rio Azul lodges,
Rossha's Restaurant, Canta Libre,
Bartholomeu Dias Point

For listings, see pages 186–8

⌂ Where to stay
1 Casa Luna Lodge
2 Complexo Turístico Hotel Seta
3 Dream Catcher Lodge
4 Dugong Lodge
5 Hotel Escola Estrela do Mar
6 Inhassoro Beach Lodge
7 Johnson's Beach Bar
8 Machiquechique
9 Pensão Inhassoro

Off map
   Billfish Lodge/Rio Azul Lodge
   Canta Libre

✖ Where to eat and drink
10 Blue Bar
11 Deep Blue Coffee & Commercial
    Johnson's Beach Bar (see 7)
12 Kito's Bar

Off map
   Rossha's Restaurant

EN1

INDIAN
OCEAN

see Inhassoro
Centre inset

Inhassoro
Centre

Craft stalls
Meta
Supermarket
School
$ BIM
Inhassoro
Information
Centre (closed)
BCI $
Monument
District
Government
Mercado
Central
Chapas
Pharmacy
Super Ana
Bakery
Football
field
Buses to
Maputo

0 ———— 200m
0 ———— 200yds

0 ———— 1,000m
0 ———— 1,000yds

infinity swimming pool, attractive bar-restaurant serving a daily home-cooked set menu, & fishing charters by arrangement. *US$100–120 5-sleeper chalets, US$200–250 8-sleeper houses, depending on season.* **$$**

Mid range
⌂ **Complexo Turístico Hotel Seta** (38 rooms)
📞 293 91000; m 82 302 0990 or 84 841 0707;
e setahotel@gmail.com; w inhassoro.org. The oldest & most central hotel in Inhassoro, the Seta stands next to the town's central junction, set in large wooded grounds running down to the beach. Accommodation is in spacious detached or semi-detached chalets with thatch roofs, veranda, fridge, AC, nets, terracotta tiling & en-suite bathroom with tub &/or shower. A pleasant beachfront restaurant with macuti roof serves various seafood & chicken dishes in the US$4–10 range.

US$110–140 family cottage sleeping 5–7; US$80 dbl with TV; US$50 twin; US$5 pp camping. **$$**

🏠 **Hotel Escola Estrela do Mar**
(11 rooms) m 82 307 9950 or 84 060 9609; e hotel.escola.estreladomar@gmail.com; 🗗 hotelescolainhassoro. Ignore the tacky signage, this hotel & training project is definitely the nicest place to stay in central Inhassoro. Accommodation options inc warmly decorated en-suite dbl chalets or family chalets that sleep up to 5 – 2 below & 3 in a wooden loft above – & all come with AC, nets & ocean views. Staffed by students & graduates of the local hotel school, it's an impressive project well deserving of support. The restaurant does meat, seafood & pizzas starting at US$5, & they can also arrange spa treatments & boat trips. US$48 dbl chalet; US$58–78 chalet sleeping 3–5; b/fast on request; rates nearly double in high season. **$$**

🏠 **Pensão Inhassoro** (12 rooms) ☎ +27 82 442 2096 (South Africa); m 84 331 4282/562 5107; e info@inhassoro.co.za; w inhassoro.co.za. Aimed mainly at the angling fraternity, this relatively central pensão is divided into 2 blocks, each comprising a square of dbl rooms set around a common area with a fully equipped self-catering kitchen, plenty of seating, Wi-Fi & DSTV. Rooms are spacious but spartan, though they do have AC & some are en suite. Indifferent value at US$50–60 dbl. **$$$**

Budget
🏠 **Canta Libre** (4 rooms) m 84 272 6603; e info@cantalibre.net; w cantalibre.net. This

attractive stilted complex stands on a cliff overlooking the beach about 3km north of the town centre. Accommodation is in wooden self-catering en-suite twin or dbl chalets with walk-in net, standing fan, safe & small private deck. There is a large deck, small swimming pool, & b/fast served on request. They offer a variety of fishing trips & excursions to the islands as well. US$44 dbl. **$$**

🏠 **Inhassoro Beach Lodge** (18 rooms) m 82 459 0820 or 84 523 2055; w inhassoro.org. This sprawling locally managed complex lies in large & rather untidy grounds stretching down from the town centre to the beach. It is friendly, relatively affordable & convenient for public transport, but there is a slightly untended feel about the place. All rooms are en suite with TV & AC. US$30 twin or dbl chalet. **$**

🏠 **Johnson's Beach Bar** (6 rooms) m 84 071 0089; e johnsonsbarinhassoro@gmail.com. Set behind the popular restaurant & bar, there are 6 clean new en-suite rooms equipped with AC, DSTV & self-catering facilities. US$50 dbl. **$$**

Shoestring
🏠 **Machiquechique** (12 rooms) m 82 441 5710. In a cheerfully dishevelled compound on the road leading through the centre of town, this place doesn't have any signposts, but look out for a gated compound scattered with potted plants, tables & plenty of coconut palms. Rooms are clean, & the eponymous owner is very kind & helpful. Excellent value. US$10 en-suite dbl; US$6 thatch rondavel dbl. **$**

✕ WHERE TO EAT AND DRINK   Map, page 187

The lodges and resorts listed previously mostly have good restaurants, with those at Billfish Lodge and the Complexo Turístico Hotel Seta most likely to appeal to non-residents. Otherwise, a popular spot for a beachfront drink, a short walk north of the Seta, is **Johnson's Beach Bar**, which also serves a limited selection of daily specials in the US$6–10 range. There are several small bars and unpretentious local eateries dotted around the market area. The **Blue Bar** has two pool tables. There is also the highly regarded **Rossha's Restaurant** (same owner as Deep Blue Coffee) about 5km north of town on the way to Bartolomeu Dias Point.

✕ **Deep Blue Coffee & Commercial** m 84 417 9802; ⏰ 07.00–17.00 Mon–Fri, 07.00–noon Sat. This friendly café-meets-grocery has cakes, coffee & Wi-Fi. They've got a variety of frozen meats & fish as well. **$**

✕ **Kito's Bar** m 84 875 0785; ⏰ 07.00–late daily. Tucked away between the main roads, this local spot has a surprisingly nice bar & does wors, beef, chicken & other standard mains. US$2.50–9. **$$**

OTHER PRACTICALITIES
Banks BCI and BIM Millennium are both represented in the town centre within a few metres of the main junction and with outside ATMs.

Marine activities Inhassoro is poorly equipped for marine activities at the time of writing, but a dive centre has been under discussion at Canta Libre for some time. This will theoretically arrange diving and snorkelling excursions to the Bazaruto Archipelago, as well as fishing charters, and it will be open to people staying at other hotels. Check the Canta Libre website (page 188) for up-to-date details.

Shopping Super Ana opposite Inhassoro Beach Lodge stocks a pretty decent selection of imported and packaged goods, including wine and frozen meat, and there is a good bakery right next door. The Meta Supermarket on the road out of town is also quite well stocked. For fresh fish and greens, the Mercado Central is a couple of blocks west of the main road, while the best place to shop for crafts is the stalls outside the entrance to the Complexo Turístico Hotel Seta.

BAZARUTO NATIONAL PARK

Comprising a string of small sandy islands lying roughly 15–25km from the mainland north of Vilankulo and south of Inhassoro, the Bazaruto Archipelago was one of the few parts of Mozambique that remained safe to visit during the closing years of the civil war, when it developed as an upmarket package-based tourist destination that functioned in near isolation from the rest of the country. That much is arguably still true today, since all the archipelago's lodges slot comfortably into the upmarket or exclusive price bracket, and their fly-in clientele consists mostly of people on a multi-country itinerary who barely set foot on the Mozambican mainland. That said, Bazaruto is also the focal point of marine activities out of Vilankulo and Inhassoro, and its islands and reefs are the target of almost all diving, snorkelling and other day excursions from these popular mainland resorts.

In 1971, the archipelago's five main islands and the surrounding ocean were gazetted as Bazaruto National Park, which extends eastward from the coastline between Vilankulo and Inhassoro to cover some 1,430km². The three largest islands were formerly part of a peninsula that is thought to have separated from the mainland within the last 10,000 years. The largest and most northerly island is Bazaruto itself: 30km long, on average 5km wide, and punctuated by a few substantial freshwater lakes near its southern tip. South of this, Benguerra, the second-largest island at 11km long by 5.5km wide, was known to the Portuguese as Santa Antonio, but was later renamed after an important local chief. South of this, the much smaller Magaruque lies almost directly opposite Vilankulo. The smallest island, Santa Carolina, also known as Paradise Island, is a former penal colony covering an area of about 2km² roughly halfway between Bazaruto and the mainland near Inhassoro. The fifth island, Bangue, is only rarely visited by tourists.

With its white, palm-lined beaches, the Bazaruto Archipelago is everything you would expect of an Indian Ocean island retreat. It is of great interest to birdwatchers, with roughly 150 species recorded, including several that are rare or localised in southern Africa, including green coucal; crab, sand and Mongolian plovers; olive and blue-cheeked bee-eaters; and a variety of petrels, gulls and waders. Lesser flamingos seen on the islands come from a nearby breeding colony, the only one known in eastern Africa south of Lake Natron in Tanzania. An estimated 45 reptile and amphibian species occur on the islands, including two endemics.

The freshwater lakes on Bazaruto and Benguerra support a relic breeding population of crocodiles, while the shores of the islands are nesting sites for at least three types of turtle including the rare loggerhead. Mammals present on one or

10

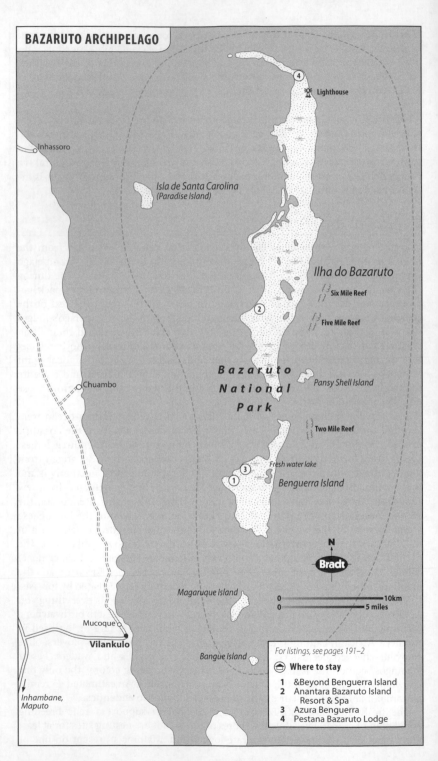

BAZARUTO ARCHIPELAGO

Inhassoro

Isla de Santa Carolina
(Paradise Island)

Lighthouse

④

Ilha do Bazaruto

Six Mile Reef

Five Mile Reef

②

Chuambo

B a z a r u t o
N a t i o n a l
P a r k

Pansy Shell Island

Two Mile Reef

Fresh water lake

③
①

Benguerra Island

Bradt

N

Magaruque Island

0 ——————— 10km
0 ——————— 5 miles

Mucoque

Vilankulo

Bangue Island

↓
Inhambane,
Maputo

For listings, see pages 191–2

🛏 **Where to stay**

1 &Beyond Benguerra Island
2 Anantara Bazaruto Island
   Resort & Spa
3 Azura Benguerra
4 Pestana Bazaruto Lodge

other island include the localised suni antelope, red duiker, bushbuck and samango monkey. An endemic butterfly species is found on Bazaruto Island.

However, the main attractions of the islands lie off their shores. The surrounding sea, warmed by the Mozambique Stream, is crystal-clear and its reefs support a variety of brightly coloured fish, making the area one of Mozambique's finest snorkelling and diving destinations. There are well-established diving centres on the north of Bazaruto Island and on Benguerra Island. Visitors to the islands frequently see marine turtles, humpback whales and bottlenose, spinner and humpback dolphins, as well as large game fish such as marlins and barracudas. The islands are also renowned for their game fishing (box, page 184).

The Bazaruto area supports what is probably East Africa's last viable population of the endangered dugong.

The Bazaruto Islands have a long history of human occupation. Prior to the Portuguese occupation of the coast, the islands were almost certainly the site of East Africa's most southerly Muslim trading settlements. By the middle of the 16th century, the islands were lorded over by Portuguese traders, and the surrounding sea was known for producing high-quality pearls. The first formal Portuguese settlement was established in 1855, on Santa Carolina. Initially an ivory trading post, the island was later used as a penal colony, but it was evidently abandoned by the beginning of the 20th century. Interesting historical relics include a ruined 19th-century fort on Magaruque and a fully intact but non-operational hundred-year-old lighthouse on Bazaruto.

Day visitors must pay an entrance fee of around US$8 in advance at the WWF Office in Vilankulo. If you are on a package deal or staying at one of the lodges on the islands, the fee will almost certainly be included in your bill.

GETTING THERE AND AWAY Most overnight visitors to Bazaruto fly from Maputo or Johannesburg to Vilankulo (page 178) and either fly to their lodge with **CR Aviation** (w *craviation.co.mz*), which operates at least one daily flight connecting Vilankulo to the various islands, or transfer there by boat. Either way, this is something that can be arranged with the company that books your accommodation (or, if you book directly, with the lodge itself). Day visitors most often come on a motorised dhow trip from Vilankulo, which can be arranged with any of the local dive operators listed on pages 184–5.

WHERE TO STAY *Map, opposite, unless otherwise stated*

Accommodation options are limited to a handful of exclusive upmarket resorts, whose prices and facilities are in line with private safari lodges in South Africa, Botswana and Zambia.

Benguerra Island

The 3 lodges on this island are all small, intimate & utterly wonderful, typifying the spirit of barefoot luxury, but they do fit firmly into the exclusive price bracket.

🏠 **&Beyond Benguerra Island** (13 rooms) \+27 11 809 4300 (South Africa); e safaris@ andbeyond.com; w andbeyond.com. Incorporated into the &Beyond collection, this popular & highly rated lodge is the oldest on the islands, founded in the early 1990s, & offers the choice of luxury

beachfront cabanas with queen-size bed, roof fan, private deck with jacuzzi/plunge pool or larger & more luxurious casitas. *US$765–1195 pp fully inclusive, depending on season & type of accommodation.* **$$$$$**

🏠 **Azura Benguerra** (20 rooms) \+27 11 467 0907 (South Africa); e reservations@ azura-retreats.com; w azura-retreats.com/azura-benguerra. Built on the site of what used to be the islands' only backpacker-friendly venue, this is now the most upmarket venue in the region, offering a choice of very spacious beachfront villas, all of which come with a king-size bed with walk-in netting, private plunge pool, AC, roof fans, indoor & outdoor bathroom, minibar & a large partly shaded deck. *US$1,310–2,990 dbl, depending on season & type of accommodation, inc all meals, most drinks & some activities.* $$$$$

🏠 **Kisawa** [not mapped] **w** kisawaltd.com. A new upmarket lodge & research centre are in the works.

Bazaruto Island

The 2 lodges on this island are both larger, more conventionally resort-like, & more impersonal than their counterparts on Benguerra, but the Anantara Bazaruto Island Resort operates to a similar standard of service & facilities. The Pestana Bazaruto Lodge is a step down, but still very luxurious & far more affordable than the archipelago's other resorts, especially if you take advantage of the seasonal website-only specials.

🏠 **Anantara Bazaruto Island Resort & Spa** (44 units) **📞** 293 91500; **m** 84 304 6670; **e** bazaruto@anantara.com; **w** bazaruto.anantara.

com. Part of the impressive Thailand-based Anantara Resorts' portfolio, this sprawling lodge lies in well-wooded grounds leading down to a beautiful swimming beach. Its chalets are attractive & well equipped, with understated contemporary décor, queen-size beds (walk-in net), AC, flat-screen DSTV, private balcony overlooking the sea, & large en-suite bathroom with tub & shower. The restaurant is very good, the dive centre arranges all the usual activities, & there's an exquisite hilltop spa offering great views over the beach. *From US$525/1,050 sgl/dbl inc meals, most drinks & non-motorised watersports.* $$$$$

🏠 **Pestana Bazaruto Lodge** (40 rooms) **📞** 213 05000; **m** 84 308 3120; **e** reservas.africa@pestana.com; **w** pestana.com. Closed indefinitely for maintenance at the time of research, this resort offers accommodation in en-suite A-frame thatched bungalows set amid tropical gardens with an ocean view. *From US$450 dbl FB, though much cheaper special offers are often offered on website bookings.* $$$$$

WHAT TO SEE AND DO All lodges on the islands can arrange excursions to the sites described below, and most are also routinely visited on day trips from the mainland.

Diving and snorkelling There are numerous dive sites dotted around the islands, but the undisputed champion is Two Mile Reef, a barrier reef that lies on the outer side of the archipelago between the islands of Bazaruto and Benguerra. Tides permitting, the best snorkelling spot is The Aquarium, a calm coral garden that lies on the inner reef and supports a dazzling selection of hard and soft corals, as well as reef fish of all shapes and colours, from tiny coral fish to the mighty potato bass and brindle bass. It is also a good spot to see reef sharks and marine turtles, though neither is guaranteed, while lucky divers might see manta rays and whale sharks. There are a host of dive sites on the seaward side of the same reef, with evocative names such as The Arches, Shark Point, Surgeon Rock, The Cathedral and The Gap. Any dive centre can advise on the site most suitable to your interests and current conditions but, if you are setting up a trip from Vilankulo, it is emphatically worth paying the extra to visit Two Mile Reef as opposed to taking the cheaper excursion of Magaruque, which has no proper reefs and thus offers vastly inferior diving and snorkelling.

Pansy Island Not so much an island as a tidal sandbar situated a short distance south of Bazaruto Island, this popular landmark can easily be visited as an extension of a trip to Two Mile Reef. It is named for the so-called pansy shells (also known as sea biscuits or sand dollars) that are abundant in its intertidal shallows. This pretty shell-like object, with a distinctive five-petalled floral pattern on its flattened face, is not a shell at all, but the endoskeleton of a burrowing sea urchin of the order Clypeasteroida. The living creature is usually black or purple in colour, and covered in bristles, but after it dies the endoskeleton is bleached white by the sun and saline water. The five petals are formed by a series of perforated pores through which the podia project from the body, and reflect the fivefold radial symmetry associated with all sea urchins. There are also 2cm slits above the floral pattern, the relicts of two grooves used for feeding. Any experienced guide will be able to find you examples of the pansy shell here, as well – with luck – as the living urchin.

Bazaruto Island A striking feature of the archipelago's largest island is the immense dunes that rise from its southern shore, and these too can easily be visited in conjunction with Two Mile Reef and Pansy Island. Reputedly the highest point on the islands, rising around 100m above the surrounding water, the steep dunes can be climbed, albeit in something of a two-steps forward, one-step back mode, and with some serious sandblasting in windy weather. Once at the top, the view in all directions is utterly exhilarating, with the open ocean and other islands stretching away to the south, and a landscape of lakes and dunes running to the north. If you are staying at one of the lodges on Bazaruto, island tours can be arranged to visit some of the lakes and other dune fields, some of which are spectacular, and to meet local communities.

Benguerra Island Like its larger and more northerly neighbour, Benguerra supports an attractive and varied landscape of marshes, lakes and tall climbable dunes, well worth exploring on a guided drive if you are staying at one of the lodges. Wildlife includes plentiful monkeys, small antelope such as red duiker and suni, some impressive crocodiles on the lakes, and a superb mix of birds, with brown-headed parrot, African hoopoe, green pigeon, crowned hornbill and various bee-eaters conspicuous, while flamingos and other waterbirds frequent the lakes. Community visits can also be arranged.

10

Part Three

CENTRAL MOZAMBIQUE

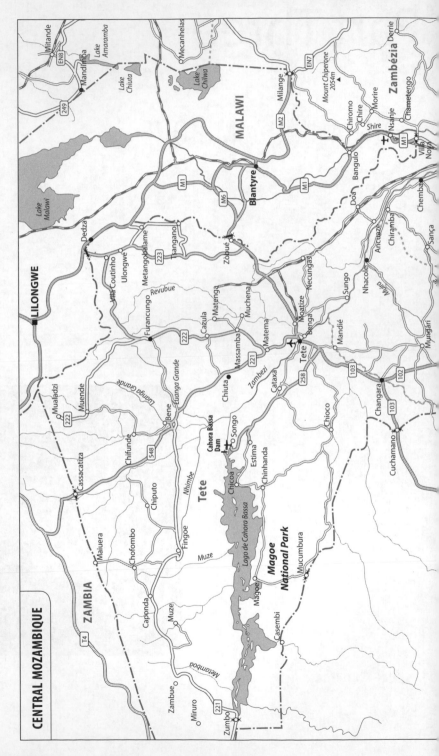

CENTRAL MOZAMBIQUE

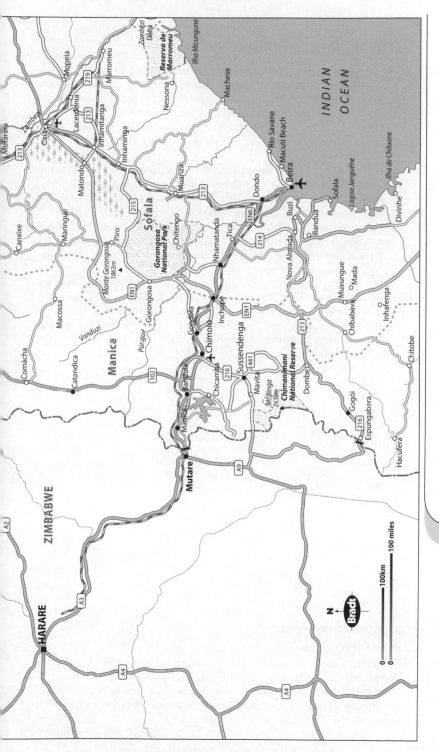

CENTRAL MOZAMBIQUE

The four chapters that follow cover central Mozambique, an area bounded by the Save River in the south and the Zambezi in the north, and which includes the pivotal EN6 through the so-called Beira Corridor (between the port of Beira and Zimbabwe), as well as the rather disjunct province of Tete to the northwest.

Chapter 11 covers the port city of Beira, which offers the only ready access to the coast in this part of Mozambique, but tends to attract more business travel than tourism.

The main focal point of *Chapter 12* is the city of Chimoio, an important route focus that also acts as the springboard for a number of worthwhile hiker-friendly attractions in the Manica Highlands, among them the Chinhamapere Rock Art Site and the remote Chimanimani National Reserve.

The renascent Gorongosa National Park, Mozambique's top safari destination, is the main subject of *Chapter 13*, which also provides details of the forested Mount Gorongosa and the main road north to Caia on the Zambezi River.

Chapter 14 covers the city of Tete, capital of the rather anomalous province of the same name, which shares longer borders with Zimbabwe, Zambia and Malawi than it does with the rest of Mozambique, and which is most often visited by travellers in transit between Malawi and Zimbabwe. The region's main attraction is the immense lake formed by the Cahora Bassa Dam on the Zambezi upriver of Tete.

NOTE TO READERS

During the period of research for this seventh edition, political instability prevented the updater from personally visiting certain parts of central Mozambique. On-the-ground sources made their best efforts to supply accurate and current information, but some details in the chapters on Beira, Chimoio and Tete might still be out of date.

11

Beira

Mozambique's busiest port and third-largest city, Beira enjoys a mixed reputation among travellers. In the immediate post-war era it was notorious as a crime hot spot, but that no longer seems to be a problem today. Even so, the city boasts no compelling tourist attractions, and not a great deal more in the way of traveller-oriented accommodation. Furthermore, it is something of a cul-de-sac, lying at the eastern terminus of the EN6, 135 pot-holed kilometres from the pivotal junction with the EN1, so there is unlikely to be a strong logistical reason for including Beira in your travel plans. Chimoio, 200km inland, is a more convenient travel pivot for crossing between almost anywhere south and north of the EN6.

Then again, approached in a spirit of 'because it's there', Beira can be a very enjoyable place to explore. The main business centre, laid out with an attention to detail rare in African cities, has plenty of architectural character, particularly in the vicinity of the two main squares. The old residential area to the southwest is also oddly appealing, lined with block after block of Portuguese villas in varying states of repair and disrepair. The area around the bus terminus and the docks is seedier, but has a definite sense of bustle and energetic commerce. And the long miles of seafront, though not exactly comparable with the likes of Tofo or Vilankulo, do much to enhance the city's rather agreeable atmosphere. So, yes, Beira lacks the overt charms of the popular resort towns to its south, but therein lies its potential interest – after a couple of weeks of beach-oriented travel, spending a day or two in this totally non-touristic port city can be a gratifyingly real and rewarding experience.

HISTORY

Sofala, a short distance south of Beira, was the medieval gateway to the south-central African interior, and an active trade centre from AD900 to the 19th century (box, page 210). By comparison, Beira itself is a modern entity, founded in 1884 on the sandy, marshy shore near the mouth of the Pungué River, as a base of operations for the rich prazero Joaquim Carlos Paiva de Andrade. In the late 1880s, the British imperialist and founder of Rhodesia, Cecil John Rhodes, attempted to annex the Beira area, but his attempts at warmongering garnered no support from the British government and in 1891 the area was formally incorporated into Mozambique. The town centre was laid out in 1887, and at the same time a permanent garrison was installed. Beira was granted city status in 1894. Serious development of the port started in 1891, when it was leased to Andrada's Mozambique Company, and it accelerated after 1898 following the completion of Rhodes' railway line to Rhodesia.

In its early days, Beira was a scruffy shanty town with a reputation as the most drunken, lawless settlement in Africa. At the start of the 20th century, the city boasted some 80 bars serving a population of only 4,000, roughly a quarter of which consisted of Europeans, mostly of Portuguese or British origin. The town did not have the most amenable of settings: the company that built the railway line to Rhodesia lost 60% of its European staff to malaria in two years, and the surrounding area was so untamed that lions were frequently seen walking through the main street. The sand on which the town was built was so deep that 40km of trolley lines had to be laid to allow residents to transport goods to their homes. The trolley lines later served as public transport, before they were torn up in 1930.

Beira's rapid expansion was curbed after rail links were completed between Rhodesia and South Africa in 1903. Nevertheless, the figures produced by the 1928 census show that by this time Beira was well established as the country's second city, with a population of 23,694 – more than half that of Lourenço Marques, and well over double that of the next-largest town in Mozambique. By 1970 the city had a population of 114,000, and it was entrenched as a popular holiday destination for residents of landlocked Rhodesia. Beira remained the country's second-largest city in 1997, according to a census taken that year, but it was overtaken sometime before the 2007 census by faster-growing Nampula, and its 2016 population was estimated at 462,000.

GETTING THERE AND AWAY

BY AIR Beira's airport [201 G1] is about 10km from the centre of town, and there are daily **LAM** flights to Nampula and Maputo, almost-daily flights to Tete, Quelimane, Pemba, Lichinga and Vilankulo, and several flights a week to Chimoio and Inhambane. Either **Airlink** or LAM will connect to Johannesburg daily, and LAM flies thrice-weekly to Harare. The LAM office [205 E5] (✆ *233 24141/2*) is on Rua Major Serpa Pinto.

BY CAR Beira is the eastern terminus of the **EN6**, situated 135km from Inchope (the junction with the EN1), 200km from Chimoio, and almost 300km from the Machipanda border with Zimbabwe. The EN6 is surfaced in its entirety but the part between Inchope and Beira has some heavily pot-holed stretches, and also carries heavy truck and chapa traffic, which makes for a relatively stressful drive. If you are driving yourself, take it easy, and bank on 2 hours to/from Inchope. Further afield, bank on a total driving time of 3 hours from Beira to Chimoio, 4 hours to Machipanda, at least 3 hours to Gorongosa National Park, and around 6–7 hours to Vilankulo or 7–8 hours to Quelimane.

BY BUS AND CHAPA Of the public transport options, most chapas and buses start or end their journeys on Avenida Daniel Napatima [205 E4], although it's just possible that you'll be dropped at the roundabout Praça 11 de Outubro, which lies on the junction of Avenida Samora Machel and Avenida Armando Tivane (near the Shoprite supermarket). Sticking with relatively local destinations, there are plenty of chapas along the EN6 between Beira and Inchope (*US$3*), Chimoio (*US$6*) and Manica (*US$8*), though it's usually easier to change in Chimoio for Manica. In either case you're not far from the central business district (CBD), and the two best hotels in this part of the city stand at the western end of Avenida Daniel Napatima. Crime is no longer the issue it was a few years back, but it is still wise to be on guard should you arrive at the chapa terminus late in the afternoon or evening.

Chapas also cover longer-haul routes, but there is also the twice-weekly **Postbus** coach to Maputo which leaves at 03.00 in either direction and takes about 16 hours, with stops at Vilankulo, Maxixe (for Inhambane and Tofo) and Xai-Xai. The full fare is around US$30, but pro-rata fares are available. **Maning Nice** (m *82 953 6795*) and **Nagi Investimentos** (m *86 400 0656*) run buses to Quelimane (*US$10*) and Nampula (*US$34*) several days a week, all leaving from Rua Capitão Duarte

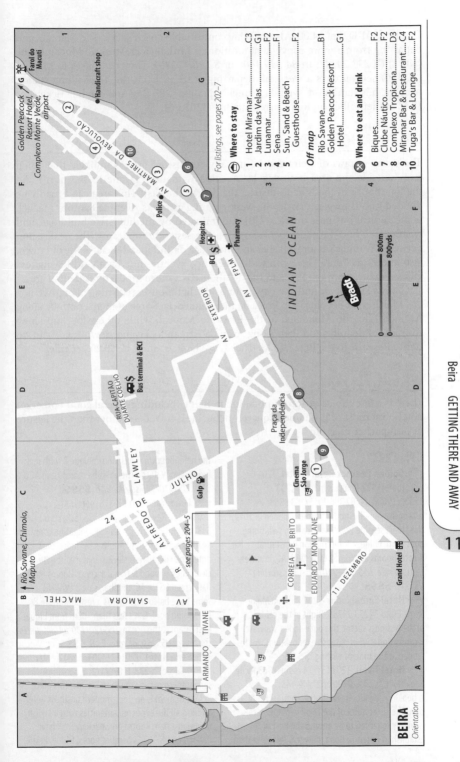

BEIRA
Orientation

For listings, see pages 202–7

Where to stay
1 Hotel Miramar..........................C3
2 Jardim das Velas.......................G1
3 Lunamar...................................F2
4 Sena.......................................F1
5 Sun, Sand & Beach
 Guesthouse............................F2

Off map
 Rio Savane...............................B1
 Golden Peacock Resort
 Hotel....................................G1

Where to eat and drink
6 Biques.....................................F2
7 Clube Náutico...........................F2
8 Complexo Tropicana..................D3
9 Miramar Bar & Restaurant........C4
10 Tuga's Bar & Lounge.................F2

INDIAN OCEAN

Coelho [201 D2] at 04.00. Also offering comfortable coach services to Maputo, and departing from a more convenient location, is **Linhas Terrestres de Moçambique (LTM)** (𝄂 *233 24141*; m *84 349 1400* or *82 186 7340*). They run buses to Maputo (*US$30*) several days a week, all departing at 03.30 from the Total filling station near the bus station on Avenida Daniel Napatima [205 E4]. You can buy tickets for LTM at their office on Rua Correia de Brito [205 F6].

ORIENTATION AND GETTING AROUND

The urban sprawl of Beira can be initially confusing, but it's unlikely that you'll stray outside the area bounded by Avenida Armando Tivane to the north and the lighthouse in the Macuti district that lies to the east. This area can broadly be divided into three sectors. To the west, running as far as Avenida Samora Machel, is the central business district (CBD), dominated by medium-rise buildings, and where you'll find the majority of shops, businesses and restaurants. The next sector, between Avenida Samora Machel and the Praça da Independência, is the old town, also known as Ponta Gea, with wide, tree-lined avenues lined with old Portuguese villas. Finally, from the Praça to the lighthouse is a more modern residential area.

Chapas run all around the city as far as the lighthouse, returning along Avenida dos Mártires da Revolução to Praça da Independência. Some of them continue along Avenida Eduardo Mondlane to the Praça do Metical, while others loop up along Avenida 24 de Julho and then along Avenida Armando Tivane, down Rua Artur do Canto Resende to the Praça do Metical. They charge around US$0.20 per ride.

WHERE TO STAY

There is a fair choice of accommodation in Beira, including several good upmarket hotels, but most of it is aimed squarely at business travellers rather than the leisure or backpacker market.

UPMARKET

Golden Peacock Resort Hotel [201 G1] (183 rooms) 172 Rua Luis Inácio; 𝄂 233 15000/15088; m 82 306 1955/303 3053; e brgprh@gmail.com; f brgprh. Opened in 2014, this smart seaside hotel has a casino, swimming pool, gym, Chinese & international restaurants, bar & café. Rooms are comfortable with AC, internet, kettle & safe. *US$156–200 dbl; suites starting US$213.* **$$$$**

Hotel Embaixador [204 D5] Rua Major Serpa Pinto; 𝄂 233 23785. Right in the centre of the business sector, this once-faded stalwart recently underwent extensive renovations. Yet to reopen at the time of writing. **$$$$**

Hotel Tivoli [204 C3] (74 rooms) 363 Av de Bagamoio; 𝄂 233 20300 or 214 84448; e bookings.tivolibeira@tdhotels.com; w tdhotels. com. The sister hotel of the Tivoli in Maputo, this is widely regarded to be among the best of the established hotels in Beira, newer & swankier than

the neighbouring Hotel Moçambique & with less fuddy-duddy décor. The en-suite rooms have AC & DTSV. *US$110/145 sgl/dbl B&B.* **$$$$**

Lunamar [201 F2] (16 rooms) Av Mártires da Revolução; 𝄂 233 13578/9; m 82 543 4528; e lunamarhotel@grupogodiba.com; w lunamarhotel.com. Another business-class hotel, the vibe here is sleek & minimalist with clean lines & wood & metal accents. Rooms have flat-screen DSTV, AC, minibar, safe & Wi-Fi, & some have balconies. There's a restaurant-bar & swimming pool, & it's less than 300m from Biques Restaurant & the ocean. *US$120/130 sgl/dbl, suites starting at US$150, all rates B&B.* **$$$$**

Sena Hotel [201 F1] (20 rooms) Av Mártires da Revolução; 𝄂 233 11070/1/2; e booking@ senahotel.co.mz; w senahotel.co.mz. This place in Macuti town is an über-modern business hotel offering all the expected amenities with a stylish, minimalist flair. Rooms are spacious & all have flat-screen DSTV, AC, parquet floors, fridge, kettle,

Wi-Fi, writing desk & plush furnishings. There's a restaurant & bar on-site. A new wing containing 50 rooms is under construction, along with a business centre, gym & spa. *US$130/151 standard/superior twin or dbl; suites starting at US$179; all rates B&B.* **$$$$**

🏠 **VIP Inn Beira** [204 A3] (54 rooms) 172 Rua Luis Inácio; 📞 233 40100; 📱 82 305 4753; ✉ hotelbeira@viphotels.com; 🖥 viphotels.com. This hotel in the heart of the CBD throws down the gauntlet to its stuffier counterparts, with its modern décor, efficient atmosphere, comfortable en-suite rooms with AC & DSTV, & 21st-century touches such as an online booking service & Wi-Fi throughout. *US$74/80 sgl/dbl B&B.* **$$$**

MID RANGE

🏠 **Aulio's Residencial** [205 H7] (19 rooms) Rua Mouzinho de Albuquerque; 📞 233 27549; 📱 82 378 8571; ✉ residencialaulios@hotmail. com; 📘 Residencial-Aulios-205804372781243. This beautifully restored old house near the cathedral has safe parking, free internet & clean stylish rooms with tiled floor, dbl or twin beds, AC, net, DTSV, fridge & large en-suite bathroom with combination tub/shower. An on-site restaurant serves typical Mozambican food for US$4–6. Good value. *US$50 dbl or twin B&B.* **$$**

🏠 **Jardim das Velas** [201 G1] (12 rooms) 282 Av FPLM; 📞 233 12209; ✉ jardimdasvelas@gmail. com. This pleasant place near the lighthouse has a Mediterranean feel, comprising apartments split over 6 double-storey villas. All units have AC, DSTV, nets, balcony & fridges, & the whole thing is less than 100m from the beach. Drawbacks are that it is some distance from the city centre & has no on-site restaurant or cooking facilities. Prices are slightly higher when paying in meticais. *US$105 dbl; US$120 family room (sleeping 4).* **$$$**

🏠 **Residencial Beirasol** [204 C3] (6 rooms) 168 Rua da Madeira; 📞 233 26420; 📱 82 388 3522/533 3337; ✉ geral@residencialbeirasol. co.mz; 🖥 residencialbeirasol.co.mz. This restored colonial villa opposite the Tivoli has a useful central location & plenty of character. The rooms are on the small side but very comfortable, & come with DSTV, AC, Wi-Fi & fridge. The ground-floor restaurant is comfortable & modern, & has been warmly recommended. *US$34–50 dbl.* **$$**

🏠 **Royal Guesthouse** [205 H6] (6 rooms) 1311 Av Eduardo Mondlane; 📞 233 24030; 📱 82 388 3522; ✉ r.guesthouse@gmail.com. This low-key gem really is a very pleasant place to stay, with an ambience all its upmarket competitors lack. It lies in the lovely old residential area near the CBD &, though recently constructed, is very similar in design to the surrounding old villas. The rooms are tiled & come with AC, net, writing desk, DSTV & large en-suite bathroom with tub & shower. Facilities inc internet area, Wi-Fi access throughout the building, & a swimming pool in the back garden. Highly recommended. **$$$**

🏠 **Sun, Sand & Beach Guesthouse** [201 F2] (6 rooms) 2196 Av FPLM; 📱 82 848 6880 or 84 519 0243; ✉ sunbeira@gmail.com. On the beachfront near Clube Náutico, 2.5km east of Praça da Independência, this guesthouse has a great location & is a pretty good bet overall, assuming you can get over the bombastic colour scheme. The large clean rooms have DSTV, AC, fridge, dressing area & en-suite hot shower, & facilities inc small swimming pool & Wi-Fi. *US$50/60 dbl/twin B&B.* **$$**

BUDGET

🏠 **Hotel Infante Residencial** [204 D6] (35 rooms) Rua Jaime Ferreira; 📞 233 26603; ✉ hinfante.beira@gmail.com. Boasting a prime location in the heart of the CBD, a few paces from Praça da Municipalia, this sober multi-storey hotel has also been a reliable & reasonably affordable bet for some years. The comfortable & rather busily furnished en-suite rooms have parquet floor, TV, fan &, in some cases, AC. There's an adequate ground-floor bar & restaurant. Unusually in this range, Visa is accepted. **$$**

🏠 **Hotel Miramar** [201 C3] (24 rooms) Rua Vilas Boas Truão; 📞 233 22283; 📱 84 729 1714; ✉ hrmmbeira@gmail.com. This has been a strong contender for Beira's best-value accommodation for some years, & it remains a great choice, albeit not all that central. The rooms are pleasant enough, & some have a view over the bay to the south. *US$20/30/36 sgl/dbl/twin, all en suite with AC.* **$**

🏠 **Pensão Catembe** [204 C6] (6 rooms) Av Eduardo Mondlane; 📱 82 578 9398; ✉ alfredodinene34@gmail.com. This bright orange pensão is set on the 1st floor of a nondescript building a couple of blocks from the Praça da

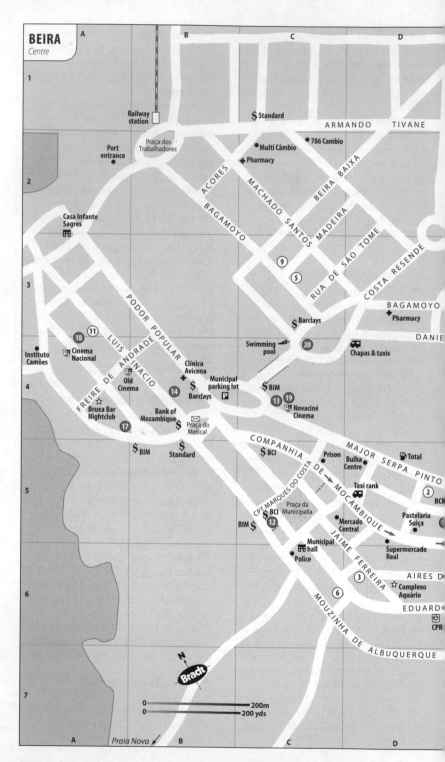

BEIRA
Centre

Railway station

Praça dos Trabalhadores

Port entrance

Casa Infante Sagres

$ Standard

786 Cambio

Multi Câmbio

✚ Pharmacy

ARMANDO   TIVANE

ACORES

BAGAMOYO

MACHADO SANTOS

BEIRA BAIXA

MADEIRA

RUA DE SÃO TOME

COSTA RESENDE

BAGAMOYO

✚ Pharmacy

DANIE

⑨

⑤

$ Barclays

PODOR POPULAR

LUIS ANDRADE

⑱ ⑪

🎭 Cinema Nacional

Instituto Camões

Swimming pool

⑳

🚌 Chapas & taxis

Old Cinema

Clínica Avicena
✚

Municipal parking lot 🅿

⑭ $ Barclays

$ BIM

⑬ ⑲ 🎬 Novaciné Cinema

FREIRE DE ANDRADE

☆ Bruxa Bar Nightclub

Bank of Mozambique $
✉ Praça do Metical

⑰

$ BIM

$ Standard

COMPANHIA

$ BCI

Prison

Bulha Centre

🚌 Total

MAJOR SERPA PINTO

CPT MARQUES DO COSTA DE MOCAMBIQUE

Taxi rank 🚌

②
BCI

Praça da Municipália

$ BCI ⑫

BIM $

Mercado Central

Pastelaria Suiça

Supermercado Real

JAIME FERREIRA

🏛 Municipal hall

Police

③

⑥

AIRES D

☆ Complexo Aquário

EDUARD

e CPR

MOUZINHA DE ALBUQUERQUE

N
🎈 Bradt

0 ____ 200m
0 ____ 200 yds

Praia Nova ↙

A   B   C   D

204

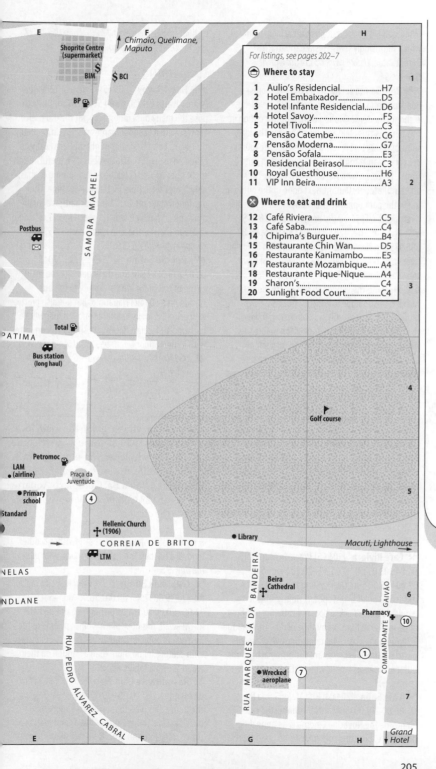

E   F ↑ Chimoio, Quelimane,   G   H
          Maputo

Shoprite Centre (supermarket)
BIM $ $ BCI

BP

For listings, see pages 202–7

🏨 **Where to stay**

1	Aulio's Residencial	H7
2	Hotel Embaixador	D5
3	Hotel Infante Residencial	D6
4	Hotel Savoy	F5
5	Hotel Tivoli	C3
6	Pensão Catembe	C6
7	Pensão Moderna	G7
8	Pensão Sofala	E3
9	Residencial Beirasol	C3
10	Royal Guesthouse	H6
11	VIP Inn Beira	A3

🍴 **Where to eat and drink**

12	Café Riviera	C5
13	Café Saba	C4
14	Chipima's Burguer	B4
15	Restaurante Chin Wan	D5
16	Restaurante Kanimambo	E5
17	Restaurante Mozambique	A4
18	Restaurante Pique-Nique	A4
19	Sharon's	C4
20	Sunlight Food Court	C4

Postbus

SAMORA MACHEL

Total

Bus station (long haul)

PATIMA

Golf course

Petromoc
LAM (airline)   Praça da Juventude
Primary school   (4)
Standard

Hellenic Church (1906)

CORREIA DE BRITO   • Library   Macuti, Lighthouse →

LTM

NELAS

NDLANE   **Beira Cathedral**

RUA MARQUES SÁ DA BANDEIRA

COMMANDANTE GAIVÃO

Pharmacy ✚ (10)

(1)

RUA PEDRO ALVAREZ CABRAL

• Wrecked aeroplane (7)

↓ Grand Hotel

Beira WHERE TO STAY

11

205

Municipalia. It's basic, but pleasant & high-ceilinged, with a surprisingly stylish restaurant attached. Decent value. *US$24 twin; US$34 dbl with AC.* **$$**

🏠 **Pensão Moderna** [205 G7] (42 rooms) Rua Mouzinho de Albuquerque; ✆ 233 29901; e shonnymoderna@yahoo.com. A newer option in this range is this pleasant guesthouse in the leafy suburbs a short walk south of the CBD. The rooms are very clean & comfortable, some are en suite & some also come with AC, DSTV & balcony. There's an unaffiliated restaurant next door, or the outdoor bar in the park opposite occasionally serves meals. Overpriced. *US$35/53 dbl or twin/trpl, B&B.* **$$**

🏠 **Rio Savane** [201 B1] ✆ 233 24855; m 82 598 9751; e riosavmoz@gmail.com. With its idyllic river-mouth location about 35km north of town, this is an excellent place to chill out for a few days enjoying the very good restaurant, deserted beach & unspoilt bush, which supports a rich birdlife. It's accessible in any saloon car: follow the EN6 towards Inchope until 300m before the main flyover to Beira Airport, then turn left on to a secondary road & follow for 34km to a safe guarded car park. From here, you cross to the resort

by boat (*the last leaves at 17.00*). *From US$25/37 sgl/dbl; US$12 pp camping.* **$$**

🏠 **Hotel Savoy** [205 F5] (9 rooms) 1299 Rua Pedro Alvares Cabral; m 84 589 0267. Unlikely to pose too many difficulties in a 'spot the difference' contest with its London namesake, this improbably timeworn hotel has what might diplomatically be called an excess of character, but it's a useful option for budget travellers taking early morning chapas, only 5mins' walk from Av Daniel Napatima. Their outdoor restaurant-bar, 'The Back Yard', is actually much nicer than you would expect. *US$13 sgl using common shower; US$21 en-suite twin; US$27–42 en-suite dbl with AC.* **$$**

🏠 **Pensão Sofala** [205 E3] ✆ 233 27048; m 82 815 9854. Off Rua de Bagamoio. The main virtue of this place is its proximity to the bus station on Av Daniel Napatima, but it is also pretty well priced, & looks habitable enough following a fairly recent facelift. Rooms are spacious & en suite, with parquet floor & fan. *US$16 sgl using common WC, US$20–34 en-suite dbl with AC & some with hot water.* **$**

✗ WHERE TO EAT AND DRINK

There is a great choice of eateries in Beira, with seafood inevitably being the main local speciality. There are also a couple of Chinese restaurants, which come as a welcome change if you've been in Mozambique a while. On the whole, eating out in Beira is cheaper than in more touristy parts of the coast. For nightlife, the most popular spots in the CBD include the Centro Hipico (north of the centre), Baixa Ba, Complexo Aquário and Imperial, while the larger Complexo Monte Verde (**f** *ComplexoMonteVerde*) lies along the road running north from Macuti towards the airport.

CBD

✗ **Café Riviera** [204 C5] Praça do Município; m 84 303 0333; ⏰ 06.30–20.30 Mon–Sat, 07.00–15.00 Sun. Overlooking the main square, this is a popular b/fast spot, & rightly so, but it would do for a snack, a boost of caffeine, or a bout of people-watching at any time of day. Their frango à Zambeziana is excellent. Inexpensive croissants, pastries & fresh espresso are the prime attractions, but it also serves a good range of sandwiches & snacks. **$$**

✗ **Café Saba** [204 C4] Rua Major Serpa Pinto; ⏰ 06.00–19.00 daily. This unsignposted café alongside the Novaciné Cinema is an appealing little place, boasting colourful décor, good espresso

& pastries, a limited range of sandwiches & other food, & a full bar. *Sandwiches & snacks with plate of the day.* **$$$**

✗ **Chipima's Burguer** [204 B4] Rua Luis Inácio; m 82 629 8852; ⏰ 08.00–20.00 Mon–Sat, 11.00–20.00 Sun. A surprisingly charming hole-in-the-wall, this busy place whips up some of the best-value burgers, sandwiches & chicken in town, with seating for no more than a handful on their wood-&-raffia tables. *US$2–4.* **$**

✗ **Restaurante Chin Wan** [204 D5] Rua Pêro de Alenquer; ⏰ 09.00–20.00 Mon–Sat. Despite the name, this place opposite the Kanimambo doesn't serve Chinese dishes but a combination of pizzas, Mozambican grills & lighter snacks. There's comfortable outdoor seating. *Most mains clock in at around US$6.* $

✖ **Restaurante Kanimambo** [205 E5] Rua Pêro de Alenquer; ☏233 23132; m 82 888 8560; ⏲ 10.30–14.30 & 18.00–22.00 daily. This long-serving Chinese restaurant contrives to look closed from the outside even when open, & the canteen ambience only furthers indifferent first impressions. That said, it's centrally located, the menu is refreshingly varied, vegetarians are well catered for, the food is very good, there's a helpful English-speaking owner-manager, & it would undoubtedly be our first culinary port of call in Beira. *Bank on around US$11–16 for a main with steamed rice.* $$$$

✖ **Restaurante Mozambique** [204 A4] Largo Luis de Camões; m 84 448 5001; ⏲ 07.30–23.00 daily. The former Cabine do Capitão looks a little timeworn on the inside, but the shady veranda is a great spot for a relaxed drink. It retains a good reputation for seafood, but when we last popped in they had precious little of it available. $$$

✖ **Restaurante Pique-Nique** [204 A4] Rua Costa Serrão; m 82 585 9907; ⏲ 07.00–23.00 daily. Bizarrely tucked away on an unpleasant street near the docks, this Beira institution might have come out of a film noir set, with its unobtrusively attentive tuxedoed waiters & no-nonsense maître d'. The food is equally memorable, not straying hugely from the traditional seafood & *prego no prato*, but produced with a flair that's so often missing, & not as expensive as you might fear. To summarise: if you're in Beira a while & don't eat here, then you've missed a trick. *Most mains are in the US$9–15 range, though prawns are steeper.* $$$$

✖ **Sharon's** [204 C4] Rua Major Serpa Pinto; m 82 580 2100. Once the hippest night venue in the CBD, this little bar tucked away at the rear left side of the Novaciné is pending reopening after years of major renovations. Expect a colourful & classy set-up, with an assortment of nightlife accoutrements inc new DJ booth, dance floor, karaoke & projector &, of course, a full bar. $$$

✖ **Sunlight Food Court** [204 C4] Rua Daniel Napatima; m 84 843 8888; ⏲ 11.00–late Mon–Sat, 15.00–late Sun. Keeping long hours & conveniently situated on the same road that effectively serves as the long-haul chapa station, this carnivalesque set-up in the middle of a roundabout sells a varied selection of Mozambican grills, Chinese noodle & rice dishes & fast foods. It's reasonably cheap, with plenty of seating & pool tables, & beer is served too. *US$4–12* $$$

SEAFRONT

✖ **Miramar Bar & Restaurant** [201 C4] Av Mateus Sansão Muthemba; ☏233 22283; ⏲ 08.00–late daily. Situated a short walk west of Praça da Independência, this beachfront spot with outdoor & indoor eating is a good place for a sundowner & serves decent meals. There is occasional live music, usually at w/ends, & a large screen for major sporting events. If you feel like a bit of a pub crawl, Beira Bar next door is a good spot as well. *US$9–20.* $$$$

✖ **Clube Náutico** [201 F2] Av FPLM; m 82 303 7016/764 8098; 🇫 ClubeNautico; ⏲ 08.00–late daily. This venerable beachfront complex 2.5km west of Praça da Independência has a well-maintained swimming pool & a bar-restaurant serving decent seafood, burgers, pizzas & other mains. $$$

✖ **Biques** [201 F2] Av FPLM; ⏲ 09.30–23.30 daily. This perennially popular sports bar 3.3km west of Praça da Independência has a very South African feel, with its pub-like décor, thatched roof & large-screen TV, & it serves good steaks as well as seafood. *Most mains are in the US$6–10 range.* $$$

✖ **Complexo Tropicana** [201 D3] Rua Brito Capelo; m 82 192 5818; ⏲ noon–late daily. Overlooking the beach about 300m east of Praça da Independência, this complex is centred on a large swimming pool & it has a shaded deck positioned perfectly to hear the waves crash & catch a sea breeze over dinner. *Tasty seafood dishes, pizzas & other mains are in the US$8–12 range.* $$$

✖ **Tuga's Bar & Lounge** [201 F2] Rua do Tenente Valadim; m 82 291 7938; ⏲ 11.00–22.00 daily. This new Portuguese restaurant has indoor & outdoor garden seating & serves up a fantastic selection of meat & seafood mains with tantalising desserts to boot. $$$$

OTHER PRACTICALITIES

BANKING AND FOREIGN EXCHANGE The usual banks are all represented, including Barclays, Standard, BCI and BIM Millennium. Most have branches with

24-hour ATMs dotted within a block of Praça do Município and Praça Metical. There is also an ATM at the Shoprite Centre [205 F1] on Avenida Samora Machel. There are only a couple of forex bureaux, including Multi Câmbio off Avenida Armando Tivane.

CINEMA The **Novaciné** [204 C4] on Rua Major Serpa Pinto sadly no longer shows films, but there are occasional events – check the fliers out front.

CULTURAL CENTRE The **Instituto Camões** [204 A4] (\ *233 23588;* e *icccp-beira@ tdm.co.mz;* w *ic-beira.blogspot.com;* f *InstitutoCamoesBeira*) on Rua António Enes puts on an impressively robust cultural calendar, including film screenings, art exhibitions, Portuguese lessons and literary readings, as well as music, theatre and dance performances. It's likely you'll see flyers around town, but events are also posted at f InstitutoCamoesBeira.

GOLF Unbelievably a golf course [205 H4] has been built on one of the swamps in the middle of the city. They have kit for hire if for some peculiar reason you neglected to include your clubs in your 20kg of luggage (\ *233 29523*).

HOSPITAL [201 E2] (\ *233 12071*) Situated on Avenida Mártires da Revolução. The private **Clinica Avicena** [204 B4] (\ *233 27990;* e *avicena.clinic@intra.co.mz*) on Avenida Poder Popular is excellent. There are also health centres on Rua General Machado, Rua Correia de Brito and two on Avenida Eduardo Mondlane, one at either end.

INTERNET Internet cafés are far fewer in number than might be expected in a city of this size, but the **Centro Provincial de Recursos Digitais** (CPRD) [204 D6] on Avenida Eduardo Mondlane is probably your best bet. There is also paid Wi-Fi at the Clube Náutico (page 207). If you need ready internet access and carry a laptop, it would make sense to book into a hotel with Wi-Fi.

POLICE (\ *233 27827*) There are police stations at Rua do Capitão Montanha, next to the Mercado do Maquinino [204 D2], Rua do Aruângua [204 C6], Rua Roma Machado and Avenida Mártires da Revolução, at the junction with Rua Paiva Couceiro [201 F2].

POST OFFICE There are a few of these dotted around town: Rua Capitão Curado [205 E3] (with Postbus), Rua General Machado just down from the Praça do Metical [204 B4], Rua Correia de Brito in the health centre on the corner with Rua dos Irmãos Bivar [205 F5], and on the corner of Rua Major Serpa Pinto and Rua 1.350 [204 B4].

SHOPPING The best supermarket is the **Shoprite** [205 F1] (*Av Samora Machel immediately north of Praça 11 de Outubro;* ⊕ *09.00–20.00 Mon–Sat, 09.00–15.00 Sun*), which stocks a vast range of fresh and processed goods, including much that is unavailable elsewhere in Beira. For fruit and vegetables, you can't beat the Mercado do Maquinino on Rua do Capitão Montanha, but the smaller **Mercado Central** [204 C5], painted bright yellow where Rua Jaime Ferreira meets Praça do Município, is likely to prove more convenient. **Supermercado Real** [204 D5] on Rua Correia de Brito is another good choice. There are plenty of other shops in the CBD, and meandering around them could also prove rewarding, while the **Bulha**

Centre [204 D5], on Rua Major Serpa Pinto, has a variety of upmarket clothing and electronics. Beira's limited appeal to tourists is reflected in the lack of craft and other touristic markets, but there is a tiny handicraft shop [201 G1] along the beach near Jardim das Velhas and craft sellers sometimes hang out near the Farol do Macuti [201 G1] or Clube Náutico [201 F2].

SWIMMING POOLS A small fee is charged to use the Olympic-size municipal pool [204 C4] (*Av Daniel Napatima, opposite the Hotel Moçambique*), which is in surprisingly good condition, and is adjoined by a 4.5m-deep pool for high diving. There are also swimming pools at the seafront Clube Náutico [201 F2] and Complexo Tropicana [201 D3], but they are less central and costlier, though worth heading out to if you feel like a seaside meal or drink after your swim.

WHAT TO SEE AND DO

If you like your entertainment planned and packaged, there isn't an awful lot to occupy yourself with in Beira, but it's a pleasant city to explore, with several notable buildings and an attractive seafront. The city centre boasts an intriguing mixture of architectural styles, ranging from early 20th-century colonial buildings – many in an advanced state of disrepair – through 1950s constructions in the Bauhaus style to some bizarre and ostentatious modern buildings.

A good place to start any exploration of the city centre is **Praça da Municipalia** [204 C5], which is ringed by old colonial buildings, notably the marble **municipal hall** and the old fort and jail, which now serves as the **central market**. A short walk away, on Rua Luis Inácio at the corner of Praça do Metical, the restored red-brick **Casa Portugal** [204 B4] is one of the best surviving examples of a turn-of-the-century Portuguese dwelling.

Praça do Metical [204 B4], named after the country's currency, is appropriately ringed by banks housed in buildings of various vintages. From Praça do Metical, walk up Avenida Poder Popular to the recently restored **Casa Infante Sagres** [204 A2], an old colonial building. Apparently it used to be covered in mosaics; if that's the case, some bright spark has ruined it by painting it brown and white. It's still fairly impressive, although from the wrong angle it looks a little like a Black Forest gateau.

Just behind the Casa Infante Sagres is the entrance to the **fishing port** [204 A2], where you can poke around the docks. If you do decide to visit (for whatever reason), it's crucial that you introduce yourself to the policemen on duty at the gate – they are very amicable but might start asking awkward questions if you fail to talk to them first.

To the right of the Casa Infante Sagres, a short and bumpy dirt road runs beside an old railway bridge to open out on **Praça dos Trabalhadores** (Workers' Square) [204 B2], the **freight port** and the adjacent **railway station** [204 B1]. Completed in 1966, the railway station has been described in the tourist literature as 'one of the most beautiful modern buildings in Africa' and by a correspondent to the previous edition as 'a hideous example of imperial overlord modern school architecture'. The latter description rings more true.

Return to Praça da Municipalia and follow Avenida República into Avenida Eduardo Mondlane. A short distance along the road is the striking **Beira Cathedral** [205 G6], which was erected between 1907 and 1925 using stones taken from the Portuguese fort at Sofala. It has a children's playground in its grounds. There is a pretty chapel a block further along the same road, as well as one a block up on Rua Correia de Brito. In addition to housing Beira's main cluster of old ecclesiastical

For centuries prior to the Portuguese occupation, the most important trading centre in what is now Mozambique was Sofala, which lay amid the shallow waterways and impermanent sandbars of the Buzi River mouth, about 50km south of present-day Beira. Founded in AD900 and described in a contemporary document by the Arab writer al-Masudi, Sofala formed the main medieval link between the inland trade route to the gold mines of present-day Zimbabwe and Manica, and the prosperous Swahili city of Kilwa (in southern Tanzania), as well as being an important trading centre in its own right. By the 15th century it probably had a population of around 10,000.

The first European visitor to Sofala was the Portuguese explorer and spy Pêro de Covilhã, who travelled there overland disguised as an Arab merchant in 1489. In 1500, Sofala was visited by Sancho de Toar, who recognised its pivotal role in the gold trade. Five years later, Portugal erected a small fort and trading factory at Sofala. Although this was done with the permission of the local sheikh, Portugal rapidly set about establishing its own local trade network, bypassing the Muslim traders. Within a year of its foundation, the Portuguese fort was attacked without any marked success by the sheikh and his allies. Portugal responded by killing the sheikh in a punitive attack, and installing a puppet ruler in his place.

The Portuguese occupation of Sofala evidently coincided with a northward migration of the main chieftaincies of Karangaland and a corresponding shift in the main inland trade routes. Combined with the increasing dominance of ivory over gold as a trading commodity, this shift in trade routes caused Sofala to diminish in importance. As early as 1530, the main captaincy of the coast moved from Sofala to Mozambique Island. By the 17th century, Sofala was a neglected backwater, with the token Portuguese occupancy largely to prevent the fort from falling to a rival European power. By the 1750s, the stone buildings of the Portuguese quarter were partially submerged, and Sofala was more or less left in the hands of a few Muslim traders. By the time that modern Mozambique came into being, Sofala's permanent buildings had mostly disappeared beneath the sea, and the ancient port was passed over in favour of Chiloane as the local administrative centre. The stone fort at Sofala was dismantled and its bricks were used to build Beira Cathedral.

Sofala still exists today, though as little more than an overgrown fishing village. It is possible to visit the site (there is reputedly even a pensão in the town), but you'll need a couple of days as it will be more than a day trip. There are two routes to Sofala. The road route is in poor condition, and entails following the EN6 northwest for 65km to Tica, then turning south along the EN214 and following it for about 60km to Nova Almada, then crossing the Buzi River by motor ferry, and continuing another 50km southeast to Sofala.

The second option, which is rather more in keeping with the spirit of old Sofala, is to go by boat. A daily ferry heads in this direction from Beira, leaving Praia Nova at 07.00. To get to Praia Nova you need to walk through the Mercado Praia Nova – the best entrance to use is the one opposite the police barracks on Rua do Aruângua. Just walk straight down the main path through the Mercado (if you come to any forks, stay on the left) and, once you reach the crossroads, carry straight on over on to the bottom end of the beach.

For the intrepid traveller willing to go well off the beaten track, it is possible to leave Beira by boat and visit the remote palm-fringed island fishing community of Chiloane, located about 60 miles (100 km) south of Beira. Ilha Chiloane is a place truly untouched by tourism, much less the outside world; a visit will provide a glimpse into a listless Arcadian lifestyle still dictated by the tides, the sun and the moon.

Fishing boats sail from Beira to Chiloane once or twice a week and leave from Praia Nova, the fishing beach in Beira located south of the port and near the Baixa neighbourhood. There are also daily boats to Nova Sofala, the historic seaport located south of Beira across the Pungué River (box, page 210). In typical Mozambican style, departures in the wee hours of the morning are likely, so you should enquire in advance and make arrangements the day before you plan to travel; you will need to do some informal asking around at the Praia Nova to locate a boat that is sailing soon. You may also wish to see the boat beforehand as not all vessels are seaworthy, as it is likely to be not much more than a large fishing boat with a motor strapped on the back.

The boat journey to Ilha Chiloane is long (*9–11 hrs*) and can be choppy, especially as you set off from Beira, where the Pungué River empties into the Indian Ocean. Once you find your legs on Ilha Chiloane, ask anyone for **Pensão Nora**, which has low-cost, basic double rooms and can arrange meals as well. There's little to do on the island besides soaking up the sun, trying your hand at some fishing, and relishing your almost-guaranteed status as the only tourist for miles around.

When it's time to leave this idyll, you can always just return to Beira by boat, or there are occasional boats through the mangrove labyrinth to one of the mainland villages facing the island, such as Divinhe or Marrupahne. It's just a short hop to Divinhe; pirogues will take you across for about US$2, or you can charter a motorised boat for about US$40. From there, it is possible to catch a twice-weekly chapa (*Tue & Fri*) to Machanga, which lies just across the Save River from Nova Mambone, where you'll find a BIM Millennium ATM and some basic pensões. Machanga and Nova Mambone are easily connected by a regular riverboat crossing, and both cities are served by daily chapas to the EN1 and beyond.

buildings, this part of town was formerly the most upmarket residential area, and there are several pleasing old houses, some beautifully maintained, others utterly derelict – you could happily pass an afternoon or two exploring this area.

A brisk 30-minute walk along Avenida Eduardo Mondlane, under a canopy of overhanging trees and over a rather rough pavement with flagstones that have been pushed up by the roots of those trees, brings you out at **Praça da Independência** [201 D3], a large open circle on the seafront. From here, you could continue 5km west, walking or catching a chapa along Avenida FPLM, to the **Farol do Macuti** (Macuti Lighthouse) [201 G1], where there is a pretty beach and a cluster of cheap eateries and bars. The lighthouse was built in 1904, stands 28m tall, and has a conical top with two red stripes. Whether the two rusting ship hulks that lie on the nearby beach are testament to the lighthouse's efficacy is unclear.

Alternatively, if you feel like heading back to the city centre from Praça da Independência, then follow the seafront Avenida Mateus Sansão Muthemba back east, with the crumbling seafront wall to your left – possibly taking a break at the Miramar Restaurant [201 C4]. A short diversion leads down to the **Grand Hotel** [201 B4]. The Grand has clearly not been a hotel since independence and is now a thriving high-rise slum. Entering the building today would be both dangerous and a little insensitive, but it's worth taking 5 minutes to observe from the outside – not because of the poverty and poor condition of the building, but more to see the people. You'll see children playing in the grounds, women doing their washing in the pool, men sitting chatting together on the entrance steps. It is, in a slightly bizarre way, a tribute to the resilience of the Mozambicans and their ability to take the little that is available to them and make the best of it.

Continuing along from the Grand Hotel, the avenue bends to the right and stops in the Largo Artur Brandão. Head directly over it on to the Rua 1 de Dezembro. This will take you through some of the swampland that the city was built on to the crossroads with Rua do Governador Augusto Castilho. Turn left and walk up past the **Mercado Praia Nova** [204 B7] back to the Praça do Município.

above The Fortaleza de São Sebastião on Ilha de Moçambique was built in 1546 to defend against marauders, and remains remarkably well preserved to this day (AVZ) pages 300–2

above The highland town of Gurué is surrounded by tea plantations and lies at the foot of Mount Namuli, making it an ideal base for hikers (AVZ) pages 270–3

left The Ilha-Fortim de São Lourenço, with its 17th-century fort, lies just offshore from Moçambique and is accessible at low tide (AVZ) page 305

below Moçambique is the oldest European settlement on Africa's east coast and remains a maze of narrow alleys lined with Portuguese-style buildings with Arabian and Indian flourishes (AVZ) pages 291–305

above   Ibo's old town is a haunting backwater, many of its grand 19th-century villas having been abandoned to strangler figs and the ravages of time (EL) pages 335–43

right   Built in 1522 by the Portuguese, the Capela da Nossa Senhora do Baluarte on Ilha de Moçambique is deemed to be the oldest European building in the southern hemisphere (AVZ) page 302

below   Built in 1776, Quelimane's old Roman Catholic cathedral overlooks the Rio dos Bons Sinais, 'River of Good Signs' (AVZ) page 258

above & left The vast and entrancing Niassa Reserve, dominated by the Lugenda River, offers as untrammelled an African bush experience as still exists (AVZ and SC) pages 366–73

below & left Gorongosa National Park has had mixed fortunes since the civil war, but is now on the road to recovery; visitors have a good chance of spotting elephant and waterbuck (AVZ and AG/S) pages 229–34

above   **Lago Niassa provides a remote freshwater alternative to the many coastal Mozambican destinations, offering its own distinct cultures and serene landscapes** (AVZ) pages 359–66

middle left   **Eastern double-collared sunbird (*Cinnyris mediocris*)** (AVZ) page 35

middle right   **Böhm's bee-eater (*Merops boehmi*)** (AVZ) page 34

lower left   **Yellow-fronted canary (*Serinus mozambicus*)** (MK/IB/FLPA) page 34

lower right   **Palm-nut vulture (*Gypohierax angolensis*)** (MBW/FLPA) page 34

below   **Horseback safaris explore the coconut groves and beaches around Tofo** (AVZ) page 171

left   Dozens of isolated villages with pristine beaches await the intrepid traveller, such as at Angoche and Pangane (AL/S) pages 285 & 350

below   Dhows in Fernão Veloso Bay, the deepest natural harbour along the east coast of Africa (AVZ) page 309

bottom A fishing village on Ilha Matemo: the lush island is one of 11 that fall within the Quirimbas National Park (IB/FLPA) pages 344–5

right   Bull shark (*Carcharhinus leucas*) (GS/B/FLPA)
page 40

below   Much of Mozambique's 2,470km coastline is
protected by offshore coral reefs, making it a
Mecca for divers and snorkellers (SS)
pages 75–82

bottom   Bottlenose dolphins (*Tursiops truncatus*)
(BT/S) page 39

12

Chimoio and the Manica Highlands

With thanks to Hannah Fagerbakke (see box, page 198)

The landlocked province of Manica is bordered by the Save and Zambezi rivers to the south and northeast, the province of Tete and Sofala to the northwest and east, and Zimbabwe to the west. The gold deposits associated with the so-called Manica Greenstone Belt along the Zimbabwean border have been exploited since medieval times, when the Monomotapa Kingdom exported gold via the Zambezi Valley to the coastal port of Sofala. The province formed the centre of the Manica Kingdom, which was most likely established in medieval times and survived into the 19th century, and several of its larger towns, including Manica itself, were founded in the pre-Portuguese era.

Few travellers spend much time in Manica, at least by comparison with coastal provinces such as Inhambane and Sofala. The province does, however, see quite a bit of passing tourist traffic, bisected as it is by several pivotal trunk roads. Most important of these is the EN6 through the Beira Corridor, which links the Indian

THE BEIRA CORRIDOR

The strategic importance of the Beira Corridor, which consists of the 300km-long EN6 and a parallel oil pipeline and railway (which now operates for freight only), grew after Zimbabwe achieved full independence in 1980, leaving South Africa and Namibia as the last bastions of white rule in southern Africa. Zimbabwe and the various other states neighbouring South Africa formed the SADCC (Southern Africa Development Co-ordination Conference), with the declared aim of reducing the region's economic dependence on the apartheid regime. For landlocked countries such as Zimbabwe, Zambia and Botswana, a crucial factor in achieving this goal was to have access to a sea port that was not under South African control.

Beira was the obvious choice on account of its proximity to the Zimbabwean border. However, by the mid 1980s, years of neglect had caused Beira's harbour to silt up to the point where it was practically unnavigable, while the rail link to Zimbabwe had become a regular target for terrorist attacks by Renamo. The Mozambican national army was too weak to protect it against these attacks, and so Zimbabwe's defence forces took responsibility for defending the Beira Corridor. After large amounts of foreign aid were used to make Beira harbour operational, Zimbabwe and Zambia steadily increased their imports via Beira during the late 1980s – although neither country ever came close to being independent of the South African transport system. (See box, page 58 for more about Mozambique's transportation corridors.)

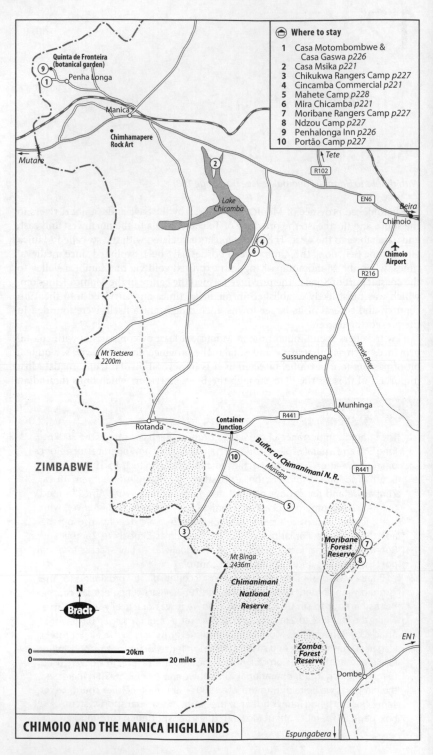

Where to stay

1 Casa Motombombwe &
   Casa Gaswa *p226*
2 Casa Msika *p221*
3 Chikukwa Rangers Camp *p227*
4 Cincamba Commercial *p221*
5 Mahete Camp *p228*
6 Mira Chicamba *p221*
7 Moribane Rangers Camp *p227*
8 Ndzou Camp *p227*
9 Penhalonga Inn *p226*
10 Portão Camp *p227*

Quinta de Fronteira
(botanical garden)

Penha Longa

Manica

Chimhamapere
Rock Art

Mutare

Tete

R102

EN6

Beira

Chimoio

Lake
Chicamba

Chimoio
Airport

R216

Mt Tsetsera
2200m

Sussundenga

Revúe River

Rotanda

Container
Junction

R441

Munhinga

Buffer of Chimanimani N. R.

Mussapa

R441

ZIMBABWE

Mahete

Mt Binga
2436m

Moribane
Forest
Reserve

Chimanimani
National
Reserve

N

Bradt

0   20km
0   20 miles

Zomba
Forest
Reserve

EN1

Dombe

Espungabera

CHIMOIO AND THE MANICA HIGHLANDS

Ocean port of Beira to Mutare (Zimbabwe). At Inchope, the EN6 intersects with the EN1, the main road connecting all coastal ports south of Beira to regions north of the Zambezi, while the only surfaced road connecting Mozambique to Malawi, the R102/3 (EN7) to Blantyre via Tete, runs north from the EN6 at Bandula.

The main regional route focus, about 200km inland of Beira, is the provincial capital Chimoio, an affably unremarkable town that lies immediately north of the EN6 between Inchope and Bandula. The other main population centre in the region is the historic town of Manica, which is bisected by the EN6 about 30km east of the Zimbabwean border. Either town can be used as a base for exploring the province's main attractions, which include the little-known but very accessible Chinhamapere Rock Art Site, the mountains around Penhalonga, the attractive Chicamba Real Dam and the remote Chimanimani National Park.

CHIMOIO

The capital of landlocked Manica Province, Chimoio (pronounced 'Shimoio') is the fourth-largest city in Mozambique, with a population estimated at 325,000, and the most important town along the EN6 between Beira and the Zimbabwean border. At 750m above sea level, Chimoio has a refreshing mid-altitude climate and a compact and well-equipped town centre, comprising a neat oval grid of roads, lined with leafy trees and two- to three-storey buildings, a few hundred metres northeast of the EN6. It's not the sort of town you'd make a special effort to visit, but it is a pleasant enough place and its significance as a route focus means that a fair number of travellers pass through. The most significant local attraction is the striking outcrop known as Cabeça de Velho, but Chimoio also forms an increasingly popular base for visits to other sites of interest covered in this chapter.

HISTORY Oral tradition has it that Chimoio is the name of a prince who was executed by a local clan chief as punishment for hunting in his territory, and buried in the area. The modern town dates to 1893, when the Mozambique Company established its district headquarters at a nearby site known as Vila Barreto, relocating to the present-day site in 1899 following the completion of the railway connecting Beira to Zimbabwe. Initially known as Mandigos, the town prospered as a transportation and agricultural centre in the early 20th century, thanks partly to the implementation of a cotton scheme in 1902.

Mandigos was renamed Vila Pery in 1916 (after the Governor of Manica, João Pery de Lind), accorded city status in 1969, and given the name Chimoio at a post-independence rally held there by President Samora Machel in 1975. A mortar strike on the town in 1974 was the only instance in which Frelimo attacked a major settlement during the war for liberation from Portugal. In November 1977, the Rhodesian Security Forces launched an aerial attack on Robert Mugabe's ZANLA (Zimbabwe African National Liberation Army) headquarters at Chimoio, killing an estimated 3,000 ZANLA soldiers.

GETTING THERE AND AWAY Chimoio is one of Mozambique's most important public transport hubs. It is the closest substantial town to the crossroads of the **EN6** between Beira and Mutare (Zimbabwe) and the **EN1** from Maputo and Vilankulo to Quelimane, as well as lying only 20km east of where the **R102/3** (EN7) branches north from the EN6 to Tete and Blantyre (Malawi). As such, Chimoio is passed through by many people travelling between southern and northern Mozambique, or crossing into or out of Malawi or Zimbabwe.

Given the resurgent conflict since 2013 between Renamo and the Frelimo government, there have been military escorted convoys on several sections of road in the central region of Mozambique, where the conflict has been most active. During the period of research (mid 2016) for this edition, three convoys were in place: two on the EN1 between the Save River and the small town of Muxungue and between Nhamapadza and Caia; and one on the EN7 between Vanduzi and Changara (Luenha River). At the end of December 2016, a truce was agreed. The convoys were suspended and remained as such until the time of research (April 2017).

In the event that convoy travel is once again instituted, travellers should consult locals as to the current safety of convoy travel – if there have been recent attacks – as well as to departure times. Historically, there have been two convoys per day, each consisting of 100–200 vehicles, including lorries and buses. For those not travelling in their own vehicle, public transport poses an elevated risk: coaches have been the target of attacks, as the government has hired out coaches to conceal the transport of troops. If you find yourself at the edge of a convoy on public transport, it is perhaps advisable to hitch a ride with a private vehicle. Once in the convoy, note that it has been known to travel rather fast, with vehicles overtaking and jockeying for their preferred position within the convoy – most aiming to be near the military escort vehicles. Soldiers have also been known to ask drivers for beverages and cigarettes.

By car For self-drivers, trunk roads in all directions are in fair to good condition, with the EN6 slated to be resurfaced by the end of 2018. Typical driving times would be around 45 minutes to Inchope junction, 3 hours to Beira, 4 hours to Tete, 1 hour to Mutare (excluding border formalities) and 6 hours to Vilankulo.

By bus and chapa Almost all public transport out of Chimoio leaves from the bus station between the Mercado Central and the disused railway station. **Chapas** to destinations along the Beira Corridor leave regularly throughout the day, as do vehicles heading for Sussundenga (for Chimanimani National Park) and other local destinations. Sample fares are US$5 to Beira, around US$2 to Manica and US$1 to Sussundenga.

All **long-haul buses** out of Chimoio leave in the wee hours. At least one bus runs daily to Tete, costing US$8, leaving at around 04.00 and arriving at 11.00. The daily bus to Quelimane costs US$14, also departs around 04.00 and arrives 10–12 hours later. One or two buses leave for Maputo daily, setting off at 03.00, taking 6 hours to Vilankulo, 10 hours to Maxixe (for Inhambane) and 19–20 hours to Maputo. The full US$26 fare to Maputo is charged, irrespective of where you disembark. Heading north, **Maning Nice** (m *82 706 2820 or 84 600 9019*) runs direct buses to Nampula three times a week for US$30. Long-haul tickets should be bought directly from the bus conductor on the afternoon before departure. Different companies cover the various routes on different days, so ask around at the bus station to locate the correct vehicle. If you stay at Pink Papaya (page 218), the management is an excellent source of current information about bus schedules (and they can also arrange an escort to the bus station for early morning starts).

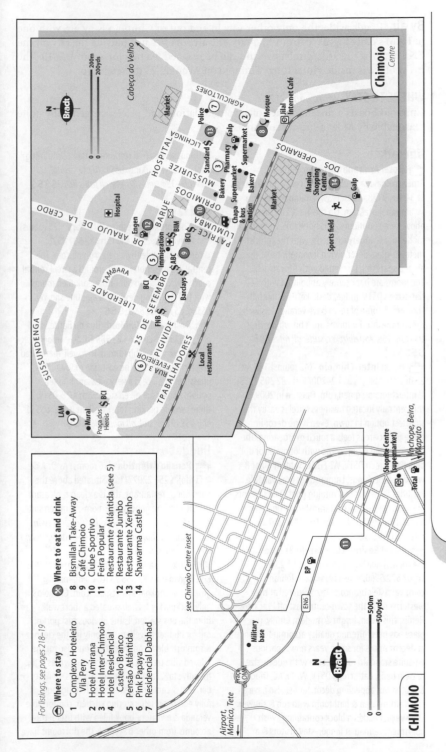

By air Roads aside, the only other way in and out of Chimoio is by air, with one of **LAM**'s daily flights to/from Maputo. The **airport** lies just outside the city off the EN6 heading towards Zimbabwe and can be reached via taxi for about US$10. The LAM office is inside Hotel Inter-Chimoio on Avenida 25 de Setembro.

WHERE TO STAY *Map, page 217*

Chimoio boasts a decent choice of accommodation, and prices are generally quite reasonable by Mozambican standards.

Upmarket

Hotel Amirana (41 rooms) Rua Dr Américo Boavida; 251 23334; m 82 333 9590 or 84 164 9178; e reservas@amiranahotel.com; w amiranahotel.com. On the 1st & 2nd floors above some boutiques, this hotel takes a swing at modernity & largely succeeds, with the futuristic metal-&-glass décor giving it something of the air of a spaceship festooned with African art. The rooms are handsomely appointed with AC, flat-screen DSTV, fridge, desk, kettle & rainfall showers, & some of them have verandas as well, though the interior rooms are a bit windowless. *US$136/166/250 dbl/exec/suite; all rates B&B.* **$$$$**

Hotel Inter-Chimoio (42 rooms) 18B Av 25 de Setembro; 251 24200/1; m 82 305 7233; e interchimoio@gmail.com. Opened in 2009, this centrally located business hotel is easily the smartest option in town, even if the décor in some public areas feels a touch overbearing. The large carpeted rooms come with king-size or dbl bed, flat-screen DSTV, Wi-Fi, AC, safe, minibar & wooden furnishings. Larger suites are available. Facilities inc terrace swimming pool, 2 restaurants, business centre & airport transfers to tie in with all LAM flights. *US$130 dbl; US$170–260 suites; all rates B&B.* **$$$$**

Hotel Residencial Castelo Branco (34 rooms) Rua Sussundenga; 251 23600/1; m 82 522 5960; e reservas@castelobranco.com; w castelobranco.co.mz. Situated at the western end of the town centre just off Praça dos Heróis, this clean, bright & modern family-run place has been offering quality accommodation at decent prices for some years now. Spacious en-suite standard rooms come with queen-size or twin beds, flat-screen DSTV, Wi-Fi, AC, fridge & muted but appealing décor. Suites also have a small sitting area & bathroom with tub & shower. They've just added a block containing swish apartments aimed at longer-stay visitors & a Portuguese-inspired restaurant. Has a swimming pool & secure parking. *US$120/137 sgl/dbl; US$166–384 suites & apts; all rates B&B.* **$$$$**

Mid range

Complexo Hoteleiro Vila Pery (26 rooms) Rua Pigivide; 251 24391; m 82 501 4520; e complexohoteleirovilapery@gmail.com. This central 3-storey hotel, built around a small central courtyard, has clean but rather dark tiled rooms with DSTV, writing desk, AC & en-suite shower. *US$60/65 sgl/dbl B&B.* **$$$**

Residencial Dabhad Rua do Bárue, nr 32; 251 23264; m 82 385 5480; e info@dabhad.com; w dabhad.com. In a well-manicured green compound on the east side of town, this unassuming place is a very pleasant budget option. Rooms are all en suite with AC & DSTV, & there's secure parking too. Excellent value. *US$35 dbl; US$39 exec dbl; all rooms B&B.* **$$**

Budget

Pensão Atlántida (16 rooms) Av Dr A de la Cerdo; 251 22027/169. Situated above the eponymous restaurant, this is a clean & pleasant pensão offering good-value rooms, some en suite, & all with fan & writing desk. *US$30 sgl or twin with common shower; US$40/50 en-suite sgl/twin with balcony & AC.* **$$**

Pink Papaya (2 rooms, 1 dorm) Casa 795, Rua Pigivide; m 82 555 7310; e anjamann@gmx.de; w pinkpapaya.atspace.com. Chimoio's only backpacker hostel, situated a short walk from the bus station, is the obvious first port of call for budget travellers, not only for the clean & comfortable accommodation, but also for the relaxed vibe created by the German owners & the friendly staff. Facilities inc hot showers, honesty bar, tent & camping gear rental, left luggage, fully equipped self-catering kitchen, comfortable veranda & a visitors' book filled with useful trip accounts from other travellers. The dbl rooms have walk-in nets & cane furniture. Beds in the 10-bed dorm also have nets. The staff is usually a good source of local travel advice & can help with public transport information & possibly visa extensions. *US$20/26 sgl/dbl; US$30/40 dbl/quad family room; US$10 dorm bed.* **$$**

✖ WHERE TO EAT AND DRINK   Map, page 217

There's no shortage of decent places to eat in Chimoio. For cheap local dishes, try one of the no-frills eateries marked on the map around the corner from Pink Papaya. There is a bar at the old railway station. Other acceptable and affordable options serving typical Mozambican fare include **Restaurante Xerinho**, **Restaurante Jumbo** and the **Clube Sportivo** (as shown on the map), all of which double as bars. Otherwise, the following stand out:

✖ **Bismillah Take-Away** m 82 023 0248; ⏱ 05.00–midnight daily. This busy place is the hub of the local Somali community & dishes up chicken & rice & a few other meals, all in record time. *US$2–4.* **$**

✖ **Café Chimoio** Av 25 de Setembro; ⏱ 08.00–23.00 daily. This pleasant central eatery keeps long hours & serves a selection of sandwiches, burgers, torrados & light meals. Also has pastries & espresso coffee. *US$3–5.* **$**

✖ **Feira Popular** Immediately south of the EN6, more or less opposite the railway station, this cluster of drinking holes & low-cost eateries is the place to head for a cheap night out, especially on Fri & Sat. **$**

✖ **Restaurante Atlántida** Av Dr A de la Cerda; ☎ 251 22027/169; ⏱ lunch & dinner daily. On the ground floor of Pensão Atlántida (page 218), this place has plenty of old-fashioned charm, with its tall ceiling, wood-panelled walls & red chequered tablecloths. The daily special is usually good value, or you can choose from the extensive menu of seafood & meat dishes. There's a good wine list too. *Mains US$6–8.* **$$**

✖ **Shawarma Castle** Inside Manica Shopping Centre; m 82 389 7410; ⏱ 08.00–22.00 Sun–Thu, 08.00–23.00 Fri/Sat. While it may be lacking in turrets, drawbridges, or other features one might expect in a castle, on the shawarma front this café does not disappoint. The menu here is wide, but the real reason to go is the delicious selection of Lebanese dishes such as hummus, falafel, manaqish & baba ghanoush. There's outdoor seating & vegetarians are well catered for. 2 for 1 pizza specials on Fri. No alcohol, but excellent fresh juices. *US$4–7.* **$$**

OTHER PRACTICALITIES

Banks and foreign exchange There are several banks, mostly clustered around the junction of avenidas 25 de Setembro and Dr A de la Cerda. The Standard, Barclays, BIM Millennium, FNB, ABC Bank and BCI all have 24-hour ATMs. There is also a BIM Millennium ATM at the Shoprite Centre on the EN6 to Beira, as well as at the Manica Shopping Centre just south of town, where you'll also find a private bureau de change. There is also a private bureau de change next to ABC Bank on Avenida 25 de Setembro. Note, too, that many private money changers hang around the park at the corner opposite the Standard Bank, as well as by the chapa stop, but they are very sharp operators and attempted robberies aren't unknown, so be careful.

Hospital (*Rua do Hospital, opposite junction with Rua Patrice Lumumba;* ☎ *251 22415*). There's a medical centre on the corner between avenidas 25 de Setembro and Dr A de la Cerda, and a pharmacy on Rua Dr A Boavida between Rua Cidade de Lichinga and Rua dos Operários.

Immigration The immigration office in Chimoio, next to the BIM Millennium on Avenida 25 de Setembro, can process visa extensions on a 30-day single-entry visa. It'll cost about US$20 and take a couple of days. If you are staying at Pink Papaya, ask there for details before you head out to the immigration office.

Internet Your best bet is the **Jilal Internet Café** (m *82 777 1690* or *84 908 6111;* ⏰ *08.00–16.00 daily*), in a green-and-white container on the east end of Avenida Trabalhadores.

Police On Rua dos Operários, just up from the junction with Rua do Bárue (☎ *251 22213*).

Shopping The **Shoprite** (⏰ *09.00–20.00 Mon–Sat, 09.00–15.00 Sun*) in the eponymous centre (on the EN6 to Beira) is very well stocked – coming from the north, it'll be the best supermarket you'll have seen in a long time. The centre also has a fast-food outlet, BIM Millennium with ATM and internet café. More centrally, there are several good supermarkets dotted around the market area and in the Manica Shopping Centre, and there's a decent enough bakery on Rua Cidade de Lichinga (though it's not as good as La Plaza).

WHAT TO SEE AND DO It has to be said that, while pleasant enough and having some startlingly pretty sunsets, Chimoio is not in itself the most interesting of towns. Within the town itself, the only real point of interest is the colourful mural of the revolution that runs around the wall of the Praça dos Heróis at the western end of Avenida 25 de Setembro. Further afield, the town makes a good base for day or overnight trips to most other sites of interest covered in this chapter, and Pink Papaya is an excellent place to catch the latest news about tourist developments in the region.

It is definitely worth heading a short way along the 3km road towards **gelho**, a vast granite outcrop that resembles an old man's face in repose. It is also possible to walk to the top of the formation's three peaks. (Theft was once an occasional problem on this hike, but there have been no reported incidents for a number of years.) To get there, walk along Rua do Bárue until it becomes dirt road and then follow it past the Restaurant os Bambus and through the market stalls. This road eventually meanders off around the mud huts, but you won't get lost – the rocks are right in front of you. Unless you really dawdle you'll be able to do all three peaks in a morning or afternoon, but (as ever) take water and a hat – there's little shelter from the sun on the route. Once at the top, the view of the surrounding countryside is impressive.

There is also a fun nightlife scene in Chimoio. If you find yourself here on a Friday or Saturday night, the Feira Popular (page 219) is full of various bars for drinking and a few places for dancing. For a more traditional discoteca experience, the club in Soalpo (any taxi driver will know where it's at) provides a fun atmosphere.

LAKE CHICAMBA

Also known as Chicamba Real, this scenic lake was created in 1968 when the colonial government constructed a new hydro-electric dam on the Revué River about 40km downstream of Manica town and a similar distance from Chimoio. Set in a distinctively African landscape of rocky hills swathed in dense brachystegia woodland, the lake extends over 160km^2 northwest from the dam wall, and numerous inlets and coves follow the surrounding contours, with the Chimanimani and Vumba mountains providing a backdrop on the Zimbabwean border. Lake Chicamba is popular with fishermen from neighbouring Zimbabwe, with Florida-strain largemouth bass being their main quarry, and accommodation tends to fill up over weekends and during Zimbabwean school holidays. At other times it is generally very quiet, and the surrounding wooded hills would be of great interest to birdwatchers, while the attractive scenery, pleasant climate and sense of isolation add up to a potentially alluring stopover for backpackers seeking a change of scene after a period on the coast.

GETTING THERE AND AWAY Casa Msika, the main tourist focus, stands on a northwestern arm of the lake, 5km – and clearly signposted – from the south side of the **EN6** some 30km east of Manica town and 40km west of Chimoio. Alternatively, a scenic and very good unsurfaced road runs all around the east side of the lake, leading south from the EN6 about 5km closer to Chimoio. After 15km, this road reaches the tiny village of Chicamba, from where it is another 1km to the bridge that spans the Revué immediately below the hydro-electric dam, then another few hundred metres to Mira Chicamba Lodge. From here, it continues southward to Rotanda and Tsetsera (page 228).

Using public transport, **chapas** from Chimoio to Manica can drop you at the junction for Casa Msika (an hour's walk further) while chapas from Chimoio to Nyamakamba (*less than US$1*) can drop you right at Mira Chicamba Lodge.

⌐ WHERE TO STAY, EAT AND DRINK   *Map, page 214*

⌂ **Casa Msika**   (30 rooms) m 82 440 4304/960 9418; e casamsika@gmail.com; ⨍ casa.msika. This long-serving (& starting to show it) lodge is aimed mainly at the Zimbabwean w/ender crowd, so the focus is firmly on fishing, though it also has a lovely location for rambling & an animal-rehabilitation project on-site with giraffes. A varied selection of thatched family, lake-view chalets, dbl rooms & self-catering units is offered, along with camping, barbecue areas, swimming pool, restaurant & Wi-Fi at the bar. Guided game drive, game walk, bird walks & canoe trips available. *US$30 dbl or twin room; US$70 self-catering dbl; US$35 pp chalet (sleeping 3 or 4); US$8 pp camping.* **$$$**

⌂ **Cincamba Commercial**   (10 rooms) Situated between Mira Chicamba & the dam wall, this place is primarily a bar, but also serves basic meals for around US$3 & offers good sunset views over the lake. *Has a few very basic rooms at the back for around US$10.* **$**

⌂ **Mira Chicamba**   (6 rooms) ☏ 239 10076; ⨍ mirachicamba.lodge. Set on the east side of the lake about 1km south of the dam wall, this pleasant resort offers clean no-frills accommodation in semi-detached cottages, all of which have a dbl bed, en-suite hot shower, writing desk & small private balcony. The open thatched bar/restaurant has DSTV & a decent selection of meat & fish dishes. **$**

MANICA

Flanking the EN6 about 30km east of the Zimbabwean border, this agreeable small town (estimated population 45,000) is today overshadowed by the provincial capital Chimoio some 70km to its west. In times past, however, it was one of the most important settlements in the Mozambican interior, serving as capital of the Manica Kingdom, and the site of a gold fair that operated intermittently from medieval times into the early 19th century. Tourist attractions fittingly include a venerable geological museum, which is unlikely to be of more than passing interest to most visitors, and the altogether more compelling Chinhamapere Rock Art Site, 5km out of town. Manica is also the springboard for visits to the mountainous Penhalonga region on the Zimbabwean border northwest of town.

HISTORY Manica's fortunes have traditionally risen and slumped with that of the regional gold trade. Chipangura, the pre-Portuguese capital of the Manica

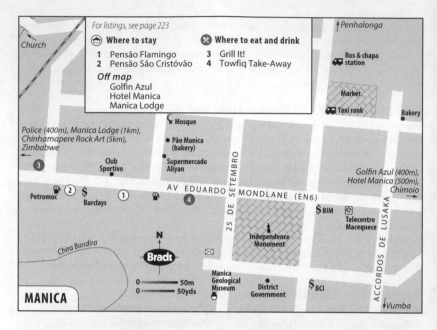

For listings, see page 223

🛏 **Where to stay**

1 Pensão Flamingo
2 Pensão São Cristóvão

Off map
　Golfin Azul
　Hotel Manica
　Manica Lodge

🍴 **Where to eat and drink**

3 Grill It!
4 Towfiq Take-Away

↑ *Penhalonga*

Church

Bus & chapa station

Market

Taxi rank

Bakery

Police (400m), Manica Lodge (1km), Chinhamapere Rock Art (5km), Zimbabwe

Mosque

Pão Manica (bakery)

Club Sportivo

Supermercado Aliyan

Golfin Azul (400m), Hotel Manica (500m), Chimoio

Petromoc   Barclays

AV EDUARDO MONDLANE (EN6)

25 DE SETEMBRO

$ BIM

Telecentro Macequece

Chira Bandira

N

Bradt

Independence Monument

ACCORDOS DE LUSAKA

0 ——— 50m
0 ——— 50yds

Manica Geological Museum

District Government

$ BCI

↓ *Vumba*

MANICA

Kingdom, stood on the same site as the present-day township, and served as one of the most important regional centres of medieval gold extraction for trade with the coastal Arabs. Chipangura was a major objective of Francisco Barreto's failed expedition to Monomotapa in the early 1570s, but Barreto's successor Vasco Homem reached it in 1575 and established good trade relations with the ruling Chicanga dynasty. From then onwards, Portuguese traders regularly visited the gold fair at Chipangura and some even settled in Manica, an amicable arrangement that endured until 1695 when the Rozvi crossed from modern-day Zimbabwe to sack the town.

In 1720, a trade fair was re-established at the site, by then known as Macequece (aka Masekesa). It soon gained official Portuguese status, and fell under the joint rule of a traditional Chicanga and a foreign captain appointed by the Portuguese administration. Gold extraction remained the exclusive preserve of the Chicanga, but many other valuable items were traded at Macequece, among them ivory, crystals, gemstones, copper, iron and livestock. From the 1790s onwards, however, Macequece fell into decline: a series of Chicanga secession disputes that created political instability in Manica and led to a decreased Portuguese presence was followed by an extended drought c1830 and then by the arrival of militant Nguni refugees from Zululand. In 1835, following a Nguni raid led by a chief called Nxaba, Macequece was abandoned.

The Portuguese attempted to re-establish a gold fair in Manica in the 1850s, but by this time ivory had replaced gold as the most important item of regional trade. Renewed interest in the region's mining potential led the Portuguese to name Manica as an administrative district in March 1884, and Macequece was established as its capital. In 1890, Fortaleza Macequece was built in the hills outside town in response to territorial tensions with Rhodes' British South Africa Company, then in the process of staking out Southern Rhodesia (Zimbabwe), and the two rival powers clashed at the fort in 1891. A year later, Manica became the inland headquarters of the Mozambique Company, a Beira-based mining company, though this role was later usurped by Chimoio. The village was chartered as a town in 1956 and upgraded to city status in 1972.

In 2015, a London-based company, Xtract Resources, purchased the Manica Gold Project, 4km out of town, a development that once again brought gold production back into Manica's economic framework. Production is set to commence by the end of 2017, once renovation of the processing plants is complete. Aside from agriculture and gold mining, the biggest local industry is the Vumba Bottling Plant, which extracts mineral water from the Vumba Mountains outside town.

GETTING THERE AND AWAY Manica town is bisected by the surfaced **EN6**. In a private vehicle, the drive from Chimoio takes about 45 minutes and from the Zimbabwean border about 20 minutes. There is also plenty of **chapa** transport along this road; the fare from Chimoio is around US$2. The chapa station, two blocks north of the EN6 behind the market, is also the place to pick up transport to Chinhamapere and Penhalonga.

WHERE TO STAY *Map, opposite*
Upmarket
🏠 **Hotel Manica** (16 rooms) ✆251 62560; m 82 509 1080; e opgrupovalymanica@gmail. com. This business hotel is about 300m out of town towards Chimoio, & offers very clean en-suite rooms with AC, flat-screen TV, writing desk & fridge. A bit short on character, but comfortable, & there's a restaurant under construction. The executive rooms are almost identical to the standard ones. *US$40/50/60 dbl/exec/suite; all rates B&B.* **$$**

Mid range
🏠 **Manica Lodge** (19 rooms) ✆251 62452; m 82 872 6668/501 5790; e anabelaching@ gmail.com. Signposted to the left of the main road to Zimbabwe, this unexpected gem lies in manicured leafy grounds 1km from the town centre. Accommodation is in attractive thatched chalets with DSTV, hot shower & (in most cases) AC. An excellent outdoor restaurant serves large tasty mains in the US$8–16 range. *US$24/50 dbl/ exec; from US$80 suites.* **$$**
🏠 **Pensão Flamingo** (10 rooms) Situated on the EN6, this pleasant pensão has clean twin rooms with 2 ¾ beds, AC, fan & parquet floors.

Some rooms have a balcony & all are en suite with hot showers. The ground-floor bar serves cheap snacks, as well as the usual Mozambican chicken, meat & fish mains in the US$4–8 range. There is a small garden bar at the back. Poor value. **$$**

Budget
🏠 **Pensão São Cristóvão** (16 rooms) A couple of doors down from the Flamingo, this sensibly priced place has bright clean twin & dbl rooms with parquet floor, clustered in 4 groups of 3, each of which shares a bathroom. The ground-floor snack bar has a limited menu of chicken & meat dishes for around US$4 apiece. **$**

Shoestring
🏠 **Golfin Azul** (16 rooms) m 82 425 2650. The 'blue dolphin' is hot pink on the outside, grey inside the rooms, & while it may be chromatically challenged, it's still the best value in town. Rooms are small but en suite & very clean, with fans & nets, & the nicer rooms have TVs & sofas. The management is friendly, & there's a restaurant attached serving Mozambican staples for US$4–7. *US$10/14–24 dbl/exec dbl.* **$**

WHERE TO EAT AND DRINK *Map, opposite*
✖ **Grill It!** ⊕ 08.00–21.00 daily. A trim little restaurant with indoor/outdoor seating, sports on TV, burgers, chicken & steaks, & probably the only ice cream & pizza in town. **$$**

✖ **Towfiq Take-Away** ⊕ 05.30–23.00 daily. Fast, cheap & with long hours, this place has all the usuals, as well as a rice & beans dish that might be vegetarian-friendly. **$**

OTHER PRACTICALITIES
Banks and foreign exchange There is Barclays Bank on the same block as the two pensões, while BIM Millennium and BCI are opposite the main praça. All have ATMs.

12

Internet The only option is Telecentro Macequece (📞 *251 62238*) on the main road a few doors down from BIM Millennium.

Police On the west side of town along the EN6 to Zimbabwe.

Shopping The **market**, to the north of the EN6, sprawls across several blocks. The best bakery is Pão Manica next to the mosque, and Supermercado Aliyan is surprisingly well stocked.

WHAT TO SEE AND DO Architectural landmarks in the town centre include the museum building and district government office opposite. The hilltop church on the northwest outskirts of town is currently being used as a school, and offers great views over the surrounding countryside; it can be reached by crossing a secondary bridge over the Rio Chirabandina, then climbing a steep staircase of around a hundred stone steps. With a 4x4, it is also possible to seek out the ruined Fortaleza Macequece, a few kilometres outside town off the road to Penhalonga. Otherwise, the main two attractions are the geological museum and rock art sites detailed below.

Museu de Geologica de Manica (*Av 25 de Setembro;* 📞 *251 62168;* e *dprmem@ teledata.co.mz;* ⊕ *07.30–15.30 Tue–Sat, 09.00–15.00 Sun; entrance free*) This unambitious but diverting museum is housed in an unusual wide-balconied colonial building that reputedly dates to 1884, the year in which modern Manica was founded, and is made primarily of corrugated iron. The main exhibition hall is given over to a collection of rocks and minerals from the town's geologically rich surrounds, including some crystal quartzite, graphite and raw gemstones such as agate and malachite. The natural history section is of interest less for its motley assemblage of bedraggled stuffed animals than for a collection of invertebrate fossils. There are also some ancient examples of *bao* games carved into rock.

Chinhamapere Rock Art Site Essentially the Mozambican extension of Zimbabwe's misty Vumba Mountains, Chinhamapere Hill, situated to the south of the EN6 about 5km from central Manica, is the site of one of the country's most important and sacred rock art shelters, submitted for consideration as a UNESCO World Heritage Site in 2008. The main shelter, a 20m-high panel, is thought to comprise paintings from three distinct eras, ranging from 6,000 to a few hundred years old. The most impressive is a well-preserved brown frieze depicting six hunters carrying bows, arrows and spears; dozens of other less distinct human, antelope and other animal figures can also be discerned. As with other rock art in southern Africa, the Chinhamapere paintings are the work of the hunter-gatherer peoples (sometimes referred to as Bushmen or San) who inhabited the entire region prior to the arrival of the first pastoralists about 2,000 years ago, and who are thought to be associated with shamanic trance states and rain-making rituals, though some pictures also appear to depict battle scenes. Unusually, however, the paintings here are considered sacred by the region's modern inhabitants, who still hold rain-making and other rituals at the site.

Practicalities Getting to Chinhamapere is very straightforward. The unsignposted junction to the base of the mountain lies on the left side of the **EN6** precisely 3.4km west of the bridge across the Rio Chirabandina on the west side of Manica town centre. Those without a vehicle could walk there in around 45 minutes, or catch a **chapa** from the station behind the market (*less than US$1*). If in doubt, ask for Escola Chinhamapere (or *pinturas respestres*). At the junction, turn left along a dirt road for about 1km until the track peters out, then enter the compound on the left (known locally as Casa Ganda) where you will find the caretaker Veronica, an official spiritual healer (with a certificate issued in Zimbabwe to prove it). Because the site is so sacred, it is unacceptable to visit it without Veronica (or, possibly, a similarly qualified local). The short but steep walk up takes about 30 minutes at the guide's leisurely pace, and includes at least two stops at other ceremonial sites to communicate with the spirits associated with the paintings. The paintings are well worth the effort, and the views from the shelter are also pretty special.

There is no official fee for visiting the site, but budget on around US$3–5 per person in fees and tips for the expedition – up to US$1 per person when you set out, a similar figure when you arrive at the paintings, and a tip on the way down. Best to carry plenty of small-denomination notes and coins, or you might find you have no choice but to hand over a few larger notes as things progress!

PENHALONGA

The Penhalonga region, which straddles the Zimbabwean border some 20km northwest of Manica town, is characterised by fertile rolling hills covered in Shona smallholdings with neatly painted huts and extensive eucalyptus plantations scattered with a few relict patches of indigenous forest. An important source of alluvial gold in pre-colonial times, this is a pleasant area for rambling, birdwatching, unforced interaction with rural Mozambicans (a fair bit of English is spoken this close to the border) or simply escaping the tropical summer heat after a period on the sticky coast. The Shona people living on either side of the border retain a strong shared identity, despite having their territory cut in half by the Anglo–Portuguese treaty of 1891. As a result, the name Penhalonga (Portuguese for 'Long Rock') evidently applies to the entire cross-border region and to the largest village on the Mozambican side, but (especially when looking at maps) do be aware that it is also the name of a larger mining town established on the Zimbabwean side of the border in 1895.

The main tourist focus, set at around 1,050m above sea level, is the Quinta de Fronteira (literally 'Border Farm'), a botanical garden (⊕ 08.00–18.00 daily; entrance around US$1 pp & per vehicle) that was seemingly founded in colonial times and now houses the slightly decrepit Penhalonga Inn. Planted mainly with non-indigenous trees, the botanical garden is a peaceful retreat, and there are still a few stands of bamboo, forest and other naturally occurring vegetation, especially along the gullies and streams that run between the slopes. The only mammals likely to be seen are vervet and possibly samango monkey, but there is a fair amount of birdlife around, and plenty of footpaths to explore the surrounding hills. There's a small waterfall in the gardens about 10 minutes' walk from reception, and a larger one about 30 minutes' walk from Casa Motombombwe (page 226) en route to Quinta de Fronteira.

GETTING THERE AND AWAY

By car The main village of Penhalonga lies about 20km from Manica along a good dirt road. To get there in a private vehicle, drive northward out of Manica, passing the market and bus station to your right before you cross a bridge leading out of town. Turn left at the junction about 2km out of town and then left again at a second junction halfway to Penhalonga. When you reach Penhalonga, follow the signpost left for Quinta de Fronteira/Penhalonga Inn, and branch to the right when you reach a fork in the road about 1km later. After another 1.2km, there's another signposted fork in the road: the right fork takes you to Quinta de Fronteira/

Penhalonga Inn after 3km, while the left fork leads to Casa Motombombwe and Casa Gaswa (below) after about 500m.

By chapa Regular chapas connect Manica to Penhalonga village, but you will need to walk the last stretch. Note that a 4x4 is not normally required to get to Quinta de Fronteira, but is absolutely necessary for the last 500m stretch to the two casas.

⌂ WHERE TO STAY, EAT AND DRINK   Map, page 214

⌂ **Casa Motombombwe & Casa Gaswa**
m 84 648 2566; e giftmashiri@yahoo.com.br. These 2 comfortable & attractively located private houses lie about 3km from Penhalonga village & 500m from the road towards Quinta de Fronteira. Either house sleeps up to 4 people in 2 rooms & also has a self-catering kitchen & lounge. If you have exacting requirements then best bring all the food you need from Manica or Chimoio, but simple meals such as chicken & potatoes can be provided with a bit of warning. Each house is rented out as a unit, & it is strongly recommended you book in advance through the helpful English-speaking caretaker Gift Mashiri (see above for contact details), or Pink Papaya (page 218) in Chimoio can arrange this as well. Gift can also arrange for somebody to meet you in Manica if required, & for local guides to take you to visit nearby waterfalls & other sites of interest. Cooks & cleaners may be hired as well. **$**

⌂ **Penhalonga Inn**   (6 rooms)
e penhalongainn@gmail.com. Set in the Quinta de Fronteira botanical garden, & offering sgl/dbl round houses & camping. Local meals can be arranged by request. A lovely spot. *US$50/80 sgl/dbl round house; US$5 pp camping.* **$$**

CHIMANIMANI NATIONAL RESERVE

The 640km² Reserva Nacional de Chimanimani is Mozambique's newest protected area, created in 2003 as part of the Chimanimani Transfrontier Park, two-thirds of which lies in Zimbabwe. It protects the eastern slopes of the Chimanimani range above an altitude of around 1,000m, rising to the 2,436m Mount Binga, the highest point in Mozambique. Dominated by brachystegia woodland and montane grassland, the reserve also harbours some impressive stands of Afro-montane forest and is cut through by numerous mountain streams and waterfalls. At least 45 of the 1,000 plant species recorded are endemic, among them five types of aloe, two proteas and a dwarf palm, and the reserve is listed as an Important Bird Area, home to a long list of specials that includes chestnut-fronted helmet-shrike, briar warbler, Chirinda apalis, boulder chat, Swynnerton's robin and Gurney's sugarbird. A significant elephant population still survives in the forests of Chimanimani, with regular sightings being had by hikers in the vicinity of **Moribane Rangers Camp** (see opposite), and other mammals include rock hyrax, bushbuck, red duiker, samango monkey, bushpig and various small predators.

Few travellers make it to Chimanimani as things stand, but the reserve is readily accessible to self-drive visitors with a 4x4 or other high-clearance vehicle, while it also makes a worthwhile goal for adventurous backpackers using public transport. With the noteworthy exception of the community-owned Ndzou Camp in the Moribane Forest Reserve (page 227), accommodation is limited to a handful of basic ranger camps, and all visitors need to be self-sufficient in terms of food.

Further information about new developments can be obtained from **MICAIA** (m *82 303 4285; info@micaia.org;* w *micaia.org*), which proposes to expand the trail network and to create a feature route called the Great Chimanimani Trek; or from Pink Papaya in Chimoio, which also rents out tents and camping gear, and can hold on to hikers' excess luggage.

Three main sectors of the reserve are open to tourists, and since each functions more or less as a self-contained unit in terms of travel logistics, they are discussed separately below.

MORIBANE FOREST RESERVE Proclaimed back in 1957, this 120km² forest reserve doesn't actually lie within the national reserve, but rather forms part of an extensive buffer zone to its east. Nevertheless, it is currently the most popular goal for visitors to Chimanimani, protecting an area of largely unspoilt lowland forest that harbours a substantial and regularly observed population of elephants, as well as a good selection of birds associated with forest and brachystegia habitats. At the time of writing, there are two main centres for exploring the forest here: **Moribane Rangers Camp** [map, page 214], which caters only to those with their own tents and camping gear; and **Ndzou Camp** [map, page 214] (m *82 303 4285;* e *info@micaia.org;* w *micaia.org*), 3km further down the road with a full range of facilities. It's been put together hand in hand with the local community, and is quite an admirable set-up, offering guided elephant-tracking excursions (*US$11 pp*), birdwatching, cultural tours and several conservation education programmes. Accommodation is in attractive thatched rondavels (*US$48 dbl B&B*) and a three-bedroom family house that sleeps up to six (*US$80*). Camping is US$6 per tent, and there's a small dorm for US$9 per person as well. The restaurant and bar on-site does a small rotating menu of Mozambican staples and their own specialities, with a focus on fresh local produce.

There are enough hikes here to keep most visitors busy, including the 7-hour round hike from the ranger camp to the rainforest where elephants are resident (most people see plenty of spoor, though the actual beasts can be more elusive), and a growing network of themed nature trails (four new trails to date) under development near Ndzou, where they can also arrange multi-day guided hikes anywhere in Chimanimani.

Practicalities The springboard for Moribane is the modest district capital Sussundenga, which lies about 40km south of Chimoio. To get to Sussundenga in a private vehicle, follow the **EN6** west out of Chimoio for about 5km, then turn left at the signpost for the airport on to the **R216** (N260), which is surfaced for the first 7km or so, then well-maintained dirt. From Sussundenga, head south for 15km to the village of Munhinga, from where you need to follow the **R441** (N260) southeast towards Dombe. Moribane Camp is clearly signposted on the west side of the Dombe road about 30km past Munhinga, and Ndzou Camp is about 3km past it.

Using public transport, regular **chapas** run from Chimoio to Sussundenga, and the trip shouldn't take longer than an hour. From Sussundenga, chapas to Dombe leave every hour or so (less frequently on Sunday), and will drop you at the signposted turn-off for Moribane, from where it is 100m to the camp.

MOUNT BINGA Mozambique's highest mountain is an obvious draw for keen hikers, and the surrounding area also protects plenty of wildlife, while some of the country's finest prehistoric rock art can be seen in a gorge near **Chikukwa Rangers Camp** [map, page 214]. The closest camp to the mountain base is Chikukwa, which can be reached from Chimoio in a day in a private 4x4, but otherwise takes two days to reach (with an overnight stop at **Portão Camp** [map, page 214]) with a combination of public transport and walking. As with Moribane, culinary self-sufficiency is required to explore Chikukwa at the time of writing, and the only option in terms of accommodation is camping, which is free, though it would be protocol to offer a small gift to the chief. Construction of the planned Binga Camp, 5km

12

from Chikukwa, has halted but there's some talk of building a community-owned camp in partnership with the **MICAIA Foundation**, and opening an activity centre offering kayaking, climbing, orienteering and horseriding among other activities. For now expect to pay around US$15 per party per day for guided walks.

About 20km east of Chikukwa, the little-visited **Mahete Camp** [map, page 214], with four simple thatched huts and bamboo platforms for campers, is the best base for exploring the bamboo forest and some of the sacred sites associated with the mountains.

Practicalities As with Moribane, the first point of call *en route* to Binga is Sussundenga, and self-drivers will need to head south for 15km from here to Munhinga. Here, instead of heading southeast along the **R441** (N260), however, you need to fork west for 25km to a signposted junction known locally as 'Container' (though the container for which it is named disappeared some years back). After heavy rains, a 4x4 may be required to cross a river along the 4km road between the junction and Portão Camp. From here, you can drive to either Mahete or Chikukwa in about 1 hour, ideally with a guide to show you the way. Using public transport, **chapas** from Sussundenga to Rotunda can drop you at Container, from where it takes the best part of an hour to reach Portão Camp. If you plan to head on to Chikukwa, it is a 10-hour walk, so you'll need to overnight at Portão, provided you are self-sufficient, as there is currently no fixed accommodation in the mountains.

MOUNT TSETSERA Situated along the Zimbabwean border at the very north of the national reserve, the 2,200m Mount Tsetsera is noted for the pristine condition of its forested slopes, which run the span from lowland brachystegia woodland at the base to Afro-montane rainforest at higher altitudes. It is a particularly popular spot with birdwatchers, as the forest hosts such regional specials as Chirinda apalis, briar warbler, red-faced crimsonwing, lemon dove and rufous-bellied tit.

Practicalities Reaching Tsetsera is only realistic with a private 4x4. The best approach is by following the dirt road around the east side of Lake Chicamba, passing Mira Chicamba Lodge to your right (page 221), and continuing for about 55km to the base of the mountain. The final ascent requires a 4x4 and takes at least an hour. There are the beginning phases of a wooden lodge/camp at the trail head; however, there's no water, power, furniture or other services yet. It is also permitted to camp in the grounds of the ruined mansion at the top of the mountain.

13

Gorongosa and the Caia Road

North of the EN6 through the Beira Corridor, the EN1 continues from the junction town of Inchope to the sleepy port of Quelimane, crossing the Zambezi at Caia. The 550km drive can easily be covered in a day – the road is surfaced all the way, and Caia is now the site of a nippy bridge rather than a ponderous ferry – but it also offers access to some of Mozambique's most worthwhile inland landmarks, and the areas could as easily keep nature lovers (and birders in particular) busy for a week. Foremost among these attractions, only an hour's drive north of the EN6, is the vast Gorongosa National Park, which is gradually re-emerging from a long period of neglect to reclaim its slumbering reputation as the country's most alluring safari destination. Further north, Mount Gorongosa protects the largest extant Afro-montane forest in southern Africa, making it a green haven for hikers and birders. Also of interest as you approach Caia is the dense and bird-rich miombo woodland of the roadside Catapu Forestry Concession, and the relatively inaccessible but inestimably lush Zambezi Delta, part of which is protected within Marromeu National Park.

GORONGOSA NATIONAL PARK

Extending over 5,250km² at the southern end of the Rift Valley, Gorongosa National Park was Mozambique's flagship conservation area in the last years of the Portuguese colonial era, when it was widely regarded as one of the finest safari destinations anywhere in Africa, rivalling the Serengeti for its prodigious concentration of wildlife. Gorongosa has been through some lean times since then, particularly during the post-independence civil war, but it is now well on the road to recovery and, following the welcome intervention of the Carr Foundation in 2004, there is some cause for optimism that it might yet reclaim its place as one of the region's finest wildlife destinations.

Realistically, Gorongosa has some way to go in attaining this goal. For aficionados of the Big Five, there is a sporting chance of encountering lion and elephant, which are both increasing in number and reasonably habituated to vehicles, but buffalos are scarce, leopards are predictably furtive and rhinos are – no less predictably – extinct. Still, even as things stand, Gorongosa is unquestionably the best non-marine wildlife-viewing destination in Mozambique, with the floodplains around Chitengo in particular supporting large and rapidly increasing herds of waterbuck, reedbuck, impala and other antelope. And if most safari-goers might need a little persuasion to give Gorongosa a try, birdwatchers should have no such qualms: the park's tangled bush and mesmerising waterways are literally teeming with avian activity, and there is the added bonus of potential day visits to nearby Mount Gorongosa and its eagerly sought endemic race of green-headed oriole.

13

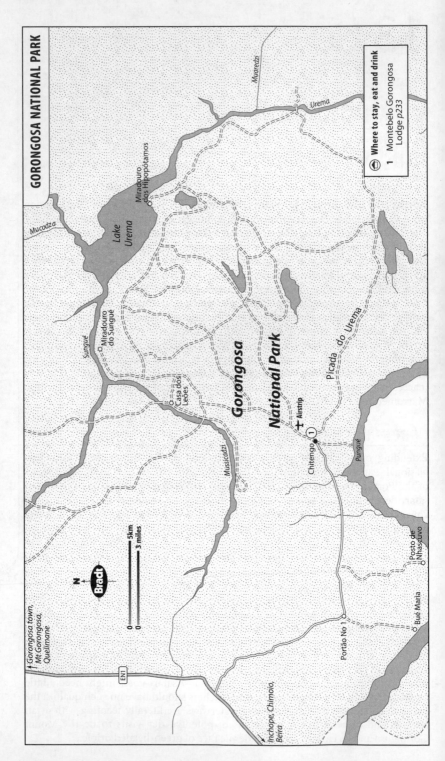

GORONGOSA NATIONAL PARK

Where to stay, eat and drink
1 Montebelo Gorongosa
   Lodge p233

Muaredzi

Urema

Mucodza

Miradouro
dos Hipopótamos

Lake
Urema

Sungué

Miradouro
do Sungué

Gorongosa

Casa dos
Leões

National Park

Picada do Urema

Airstrip
1

Chitengo

Pungué

Mussicadzi

N
Bradt

0   5km
0   3 miles

Gorongosa town,
Mt Gorongosa,
Quelimane

EN1

Posto de
Nhasücuvo

Portão No 1

Bué Maria

Inchope, Chimoio,
Beira

230

For independent travellers, especially self-sufficient campers with their own wheels, Gorongosa also has in its favour its relative affordability and accessibility, with the main camp situated perhaps an hour's drive north of the pivotal junction of the EN1 and EN6. Bigger-spending Africa addicts may have to hold off for the time being, as the park's only exclusive tented camp closed its doors in 2012, and plans for another luxury operator to step in have stalled since 2013.

ECOLOGY AND VEGETATION Bounded by the Pungué River in the south and the Mucombeze in the north, the park is set within the Zambezi Basin and much of the terrain is low-lying, typically below 50m. It is traversed by a series of east-flowing waterways and associated floodplains that empty into a large seasonally fluctuating sump called Lake Urema, which lies at the heart of a 7,850km² catchment area on the park's eastern border. Several of these rivers rise on Mount Gorongosa, whose forested peak is prominent on the park's northern horizon, while others cross into the country from the highlands of eastern Zimbabwe. As with so many African parks, the ecology of Gorongosa is highly seasonal. During the rainy summer months of November to March, the park essentially comprises a vast partial wetland of which up to 200km² is completely submerged and much of the rest is waterlogged and all but inaccessible to landlubbers. The floodwaters usually retreat over April and May, and by the end of the dry season, over August to October, the park has a more parched appearance, comprising large tracts of dry grassland and savannah interspersed with a few precious perennial water sources. The main vegetation type is mixed savannah, dominated by typical miombo species of the *Brachystegia* genus, but there are also large tracts of grassland, particularly along the floodplains, and some 14% of the park supports a cover of closed-canopy miombo or riparian woodland.

HISTORY Gorongosa National Park has its roots in a 1,000km² hunting reserve set aside in 1920 for the amusement of management and guests of the Mozambique Company, which controlled this part of the country by charter until 1940. In 1935, the reserve was enlarged by another 2,000km², partly to preserve its dwindling trophy herds of black rhinoceros and nyala antelope. The first tourist facility (the so-called Casa dos Leões or 'Lion House') was built on the Mussicadzi floodplain in 1940 but abandoned a year later after heavy flooding, leading to the construction of Chitengo Camp at its present-day site in 1941. In July 1960, the former hunting reserve was gazetted as a national park and expanded to cover its present-day area. By this time, Gorongosa was one of the most popular safari destinations in southern Africa, attracting more than 50,000 guests annually, and in the mid 1960s Chitengo was expanded to sleep more than a hundred overnight guests.

The first aerial survey of the park, undertaken by Kenneth Tinley in 1972, counted 13,300 buffalo, 6,500 wildebeest, 3,500 hippo, 3,500 waterbuck, 3,300 zebra, 2,000 impala, 1,000 greater kudu, 800 hartebeest, 700 sable antelope, 500 eland, 200 lions and 100 spotted hyena. Then came the civil war and, following a Renamo attack on Chitengo in 1983, the park effectively ceased to function as a protected area and instead became the site of frequent battles between the two opposing forces. Elephants were shot for their valuable ivory, antelopes and other ungulates were harvested as a source of meat, and although large predators such as lions and leopards were probably not directly targeted by the combatants, their numbers dwindled dramatically with this loss of suitable prey. Two years after the war ended, a 1994 survey indicated that the number of hippo, wildebeest and buffalo stood at fewer than 50 each, the elephant population at around 100 and waterbuck at 130.

13

Since then, rehabilitation of Gorongosa has been a gradual but steady process. In 1994, a joint initiative by the IUCN and African Development Bank attempted to re-establish the park by reopening some 100km of internal roads, clearing landmines, and appointing a team of former soldiers to help curb illegal hunting. This, however, was a relatively low-key initiative by comparison with the three-year agreement signed between the Mozambican government and the American entrepreneur and philanthropist Greg Carr in 2004, which led to the Carr Foundation's investment of more than US$10 million into the restoration of the park's battered infrastructure and diminished wildlife populations. By now, animal populations were visibly on the road to recovery, and a 2007 aerial survey counted 4,930 waterbuck, 3,830 warthog, 300 elephant, 300 sable antelope and 150 hippo, while buffalo and wildebeest numbers, partially boosted by a programme of reintroductions, both stood at around 200 head.

The Carr Foundation recommitted to Gorongosa in 2008 when it signed a fresh agreement undertaking to manage development of the park on behalf of the Mozambican government before handing it back to them at the end of a 20-year period. Overall, Gorongosa had much to celebrate when it reached its 50th anniversary as a national park in July 2010, just months after *Africa's Lost Eden*, an acclaimed documentary about the park, debuted on the National Geographic to give it the publicity boost of its lifetime. In another auspicious development that year, the Mozambican government announced that all of Mount Gorongosa above the 700m contour would be incorporated into the national park, as well as a plan to create a buffer zone that would extend the greater protected ecosystem by 3,500km². Furthermore, wildlife counts undertaken in 2014 indicate that the elephant population has topped the 500 mark, lion numbers have recovered to more than 50, and the sheer volume of ungulates on the floodplains is starting to evoke the park's pre-war heyday.

More recently, the park's only extant accommodation – formerly the state-run Chitengo Safari Camp – has been revamped, privatised and rebranded as Montebelo Gorongosa Lodge (page 233). Unfortunately, however, Gorongosa Adventures, an exclusive tented camp located close to Chitengo, closed in 2012, and little progress has been made with regard to long-standing plans to carve up the park into eight sectors, one of which (essentially the existing game-viewing circuit) will continue to be utilised as a public sector, while the others will be leased to private concessionaires for the creation of exclusive upmarket camps. The main stalling point for tourist development in Gorongosa has been Renamo-related instability so, assuming that the December 2016 truce with Frelimo holds, things may well come back on track during the lifespan of this edition.

FEES Gorongosa National Park is shut during the rainy season, closing mid-December and reopening around 13 April, when the main tracks have been repaired. There's a daily park fee of US$20 per person for international guests and US$10 for SADC resident guests. As of 2015, the park has suspended self-drive safaris. However, Montebelo Gorongosa Lodge (page 233) offers guided 3-hour game drives in open 4x4s for US$35 per person. It is possible fees will rise significantly as tourism is re-established, so check the park website (w *gorongosa. org*) for the latest details.

GETTING THERE AND AWAY
By air Charter flights can be hired through **CR Aviation** (m *84 490 9734;* e *reservations@craviation.co.mz;* w *craviation.co.mz*).

By car Gorongosa National Park lies to the north of the **EN6** and the main entrance gate can be accessed by heading along the **EN1** north from Inchope for 40km until you reach the clearly signposted turn-off to the right. From here it is 10km to the entrance gate, where you need to stop to pick up a gate pass before driving another 18km to Chitengo, the site of the park headquarters and Montebelo Gorongosa Lodge, where the gate pass must be shown and entrance fees paid at reception. Except after heavy rain, Chitengo can be reached in most vehicles, but take it easy on the bends – there are some very corrugated stretches. A high-clearance vehicle, or better a 4x4, may be required to explore deeper in the park for a couple of months after the park reopens at the end of the rainy season. Note that while fuel may sometimes be sold to guests at Chitengo, this is not a formal service and it is best to arrive with a full tank (last fill-up points coming from north and south respectively are Vila Gorongosa and Inchope).

By transfer For those without private transport, road transfers can usually be arranged through the reception desk at Montebelo Gorongosa Lodge (below), ideally with a few days' notice, but this will depend on vehicle availability. Transfers cost the equivalent of US$15 from the main junction on the EN1 (accessible by chapa from Inchope or from Vila Gorongosa), US$37 from Inchope, US$74 from Chimoio or US$88 from Beira.

WHERE TO STAY, EAT AND DRINK *Map, page 230*

🏠 **Montebelo Gorongosa Lodge** (45 units) 📞235 80122; e reservasgirassol@visabeira.co.mz; w girassolhoteis.co.mz. Situated 18km past the main entrance gate, this venerable rest camp opened back in 1941, was destroyed & closed in 1981, but reopened in 1995, since when it has seen immense developments funded partially by the Carr Foundation. Girassol Hotels took over in 2012 but management has since been assumed by Montebelo Hotels, signalling a shift in focus from the traditional safari experience to the conference market. Accommodation is in comfortable semi-detached bungalows with thatched roofs, twin or king-size beds, AC, netting & en-suite hot shower.

There are also serviced platform tents using common ablutions, as well as a large campsite. Facilities inc 2 swimming pools, a small gift shop selling T-shirts, lip balm & not much else, Wi-Fi in the common areas, & a selection of activities aimed at travellers without their own 4x4. The on-site Restaurant Chikalango has comfortable indoor & outdoor seating, a good selection of drinks, & à la carte meals in the US$8–12 range. Surprisingly, Visa cards are accepted. *US$110/143 sgl/dbl B&B; US$138/171 sgl/dbl bungalow B&B; US$176/209 exec bungalow; US$50/70 sgl/twin serviced platform tent B&B; US$12 pp camping.* **$$$$**

EXPLORING GORONGOSA Visitors to Montebelo Gorongosa Lodge and Safari (Chitengo Camp) can sign up for reasonably priced guided game drives for US$35/35/40 per person every morning, midday and afternoon, respectively. Other tours on offer include a guided waterfall hike for US$70 per person, canoe safari on the Pungué River for US$50 per person (*min 2 people*), walking safari for US$50 per person (*min 2 people*), boat safari on Lake Urema for US$100 (*min 3 people*), and a Vinho Community visit for US$14 per person.

While it used to be permissible to explore the park with your own 4x4, such access was suspended in 2015. Should self-drive permission return during the lifespan of this edition (potentially in 2017), exploration of the public part of the park – bounded by the Sungué River to the north and Pungué to the south – is possible along a network of roads that are clearly numbered for use in conjunction with a map available at Chitengo's reception. Some of these roads may be closed after the rainy season, especially the approaches to Lake Urema,

13

With Keith Barnes & Josh Engel (w tropicalbirding.com)

Gorongosa National Park is one of the most rewarding destinations in Mozambique, with more than 500 species recorded, and what it lacks in terms of the sort of forest specials associated with Mount Gorongosa, it compensates for in terms of variety, with waterbirds in particular being very well represented. The open woodlands, grassland and huge wetlands of this national park make for easy and highly rewarding birding.

The road into Chitengo passes through many grassy areas (keep an eye out for moustached grass warbler and a wide variety of finches) as well as extensive miombo woodlands, with thick-billed and barred long-tailed cuckoos, racket-tailed roller, Arnot's chat, southern hyliota, purple-banded sunbird, broad-tailed paradise whydah and Cabanis's bunting heading a list of local specialities. The localised sooty falcon is among the many raptors that can be seen along the road, and bronze-winged coursers are present, but probably seasonal.

The area around the campground has quite good birding. Collared palm thrush is fairly common, but black-and-white flycatcher is more difficult to find, though it is often seen calling from the tall trees around the cabanas. Dickinson's kestrel, red-necked falcon and racket-tailed roller all occur here too.

The most important seasonal wetlands accessible from Chitengo are the Mussicadzi and Urema floodplains. There's always a fair amount of avian activity at these floodplains, and sometimes they host fantastic numbers of pelicans, storks and other large waterbirds, alongside such sought-after species as Baillon's crake, long-toed lapwing, wattled crane and greater painted snipe.

A useful checklist of birds recorded in the park can be downloaded at w gorongosa.org/explore-park/wildlife/gorongosas-birds.

in the northeast of the public area, but they usually reopen as the floodwaters recede and the dry season takes grip.

Again, should self-drive permission return, an excellent short drive from Chitengo follows Road 1 north to the Mussicadzi floodplain, from where you can follow Road 4 up the east side of the plain or Road 9 up the west side. While you are heading out this way, be aware that the pan alongside Road 1 between the junction with roads 2 and 3 is a favoured drinking hole for the shy but beautiful nyala and sable antelope. On the floodplain, you'll see plenty of waterbuck, reedbuck, impala, oribi and warthog in this area, as well as a dazzling selection of waterbirds, and most likely a few troops of baboon (officially listed as yellow baboon, but some experts believe that the population here is intermediate with the Chacma baboon and may warrant a unique subspecific status). You'll also pass the legendary Casa dos Leões, the ruins of the original tourist accommodation built here in 1949, and so named because its roof was a favoured resting place for lions in the 1970s. You could return via Road 6 and roads 2 or 3; there is generally less wildlife in this area, but the thickets are good for greater kudu, nyala, bushbuck and the pretty samango monkey. For a longer game drive, return along Road 4 via Lake Urema, which is known for its waterbird concentrations and forms the main foraging ground for the park's 500-odd elephants. A short diversion up Road 11 leads to a hippo pool at the southeast end of the lake. From here you can return to Chitengo via roads 8 and 2.

MOUNT GORONGOSA

Towering above the northwest horizon of the namesake national park, the Serra de Gorongosa is a wide isolated massif that rises almost 1.5km above the surrounding plains to a 1,862m peak called Gogogo. The mountain has long been legendary among birders as the only southern African location for the green-headed oriole, a spectacular and vociferous forest dweller whose main range is centred upon the Eastern Arc Mountains of Tanzania. However, this eagerly sought bird might be most significant as a flagship species for what is probably the largest continuous area of Afro-montane south of the Zambezi, a magnificent stand of tall evergreen trees and tangled undergrowth alive with birdsong and the chattering of monkeys. Threatened by encroaching cultivation and charcoal production, these forests

BIRDING MOUNT GORONGOSA

With Keith Barnes & Josh Engel (w tropicalbirding.com)

More than 250 species have been recorded on the mountain and in its immediate vicinity, including several specials. The best known of these is the green-headed oriole, an isolated population regarded as a distinct endemic subspecies. Another subspecies confined to the mountain is an isolated sunbird population that was originally listed as Miombo double-collared and is now officially listed as greater double-collared, but may in fact be an endemic species. The forests of Gorongosa are also thought to harbour the world's largest single population of the localised and very attractive Swynnerton's robin.

Experienced birders have recorded a total of 100 species on the mountain in one day, not all of them associated with forests. The trail from Nyankuku passes first through agricultural areas, then a patchwork of thickets and farmland. These open areas are excellent for finches, and as well as the bronze and red-backed mannikins, Jameson's fire-finches, red bishops and other common species, keep an eye out for magpie mannikin, orange-winged pytilia, and grey-and-yellow-bellied waxbills. This is also the favoured habitat of the mystery double-collared sunbird and the localised moustached warbler, while thickets and forest patches can be rewarding for birds such as blue-spotted wood-dove, Anchieta's tchagra, pale batis, Vanga flycatcher and red-throated twinspot.

The endemic race of green-headed oriole is occasionally seen in the forested ravine below Morrumbodze Falls, but this is a long shot and anybody who is serious about seeing this bird will need to hike into the forest proper. Fortunately, it is not uncommon, and its presence is often betrayed by a typically fluid oriole call, but the odds of seeing it are highest if you get to the forest edge before 08.30 or so. Other notable forest species here include silvery-cheeked hornbill, trumpeter hornbill, Livingstone's turaco, eastern bronze-naped pigeon, Narina trogon, pallid honeyguide, white-tailed blue flycatcher, Chirinda apalis, Swynnerton's robin, thrush-nightingale, white-starred robins and black-fronted bush-shrike. If you hike to the peak, you might well see the endangered blue swallow, and at all altitudes keep an eye out for raptors, which include Ayres's hawk-eagle, African cuckoo-hawk, lizard buzzard, African goshawk and African crowned eagle.

swathe the upper slopes of the mountain, a major regional watershed that feeds five rivers, including three that drain into Lake Urema and two that empty into the Pungué River on its southern boundary.

Mount Gorongosa was not accorded any official protection until 2010, when the boundaries of the national park were redefined to incorporate the dwindling forests above the 700m contour. Shortly after this, unfortunately, political conflict rendered the mountain off-limits to tourism. As and when that changes (which seems a distinct possibility following the signing of a truce in December 2016), day or overnight hikes out of the national park should be offered by Montebelo Gorongosa Lodge (page 233), and it should also be possible to visit independently from Vila Gorongosa (page 237) or from the Nyankuku campsite at the base of the mountain, though the last is difficult without a private 4x4. Long-term plans include the establishment of a formal ecotourism programme to help benefit the estimated 2,000 people who inhabit the lower slopes and depend on the mountain for their livelihood, training suitable individuals as guides, and implementing a fee structure to boost community coffers.

Several hiking options are possible, all starting at Nyankuku, which doubles as the site of a community-based reforestation project. An attractive short walk, about an hour in either direction, and without too many steep gradients, leads to the Morrumbodze Falls, a spectacular sight as it crashes over a series of ledges into the base of a ravine about 100m below. For dedicated birders, the most popular option is to head to the forest edge about 2 hours' walk from Nyankuku, a steepish hike that requires the earliest possible start to boost your chances of seeing green-headed oriole, and then to return via the waterfall, which takes about 2 hours. It is also possible to hike through the forest all the way to the summit, which lies on a plateau of heath-like vegetation dotted with proteas, strelitzias and other species reminiscent of Cape fynbos. The summit can be reached on a very long day trip (bank on at least 6 hours up, and 2 hours down) or as an overnight hike, carrying all camping gear, food, etc.

GETTING THERE AND AWAY The normal trail head for hikes is a campsite called Nyankuku (literally 'Place of the Chicken'), where facilities amount to a patch of cleared lawn surrounded by invasive eucalyptus trees, and a drop toilet. To get there, follow the **EN1** north from Vila Gorongosa for about 10km, then turn right on to an unsignposted dirt road surrounded by huts near the top of a rise, a short distance before a bridge across the Morrumbodze River. It's about 12km from this junction to the campsite along a rough intersecting track (if in doubt, stick to the right), so it requires high clearance (possibly a 4x4 after rain) and the best part of an hour to get there. There is safe parking at the campsite for day or overnight visitors and guides can be hired from here.

For travellers without a vehicle, the easiest option is to arrange a formal day trip from Montebelo Gorongosa Lodge (Chitengo) once they resume offering the trip. Alternatively, it might be possible to rent a car or bicycle in Vila Gorongosa, or you could walk in with all the gear you require and camp overnight at the Nyankuku.

So far as we can ascertain, it is easy enough to arrange a day hike into the forest informally and to find a guide locally. However, it is not technically clear whether this is permitted or you are obliged to make all arrangements through Chitengo or Mangwana. Either way, a more structured approach to hikes and ecotourism seems likely now that the upper slopes of the mountain fall within Gorongosa National Park. The local Chigorongosa people hold the mountain sacred and it is our understanding that summit hikes may be undertaken only with the ceremonial blessing of the local chief (known as the *régulo*). You don't need to attend this ceremony yourself, unless of course you want to, but some advance warning may be required and you will need to provide a bouquet of tobacco, alcohol and other goodies to ensure all goes well.

THE EN1 FROM INCHOPE TO CAIA

The surfaced 550km road running northeast from Inchope on the EN6 to the port of Quelimane, crossing the Zambezi using the Armando Emilio Guebuza Bridge at Caia, is the most important through-route connecting northern and southern Mozambique, and it will be used by almost all travellers heading between these two halves of the country. The drive, though long, is not too demanding, as the road is in good condition for most of its length and traffic volumes are quite low. For those using public transport, chapas cover the route in stages, with the most likely places you'll need to change vehicle being Vila Gorongosa (60km from Inchope), Caia (320km from Inchope), and Nicoadala (about 40km before Quelimane). The Maning Nice and Nagi Investimentos coaches between Nampula and Beira or Chimoio (a 14-hour trip stopping in Quelimane) also follow this road most days of the week, departing between 03.00 and 04.00 in either direction.

The southern part of this road offers access to Gorongosa National Park and Mount Gorongosa, the turn-offs to which lie about 40km and 70km north of Inchope respectively. The drive can also be broken up at the Catapu Forestry Concession, a favourite with birdwatchers, or at the riverside town of Caia, which provides a useful base for several motorised excursions upstream or downstream along the Zambezi.

INCHOPE Situated at the junction of the EN1 and the EN6 between Chimoio and Beira, Inchope is arguably the single most important road pivot anywhere in Mozambique, though that's about as far as it goes in the superlatives stakes. Spreading for a couple of hundred metres along the EN6 east of the main intersection, it has a bustling little market – cashews and pineapples are the local specialities – and a few shops and local restaurants, and there is plenty of chapa transport available in all directions. The only accommodation here is of the hourly variety, but if you need a pick-me-up of a different sort, **Bismillah Take-Away** on the EN6 east of the junction has good cheap meals. There's no bank or ATM, and private money changers tend to offer a lousy rate. Otherwise, facilities are limited to a pair of filling stations along the EN1, with BP north of the junction and Petromoc south.

VILA GORONGOSA Straddling the EN1 about 60km north of Inchope, Vila Gorongosa is a substantial town of around 15,000 people set at an altitude of 380m in the shadow of the eponymous mountain. Prior to independence, the town was known as Vila Paiva de Andrade (after a 16th-century Portuguese philosopher) and it had a reputation as being rather pretty, an adjective that doesn't really seem apt today. It is potentially a useful springboard for visits to Gorongosa National Park and even more so to Mount Gorongosa; the turn-off to the former lies 20km south along the EN1 towards Inchope, while the latter can be reached along a dirt road that branches eastward from the EN1 about 11km north of town. The town is notable for its busy agricultural market, at the main intersection, which sells fresh produce from the nearby mountain slopes. The chapa station opposite this is the place to pick up chapas to Inchope, Beira or Caia. Other facilities include a BIM Millennium bank with two ATMs about 500m back along the Inchope road, and a rather inconspicuous filling station alongside the EN1 north, immediately after the turn-off to Inhaminga.

If you need a room or bite to eat, the place to head for is the **Pousada Azul**, which lies about 200m from the main intersection along the side road running northeast past the market. Here you'll find a selection of neat single rooms using common showers, en-suite double rooms, safe parking and a pleasant balcony where you can enjoy a cold beer or typical Mozambican meal – or both!

CATAPU FORESTRY CONCESSION This 250km² private concession, bisected by the EN1 some 30km south of Caia, is managed by TCT Dalmann, an advocate of sustainable forestry of indigenous tress, in particular the African blackwood (*Dalbergia melanoxylon*). The trees here are harvested using a traditional method of woodland management called coppicing, which entails the cyclic felling of trees in a manner that allows them to regrow from the original stumps to attain maturity about four times faster than they would from seedlings. As a result, the miombo woodland here feels more like wild bush than artificial plantation, and supports a varied fauna, including various medium–small mammals (red duiker, warthog, vervet monkey) as well as offering some of the finest miombo birding in Mozambique along a great network of walking trails. This is perhaps the best place in Mozambique to see the localised chestnut-fronted helmet-shrike, alongside the likes of Narina trogon, Angola pitta, Livingstone's flycatcher, Vanga flycatcher, Woodward's batis and Arnot's chat, while patches of riparian woodland host silvery-cheeked hornbill, crested guinea fowl and African broadbill. Catapu is also a popular base with dedicated birdwatching tours wanting to explore the bird-rich Zambezi floodplain 20 minutes' drive north, and it can be used as a base to visit Mary Livingstone's grave at Chupanga.

Where to stay, eat and drink

Mphingwe Camp (11 rooms) m 82 301 6436; e mphingwe@dalmann.com; w mphingwe. com. Mphingwe is the Sena name for the African blackwood, one of many varieties of tree that grow wild around this lovely bush camp set in the Catapu Forestry Concession. A couple of hundred metres from the EN1 & clearly signposted, it is staffed by English speakers & offers accommodation in neat wood cabins, some en suite, & a shady outdoor restaurant-bar serves meals in the US$6–13 range. Great value. *US$12/18 sgl/dbl; US$23/33 en-suite sgl/dbl; US$31/59 family cottages (sleep 4/6).* **$$**

CAIA Situated 320km past Inchope, Caia is an inherently unremarkable town, though it does have a rather attractive setting on the banks of the Zambezi, and it seems set for some economic expansion following the long-awaited opening of the 2,376m-long Armando Guebuza Bridge to replace a tired old ferry service in August 2009. Built at a cost of around US$80 million, this is the longest road bridge anywhere along the Zambezi's length (though it is shorter than the rail bridge at Sena). Downriver from the bridge it is also the only place where drivers can cross between northern and southern Mozambique. The biggest focal point for passing traffic seems to be the Petromoc filling station alongside the main road, which is attached to a good supermarket, clean toilets and a Standard Bank with ATM. A couple of interesting days out from Caia can be had (page 240), although you'll need your own wheels.

Where to stay, eat and drink
Arguably the nicest place to stay in the Caia region, and certainly the best value, is Mphingwe Camp (above), 30km south along the EN1, but there are a few other options closer to town.

Caia Lodge m 82 773 8770. Sited about 2.5km down the road between Caia & Sombreiro, the accommodation is either camping or in casas. On-site restaurant & bar; self-catering allowed. **$**

Cuácua Lodge (9 units) m 82 312 0528/960 1198; e cuacualodge@gmail.com. Situated on a rocky wooded hill overlooking the Zambezi about 1km north of the Caia Bridge, this attractive lodge offers good birding & fishing, free bicycle use, a decent restaurant specialising in meat dishes (beef & lamb from an associated ranch), & a swimming pool. There is the choice of 1- or 2-bedroom houses, the latter sleeping up to 5, spaced out along the thickly wooded slopes, with AC, en-suite hot shower & veranda, or camping. **$$**

Hotel Caia (20 rooms) 237 10026. Situated about 1.5km from the town centre (turn left immediately after the Petromoc) where it overlooks a seasonal inlet of the Zambezi, this adequate but characterless hotel is housed in a large pink building with rooms arranged around a courtyard. Clean en-suite rooms come with TV, AC & en-suite hot shower, & a restaurant is attached. Decent value. **$**

BIRDING CHINIZUIA FOREST AND THE ZAMBEZI DELTA

With Keith Barnes & Josh Engel (w tropicalbirding.com)

The Chinizuia Forest, which lies along the old 4x4-only route from Dondo to Caia (passing along the east side of Gorongosa National Park), is famous among birdwatchers as the site to see a slew of local specialities while offering some of the best miombo and forest birding in all of southern Africa. The area remains unprotected and under severe logging pressure, but there is still excellent forest, both along the road from Dondo to Muanza, and from the turn-off (11km north of Muanza, towards Chenapamima) to the Chinizuia River. Take the turn-off on the left about 35km after leaving the main road to find a camping area and a forested stream.

The birding is outstanding, and a wide variety of uncommon and local species are regularly seen. Among the numerous common miombo species are the localised southern banded snake-eagle, Ayres's hawk-eagle, racket-tailed roller, black-and-white flycatcher, chestnut-fronted helmet-shrike (alongside Retz's and white helmet-shrikes), yellow-bellied hyliota, red-throated twinspot and lesser seedcracker. Near the camping area and stream, East Coast akalat, white-breasted alethe and barred long-tailed cuckoo are common but very difficult to see, and African pitta is uncommon and also difficult to see. Also in this area are eastern bronze-naped pigeon, silvery-cheeked hornbill, African broadbill, Narina trogon, speckle-throated woodpecker, tiny greenbul, black-headed apalis, and plain-backed and western violet-backed sunbirds. Camping will be anything but quiet, as African wood-owl, barred owlet, Verreaux's eagle-owl and fiery-necked nightjar create a night-time chorus.

Perhaps even better than Chinizuia, because of its better roads and easier accessibility, the Zambezi Coutadas (hunting concessions) offer a very similar birdlife to Chinizuia but with the added excitement of abundant big game. The area is best accessed from Mphingwe Camp in the Catapu Forestry Concession (see opposite), where up-to-date access and road condition information should be sought. It contains an exceptional diversity of habitats, including outstanding coastal forest, savannah and wetlands. The forest birding, including such gems as white-chested alethe and East Coast akalat, is very similar to Chinizuia. However, it also contains grasslands and wetlands with birds such as wattled crane, lesser jacana and huge flocks of African openbill and other waterbirds.

Excursions from Caia

Mary Livingstone's grave Mary Moffat was the daughter of Robert Moffat, a Scottish missionary also known for his prowess as a gardener. Moffat worked at Kuruman in South Africa for most of his life and during his infrequent visits back to Britain gave lectures on the work that the Missionary Society was doing in Africa. It was at one such lecture that the young David Livingstone, then on the verge of leaving for China, changed his mind and decided to work in Africa. In 1844, Livingstone married Moffat's daughter Mary, who accompanied him on several of his journeys (much to the disapproval of her parents) and died in 1862 at Chupanga. Her grave can still be seen in the Catholic Mission grounds at Chupanga, which lies about 25km downriver of Caia along a dirt road that may require a 4x4, especially during the rainy season.

Marromeu Buffalo Reserve Nominally protecting a 1,500km² area of grassland and seasonal swamps on the southern side of the Zambezi Delta, this special reserve was set aside during the colonial era to protect one of the world's densest populations of buffalo, estimated to stand at 30,000–60,000 at its peak. Unfortunately, however, the ecology of this seasonally inundated delta has changed greatly in recent decades as the result of the multiple dams built along the Zambezi, which have collectively controlled and contained the river's flow to reduce the natural flooding that occurs during the rains and open the area up to hunters. The area also suffered badly during the civil war, and by 1994 it was estimated that around 1,000 buffalo remained, while waterbuck numbers were reduced from around 50,000 in the 1970s to fewer than 200, and the hippo population crashed from almost 3,000 to about 250.

Wildlife numbers have reputedly increased since the end of the war, and the delta still holds significant numbers of elephant, Lichtenstein's hartebeest, sable antelope and predators such as lion and leopard. The reserve also still supports the country's densest waterbird populations, including 100 breeding pairs of the endangered wattled crane. As such, it was designated as Mozambique's first Ramsar Wetland of International Importance in 2004. Marromeu is currently undeveloped for tourism but it is possible to drive there from Caia, following a 100km track (N283) that runs southeast from Chupanga. About 34km along this road you reach Vila Marromeu, the site of Mozambique's largest sugar refinery and a couple of adequate small hotels. The road is good as far as Vila Marromeu, but a 4x4 will almost certainly be necessary as you approach the reserve itself.

Sena Railway Bridge Heading west from Caia for around 60km brings you to Vila de Sena, which was one of the most important outposts on the Zambezi throughout the Portuguese colonial era, and may well stand on the site of the Swahili trading post of Seyouna mentioned in a 12th-century Arab document by Abu al-Fida. It is also the site of the 3,670m Dona Ana Bridge, built by the Portuguese in 1934, and the longest railway bridge in the world at the time of its construction. The bridge was blown up and rendered unusable by Renamo in the 1980s, but it reopened as a single-lane car bridge following repairs in 1995. It closed again in 2006, and has functioned exclusively as a railway bridge since 2009. With a decent 4x4 it is possible to continue along the Zambezi all the way to Tete, a little-used route that's best explored in the dry season.

14

Tete

With thanks to Sterling Jarrett (see box, page 198)

Seen from a bus window, Tete is not the most inviting province of Mozambique: the dry, dusty badlands are covered in puny acacia scrub punctuated by the occasional thatched village whose inhabitants do well simply to subsist in this harsh, arid climate. The main tourist focus, if you can call it that, is the city of Tete, which lies at a low altitude on the south bank of the Zambezi, in a climate that contrives to feel both dusty and almost intolerably muggy. In the harsh light of the day, the town has little to no aesthetic appeal, though in the softer light of dusk its riverbank takes on an altogether more pleasing hue. An ongoing influx of mining investment has clearly given its restaurants and hotels a facelift, so that the town appears far less run-down than it did a few years back.

Mozambique's most westerly province, Tete ranks among the most peculiar relics of the colonial carve-up of Africa. Following four centuries of intermittent Portuguese settlement, Cecil Rhodes tried to append the region to Britain's so-called 'red corridor' between Cape Town and Egypt in the 1870s. This claim was thwarted when the French politician Patrice Mac-Mahon formally awarded Tete to Portugal (earning himself bar-room posterity in the name of the Mozambican beer 2M), even though most bordering territories went to Britain. As a result, the wedge-shaped province, which juts northwest from Manica into what was formerly the British Central African Protectorate, shares longer borders with three other countries (Zimbabwe to the west, Zambia to the north and Malawi to the east) than it does with the rest of Mozambique.

Looking at a map, one would most likely classify Tete as part of northern Mozambique. In reality, however, it has long been isolated from the other four provinces of the north by Malawi and the Shire River, and both the province and its capital enjoy far closer economic links to south-central Mozambique, and thus is classified as such. Indeed, the only surfaced road that connects Tete to the rest of Mozambique, the **EN102** (N7) from Chimoio, is far less busy than the **EN103** (N7/N8; or Tete Corridor) that links Blantyre (Malawi) to Harare (Zimbabwe) via the city of Tete.

The province has a population of around 1.8 million, and the main ethnic groups are the Nyanja, the Nyungue and the Sena. Its virtual separation from the rest of Mozambique and its importance as the most straightforward route between Zimbabwe and Malawi have resulted in several mild anomalies, such as the fact that considerably more English is understood in Tete than in most other parts of the country.

In the 1990s, when Zimbabwe was enjoying its heyday as a backpacker hub and Mozambique was still emerging from decades of turmoil, the Tete Corridor (known as the 'Gun Run' during the civil war) probably saw more traveller through-traffic than the rest of Mozambique's provinces combined, even if few spent longer in the country than the few hours required to drive between Blantyre and Harare. This backpacker traffic has of course diminished greatly over the past decade, though the route through Chimoio and Tete is still the quickest and easiest option between southern Mozambique and Malawi. But while it has fallen off the travel map, Tete is experiencing a local economic boom thanks to the discovery of several rich coal seams in the province and a spate of multi-national investment.

Away from the main road, Tete Province offers at least one worthwhile and straightforward excursion in the form of the vast Cahora Bassa Dam and the nearby town of Songo – the latter with a remarkably fresh highland climate after the claustrophobic humidity of Tete. Further off the beaten track, but also of interest, is the attractive mission at Boroma, which lies on the west bank of the Zambezi some 60km upriver from Tete.

In a heartening victory for conservation in a province otherwise largely given over to mining concessions, Tete province's first national park was proclaimed in October 2013. Magoé National Park now covers 350,000ha along the southern shore of Lake Cahora Bassa, and while tourism development is nearly non-existent and game densities are likely to be quite low until comprehensive protections are put into place, this remains one of Mozambique's most remote regions and a tempting new diversion for visitors to Tete.

TETE

The eponymous capital of Tete Province, often and with some justification claimed to be the hottest town in Mozambique, is situated on the southwest bank of the Zambezi roughly 650km upriver from its mouth, at an altitude of only 175m above sea level. It is an important transport hub, thanks to its position on the Tete Corridor between Malawi and Zimbabwe. The city expanded greatly during the construction of the Cahora Bassa Dam, and it is now the third-largest town in the Mozambican interior after Nampula and Chimoio, with a population estimated at 170,000.

Tete became very run-down during the civil war, and plenty of ruinous old buildings still evoke the city's moribund aura at the start of the millennium, but today the overall impression (at least compared with ten years ago) is of rejuvenation and rehabilitation. For this writer, the definitive moment was walking into the renovated Hotel Zambeze and trying to absorb the fact that this plush establishment was the same dump that had reduced several of my tour clients to tears back in 2001. But everywhere in town there are neatly painted facades, tarred roads and other encouraging signs of urban renewal, much of it associated with the region's emergent coal-mining industry, which, if the markets hold, is in the midst of a full-fledged boom.

HISTORY Tete is a settlement of some antiquity. Even before the Portuguese arrived in East Africa, it lay at the junction of the Zambezi and three of the four main trading routes from the Sofala area into the African interior. The site of the modern town was probably occupied by Muslim traders in the 15th century, when it formed the main link between the coast and the gold fairs of Karangaland. Tete was settled by a few Portuguese adventurers in 1531, and by 1630 it supported around 20 mazungo households.

Contemporary reports suggest that Tete was rather makeshift in appearance until around 1767, when it was made the seat of administration for the Zambezi Valley and a permanent garrison of 100 soldiers was posted there. By the end of the 18th century, Tete's city centre consisted of roughly 30 stone houses enclosed by a 3m-high wall, as well as a hospital, trade factory, governor's residence and council building.

Today the concrete part of Tete is on the southern side of the river, linked to the northern side, Bairro Matundo, by the Samora Machel Bridge. As with the other provincial capitals, there are very few buildings remaining that pre-date World War II.

GETTING THERE AND AWAY

By air The **airport** is 5km out of town towards Zóbuè and any bus travelling between Tete and Moatize, a small town and mine site 20km to the east, can drop you at the entrance. **LAM** (w *lam.co.mz*) flies daily between Tete and Beira, Nampula, Maputo and Johannesburg; it also operates flights several times a week to/from Chimoio, Lichinga and Quelimane. Their office is on Avenida 24 de Julho (✆ 252 22056). **Airlink** (w *flyairlink.com*) also has direct flights to Johannesburg most days of the week.

By car Tete lies about halfway along the **EN103** (N7/N8) (Tete Corridor), a 280km road that connects the Zimbabwean border at Cuchamano to Zóbuè on the Malawian border. This road is surfaced and in good condition all the way, although owing to the amount of heavy traffic you may come across the odd pot-holed section. The drive to Tete from Blantyre (Malawi) usually takes about 3–4 hours, not allowing for border crossings, and the drive from Harare (Zimbabwe) about an hour longer. About 16km before Zóbuè, the **EN223** (N304) heads north from the **EN103** (N7) heading for the other major border with Malawi at Dedza, which is a little closer to Lilongwe. The road is of a similar quality to the **EN103** (N7), but it adds another 150km or so to the journey. Another option is the surfaced **EN221/548** (N9) from Tete via Bene to the Zambian border at Cassacatiza, though this is seldom used by travellers. The main access road to Tete from within Mozambique is the **EN102** (N7) from Chimoio, a 430km stretch of well-maintained asphalt that shouldn't require more than 5 hours' driving time.

By bus and chapa The long-distance and local **bus terminal**, referred to as TTA or Mpadue, is located just outside of the city on Avenida 25 de Junho. From here you'll find buses heading in all directions, as well as buses to Zimbabwe (Cuchamano) and Malawi. At least one bus daily travels between Chimoio and Tete, costing US$8, leaving at around 04.00 and arriving at 11.00 in either direction. This gives Malawi-bound travellers from Chimoio plenty of time to head on to Blantyre: there are **chapas** to Zóbuè (*or Ulongué/Dedza/Angonia for Lilongwe-bound travellers US$5*) and, once across the border, there is lots of transport from Mwanza to Blantyre.

Postbus (✆ 214 30061/2; m 82 305 7378 or 84 312 3102/3/4; w *correios.co.mz*) has a weekly bus to Maputo that leaves at 03.00 on Saturday for US$34. **Maning Nice** (m 84 363 5699 or 86 288 4154) runs coaches daily to Beira (*US$12*) via Chimoio (*US$8*), departing at 05.00 from the TTA bus station. If you are heading to Songo or Estima (also known as Chitima), these buses are also found at the TTA bus station and cost around US$2. If you are heading to Boroma, then head to the TTA station. It is also reputedly possible to get to the Zambian border at Cassacatiza by chapa, but you'll probably have to change vehicles at Matema, and possibly once after that – ask around at the main bus terminal on the north side of town, across the Samora Machel Bridge, called Matema Cruzamento.

Chapas for Moatize (and the airport) park below the Samora Machel Bridge at the junction of Avenida Julius Nyerere and Rua Unidade Africana and cost less than US$1.

⊣ WHERE TO STAY *Map, page 244*
Tete has a fair range of accommodation, although it is rather short on budget options. Most of the action is in the city centre south of the river, but several new upmarket lodges are across the bridge in Bairro Matundo. If you're **camping**, options are limited, with Jesus é Bom being the primary camping location – there

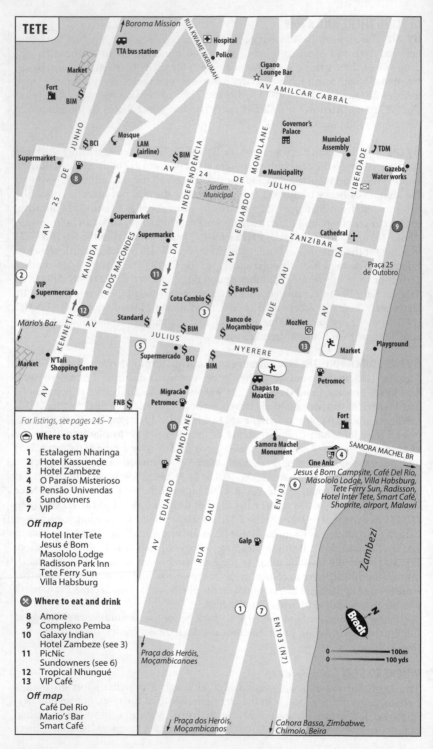

TETE

Boroma Mission

RUA KWAME NKRUMAH

Hospital

TTA bus station

Police

Market

Cigano
Lounge Bar

Fort

BIM

AV AMILCAR CABRAL

BCI

Mosque

Governor's
Palace

LAM
(airline)

BIM

Municipal
Assembly

TDM

Supermarket

AV

24

DE

JULHO

Municipality

Gazebo,
Water works

Jardim
Municipal

LIBERDADE

Supermarket

Supermarket

Cathedral

ZANZIBAR

VIP
Supermercado

Praça 25
de Outobro

Mario's Bar

Standard

Cota Cambio

Barclays

Market

N'Tali
Shopping Centre

BIM

Banco de
Moçambique

MozNet

Playground

JULIUS

Supermercado

BCI

NYERERE

BIM

Migração

Chapas to
Moatize

Petromoc

Petromoc

FNB

Fort

Samora Machel
Monument

SAMORA MACHEL BR

Jesus é Bom Campsite, Café Del Rio,
Masololo Lodge, Villa Habsburg,
Tete Ferry Sun, Radisson,
Hotel Inter Tete, Smart Café,
Shoprite, airport, Malawi

Cine Aniz

Galp

Zambezi

For listings, see pages 245–7

🛏 **Where to stay**
1 Estalagem Nharinga
2 Hotel Kassuende
3 Hotel Zambeze
4 O Paraíso Misterioso
5 Pensão Univendas
6 Sundowners
7 VIP

Off map
   Hotel Inter Tete
   Jesus é Bom
   Masololo Lodge
   Radisson Park Inn
   Tete Ferry Sun
   Villa Habsburg

❌ **Where to eat and drink**
8   Amore
9   Complexo Pemba
10 Galaxy Indian
    Hotel Zambeze (see 3)
11 PicNic
    Sundowners (see 6)
12 Tropical Nhungué
13 VIP Café

Off map
   Café Del Rio
   Mario's Bar
   Smart Café

Praça dos Heróis,
Moçambicanoes

Praça dos Heróis,
Moçambicanos

Cahora Bassa, Zimbabwe,
Chimoio, Beira

0 ——— 100m
0 ——— 100 yds

are other places that will let you camp, but it's clearly a matter of their just using whatever space they happen to have available rather than actually setting up a campsite.

Exclusive

🏠 **Radisson Park Inn** (117 rooms) Estrada da Zambia; ☎ 252 27900; e info.tete@rezidorparkinn. com; w parkinn.com/hotel-tete. Perhaps nothing is as emblematic of Tete's new-found hub status as the opening of its first international hotel. It's the most modern place in town & has all the bells & whistles you would expect from a Radisson anywhere – AC, DSTV, minibar, etc – & its location 4km from the town centre would be great for anyone working in Moatize, but it feels a bit removed from the city itself for a casual visitor. There's an on-site bar & grill, swimming pool, gym facilities, & Wi-Fi throughout the hotel. *US$255/290 std/exec dbl; from US$405 suites; all rooms B&B.* **$$$$**

Upmarket

🏠 **Hotel Zambeze** (81 rooms) Av Eduardo Mondlane; ☎ 252 23100/1; e hz@tvcabo.co.mz; 📘 pages/Hotel-Zambezi-Tete-Mozambique/195000063846632. This 5-storey colonial-era landmark in the heart of the city had become seriously seedy & run-down prior to a 2007 makeover that re-established it as one of Tete's most prestigious addresses. The spacious, tastefully refurbished rooms have tiled floors, DSTV, AC & en-suite hot shower, & suites are available. There's also a chic bar & restaurant (page 246) on the very top floor offering fabulous views over the city towards the river. Wi-Fi is available at the restaurant. *US$70 budget dbl; US$90 standard dbl; from US$160 suites; all rates B&B.* **$$$**

🏠 **Tete Ferry Sun** (143 villas) Bairro Matundo; m 84 251 1010; e mendes@teteferrysun.com; w teteferrysun.com. Boasting a 9-hole golf course, 20m pool, restaurant, gym & spa to complement its stunning location on the Zambezi, this new resort offers accommodation in 1-, 2- & 3-bedroom villas equipped with kitchenette, lounge, writing desk, TV, private veranda & (2- & 3-bedroom units only) plunge pool. Prices vary according to location & occupancy. *US$79–115 1-bedroom; US$125–280 2-bedroom & US$185–340 3-bedroom villa; all rates B&B.* **$$$$**

🏠 **Villa Habsburg** (6 rooms) Bairro Matundo; ☎ 252 20323; m 84 724 6435; e monhabsburg@

gmail.com. Hidden away 1km downstream from the bridge on the far side of the river, Villa Habsburg is without a doubt the most delightfully incongruous accommodation in Tete. It's a misplaced corner of Victorian Europe planted on the sweltering banks of the Zambezi, replete with plaster busts, heroic portraits & a classical library unrivalled for miles around. Rooms are each individually decorated, but they're all en suite with nets, writing desks & Wi-Fi. There's a swimming pool too, & the sunsets over the bridge are magnificent. *US$90/100 sgl/dbl; B&B.* **$$$**

🏠 **VIP Hotel** (120 rooms) Av da Liberdade; ☎ 252 22630; m 84 426 5238; e res.tete@viphotels.com or hoteltete@viphotels.com; w viphotels.com. One of the newer hotels catering to the business market, this has comfortable en-suite rooms with AC, twin or dbl bed, TV, safe & Wi-Fi overlooking the Zambezi. Executive rooms have a kitchenette. Facilities inc swimming pool, gym, gardens, restaurant & secure parking. *US$182/263 standard/exec dbl; all rates B&B.* **$$$$**

Mid range

🏠 **Hotel Inter Tete** (71 rooms) Estrada da Zambia; ☎ 252 20049; m 84 692 0565; e reservastete@interhotels.co.mz; 📘 Hotel-Inter-Tete/1566450020255552. Another new business-style hotel offering comfortable rooms with AC, writing desk, safe, TV, kettle, minibar & Wi-Fi. Facilities inc swimming pool, gym & restaurant (*meals around US$20*). *US$130 standard dbl; suites starting at US$170, B&B.* **$$$$**

🏠 **O Paraíso Misterioso** (80 rooms) Off the N7 past Sundowners; m 84 830 6687. Though it's not quite as enigmatic or heavenly as the name suggests, this is definitely the most pleasant option in this price range, with a great waterfront position in view of the bridge & large green grounds centred on a swimming pool & amusement complex with bumper cars! Comfortable dbl rooms have AC, nets, flat-screen DSTV & en-suite hot shower, a good restaurant is attached & it is home to the Cine Aniz (page 247).

Tete TETE

14

US$84 dbl; US$117 dbl in new wing; all rates B&B. **$$$$**

Budget

🏠 **Estalagem Nharinga** (16 rooms) Rua Agostinho Neto; \252 24638; m 84 301 9581. This is a pleasant enough option, set in a low-slung compound next to Hotel Nhungué. Recently renovated, all rooms are en suite & have AC & TV. There's an attached restaurant & bar, which could be noisy depending on the night. *US$30/50 sgl/dbl, B&B.* **$$**

🏠 **Masololo Lodge** (9 rooms) Bairro Matundo; m 84 301 9165/546 1190. Situated on the Matundo side of the river about 400m upstream from the bridge, this leafy compound of cosy wood-&-thatch bandas is a welcome antidote to the impersonal business hotels that proliferate in this price range. En-suite rooms are on the small side, but come with AC, DSTV, fridge, nets & verandas. The attached restaurant & bar serves mains for US$10–14 & the outdoor seating makes for an excellent place to watch the Zambezi slink by. *US$30 budget dbl; US$50 standard dbl, B&B inc Wi-Fi.* **$$**

🏠 **Pensão Univendas** (20 rooms) Av da Independência; m 84 456 6237 or 82 176 0568. Set above the Univendas store on the junction with Av Julius Nyerere, this can be identified by a set of stairs with 'Flats, Suites, Quartos' on the window

above the entrance. The twin rooms are quite nice, & have AC, TV & even balconies, but steeply priced given that they all use common bathrooms. *US$44/59 sgl/dbl.* **$$$**

🏠 **Sundowners** (13 rooms) N7 about 200m from Samora Machel Bridge; m 82 568 1568 or 84 821 9830. Set at the back of a large thatched sports bar, the rooms here are potentially noisy but otherwise seem pretty decent, & come with en-suite hot shower, DSTV & AC. *US$30 dbl.* **$**

Shoestring and camping

🏠 **Hotel Kassuende** (30 rooms) Av 25 de Junho. This place isn't the smartest, but it's about the cheapest option in Tete, & the better rooms come with balcony, TV & fan. Convenient location near the supermarket, central market & restaurants. *US$26/40 sgl/dbl using common showers.* **$**

🏕 **Jesus é Bom** Bairro Matundo; e jesusebomcamp@gmail.com. The only official campsite in Tete, it is owned by the reformed church. It is set on the river about 500m downstream from the bridge. With recent renovations to the kitchen & toilets, the facilities are kept relatively clean. There's hot water, braai, a swimming pool & 2 self-catering rooms. The area can be unsafe, so keep your possessions with you. *US$36/40 sgl/dbl, US$6 pp camping.* **$$**

✖ WHERE TO EAT AND DRINK *Map, page 244*

Tete has a wide selection of restaurants and bars, and the influx of mining capital means that new places are opening all the time.

✖ **Amore** Av 25 de Junho; m 86 011 5577; ⏱ 07.00–23.00 daily. This new restaurant is a great place to break away from the Tete heat. The menu inc salads, sandwiches, pizzas, chicken & more, plus a wide selection of pastries & ice cream. *US$5–15.* **$$$**

✖ **Café Del Rio** Barrio Matundo; m 84 749 2380; w cafedelrio.co.za; ⏱ 08.00–midnight Tue–Sun. A stunning location on the Zambezi, this popular restaurant-bar is a favourite among expats & Peace Corps. The sunsets, along with the rotating menu of freshly prepared seafood, salads, nachos & meat specials keep people coming back for a relaxing, riverside evening. The perfect location for a sundowner. Live music at w/ends. *US$8–20.* **$$$$**

✖ **Complexo Pemba** Rua Poder Popular; m 82 710 2762; ⏱ evenings Tue–Sun. A great riverside setting, shady seating & an attractive garden make this a good place to sip a beer as the sun goes down. Live music at w/ends. *Large helpings of typical Mozambican fare around US$6.* **$**

✖ **Galaxy Indian Restaurant** Av Eduardo Mondlane; \252 22821; m 84 722 2087/110 4904. Serves lunch & dinner daily. Serves up a long menu of authentic Indian fare, inc naan, lassis & a healthy complement of vegetarian options. Indoor & outdoor seating available, plus they deliver for a small fee. *US$8–12.* **$$$**

✖ **Hotel Zambeze** Av Eduardo Mondlane; \252 23100/1; ⏱ 07.00–10.30, noon–13.30 & 17.00–22.00 daily. The 5th-floor restaurant here is the finest in town, & priced accordingly, with a tempting selection of seafood & steaks. The view over town is immense, especially after dark. Wi-Fi available. *US$10–50.* $$$$

✗ **Mario's Bar** Rua 7 de Setembro; m 82 502 0530/1; ⏱ 10.00–late Mon–Fri, 17.00–late Sat. This recently renovated establishment functions as a sports bar, disco & restaurant, offering live music, TVs & a menu of seafood, steaks, chicken & local Mozambican food & an extensive wine list to match. The party goes late here. *Snacks & meals range from US$6 to US$30.* $$$$

✗ **Smart Café** Barrio Matundo, EN6; m 84 243 9125; ⏱ 06.00–22.00 daily. An expat favourite, Smart Café has a well-rounded menu with a tempting selection of pastries. Wi-Fi available. *Meals US$5–10.* $$

✗ **VIP Café** Av de Liberdade; m 84 477 4374. This delightful new café offers fresh pastries

alongside the typical Mozambican café menu. There is free Wi-Fi & a TV. *Mains from US$3–10.* $$

♀ **PicNic** Av da Independência. This is more a bar than an eatery & has a slightly seedy air, but it's a good place to sit & people-watch or play some billiards. Light meals are served for around US$3. $

♀ **Sundowners** N7; m 84 583 7830. The thatched sports bar here is one of the liveliest in town, especially when big matches are shown on the flat screen. *Serves decent steaks & seafood in the US$6–10 range.* $$

♀ **Tropical Nhungué** Av Julius Nyerere; ⏱ 07.30–22.00 daily, later at w/ends. Thatched restaurant & bar with large-screen DSTV for big sporting events, occasional live music & a lively atmosphere at w/ends. *US$4–8.* $

OTHER PRACTICALITIES

Banks and foreign exchange The usual banks are all represented in Tete. There are ATMs at Barclays, Standard, BIM Millennium and BCI. **Cota Câmbio** is the only forex bureau, located at Hotel Zambeze. It's also easy enough to change US dollars or Malawian kwacha with private money changers either in town or at the borders.

Hospital Situated on Rua Kwame Nkrumah (✆ 252 22150/2).

Internet The best internet café is **MozNet** (✆ 252 20324; ⏱ 07.30–21.30 Mon–Fri, 07.30–12.30 Sat) on Avenida da Liberdade next to VIP Café. It's a bit pricey at US$3/hour, but the air conditioning feels worth the cost. If you have your own device, head to VIP Café or Smart Café for free Wi-Fi.

Police On the corner of Avenida da Independência and Rua Kwame Nkrumah.

Post office On the corner of avenidas da Liberdade and 24 de Julho.

Shopping Tete has plenty of **supermarkets**, most notably the recently opened **Shoprite** in Barrio Matundo, with more of them along Avenida 25 de Junho, Avenida Kenneth Kaunda and Avenida da Independência. There are two **markets** selling food, both on Avenida 25 de Junho. One is on the road towards Boroma, and the other in the opposite direction just past the junction with Avenida Julius Nyerere. Craft shopping in Tete is limited to say the least, but you'll usually find a handful of sellers plying their wares next to Tropical Nhungué. There is also the new Tete Mall with a Shoprite, Woolworths, KFC and a selection of other stores.

Swimming pool O Paraíso Misterioso charges a day fee equivalent to around US$5 to swim in its pool.

Cinema The unexpectedly smart new Cine Aniz (🛈 *cineaniz*) in O Paraíso Misterioso shows recent Hollywood movies.

WHAT TO SEE AND DO Tete is a town of limited interest to tourists, and for many its few attractive qualities will be outweighed by the oppressive humidity of the Zambezi Valley. The old part of town is not without a certain decrepit charm: there are some beautiful old houses here, though most are in urgent need of restoration.

The oldest building is the disused **cathedral**, which reportedly dates back to 1563. The most unlikely is a **domed gazebo** on the riverfront. It's been suggested that it was a bar where the Portuguese used to drink sundowners, but the inside is dominated by some form of water pump with associated pipes, so it appears that it's actually part of the water system. Either way, it is now fenced off and can only be admired from a distance.

Also worth a look is the old **slaving fort** near the municipal market, though it now protects a couple of water tanks so it may be difficult to get inside. A second fort, situated on the riverfront below the bridge, is now used as a football training ground.

Tete's best-known landmark is the **Samora Machel Bridge**, the kilometre-long multi-span suspension bridge that spans the Zambezi immediately northwest of the town centre. Built in the 1960s, this was the only permanent crossing of the Zambezi anywhere in Mozambique prior to the opening of the Caia Bridge in August 2009. A new toll bridge (*US$1 per standard vehicle*) was completed in 2014 at the mining settlement of Benga, 6km downstream from Tete.

An attractive feature of Tete is the row of bars and restaurants that lines the riverfront – this is, after all, the one place in Mozambique where the Zambezi is readily accessible to casual visitors and, even if the riverbank around Tete itself is somewhat denuded of natural vegetation, it would be a shame to visit Mozambique and not spend at least one evening drinking in sight of Africa's fourth-largest river. More adventurously, you could ask around to find a fisherman to paddle you along the river in a dugout: the papyrus beds near the town support a good variety of birds, and you wouldn't need to go more than 1km or so upriver to stand a chance of seeing hippos and crocs.

AROUND TETE

Sightseeing opportunities in Tete Province are rather sparsely distributed and, for the most part, time-consuming to reach without private transport. The main attraction in the region is the **Cahora Bassa Dam**, but **Boroma** and **Zumbo** are both of some historical interest.

CAHORA BASSA DAM Situated on the Zambezi in the north of Tete Province, Cahora Bassa confines one of Africa's ten largest bodies of water, covering an area of 2,660km². Construction of the 300m-wide, 160m-high concrete wall started in 1969 and, despite Frelimo's attempts at sabotage, it was completed in 1974.

Cahora Bassa is potentially Africa's largest supplier of hydro-electric power and a vital source of foreign revenue for Mozambique. The five turbines, housed in a rock-hewn cavern of cathedralesque dimensions, have a total capacity of 2,075MW, roughly ten times the power requirement for the whole of Mozambique. When the dam was built, the idea was that it would supply large amounts of hydro-electric power to South Africa. Sadly, by the end of the civil war only two of the dam's turbines were still functional, and no electricity from Cahora Bassa had reached South Africa since part of the power line was destroyed by Renamo in 1986. Nowadays, since the rehabilitation of the dam in 1997 and the beginning of construction of a new plant some 70km downstream of Cahora Bassa, Mozambique can expect to earn a considerable amount of its foreign exchange from the export of electricity to South Africa and other neighbouring countries.

CAHORA BASSA RAPIDS

Now partially submerged by a namesake dam, the Cahora Bassa Rapids were the obstacle that prevented Livingstone's Zambezi expedition from opening up the Zambezi as 'God's Highway' into the African interior, and which led to the explorer turning his attention to the Shire River in what would eventually become the British enclave now known as Malawi. Covering a distance of roughly 80km, and marked by two near-vertical drops of 200m, the rapids had been known to the Portuguese and other traders for several centuries before Livingstone arrived at the Zambezi – the phrase 'Cahora Bassa' means 'where the work ends' in the local dialect, a reference to the fact that the rapids were an impassable obstacle for boatmen sailing up the Zambezi.

Livingstone had used a path that arched around the rapids in the course of his epic trans-African hike, the journey that preceded and inspired the Zambezi Expedition, so it is something of a mystery why he never thought to look at the rapids for himself, and steadfastly dismissed local advice that they would be impassable. Even when his boat, the *Ma-Robert*, was confronted by the rapids on 9 November 1858, Livingstone refused to believe they couldn't eventually be surmounted, though he was finally persuaded of this in November 1860 when he attempted to ascend the rapids with five dugout canoes, a number of which overturned, taking many of the expedition's notes and drawings with them.

Probably the first person to navigate the rapids was a rather enigmatic and obscure figure remembered in the annals of the Royal Geographical Society by the name of Mr F Monks (though his real surname was evidently Foster). In 1880, Monks made a solo canoe trip between the confluence of the Gawayi and Zambezi rivers and the port of Quelimane. Although he left no substantial journal of this trip, he did leave behind an impressively accurate topographical map of the Zambezi and several of its tributaries as far downriver as Tete. Monks disappeared into the African interior a few years after this, never to be heard of again. As a footnote, the first people known to have kayaked the full length of the Zambezi from its source near the borders of Zambia, the Democratic Republic of Congo and Angola are two young British travellers, Rupert FitzMaurice and Justin Matterson, who did the trip to raise money for charity towards the end of 1996.

An interesting story associated with the rapids is that of the legendary silver mines of Chicova, which were shown to Portuguese explorers in the early years of the 17th century. In 1617 and 1618, the period when Madeira occupied the fort at Sena, an estimated 450kg of silver was brought there, allegedly from Chicova. The odd thing is that the mines were 'lost' shortly after Madeira left Sena, and despite the subsequent attempts of several fortune hunters, they have yet to be relocated. If the mines ever did exist, they are probably now submerged by Cahora Bassa, or close to its southern shore.

14

The closest town to the dam, **Songo**, was purpose-built in the style of a Portuguese village while the dam was under construction. By 1974 it had a population of almost 15,000. Located in the cool, breezy highlands immediately south of the dam, Songo is well worth visiting in its own right, with a spacious layout and green, flowering gardens that blend attractively into the surrounding woodland. It's unique in Mozambique in that it doesn't really have an identifiable centre – it's more a series of *barrios* (neighbourhoods) connected by roads. It's also the only town in Mozambique where it's safe to drink the water straight from the taps as it comes direct from the company's processing plant on the lake – the pipes run alongside the road between Songo and the dam.

The approach road to Songo is one of the most spectacular in Mozambique, and the well-wooded, boulder-strewn hills that surround the town offer a refreshing contrast to the humid air and stark landscape of Tete. The Songo area also promises excellent birdwatching, and there are plenty of roads along which you can explore it.

Songo's most unexpected attraction comes in the form of two captivating monuments: *Reversão* and *Sandwana*, crafted by Tete-born painter and mosaicist Naguib Elias in 2012. These jaw-dropping mosaics, each approaching 2ha in size, were commissioned by Hidroeléctrica de Cahora Bassa (HCB) to commemorate Mozambique taking ownership of Portugal's last remaining stake in the Cahora Bassa Dam. *Reversão* depicts the human history of Mozambique and the dam from ancient times to the present day (with excellent, though Portuguese-only, information panels), and *Sandwana* invokes local cosmologies in the shape of a 120m-long mythical serpent believed by some to reside deep in the waters of Lake Cahora Bassa.

Also of interest is the remains of a Zimbabwean-style stone enclosure, dating from the 18th or 19th century, right in the heart of Songo, in an open field about 200m south of the central shopping plaza. In the plaza itself you'll find Songo's only real services: BIM and BCI ATMs, an impressively well-stocked supermarket and bakery, the town pharmacy, and even a diminutive but fully functional post office.

You no longer need to get specific authorisation in Tete before visiting Songo and Cahora Bassa, but the dam and its turbine rooms can only be visited on a (free) tour arranged through the Songo office of HCB. Anybody in Songo can point you there, or else you can ring in advance (♦ *252 82157*).

Getting there and away

By car Songo lies 150km from Tete along an excellent surfaced road. The junction for the scenic **EN258** (N301) to Songo is roughly 25km from Tete along the **EN103** (N7) towards the Zimbabwean border. The signage is a bit whimsical, but it's the only major junction along this stretch of road. The drive from Tete to Songo can comfortably be done in 2 hours in a private vehicle.

By chapa Chapas run to Songo daily, leaving from outside the post office on Avenida da Liberdade in Tete. You could also take a chapa to Estima (also known as Chitima), a small town at the base of the mountains about 15km from Songo, and pick up a lift to Songo from there. They cost around US$4 and the journey takes up to 4 hours. Given the lack of a town centre at Songo, getting back to Tete requires some organisation, but since there's really only one road, position yourself at the edge of town and you shouldn't have too much trouble finding a lift back. Barring that, you could always arrange with the driver of the chapa that brought you here.

🏠 Where to stay, eat and drink

🏠 **Acomodação Mangueiras** (25 rooms) ♦252 82570; m 82/84 305 6100; e acomodacao. mangueiras@gmail.com. Set in a wide, grassy compound, the uniformly priced en-suite rooms here are in detached brick bungalows with TV, fridge & hot showers. Older rooms have a kitchen, while newer rooms lack the kitchen but have larger (king-size) beds. Wi-Fi available. You'll also find one of Songo's liveliest eateries, dishing up Mozambican favourites for US$6–8. It's the place in town to catch a football match, & there's even an inflatable pool in front if you're desperate for a dip. *US$50 dbl or bungalow B&B.* **$$**

🏠 **Casindira Lodge** (5 rooms) Magoé; m 84 618 6599/599 9871; e casindiralodge@gmail. com; 🇫 CasindiraLodge. About 160km from Songo near the town of Magoé & its eponymous national park, this decidedly remote lodge on the southern shores of Lake Cahora Bassa is catnip for fishing enthusiasts, but the cliffside luxury chalets, terrace restaurant & bar with DSTV, Wi-Fi & swimming pool ought to keep even the least piscatorial guests pleased as well. Call ahead. *US$120 pp FB, US$165 pp, FB fishing package.* **$$$$**

🏠 **Montebelo Songo Hotel** (14 rooms) ☎252 82704/7; e songohotel@montebelohotels. com; w montebelohotels.com. Formerly known as The Club, this Songo institution has been fully revamped in recent years. It's very nicely done, & the well-equipped en-suite rooms all boast DSTV, Wi-Fi & chic modern décor. The swimming pool & attached bar make for a very pleasant way of

passing an afternoon, & the restaurant is the best in town, serving mains for US$12–20. *US$89/104 sgl/dbl; from US$125 suites; all rooms B&B.* **$$$$**

🏠 **Pensão-Residencial** 7 Montes (5 rooms) ☎252 82341; m 82 014 4423. Your only option for budget accommodation in Songo, this place has basic but clean en-suite rooms with hot water in a compound near the *Reversão* monument. There's 1 room with AC which goes for the same price. *US$34 twin.* **$$**

🏠 **Ugezi Tiger Lodge** (16 units) ☎+27 15 318 4381 or +27 82 809 1407 (South Africa); m +27 84 599 8410 (South Africa); e zrb@mweb.co.za; w ugezitigerlodge.co.za. Aimed mainly at keen anglers, this pleasant lodge lies on the lakeshore about 3km south of the dam wall, an area rich in birdlife & fishing opportunities. Accommodation is in comfortable en-suite chalets with AC, & there is a nice campsite. *Rates start at US$86 dbl.* **$$$**

BOROMA MISSION Situated along the Zambezi about 25km upriver of Tete, the Missão de São José de Boroma, founded in 1891, is one of the country's most attractive missions. Its centrepiece is a large and beautiful church on a hill overlooking the river. This building was abandoned by the missionaries shortly after independence, and the complex now seems to house a school. The site was reputedly an important source of alluvial gold even before Portuguese times, but this resource had been exhausted long before the mission was founded. The Boroma area is also a good place to see hippos and crocs, and offers good birdwatching.

Getting there and away
By car Although Boroma is only 25km northwest of Tete, the road there is in variable condition, crossing several seasonal watercourses, and certain sections may require a 4x4, especially after rain. To get there, follow Avenida 25 de Junho out of town northwest for about 1.5km past the old slave fort until you see a large blue signpost pointing left to Boroma. From here the road follows the Zambezi closely, passing through the villages of Dege and Mufa, and it offers some excellent views over the water, as well as a good chance of encountering monkeys, hippos and crocodiles.

By chapa A few chapas run between Tete and Boroma daily. They start and end in the huge local market to the south of Avenida 25 de Junho, but it's a very confusing walk through the huts and you'd be ill advised to try it without a guide. Better perhaps to walk out along Avenida 25 de Junho to the signpost mentioned above; the chapas reach this junction about 5 minutes after they leave the market. The journey will cost around US$1.50 and it takes around 90 minutes. Every now and again someone coming in the opposite direction will give a little signal to the driver, and he'll drop a few people off who vanish into the bush. The signal means that there is a police roadblock a little further on; the people being dropped off will not have their identity papers so will be skirting around it, to be picked up later on.

Where to stay, eat and drink There is no formal accommodation at Boroma, and it's easy enough to visit the mission as a day trip out of Tete. You may be able to camp near the mission, and there are several bars in Boroma where you'll be able to get food and drink.

ZUMBO The most westerly town in Mozambique is Zumbo, which lies on the Zambian border at the confluence of the Zambezi and Luangwa rivers near the western end of Lake Cahora Bassa, 240km west of Songo. Well off any beaten track today, Zumbo was once the site of an important gold fair, reputedly founded in 1715 by Francisco Pereira, a Goan trader and refugee from the Rozvi attack on Dambarare. By 1750, a lively trade in gold with the Rozvim, supported by ivory potted in the Bangweulu Basin (in what is now northern Zambia), had made Zumbo the largest Portuguese town on the Zambezi, with a Christian population of almost 500 including 80 Europeans. By 1764, when it was granted municipal status, Zumbo was possibly the most prosperous settlement in Portuguese Africa.

Zumbo's decline can be linked to the political tensions that gripped the upper Zambezi in the late 18th century, combined with the great drought that started in 1832. After being attacked several times, Zumbo was fortified in 1801, and at the same time a Portuguese garrison moved in. This was not enough to prevent further attacks, so the town was evacuated in 1813. The fair was reoccupied in 1820 but, following the resurgence of drought conditions and the looming threat of the Nguni after they deposed the Rozvi dynasty in 1836, Zumbo was permanently abandoned by Portugal.

In 1859, the British explorer Richard Thornton passed through the ghost town that had once been described as the metropolis of the whole trade of the rivers. Thornton recorded seeing the ruins of some 200 stone houses lining the riverbank over a distance of 3km. A more recent report confirms that a fort of unknown antiquity, built around a 500-year-old fig tree, was still in use at Zumbo during World War II. It is still a reasonably sizeable town, serving as district capital and supporting a population of around 35,000, but it remains very isolated from the rest of the country.

Getting there and away

By road Getting to Zumbo requires a bit of determination. By road, you need to follow the **EN221** (N9) north for about 135km to Bene, where the 325km dirt road (N303) to Zumbo, via Fingoe and Caponda, branches to the right. This has never been a very good road and it suffered considerable flood damage in 2001. We have no recent reports regarding its condition, but there is certainly no public transport along it, and self-drivers should only consider trying it if they have a solid 4x4 and feel up for a genuine adventure.

By ferry Another option is a pontoon ferry called the *Kuza*, which theoretically makes a return passage along the length of Cahora Bassa from Songo to Zumbo every 10–14 days. By all accounts, however, this boat is old, unreliable and in less than shipshape condition, so delays are frequent and it might be a risky trip, especially in the rainy season. If you decide to risk it, be prepared for a journey of some days and carry all your own food.

Where to stay, eat and drink
There is at least one basic lodging and restaurant in Zumbo. The only other option is **Chawalo Safari Camp** (w *safari-international. com*), a hunting and fishing camp set in a private concession on the north bank of the Zambezi 15km northeast (downstream) from Zumbo.

Part Four

NORTHERN MOZAMBIQUE

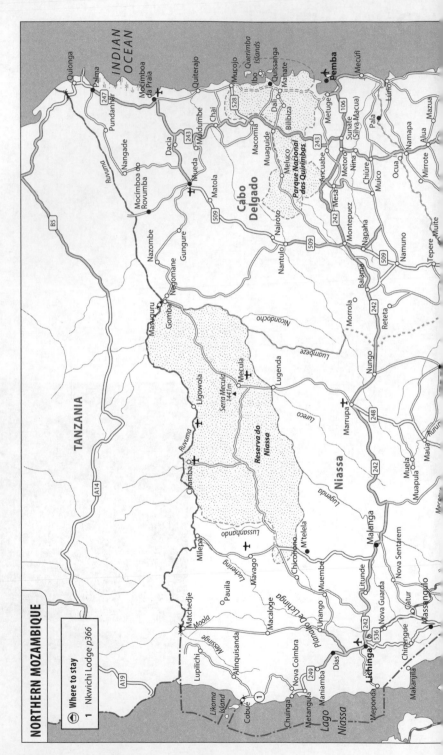

NORTHERN MOZAMBIQUE

Where to stay
1 Nkwichi Lodge *p366*

INDIAN OCEAN

TANZANIA

Quionga
Palma
Pundanhar
Nangade
Mocímboa da Praia
Quiterajo
Mucojo
Querimba Islands
Ibo
Quissanga
Mahate
Pemba
Mecufi
Dacia
Mucojo
Chai
Macomia
Muaguide
Dali
Bilibiza
Metuge
Sunate (Silva-Macua)
Pala
Lúrio
Mueda
Matola
Mocímboa do Rovuma
Meluco
Parque Nacional das Quirimbas
Ancuabe
Metoro
Nina
Chiúre
Muico
Ocua
Namapa
Alua
Mazua
Mirrote

Cabo Delgado

Matchedje
Nazombe
Negomane
Gungure
Nairoto
Nantulo
Montepuez
Napaha
Namuno
509
509
242
242

Masuguru
Gomba
Ligowola
Serra Mecula 1441m
Mecula
Lugenda
Morrola
Reteta
Nungo
Nicondcho
Luambeze
Lureco
Marrupa
248

Chamba
Reserva do Niassa
Lussanhando
Lugenda
Mavago
Muembe
Muela
Muapula
242

Milepa
Luchering
Chiconono
Mtelela
Litunde
Malanga
Nova Santarém

Niassa

Matchedje
Moola
Macaloge
Pauila
Unango
Planalto de Lichinga
Nova Guarda
Catur
Massangulo
536

Lupilichi
Alinquisanda
Nova Coimbra
Dias
Lichinga
Chirenguе
Makanjila

Lago Niassa
Cóbuè
Likoma Island
Chuinga
Metangula
Maniamba
Meponda

A14
B5
A19
247
243
243
509
528
106

254

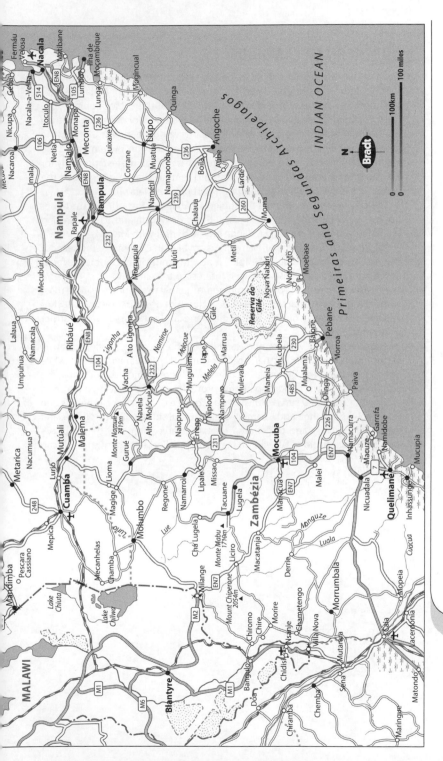

NORTHERN MOZAMBIQUE

The last six chapters in this guidebook are dedicated to the far north of Mozambique, a region bordered by Tanzania to the north, Malawi to the west and the Zambezi River to the south. Like southern Mozambique, the region has a long coastline and, though less developed for mass tourism than the south, it boasts several worthwhile resorts and focal points, notably the time-warped Ilha de Moçambique, the more modern port of Pemba and the stunning Quirimbas Archipelago. The interior is also of interest, primarily for the mountains around Gurué, the vast and remote Niassa Reserve and the beautiful Lago Niassa (the Mozambican part of Lake Malawi).

The province of Zambézia is the subject of *Chapter 15*, starting at the rather ho-hum provincial capital Quelimane, then moving inland to the bracing highlands around Gurué and Milange on the border with Malawi.

Another provincial capital, Nampula, is covered in *Chapter 16*. The second-largest city in Mozambique, Nampula is also the most important route focus in the north, but otherwise of limited interest to travellers.

Chapter 17 covers Ilha de Moçambique, arguably the country's single most compelling urban attraction, as well as a clutch of other interesting beaches and historic villages on the facing mainland around Mossuril and further north at Nacala.

Chapter 18 deals with Pemba, capital of Cabo Delgado Province, as well as the mainland coast further north towards the Tanzanian border, while *Chapter 19* covers the Quirimbas – both the offshore archipelago of that name and the eponymous national park that protects part of the facing mainland.

Finally, *Chapter 20* surveys the inland province of Niassa, including its two major towns Lichinga and Cuamba, the beautiful shores of Lago Niassa, and the thrillingly vast and underrated Niassa Reserve, home to the country's largest concentrations of wild animals such as lion, elephant and African hunting dog.

15

Zambézia

Flowing southeast along the boundary of Sofala and Zambézia provinces, the final seaborne stretch of the mighty Zambezi forms the closest thing there is to a tangible border between southern and northern Mozambique. True, the transition from south to north is less emphatic now that the time-consuming ferry crossing at Caia has been rendered redundant by the nippy 2.4km Armando Emilio Guebuza Bridge, which opened in August 2009. Nevertheless, crossing into Zambézia at Caia feels almost like journeying into another country. The goods sold at the roadside change, with fresh fruit and vegetables taking the place of the more processed and packaged foods available in the south. The quality of the vehicles falls, the chapas being more battered. The road network is worse too, with a higher proportion of dirt roads than you'll find in the south and a greater likelihood of damage during the rainy season. And Zambézia is the province where the eternal problem of getting change ceases to be a slightly charming affectation and becomes a serious annoyance.

Extending inland from the Indian Ocean to the Malawian border, Zambézia is the country's second-largest province at 105,008km², and the second most populous, with an estimated 4.5 million inhabitants, the main ethnic groups being the Macua, the Chuabo and the Lomwe. It is also the most topographically varied and agriculturally rich, with habitats ranging from coastal mangroves and savannah to the cultivated Rift Valley foothills, where extensive tea and cotton plantations flank isolated islands of evergreen forest on the slopes of mounts Namuli, Mabu and Chiperone. The coastline has more in common with the swathes of mangroves around Beira than the extended beaches in the south of the country, and a glance at any decent map will show a far higher number of rivers running into the Indian Ocean.

Zambézia's delights aren't immediately apparent. The province lacks the beach culture of the south, the extensive wilds of the north, or any settlement as captivating as Ilha de Moçambique or Inhambane, and most travellers simply treat it as a corridor between north and south (or to a lesser extent between Mozambique and Malawi). But there are bright points that deserve some attention. The provincial capital Quelimane is a quirky, timeworn riverside town whose history in some ways mirrors that of Mozambique itself. And the highland town of Gurué is extremely pleasant, with good walking opportunities in the surrounding hills including the possibility of walking up the country's second-highest peak, the 2,419m-high Mount Namuli.

QUELIMANE

The capital of Zambézia and the most important settlement along the 1,000km road between Beira/Chimoio and Nampula, the riverport of Quelimane is Mozambique's seventh-largest town, with a population estimated at around 245,000 in 2016. It is also one of the oldest towns in Mozambique, founded near the Cuácua River mouth in medieval times, probably by Swahili traders from Kilwa (in southern Tanzania), and it has remained a settlement of some significance throughout the Portuguese era to the present day.

Oddly, perhaps, the modern city centre, a curious mishmash of outmoded 20th-century architectural styles, is almost totally lacking in relics of its early days, the nearest contender being a disused 18th-century cathedral on the waterfront. Quelimane today is looking better than it has in years, however, thanks to an initiative to resurface all of the roads in the town centre. Gone are the 'pot-holes of such a magnitude they could hide a family of wallowing buffalos in the rainy season' that bedevilled residents and visitors alike for years. Today getting around Quelimane is a breeze, and while visitors still have to contend with the sweltering coastal heat, unrelieved by the oceanic breeze associated with ports on the open sea, a stop in Quelimane is no longer the ordeal it once was and, with a growing number of good food and accommodation options, it may not be the most compelling, but it's a perfectly agreeable place to break up the long overland trek between northern and southern Mozambique. If you're simply looking for a place to break the journey, though, the accommodation in Mocuba may be better value overall.

HISTORY The settlement that eventually became Quelimane was almost certainly founded by Muslim traders, probably at around the same time as Tete and Sena. The site on the north bank of the Cuácua, about 25km upstream of its mouth, was chosen after it was discovered that this relatively small waterway formed part of a navigable channel that opened into the Zambezi, merging near modern-day Mopeia (a far more manageable and safe prospect than entering the vast and labyrinthine Zambezi Delta to the south). It is assumed that this waterway formed an important link on one of the various transport networks that connected the goldfields of the interior to the ports of the Swahili coast.

Vasco da Gama stopped at Quelimane on his pioneering 1498 voyage to East Africa. When he saw that some locals were dressed in Arab-style robes, he realised he was almost certainly on track to his ultimate goal of India, and gave the Cuácua its Portuguese name Rio dos Bons Sinais ('River of Good Signs'). One local tradition has it that the name Quelimane was inadvertently coined by da Gama, based on the response of local labourers who misunderstood his query and replied 'kuliamani' (we are cultivating). An even more improbable (and anomalously Anglocentric) explanation is that Quelimane derives from the phrase 'Killer of Men', in reference to the high incidence of malarial deaths in the area. Far more likely is that the name pre-dates any European influence and is simply a variant spelling of the KiSwahili 'Kilimani', which means 'On High Ground'.

A Portuguese trading factory was established at Quelimane in 1530, and the town appears on Portuguese maps dating from 1560. Quelimane grew in importance as the ivory-trading routes up the Zambezi replaced the older gold-trade routes out of Sofala. Reports dating to the 1590s depict it as an attractive small town, surrounded by plantations and protected by a wooden fort. In common with many other coastal settlements, Quelimane benefited from the growth in the slave trade from the interior during the latter part of the 18th century. It also became a major supplier of food to Mozambique Island during this period. Quelimane's oldest stone buildings date to the 1780s, and in 1812 the town was made a separate captaincy with its own customs house.

By the 1820s, Quelimane was the most important slaving port in East Africa, but lost its municipal status in 1826 on account of the lack of government control over the trade in slaves. The main results were that the local slave trade was driven underground, and that many visiting ships avoided Portuguese settlements

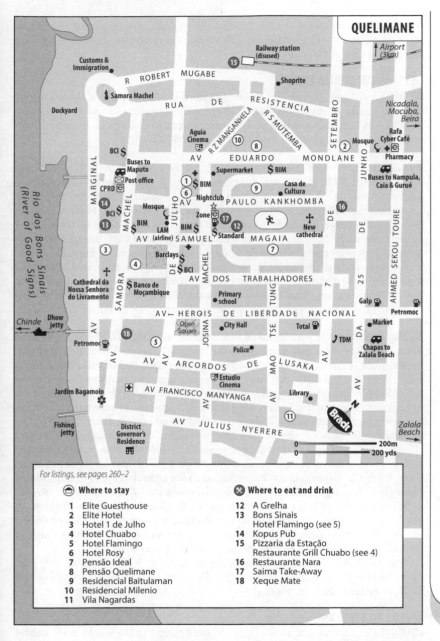

QUELIMANE

Airport (3km)

Railway station (disused)

Customs & Immigration

R ROBERT MUGABE

Shoprite

Dockyard

Samora Machel

RUA DE RESISTENCIA

RS MUTEMBA

Nicadala, Mocuba, Beira

Aguia Cinema

Rafa Cyber Café

Mosque

BCI

AV EDUARDO MONDLANE

Pharmacy

Buses to Maputo

Post office

Supermarket

BIM

Buses to Nampula, Caia & Gurué

CPRD

Mosque

Casa de Cultura

PAULO KANKHOMBA

BCI

BIM

Nightclub

Zone

Standard

LAM (airline)

BIM

SAMUEL MAGAIA

New cathedral

Barclays

BCI

AV DOS TRABALHADORES

AHMED SEKOU TOURE

Cathedral da Nossa Senhora do Livramento

Banco de Moçambique

Primary school

Galp

Petromoc

Chinde

Dhow jetty

AV HEROIS DE LIBERDADE NACIONAL

Petromoc

Open Square

City Hall

Total

Market

TDM

Chapas to Zalala Beach

Police

AV ARCORDOS DE LUSAKA

Jardim Bagamoio

Estudio Cinema

AV FRANCISCO MANYANGA

Library

Zalala Beach

Fishing jetty

District Governor's Residence

AV JULIUS NYERERE

Brandt

0   200m
0   200yds

Rio dos Bons Sinais (River of Good Signs)

For listings, see pages 260–2

🛏 **Where to stay**

1 Elite Guesthouse
2 Elite Hotel
3 Hotel 1 de Julho
4 Hotel Chuabo
5 Hotel Flamingo
6 Hotel Rosy
7 Pensão Ideal
8 Pensão Quelimane
9 Residencial Baitulaman
10 Residencial Milenio
11 Vila Nagardas

✖ **Where to eat and drink**

12 A Grelha
13 Bons Sinais
    Hotel Flamingo (see 5)
14 Kopus Pub
15 Pizzaria da Estação
    Restaurante Grill Chuabo (see 4)
16 Restaurante Nara
17 Saima Take-Away
18 Xeque Mate

altogether, preferring to enter into clandestine trade with Muslim settlements elsewhere on the coast. The town's strategic importance also declined after the late 1820s, when the channel connecting the Cuácua to the Zambezi silted up as a result of drought, never to reopen.

Quelimane nevertheless remained a prosperous settlement throughout the 19th century, mainly as a supplier of agricultural produce to other Portuguese ports. The town was the end point of David Livingstone's pioneering 1856 crossing of south-central Africa from west to east. Livingstone was officially appointed the British Honorary Consul to Quelimane in 1858, though his main interest in the town was as a base to explore the Zambezi.

GETTING THERE AND AWAY

By air Quelimane Airport lies about 3km from the town centre at the northwest end of Avenida 25 de Junho, and a cab from the city centre should cost around US$6. **LAM** flies to Quelimane several times a week from Maputo, Beira and Tete, and has an office on Avenida 1 de Julho (✆ *242 12800/1*).

By car Quelimane lies about 40km southeast of the **EN1** and can be reached along the surfaced **EN470** (N10), which branches from it at the small but expanding junction town of Nicoadala. Coming from the south, it is about 660km to Quelimane from Beira and 600km from Chimoio via the junction town of Inchope and the Caia Bridge. The surfaced road is in fair to good condition all the way and either drive can be completed in a day, ideally with an early start, though that is not quite so important now the old ferry at Caia has been replaced by a bridge.

For those with no particular interest in diverting to Quelimane from Nicoadala, it is possible to continue 115km north to Mocuba, the springboard for more northerly destinations such as Milange (on the Malawian border), Gurué or Alto Molócuè (all covered in greater detail in this chapter), as well as Nampula.

By bus and chapa Chapas to Zalala Beach (*45 mins; US$0.60*) and other more local destinations leave from outside the market on Avenida Heróis de Liberdade. For chapas to Nicoadala (*45 mins; US$0.80*), Mocuba (*2–3 hrs; US$6*), and all other destinations reached via the EN1/EN7, you need the Romoza Terminal next to BP on Avenida Eduardo Mondlane. This terminal is unusually well organised, with signs indicating the queues for the various destinations, but it is about 30 minutes' walk from the waterfront and several sections are unlit at night, so you might want to catch a taxi.

Heading to Milange, there's one direct minibus daily, leaving at 05.00 and charging US$9. If you miss that, get yourself to Mocuba and pick up onward transport there. You could do the same thing if your goal is Alto Molócuè or Gurué, though there is also one direct daily minibus to the latter, leaving at 05.00, taking 6 hours and charging US$7. The **Nagi Investimentos** (m *84 101 6738/955 1669/449 3730*) bus to Nampula leaves at 04.30, costs US$12 and takes up to 10 hours. A few buses leave daily for Beira, including **Maning Nice** (m *84 635 1218* or *86 363 8932*), whose buses depart at 04.00 from their own terminal on Avenida Eduardo Mondlane about 1km beyond the Romoza Terminal, and cost US$14.

Postbus (✆ *214 30061/2*; m *82 305 7378* or *84 312 3102/3/4*; w *correios.co.mz*) runs buses to Maputo on Sunday, returning on Thursday for US$40, departing at 03.00 and leaving from the post office.

🏠 WHERE TO STAY *Map, page 259*
Upmarket

🏠 **Elite Guesthouse** (7 rooms)
Av 1 de Julho; ✆ 242 18294; m 82/84 592 6910;
e eliteguesthouse@gmail.com; w elitehoteis.com.
Opened in 2012, this place has sleek tiled rooms that are short on windows, but otherwise seem quite comfortable, sporting AC, flat-screen TV, Wi-Fi, kettle & fridge. The vibe here is meant to be

cool & modern, & it largely succeeds. Also available is their VIP guesthouse, opened in 2015, which is more like a proper house than a hotel set-up. Decent value. *US$78/90 dbl/twin, US$84–114 VIP guesthouse, B&B.* **$$$**

🏠 **Elite Hotel** (22 rooms) Av 7 de Setembro;
✆ 242 19900; m 82/84 592 6910; e hotelelite.
moz@gmail.com; w elitehoteis.com. Opened in

2016, this sleek modern hotel is an extension of the Elite Guesthouse. En-suite rooms with AC, flat-screen TV, Wi-Fi, kettle & fridge are priced according to size. There is a pool with loungers & an outdoor sitting area. The energetic owner-manager is most helpful as well. *US$84–114 dbl B&B.* **$$$**

🏠 **Hotel Chuabo** (64 rooms) Av Samora Machel; 📞 242 13181/2; e hotelchuabo@tdm. co.mz. Given the limited attractions on offer in Quelimane, it seems somewhat bizarre that the city centre is graced with a relatively plush hotel of skyscraping dimensions. Nevertheless the Chuabo is exactly that – & deliciously retro to boot – with comfortable rooms with DSTV & AC, reasonably well maintained, but rather impersonal. The view from the top-floor restaurant is impressive. *US$70/86 standard sgl/dbl; US$76/92 executive sgl/dbl; from US$118 suites; all rates B&B.* **$$$**

🏠 **Residencial Milenio** (21 rooms) 84 Av Zedequias Manganhela; 📞 242 13314; m 82/84 305 6331; e milenio_hotel@hotmail.com. Another pleasant option aimed at business travellers, this is a converted old Portuguese house with a range of en-suite rooms with AC, DSTV, tea/coffee, twin beds & large bathroom with hot shower. The well-maintained buildings & neat grounds stand in sharp contrast to the rather dingy street outside. *US$70/76/80 sgl/twin/dbl; US$84/96 exec sgl/dbl.* **$$$**

🏠 **Vila Nagardas** (13 rooms) Praça do Bonga; 📞 242 12046; m 82 712 3489 or 84 611 1448; e villanagardas1e2@gmail.com. Often fully booked & with good reason, this secluded hotel has some of the best rooms in Quelimane. The main house has a classic, colonial feel, with parquet floors & finely appointed, high-ceilinged guestrooms with TV, AC, Wi-Fi, minibar, kettle & safe. The newer chalet rooms sit in the garden opposite the terrace restaurant & offer much the same in terms of amenities. The staff are warm & adept, & it's a commendable set-up overall. Highly recommended. *US$84/96 sgl/dbl; US$102/114 chalet sgl/dbl, all rooms B&B.* **$$$**

Mid range

🏠 **Hotel Flamingo** (24 rooms) Av 1 de Julho; 📞 242 16800/15602; m 82 552 7810; e hotelflamingo.qlm@tdm.co.mz; w hotelflamingoquelimane.com. Something of a focal point for volunteers & expats based

in Zambézia, this well-run hotel is set around a private courtyard with parking, swimming pool & a very good bar/restaurant. The rooms are all well appointed, with DSTV, AC, private bathrooms & fridges, & Wi-Fi throughout. Very good value. *US$44/56 sgl/dbl; US$58/70 executive sgl/dbl; all rates B&B.* **$$$**

Budget

🏠 **Hotel 1 de Julho** (21 rooms) Av Filipe Samuel Magaia; 📞 242 13067; m 82 894 3950. This likeable multi-storey hotel, half a block back from the waterfront, has distinctive if idiosyncratic décor & brightly painted clean twin rooms with TV, AC, fan & balcony. The only drawback is that rooms are not en suite, though each has a washbasin. *US$30 twin.* **$**

🏠 **Hotel Rosy** (15 rooms) Av 1 de Julho; 📞 242 14969. Central but rather grotty & loud, this should be considered only as a fall-back. Poor value. *US$29/36 twin/dbl.* **$$**

🏠 **Residencial Baitulaman** (7 rooms) Av Paulo Kankhomba; m 82 187 0849 or 84 442 9450. Walking in through the compound of broken down cars doesn't give the best first impression here, but the tiled en-suite rooms are well taken care of & have AC, TV, kettle, fridge & hot water. *US$26 dbl B&B.* **$**

Shoestring

🏠 **Pensão Ideal** (41 rooms) Av Filipe Samuel Magaia; 📞 242 12731; e p.ideal@hotmail.com. A long-standing backpacker's bolthole, this large pink building just down from the cathedral is the best-value cheapie in town, especially following the addition of a newer wing. It has a quiet location, rooms are clean & all come with a fan, & a restaurant is attached. *US$11 twin using common shower; US$16 en-suite dbl with AC & TV; US$30/40 en-suite sgl/dbl with AC & TV in newer wing.* **$**

🏠 **Pensão Quelimane** (24 rooms) Av Eduardo Mondlane; 📞 242 17007; m 82 592 9510. This faded old hotel on the periphery of the town centre looks nice enough from the outside but the interior is gloomy & some rooms have a pervasive toilet smell. A real step down from the Pensão Ideal (above). *US$10/14 dbl/twin using common shower; US$20/30 en-suite dbl/twin with AC & TV.* **$**

✗ WHERE TO EAT AND DRINK *Map, page 259*

✗ **A Grelha** Av Samuel Magaia; m 82 392 4240 or 84 271 5859; ⏰ 08.00–midnight Mon–Sat. The best restaurant in town is this owner-managed place with a good selection of Portuguese/ Mozambican seafood & meat dishes in the US$8– 12 range, along with cheaper snacks. **$$$**

✗ **Bons Sinais** Av Marginal; m 84 277 7775; ⏰ noon–22.00 Tue–Sun, later at w/ends. With its thatched roof & cheerful outdoor feel, this waterfront bar, restaurant & swimming pool complex is well worth a try. They've got a big menu with pizza, pasta & the usual meat & seafood dishes. There's live jazz on Fri & swimming costs US$10. *Pizzas & other mains for US$9–13.* **$$$**

✗ **Hotel Flamingo** Av 1 de Julho; ☏242 15602; ⏰ 07.00–22.00 daily. The courtyard restaurant at the Flamingo has a relaxed atmosphere & a varied menu with soups & pasta alongside more typical Mozambican meat & seafood dishes. An added bonus is free Wi-Fi for diners. *Mains US$5–9.* **$$**

✗ **Pizzaria da Estação** Rua Robert Mugabe; m 84 412 4500; ⏰ 08.00–midnight daily exc Tue. Known for having some of the best pizza in town, this unsignposted house on the edge of the centre does the standard range of Mozambican dishes as well. *Mains US$6–9.* **$$**

✗ **Restaurante Grill Chuabo** Av Samora Machel; ☏242 13181; ⏰ lunch & dinner daily. Situated on the 8th floor of the Hotel Chuabo (page 261), this place is more notable perhaps for the spectacular views than the food, which is still among the best in town & surprisingly affordable. *Most dishes around US$9. There's a cheaper snack bar on the ground floor.* **$$**

✗ **Restaurante Nara** Av 7 de Setembro; ☏242 17833; m 82 777 0303; ⏰ 07.00–22.00 Mon–Sat. The décor here is oddly alpine but the food is distinctly Levantine, with shawarma, falafel & hummus all making an appearance on the menu next to more standard mains such as pizza & pasta. You can even smoke a hookah pipe on the shaded terrace out front. *Sandwiches US$1–3, mains US$7–12.* **$$$**

✗ **Saima Take-Away** Av Josina Machel; m 84 297 5684; ⏰ 07.00–21.00 Mon–Sat. This busy pastelaria has a long menu of sandwiches, burgers, pizzas & Mozambican dishes, with a good plate of the day special as well. *Mains starting around US$6.* **$$**

✗ **Xeque Mate** Av Samora Machel; m 84 297 6930/303 1311; ⏰ 09.00–21.00 Tue–Sun. This hidden Portuguese hangout is easily missed, but definitely worth keeping your eye out for. The rotating daily menu of pork, squid, steaks & more is chalked up on the board out front, & the cool, cosy interior is covered in local artwork for sale. There's an outdoor patio & a full bar with football on the TV. *Mostly in the US$3–5 range.* **$**

♀ **Kopus Pub** Av Marginal; m 82 590 1525; ⏰ 18.00–midnight Sun & Tue–Thu, 18.00–06.00 Fri/Sat. The undisputed party spot in Quelimane, & it's actually quite stylish, with a proper dance floor, DJ booth, pool table & disco lights galore. The music goes all night at w/ends &, given what time the sun rises, you're almost guaranteed to see it. Depending on the night, there may be a cover charge.

OTHER PRACTICALITIES

Banks and ATMs Barclays, Standard, BIM Millennium and BCI are all present and correct, with 24-hour ATMs attached.

Hospital On Avenida Accordos de Lusaka, between avenidas 1 de Julho and Samora Machel (☏ 242 13000).

Internet The Zone Internet Café (⏰ 08.00–noon & 14.00–18.00 Mon–Fri, 08.00–noon Sat) on Avenida Josina Machel is probably your best bet as, even though they've only got two computers, the connection is usually quite good. Alternatively, the Centro Provincial de Recursos Digitais (CPRD; ☏ 242 17218; ⏰ 07.00–19.00 Mon–Fri) at the post office has at least seven machines and keeps longer hours. If you've got your own device, there's Wi-Fi at the Hotel Flamingo and Villa Nagardas restaurants.

Police The police station is on Avenida Heróis de Liberdade, next to City Hall (📞 *242 13453*).

Post office On Avenida Samora Machel opposite Avenida Paulo Kankhomba.

Shopping Significantly boosting the provisions department in Quelimane, a new **Shoprite** should have opened near the old railway station on Rua de Resistência by the time you read this. The **market** on Avenida Heróis de Liberdade is good for fruit and vegetables, and there are **supermarkets** on avenidas 1 de Julho and Eduardo Mondlane. The best **bakery** in town is the Pastelaria Nacional on Avenida Eduardo Mondlane, but the Pastelaria Saima and Pastelaria Kassif also look good. There's typically a handful of craft sellers along Avenida Samora Machel in front of the Hotel Chuabo.

Swimming pool The Piscina on Avenida Marginal (see Bons Sinais, page 262) charges a rather steep US$10 per person to swim. The swimming pool at the Hotel Flamingo is open to non-guests for a similar price.

Taxis Taxis in Quelimane are nearly all bicycles and you'll have to perch yourself on the parcel shelf. If you're lucky then you'll get one with a bit of cushioning. Trips around town should cost you no more than a couple of dollars and the taxis can be most easily found at the market, the bus terminal and outside the city hall.

WHAT TO SEE AND DO The entertainment options open to you in Quelimane are truly limited. There is little left of the city from before the 20th century, and the old port buildings have long disappeared. The twin-towered **Cathedral da Nossa Senhora do Livramento**, built in 1776 and situated on the Avenida Marginal around the corner from the Hotel 1 de Julho, is worth a look. From the outside it looks in reasonable condition, but peek through the doors (which seem to have disappeared) and it's a very different situation. The building is empty, the only furniture being the remains of the wooden altar, in front of which are the memorial stones of some of the old priests. At the back of the church is a gallery which you can climb up to, although you'd have to be brave or lightly built (preferably both) to try to cross it.

The **new cathedral** on Avenida 7 de Setembro is far less attractive – it looks more like a nuclear plant than a religious building. The old **District Governor's Residence** near the jetty dates to 1895, but otherwise most of the town centre's older buildings date to the early 20th century, with plenty of Art Deco on show, while the most attractive building anywhere in town is probably the well-maintained 1936 **primary school** on Avenida Josina Machel a block down from the city hall.

The walk along the Avenida Marginal is pleasant enough, particularly as the sun goes down. There is a variety of abandoned boats next to the jetties. Once night has fallen the only real options are the bars, although the **Aguia Cinema** on the corner of avenidas Eduardo Mondlane and Zedequias Manganhela may show occasional martial arts films or Bollywood epics, though it's looking pretty inactive these days. There are also occasional events, including live **music**, at the Casa de Cultura on Avenida Paulo Kankhomba; the easiest way to find out what (if anything) is on is to pop in and ask. Alternatively you could head for the **basketball** courts – there's one on the corner of avenidas Josina Machel and Francisco de Manyanga and another on Avenida Samora Machel between avenidas Heróis de Liberdade and Accordos de Lusaka.

THE COAST NORTH OF QUELIMANE

Zalala Beach Situated about 40km northeast of town along a road that passes through a vast coconut plantation, Zalala is the closest swimming beach to Quelimane and, while it doesn't compare to the finest beaches in the south of the country, it is a pretty enough spot, fringed with casuarina trees that separate it from the small village of Suphino. The road there is good fast tarmac, but very narrow – only big enough for one vehicle at a time, so expect to have to pull off to let something bigger past. It's also littered with bicycles, some of whose riders seem to have a death wish. Regular chapas from Quelimane leave from outside the market on Avenida Heróis de Liberdade, take 45 minutes, and cost less than US$1.

 Where to stay, eat and drink

Ocas Beach Hotel (24 rooms) ☏ 242 18764; m 84 490 3770/786 5607; e ocasbeachhotel@gmail.com. Slightly cheaper than Zalala, but lacking the comfort & atmosphere, this new hotel has en-suite rooms with AC, DSTV, fridge & kettle, as well as 2 4-/6-sleeper houses. There is a swimming pool & a restaurant. Overpriced. *US$80/120 sgl/dbl B&B; US$200 6-sleeper house.* **$$$$**

Zalala Beach Lodge (10 rooms) ☏ 242 17055; m 84 390 1630/3; e info@zalalabeach.com; w zalalabeach.com. The only resort-style accommodation near Quelimane, this place opened in mid 2010 & offers accommodation in smart beachfront bungalows with walk-in nets, fridge, ceiling fan & writing desk. The restaurant does seafood & local specialities such as frango à Zambeziana, & has live music by the pool on Sun. They do a variety of activities, inc kayak & canoe trips, as well as excursions to the little-visited Nhafuba hot springs. It's really an admirable set-up, & they are deeply involved with the local community, spearheading a number of development schemes in the area. *US$100/150 sgl/dbl B&B; HB & FB also available.* **$$$$**

Pebane Situated on the east bank of the Moniga Estuary, about 150km northeast of Quelimane as the crow flies, the historic riverport of Pebane was a popular resort area in the colonial era but these days it sees few visitors and has an appealingly isolated character. The main attraction, aside from the sense of just getting away from it all, is the idyllic palm-lined beaches, which can be a little murkier than their more southerly counterparts (as a result of silt washed down by the Rio Moniga and other rivers), but offer good swimming and fishing, and some of the best surfing in the country. Of historical interest is the Ponta Matirre Lighthouse, which dates to 1913 and was recently restored, as well as the old Catholic cathedral and a colonial Portuguese cemetery.

The shortest reliable route to Pebane from Quelimane is about 300km and entails following the EN7 northeast of Nicoadala for 35km, then turning left at Namacurra and following dirt roads (N324) through Olinga and Mucubela. Patient travellers could follow this route using chapas to hop between towns, but be prepared for a long day. Another possible approach road (R646/651) leads southeast from the EN232, about 40km north of Mocuba, to Mucubela. A more northerly route entails driving via Gilé town and the Gilé National Reserve (N323/R1108) to/from Alto Ligonha on the EN232 between Alto Molócuè and Nampula.

Where to stay, eat and drink There are a couple of inexpensive places to stay (Pensão Jemayma and Complex Miramar have been recommended), but the main focal point of tourist activities is:

Pebane Fishing Lodge (10 units) m 82 950 2605 or 84 407 5124; e pebanefishing@gmail.com; w pebane.com. Has beachfront chalets, a small restaurant & boats for fishing charters. *US$250 dbl FB.* **$$$$**

THE QUELIMANE–NAMPULA ROAD

The most important trunk route through Zambézia is the 525km road connecting Quelimane to Nampula via Nicoadala, Mocuba and Alto Molócuè. Although it is clearly the main road through the region, it has no definite name. Connected to Quelimane by a feeder road called the EN470 (N10), Nicoadala is officially the most northerly point on the EN1, which runs south from here all the way to Maputo. North of Nicoadala, the EN1 becomes the EN7 for 65km, as far as the junction town of Malei, where the EN7 (N11) veers westward to Milange and the road towards Nampula becomes the EN104 for another 45km. At Mocuba it changes to the EN232, the name by which it is known all the way to Nampula. To add to the confusion, around 2010 the Administração Nacional de Estradas introduced a new nationwide numbering system (listed in parentheses after the original road numbers throughout this guide) on its maps, but these changes may not be reflected in signage on the ground for some time. According to the new system, however, the entire Quelimane–Nampula road is now part of the EN1, which will have its northern terminus in Pemba, while the roads to Quelimane and Milange will be the N10 and N11 respectively. For most of its length the road is in good condition, but there are some abysmal stretches, particularly the 70km immediately north of Mocuba. With an early start, the trip from Quelimane to Nampula can be done in a day, but it is possible to break it at two points, Mocuba and Alto Molócuè.

MOCUBA Set on the southwest bank of the wide and muddy Licungo River, Mocuba is one of the largest towns in the Mozambican interior, with an estimated population of 70,000, and a strategic location on the main north–south road through Zambézia, immediately south of the 300m road bridge over the Licungo. It is a neatly laid-out town, and pleasant enough, with a few moderately interesting examples of colonial architecture, a fabulously busy market and a relatively fresh and airy climate by comparison with a sweltering summer day in Quelimane. Mocuba is of interest mainly as an inland alternative to Quelimane for breaking up the long trip between Beira/Chimoio and Nampula, or as a springboard for visits to Gurué or the border town of Milange. Sightseeing options in the immediate vicinity are practically non-existent, though the river itself is quite a hive of human activity, and it can be interesting to sit on the banks or the bridge and watch the day's business unfold.

Getting there and away Mocuba is something of a route focus, situated at the junction of the main north–south road through Mozambique and the **EN7** (N11) west to Milange (the main border crossing between Zambézia and Malawi). The surfaced 85km **EN7/EN104** (EN1) between Nicoadala and Mocuba can be covered in under an hour, and there are loads of **chapas** between Quelimane, Nicoadala and Mocuba. By contrast, bank on 3–5 hours' driving along the 200km **EN7** (N11) to Milange, which is unsurfaced and may be rough in parts, especially after rain, and aim for the earliest possible start if you are covering this road by chapa, as these tend to leave before 05.00 and might take up to 8 hours in bad weather. For destinations further afield, both **Maning Nice** (m *82 012 1011, 84 295 3808 or 86 520 5699*), **Etrago** (m *84 039 5196 or 86 353 6971*) and **Nagi Investimentos** (m *82 614 1820, 84 698 4238 or 86 318 2876*) buses regularly pass through Mocuba heading everywhere from Maputo (*US$26*) to Pemba (*US$20*). Their ticket offices are at Ramada Take-Away on Avenida Eduardo Mondlane, but tickets can also be purchased from where the buses depart (see map, page 266), also on Avenida Eduardo Mondlane.

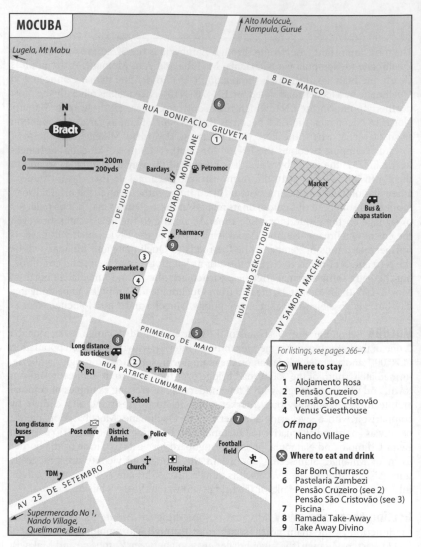

MOCUBA

Lugela, Mt Mabu

Alto Molócuè,
Nampula, Gurué

N

Bradt

0 _____ 200m
0 _____ 200yds

RUA BONIFACIO GRUVETA

8 DE MARCO

Barclays $ Petromoc

Market

Bus &
chapa station

AV EDUARDO MONDLANE

1 DE JULHO

Pharmacy

Supermarket

BIM $

RUA AHMED SÉKOU TOURÉ

AV SAMORA MACHEL

PRIMEIRO DE MAIO

Long distance
bus tickets

RUA PATRICE LUMUMBA

$ BCI

Pharmacy

School

Long distance
buses

Post office

District
Admin

Police

TDM

AV 25 DE SETEMBRO

Church

Hospital

Football
field

Supermercado No 1,
Nando Village,
Quelimane, Beira

For listings, see pages 266–7

⌂ Where to stay

1   Alojamento Rosa
2   Pensão Cruzeiro
3   Pensão São Cristovão
4   Venus Guesthouse
Off map
    Nando Village

✕ Where to eat and drink

5   Bar Bom Churrasco
6   Pastelaria Zambezi
    Pensão Cruzeiro (see 2)
    Pensão São Cristovão (see 3)
7   Piscina
8   Ramada Take-Away
9   Take Away Divino

⌂ Where to stay, eat and drink *Map, above*

Mocuba turns out to have some of the best-value accommodation in the north of Mozambique, reason enough perhaps to choose it over Quelimane as a place to break up the trip from south to north. The restaurants at the two pensões listed on page 267 are about the best in town, but for cheaper eats you could try the **Pastelaria Zambezi** or **Take Away Divino**, both on Avenida Eduardo Mondlane.

⌂ **Alojamento Rosa** (14 rooms) Rua 1 de Maio; m 82 561 3000 or 86 998 2676. A significant step down from any of the below, but cheaper & closer to the bus station, this place has small tiled rooms with dbl bed using shared ablutions. *US$10 dbl; US$20 dbl with AC.* **$**

⌂ **Nando Village** (20 rooms) EN7/EN104 (EN1), signposted 'Venus Guesthouse'; ☎ 248 10049; m 82 509 6430; e nandovillagemocuba@ tdm.co.mz. Located about 4km south of town, this new extension of the central Venus Guesthouse offers en-suite accommodation in dbl suites & self-

266

catering chalets with AC & DSTV. A good option for self-drivers as there is secure parking. *US$60/70 suite/chalet.* **$$$**

🏠 **Pensão Cruzeiro** (14 rooms) Av Eduardo Mondlane; m 82 267 7081/305 3173. The pick of several good budget options in Mocuba, this family-run 1st-floor guesthouse is reached via a stairwell littered with potted plants. The pleasant ground-floor café has indoor & outdoor seating, & serves fresh bread & pastries, along with a typical selection of Mozambican mains from US$6. The big airy rooms have en-suite bathrooms, fans, twin beds & parquet floors that are clearly polished on a regular basis. *US$27 dbl or twin.* **$**

🏠 **Pensão São Cristóvão** (10 rooms) Av Eduardo Mondlane; ☎ 243 10954; m 82 014 5125 or 86 303 1809. This is another clean & reasonably priced lodging, with a restaurant serving meat & seafood dishes in the US$5–10 range, & comfortable en-suite rooms with AC & TV. *US$20/26 dbl/twin.* **$**

🏠 **Venus Guesthouse** (10 rooms) Av Eduardo Mondlane; ☎ 248 10684; m 82 560 5476. The classiest option in town, this newer hotel on the main drag offers 10 celestially named en-suite rooms that are cool & comfortable, with AC, TV, kettle, fridge & a bit of African décor. There's a restaurant & beauty salon attached. *US$30/36/40 sgl/dbl/suite B&B.* **$$**

✖ **Bar Bom Churrasco** Primeiro de Maio; m 84 675 3532/051 2461; ⊕ 08.00–late daily. A new & popular addition to the eateries in Mocuba, this Brazilian-style grill & bar serves up chicken & meat by the kilo along with the traditional side options. *Expect to pay around US$8 per plate.* **$$**

✖ **Ramada Take-Away** Av Eduardo Mondlane; m 82 654 9630; ⊕ 05.00–late daily. This place has the standard chicken, fish or meat dishes with rice, xima or pasta, along with some baked goods. Also home to the long-distance bus offices. *US$2–4.* **$**

☆ **Piscina** Av Samora Machel. Set around a fantastic blue-&-yellow Art Deco building worth a look in itself, this former swimming pool complex features several long-dry basins & acts as the local nightclub, where the party really kicks off in the wee hours.

Other practicalities There are several **banks** on Avenida Eduardo Mondlane, including a Barclays, BCI and BIM Millennium, all with ATMs. For **shopping**, a new supermarket, **Super Mercado No. 1**, has opened up less than 2km south of town, and there's still a sprawling market near the bus station. There is no public internet in Mocuba at present.

ALTO MOLÓCUÈ The mid-altitude town of Alto Molócuè sprawls northward from the EN232 (EN1) all but midway along the 370km road that separates Mocuba from Nampula. It is a town of three distinct components: there's the bustling junction area where the unsignposted feeder road to the town proper runs northward from the EN232 (EN1); the compact triangle of roads that comprises the old commercial town centre about 1km north along the feeder road; and the administrative centre about 1km northeast of the old town centre and separated from it by the Molócuè River.

Unless you're looking for somewhere to break up the drive between Mocuba and Nampula, Alto Molócuè is about as missable as a Mozambican town can get. The sedate administrative centre is of minor architectural interest, centred on a ludicrously opulent city hall with evident pretensions to being part of the senate in ancient Rome, and an equally anomalous governor's residence built in pseudo-fortified style. The old town centre, by contrast, is quite down to earth (or, less charitably, plain run-down), and the lily-covered pond a short walk away might be interesting for birding. But one senses that the real action in Alto Molócuè has drifted southward, to the junction with the EN232 (EN1), where a busy little market thrives on the passing truck and bus traffic. Hikers and climbers with some time to spare ought to check out Monte Rupi, 17km west of town.

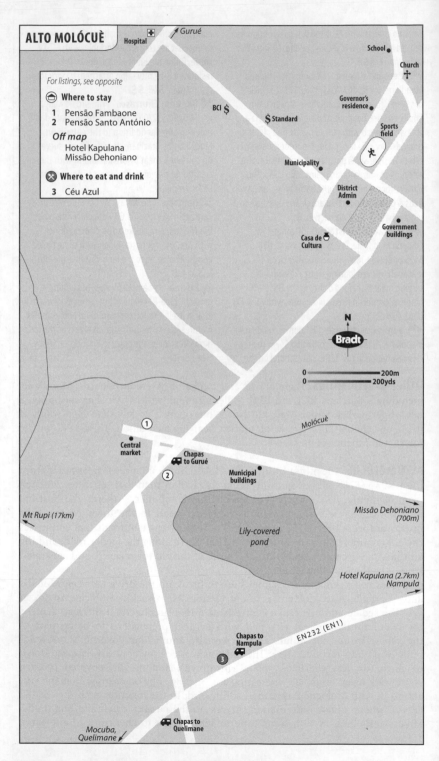

ALTO MOLÓCUÈ

Hospital

Gurué

School

Church

For listings, see opposite

⌂ Where to stay
1 Pensão Fambaone
2 Pensão Santo António

Off map
    Hotel Kapulana
    Missão Dehoniano

✕ Where to eat and drink

3 Céu Azul

BCI $

$ Standard

Governor's
residence

Sports
field

Municipality

District
Admin

Government
buildings

Casa de
Cultura

N
Bradt

0 ——————— 200m
0 ——————— 200yds

Molócuè

1

Central
market

Chapas
to Gurué

2

Municipal
buildings

Mt Rupi (17km)

Missão Dehoniano
(700m)

Lily-covered
pond

Hotel Kapulana (2.7km)
Nampula

Chapas to
Nampula

EN232 (EN1)

3

Chapas to
Quelimane

Mocuba,
Quelimane

Where to stay, eat and drink   *Map, opposite*

Generally speaking, Mocuba has a better overall selection of accommodation than Alto Molócuè, but the options in Alto Molócuè have improved significantly in recent years.

🏠 **Hotel Kapulana** (10 rooms) 📞213 07320/1; m 84 545 8597, 86 168 0030 or 82 848 8100; e r.tricanji@live.com; 📘 hotelkapulanamolocue. On the south side of the EN232 (EN1) 2.7km east of the main junction for Alto Molócuè, this is the best accommodation in town, with clean en-suite tiled rooms in a bright compound with safe parking & a highly regarded restaurant. *From US$35 dbl.* **$$**

🏠 **Missão Dehoniano (Padres of the Pista Velha)** 📞246 30024; m 86 669 1220. This Catholic mission, operated by the Dehonian order of priests, runs a number of community programmes inc school & library, & rents out simple, clean rooms as well. They don't have a restaurant, but there are fixed daily meals available to guests. Follow the road from the triangular junction for 1km & make a left. The compound is 300m further down & there is safe parking.

Rates are budget-friendly, around US$20 – call to enquire. **$**

🏠 **Pensão Fambaone** m 84 829 6538/054 3155. The better of the 2 pensões in the old town centre, this 2-storey hotel has reasonably clean rooms with net, TV, fan & a shared bathroom with no running water. The friendly ground-floor bar & restaurant serves a good plate of chicken & chips (allow an hour to prepare), & there is safe parking. *US$14–20 dbl.* **$**

🏠 **Pensão Santo António** (8 rooms) This is about as basic & grubby as functional hotels get, but at least the prices reflect this. *US$10 sgl using common shower; US$14 en-suite sgl with ¾ bed.*

✗ **Céu Azul** Offering the usual range of Mozambican eats & a pool table too, this casual place at the main junction is a favourite of local Peace Corps volunteers. *US$2–5.* **$**

Other practicalities Both Standard Bank and BCI have ATMs, though they're well hidden on the road connecting the administrative centre to the hospital. There are few other facilities of interest to tourists, though the market area around the junction with the EN232 (EN1) has a pretty good selection of goods on offer.

What to see and do There's precious little for tourists in Alto Molócuè itself, but an interesting side trip for keen hikers and climbers would be a visit to Monte Rupi, a granite outcrop whose highest peak is reputedly almost 1,300m, on a dirt track 17km northwest of town. There's really only one road to get there; just be sure to take the right fork at the first junction after leaving the main road. It's entirely undeveloped, but there are some Italian priests living at the base of the mountain (✪ *15°34'56.83"S, 37°34'12.91"E*) who might be of help if you needed a place to stay.

GILÉ NATIONAL RESERVE This 2,100km² reserve, the only protected area in Zambézia, lies about 100km south of the EN232 between Alto Molócuè and Alto Ligonha. Bounded by the Molócuè and Melela rivers to the east and west respectively, and bisected by the Malema River, it protects an area of low-lying hilly country swathed in dense brachystegia woodland interspersed with strips of riverine forest and patches of seasonal flooded grassland known as *dambos*. Somewhat neglected and undeveloped for tourism at the time of writing, the reserve is nevertheless reasonably accessible to self-sufficient travellers with a private 4x4.

A survey undertaken in 2007 by the IGF Foundation indicates that a fair amount of wildlife remains, and there are plans to rehabilitate the reserve and reintroduce further animals, starting with some 50 buffalo translocated from Niassa as of late 2013. Some 40 mammal species were recorded during the survey, among them leopard, elephant, buffalo, eland, greater kudu, sable antelope, bushbuck and waterbuck, and it is possible that small numbers of lion and African hunting dog still haunt the area. The reserve also has immense potential as a birding destination, and the current checklist of 113 species (based on a short survey in 2000) would most likely double were further studies undertaken.

Best visited in the dry season, when roads are less likely to be washed away and wildlife is more visible, Gilé National Reserve can be approached along an 80km dirt road (N323) that leads south from the **EN232** (EN1) at Alto Ligonha to the small district administrative centre of Gilé. From here, a single dirt road (R1108) runs south to the reserve's northern entrance, then passes through its western half for about 50km, before continuing on south to Pebane. It is not clear what, if any, entrance fees are charged at the time of writing, but camping is permitted at the Musseia Ranger Post, and there is limited accommodation at Pebane (page 264) and reputedly at least one basic pensão in Gilé.

THE WESTERN HIGHLANDS

Nudging up towards the border with Malawi, western Zambézia lies at a much higher elevation than the east, and it is studded with impressive mountains that form part of the Rift Valley's eastern foothills. These include the 2,419m Mount Namuli, the country's second-highest peak and the sole refuge of its only endemic bird species, the Namuli apalis. The largest town in the region, and main tourist focus, is Gurué, which lies close to the base of Namuli and is the obvious urban base for hikes and birding expeditions to the mountain. The only other place that sees much in the way of traveller through-traffic is Milange, site of a moderately busy border crossing into Malawi. For more adventurous travellers, however, there is also the possibility of checking out Mount Mabu and Mount Chiperone, isolated peaks whose slopes were recently found to support extensive patches of evergreen montane forest.

GURUÉ Surrounded by orderly tea plantations and immense granite protrusions, the breezy market town of Gurué sits at an altitude of 720m in the fertile green foothills of the southern Rift Valley. It is the tenth-largest town in Mozambique, with a population estimated at 130,000, a comparatively moist and cool climate, and an energised, bustling mood absent from many of its more torpid coastal cousins. Gurué's relatively temperate climate is a refreshing change from the coastal heat, and the immediate environs offer some good opportunities for relaxed rambling in scenic surrounds (recalling the Mulanje and Thyolo districts of neighbouring Malawi), but the major attraction here is Mount Namuli, one of Mozambique's premier hiking and birding destinations. The town itself is of limited architectural interest, mostly dating to the post-World War II era, but there is a rather pretty small chapel, with some colourful murals inside, at the northeast end of Avenida República.

Founded by the Portuguese in the late 19th century, Gurué is named after a Lomwe chief who previously inhabited the area. Though renamed Vila Junqueiro in 1959, after the local tea magnate Manuel Junqueiro died in a plane crash, it reverted to its original name at independence. The district is renowned as a production centre for tea, which was first planted in the vicinity in the 1920s. Tea production reached a commercial peak in the years after World War II, when a quartet of vast estates around Gurué comprised what was reputedly the largest tea plantation in the southern hemisphere and the local economy boomed on exports to Europe and North America. Despite a major slump in production after independence, tea remains the mainstay of the local economy to this day, though the fertile soils and

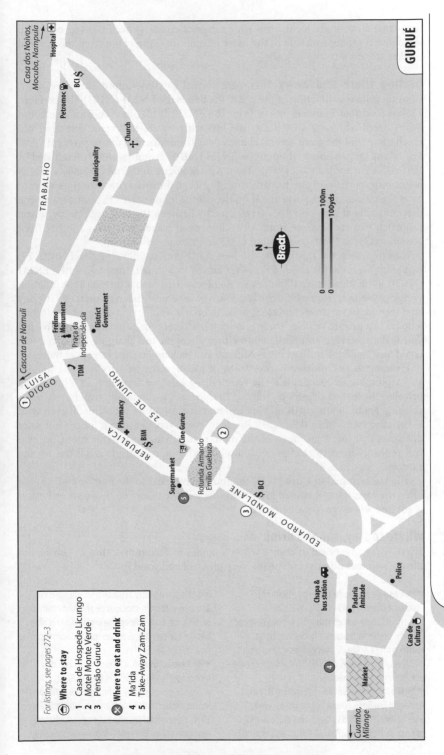

GURUÉ

For listings, see pages 272–3

Where to stay
1 Casa de Hospede Licungo
2 Motel Monte Verde
3 Pensão Gurué

Where to eat and drink
4 Ma'ida
5 Take-Away Zam-Zam

Casa dos Noivos,
Mocuba, Nampula

Hospital

Petromoc
BCI $

Municipality

Church

TRABALHO

Cascata de Namuli

LUISA
DIOGO

Frelimo
Monument

Praça da
Independência

TDM

District
Government

25 DE JUNHO

REPUBLICA

Pharmacy
BIM $

Cine Gurué

Supermarket

Rotunda Armando
Emílio Guebuza

EDUARDO MONDLANE

BCI $

Chapa &
bus station

Padaria
Amizade

Police

Casa de
Cultura

Market

Cuamba,
Milange

0 100m
0 100yds

temperate climate are ideal for a wide range of crops – check out the bountiful agricultural produce on sale in the maze of stalls that sprawl out from the covered market at the south end of town.

Getting there and away There are several possible approaches to Gurué. Coming from the direction of the coast, the best is the **EN231** (N103), the surfaced 135km road that branches north from the EN232 (EN1) to Alto Molócuè about 70km north of Mocuba. At least one **bus** daily covers this route directly from Quelimane, and there are several **chapas** daily from Mocuba, costing around US$6 and taking up to 4 hours. Though the EN231 (N103) is quite scenic, it is eclipsed by the less well-travelled road (R655) from Alto Molócuè to Gurué via Nauela, which is stunning, particularly in the early morning when the mists rise from the valleys to meet the clouds sinking over the shoulders of the mountains. On public transport, there's usually at least one daily truck directly between the two, but otherwise you can catch two chapas, one from Alto Molócuè to Nauela and then another from Nauela to Gurué (both cost around US$2 and take up to 3 hours).

Coming from the northwest, the best route entails following the **EN8** (N13) east from Cuamba for about 65km (via Lurio) to Mutuali, then taking the **EN231** (N103) south for another 100km or so via Lioma. This road is dirt until the junction village of Magige, from where the last 35km have recently been resurfaced. The dirt stretches are in variable condition, so bank on the whole trip taking a bit less than 4 hours in a private vehicle. There is at least one direct chapa between Cuamba and Gurué daily, leaving around 05.00 in either direction and charging US$6, but you could also catch the train as far as Mutuali and pick up onward transport there.

Heading to or from the border town of Milange, the best route is via Magige and Molumbo, a 200km ride along rough dirt roads that takes at least 4 hours in a private vehicle. Self-drivers be warned that there is a potentially treacherous river crossing about 30km north of Milange, one that might be problematic even with a 4x4 after rain – if in doubt, ask locals to point you to a much longer but safer diversion that loops southeast of the main road. Chapas cover this route, but you will probably need to change at Molumbo and should set aside a full day for the exercise.

The bus terminal in Gurué is off the roundabout next to the market and, as is so often the case, the majority of long-haul chapas leave before 05.00, so an early start is advised wherever you are headed.

🏠 Where to stay, eat and drink *Map, page 271*
There isn't a great deal of choice when it comes to accommodation in Gurué, but the options that do exist are mostly very pleasant and good value.

🏠 **Casa de Hospede Licungo** (8 rooms) Rua Luisa Diogo; ☎249 10441; m 82 253 0317. This small family-run guesthouse, set in a restored colonial house with parquet floors, has clean rooms with TV & fan, & a very pleasant feel about it. It's very good value, too. *US$9/14 sgl/dbl or twin using common bathroom.* **$**

🏠 **Motel Monte Verde** (20 rooms) Rotunda Armando Emilio Guebuza; ☎249 10245; m 82 516 1030/724 0624/539 0053. Not quite so nice as Casa de Hospede & Pensão Gurué, this central

motel is still a pretty attractive set-up, offering accommodation in spacious clean rooms with dbl bed, TV, fan & tiled floor. The veranda bar is often busy in the evening, & serves good Mozambican fare. *US$24 dbl.* **$**

🏠 **Pensão Gurué** (14 rooms) Av Eduardo Mondlane; ☎249 10050; m 84 297 4202; e pensao.gurue@gmail.com; 🅵 Pensao.Gurue. Mozambique. Under Austrian management since 2010, this popular pensão has enjoyed a happy resurgence in recent years, & is today essentially the hub of all things travel-orientated in Gurué. The recently refurbished rooms are all simple & quite pleasant, with parquet floors & splashes of African décor. There's space to camp in the back garden & safe parking as well. The ground-floor restaurant has benefited from a thorough overhaul to make it easily the most alluring eatery this side of Quelimane, Nampula or Cuamba, serving a selection of tasty snacks in the US$2–4 range & exquisite full meals for around US$6–11. There's free Wi-Fi & it's the best place to arrange hiking, camping & bicycling excursions to the tea plantations, Mount Namuli & other local attractions. A bar/disco has also been added to the grounds, making this essentially a one-stop shop. *US$44 dbl using common showers; US$56 en-suite dbl.* **$$**

✗ Ma'ida Restaurant m 84 921 2600; ⊕ 06.00–late daily. For cheap eats & football on the TV, this Somali hangout near the market should be your first stop. They've got chicken & rice done in a biryani style, sweet Somali tea & some of the longest hours in town. *US$2–3.* **$**

✗ Take-Away Zam-Zam On the main square opposite the Motel Monte Verde, this place was looking a bit worse for wear on our last visit, but still offers the usual range of dishes. *US$3–6.* **$**

Other practicalities

Banks and ATM BIM Millennium has an ATM on Avenida República just around the corner from the cinema, and BCI has two, one across from the Petromoc on the east side of town and one across from Pensão Gurué.

Entertainment Gurué has a cultural centre that holds occasional events, although the only real way of finding out what's happening is to go and read the posters there. Just behind it is a very dilapidated tennis court and just behind that a swimming pool whose murky green water is evidently used as a local laundry. The **Cine Gurué** (*Rotunda Armando Emilio Guebuza*; m *82 395 1560;* e *cinegurue007@hotmail.com*) primarily functions as a bar, but it does still show an eclectic and erratic selection of martial arts films and/or Hollywood/ Bollywood epics; tickets are about US$2.

Hospital At the top end of town on the road leading to Mocuba.

Internet There didn't seem to be any public internet in Gurué on our last visit, but the free Wi-Fi at Pensão Gurué is excellent for those with their own devices.

Police The police station is just off the roundabout next to the market.

Shopping Though it doesn't cater specifically to tourists, the market at the south end of town is one of the largest in the country, and particularly good for fresh agricultural produce.

AROUND GURUÉ Gurué's biggest attraction is the surrounding countryside, which offers probably the best walking you'll find in Mozambique. A nice easy walk is to tour the tea plantations that surround the town. Head out to the hospital and then take the road off to the left and within 5 minutes you'll be surrounded by tea bushes. It's an extremely pleasant walk and very photogenic. A more serious walk is the hike up Mount Namuli, which requires three days/two nights on foot from Gurué, as well as a good head for heights for the final ascent, though theoretically it could be done in a (very rushed) day with a private 4x4 to get you to the base camp. While Namuli is not a peak along the lines of Kilimanjaro or K2, it shouldn't be undertaken lightly and you'd be well recommended to check conditions locally before you head out. Pensão Gurué is a good source of information and can also arrange guides.

Mount Namuli Mozambique's second-highest peak at 2,419m, Namuli is a massive granite dome that protrudes a full kilometre above a grassy rolling plateau incised with numerous streams and gorges. The main peak of Namuli lies only 12km northeast of Gurué, but is not visible from the town itself. Several other tall domes stand on the same plateau, and the entire massif comprises almost 200km² of land above the 1,200m contour. Popular with hikers for its lovely green upland scenery, Namuli is also a mountain of great biological significance, supporting a variety of montane habitats including some 12km² of moist evergreen forest that shows some affiliations to the Eastern Arc Mountains of Tanzania. Two main patches of forest remain: the larger but relatively inaccessible Manho Forest, which borders the Muretha Plateau about halfway between Gurué and Namuli Peak, and the more accessible Ukalini Forest at the southwest base of the granite cliffs below Namuli Peak. Vincent's bush squirrel, listed as Critically Endangered by the IUCN, is endemic to these forests, which also support samango and vervet monkey, red and blue duiker, various small carnivores and at least one endemic but as yet undescribed species of pygmy chameleon.

The forests of Namuli are of particular interest to ornithologists for the presence of one endemic and several very localised species. The mountain is the only known location for the Namuli apalis (*Apalis lynesi*), a pretty green, yellow, black and grey warbler that was first described on the basis of a specimen collected by Jack Vincent in 1932 and went unrecorded for more than 60 years thereafter, largely because no other ornithological party visited the area until 1998. Namuli also supports what is probably the largest extant population of two other range-restricted species: the enigmatic and little-known dapple-throat (first collected at Namuli in 1932, also by Jack Vincent, and otherwise restricted to a handful of Tanzanian forests), and the Thyolo alethe (otherwise known only from southern Malawi). Though they have been seen by very few African birders, all three of these key species are common in the Ukalini Forest, along with the likes of bar-tailed trogon, green barbet, white-starred robin, olive-flanked robin-chat and many more.

Whether you are there for the scenery or the fauna, the normal springboard for exploring Namuli is the village of Mukunha (also known as Muguna Sede), which lies on the southeast footslopes about 30km from Gurué. A rough road leads from

Gurué to Mukunha, heading north from the Mocuba road just past the hospital, but there is no public transport so, unless you have a private 4x4, the only option is to hike, a beautiful but long trek that takes 8–10 hours and requires a guide (a local student nicknamed Rambo has been recommended by local Peace Corps volunteers, and he or another guide can be arranged through Pensão Gurué).

At Mukunha is a rather rudimentary base camp operated by a female spiritual leader (also known as the *régulo* or queen) whose permission is required to climb the mountain, which is still held sacred by the local Lomwe people. It is conventional to offer the queen a few gifts (a bottle of gin, and some sugar and ncima), to pay her a fee equivalent to around US$20, and to take a member of her family along as a guide (another US$10). In return, the queen will hold a ceremony to bless the climb, prepare a basic evening meal, and allow you to sleep in a small hut set aside for climbers (no bedding provided, so bring plenty of warm clothing in winter). From the base camp, the ascent to Namuli Peak is a 6–8-hour round trip, so you will need to spend a second night at camp after you descend. The base camp is also a pretty useful base for exploring Ukalini Forest.

For more information on Namuli's birdlife (and other fauna), check out the online report of the 1998 expedition (w *africanbirdclub.org/feature/namuli.html*). Better still are the downloadable PDFs of Françoise Dowsett-Lemaire's 2007 bird survey of Namuli (w *kew.org/science/directory/projects/annex/namuli-birds-Dowsett.pdf*), and the broader-ranging 115-page survey *Mt Namuli, Mozambique: Biodiversity and Conservation* compiled by 11 biologists (w *kew.org/science/directory/projects/annex/Namuli_report_FINAL.pdf*).

Cascata de Namuli The best known of several spectacular waterfalls on the western side of the massif, the Cascata de Namuli is formed by the Licungo River as it cascades about 100m down a sloping rock face north of Gurué. It is an excellent goal for a day walk, a 5–6-hour round hike out of Gurué that passes through a variety of habitats, including the tea plantations of the Chá Zambezi Estate, stands of bamboo and small patches of indigenous forest, and you can swim in a pool above the waterfall. The riverine forest above the waterfall reputedly shelters the Namuli apalis and other rare birds, but it is unclear whether these range as far down as the waterfall itself.

To get there, follow the road past the Casa de Hospede Licungo out of town and keep going – you can't really go wrong, and if in doubt anybody will point you in the right direction (just ask for '*cascata*'). The road to the waterfall passes through the tea estate and although no charge is levied to walk to the waterfall, nor is any prior permission required, people driving may be required to park at the estate entrance gate and to do the last stretch on foot (about 1 hour each way).

Casa dos Noivos Situated in the hilly countryside north of Gurué, the Casa dos Noivos is an abandoned hilltop dwelling that must have been very beautiful in its prime, and that still offers one of the most spectacular views in the region, over a rolling series of verdant valleys below Mount Namuli. The origin of its name (literally 'House of the Bride and Groom') is unclear: it may be that the house was built for a newlywed couple or simply that it is known locally as a place for romantic assignations. On foot, the casa can be reached by following the Mocuba road out of town past the hospital, then taking the second road to the left and heading more or less north for about 90 minutes, passing through scenic tea estates *en route*. If you are thinking of driving, the road is very winding with some vertical drop-offs, so a 4x4 may be necessary, especially after rain.

MILANGE This small town on the Malawian border west of Mocuba is of little interest except as a crossing point to or from the Malawian towns of Mulanje and Blantyre. Architecturally, it is notable for the district government building, an anomalously overblown edifice at the east end of Avenida Eduardo Mondlane, perched at the foot of Monte Tumbine and offering good views towards the 3,001m Mount Mulanje, which is the tallest point in central Africa, but set entirely within Malawi. There is a busy market in the commercial centre, stocked with plenty of goods that have presumably slipped across the border and, if you are trying to dispose of spare meticais or Malawian kwacha, more money changers per square metre than in any other town in Mozambique operate here. Other facilities include a BIM Millennium bank with ATM.

Getting there and away Milange lies 200km west of Mocuba along the **EN7** (N11), a decent dirt road. A few **chapas** run here from Mocuba daily, mostly leaving in the morning, taking about 4 hours and charging around US$6. There's also a once-daily minibus from Quelimane that charges US$10. The only other viable Mozambican approach road, from Gurué via Molumbo, is covered on page 272. The **border crossing** is at Melosa, 3km from town along a good asphalt road, and plenty of bicycle taxis can be found waiting at either end. The border is open from 06.00 to 18.00 daily.

'LOST EDENS' OF ZAMBÉZIA

The EN7 (N11) between Mocuba and Milange flanks a pair of isolated granite inselbergs that, until recently, ranked among the least-studied wilderness areas anywhere in south-central Africa. These are mounts Chiperone and Mabu, respectively situated about 10km northeast of the EN7 (N11) near Tacuane and 30km southwest of the same road near Liciro, and home to extensive tracts of moist evergreen forest.

Rising to 2,054m, Chiperone lends its name to the misty *chiperone* weather conditions that are said to form around its slopes before drifting to Malawi's Mount Mulanje, 60km further north. Jack Vincent, whose 1932 expedition to Namuli collected several previously unknown species there, trekked past Chiperone during the course of the same trip and noted that it 'should hold much interest to the naturalist', but left it at that. Indeed, the only known scientific exploration of the mountain in the 20th century was Jali Makawa's 1950 ornithological expedition, which produced eight new bird records for Mozambique.

In December 2005, Claire Spottiswoode, Hassam Patel, Eric Herrmann and Julian Bayliss undertook the most comprehensive survey of Chiperone to date, and discovered that it still supported around 15km^2 of montane forest and a rich avian diversity comprising two globally threatened species, Thyolo alethe and white-winged apalis, alongside green-headed oriole, olive-headed weaver and Bertram's weaver. Other wildlife recorded in the forests included leopard, buffalo, samango monkey, an unidentified duiker, and one lizard and one butterfly species previously thought to be endemic to Mulanje.

Possibly the most remarkable recent biological discovery in Africa is the existence of a full 70km^2 of moist evergreen forest on the slopes of the 1,710m Mount Mabu. So far as can be ascertained, this is the largest tract of rainforest in

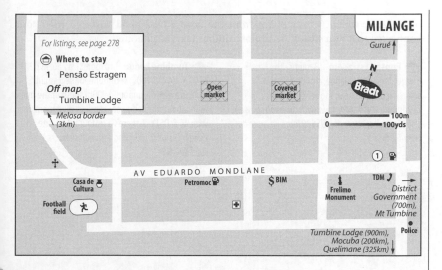

For listings, see page 278

🏨 **Where to stay**

1 Pensão Estragem

Off map
   Tumbine Lodge

MILANGE

Gurué ↑

Melosa border
(3km)

Open market

Covered market

0 ▬▬▬▬▬ 100m
0 ▬▬▬▬▬ 100yds

① 🖴

AV EDUARDO MONDLANE

Casa de Cultura

Petromoc 🖴

$ BIM

Football field 🏃

➕

Frelimo Monument

TDM ♪ →

District Government (700m), Mt Tumbine

Tumbine Lodge (900m), Mocuba (200km), Quelimane (325km) ↓

Police

Where to stay, eat and drink   *Map, above*

Unless you absolutely have to stay on this side of the border, it is worth knowing that a far better range of accommodation can be found at the Malawian town

southern Africa, yet it went completely undocumented until 2005, when Julian Bayliss picked up a vast swathe of undulating green vegetation at Mabu using Google Earth, and joined the aforementioned Chiperone expedition on a five-day visit. In this short time, the team discovered that Mabu harboured what is almost certainly the largest single population of the endangered Thyolo alethe, along with the globally threatened East Coast akalat.

Since then, the scientific press has labelled Mabu a 'Lost Eden' as subsequent expeditions, covering little more than 10% of the forest's area, have already collected three butterfly, two chameleon, one adder and three other reptile species new to science, and confirmed the presence of half a dozen globally threatened bird species, including Swynnerton's robin and the first record of a Namuli apalis away from Mount Namuli, along with mammals such as samango monkey, blue duiker and a species of elephant-shrew.

The combination of steep slopes, local taboos and extensive brachystegia buffer zones has discouraged large-scale local exploitation of the forests on Mabu and Chiperone, with the former in particular being in near-pristine condition. All the same, like their counterparts on Namuli, these forests are not officially protected, though the Mozambican government agreed to bar logging in Mabu in 2009, and it is to be hoped that eventually both sites will be accorded fuller protection.

For further details of the 2005 expeditions to Chiperone and Mabu, download the reports *Threatened Bird Species on Two Little-known Mountains (Chiperone and Mabu) in northern Mozambique* (w *131.111.101.93/zoostaff/bbe/ Spottiswoode/Papers/Ostrich_Spottiswoode2008.pdf*) and *The Biodiversity and Conservation of Mount Chiperone* (w *kew.org/science/directory/projects/annex/ ChiperoneTechReport.pdf*).

Zambézia **THE WESTERN HIGHLANDS**

15

of Mulanje, which is only 30km from the border by a good surfaced road, and connected to it by a steady stream of minibus taxis at all hours.

Pensão Estragem (8 rooms) The best budget option in Milange, this place has a selection of quite clean rooms & a decent restaurant. *US$9 sgl or twin with common showers; US$11 small en-suite dbl; US$20 large en-suite dbl with TV.* **$**

Tumbine Lodge (10 rooms) m 86 381 6700 or 84 411 7006; e tumbinelodge@gmail. com. In a gated compound 900m south of the main roundabout, this lodge has modern tiled rooms with AC & DSTV, & there's a restaurant on-site. *From US$36/50–60 using common showers/en-suite dbl.* **$$**

16

Nampula

The eponymous capital of Nampula Province is the commercial hub of northern Mozambique and the main regional route focus, situated at the junction of the EN8 between Mandimba (on the Malawian border) and the port of Nacala, and the main trunk road running south to Maputo. One of the country's fastest-growing towns, Nampula overtook Beira as Mozambique's second-largest city, with a population currently estimated at 638,000. For all that, by comparison with Beira or even Quelimane, Nampula feels more like a large modern town than a city proper, and there is little, aside from the linguistic dominance of Portuguese, to distinguish its spacious, low-rise centre from those of a dozen other moderately sized towns in Zimbabwe or Malawi.

It would be practically impossible to travel through northern Mozambique without stopping over in Nampula at some point, and while the city boasts few tourist attractions it has a lively and prosperous feel, and there are plenty of good shops and other facilities for visitors. It is also an agreeably compact city, with everything that matters happening in a few streets on either side of Avenida Paulo Samuel Kankhomba, the main road that connects the railway station to Praça da Liberdade. If you have an afternoon to spare here, the early 20th-century cathedral is interesting in a vaguely bland way, and it is definitely worth popping into the Museu Nacional de Etnologia and associated Makonde Collective on Avenida Eduardo Mondlane.

Whether one arrives by train from the west or by road from the south, Nampula is the best base for exploring the country's most populous province (estimated population 5.13 million in 2016). Bounded by the rivers Lúrio to the north and Ligonha to the south, the interior of Nampula comprises largely open savannah broken up by any number of isolated and imposing rocky outcrops, mesas and plateaux (these reputedly offer some of the best free-face rock climbing in southern Africa but, pending further tourist development, this is of interest only to experienced and fully equipped rock climbers). One such basalt outcrop just outside Nampula town resembles a profile of a face looking at the sky. Known as 'the old man', local legend has it that this outcrop materialised upon the death of an old king of Monomotapa in 1570.

GETTING THERE AND AWAY

SOUTH

By air There are daily **LAM** (w *lam.co.mz*) flights to Nampula from around Mozambique and twice-weekly flights from Dar es Salaam, while **Airlink** (w *flyairlink.com*) flies daily to Johannesburg and **Kenya Airways** (w *kenya-airways. com*) flies several times a week to Nairobi. The **airport** is on the road towards Nacala. The LAM office is on Avenida Francisco Manyanga (\ *262 13011/311*).

By road The **EN232** (EN1) connects Nampula to Alto Molócuè, Mocuba and Quelimane in Zambézia. The road south to Quelimane is mostly good-condition tarmac, though the stretch immediately north of Mocuba remains in poor condition at the time of writing. Still, it is easy enough to drive through from Quelimane in a day. **Chapas** cover all stretches of this road, leaving either from the terminus on Avenida de Trabalho, 5 minutes away from the railway station, or from directly in front of the railway station.

For destinations further south, **Maning Nice** (m *82 456 5760, 84 450 0095 or 86 401 8491*) and **Nagi Investimentos** (m *86 400 0651/2/3*) alternate running direct buses to Maputo most days of the week for US$62, leaving at 03.00 from the main terminal on Avenida de Trabalho. They also run daily buses to Quelimane (*US$14*), and several times weekly to Beira (*US$34*) and Chimoio (*US$32*). They will pro-rate your fare if you're not going all the way through, and all tickets are best bought a day in advance from the respective offices at the main terminal.

WEST
By car The main trunk road west is the **EN8** (N13), which connects to the Mandimba border post with Malawi (*about 500km*) via Cuamba (*360km*). This road is unsurfaced almost in its entirety and some stretches require a 4x4, or may be impassable during the rains. From Nampula, the first 200km to the west is surfaced, but past that the road condition drastically deteriorates.

By train Here, for once, people using public transport have the upper hand, as Cuamba and Nampula are connected by the north's only long-distance passenger train, a service that may fall short of attracting superlatives but is a whole lot more comfortable than the corresponding road. The trains run from Nampula to Cuamba on Tuesdays and Saturdays and from Cuamba to Nampula on Thursdays and Sundays, leaving at 05.00 sharp and arriving 10–12 hours later. Tickets should be bought from the train itself on the evening before departure. The relatively new carriage is air conditioned and has executive (*US$12*) and second-class (*US$4*) seating options. Executive class consists of comfortable reclining cloth seats while second class is plastic seating. You may want to carry some provisions to supplement the trackside vendors and simple fare produced by the restaurant carriage. Needless to say, the usual rules about not leaving your luggage unguarded apply. When the train arrives at Cuamba, it is met by buses on to Mandimba, Entrélagos and Lichinga. For updates on the train schedule visit w cdn.co.mz/en/passengers-transport, or call the Nampula office (📞 *213 44800*) for the latest on train transport in the north.

NORTH AND EAST The 440km road to Pemba via Namialo is surfaced in its entirety and can be covered in around 5 hours. Regular **chapas** to Pemba cost around US$8, while regular chapas to Nacala and Ilha de Moçambique cost US$4 and take about 4 hours. **Maning Nice** also runs daily buses to Mocímboa da Praia (*US$12*), departing from the terminal at the west end of Avenida de Trabalho at 03.00.

WHERE TO STAY   *Map, page 282*

UPMARKET
🏠 **Hotel Lúrio** (63 rooms) Av da Independência; 📞262 18631; m 82 827 8587; e hotelurio@gmail. com. Following extensive renovations in 2009, this modern 5-storey hotel comes close to giving

the Nampula Hotel a run for its money. Clean international-style rooms come with dbl bed, DSTV, AC, fridge & en-suite hot shower. A good restaurant is attached & rates are negotiable. *US$65/72/80 sgl/ dbl/suite; all rooms B&B.* **$$$**

Hotel Milenio (40 rooms) Av 25 de Setembro; 262 18877; e hotelmilenio@tdm.co.mz. This smart newer hotel is a favourite with business travellers, thanks to the efficient English-speaking staff, good restaurant, free Wi-Fi & comfortable en-suite rooms, which come with twin or king-size bed, balcony, AC, DSTV, combination bath/shower & décor that is maybe a touch old-fashioned but easy enough on the eye. *US$78/98 dbl/exec dbl B&B.* **$$$**

Nampula Hotel (28 rooms) Av Eduardo Mondlane; 262 16000; e reservasmontebelo@montebelohotels.com or recepcaonampula@visabeira.co.mz; w montebelohotels.com. Formerly the Girassol Nampula, this 4-star hotel housed in the Centro Comercial Nampula is one of the classiest in town, with professional staff who speak fluent English, a small guest lounge, free internet access & modern tiled rooms with en-suite tub/shower, DSTV, AC & minibar. Aside from being on the bland side, it's everything you could ask of an international hotel in a major business centre. *US$75/89/119 sgl/dbl/suite B&B.* **$$$**

New Hotel (134 rooms) Av Eduardo Mondlane; 262 19050; m 84 845 2911; e reservas@newhotel.co.mz; w newhotel.co.mz. As shiningly new as its name suggests, this reputable business hotel has Wi-Fi throughout, a restaurant-bar with an extensive international menu, & a swimming pool. The décor can be a bit much with shiny black, white & silver being the motif (though some of the standard rooms are incongruously earthen), but nonetheless it provides comfortable, spacious rooms with all of the amenities. *US$78/82/98 sgl/dbl/suite B&B.* **$$$**

Residencial Primavera (20 rooms) Rua Macombre; 262 14600; e residencial.primavera@tvcabo.co.mz or residencial.primavera.nampula@gmail.com; residencialprimaveranampula. This attractive business hotel near Restaurante Copacabana is one of the best options in this range, with a swimming pool, gym & restaurant all on-site. Rooms are modern & understated, all with AC, DSTV, safe, writing desk, minibar, kettle & Wi-Fi. *US$79/99 dbl or twin/exec dbl; all rooms B&B.* **$$$**

Seasons Hotel (34 rooms) Rua dos Continuadores; 262 14481; m 82 577 3886; e seasonshotel.nampula@outlook.com; w seasonshotelandspa.co.mz. This new business hotel offers elegant accommodation in tastefully appointed rooms & suites with fridge, kettle, AC, Wi-Fi & balcony. Facilities inc spa, pool & restaurant serving continental & Indian cuisine. *US$78/90 dbl or twin/suite; all rooms B&B.* **$$$**

MID RANGE

Butik Hotel (21 rooms) Av Paulo Samuel Khankhomba; m 84 786 0090 or 86 786 0091; e butikhotel.npl@gmail.com; hotelbutik. Clean & classy, this is a great option & close to the bus & train stations. En-suite rooms have AC, TV, Wi-Fi, fridge & hot water. Great value. *US$58/70 dbl or twin/exec.* **$$$**

Residencial a Marisqueira (20 rooms) Av Paulo Samuel Kankhomba; 262 13611; m 84 591 9996. This centrally located lodge has spacious airy rooms with 1 sgl & 1 dbl bed, fridge, TV, AC & hot showers. *US$37 used as a dbl; US$43 as a twin.* **$$**

Residencial Hanna (11 rooms) Av da Inpendência; 262 18808; m 84 615 6455/276 4999; e residencial.hanna@gmail.com. A sister company to Residencial Primavera, this modest establishment offers the basics with en-suite standard rooms fitted with AC, Wi-Fi & TV. The 7 apartments also have a kitchenette. *US$55/59 standard/apt.* **$$$**

Residencial Universidade Pedagógica (22 rooms) Av 25 de Setembro; m 84 870 2623. Among the nicer options in this range, this has safe parking & large, clean, secure en-suite rooms with fan, AC & hot water. *US$46/52 dbl/twin.* **$$**

BUDGET

Pensão Brasilia (23 rooms) Rua dos Continuadores; 262 12126/7; m 84 700 0454. This multi-storey hotel with a selection of newer rooms, a few doors up from the Shoprite supermarket, has decent (albeit slightly run-down) en-suite rooms with AC, TV, hot shower & in some cases a balcony. It's rather a long way from the railway & chapa station should you have an early morning departure. *US$40/50 old/new dbl.* **$$**

Pensão Estrella (15 rooms) Av Paulo Samuel Kankhomba; m 86 522 6495. This is a likeable lodge with a range of rooms that are reasonable value, with fans or AC, TV & fridges. *US$34–38 dbl.* **$$**

Ruby Backpackers Nampula (3 rooms, 2 dorms) Av Daniel Napatima; m 82 717 9923 or

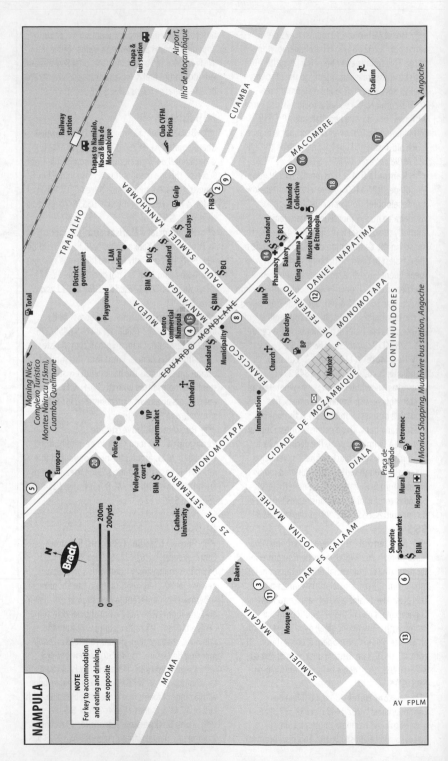

NAMPULA

NOTE
For key to accommodation and eating and drinking, see opposite

NAMPULA
For listings, see pages 280–4

Where to stay
1 Butik
2 Hotel Lúrio
3 Hotel Milenio
4 Nampula
5 New
6 Pensão Brasilia
7 Pensão Estrella
8 Residencial a Marisqueira
9 Residencial Hanna
10 Residencial Primavera
11 Residencial Universidade Pedagógica
12 Ruby Backpackers Nampula
13 Seasons
Off map
    Complexo Turístico Montes Nairucu

Where to eat and drink
14 Bar-Pub Bagdade
15 Café Atlântico
    New Marisqueira Café (see 8)
16 Restaurante Copacabana
17 Restaurante Lua
18 Sporting Clube
19 Taymã
20 Tia Maria
Off map
    Monica Shopping

84 206 7756; **e** rubybackpackers@outlook.com. Formerly under the same ownership as Ruby on Ilha de Moçambique, Nampula's best budget lodge is set in an old house with a terrace & garden. The high-ceilinged rooms are colourful, spotlessly clean & use a common bathroom. There are kitchen facilities, an honesty bar, Wi-Fi & evening film screenings on Thu. Expensive for a dorm bed, but still the cheapest option in town. *US$28 dbl; US$12 dorm bed; all rooms B&B. US$7 pp camping.* **$**

CAMPING
Complexo Turístico Montes Nairucu (4 rooms) Off the EN8 towards Cuamba, 15km out of town; 262 15297; **m** 82 669 3680 or 82/84 601 2840; **e** montesnairucu@teledata.mz. Situated on a scenic farm, overlooking a small dam & surrounded by granite outcrops, this friendly owner-managed excellent camp is justifiably popular with self-drivers. It comprises a good restaurant, a campsite with a clean ablution block, barbecue facilities, & 4 en-suite rooms. **$$**

WHERE TO EAT AND DRINK *Map, opposite*

Aside from the establishments listed below, street vendors, such as **King Shwarma** near the Museu Nacional de Ethnologia, offer a quick bite from pizzas to shwarma to noodles to burgers.

Restaurante Lua Av Eduardo Mondlane; **m** 82 226 5520 or 87 450 5001; 09.00–21.30 daily exc Wed. Tucked behind a rather grotty shopping arcade & characterised by a total lack of pretence, this workaday Chinese restaurant nonetheless serves up a huge variety of authentic Chinese cuisine – this is the place to get your noodle fix. There's a rather unglamorous balcony with a few chairs on it, a full bar & a TV blaring news of the day straight from China. *Most mains in the US$6–9 range.* **$$**

Taymã Av Paulo Samuel Kankhomba; **m** 84 217 5973/390 2088; 06.00–22.00 daily. Far more inviting than the run-down pensão of which it forms part, this covered terrace restaurant serves a rather greasy selection of fast foods such as fried chicken, burgers & pizzas, but they've got a few Indian dishes & breads as well. *Mains US$4–8.* **$$**

Restaurante Copacabana Rua Macombre, opposite the Hotel Tropical; 262 17510; 07.00–21.00 daily. A big favourite among the expat community, this large thatched restaurant

concentrates on buffets &, though it seems reasonably priced, the food can start to look a little tired by late afternoon. *US$5–12.* **$$$**

Monica Shopping Rua de Quelimane Muahivire. This new shopping complex has a selection of restaurants alongside banking & shopping facilities. **Restaurante Istanbul** offers Turkish-style pizza & local food, **Luistano Restaurante** serves up Portuguese-style food, & **DD Pub** has a limited bar menu & well-rounded cocktail selection to complement the live music. **$$–$$$$**

New Marisqueira Café Av Eduardo Mondlane; **m** 84 587 4621/390 2088; 06.00–22.00 daily. A varied selection of pizzas, meat & seafood meals, & a tempting array of pastries & sandwiches to be washed down with fresh espresso, make this an excellent place to stop for b/fast, lunch or dinner. *Around US$7.* **$$**

Sporting Clube Av Eduardo Mondlane; **m** 84 019 8808; 10.30–2.00 daily. This brightly painted outdoor venue next to the museum is

16

about as funky as it gets in Nampula, making it a popular evening rendezvous with expats & volunteers. The menu comprises a standard selection of Mozambican seafood & meat dishes, but it is all very tasty & good value. The club itself has been turned into a school, just in case you were wondering what all the children are doing here. *Mains in the US$6–11 range, & cheaper sandwiches & snacks.* $$$

✕ **Tia Maria Restaurante** Av Eduardo Mondlane; m 84 478 3968; ⊕ 10.00–22.30 daily exc Mon. This new restaurant with pleasant indoor & outdoor seating is popular among businessmen for its tasty & fast daily lunch specials, as well as a selection of Portuguese dishes & wines. *Mains US$4–10; snacks US$2–4; lunch special US$7.* $$$

🍽 **Café Atlântico** Av Eduardo Mondlane. This modern AC café on the ground floor of the Centro Comercial Nampula dishes up the best coffee, fruit juice, croissants & pastries in town.

🍷 **Bar-Pub Bagdade** Av Eduardo Mondlane; ⊕ 10.00–late. Probably the nicest drinking hole in the city centre after the Sporting Clube.

OTHER PRACTICALITIES

BANKS AND ATMS The main banks are all represented by at least one branch with an ATM in the city centre. Most are within a block or two of the junction of avenidas Paulo Samuel Kankhomba and Eduardo Mondlane, but there is also a BIM Millennium ATM in the Shoprite Centre, and one across from the main bus terminal.

CAR RENTAL There's a **Europa Car** (✆ *262 14883* or *214 97338*) on Avenida Eduardo Mondlane and at the airport.

HOSPITAL On Avenida Samora Machel just down from the Praça da Liberdade (✆ *262 13001/16539*).

INTERNET The fastest and most reliable option is the Teledata Internet Café in the Centro Comercial Nampula. Ruby Backpackers and several of the better hotels offer free Wi-Fi to guests.

PHARMACY Farmácia Calendula (⊕ *08.00–20.00 daily*) is on Avenida Eduardo Mondlane just up from the Museum of Ethnology.

POLICE The police station is on Avenida 25 de Setembro, opposite the junction with Avenida Eduardo Mondlane (✆ *262 13759*). Be aware that the police in Nampula have a reputation for enforcing the ruling that travellers must carry ID on them at all times (or, more accurately, for abusing this law to intimidate travellers into offering them a bribe). So carry your passport, or better still a certified copy of it, at all times.

POST OFFICE On Avenida Paulo Samuel Kankhomba, on the corner with Rua Cidade do Mozambique.

SHOPPING The **market** on Avenida Paulo Samuel Kankhomba is good for fruit and vegetables, though you might find the children selling plastic bags irritating after a while. By far the best supermarket is the **Shoprite** on Rua dos Continuadores, along from the Praça da Liberdade. Also good is the **Supermercado Ideal** in the Centro Commercial Nampula, which also houses a good gift and bookshop called **Mabuko**. The new **VIP Supermarket** on Avenida Eduardo Mondlane has a good selection. For craft shopping, head to the **Makonde Collective** behind the museum.

SWIMMING The Club CVFM Piscina on Rua 3 de Fevereiro has a large pool with diving boards set in pleasant green gardens. Swimming costs around US$6 for adults or US$3 for children, and a decent restaurant-bar is attached. Day visitors are welcomed at the New Hotel swimming pool for US$8 per person.

WHAT TO SEE AND DO

MUSEU NACIONAL DE ETNOLOGIA (*Av Eduardo Mondlane;* ⏰ *09.00–17.00 Tue–Fri, 14.00–17.00 Sat/Sun; entrance US$2; photography forbidden*) This ethnological museum is well worth a visit. The ground floor houses a collection of traditional ethnic artefacts, mostly from the northern provinces of Nampula and Cabo Delgado, including copper and bead bracelets, earplugs, metre-high drums and other musical instruments, bao games, basketwork, and a couple of dozen garish Makonde masks (one of which bears a striking but presumably unintentional resemblance to former US president Ronald Reagan). There's more of the same upstairs, notably some wonderfully grotesque Makonde sculptures, a few sculpted metal penises that look like (but surely aren't) Iron Age dildos, and more contemporary artefacts including some excellent examples of the toy cars and bicycles you sometimes see sold on the roadside.

In the same compound as the museum is a **Makonde Collective** where you can watch the carvers at work and buy some of their output. Haggling here will be of limited value, as many of the pieces have price tags on them. Similarly if you just want to take photos without buying anything, you'll probably be expected to pay. If you want to visit the collective but not the museum itself, you need to pass through the museum's entrance hall but won't be asked to pay the entrance fee.

AROUND NAMPULA

The main attraction in the vicinity of Nampula, set on the coast 170km to the east (and covered in the next chapter; pages 291–305), is the historic town of Ilha de Moçambique (Mozambique Island), an absorbing and atmospheric warren of dense alleys and colonial buildings dating to the earliest years of the Portuguese occupation. Also of interest is the ancient Muslim port of Angoche, the offshore Primeiras and Segundas archipelagos, and the junction town of Namialo, all described as follows.

ANGOCHE Set on the Mluli River mouth, 120km southeast of Nampula as the crow flies and a similar distance southwest of Ilha de Moçambique, the port of Angoche is one of the country's most venerable towns, having first established trade links to the Arabian Peninsula in medieval times and retained these until its sultan was deposed by Portugal in 1910. Oddly, however, it seems there are no pre-20th-century buildings in the modern town, which has a very peculiar character – the long wide main avenue is lined by abandoned office blocks, warehouses and shops that hint at its former prosperity, while the residential area to its southeast is studded with attractive colonial villas fallen into disuse. An estimated population of 85,000 ensures that Angoche isn't quite a ghost town, but as you wander around the surreally sleepy old town centre, you keep thinking it must be a Sunday or public holiday.

Angoche sees few visitors, but it is a worthwhile diversion for travellers with enough time, and it does have two key draws – Praia Nova, a long wide sandy beach fringed with mangroves to the east of the town centre, and a busy little dhow harbour and fishing market to the west. It is also the best port to get to the

Ilhas Primeiras and Segundas, a chain of islands similar to the Quirimbas but with virtually no tourist development. It's an altogether beguiling place, and if you find yourself – as this author did – spending more time in Angoche than you had planned, the silent walk through the mangroves and the creaky rowboat crossing to windswept Praia Thamole on the other side of the estuary are nothing short of dazzling. The Portuguese *azulejo* tiles at the top of Rua do Parapato date back to 1956 and are worth a look, along with the excellent views over the town.

History Angoche is thought to have formed a minor stop along the medieval gold-trade route that connected Sofala to Kilwa (the most important medieval trading port along the Swahili coast, in what is now southern Tanzania). However, it first came to prominence after 1485, following the foundation of the Sultanate of Angoche (covering the cities of Angoche and Moma) by an offshoot of the ruling family of Kilwa. This event coincided with the reorientation of the gold-mining

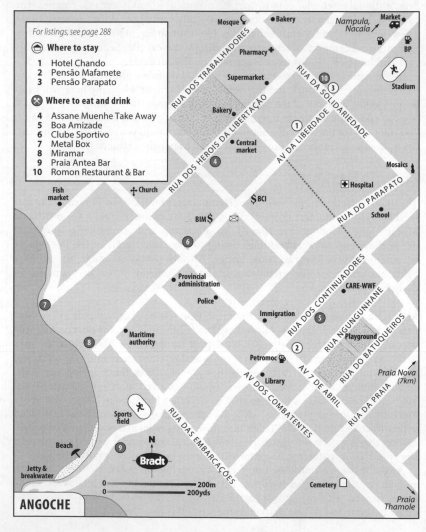

For listings, see page 288

🏠 **Where to stay**

1 Hotel Chando
2 Pensão Mafamete
3 Pensão Parapato

🍴 **Where to eat and drink**

4   Assane Muenhe Take Away
5   Boa Amizade
6   Clube Sportivo
7   Metal Box
8   Miramar
9   Praia Antea Bar
10 Romon Restaurant & Bar

ANGOCHE

industry in the southern interior, and as a result Angoche became the terminus of a new trade route from Sena on the Zambezi.

Like the Quirimba Islands, Angoche became an important refuge for Islamic traders in the early years of the Portuguese occupation. The town enjoyed an economic boom between 1505 and 1511, when the route from Sena was favoured as a clandestine way of getting gold to the coast without Portuguese knowledge, and its population may have stood at around 10,000. In 1511, however, Angoche was bombarded by Portuguese ships and burned to the ground, and the sultan was taken into captivity. The town slid into relative obscurity after the 1530s, when ivory replaced gold as the major trading commodity along the coast and Portugal established a greater presence along the Zambezi. It was dealt a further death blow when Barreto's army massacred the Islamic traders at Sena in 1572.

Angoche enjoyed a major revival in the early 19th century, largely due to the emergence of the slave trade off the Swahili coast, which led to its re-emergence as a thriving trade centre by 1830. Angoche assumed a greater importance after Portugal abolished the slave trade, as its inaccessibility to large ships made it a good place for Islamic merchants to operate an illegal trade, undetected by the British boats that started policing the coast in 1842. In early 1847, a Portuguese warship attempted to impose an anti-slaving treaty on the Sultanate of Angoche, but it was driven away. Later in the same year, Britain and Portugal bombarded the town from the sea, causing great damage to its buildings, but were unable to occupy it.

Angoche fell briefly to Portugal in 1862, following a bloody battle which caused its sultan to flee inland, but ultimately this led to the strengthening of its links with the interior and increased control over the slave trade at its source. The clandestine slave trade out of Angoche continued into the early 20th century, and the sultanate effectively retained independence from the rest of Mozambique until 1910, when the Portuguese overthrew the sultan and renamed the town António Enes (in remembrance of a former Commissioner of Mozambique who died in 1901 after returning to Portugal).

The town has since sunk into relative obscurity again, although it enjoyed a brief resurgence in the late 20th century as a major processing and export centre for cashew nuts, prior to the closure of its two main processing factories in 1999. The channel that was dug in its cashew-exporting heyday has since silted up, though Angoche may be due another resurgence thanks to a pending multimillion-dollar project to mine and process heavy sand (a mixture of titanium and zircon ores) in the area.

Getting there and away From Nampula, the best road to Angoche is the well-maintained dirt **EN239** via Namétil and Biola, a drive of around 160km that should take under 3 hours. A few **chapas** and **buses** run between Angoche and Nampula daily, costing around US$4. They leave Nampula from the Muahivire bus station on Avenida Samora Machel. The journey takes around 4 hours, so you should assume that you will be staying overnight.

A 170km dirt road called the **EN236** (R689) connects Angoche to Liúpo and on to Monapo, on the EN8 about 45km west of Ilha de Moçambique. This is also in pretty good condition, though rough in patches, so best allow 4 hours. There is not much chapa transport between Angoche and Liúpo, but it's worth asking around the station. Alternatively, it may be possible to find a **boat** to Mossuril, on the mainland opposite Ilha de Moçambique. The best way to find out about this option in Angoche is at the maritime authority, which will have a good idea of what boats are in port and where they are heading.

Where to stay, eat and drink *Map, page 286*

⌂ **Hotel Chando** Av 7 de Abril; m 84 576 3991; e hotelchando@gmail.com. The newest establishment in town, Hotel Chando offers clean & comfortable en-suite rooms with AC, hot water & a bit of Mozambican flair. There is a restaurant, bar & conference room. A discoteca & pool are in the works. *US$40/50 dbl or twin/exec, B&B.* **$$**

⌂ **Pensão Mafamete** Av 7 de Abril; m 84 487 1489 or 86 159 7400. Set in an old colonial building overlooking the central plaza, this was under renovation at the time of research, but the clean (mostly en-suite) rooms with parquet floors but no hot water or nets should be boosted with AC when it reopens. Good value. *US$12/20 dbl/twin.* **$**

⌂ **Pensão Parapato** Av da Liberdade; m 82 777 4283 or 84 551 0530. On the main avenue into town, this place has en-suite rooms with nets & fans, & the attached restaurant is a favourite with local Peace Corps volunteers, known for its excellent matapa. It's not as breezy as the Mafamete, but also good value. *US$13 twin or dbl.* **$**

✕ **Assane Muenhe Take Away** Rua dos Heróis da Libertação; m 86 048 0783; ☉ 07.00–late daily. This marketplace eatery is popular with locals, especially in the evening when everyone is strolling around & socialising. From popcorn to chicken or shrimp, snacks & meals range from US$0.50 to US$7. **$**

✕ **Boa Amizade** Rua dos Continuadores; m 82 628 4730 or 84 547 0247; ☉ 08.00–19.00 daily. Its name means 'good friendship' in Portuguese, & this amiable place lives up to its billing with a warm welcome & good (if slow) Mozambican dishes. They also probably keep the longest hours of any restaurant in Angoche. *US$2.50–6.50.* **$**

✕ **Clube Sportivo** Av da Liberdade; m 82 384 1776. Known simply as 'sporting' around town, this Angoche stalwart hosts occasional concerts & serves decent food & beers in the evening. **$**

✕ **Miramar** Av da Liberdade; m 84 413 5081. This corrugated tin building on the Praça dos Heróis Moçambicanos is painted bright yellow & has simple meals, good chamussas, cold beers & one of the best locations in town, on the sea wall & under the praça's whitewashed trees. *US$5–10.* **$$**

✕ **Romon Restaurant & Bar** Rua da Solidariedade; m 84 563 3169 or 86 789 0578; ☉ 08.00–late Tue–Sun. Offering up the typical Mozambican menu with fish, chicken & beef options, this establishment has a gregarious owner well versed in the history of Angoche. *US$4–7.* **$**

♀ **Metal Box** Rua dos Heróis da Libertação. Claustrophobically named after the fish market next door, this open-air bar is actually quite the opposite, perched under a thatched roof just steps from the mangroves. The place to be for sundowners.

♀ **Praia Antea Bar** Rua do Parapato. The closest bar to the beach serving up the usual bottled cool drinks.

Other practicalities

Bank There's a BIM Millennium with an ATM on the main road.

Internet There's currently no public internet in Angoche. The café on the main road left its signs up, but is very much closed.

Hospital Near the top of Rua do Parapato.

PRIMEIRAS AND SEGUNDAS ARCHIPELAGOS The ecologically important Primeiras and Segundas (literally 'First' and 'Second') archipelagos off Angoche consist of two groups of five large islands and numerous smaller islets. The area contains the most abundant and diverse coral communities in Mozambique, possibly anywhere in Africa, along with sea-grass beds of the type classically associated with dugong, that also form the nesting grounds for green, loggerhead and hawksbill turtles. The island of **Puga-Puga** is a nesting site for the sooty tern, and the area as a whole is known for its abundance of shrimp. The archipelagos were declared a marine protected area in November 2012 and, at 10,400km², they comprise the largest marine protected area anywhere in Africa. Overseeing this transformation is the Primeiras and Segundas Project, which was established in 2008 by the World Wide Fund for Nature, and it is worth visiting their blog (**w** *primeirasesegundas.net*) for information on new projects.

Tourist development on the islands is non-existent. The islands have little or no tourist infrastructure, although there are thriving communities on a couple of the northern ones and it is possible to visit providing you are prepared to rough it. For now, the best source of information on getting to the islands is the CARE-WWF office (*267 20130*) on Rua dos Continuadores, or the Angoche maritime authority. If you want to visit the islands, they should be able to point you in the direction of a suitable boat. For obvious reasons the price of boats to the islands isn't fixed – it'll be down to your haggling ability – but expect to pay around US$100 for the boat rental, US$65 for the hire of the skipper, and also to pay the cost of fuel and oil. The 12-nautical-mile journey from Angoche to Quelelene should cost around US$200, while the 18-nautical-mile journey from Angoche to Mafamede should be around US$250.

NAMIALO The small town of Namialo lies at the junction of the EN8 between Nampula and Nacala and the EN106 (N1) north to Pemba. As you'd expect it's an unpretentious little place, and surprisingly lively – one side of the road is made up of almost continuous market. The Maning Nice buses heading up to Mocímboa da Praia stop here around 05.00, so if you are heading from Ilha to Pemba and can't bear the idea of going to Nampula again, you could overnight at Namialo and meet them here. If you do decide to take this option, don't expect to get a seat; and for Pemba you'll have to transfer again at Metoro or Sunate. BCI and BIM both have ATMs in Namialo.

There are two inexpensive lodges, of which the **Pousada Hotel** (**m** *84 500 5672*) is the better, charging around US$30 for clean, comfortable rooms with bedding. It does food, but the **Restaurante Tropical** (**m** *84 707 2455*) also looks good and has been recommended, and **Arahman Take-Away** is the spot for something quick on your way out of town. Given that one half of the town has been given over to market stalls, you shouldn't have too much trouble finding fruit and vegetables. You could also stop at Monapo, 38km east of Namialo, 3km before the roads to Nacala and Ilha de Moçambique diverge, and noted for its cashew factory.

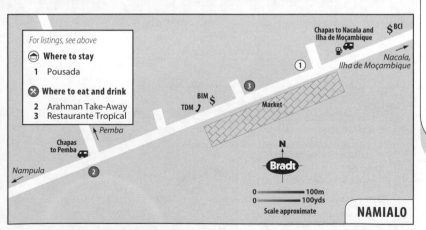

For listings, see above

🏠 **Where to stay**
1   Pousada

❌ **Where to eat and drink**
2   Arahman Take-Away
3   Restaurante Tropical

Chapas to Nacala and Ilha de Moçambique $ BCI

Nacala, Ilha de Moçambique

BIM $
TDM

Market

Pemba

Chapas to Pemba

Nampula

N

Bradt

0 ——— 100m
0 ——— 100yds
Scale approximate

NAMIALO

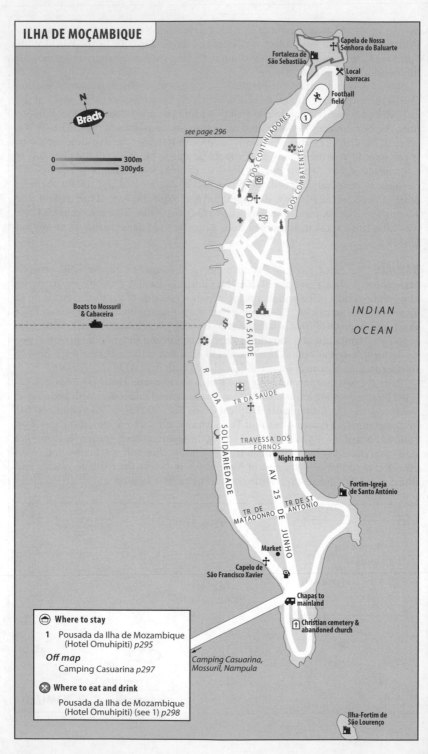

ILHA DE MOÇAMBIQUE

Capela de Nossa Senhora do Baluarte

Fortaleza de São Sebastião

Local barracas

Football field

1

see page 296

AV DOS CONTINUADORES

R DOS COMBATENTES

Boats to Mossuril & Cabaceira

INDIAN OCEAN

R DA SAUDE

R DA SOLIDARIEDADE

TR DA SAUDE

TRAVESSA DOS FORNOS

Night market

Fortim-Igreja de Santo António

TR DE MATADONRO

AV 25 DE JUNHO

TR DE ST ANTONIO

Market

Capelo de São Francisco Xavier

Chapas to mainland

Christian cemetery & abandoned church

Camping Casuarina, Mossuril, Nampula

Ilha-Fortim de São Lourenço

⊖ Where to stay

1 Pousada da Ilha de Mozambique
(Hotel Omuhipiti) p295

Off map
Camping Casuarina p297

⊗ Where to eat and drink

Pousada da Ilha de Mozambique
(Hotel Omuhipiti) (see 1) p298

17

Ilha de Moçambique and Surrounds

The town of Moçambique, which occupies the small offshore coral island of the same name in Mossuril Bay, is the oldest European settlement on the east coast of Africa, and also perhaps the most intriguing and bizarre. Measuring about 3km from north to south and at no point more than 600m wide, crescent-shaped Ilha de Moçambique (Mozambique Island) was the effective capital of Portuguese East Africa and the most important Indian Ocean port south of Mombasa for almost four centuries prior to the emergence of Maputo, peaking in prosperity during the 18th century when it handled some 70% of the ivory exported from the Mozambican coast. It houses several of the southern hemisphere's oldest extant buildings, including the Fortaleza de São Sebastião, the former Convent of São Paulo and a trio of handsome churches. In 1991, the entire island was inscribed as Mozambique's first (and thus far only) UNESCO World Heritage Site, in recognition of its numerous old buildings and singular architectural cohesion, and it surely ranks as the country's most alluring urban destination for travellers.

Often referred to locally as Ilha (pronounced *Ilya*), Moçambique drifted towards backwater status over the course of the 20th century, a trend that goes a long way towards explaining why the town centre, a maze of narrow alleys lined with old colonial buildings, has barely changed shape in centuries. But while the architectural landscape is overtly Portuguese, the overall mood of the island has greater affiliations to old Swahili ports such as Lamu or Zanzibar, a kinship underscored by the predominantly African/Muslim human presence.

In the early 16th century, when Ilha de Moçambique became the Portuguese regional capital, the original Muslim population was forced to relocate to the mainland. And there they stayed for four centuries, only starting to drift back across the water after the capital relocated to Lourenço Marques (now Maputo) in 1898, and again, in greater numbers, in the wake of the Portuguese evacuation of 1975, to give Ilha de Moçambique a strong but deceptive sense of historical continuity, one that has the odd effect of reducing 400 years of Portuguese rule to something of a passing episode.

By comparison with its lamentably run-down state when the first edition of this guidebook was researched, Ilha de Moçambique is currently enjoying a fresh lease of life as a low-key tourist destination. A number of derelict houses have been rehabilitated to serve as hotels, backpackers or restaurants, while the Fortaleza de São Sebastião and other key public buildings have been renovated by UNESCO or affiliated organisations. And where in 1996 there was only one hotel and two restaurants on the entire island, today there are enough cafés, restaurants, boutique shops and lodgings to make the old town a genuinely pleasant place to hang out for a few days.

And yet the overall feel of Moçambique remains isolated, old-world and not at all touristy. Indeed, from that perspective, there may never be a better time to visit

Ilha de Moçambique, poised as it is at a most appealing point along the trajectory between the half-forgotten and rather moribund backwater it had become at the end of the long years of civil war, and the fully developed tourist hub – a kind of southern African counterpart to Zanzibar or Gorée – one senses it will be in the not-too-distant future.

HISTORY

Ilha de Moçambique, like Sofala and Angoche, was an important Muslim trading centre even before the Portuguese arrived on the east coast of Africa. When Vasco da Gama first landed on the facing mainland in 1499, he noted that the island supported a 'collection of dark huts dominated by white verandas of the sheikh's residence and mosque'. The name 'Moçambique' probably derives from that of a local sultan Moussa Ben Mbiki, said by some to have been incumbent when da Gama reached the area, and by others to have been the founding father of the island's Muslim settlement. Back then, the island was a renowned centre of shipbuilding; indeed, the records show that the Portuguese navigator Vincente Soares had a boat assembled here in 1512.

In 1507, two years after Portugal had occupied Kilwa and Sofala, it added Ilha de Moçambique to its list of East African conquests, and built a hospital, church and small fort here. Easily defensible and positioned at the junction of the all-important trade route from Africa to Goa, the island soon replaced Kilwa as the favoured base for India-bound ships awaiting the monsoon winds, and as the main regional focus of Portuguese naval activities. As a result, Portugal abolished the Captaincy of Kilwa in 1513, then in 1530 it renamed the Captaincy of Sofala the Captaincy of Moçambique and Sofala, and the 'Praça de Moçambique' island became the ipso facto capital of Portuguese East Africa, a status it would retain for close on four centuries.

In 1562, the first Dominican monks settled on Ilha de Moçambique. By this time, more than 70 Portuguese officials, ranging from a judge and doctor to priests and soldiers, were listed on the island's official payroll. Depending on how many ships were docked at the island, it supported up to a thousand Portuguese inhabitants at any one time. The main activity at this time was commerce: gold, silver and ivory carried to the coast from the Zambezi Valley and elsewhere in the interior were traded for exotic spices, cloths, spirits and other items shipped from India and Arabia. Food was in short supply, and some provisions were sourced from the Muslim traders who had abandoned the island for Sancul on the facing mainland following the Portuguese occupation, while others were imported from the Comoros Islands and Madagascar. High taxes were imposed on all commercial activity following the establishment of an excise office in 1593, and most of the wealth generated on the island was diverted elsewhere: either into the overflowing coffers of the Portuguese crown, or to support the high lifestyle of the administration at Goa.

Ilha de Moçambique was the site of the earliest battle between European powers to take place in Africa, when the Netherlands attempted to seize it as an East African base for the Dutch East India Company in 1607–08 (box, page 302). In 1671, the island was attacked by Omani Arabs, again without success. During the early 18th century, the Portuguese economic hegemony was curtailed by an influx of Indian traders, known as Baneanes, who soon came to dominate commercial activity and own a significant proportion of property on Ilha de Moçambique. The Portuguese traders based on the island resented this economic intrusion and attempted to force out the interlopers, sometimes violently, but ultimately without success.

MOÇAMBIQUE AND THE SLAVE TRADE

Over the second half of the 18th century, commerce along the Indian Ocean coast of Africa focused increasingly on the slave trade. Ilha de Moçambique was no exception, though the main local slave markets were actually centred on Mossuril on the facing mainland, which lost ground to the emergent slave ports of Ibo and Quelimane, especially after 1787, when the Portuguese legalised the sale of firearms to indigenous Africans. Caravan routes via the southern shores of Lago Niassa were established to link ports such as Moçambique, Kilwa and Ibo with the interior of present-day Malawi and Tanzania, whose inhabitants were terrorised by murderous Yao and Arab slave raiders.

By the 1790s, around 5,000 captives passed through the warehouses of Mossuril or Ilha de Moçambique every year, with numbers peaking above 30,000 annually in the late 1820s. Some of these captives were sold into bondage to local merchants, others to Portuguese landowners in Brazil, but the vast majority ended up on the sugar plantations of Mauritius, Réunion and the other islands of the Mascarenes. The few available records indicate that only half the Africans captured in the interior ever arrived alive at their intended destination; the other half died along the inland caravan route, while held captive on the coast or in transit to Brazil or to the Mascarenes, a reflection of the harsh and insanitary conditions in which they were kept.

After Portugal abolished the transatlantic slave trade in 1836, traffic out of Mozambique declined somewhat, or was at least conducted more discreetly, with labourers exported to the Mascarenes given the nominal title of contract workers or recruits. It was only in 1869 that slavery was properly outlawed in Portugal's African colonies. This effectively terminated the slave trade out of Ilha de Moçambique, but a clandestine trade continued to operate out of nearby Angoche, which remained an independent sultanate until 1910.

It was largely in order to curb Indian activity on Moçambique that the island was declared an independent entity from Goa in 1761, with its own captain-general and town council. In 1810, it was granted the status of a city. The earliest-known census, taken in 1882, shows that the island and associated mainland settlements of Mossuril and Cabaceira then supported a population of 8,500, of which 125 were classified as Portuguese or 'white', 650 as *mestizos* (mixed race), 380 as Canarins (Goans) or Baneanes, 500 as Arab and 800 as *cafres forros* (free Africans). The remaining 6,000 were slaves.

Ilha de Moçambique slid into economic decline during the late 19th century. This phenomenon was rooted in two causes: the general southward drift of the economy towards Lourenço Marques and the Portuguese discovery of the superior natural harbour at nearby Nacala. The declining importance of the island was acknowledged as early as 1898, when it was superseded as national capital by Lourenço Marques, even though it was still handling roughly 20% of the total goods shipped out of Mozambique. The former capital was granted a lifeline in 1913, when it was agreed that a proposed railway line to the interior would terminate at Lumbo, on the mainland directly opposite Ilha de Moçambique, but the intervention of World War I delayed construction until the late 1920s, with the line reaching as far inland as Nampula in 1930.

As that time, Ilha de Moçambique was still one of the five largest urban centres in the country, supporting a population of 7,000. However, its significance dwindled further following the completion of the more modern port at Nacala. In 1935, the reins of local government were handed over to the new provincial capital of Nampula, while the railway connection to Lumbo was superseded by a new line to Nacala in 1947. Today, Ilha de Moçambique probably ranks outside the country's 50 largest towns, supporting a population estimated at 14,000.

GETTING THERE AND AWAY

BY AIR The closest airport with scheduled **LAM** flights is at Nacala. However, the better option is to fly to Nampula, as the Nacala airport only has three weekly flights from Maputo, whereas Nampula has LAM flights daily from around Mozambique, as well as flights from Dar es Salaam, Nairobi (Kenya Airways) and Johannesburg (Airlink) several times a week.

BY CAR Ilha de Moçambique lies in Mossuril Bay about 170km east of Nampula. It can be reached by following the **EN8** (EN1) east towards Nacala as far as Monapo, then turning right on to the **EN105** and following it for 45km to its mainland terminus at Lumbo. From here, you can cross to the southern end of the island along a recently renovated 3.5km-long concrete bridge built by the Portuguese in 1969. The bridge is single-lane for most of its length, but it has been widened in about half a dozen places to allow oncoming traffic to pass. A pick-up or similarly sized vehicle won't have any problems crossing, but anything wider than a minibus may not make it. The charge for the bridge is about US$0.20 per vehicle, but there's no charge for foot passengers.

BY BUS AND CHAPA If you're planning to use public transport, local **chapas** run between Nampula and Ilha de Moçambique daily. These leave Ilha de Moçambique from next to the bridge between 03.00 and 05.00 and from Nampula between 09.00 and noon. Tickets cost US$4 and the run takes about 4 hours in either direction. Leaving Ilha de Moçambique after 05.00, you may need to catch a chapa to Monapo, on the junction with the **EN8** (EN1), and to change vehicles there. In either direction, transport tends to peter out after midday. Heading northward to Pemba, you will need to change vehicles at Namialo and should aim for the earliest possible start to connect with passing buses from Nampula.

BY BOAT The only real option for arriving on Ilha by boat is to head to Mossuril on the mainland and catch a boat from there. It'll cost around US$0.60. There are also occasional boats from Ilha to Cabaceira Pequena and Cabaceira Grande.

 WHERE TO STAY *Map, page 296, unless otherwise stated*

Ilha de Moçambique is now serviced by a good selection of lodges catering to most tastes and budgets, much of it very good value compared with the more resort-like parts of the country, though it's worth noting that the most upmarket beach resort in the vicinity is situated on the facing mainland at Cabaceira Pequena.

EXCLUSIVE/LUXURY
Terraço das Quitandas (6 rooms)
Av da República; **m** 84 613 1243; **e** terraco.das.

quitandas@gmail.com; **w** terracodasquitandas. com. This restored waterfront mansion next to the Restaurante Reliquias is Ilha's most esteemed boutique guesthouse, comprising 6 spacious suites with king-size or twin beds, AC & Wi-Fi, as well as a large internal courtyard overlooked by 2 balconies & 3 recreation rooms. Actor Kevin Costner is one of its past guests. *US$175/200/250 sgl/dbl/twin; all rates B&B.* **$$$$**

🏠 **Villa Sands** ☎266 10160; m 82 744 7178/418 0321; e info@villasands.com; w villasands.com. Built out of 3 once-derelict warehouses, this recent addition to the hotels in town has raised the bar on boutique accommodation on the island. Swedish-run & designed around an open courtyard in a cool Mozambique-meets-Scandinavia style, rooms here are whitewashed & floored in dark wood, with flat-screen TV, walk-in nets & rainfall showers, though some are a bit short on windows. There's an oceanfront terrace with swimming pool, a restaurant serving fine seafood dishes for US$11–24, & a full range of aquatic activities. *US$200–300 dbl; all rooms B&B.* **$$$$**

UPMARKET

🏠 **Jardim dos Aloés** (3 rooms) m 84 213 1488 or 87 827 4645; e jardim.aloes@gmail. com; w jardim-dos-aloes.com. The island's newest boutique B&B does both equally well: the atmosphere is enchanting & the b/fast a renowned feast. It is restored from a ruined old house in Stone Town, & the spacious & charmingly appointed en-suite rooms are complemented by terraces, verandas & gardens. Choose between 2 suites or a 2-bedroom self-catering apartment, all with AC, fan, hot shower & net. *US$170–180 dbl apt or suite; low-season & package discounts available; B&B.* **$$$$**

🏠 **Rickshaws Pousada** (4 rooms) Rua da Solidariedade; m 82 678 0098; e orgulhodailha@ gmail.com; 📘 mozambiquerickshaws. With a stunning location overlooking Mossuril Bay, this new boutique hotel is still a bit of a work in progress, but so far it is shaping up to be a promising addition to the island's boutique accommodation. En-suite rooms with bed, net & AC, as well as one of the best cafés (page 298) in town. *US$100 standard dbl; US$200 suites.* **$$$$**

MID RANGE

🏠 **Casa Azul** (4 rooms) m 82 794 2540/1; e imf_zico@gmail.com or contact@casaazul-guesthouse.com; w casaazul-guesthouse.com.

Lovingly restored over 4 years, this unsignposted casa next to Ruby Backpackers has spacious en-suite rooms with timber floors, wooden beam ceilings, AC & hot shower. There is an attractively decorated living & dining room with DSTV, & a roof terrace with views over the island. *US$50 dbl.* **$$**

🏠 **Casa Branca** (7 rooms) Rua João Deus; ☎266 10076; m 82 454 3290 or 84 398 7307; e pmaga@hotmail.com. Set around a private courtyard & living room, this set of restored old casas has large en-suite rooms only 20m from the sea at high tide. AC available. *US$50 dbl with fan; B&B.* **$$**

🏠 **Casa Paula** Rua dos Arcos (4 rooms) m 82 317 4160; e paula.elina.oksanen@gmail. com. This delightful guesthouse opposite the Missanga Craft Shop is as charming as they come. Airy rooms frame a rooftop terrace green with lush potted plants. 2 rooms share a bathroom, while the others have private or en-suite bathrooms; all come with nets, fan & Wi-Fi. *US$50/60 dbl using shared facilities/private bathroom.* **$$**

🏠 **Mooxeleliya** (7 rooms) ☎266 10076; m 82 454 3290; e flora204@hotmail.com. The central & attractively restored old homestead has plenty of character, enhanced by antique furniture, & all en-suite rooms come with TV, standby light for power cuts, 4-poster bed with netting, & writing desk. Good value. *US$30/40 dbl with fan/AC.* **$$**

🏠 **O Escondidinho** (11 rooms) Av dos Heróis; ☎266 10078; m 84 389 8628; e escondidinho. reservas@gmail.com; w oescondidinho.net. This converted old Portuguese mansion has a range of spacious cool rooms set around a private courtyard with swimming pool. It's probably the best-value accommodation in this range. There is an excellent restaurant on the ground floor, & reception can arrange a variety of excursions. *US$50–58/120–128 sgl/dbl, depending on whether the room is en suite.* **$$$$**

🏠 **Pousada da Ilha de Mozambique (Hotel Omuhipiti)** [map, page 290] (22 rooms) Rua dos Combatentes; ☎266 10101/3; m 82 696 5500; e pousada.ilhademocambique@gmail.com. Now under new ownership, this architecturally misplaced Art Deco relic on the northeast end of the island is the town's oldest hotel. The en-suite rooms, though a little frayed at the edges, are light & airy, & come with sea view, AC, DSTV & hot shower. It has a classy restaurant too. Decent value. *US$52/56 sgl/dbl; from US$60 suites.* **$$$**

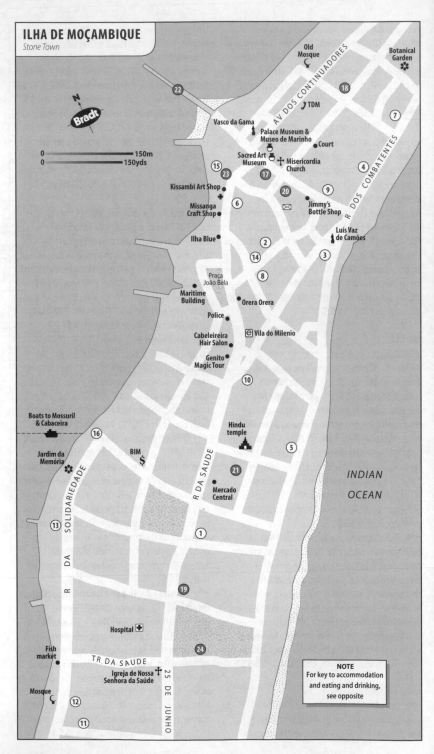

ILHA DE MOÇAMBIQUE
Stone Town

N

Bradt

0 ——————— 150m
0 ——————— 150yds

Old Mosque

Botanical Garden

AV DOS CONTINUADORES

22

18

7

TDM

Vasco da Gama

Palace Museum & Museo de Marinho

Court

Sacred Art Museum

Misericordia Church

15

23

17

20

4

R DOS COMBATENTES

Kissambi Art Shop

9

Missanga Craft Shop

6

Jimmy's Bottle Shop

Luís Vaz de Camões

Ilha Blue

2

3

14

8

Praça João Bela

Maritime Building

Orera Orera

Police

Cabeleireira Hair Salon

Vila do Milenio

Genito Magic Tour

10

Hindu temple

5

Boats to Mossuril & Cabaceira

16

BIM

INDIAN

Jardim da Memória

R DA SOLIDARIEDADE

R DA SAÚDE

21

OCEAN

Mercado Central

13

1

19

Hospital

Fish market

TR DA SAÚDE

24

25 DE JUNHO

Igreja de Nossa Senhora da Saúde

Mosque

12

11

NOTE
For key to accommodation and eating and drinking, see opposite

ILHA DE MOÇAMBIQUE Stone Town
For listings, see pages 294–8

Where to stay
1 Casa Amy
2 Casa Azul
3 Casa Branca
4 Casa das Ondas
5 Casa Kero
6 Casa Paula
7 Casa Yasmin
8 Jardim dos Aloés
9 Mooxeleliya
10 O Escondidinho
11 Omakthini Guesthouse
12 Pátio dos Quintalinhos
13 Rickshaws Pousada
14 Ruby Backpackers
15 Terraço das Quitandas
16 Villa Sands

Where to eat and drink
17 Café-Bar Âncora d'Ouro
18 Celda's (Yoyo's)
19 Flor de Rosa
20 Karibu
   O Escondidinho (see 10)
21 O Paladar
22 O Pontão
23 Restaurante Reliquias
   Rickshaws Café (see 13)
24 Sarah's

Pátio dos Quintalinhos (6 rooms) Rua dos Trabalhadores; \266 10090; m 82 419 7610; e gabrielemelazzi@hotmail.com; w patiodosquintalinhos.com. Also known as Casa do Gabriel after its Italian owner, this lovingly restored house lies on the boundary of the stone town & the reed town, immediately opposite the main mosque. The rooms are tastefully furnished, some with AC, & each one is completely different. They're all cool & comfortable, with clever architectural touches, eg: lofts & hanging beds. There's a swimming pool, the lovely rooftop b/fast area overlooks the beach, & you can arrange boat trips, bicycles & canoe rental & fishing. One drawback for those fond of a lie-in is the morning mosque call, which is so loud you could be forgiven for thinking the muezzin is lurking in your bathroom. *US$33/43 sgl/dbl using shared ablutions; US$70 en-suite dbl; US$75 large dbl with private courtyard & roof terrace; rates slightly higher during peak season, all rates B&B.* **$$$**

BUDGET
Casa das Ondas (2 rooms) m 82 438 6400. This waterfront homestead on the north end of the island has a quiet location & the clean rooms have nets & fans. *US$34/40 twin/dbl.* **$$**

Casa Kero (3 rooms) m 82 675 5890. Signposted 'Hospedagem' & owned by a friendly Mozambican family, this casa on the eastern waterfront feels more like a homestay than a guesthouse, & the rooms seem very comfortable. *US$16 dbl with fan; US$20/30 dbl with AC/en suite; all rates B&B.* **$**

Casa Yasmin (6 rooms) m 84 035 4689. Run by a local Indian family with ties to the island stretching back over generations, this local guesthouse feels like a homestay. *US$30/50 dbl with fan & shared facilities/AC, en suite.* **$$**

Ruby Backpackers (2 rooms, 2 dorms) m 82 467 0524 or 84 866 0200; e ruby. backpackers@gmail.com. This superlative backpackers is housed in a beautifully restored homestead, parts of which date back 400 years. Facilities inc fully stocked & sociable bar, well-equipped kitchen with fridge, & rooftop & courtyard seating. Showers & toilets are not en suite but clean & plentiful. Rooms are simply but tastefully furnished with nets & fans. *US$31 dbl; US$13 pp dorm bed; all rates B&B.* **$**

SHOESTRING
Casa Amy (6 rooms) Rua da Saúde m 84 854 0403. A friendly option offering clean, basic accommodation. Rooms are short on windows. *US$20/30 dbl or twin fan/AC & en suite.* **$**

Omakthini Guesthouse (3 rooms, 1 dorm) Barrio do Esteu, off Travessa dos Fornos; m 82 436 7570/540 7622. Also known as Casa Luis, this family-run place has long been a favourite with budget-conscious backpackers. The dbl or twin rooms are small but clean & come with nets & fan, as do the bunks in the 8-bed dorm, & there is a pleasant garden area, kitchen, & a lounge with DSTV & a library. AC available in rooms, but not the dorm. *US$30/40 sgl/dbl; US$11 per dorm bed.* **$**

CAMPING
Camping Casuarina [map, page 307] At the other end of the causeway in the town of Lumbo; m 84 616 8764; e casuarina.camping@gmail.com. You'll have noticed a lack of camping on the island itself & this is currently the only site. The facilities inc restaurant & bar with a pizza oven & a kitchen if you're self-catering. *US$40 en-suite dbl; US$7 pp camping.* **$**

The choice of restaurants has improved greatly in recent years, and you could now spend several days on the island without eating at the same place twice. There are also a few local barracas on the north end of the island serving up seafood and local dishes that are popular at the weekends.

✖ **Café-Bar Âncora d'Ouro** ☏266 10006; m 82 692 3930; ⊕ 08.00–late daily exc Wed. A restaurant of this name has stood here since the first edition of this guide was researched, but the similarities between this airy European café & its dank & uninviting 1996 incarnation end there. The menu inc fresh coffee, juices, fruit salad, pizzas & a fair choice of b/fasts, while the rotating lunch & dinner menu, chalked up on a board, usually inc filling soup of the day with bread & imaginative seafood mains for US$6–10. There's indoor & outdoor seating, a full bar, & it will usually stay open late if there's sufficient custom. *US$2–10.* **$$$**

✖ **Flor de Rosa** ⊕ 17.00–midnight Mon–Sat. This Italian restaurant diagonally opposite the hospital serves great pasta dishes & seafood grills. Eat downstairs & enjoy the simple but stylish décor, or better still grab a rooftop table & soak up the sea breeze, mosque chants & nocturnal gossip drifting up from the streets. *US$6–8.* **$$**

✖ **Karibu** m 84 380 2518; ⊕ 11.00–15.00 & 18.00–21.00 Tue–Sun. A Portuguese-fusion seafood-dominated restaurant offering a daily menu of starters, mains & desserts expertly crafted with seasonal local ingredients. *US$3–9.* **$$$**

✖ **O Escondidinho** (page 295) ⊕ 08.00–21.00 daily. On the ground floor of the namesake hotel, this has an excellent terrace-like restaurant facing the swimming pool. *Salads, steaks & prawns are particularly recommended – mains are in the US$6–10 range.* **$$$**

✖ **O Paladar** m 82 455 9850; ⊕ 07.00–17.00 Mon–Fri. Situated at the back of the covered market, this likeable local place is among the cheapest eateries in town, & the freshly prepared food – a varied selection of seafood & chicken dishes – is excellent. Best, however, to order an hour or 2 in advance, or settle in for a bit of a wait. *Mains up to US$6.* **$**

✖ **O Pontão** m 84 763 2211; ⊕ 09.00–22.00 daily, later at w/ends. Halfway down the main pier near the Vasco da Gama statue, this place does a few bar snacks & cold beverages, & it's

arguably got the best view in town. Great place for a sundowner. **$**

✖ **Pousada da Ilha de Mozambique (Hotel Omuhipiti)** [map, page 290] (page 295) ⊕ noon–22.00 daily. The ground-floor restaurant at this stalwart hotel is as formal as it gets on Ilha, & as green (not as in 'eco-friendly', but as in 'somebody really likes the colour green'). *Serves tasty seafood dishes & curries in the US$6–10 range.* **$$$**

✖ **Restaurante Reliquias** Av da República; ⊕ 09.00–22.00 Fri–Wed. This popular eatery is set in an attractively restored old house adorned with assorted flotsam & monochrome photos from the early 20th century. You can eat indoors or in the green garden, which offers views over the water & is very pleasant at lunch. *A varied selection of local dishes, seafood & poultry is served in the US$8–14 range.* **$$$$**

✖ **Rickshaws Café** Rua da Solidariedade; m 82 678 0098; ⊕ 09.00–22.00 Tue–Sun. One of the newest eateries in town, this café offers a tasty menu with views to match, using the freshest of ingredients to make appetising seafood, chicken & meat dishes ranging from light appetisers to full meals. Bruschetta & pizzas are popular picks. *US$4–12.* **$$$**

✖ **Sarah's** m 82 798 2774; ⊕ 08.00–22.00 daily exc Tue, later at w/ends. There's no sign, but this is the middle of the 3 container bars just around the corner from the hospital. Go behind the container & there's a surprisingly stylish seating area, where you can order the house speciality, matapa de siri-siri, which is a matapa recipe unique to Ilha, made with seaweed & cashews. Highly recommended. *US$5–10.* **$$**

♀ **Celda's (Yoyo's)** m 84 877 9015; ⊕ 09.00–22.00 Tue–Sun, later at w/ends. Probably Ilha's most characterful bar, this tiny tavern is unsigned, tucked into a whitewashed building just north of the centre. The playlist is eclectic, the walls are covered in masks, & the whisky selection is ample. **$**

SHOPPING

The covered central market opposite the hospital is a good place to buy fruit and vegetables, while fish and fresh bread are usually on sale at the smaller beachfront market on Rua das Trabalhadores next to the main mosque, and there's Jimmy's Bottle Shop for those seeking to imbibe. It does have to be said that the range here is limited, so serious self-caterers might want to do their shopping in the market in Nampula before they arrive. Shops catering largely to tourists include the following:

Kissambi Art Shop Av da República; ⊕ 08.00–18.00 Tue–Sun; m 84 693 9895; e sugarcia.svg@gmail.com; ◻ Kissambi-Art-Designer-234136776786162. For tailor-made, fashionable capulana clothing, this is the shop to visit.
Missanga Craft Shop Av da República; ⊕ 08.30–17.30 Tue–Sun. This well-stocked craft shop, a couple of doors down from Kissambi Art

Shop, has a nice selection of above-avg-quality Makonde carvings, basketwork, fabrics, wooden chests & other locally crafted goods.
Orera Orera Av dos Heróis; m 82 601 3440. Affiliated to Maputo's Centro de Estudos e Desenvolvimento de Artesanato (CEDARTE), this small shop sells a range of brightly coloured African-style clothes & fabrics.

OTHER PRACTICALITIES

BANKS AND ATMS There is a BIM Millennium branch with an ATM on the corner of Travessa da Saudade and Avenida Amilcar Cabral.

BOAT TRIPS Ilha Blue (m 84 124 7161/387 2168; e info@ilhablue.com; w ilhablue. com) offers dhow trips to the mainland and other islands and whale watching in season, as well as kayak trips, at a cost of around US$40 per person for a day trip, and US$300 per day for custom adventures; check its informative website for details. For cheaper transfers in local boats, a useful contact is Genito (Harry Potter) of Magic Tour (page 300).

DIVING AND SNORKELLING There is no dive operation on Ilha following the folding of the long-established Dugong Dive Centre. For snorkelling, contact Ilha Blue (page 300) or Magic Tour (page 300). Diving is now offered by Coral Lodge at Cabaceira Pequena, a short distance by boat from Ilha (page 306).

HAIR AND BEAUTY Try Cabeleireira Hair Salon on Avenida dos Heróis next to the former Saquina Take-Away (m 82 742 8783), now operating as a bar.

HOSPITAL Situated in the magnificent old colonial administration building on Rua da Saúde (✆ 266 10173).

INTERNET There is a TDM office with internet access on Avenida dos Continuadores just along from the Palace Museum, or Vila do Milenio (⊕ 08.00–17.30 Mon–Fri) near the police station has lots of computers as well. There's Wi-Fi at Ruby Backpackers.

POLICE The police station is in the colonnaded building at the top of Praça João Belo.

POST OFFICE On the corner of Travessa do Teatro and Rua Pedro Alvares Cabral.

TOURS In addition to boat and kayak excursions, **Ilha Blue** (page 299) has a fantastic set of cultural tours, all led by locals. There's one where you'll hunt for *missanga*, the ancient bits of porcelain, beads and metals that wash up on Ilha's shores from long-ago shipwrecks, and another where you'll head into the alleys of macuti town and trace the history of *capulana* cloth with a local designer. They've also got bicycles for rent if you'd rather explore the island on your own. Another local tour operator is Genito, or Harry Potter as he is locally known, with **Magic Tour** (m *84 546 4817/059 8731;* e *genitoharrypottermagictour@gmail. com;* w *genitomagictour.com;* f *genitomagictour*). Offering guided walking tours, boat trips, local fishing trips, motorbike tours and camping excursions alongside cooking, language and dance lessons, Genito comes highly recommended.

EXPLORING ILHA DE MOÇAMBIQUE

The island can be divided into two parts: the **stone town** to the northeast and the **macuti (reed-hut) zone** to the southwest. Most of the historical buildings lie in the old town, which can be divided into several sectors, of which the oldest lies in the extreme northeast, under the protective cast of the Fortaleza de São Sebastião, the only survivor of the Dutch sieges of 1607–08. A map dating to 1754 shows that by then the developed part of the town comprised a cluster of perhaps 50 buildings, including the former Jesuit Convent of São Paulo, the neighbouring Church of the Misericórdia and São Domingo's Convent (now the courthouse), on the northwest shore between the present-day TDM Building and the police station.

The road layout of the 1752 map is still clearly recognisable, with the open space in front of the present-day Restaurante Reliquias being the former Largo do Pelourinho (Pillory Square), where a whipping post then stood. By 1800, the northwest shore as far south as the present-day hospital had also been developed: the area around the shipping market was lined with granaries and warehouses, and the Largo do Pelourinho and market were relocated to the square where the covered market stands today. The macuti town started to take shape in the early 19th century as a disease-ridden slum inhabited by several thousand slaves.

FORTALEZA DE SÃO SEBASTIÃO (⊕ *08.00–16.30 daily; entrance fee of US$4 foreign tourist (with discounts for residents) to be paid at the Palace Museum; photography permitted*) Dominating the northern tip of the island, the Fortaleza de São Sebastião (Fortress of Saint Sebastian) is arguably the most formidable edifice of its type in Africa. Measuring up to 20m high, it was built of dressed limestone shipped from Lisbon between 1546 and 1583 as a response to the Turkish threat of 1538–53. The shape of the fort has changed little over the intervening centuries, though all but one of the three original entrances, the impressive extant gate beneath the buttress of Santa Barbara, were walled up before 1607. Overall, its condition is remarkably similar to that noted by the English sailor Henry Salt in the 1800s. The fortress was in active use as recently as the liberation war, when it served as a Portuguese barracks.

Aside from the Dutch siege of 1607 (box, page 302), São Sebastião has witnessed several important events in Mozambican history. In February 1618, the acting captain of Moçambique and Sofala was stabbed fatally on the steps of the fort by his eventual successor, a culmination of the ongoing intrigues that surrounded the three-yearly appointment to this most profitable of the various postings available in Portugal's Indian Ocean empire. In 1671, an Omani naval attack on Ilha de Moçambique followed a similar course to the earlier Dutch attacks, as the Omanis occupied the island for several weeks but were unable to drive the Portuguese out

It has an ancient fortress, but a very fine new one is now being built, on which large artillery which we brought from [Portugal] will be mounted. There is a ruined Moorish village. The Portuguese village has about 100 inhabitants, and of people of that country... there are about 200. Different refreshments are sent from gardens on the [mainland] and a certain quantity of orange and lemons. Many deaths take place from the ships that arrive from [Portugal].

Father Monclaro, 1576

I saw lemon, orange and fig trees like those of Portugal... a very good fortress with four bastions against the sea... a customs house that yields 50,000 cruzados a year by the sale of ivory, with which I saw the shores covered, and ambergris and gold. It also has a royal hospital, served by the religious of São João de Deus... to whom the king gives 250 reis a day and clothes and 500 cruzados for expenses... It has a Misericórdia, a collegiate church which they call a cathedral... a parish church of São Sebastião within the fortress, a beautiful chapel of our Lady of Health, and another of São António who protects the health and safety of the Indian ships.

Anonymous Jesuit priest, 1688

There is neither the noise nor bustle of [economic] life... no specific diseases... except ennui. Were I to remain here, I should die of it in three months... There are narrow streets and high houses, the former not remarkable for cleanliness, the latter partly of a dirty yellow colour impaired by neglect and decay. The windows are barred with lattices as if the town abounded in thieves... The exterior [of the Governor's Palace] appears more like an old warehouse than the mansion of the first personage... We were led to it by the clashing of billiard balls and the confused clamour of contending voices, so that we first took it to be a tavern or gambling house. [The macuti town] consists of a line of huts, formed of hurdles or bamboos, fixed in the ground and connected by wicker work, with sod or dry grass for the roofs... It is filled with strong, healthy, active inhabitants whose numerous children... displayed ample proof of health and vivacity.

James Prior, 1812

A beautiful city [of] noble houses, some of them so vast and well constructed they could rival the palaces of large cities.

Bartolomeo dos Mártires, 1822

of the fort – an outcome that had a strong influence on the modern-day boundary between Mozambique and Tanzania.

The fort remains in remarkably good condition, and its wells are still the only source of fresh water on the island. However, it has to be said that recent renovations, undertaken prior to the fortress reopening in mid 2010, seem to have been executed with remarkable architectural insensitivity. Possibly they were required for structural reasons, but the concrete slabs that now form large parts of the roof possess little aesthetic merit. Furthermore, the renovations appear to have been halted without ever being completed (the story we heard locally is that a large portion of the foreign funding was diverted into various officials' pockets), and parts of the fortress compound now look more like a construction site than a historic monument. The effect is exacerbated by the two satellite towers that have been erected right outside the fortress and now dominate the skyline.

Few other buildings have played such a decisive role in shaping the course of a subcontinent's history as the Fortaleza de São Sebastião. On 29 March 1607, nine Dutch ships appeared off the shore of Ilha de Moçambique, causing the Portuguese inhabitants to withdraw to the fort. The Dutch navy landed on the island and occupied it for about a month, but were unable to capture the fort and eventually withdrew on 13 May. Meanwhile, the Portuguese, cloistered within their fortress, survived thanks to the presence of a good well within its walls, and the assistance of their African allies on the mainland, who canoed across to the island at night to drop food and other essential supplies at a point that could not be reached by the larger Dutch boats. A year later, the Dutch returned to Ilha de Moçambique with a formidable fleet of 13 ships carrying 377 guns and 1,840 men. Again the Dutch seized the island, and again, three months after landing, they were forced to withdraw, incapable of capturing the fort.

One can only speculate but, had São Sebastião been a less imposing building, Ilha de Moçambique would almost certainly have fallen into Dutch hands in 1607–08, a power shift that would have had incalculable ramifications on the eventual course of southern African history. By the early 17th century Portugal was a waning naval power, and it seems improbable that it would have retained a significant influence in the region had it been evacuated from its headquarters at Ilha de Moçambique. Furthermore, had the Dutch East India Company decided to adopt Ilha de Moçambique as a regional base c1607, then it seems unlikely that it would have established the outpost on Table Bay that eventually became Cape Town… in a very real sense the 'Mother City' of South Africa as we know it today.

Protected within the fortress, the **Capela da Nossa Senhora do Baluarte** (Chapel of Our Lady of the Ramparts) is the island's only other 16th-century building to have survived to the present day. Built in 1522, this small church is the oldest standing European building in the southern hemisphere. The main body of the church has changed little since the 16th century, though the covered porch and pulpit both date to the 18th century. The eminent archaeologist James Kirkman, writing in the 1960s, remarked that Senhora do Baluarte is notable for its several gargoyles as well as a Manueline frieze around the roof and the royal arms of Portugal situated above the entrance. The first two are still clearly visible, but the coat of arms, while still there, has been very badly damaged by the passage of time. On the floor of the church, a stone plaque marks the tomb of the Portuguese Bishop of Japan, who was buried there in 1588. There are several other graves of bishops outside the main building, dating from between 1592 and 1969. Several human bones of unknown origin are stored in a box in the church.

PALACE OF SÃO PAULO (PALACE MUSEUM) (\ 267 10047; ⊕ 08.00–16.30 daily; entrance US$2 non-residents; knowledgeable guides available; photography restricted) When the Dutch evacuated Ilha de Moçambique in 1607, they burned the old town to the ground, destroying the Muslim quarter as well as two churches and the hospital, and sparing only the Portuguese-held fortress of São Sebastião and the church that is protected within its walls. In 1671, the Omani Arabs again razed much of the old town following their short-lived occupation of the island, for which reason the only extant 17th-century building in the old town is the former Jesuit College of São Paulo.

Situated near the jetty, the college was erected in 1619 on the site of the small Fortress of São Gabriel built to protect the first Portuguese trading post established here in 1507. A large red building with an impressive spire, it served as a college until 1759, when the Jesuits were banned from Portugal and its overseas territories. Two years later, following the decision to make the Viceroy of Moçambique independent of Goa, the building was converted to a governor's palace. It retained that role until the relocation of the capital to Lourenço Marques in 1898, after which it served as the official residence of the District Governor right up until 1975. The first indigenous African to sleep in the palace as a guest was reputedly President Hastings Banda of Malawi, back in 1971. The second and last was Samora Machel, who stayed here four years later on his first presidential tour of newly independent Mozambique, and decided it should be reinvented as a museum.

Still a museum today, the former palace is a fascinating place to explore. The original church, which was formally opened in 1640, is worth looking at for its garish pulpit, a cylindrical wooden protrusion decorated with some beautiful carvings of the Apostles, below which is a chaotic assemblage of rather less lovable but arguably more compelling creatures, a mixture of gargoyles, angels and dragons. Also notable are the copper-plate altar and the dozen or so religious paintings that decorate the otherwise bare walls. The courtyard separating the church and the palace also has several large statues, for some reason painted in a rather fetching shade of green.

The interior of the palace is a revelation. The 20-odd rooms are all decorated in period style, allegedly with furniture left behind when the governor moved to Lourenço Marques, though it's perfectly possible that some of it was accumulated more recently (witness the Kenwood Magimix and other state-of-the-art 1970s gadgetry gathering dust in the kitchen). In addition to any number of four-poster beds and antique chairs and tables, most of which are Goan in origin, the rooms are liberally decorated with vases and other porcelain artefacts from China. There is something strange and disorientating about walking from the ostentatious riches of the palace back out into the dusty, run-down alleys of the old town.

MUSEO DE MARINHO (⏲ 08.00–16.30 daily; entrance inc in the ticket for the Palace Museum; page 302) Formerly the Naval Museum but reopened under a new name in August 2009, the Maritime Museum, reached through a door to the right as you leave the Palace Museum, now focuses on a fascinating collection of artefacts recovered from the Espadarte and Nossa Senhora da Consolação, shipwrecked in the waters off Fortaleza de São Sebastião in 1558 and 1608 respectively, and rediscovered in 2001. The displays includes the richest stash of Ming porcelain ever salvaged in Africa, comprising more than 1,500 pieces, many still in mint condition, whose motifs have been dated to the reign of the Chinese emperor Jiajing (1521– 66). Also on display is a hoard of 16th-century gold and silver coins and other material from the two wrecks.

SACRED ART MUSEUM (⏲ 08.00–16.30 daily; entrance inc in the ticket for the Palace Museum; page 302) Situated in the same block as the Palace Museum but entered from around the corner (opposite Café-Bar Âncora d'Ouro), this small museum is housed in a wing of the Church of the Misericórdia, which still opens for Mass on Sunday mornings. The Misericórdia (House of Mercy) was a religious organisation with nominally charitable aims and a gift for raising revenue through bequests and later from a large prazo in Zambézia. The church that houses the Sacred Art Museum served as the island headquarters of the Misericórdia from when it was built in 1700 until the organisation was disbanded in 1915, and the majority of artefacts it contains are the former property of the Church. It might be difficult to get excited about the dozens of statues of saints displayed in the museum, especially after having spent time in the palace next door. The most unusual artefact is a Makonde carving of Jesus. It would be interesting to know when and how this statue was acquired, since it is very different in style and subject from most other Makonde carvings.

OTHER LANDMARKS Aside from the fortress and museums, the old town contains several buildings of considerable antiquity and/or architectural merit – indeed, most houses in this part of town are several hundreds of years old, and many have been restored to something approaching their former glory since the turn of the millennium. A feature of these houses is their homogeneity: over a 400-year period, generation after generation of builders have used the same materials (limestone and wood with lime-treated facades) and very similar construction methods and floor plans to create a distinct architectural style rooted in the Algarve region of southern Portugal, but with Arabian and Indian flourishes.

The **old customs house** on the Praça João Belo has an impressive entrance complete with a couple of anchors and a cannon. There's a rather stylised **statue** of the 15th-century Portuguese navigator **Vasco da Gama** in the Praça da República outside the Palace Museum, while on the east side of the island, about 300m further south, is a similar statue of his approximate contemporary, the poet **Luís Vaz de Camões**, who is regarded as the Portuguese equivalent of Shakespeare (but had no direct links with Mozambique).

A recent addition to the northern waterfront, inaugurated in August 2007, the **Jardim da Memória** (Garden of Remembrance) (*entrance free*) stands next to the old dhow jetty about 800m southwest of the Palace Museum. This small UNESCO-funded garden is the one site on Ilha de Moçambique to pay tribute to the hundreds of thousands of African slaves interred here *en route* to a life of bondage on the sugar plantations of the Mascarenes. The garden hosts a few information boards discussing the slave trade, and a dozen or so statues of human figures in ethnic style. Echoing the notorious Gates of No Return that stare out to sea from Cape Coast Castle and Gorée Island (West African sites that had strong links with the transatlantic slave trade), a stark gateway opens out at the seaward end of the garden.

The **macuti (reed) town** that occupies the southwestern part if the island is inherently less interesting than the grandiose old town in architectural terms, though it does possess more of a bustling lived-in quality. Predominantly Muslim today, this part of town is scattered with several **mosques**, the most important of which lies on the border of the old town opposite the Pátio dos Quintalinhos. Next to the mosque is the main **fishing beach**: here you can watch dhows launch and return from fishing expeditions, or buy a fresh catch in the market.

A block inland from this beach, arguably the single most imposing building on the island is the **hospital**, housed in a large and very grand whitewashed 18th-century building that once served as the administrative headquarters of the colonial government. Opposite this, the **Igreja de Nossa Senhora da Saúde** (Church of Our Lady of Health) is the third-oldest building in Mozambique, built in 1633 as part of the then rather isolated Convento-Hospital de João de Deus, but extensively renovated in 1801, which makes it difficult to say how much of the original church is intact.

One important historical landmark in this part of town is the whitewashed **Fortim-Igreja de Santo António**, which has stood on a palm-covered peninsula on the widest part of the island since before 1754. On the beach in front of this church,

A TELLING TABLEAU

One of the most remarkable artefacts in the Palace Museum is the large tableau that hangs in the banquet hall, a depiction of one of the shipwrecks which, in the 16th century alone, stranded or killed many thousands of Portuguese along the east coast of Africa. The right-hand side of the tableau depicts a ship swirling upward through the clouds, while on the beach below a solitary grey-bearded mariner, the picture of thirst and exhaustion, is desperately dragging his tired limbs towards shade. In the left half of the tableau, a group of semi-naked Portuguese maidens sits in a huddle below the trees, subjected to the surreptitious scrutiny of two Africans whose expression is open to interpretation: does it signify innocent curiosity, recognition of an easy meal or wide-eyed lust?

Assuming this tableau is of some antiquity, it pays resonant testament to the fears, prejudices and bravery of these first Europeans to settle in East Africa, one that is somehow made more vivid by its touches of the fantastic: the line of wooden crosses erected on the beach below the airborne ship, or the manner in which the maidens' breasts are spared the immodest realism of nipples and dangle unnaturally from below their armpits. For all the architectural prowess of Ilha de Moçambique's old buildings, it is this solitary tableau that offers the one real glimpse into the psyche of their constructors: pale, God-fearing immigrants who, for all their cruelty, greed and arrogance, had more than enough demons to feed their nightmares.

shipbuilders still practised the craft for which Ilha de Moçambique was famous even before the Portuguese arrived as recently as the late 1990s, but this no longer seems to be the case – though the open area in front of the church is a popular spot for informal football matches.

On the southern tip of the island, past the bridge to the mainland, the island's **Christian cemetery** is scattered with dozens of elaborate tombstones. The disused church here has a haunting atmosphere, created as much as anything by the psychedelic array of mosses that colour the wall behind the pulpit. Behind it lies the old Hindu crematorium, while the original Muslim cemetery lies a couple of hundred metres to the northeast. Other landmarks in the southwest include the small **Capela de São Francisco Xavier** and the venerable **Ponta da Ilha Well**.

Facing the old cemetery, the **Ilha-Fortim de São Lourenço** consists of a tiny mushroom-shaped coral outcrop that can be reached on foot at low tide. The small island is entirely taken up by a 17th-century fort, now rather overgrown but still in good shape, with several cannons in place. If you want to walk across, check the tides in advance, since the island is accessible by foot for no longer than an hour. Despite the presence of a couple of rusty iron ladders in front of the fort, the best way to climb up to the island is through a gap in the coral overhang, which can be reached by walking around the right side of the island for about 100m. Look out for the many starfish and other marine creatures that inhabit the pools between the two islands at low tide.

MOSSURIL BAY

The mainland opposite Ilha de Moçambique, though relatively little visited by travellers, is well worth exploring. As with the island itself, settlements such as Lumbo, Mossuril, Cabaceira Grande and Cabaceira Pequena are steeped in history, while the sleepy town of Chocas Mar is a gateway to a succession of idyllic beaches running east on either side of the peninsula that terminates 10km further east at the superb Coral Lodge 15.41. Most sites on the mainland can be visited in isolation as a day trip from the island, but it is also worth thinking about dedicating a few days to the area.

GETTING AROUND

By car The easiest way to explore this area is in a private vehicle, following an unsurfaced road (R699) that runs northward from the 45km **EN105** at almost the exact midway point between Monapo and Ilha de Moçambique. From here it is 21km to Mossuril and another 12km to Chocas Mar along a road that can be tackled in pretty much any vehicle.

The Cabaceiras lie to the east of Chocas Mar along a very sandy road that may require a 4x4. It's about 3km from Chocas Mar to the unsignposted junction south to Cabaceira Grande, then another 2km to the village itself, along a dirt track that you shouldn't have any problem navigating if you got as far as the junction. The junction for Cabaceira Pequena is another 5km past this, just before the entrance to Coral Lodge but, although it is only 1.5km from here to the village, the road may be impassable at high tide and will most likely require a 4x4 at other times.

By chapa Using public transport, there are fairly regular chapas between Lumbo (on the mainland opposite Ilha de Moçambique) and Mossuril, or you could hop on any vehicle travelling between Lumbo and Monapo, hop off at the junction, and wait there. Chapas between Mossuril and Chocas Mar are somewhat less frequent, but they do exist. There is no chapa transport from Chocas Mar to the Cabaceiras, but it is possible to catch a cheap public **boat** (an erratic service dependent on tides) across the 5km channel between Ilha de Moçambique and either of the Cabaceiras, or to Mossuril. You could also arrange a more costly private boat transfer through Ruby Backpackers (page 281) or Genito's Campsite (page 308). If you want to spend a night or two in the area, it is only a 3km walk from Cabaceira Pequena to the Carrusca Resort or Genito's Campsite.

🏠 WHERE TO STAY, EAT AND DRINK *Map, opposite*

In addition to the formal options listed below, it is usually quite easy to arrange self-catering accommodation in one of the many private holiday homes dotted around Chocas Mar. Expect to pay around US$60–70 per night for a house; you can contact Genito's Campsite (page 308) for further details.

Exclusive/luxury

🏠 **Coral Lodge 15.41** (10 chalets) ✆266 60003; m 82 902 3612; e info@corallodge1541. com; w corallodge1541.com. Officially opened in Jun 2010, this stunning 5-star lodge sets high standards for the northern Mozambican mainland. The location alone is marvellous, overlooking a quiet creek & a bone-white beach in a private reserve on the far tip of the peninsula east of Chocas Mar. The large thatched chalets have roof fan, 4-poster beds with nets & silent built-in AC, minibar, large sitting area, en-suite bathroom with tub & shower, & simple but stylish décor

with an ethnic feel. Other features inc infinity pool with views across to the Fortaleza de São Sebastião (only 3km distant as the crow flies), a quality seafood restaurant & a health spa using local products, while the dive centre is the only one in this part of Mozambique to offer wreck & reef dives, snorkelling, canoeing, dhow excursions to Ilha de Moçambique & historic walks to nearby Cabaceira Pequena. *Rates start at US$250 pp sharing inc all meals, house wines & most other drinks, & all non-motorised activities & tours.* **$$$$**

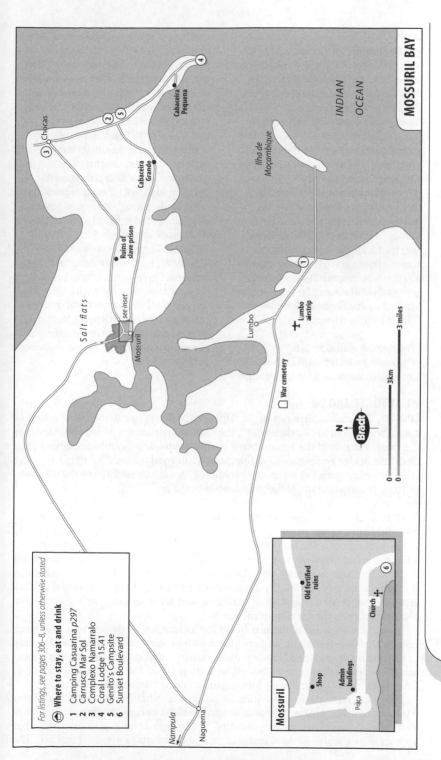

MOSSURIL BAY

For listings, see pages 306–8, unless otherwise stated

Where to stay, eat and drink
1. Camping Casuarina *p297*
2. Carrusca Mar Sol
3. Complexo Namarralo
4. Coral Lodge 15.41
5. Genito's Campsite
6. Sunset Boulevard

Nampula

Naguema

Salt flats

see inset

Ruins of slave prison

Mossuril

Chocas

Cabaceira Grande

Cabaceira Pequena

Lumbo

Lumbo airstrip

War cemetery

Ilha de Moçambique

INDIAN OCEAN

N

Bradt

0 ___ 3km
0 ___ 3 miles

Mossuril

Old fortified ruins

Shop

Admin buildings

Praça

Church

Budget

⌂ **Carrusca Mar Sol** (7 units) ☎262 13302; m 82 516 0173 or 84 814 8654; e anibalcarrusca@ hotmail.com. Situated 4km east of Chocas Mar along the road towards Cabaceira Pequena, this wonderful retreat has an idyllic location on a sandy rise overlooking a lovely white beach, a highly praised seafood restaurant, & the choice of small houses sleeping 2 or larger houses sleeping 4, the latter with AC, nets, barbecue area & balcony with hammocks. Camping is permitted. **$$**

⌂ **Complexo Namarralo** (8 rooms) ☎256 60049; m 82 673 0590 or 84 618 1815. This peaceful complex is situated in Chocas Mar about 100m to the left of the main roundabout as you enter town, & a similar distance from the sea. Accommodation is in simple thatched rondavels with twin beds, en-suite hot shower & screened private balcony with seating. The terrace restaurant has a seafood-dominated menu with most dishes falling in the US$6–8 range. **$$**

Shoestring and camping

⌂ **Sunset Boulevard** m 84 299 5697; e info@hotelsunsetboulevard.com or lisadeteran@ gmail.com; w hotelsunsetboulevard.com. The only accommodation in Mossuril, this community-run guesthouse stands in 3ha of gardens about 200m from the sea. To get here, follow the main road into Mossuril to where it terminates at a roundabout, turn left next to the district government office & continue for about 800m passing a church to your right. Most of the staff graduated at the College of Tourism here, so service is slicker than you might expect. The restaurant has a reputation for good seafood, Macua dance performances can be arranged with notice, & accommodation is in simple but clean rooms, some en suite & others using common bucket showers & toilets. *US$22/20 dbl shared ablutions/en suite.* **$**

▲ **Genito's Campsite** (1 room) m 84 546 4817/059 8731; e genitoharrypottermagictour@ gmail.com. Situated next to Carrusca Mar Sol & still in the development phase, this consists of 1 very basic reed hut with sandy floor & dorm beds, & a campsite. The location is great & food can be arranged on demand. It's advisable to make contact in advance. *US$5 pp camping; slightly more for the room.* **$**

WHAT TO SEE AND DO

Lumbo The coastal terminus of the railway to Malawi prior to the construction of a new branch line to Nacala in 1947, the scattered settlement of Lumbo stands on the mainland side of the 3.5km motor bridge to Ilha de Moçambique. About 5km from the bridge and signposted along the main road towards Nampula is a war cemetery containing the graves of 80 soldiers killed at Lumbo fighting the Germans in 1918. It is also the site of the only airstrip in the area.

Mossuril This small town on the mainland about 10km northwest of Ilha de Moçambique was the main regional centre of the Muslim-dominated slave trade in the 19th century. The town itself houses few relics of that era, though there are a few discarded cannons on the main roundabout overlooking the mangrove-lined bay, and the large church about 500m to the east certainly looks like it was built in the 19th century or earlier. The coast around Mossuril, though not as beautiful as around Chocas Mar, is also quite attractive, and some striking salt flats flank the road as you enter the town from the north.

Mossuril is the home of **Belmoz** (m *84 266 3934;* e *belmoz@gmail.com;* w *belmoz. com*), a unique eco-friendly Belgian-Mozambican enterprise that produces a variety of organic products (fruit brandies, aloe cosmetics and digestives, etc) using local materials. Its products can be bought at a shop called Heroina in Mossuril or at Missanga Craft Shop on Ilha de Moçambique, and at Nampula Airport.

Two significant slaving-era ruins lie on the right-hand side of the road from Mossuril to Chocas Mar. The first, a fortress-like structure 600m past the main roundabout, comprises a compound of 3–4m-high coral rag walls, with what appears to be a sealed turreted entrance on one corner and a well built inside it. The second and less substantial ruin, situated about 2.5km further towards Chocas Mar, is reputedly the remains of an old slave prison and can be recognised by the twin turrets close to the road.

Chocas Mar This pretty village has an idyllic location on a low coral cliff overlooking a beach as attractive as any in this part of the country. There are lots of private holiday cottages in the village, as well as a *complexo turístico* with rooms and a restaurant, but most travellers head on out of town to Carrusca Mar Sol, 4km east of town, or the stunning Coral Lodge 15.41.

Cabaceira Grande One of the earliest Portuguese settlements on the Mozambican mainland, Cabaceira is the site of what must be the oldest actively used church in sub-Saharan Africa, the well-preserved Nossa Senhora dos Remédios, constructed in 1579 for Pedro de Castro, the Captain of Sofala and Moçambique, which still hosts occasional services today. It is a rather bizarre apparition, standing perhaps 12m tall in buttressed isolation on the edge of this mangrove-lined backwater, and arguably of greater note for its antiquity than any great architectural merit, though the heavy wooden Goan-style door is very impressive and there is a gold-flecked altar similar to that in the church attached to the island's Palace Museum.

Also of interest is the old **Governor's Palace**, reputedly built in the early 19th century as a summer retreat for the island's governor. Behind this, the former **Naval Academy of Cabaceira** was restored as a Colégio de Turismo e Agricultura, founded by author Lisa St Aubin de Terán in 2004. The building has now been handed back to the government, but the college, now operating at Sunset Boulevard in Mossuril, continues to train up to 40 locals annually to work in the tourist sector (see w teranfoundation.org, or get hold of her book *Mozambique Mysteries*).

Cabaceira Pequena Local legend has it that this tiny palm-fringed village, situated on a marshy spit about 3km north of Ilha de Moçambique, is where Vasco da Gama landed in 1498, and that it was also the capital of the mysterious Moussa Ben Mbiki, after whom Mozambique is named. True or not, Cabaceira Pequena is clearly a settlement of genuine antiquity, scattered with the ruins of Swahili-style houses that reputedly pre-date the Portuguese occupation, while its main well – still in use today – is said to be the very same one that da Gama drank from all those centuries ago.

NACALA

Some 70km north of Ilha de Moçambique as the crow flies, Nacala is a purpose-built port town situated at the southern end of Fernão Veloso Bay, which is the deepest natural harbour along the east coast of Africa. The construction of Nacala in 1947, and simultaneous opening of a new rail link to the 900km line through Nampula to Malawi, sealed the declining fortunes of Ilha de Moçambique by diverting the majority of oceanic and terrestrial transport away from the old capital. The importance of Nacala extends beyond Mozambique to Malawi and Zambia, which made extensive use of the so-called Nacala Corridor prior to the collapse of apartheid in 1994, and effectively bankrolled its maintenance during that period.

Now operated by a multi-national consortium with US, South African and Portuguese investors, Nacala is the third-busiest port in Mozambique, handling about 200 cargo ships annually. It is also the site of several manufacturing concerns, including a large cement factory, and its significance will most likely be boosted when the recently privatised and expanded airport outside town starts to receive international flights. One result of all this activity is that the town has grown immensely since its foundation: with a population estimated at 244,000 it is now the country's seventh largest.

For all that, Nacala is of little interest to travellers, certainly by comparison with Ilha de Moçambique, and this is reflected in the rather poor (though growing) selection of places to stay and eat in town. For adventurous travellers, a possible goal for an excursion would be the tiny island of Somana, a few hundred metres offshore near the entrance of Nacala Bay, which supports one of the few remaining pre-Portuguese Swahili ruins in Mozambique, comprising the coral walls of a merchant's dwelling and an associated cistern. A far more enticing prospect than Nacala itself is Fernão Veloso, a short drive out of town and a very attractive area for beach and watersports enthusiasts; the protected deep bay is perfect for snorkelling and diving, providing a tempting weekend getaway spot for residents of Nampula.

GETTING THERE AND AWAY

By car Nacala and Nampula are connected by the surfaced eastern 200km of the **EN8** (EN1/N12), a good road that can be covered in 2 hours or so.

By chapa There are regular chapas between Nacala and Nampula, and less frequent ones between Nacala and Ilha de Moçambique. They leave from outside the TDM office in the Cidade Baixa and outside the petrol stations in the Cidade Alta (below). If you're heading to Fernão Veloso, then you may be able to get a chapa from the TDM office, but your best bet is to head to the market and look there; the journey takes around 45 minutes and costs US$0.50.

By train The rail link between Nampula and Nacala has been refurbished in anticipation of increased freight traffic, but no passenger services run along the line.

By air The planned international airport outside town should open to scheduled international flights during the lifespan of this edition, though it's been delayed before. There are **LAM** (w *lam.co.mz*) flights from Maputo three times a week.

ORIENTATION The town has a split personality: the main residential area, known as Cidade Alta (uptown) and made up of a mixture of mud huts with some concrete buildings, is on top of the hill overlooking the bay, while the Cidade Baixa (downtown) is a more business-oriented concrete town near the docks at the bottom of the hill. The two are linked by a long curving avenue. Chapas around town seem to follow a loop from the TDM office in Baixa, up the avenue, around the market in Alta, back to the petrol stations and then back down the avenue again.

 WHERE TO STAY *Map, opposite*
If you are stuck for budget accommodation in town, the choice is between the **Residencial Canal** and **Residencial Bella Vista**, both of which are tucked away in the Cidade Alta and have rooms for around US$40.

Upmarket
Afrin Nacala Hotel (24 rooms) ✆265 26500; m 82 000 8009 or 84 336 6000; e nacala. reservas@afrinhotels.co.mz; w afrin-hotels.com. Under the same ownership as the Afrin Prestige in Maputo, this business hotel provides modern tiled rooms with all the facilities you would expect. Rooms are bright & comfortable, with flat-screen TV, writing desk, kettle & Wi-Fi. There's a slick business centre & lounge with classic photos of Mozambique on the walls, but no restaurant. *US$75/85 sgl/dbl B&B.* **$$$**

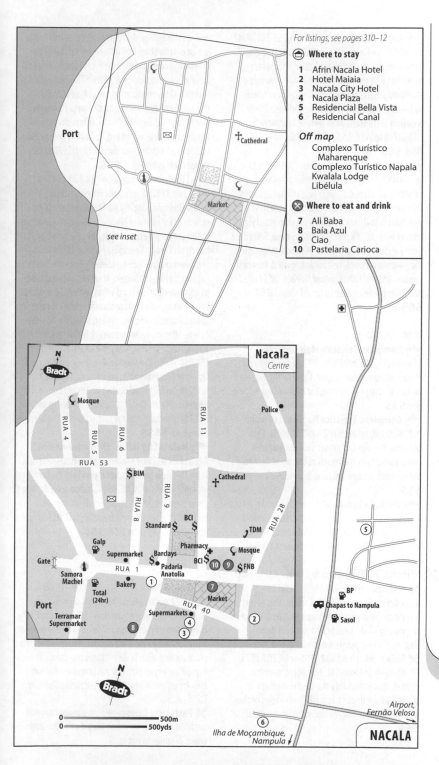

For listings, see pages 310–12

⌂ Where to stay

1 Afrin Nacala Hotel
2 Hotel Maiaia
3 Nacala City Hotel
4 Nacala Plaza
5 Residencial Bella Vista
6 Residencial Canal

Off map
Complexo Turístico
  Maharenque
Complexo Turístico Napala
Kwalala Lodge
Libélula

✖ Where to eat and drink

7 Ali Baba
8 Baía Azul
9 Ciao
10 Pastelaria Carioca

Nacala
Centre

Mosque

Police

RUA 4
RUA 5
RUA 6
RUA 53
RUA 11
RUA 9
RUA 8

BIM

Cathedral

Standard

BCI

TDM

RUA 28

Galp

Pharmacy

Mosque

Supermarket

Barclays

BCI

Gate

Padaria
Anatolia

FNB

Samora
Machel

RUA 1

Bakery

Total
(24hr)

1

Market

7

Port

RUA 40

Terramar
Supermarket

Supermarkets

4

8

3

2

BP

Chapas to Nampula

Sasol

5

Airport,
Fernão Velosa

6

Ilha de Moçambique,
Nampula

NACALA

0 ——— 500m
0 ——— 500yds

🏠 **Hotel Maiaia** (30 rooms) 📞265 26827/42; 📱 82 601 5440; e reservas.hotelmaiaia@gmail. com or maiaia.hotel@gmail.com. This central hotel has lost the bit of lustre it had in terms of standard when compared with the new hotels in Nacala. However, rooms are comfortable & a decent restaurant with terrace is attached. *US$62/70 sgl/dbl; US$78/84 sgl/dbl suite; all rates B&B.* **$$$**

🏠 **Nacala Plaza** (41 rooms) 📞265 26021; 📱 84 453 7686; e reservas@nacalaplaza.com or info@nacalaplaza.com; w nacalaplaza.com. Opened in 2015, Nacala's premier hotel has chic, spacious & stylishly appointed business-style rooms with AC, TV, Wi-Fi, writing desk & kettle. Some rooms have a private veranda. Amenities inc swimming pool, restaurant, gym & business centre. *US$99/107 standard sgl/dbl, US$119–240 dbl villa, prime or exec suite; all rooms B&B.* **$$$$**

Mid range

🏠 **Complexo Turístico Maharenque** (7 rooms) 📞265 20737; 📱 82 322 6551; e ctnherenque@tdm.co.mz. Close to the Napala (see next entry) & very similar in standard. *US$84 dbl.* **$$$**

🏠 **Complexo Turístico Napala** (14 rooms) 📞265 20608; 📱 82 601 2760/322 6551. This pleasant enough but rather soulless complex is situated above the beach at the tip of Fernão Veloso with accommodation in rondavels with AC. **$$$**

🏠 **Kwalala Lodge** (14 rooms) Fernão Veloso Bay; 📱 82 310 7040 or 84 815 4582; e info@ kwalala-lodges.com; w kwalala-lodges.com. Home to the Thirsty Whale Restaurant & Bar, as

well as the Pelago Adventure Centre, this lodge is a one-stop shop like its neighbour, Libélula. En-suite stone chalets & self-catering houses all have a veranda, fridge & kettle. The restaurant serves a tasty menu with meat & seafood at the forefront & homemade desserts to finish. The Pelago Adventure Centre offers diving, kayaking, whale watching, fishing & snorkelling. *US$90/120 sgl/dbl standard B&B; US$100/150 sgl/dbl self-catering.* **$$$$**

🏠 **Libélula** (6 rooms) 📱 84 220 7343 or 86 788 3792; e info@divelibelula.com; w divelibelula.com. By far the nicest place to stay in the vicinity of Nacala is this dive-oriented lodge set on an escarpment above a small private beach on Fernão Veloso Bay about 10km from the town centre. Run by friendly English-South African owner-managers, it offers a varied range of accommodation from villas with AC & rooftop terraces to stone cottages, dormitories & camping space. Facilities inc swimming pool, on-site dive centre offering various snorkel & dive packages, a restaurant serving tasty meals for around US$8, DSTV in the lounge, & a book exchange. Using public transport, you'll need to walk the last 2km of dirt road or ring in advance for a lift from Nacala. *US$90/150 sgl/dbl terrace room; US$75/110 stone cottage dbl; US$230 family room (sleeps 4).* **$$$$**

🏠 **Nacala City Hotel** (34 rooms) 📱 82 620 4278 or 84 912 8043; e nacala.city.hotel@gmail. com. This new business hotel provides modern en-suite rooms with AC, DSTV, fridge & Wi-Fi. Don't come here expecting inspiring views, but it's a comfortable set-up with friendly staff. *US$70 sgl/ dbl/twin, US$85 suite; B&B.* **$$$**

✖ WHERE TO EAT AND DRINK *Map, page 311*

✖ **Ali Baba** 📱 82 679 6661; ⏲ 08.00–11.00 daily. Across from Pastelaria Carioca, this eatery has a wide range of snacks & mains inc pizza, burgers, & a variety of chicken, beef & seafood dishes. *Snacks US$2–4; pizzas & mains US$4–8.* **$$**

✖ **Baía Azul** 📱 82 302 4995 or 84 207 1873; ⏲ 07.30–late Mon–Sat. Just down near the market, this is probably the best restaurant in town. Sadly it doesn't actually have views of the bay, but there is a dance floor. *Mains around US$8.* **$$$**

✖ **Ciao** 📱 86 492 5686; ⏲ 11.00–15.00 & 18.00–22.00 Tue–Sun. There's no sign posted, but this casual spot is just downhill from the FNB bank. Most of the seating is on an outdoor terrace with flat-screen TV, & it's almost certainly the only place around with bruschetta on the menu. There's a good variety of pizzas & pasta dishes, & a full bar. *Appetisers & snacks US$2–4; pizzas & mains US$6–8.* **$$**

✖ **Pastelaria Carioca** Has the usual range of pastries & drinks, although they don't have any chairs & tables to eat at. **$**

OTHER PRACTICALITIES

Banks Most banks, all of them with ATMs, are represented on or near Rua 1, but you'll find BIM Millennium a block back from the main drag on Rua 53.

Hospital Off the main road between the Alta and Baixa parts of the town (*265 20880*).

Internet At the time of writing, there is no functioning internet café but most of the hotels offer free Wi-Fi or have a business centre for guests.

Shopping The market itself is good for fruit and vegetables, and there are several grocery shops running down the main road to the dock. The **Terramar Supermarket** has a decent selection.

UPDATES WEBSITE

You can post your comments and recommendations, and read the latest feedback and updates from other readers online at **w** bradtupdates.com/mozambique.

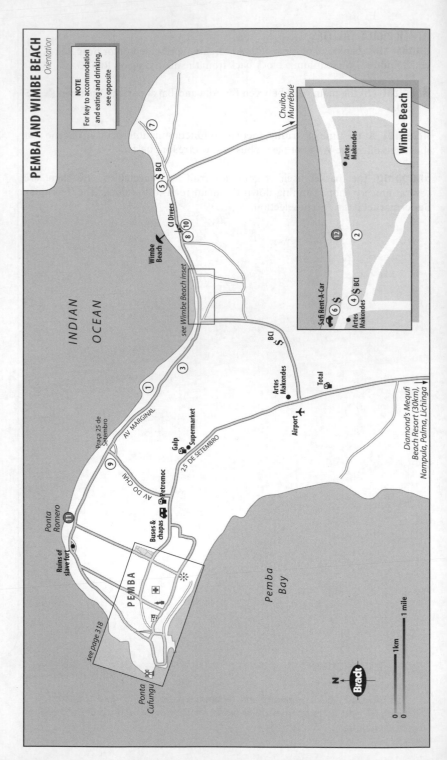

PEMBA AND WIMBE BEACH

Orientation

NOTE
For key to accommodation and eating and drinking, see opposite

INDIAN OCEAN

Wimbe Beach

see Wimbe Beach inset

Chuiba, Murrébué

5 $ BCI

CI Divers

8 10

3

1

Praça 25 de Setembro

AV MARGINAL

9

Ponta Romero

Ruins of slave fort

see page 318

PEMBA

Buses & chapas

Petromoc

Galp

Supermarket

25 DE SETEMBRO

Artes Makondes

BCI $

Total

Airport

Diamond's Mequfi Beach Resort (30km), Nampula, Palma, Lichinga

Pemba Bay

Ponta Cufungu

N

Bradt

0 1km
0 1 mile

Wimbe Beach

Artes Makondes

12

2

Safi Rent-A-Car

6 $

4 $ BCI

Artes Makondes

18

Pemba and the Northeast

Pemba is the capital of Cabo Delgado ('Thin Cape'), Mozambique's most northeasterly province, bounded by Tanzania to the north, a long Indian Ocean coastline to the east, the Lúrio River to the south and Niassa Province to the west. The most important Mozambican port north of Nacala, Pemba is also the site of an international airport with good connections to East and southern Africa, and acts as the nerve centre for Mozambique's burgeoning gas industry. While Pemba is significant as a travel hub, however, and pleasant enough as Mozambican towns go, the greater attraction for most visitors is the surrounding Pemba Bay, where beaches such as Wimbe and Murrébué offer a good range of marine activities, including diving, snorkelling, kitesurfing and seasonal whale watching. Further afield, Pemba is also the usual springboard for fly-in safaris to the Niassa Reserve (pages 366–73) in the province of the same name, and the Quirimbas Archipelago (pages 333–50), site of the historic town of Ibo and some of the country's finest beach lodges.

Few people explore the Cabo Delgado mainland beyond Pemba unless they are in transit somewhere further afield. Montepuez, for instance, is of interest solely as the starting point of the tough road crossing west to Lichinga via Marrupa. The attractive small ports of Mocímboa da Praia and Palma lie along the coastal overland route north to Mtwara in southeast Tanzania. And Mueda, the unofficial capital of the Makonde Plateau, a relatively cool highland area inhabited by the Makonde people, is the last substantial Mozambican town along the bridged inland route to Newala in the same country.

The main ethnic groups in Cabo Delgado Province are the Makonde, the Macua and the Mwani, and the total population is now approaching the two million mark.

PEMBA

This attractive old port is situated on the northwest tip of the peninsula that forms the southern entrance to Pemba Bay. The town itself is of less interest than its location, a large, deep, semi-enclosed natural harbour on a stretch

---

PEMBA AND WIMBE BEACH
For listings, see pages 319–21

Where to stay

1 Avani Pemba Beach Hotel & Spa
2 Complexo Turístico Caracol
3 Hotel Sarima
4 Hotel Wimbi Sun
5 Kauri Resort
6 The Nautilus
7 Pemba Magic Lodge
   Pemba Magic Lodge
   (Russell's Place) (see 7)
8 Pieter's Place
9 Raphael's
10 Residencial Reggio Emilia

Off map

Chuíba Bay Lodge
Diamonds Mequfi Beach Resort
Il Pirata
Nzuwa Lodge
Ulala Lodge

Where to eat and drink

Clube Naval (see 1)
11 Esplanada Marginal
12 Pemba Dolphin
   Restaurant Quirimbas (see 1)

In Pemba, Ibo and elsewhere in Cabo Delgado, you'll frequently see Macua women wandering around with what appear to be white masks, the result of plastering their faces with *musiro*, a paste created by grinding the bark of the *Olax dissitiflora* tree in water. Unlike adornments in many other parts of Africa, these masks have no ritual significance. The white paste is merely a skin softener, serving a similar purpose to the face masks used in private by many Western women, but also protecting the skin against the sun when working outdoors. It is conventional for a bride to apply musiro to her entire body before her wedding, and married women sometimes wear it to demonstrate their status, especially when their husband is away for a long period. Interestingly, there's a similar custom in the Comoros Islands, 200km away in the Indian Ocean.

of coast renowned for its wide, sandy and clean palm-lined beaches, protected by a coral reef that guarantees safe swimming as well as good snorkelling. The area's enormous potential as a tourist resort has been partially realised in recent years, but by most standards it remains somewhat off the beaten track for tourists, though it now hosts a sizeable contingent of foreigners involved in offshore gas field development.

Pemba is a town of several parts. The modern CBD, focused on the junction of Avenida 25 de Setembro and Avenida Eduardo Mondlane, is undeniably on the bland side, but well equipped with shops, banks and restaurants. About 500m west of this, adjacent to the port, the old colonial town centre comprises a small grid of pot-holed roads lined with some run-down but mostly still attractive colonial buildings. Altogether different in character, running northward from Avenida 25 de Setembro, the neat reed-hut village called Paquitequete sprawls across an area of sandy ground that sometimes floods at high tide.

Facing seaward from the entrance of Pemba Bay, about 5km east of the town centre, is Wimbe (or Wimbi) Beach. While it was once a separate entity, these days Wimbe is linked to Pemba by a near-continuous belt of suburbia. A tourist resort in the colonial era, it never entirely shut down even during the civil war, and in the past few years has enjoyed a genuine resurgence, so that the waterfront is now lined with small hotels, restaurants, dive shops and other tourist-oriented facilities. The beach itself is very pleasant and can be quite busy during the weekends – refreshingly it's not frequented just by expats, but is one of the few places in the country where Mozambican tourists can be seen in large numbers. For those seeking a quieter beach experience, Murrébué, about 12km out of town, is currently a hot spot of low-key tourist development.

The best time to visit Pemba is from April to October, when the cooling trade winds blow. In the rainy season, the monsoon blows from the northeast, which can make the beach very unpleasant. Pemba is the most easterly place using Central African Time (the same as South Africa) so daybreak is very early (04.15 in midsummer) and the sun sets before 18.00 most of the year.

HISTORY Little information is available about Pemba Bay prior to the 20th century. The ruins of an Arabic-style fortress on Ponta Romero, at the north end of the reed town, are said to be a relict of an early 19th-century slave-trade depot. This fort, presumably, was no longer operational by 1856, when Portugal granted land

CASHEW APPLES

Cashew nuts are widely available and cheap throughout Mozambique, but Pemba is a good place to look out for the same tree's fruit – sometimes known as the cashew apple (*maça do caju*) or by its South American name *marañón*. Shaped like a pear, sweet smelling, and with a yellow or red waxen casing, the fruit is slightly astringent and quite refreshing, though you probably won't want to eat more than one at a sitting. In the spirit of health and safety, it should be noted that the greenish shell of the nut contains a toxin that is a skin irritant, so it's best not to chew that (and if you're allergic to nuts it might be best not to try it at all). In northern Mozambique and southern Tanzania, sun-dried cashew apples reconstituted with water form the basis of a strong liquor known as *gongo* or *aguardente* (firewater).

concessions to 36 settlers in an unsuccessful attempt to establish an agricultural centre on the same site. The modern town was founded in 1904 as an administrative centre for the Niassa Company, and named Porto Amélia after Queen Maria Amélia, a British-born French princess who married the Portuguese king Don Carlos I in 1886 and served as Queen Consort of Portugal for two years between the assassination of her husband in 1908 and the overthrow of the monarchy in 1910.

By the late 1920s the old town centre had more or less taken its present shape, and supported a population of more than 1,500. After the dissolution of the Niassa Company in 1929, Porto Amélia continued to serve as the capital of Cabo Delgado, though it was renamed Pemba after independence in 1975. The town was largely untouched during the liberation war and civil war, despite its strategic location in one of the country's most unsettled provinces, and emerged from the wars looking less run-down than most other Mozambican towns (though it has arguably made up for this in the meantime). Today, it is ranked the tenth-largest town in Mozambique, with an estimated population of 208,000.

GETTING THERE AND AWAY

By air Most international visitors to Pemba arrive at the international airport about 3km from the town centre. **LAM** (w *lam.co.mz*) flies here from Maputo daily, twice weekly from Nampula, and several times a week from Beira. Internationally, LAM flies to Johannesburg daily, to Dar es Salaam twice a week, and to Nairobi several times a week. **Airlink** (w *flyairlink.com*) operates a direct 3-hour flight from Johannesburg to Pemba five days a week. The airport lies on the EN106 (EN1) and, while there aren't any direct chapas as such, any vehicle heading into Pemba town will stop if you flag it down. If you're staying at one of the more expensive hotels, see if they have a pick-up service. Alternatively, taxis to the town centre or Wimbe cost around US$4. The LAM office is on Avenida 25 de Setembro (✆ *272 21251*).

By car Coming from the south, Pemba is 440km from Nampula along the **EN8** and **EN106** (EN1) via Namialo and Metoro. It's good tarmac all the way, and you should get through in about 5 hours in a private vehicle.

By bus, chapa and taxi Leaving Pemba, all **buses** and **chapas** run along Avenida 25 de Setembro from the junction with Avenida Eduardo Mondlane so, if you wait outside the mCel office before 05.00, you should have your choice of buses and chapas heading in the direction you want. There will be direct transport to

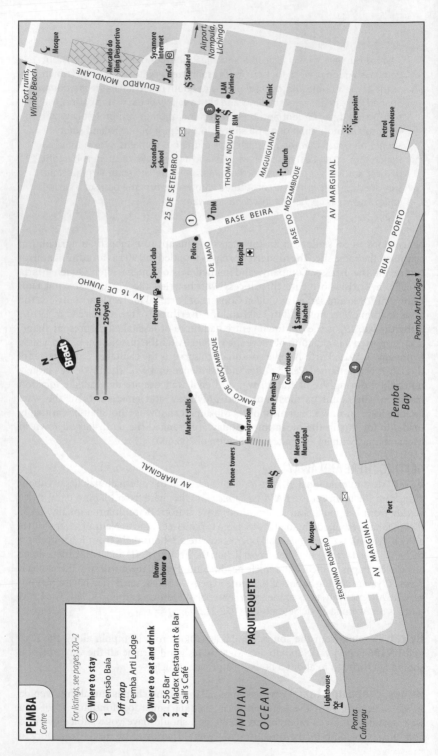

PEMBA
Centre

For listings, see pages 320–2

Where to stay
1 Pensão Baía

Off map
Pemba Arti Lodge

Where to eat and drink
2 556 Bar
3 Madex Restaurant & Bar
4 Sail's Café

INDIAN OCEAN

Ponta Cufungu

Lighthouse

PAQUETEQUETE

Dhow harbour

AV MARGINAL

Mosque

JERONIMO ROMERO

Mercado Municipal

BIM $

Phone towers

Immigration

Market stalls

BANCO DE MOÇAMBIQUE

Cine Pemba

Courthouse

Samora Machel

Port

AV MARGINAL

Pemba Bay

RUA DO PORTO

Pemba Arti Lodge

AV MARGINAL

Petrol warehouse

Viewpoint

Church

MAGUIGUANA

Clinic

LAM (airline)

Standard $

Airport, Nampula, Lichinga

mCel

Sycamore Internet

Mercado do Ring Desportivo

Mosque

Fort ruins; Wimbe Beach

EDUARDO MONDLANE

Pharmacy

BIM $

THOMAS NDUDA

Secondary school

25 DE SETEMBRO

TDM

BASE BEIRA

BASE DO MOÇAMBIQUE

Hospital

1 DE MAIO

Police

Sports club

Petromoc

AV 16 DE JUNHO

N

Bradt

0 250m
0 250yds

318

Mocímboa da Praia, Nampula and Montepuez, while travellers bound for, or coming from, Ilha de Moçambique will need to change vehicles at Namialo. **Nagi Investimentos** (m 86 400 0657/8) buses go directly between Nampula and Mocímboa da Praia without diverting to Pemba, so if you caught one of these you could be dropped off at the Sunate (also called Silva Macua) junction and get a chapa onwards to Pemba without too much trouble.

You could walk between the town centre and Wimbe, but it's a fair old hike and absolutely not recommended after dusk. **Taxis** can be found near the roundabout at the junction of avenidas Eduardo Mondlane and 25 de Setembro. Fares range from US$3 to US$10 depending on where exactly you are headed (Russell's Place is more than twice as far as Pemba Beach Hotel) and time of day (prices rise late at night or early in the morning).

For further details of transport to Montepuez, Mocímboa da Praia and Ibo, see pages 325, 326 and 335 respectively.

WHERE TO STAY *Map, page 314, unless otherwise stated*
Exclusive/luxury
Avani Pemba Beach Hotel & Spa
(179 rooms) Av Marginal; ☏272 21770; m 82 722 1770; e pemba@avanihotels.com; w minorhotels. com/en/avani/pemba. Set in a vast beachfront compound about halfway between the town centre & Wimbe Beach, this 5-star resort is the largest & smartest hotel on this side of Pemba Bay. The architecture displays Arabic & Mediterranean influences, with terracotta buildings laid out spaciously in green palm-studded lawns that lead down to an idyllic beach. Facilities inc world-class spa, 2 swimming pools, 2 restaurants, gym, gift shop, a superb buffet b/fast & free Wi-Fi throughout. Spacious tiled rooms come with king-size bed, AC, DSTV, balcony & large bathroom with separate tub & shower. There's a complex of 82 long-term apartments as well. *US$264/310 sgl/ dbl; US$310/365 sgl/dbl garden room; US$366/430 sgl/dbl ocean room; from US$625 suites; all rates B&B.* $$$$$
Diamonds Mequfi Beach Resort
(50 units) Mecufi Road; m 84 848 4299/313 1314; e info.mequfi@diamonds-resorts.com; w mequfibeach.diamondsresort.com/eng. This new luxury resort about 30km from Pemba offers de luxe beachfront rooms with dbl or twin beds, nets, AC, Wi-Fi, flat-screen TV, sofa, desk, minibar, kettle, private terrace & outdoor shower. There are also spacious suites with separate bedroom, living room, large terrace & 2 bathrooms with open-air showers. Amenities & activities inc spa & wellness centre, 3 restaurants, bar, swimming pool, horseback riding, kitesurfing, kayaking, snorkelling, sailing, bike tours & a range of local excursions. *US$525/630 de luxe room/suite HB, FB rates available.* $$$$$

Upmarket
Chuíba Bay Lodge (6 units); Chuiba; m 82 305 0836/8; e reservations@ chuibabaylodge.com; w chuibabaylodge.com. Set on an exquisite beach just 10mins from Pemba, this boutique lodge offers spacious & tastefully appointed en-suite bungalows with African décor, private patio, AC, minibar, satellite TV & sitting area. There's a gym, 2 swimming pools, lovely gardens & terraces with daybeds. Activities of all sorts can be arranged. *US$200/300 sgl/dbl; B&B.* $$$$
Il Pirata (4 rooms) m 84 456 4450; e info@ murrebue.com or info@kitesurfingmozambique. com; w murrebue.com. Also situated on peaceful Murrébué Beach, this highly praised Italian owner-managed boutique lodge offers the choice of en-suite beach bungalows built entirely from local materials, or a larger stone house set in a private garden above it. The Italian restaurant is one of the best in the vicinity of Pemba. Known as a prime kitesurfing location, lessons, from beginner to expert, are available with prior arrangement. *US$117/170 sgl/dbl beach bungalow; US$128/191 sgl/dbl stone house; all rates FB.* $$$$
Kauri Resort (42 units) ☏272 20936; m 82 151 4222 or 84 023 9882; e reservas@ kauriresort.com; w kauriresort.com. At the far end of Wimbe near the turn-off for Murrébué, this shockingly orange complex sits right on the beach, with long-stay apartments on the other side of the road. Rooms here are more business

18

than resort-like, but they are well appointed & all come with AC & Wi-Fi. There's a terrace restaurant attached with a long Asian menu & a fantastic view. *US$100–250 dbl B&B.* **$$$$**

🏠 **The Nautilus** (21 rooms) Wimbe Beach; 📞272 21407; m 86 922 5146; e reservations@ thenautiluspemba.com; w thenautiluspemba. com. This is the first resort you reach approaching Wimbe Beach from town or the airport &, like most such places in Pemba nowadays, it is aimed primarily at the oil & gas market. Most rooms were booked out long-term when we stopped in but, if you can get one, the newly renovated beach bungalows come with AC, DSTV, Wi-Fi, net, fridge, en-suite hot shower & complimentary laundry. There's a reasonably good on-site restaurant & a swimming pool. *US$152/234 sgl/ dbl; B&B.* **$$$$**

🏠 **Ulala Lodge** (6 rooms, 2 under construction) m 82 741 5104; e contact@ulala-lodge.com; w ulala-lodge.com. Attractively located on sandy Murrébué Beach about 20mins' drive from town, this beachfront lodge offers earthy accommodation in en-suite bungalows with teak decks, macuti thatch roofs, king-size or twin beds with walk-in nets & a private terrace. The beach is ideal for swimming, snorkelling or long walks, & the restaurant serves seafood set menus. To get there follow the EN106 out of town for about 10km then turn left on to the Mecufi road, left again at the blue sign reading 'Distrito de Mecufi', then right at a crossroads with white stones & a street lamp, & left after about 200m at the large driftwood mask after crossing a riverbed. *US$75/85 sgl/dbl bungalow; US$138/149 sgl/dbl stilt bungalow; all rates B&B; HB & FB also available.* **$$$$**

Mid range

🏠 **Complexo Turístico Caracol** (24 units) Wimbe Beach; 📞272 20147; m 82 688 7430; e sulemane65@hotmail.com. This architecturally uninspired double-storey apartment block facing Wimbe Beach has a useful location for beach-lovers & offers a variety of good-value rooms, all clean & tiled with AC, fridge, kettle, TV & en-suite bathroom. *US$50/56 sgl/dbl with veranda; US$60 suite; US$80 2-bedroom apt; all rates B&B.* **$$$**

🏠 **Hotel Wimbi Sun** (56 rooms) 📞272 21946; m 82 318 1300; e bookings@wimbisun.co.mz. Situated diagonally opposite the Nautilus, this

well-run guesthouse-turned-hotel has large en-suite rooms that probably represent the best value on offer at this end of the beach road. *US$80/90 sgl/dbl; B&B.* **$$$**

🏠 **Nzuwa Lodge** (7 units) Murrébué Beach; m 82 730 6365/589 4692; e nzuwalodge@gmail. com or reservations@nzuwa.com; w nzuwa.com. This new eco-friendly lodge sits on a pristine beach & offers en-suite bungalows, vista rooms with stunning views from the veranda, self-catering suites, safari tents & camping. A beach dorm, more bungalows & a pool are in the works. Rooms are fitted with king-size beds, nets & fans. Amenities inc kayaking, a children's playground & a restaurant famed for its burgers, fish & b/fast muffins. *US$100/120 dbl bungalow, US$150 dbl self-catering suite, US$80 dbl vista room; US$20 dbl safari tent; all rates B&B; US$8 pp camping. Expect the dorms to be about US$16.* **$$$**

🏠 **Pemba Arti Lodge** [map, page 318] (11 units) m 84 638 1759/388 3147; e pembaartilodge@gmail.com; w pembaartilodge. com. Situated on the northern shore of Pemba Bay, 15mins by boat from the Pemba Beach Hotel, this boutique lodge is among the most alluring options near Pemba. It is set in a patch of indigenous coastal scrub on a coral cliff overlooking a small private beach whose incline (unlike most in Mozambique) is so steep & well protected you can usually enjoy excellent snorkelling in crystal-clear water right from the shore. There's an open-air restaurant & bar, & the French owner-managers make sure that the food on offer is top notch. Accommodation is in individual villas with thatched roof & verandas overlooking the sea, as well as a block of rooms for backpackers using common showers. There's an on-site dive centre offering a full range of marine activities. *US$100 bungalow dbl; US$35 pp backpacker room; all rates B&B & inc transfers from Pemba.* **$$$**

🏠 **Pieter's Place** (5 rooms, 2 under construction) Wimbe Beach; 📞272 20102; m 82 682 2700; e cidiversmozambique@gmail.com; w pietersdiversplace.co.za. Affiliated to CI Divers & situated next door to Residencial Reggio Emilia, this is basically an extension of the owner's private house, offering accommodation in earthily decorated en-suite rooms with fridge, AC, Wi-Fi & kettle centred on a massive centuries-old baobab tree complete with a tree-house – ideal for sundowners. *US$60–100 dbl.* **$$$**

⌂ **Raphael's Hotel** (84 units) Praça 25 de Setembro; ☎ 272 25555; e info@raphaelshotel.com; w raphaelshotel.com. This new hotel offers business-style accommodation with African décor, & has a swimming pool, gym, spa & restaurant. As a whole, it feels unfinished, but the en-suite rooms are comfortable & have AC, Wi-Fi, DSTV, kettle & writing desk. Apts available. *US$100 dbl or twin.* **$$$**

⌂ **Residencial Reggio Emilia** (12 rooms) Wimbe Beach; ☎ 272 21297; m 82 888 0800/928 5660; e residencial.reggio.emilia@gmail.com; w akeelz.wix.com/residencial-reggio-emilia. Named after a town in northern Italy that supplied aid to the Frelimo during the civil war & run by an Italian agronomist, this agreeable place lies in green gardens just across the road from the beach about 1km past the main cluster of activity on Wimbe. The self-catering accommodation has AC, DSTV, Wi-Fi & en-suite hot shower. B/fast is offered by request at its new on-site restaurant. *US$80 dbl.* **$$$**

Budget

⌂ **Hotel Sarima** (24 rooms) ☎ 210 82387; m 84 712 0066; e hotel.sarima@gmail.com. The simple clean en-suite rooms here are a bit on the small side but have AC, TV, Wi-Fi, fridge & hot water. *US$50–60 dbl.* **$$**

⌂ **Pemba Magic Lodge** (6 rooms) ☎ 272 21429; m 82 686 2730; e pembamagic@gmail.com; w pembamagic.com. Also known as Russell's Place or *campismo* (see below), & the only accommodation on Wimbe Beach that really caters to the budget traveller, with a choice of chalets, dorm beds or camping at the far end of the beach about 3km past the Nautilus. The bar in the middle is one of the most popular w/end watering holes in town, which means that you'll meet a fair old number of people, but it can make for some late (potentially noisy) nights. *US$7/104 sgl/dbl chalet B&B; US$20 pp dorm bed or camping in their tent; US$14 pp camping in your own tent.* **$$$**

Shoestring

⌂ **Pensão Baía** [map, page 318] 289 Rua 1 Maio; m 82 407 4401 or 87 564 3902. This unsignposted place opposite the TDM telecoms centre looks pretty grim, but it's actually relatively comfortable, & there's an outdoor restaurant in front serving all the Mozambican basics. *US$18/24 dbl/trpl using common showers; US$24 en-suite sgl/dbl with AC.* **$**

Camping

⚠ **Pemba Magic Lodge (Russell's Place)** (see above) The best option here for camping. *US$14 pp.* **$**

✖ WHERE TO EAT AND DRINK *Map, page 314, unless otherwise stated*

✖ **556 Bar** [map, page 318] Rua Número 3; ☎ 272 21487; m 82 301 2380 or 84 235 5475 ⊕ kitchen 10.00–22.00 daily, bar until late. On a cliff overlooking the harbour just behind the Casa da Justiça, this South African sports bar serves very good steaks & seafood. Satellite TV makes it a popular venue for big rugby matches & other international fixtures. Comfortable accommodation is also available at an off-site location. *US$10–20.* **$$$$**

✖ **Clube Naval** ☎ 272 21770; ⊕ 11.00–midnight daily. Set in the grounds of the Avani Pemba Beach Hotel, this recently remodelled beachfront restaurant has a breezy open layout & serves good filling seafood & other meals. *From US$8.* **$$$**

✖ **Esplanada Marginal** Av Marginal; m 82 397 2659; ⊕ 11.00–late daily. This beachfront terrace bar-restaurant at the north end of the reed town is a great place for a sundowner & it also serves a no-nonsense menu of seafood & chicken grills. *Around US$5.* **$**

✖ **Madex Restaurant & Bar** [map, page 318] Av Eduardo Mondlane; m 82 666 2370; ⊕ 09.30–22.00 Mon–Sat. Bright & fashionably retro, this old-school restaurant-bar in the town centre is done up in wood & marble, with a full bar & good selection of snacks, sandwiches & typical Mozambican dishes. *Sandwiches US$4, mains US$5–8.* **$$**

✖ **Pemba Dolphin Restaurant** Av Marginal; ☎ 272 20937; m 82 315 4830; ⊕ 07.00–22.30 daily. This popular stilted eatery on Wimbe Beach has a varied menu of food & cocktails, crunchy pizzas, & occasional live music. *Seafood, meat & pizzas for around US$6–12.* **$$$**

✖ **Restaurant Quirimbas** ☎ 272 21770; ⊕ b/fast, lunch & dinner daily. The more formal of the restaurants housed in the Avani Pemba Beach Hotel, this is in the main building. *Serves set menus & light meals in the US$7–12 range.* **$$$**

✖ **Sail's Café** [map, page 318] Rua do Porto; m 84 546 8631; ⊕ 10.00–18.00 Mon–Fri, 08.00–13.00 Sat. A new favourite among expats, this café has a lovely deck overlooking the port & an ever-expanding menu inc coffee, juices, smoothies, pastries, b/fasts, burgers, salads & wraps. Attached is a small but well-stocked supermarket selling imported goods, meats, cheeses & other produce. Self-catering accommodation is available. *US$5–8.* $$

OTHER PRACTICALITIES

Banks and ATMs All the usual banks have branches with ATMs in the town centre, mostly along Avenida Eduardo Mondlane. The only ATMs on Wimbe are the BIM Millennium in the car park of The Nautilus, and BCI at Kauri Resort.

Car rental Kaskazini (page 43) has a fleet of 4x4s available for rental. Alternatively, try Safi Rent-A-Car (m *82 380 8630/684 7770;* e *safirentals@gmail. com;* w *pembarentacar.com*) at Wimbe Beach, or the international agency Sixt (\ *272 21821;* w *sixt.com*), which has an office at the airport.

Hospital On Rua 1 de Maio opposite the police station (\ *272 20348*). The private Cabo Delgado clinic on Rua Modesta Neva is in the old Hotel VIP (\ *272 21447/272/452*).

Internet The best option is Sycamore Internet (\ *272 20749;* m *84 714 3834;* ⊕ *07.00–20.00 Mon–Sat, 07.00–noon Sun*), which stands just east of Avenida Eduardo Mondlane on Avenida 25 de Setembro.

Police The police station is on Rua 1 de Maio on the corner with Rua Base Beira (\ *272 21006*). There is also one next door to the Wimbi Sun.

Post office On Avenida 25 de Setembro, just up from the junction with Avenida Eduardo Mondlane. There is also one just opposite the port entrance.

Shopping The best market for fruit and vegetables is the one just down from the roundabout (known as the **Mercado do Ring Desportivo**), although it is also worth checking out the **Mercado Municipal** in the old town. A well-stocked supermarket is at **Sail's Cafe** on Avenida 25 de Setembro, although there are a number of others dotted around town, notably along Rua Jerónimo Romero in the old town. For art and handicrafts, try **Ujamaa** (e *ujamaa.mz@gmail.com*) at the airport, which has an impressive array of jewellery, carvings and textiles, all made in Cabo Delgado.

Tour operators and travel information An excellent tour operator, booking agent and general travel outlet called **Kaskazini** (m *82 309 6990;* e *info@kaskazini. com;* w *kaskazini.com;* ⊕ *09.00–15.00 Mon–Fri*) is based at the Avani Pemba Beach Hotel (page 319). The knowledgeable hands-on staff can organise most things in Cabo Delgado, Nampula and Niassa provinces, including personalised programmes, accommodation and reliable, safe road transfers.

WHAT TO SEE AND DO The most popular excursion from Pemba is to Ibo and the other islands of the Quirimba Archipelago, which are covered in the next chapter. Other local sites of interest are as follows:

Around town There's not a huge amount to do in Pemba itself, but it is a pleasant town to explore haphazardly. The old quarter, down by the docks, has some

The Makonde of northeastern Mozambique and southeastern Tanzania are among Africa's best-known craftsmen, and their intricate carvings follow a tradition dating back several hundred years. Makonde society is strongly matrilineal, and the carvings in their purest form celebrate a cult of femininity. The carvers are always male and the carvings are mother figures carried for protection. Oral history links the origin of the carving tradition to the Makonde's original appearance on the plateau that bears their name. The progenitor of the first Makonde, so tradition goes, was a genderless being living alone in the bush who one day carved a statue in the shape of a woman, left it outside its hut overnight, and awoke to find it transformed into flesh and blood. The carver, apparently also transformed from his formerly genderless state, married the woman and they conceived a child, which died three days after its birth. They moved to higher ground, and again conceived, and again the child died after three days. When they finally moved to the top of the plateau, the woman gave birth to a child who survived and became the first Makonde.

In their purest form, the intricate, stylised carvings of the Makonde relate to this ancestral cult of womanhood, and are carried only by men, as a good luck charm. Traditional carvings almost always depict a female figure, sometimes surrounded by children. The large demonic masks that are also carved by the Makonde, more so perhaps in Mozambique than in Tanzania, are central to the traditional sindimba stilt dance, which is performed by men and women together. Makonde sculptures were practically unknown outside Tanzania and Mozambique until a carving workshop was established in suburban Dar es Salaam during the 1950s, but today there are also workshops in Nampula and Pemba in Mozambique. Subsequently, like any dynamic art form, Makonde sculpture has been responsive to external influences and subject to changes in fashion, with new styles of carvings becoming increasingly abstract and incorporating wider moral and social themes. Today, the finest examples of the genre fetch prices in excess of US$5,000 from international collectors.

rather dilapidated colonial buildings. The reed huts of Paquitequete also make for interesting meandering, and the beach is lively with kids playing football, though you need to watch your step – hygiene here revolves around the sea. The fishing boats leave from around the lighthouse on Ponta Cufungu, and watching them return in the afternoons with the day's catch is interesting enough. Paquitequete served as an Arab slave-trade depot in the early 19th century, and you can still see the remains of a small fortified hexagonal building – said locally to be an old slave prison – within a traffic island on Avenida Marginal at Ponta Romero, about 250m northwest of the intersection with Avenida Eduardo Mondlane.

The sprawling **Mercado de Mbanguia** is an interesting place to wander around – keep an eye open for the string made by cutting old tyres into short strips – although it's probably best avoided after dark. There is a Makonde carving collective (**Artes Makondes**) along similar lines to that in Nampula, based here, but rather than just the one outlet they have four. The main collective is on Avenida do Chai, but there are other outlets on Avenida 25 de Setembro (next to the Catholic cathedral), at the airport and next to the Caracol on Wimbe Beach.

Marine activities Wimbe is pretty much an archetypal beach resort, where activities all revolve around the sea. The diving off Wimbe is among the best on the East African coast, particularly below about 20m. Snorkelling is also excellent, especially in the Londo area in the north of the bay. You can also hire boats for cruises or fishing trips through Kaskazini (page 43).

CI Divers 272 20102; **m** 82 682 2700; **e** cidiversmozambique@gmail.com; **w** pietersdiversplace.co.za. The oldest of the operators (based here for more than 20 years) & an established PADI training centre complete with swimming pool. It's also active in environmental protection of the area. Single dives from US$70 with PADI Open Water Courses, snorkelling & whale watching available.

Lake Nikwita Situated about 45km north of Pemba, this perennial lake has a scenic location in a patch of coastal bush studded with baobabs, and it supports a varied selection of resident and migratory waterbirds. It's best to get here early if birding is your main interest, and you can also arrange to be poled on to the water in a local dugout canoe. Self-drivers need to head north for about 40km along the Quissanga road to Metugé, from where it is another 5km to the lake along rough tracks (if in doubt, ask locals to point you towards '*lago*').

MONTEPUEZ

Founded in 1904 as a regional administrative centre for the Niassa Company, Montepuez is the second-largest town in Cabo Delgado, with a population of 80,000. It shares its name with a river that rises in the mountains to the east and eventually joins the Indian Ocean just south of Ilha do Ibo, and it is also the name of a form of grey marble found in the region. The town was the setting of a terrible massacre in 2000, after 500 Renamo supporters, demonstrating against what they claimed were fraudulent results in the previous year's elections, occupied the district administration, police station and jail for 24 hours on 9 November. Seven police officers and 14 protesters died in the clash, and the surviving policemen retaliated by detaining all alleged demonstrators on 21 November, and cramming them into a tiny cell where at least 83 people died of asphyxiation. Despite this,

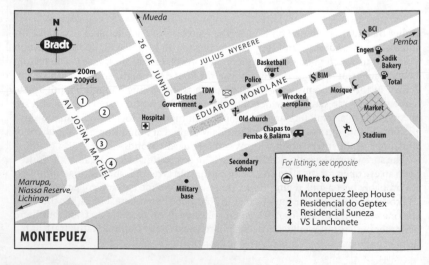

For listings, see opposite

Where to stay

1 Montepuez Sleep House
2 Residencial do Geptex
3 Residencial Suneza
4 VS Lanchonete

MONTEPUEZ

Montepuez today is a peaceful town, set attractively among granite inselbergs and with something of a dead-end feel about it, though the discovery of rich ruby deposits in the vicinity in 2009 has brought some business to the area.

GETTING THERE AND AWAY Montepuez lies 205km west of Pemba along the **EN106** (EN1) and **EN242** (EN14). It is a good surfaced road and self-drivers should get through within 3 hours. Chapas to and from Pemba leave from the large square next to the market. The journey takes around 3 hours and costs around US$4. For details of travel west to Marrupa and the Niassa Reserve, see box, page 371, and be aware that the filling stations here are the last reliable fuelling points before Marrupa.

WHERE TO STAY, EAT AND DRINK *Map, opposite*

🏠 **Montepuez Sleep House** (7 rooms) Av Julius Nyerere; ☎272 51149; m 84 457 5351; e sleephouse01@hotmail.com. The smartest option around, this was full when we were last in town, but the en-suite rooms with AC are reputedly very pleasant. The Libya-themed 'Tripoli Bar' & restaurant has indoor & outdoor seating, & can be recommended for its tasty Mozambican-style chicken & seafood grills in the US$6–10 range. *US$50 dbl.* **$$**

🏠 **Residencial do Geptex** (15 rooms) Av Julius Nyerere; ☎272 51114; m 86 448 0332. Diagonally opposite Montepuez Sleep House, this place consists of a row of dingy but otherwise adequate en-suite rooms. Difficult to take issue with at the price. *US$20/30 twin/dbl.* **$**

🏠 **Residencial Suneza** Av Josina Machel; m 86 312 8482. Another clean, simple option with en-suite rooms, hot water & fan. *US$40 dbl.* **$$**

🏠 **VS Lanchonete** (12 rooms) Av Eduardo Mondlane; ☎272 51051; m 82 485 7280 or 84 362 2928. This sharp place is the only business-class hotel in town, & has en-suite rooms with the usual trimmings such as AC, flat-screen TV, fridge, kettle & secure parking. Out front is a modern fast-food joint serving up fried chicken, fried fish, burgers & other healthy fare. *US$70 dbl B&B.* **$$$**

OTHER PRACTICALITIES

Banks and ATMs Both BCI and BIM Millennium are represented with ATMs along Avenida Eduardo Mondlane. Westbound travellers should be aware that this will be their last but one opportunity to draw cash before Lichinga, with one ATM in Marrupa.

Shopping A few decent supermarkets line Avenida Eduardo Mondlane, a good market lies two blocks south of this, and the excellent Sadik Bakery can be found on the road leading down to it.

TOWARDS TANZANIA

The Tanzanian border at the Ruvuma mouth lies about 250km north of Pemba as the crow flies, and it is probably fair to say that most travellers who pass through to the far north of Cabo Delgado are *en route* to or from here. There are two through-routes to Tanzania in Cabo Delgado, both of which entail following the EN6 (EN1) inland of Pemba for about 80km to the small junction town of Sunate (also called Silva Macua), then turning north on to the EN243 (N380) and following it for 220km to the junction at Awasse (10km west of Diaca). From here, the more established coastal route passes through the substantial port of Mocímboa da Praia and the smaller town of Palma to Namuiranga, where a ferry service crosses the Ruvuma mouth to Mwambo, 30km south of Mtwara, the largest port in southern Tanzania. This ferry sank in 2008, leading to several years of improvised dugout crossings and reports of price-gouging, but the Tanzanian government pressed a brand-new ferry into service in 2013, making this

18

once again the preferred river crossing. The Unity Bridge, opened in 2010, is upstream and accessible via Mueda and Mocímboa da Ruvuma, connecting to the Tanzanian town of Newala, but getting to the bridge itself can be a challenge as transport links are poor.

MACOMIA This small junction town lies on the EN243 (N380) about 200km northwest of Pemba and 150km southwest of Mocímboa da Praia. In itself it's an unprepossessing place, bustling and no-nonsense, and of interest to travellers solely on account of its position. For northbound travellers coming from Pemba, it lies at the end of the good surfaced road to which you'll have become accustomed, and it is also where the EN528 (R766) to coastal Pangane branches off the main road. For that reason, you may end up getting stuck here in transit.

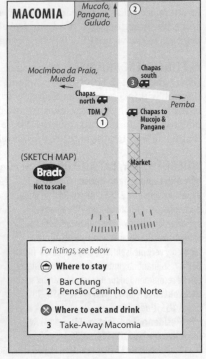

MACOMIA

Mucofo,
Pangane,
Guludo

②

Mocímboa da Praia,
Mueda

Chapas
south

③

Chapas
north

Pemba

TDM

①

Chapas to
Mucojo &
Pangane

(SKETCH MAP)

Market

Bradt

Not to scale

For listings, see below

🏠 **Where to stay**
1   Bar Chung
2   Pensão Caminho do Norte

❌ **Where to eat and drink**
3   Take-Away Macomia

Getting there and away The **EN106/243** (EN1/N380) coming from Pemba is surfaced and well maintained in its entirety, and private vehicles should get through in about 2½ hours. North of Macomia, the **EN243** (N380) is more erratic and there are some rough patches, so bank on an average driving time of around 50km/h, certainly along the 100km stretch to Awasse (Dacia). The main **buses** between the north and the south all pass through Macomia, stopping at the market next to the junction for around 20 minutes to give the drivers a break and to drop off and pick up passengers. Most buses come past between 09.00 and 11.00. From here to Pemba will cost US$4, and takes around 3 hours. To Mueda or Mocímboa da Praia costs about US$6 and takes up to 5 hours.

🏠 **Where to stay, eat and drink** *Map, above*

🏠 **Bar Chung** On the corner of the square & run by an old Chinese chap, this seems to be the closest Macomia has to a nightspot, & can rustle up meals on request. Rooms are nice & clean & surprisingly cheap. **$**

🏠 **Pensão Caminho do Norte** Also close to the junction, this pensão has basic but clean rooms & generator electricity that runs until 22.00. **$**

❌ **Take-Away Macomia** There's no signpost, but look out at the main junction for the deep-sea scene painted on the exterior. Dive inside, & you'll find Mozambican favourites & cold beers. **$**

CHAI Lying about 40km north of Macomia and 60km south of Awasse (Dacia) along a stretch of road that is in dire need of upgrading, Chai is a town that you'll pass through almost without noticing, but if you mention it to Mozambicans you'll find that it holds a very special place in the nation's history. It was here, on 25 September 1964, that the first shot of the revolution was fired, when Frelimo, then still led by Eduardo Mondlane, attacked the town's administrative headquarters. The Frelimo battle plan for the raid can be seen in the Revolutionary Museum in Maputo (page 113). The only local memorial to this pivotal event is a small mural roughly in the centre of town by one of Mozambique's most celebrated artists, Malangatana Ngwenya, a Frelimo veteran arrested by the Portuguese security police a year after this raid took place, who served as a UNESCO goodwill ambassador until he passed away in 2011. Oddly, the mural doesn't depict the raid on Chai, but the Mueda Massacre.

MUEDA Mueda is the principal town on the Mozambican part of the Makonde Plateau, the only part of the country that still remained unconquered by Portugal at the start of World War I. Even after the plateau was quelled in 1919, the Makonde people after whom it is named retained a tradition of resistance. This was intensified after an infamous massacre on 16 June 1960, when Portuguese soldiers fired on an officially sanctioned meeting of peasant farmers in Mueda, killing an estimated 600 people. Partly in reaction to this massacre – though also because of their proximity to independent Tanzania – the Makonde gave Frelimo strong support during the war of liberation. Most of the plateau was under Frelimo control after 1964, though Mueda itself remained in Portuguese hands. After the operation

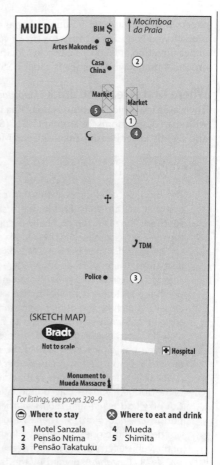

MUEDA

BIM $ ↑ Mocímboa
         da Praia

Artes Makondes •

Casa
China •   ②

Market   Market
  ⑤   ①
ç   ④

†

♪ TDM

Police •   ③

(SKETCH MAP)
Bradt
Not to scale   ✚ Hospital

Monument to
Mueda Massacre ⚑

For listings, see pages 328–9

🛏 **Where to stay**   🍴 **Where to eat and drink**
1 Motel Sanzala   4 Mueda
2 Pensão Ntima   5 Shimita
3 Pensão Takatuku

known as Gordian Knot, in which 350,000 Portuguese soldiers drove Frelimo underground in Cabo Delgado, roughly 300,000 people in the Mueda area were resettled into *aldeamentos*, collective villages that were wired off to prevent contact with Frelimo. Needless to say, the fact that many of these were arbitrarily placed in arid areas did little to help Portugal win the hearts of Cabo Delgado's people.

Mueda today is about as close as it gets to a one-street town, with little to see aside from a small memorial to the massacre, and the mass grave in which its victims were buried. Set at an altitude of around 800m, the town has an unexpectedly bracing climate – a refreshing contrast to the sticky coast – and the surrounding area is very scenic. There's also a small Artes Makondes hut, though this really doesn't bear comparison with the larger co-operatives in Pemba and Nampula. If you explore a little, then you may find some Makonde carvers sitting outside their houses, but this is one of those occasions when the journey is its own reward, with the views as you approach the escarpment ringing the plateau possessing a real 'Lost World' atmosphere.

You'll be able to change US dollars (or Tanzanian shillings) at the small Barclays Bank, and there are three ATMs in Mueda: a BCI, a Barclays and a BIM Millennium.

Getting there and away Mueda lies about 350km from Pemba and the road is tarred for most of the way, but with sporadic rough patches, so self-drivers should expect it to take at least 5 hours. **Chapas** to and from Pemba leave daily from the market, and **Nagi Investimentos** (m *86 400 0661*) also runs a **bus** which departs in either direction at 05.00. The trip to Mocímboa da Praia costs about US$2 and takes around 4 hours, while Pemba is about US$10 and will take 8 hours.

🏠 **Where to stay, eat and drink** *Map, page 327*
There are a few basic guesthouses along Rua 1 de Maio, all offering basic accommodation with shared bathrooms for around US$15 (**$**). These are the good-value **Pensão Ntima** and slightly lesser **Pensão Takatuku** and **Motel Sanzala**. If you don't eat at your hotel,

CROSSING INTO TANZANIA

The biggest travel news in this part of Mozambique was the long-awaited opening of the Unity Bridge, the first road bridge across the Ruvuma to southern Tanzania, which finally occurred in May 2010. The bridge crosses the river at Negomane, linking Mueda to the Tanzanian town of Newala.

The road distance between Mueda and the Unity Bridge is about 170km, and from there it is another 60km to Newala, passing through some spectacular scenery as you descend into the Ruvuma Valley then climb back on to the plateau on the Tanzanian side. This stretch of road doesn't come close to matching the bridge in the modernity stakes and parts can be quite tricky in the rainy season, even with high clearance, though this is likely to change when planned upgrades are complete, whenever that may be. For the time being, however, expect the drive from Mueda to Newala to take around 5–6 hours, allowing for border formalities.

It's all very low-key, but there is full immigration and customs on both sides of the bridge. If you need accommodation in Newala, two places stand out: the **Country Lodge** (*en-suite rooms with net, fan & TV;* **$**) and the cheaper **Plateau Lodge** (*en-suite rooms;* **$**). There is also plenty of accommodation in Masasi.

The second-biggest travel news in this part of Mozambique was the return of the vehicle ferry at the mouth of the Ruvuma in 2013. The ferry (m *+255 78 772 4928 (Tanzania)*), owned by the Tanzanian government, can only run at high tide and holds up to six vehicles at a time. It charges US$50–75 per vehicle and US$5 for foot passengers, and the crossing takes about 20 minutes.

There is still no public transport between Mueda and Newala via the Unity Bridge, though this will surely come as soon as the road has been upgraded. Until it does, however, backpackers must cross between Mozambique and Tanzania along the coastal route from Palma to Mtwara. Coming from Palma, the 40km to the Namoto border post takes 2 hours by chapa, along a road that is as bad as the surrounding scenery is beautiful. The immigration office here is easy-going, and there's a little shop selling water, sweets and such. Once formalities are complete, the same chapa will continue to the banks of the Ruvuma River, where you can expect a bit of a feeding frenzy among the motorboat pilots and money changers! If you've missed the ferry for the day, you shouldn't have too much trouble arranging a motorboat launch, and if you have leftover Mozambican money, this is your last chance to get rid of it, though do be aware that the rate on offer is rather poor. Otherwise, just ignore these folks and wait for the ferry. Pick-up trucks wait on the Tanzanian side to take you to Mtwara, stopping first at the border post at Singa.

For information on the Unity II Bridge in Niassa Province, see page 48.

the **Shimita Restaurante** ($$) and **Mueda Restaurante** ($$) face each other across the same road, and serve whatever they happen to have that day.

MOCÍMBOA DA PRAIA Mocímboa da Praia was once the last established overnight stop for travellers on the coastal route to Tanzania, before the recent growth of Palma in anticipation of the offshore natural gas development. It has a rather lawless frontier feel about it (the 2005 elections were marred by violence), but is otherwise quite appealing, in many ways reminiscent of a warmer Lichinga, and its location along the main trade route between Pemba and southern Tanzania ensures it bustles with commercial activity. There is also a fishing harbour, unique in Mozambique, from where hundreds of boats leave at around 05.00 in the extraordinary colours of sunrise.

On a more practical note, you'll find that there is a bit more English spoken in Mocímboa da Praia, thanks to the number of Tanzanians and Somalians living there, and a whole lot more Swahili. It's also the site of Mozambique's northernmost post office, though it seems to be out of service for the time being. Barclays Bank, BIM Millennium and BCI are all represented here with ATMs, and there's an internet café in the town centre. As the closest (relatively) urban centre to the offshore Rovuma gas field, there are already a number of Brazilian, American and other energy firms based in town (which can sometimes make it challenging to find

MAPIKO DANCES

The area between Mueda and Mocímboa da Praia is a good base for exploring Makonde culture, the highlight of which is the traditional *mapiko* dances that are held at practically every village in the region as part of the *likumbi* (male initiation/circumcision) season of December to January. This is one of the most elaborate masked-dance traditions in East or southern Africa, not only associated with initiation rituals but also reflecting broader aspects of Makonde social life and human nature, as well as tackling more contemporary concerns. Indeed, during the liberation war, the Makonde – whose homeland was a staunch Frelimo stronghold – invented several new masquerades dealing directly with the hardships they faced under the last oppressive decade of Portuguese rule.

The term mapiko is the plural of *lipiko*, the central figure in the dance, representing a malicious spirit that the community must protect itself against. Every person involved in a dance performance will drape his body in cloths until it is completely disguised, before donning an outsized wooden lipiko mask distinguished by its wild hair and grotesquely distorted facial features. Only men are allowed to perform the dance, and the masks cannot be viewed by women or by uncircumcised boys except when the dance is under way. These lipiko masks are also among the most collectible of traditional African artworks, which means that many fine examples have been exported to foreign collections, though an interesting selection can be seen in the ethnological museum in Nampula.

If you want to see the dancers in action, it shouldn't be too difficult to locate an event in the countryside between Mueda and Mocímboa da Praia during the likumbi season – just listen out for the drums, especially on a Saturday or Sunday afternoon. At other times of year, bespoke dances can be arranged with advance notice through Kaskazini in Pemba (page 43).

accommodation), and you should expect rapid changes here as the offshore gas fields are developed further.

Getting there and away Mocímboa da Praia lies about 360km from Pemba and the road is tarred until Macomia but highly variable thereafter, so self-drivers should expect it to take at least 5 hours. **Chapas** between Mocímboa da Praia and Mueda (*US$2*) leave throughout the day from opposite the Exito filling station and take about 2½ hours. For Pemba (*US$6*) and Nampula (*US$10*), a handful of **buses** including **Maning Nice** (m *82 706 2820/456 5760*) and **Nagi Investimentos** (m *86 400 0659*) leave at 03.30 daily from in front of the Movitel store.

If you're heading to the border from here, plan for an even earlier start – chapas leave for Palma (*US$2*) and the border from between 02.00 and 04.00 in the morning. While you will be able to get something after this, you may not be able to get a connection on from the border. Chapas to the border cost US$7 and the journey takes up to 4 hours.

There is an airport in Mocímboa da Praia as well. It only serves charter flights as of 2016, though, given the town's growing importance, this is likely to change.

🏠 **Where to stay, eat and drink** Vumba has the highest-calibre restaurant in town, but the Tanzanian-owned places on the road between the beach and the hospital are known for serving up goat curry, rice dishes, chapatis and, according to at least one Mocímboa resident, a selection of 'mind-blastingly delicious' fresh juices. It might be a good idea to pop in and order in advance, agreeing on a time when you can come and eat.

🏠 **Complexo Vumba** (28 rooms) m 86 315 0901; e ilhavumba.mocimboa@yahoo.com.br. On the beach road to the right of the main route into town, this established place comes with a swimming pool & a view, & the restaurant-bar has become the go-to spot for Mocímboa's movers & shakers. It's often fully booked by the gas companies or government folks, but worth checking regardless. An extension of the hotel is also to be built on Vumba Island, though at the time of writing its opening date is uncertain. *Rooms US$70 dbl, B&B.* **$$$**

🏠 **Sunset Guest House** (7 rooms) Located in the centre of town, this new guesthouse has simple en-suite rooms with hot water, DSTV, AC, Wi-Fi, nets & a restaurant that serves local mains & pizza. *Rooms US$20.* **$**

🍺 **Kharibu** In the centre of town, this is first on the (admittedly short) list of nightspots in Mocímboa, & pumps the music until late at w/ends.

PALMA The small but beautiful town of Palma, situated about 60km north of Mocímboa da Praia, lies on an attractive natural harbour that is thought once to have been a mouth of the Ruvuma River. The government buildings and hospital are up on the hill with a staggeringly beautiful view overlooking a coconut-palm-fringed lagoon and private residences by the sea. The very definition of a backwater for many years, Palma today is in the process of dramatic change, as this is the epicentre of Mozambique's nascent gas industry – the Rovuma Basin gas field, home to a possible 175 trillion cubic feet of natural gas, lies just offshore. Given the recent changes, Palma has become the last established overnight stop for travellers on the coastal route to Tanzania. An ATM is located at the petrol station and there are plans to open a supermarket. Palma itself is worth exploring, if only to see this once-bucolic fishing village before industry renders it entirely unrecognisable.

If you are looking for transport to either Quionga and the Tanzanian border at Namoto or Mocímboa da Praia, you'll need to wait in the upper part of town. Chapas to the border cost US$5 whereas a private taxi fare will be about US$50.

The ferry costs US$2 per foot passenger and US$20 per vehicle. As per the tides, if the ferry is not operating, local boats take foot passengers most of the way for US$5, but the trip involves a bit of walking with the lack of water. The manager at Palma Residence is a useful source of information regarding border crossings and happenings in Palma.

Where to stay, eat and drink For a place to stay, there are an increasing number of options as investors gear up for the impending gas industry boom. A pleasant range of accommodation is now available, most with on-site restaurants. The more established are listed below and a few more are in the works, notably **Amarula Lodge** at the north end of town. Alternatively, the reed town is down below between the hill and the beach, and you might be able to arrange a stay with some locals here, either in a home or by pitching a tent in someone's compound.

🏠 **Karibu Palma Hotel** (12 rooms) m 87 274 5982; e info@karibupalmahotel.com; w karibupalmahotel.com. Located in the centre of town, this quaint hotel offers comfortable & tastefully appointed business-style en-suite rooms & self-catering apartments with balcony/terrace, AC, Wi-Fi, satellite TV, writing desk & kettle. *Rooms start at US$107 dbl, B&B.* **$$$**

🏠 **Sunset Guest House** (7 rooms) m 84 279 8101. Owned by the same woman as the Sunset in Mocímboa da Praia, this central guesthouse offers simple accommodation with AC, TV & fridge. The associated Tipyku's restaurant stands a bit down the road. *Rooms US$39 sgl with shared facilities; US$59/86 sgl/dbl en suite; all rates B&B.* **$$$**

🏠 **Palma Inn** (30 rooms) ☎ 272 88001; m 84 765 0211; e afonseca@patamar.co.mz. On the north side of town & catering primarily to the oil & gas market, this comfortable place has en-suite rooms with AC, TV, Wi-Fi, kettle & writing desk, as well as private parking, restaurant, bar & pool. **$$$**

🏠 **Palma Residences** (57 rooms) m 84 321 2817/8; e palma@africancentury. co.mz; w palmalodge.com. Marketing itself as an apartment-style hotel, Palma's largest complex has a restaurant, swimming pool & secure fenced parking. En-suite rooms adorned with locally manufactured *umbila* furniture & African art come with veranda, kitchenette, writing desk, AC, DSTV, Wi-Fi & free laundry. *Rooms US$145/165 sgl/dbl standard suite, US$195/295 1 bedroom/2-bedroom villa.* **$$$$**

🏠 **Pensão Mustafa** (6 rooms) m 84 363 5303 or 86 624 7146. Centrally located & cheap, this otherwise unremarkable establishment uses shared facilities – a long drop toilet & bucket shower stall. *US$10 dbl.* **$**

🏠 **Pensão Wivo** (28 rooms) m 82 070 2700 or 86 679 3598. Located near the roundabout at the southern entrance to town, this established pensão offers en-suite accommodation with hot water & AC. No frills with a friendly staff. *US$30/50 sgl/dbl.* **$$**

Pemba and the Northeast   TOWARDS TANZANIA

18

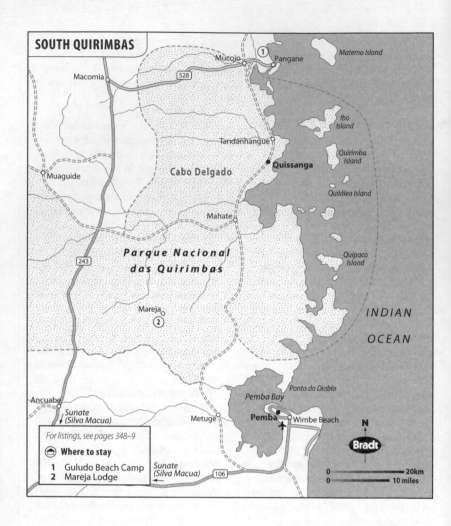

SOUTH QUIRIMBAS

Matemo Island

Mucojo ① Pangane

Macomia

528

Ibo
Island

Tandanhangue

Cabo Delgado

Quissanga

Quirimba
Island

Muaguide

Quilálea Island

Mahate

243

Parque Nacional
das Quirimbas

Quipaco
Island

INDIAN

Mareja
②

OCEAN

Ponta do Diablo

Pemba Bay

Ancuabe

Sunate
(Silva Macua)

Metuge

Pemba
Wimbe Beach

N

For listings, see pages 348–9

🏠 **Where to stay**
1 Guludo Beach Camp
2 Mareja Lodge

Sunate
(Silva Macua)

106

Bradt

0 _____ 20km
0 _____ 10 miles

19

The Quirimbas

The most important tourist attraction in the far north of Mozambique is the Quirimba Archipelago, which consists of 32 small offshore islands strung out along the 250km of Indian Ocean coastline that stretches northward from Pemba to the small town of Palma. It is an area of great scenic beauty, boasting high levels of marine and terrestrial biodiversity, some of the most significant unspoilt reef ecosystems anywhere in the Indian Ocean, and a rich history and culture whose blend of indigenous African and exotic Arabic and Portuguese influences is epitomised by the historic town of Ibo on the island of the same name. In 2002, the most southerly 11 islands, together with the surrounding waters and a large tract of the facing mainland, were gazetted as the 7,506km² Quirimbas National Park (*entrance US$12*), of which some 20% comprises marine habitats while the remainder is terrestrial. In 2008, the entire archipelago was nominated as a tentative UNESCO World Heritage Site.

The closest thing to a tourist hub in the Quirimbas, and the only island that is reasonably accessible to travellers on a budget, is Ibo, which lies within the national park and is best known for the tiny but fascinating old town that shares its name. Elsewhere in the archipelago, honeymoon-friendly idylls such as Matemo, Medjumbe and Quilálea host some of Mozambique's finest and most exclusive beach resorts, all of them connected to Pemba by daily light aircraft flights. Ibo aside, the island retreats of the Quirimbas are aimed squarely at the fly-in 'barefoot luxury' market, so for practical purposes this chapter also includes a smattering of comparably upmarket beach lodges that technically lie outside the Quirimbas, as well as the handful of tourist developments that exist within (or close to) the vast mainland sector of the national park.

The archipelago itself is a classic fringing reef, but one that runs along the Mozambican coast for hundreds of kilometres. The individual islands are essentially those points where the reef protrudes above sea level, and the waters that separate them from the mainland are very shallow. Indeed, as seen from the air – as most visitors first see it – this entire coastline forms a beguiling network of dark green mangroves and narrow channels, bright azure shallows whose sandy floor is clearly visible through the translucent waters, and small wooded islets fringed by white beaches and rows of coconut palms. The substrate of these islands is composed of coral rag – coral and sand that has been bonded into a pockmarked black rock that is razor-sharp (don't try to walk over it in bare feet) and yet brittle enough to break off with ease.

The islands are mostly lushly vegetated, and the surrounding shallows support extensive mangrove swamps and a wide range of wading birds, including an important breeding colony of sooty terns. Wandering across the intertidal areas is highly recommended (though be sure to wear a stout pair of sandals), as the pools host the likes of octopus, sea cucumber, lobster and mantis shrimp. The sandy beaches on seven of the 11 islands within the national park are used as breeding sites by hawksbill, green and olive ridley turtles, and loggerhead and leatherback turtles are also present in these waters. Several other species listed as threatened by the IUCN are resident or regular migratory visitors, among them the dugong, bottlenose dolphin, humpback whale, and grey-nurse, great white and whale shark. The offshore reefs support an incredible wealth of marine wildlife, including 52 coral and 375 fish species, making for some of the country's finest diving and snorkelling.

Most of the islands are inhabited and, while there is some industrial-scale agriculture on Quirimba Island, the predominant occupation is subsistence fishing, not only by Mozambicans but also by itinerant semi-nomadic Tanzanian fishermen, who move from island to island every month or so, drying their catch and sending it in big sacks to market in Mtwara or Pemba.

HISTORY

Little is known about the history of the Quirimbas prior to the arrival of the Portuguese, but they were certainly occupied by Arabic traders by the 13th century, and possibly even as early as the 7th century. They are assumed to have formed an important link in the medieval coastal trade network between Kilwa and Sofala. The Quirimbas were originally known to the Portuguese as the Maluane Islands, after a type of cloth manufactured in the vicinity from pre-Portuguese times until well into the 17th century.

When the Portuguese first landed in the archipelago, the main trading centre was on Quirimba Island, immediately south of Ibo. In 1507, when the more northerly island city of Kilwa was occupied by Portugal, many of its Muslim merchants fled to Quirimba and continued operating from there, refusing to enter into trade with the Christian Portuguese. As a result, Portugal attacked Quirimba in 1522, killing about 60 of its Muslim residents and looting large amounts of ivory and other merchandise before they burned the town down. This massacre had little long-term effect in subduing the Muslim trade, however, so Portugal switched tactics and attempted to gain control over the islands by leasing them to Portuguese citizens.

By the end of the 16th century, seven of the nine largest islands in the archipelago were ruled by Portuguese traders and the other two by Muslims. Islanders were forced to pay a tribute of 5% of their produce to the island's ruler, as well as a tithe to the Church. By this time, the most important island in the archipelago was Ibo, said locally to be an acronym of the Portuguese Ilha Bem Organizado ('Well-Organised Island'), a claim we've been unable to verify elsewhere. A description dating from 1609 reveals that Ibo was substantially fortified, and that the islands were reasonably prosperous and a major source of food supplies for Ilha de Moçambique. By the 18th century, prazos had been established on all the main islands, and the archipelago was lorded over by two mazungo (white-skinned) families: the Meneses and Morues.

Ibo came into its own in the second half of the 18th century as the major supplier of slaves to the sugar-plantation owners of France's Indian Ocean islands. Portugal resented the prosperity of the islands' independent traders and, fearing that the archipelago might fall into Omani or French hands, granted Ibo municipal status in 1763. By the end of the 18th century, Ibo is thought to have been the second most important Portuguese trading centre after Ilha de Moçambique. It was still a major trading and administrative centre when it was leased to the Niassa Company in 1897 but, as it transpired, the shallow, narrow approach to the island wasn't suitable for modern ships. In 1904, the Niassa Company relocated its base to Porto

Amélia (Pemba), three-quarters of Ibo's population followed, the islands faded into economic insignificance and its old towns fell into gradual decline.

IBO

Situated on the island of the same name, the small town of Ibo ranks among Mozambique's most ancient settlements. Founded prior to the Portuguese era, it was the most important coastal port after Ilha de Moçambique up until the turn of the 20th century. By mainstream tourism standards, Ibo today is also one of southern Africa's best-kept travel secrets. Tourist facilities are limited, though steadily improving, and access is not exactly straightforward (unless, of course, you fly from Pemba, which takes all of 20 minutes). Yet for the select few visitors who do make it, wandering around the timeworn alleys of Ibo's old town and interacting with its fewer than 4,000 inhabitants invariably forms a highlight of their time in Mozambique.

The old town of Ibo, though run-down, is utterly compelling: a strangely haunting backwater that vaguely recalls Kilwa Kivinje on the south coast of Tanzania. As the UNESCO World Heritage Site tentative list notes: 'The architectural character of the stone-built town, created through several hundreds of years, is remarkable for its homogeneity… the town, the fortifications and many fine buildings are an outstanding example of architecture in which local Swahili traditions, Portuguese influences and Indian and Arab influences are all intertwined.'

Today, many of the palaces and villas built in Ibo's 19th-century heyday have been abandoned and lapsed into disrepair, with clay tiles falling from the roofs, walls layered in moss and foundations undermined by the vast sprawling tendrils of strangler figs. The exposed rag coral walls and fading whitewash of the crumbling buildings give the town a washed-out pastel air that is strangely at odds with the deep blue tropical sky and the bright red flame trees, and the lush greenery that lines the streets in which mangrove kingfishers sing at dawn.

If there is an obvious point of comparison, it is Ilha de Moçambique, but Ibo is far from being a miniature of Ilha – which may have been the Portuguese capital for four centuries, but is more evocative of the Muslim world than of anything European. Paradoxically Ibo, which was frequently a base for clandestine Muslim trade during the Portuguese era, has an uncluttered and overwhelmingly Mediterranean character, its wide roads lined with opulent high-roofed buildings boasting classical facades and expansive balconies supported by thick pillars. And while Ibo is also in a more advanced state of decay than Ilha de Moçambique, this is steadily changing. An idea of Ibo's past grandeur can be seen at the Ibo Island Lodge, where three previously ruined mansions have been lovingly and sensitively restored to their former glory, and several other buildings are also in various stages of rehabilitation.

A number of organisations and investors have identified the importance of Ibo's history, culture and biodiversity, and community and conservation projects are already under way. A community tourism programme, a Montessori English School, a silversmiths' programme and several other community-based alternative-enterprise projects are operated and managed by Ibo Island Lodge (page 339), and can be visited by the lodge's guests as well as by other visitors.

GETTING THERE AND AWAY

By air The easy way to get to Ibo is by air. **CR Aviation** runs at least one daily flight connecting Pemba to Ibo and all other islands with lodges, though times and schedules are flexible depending on the bookings for that day. Bookings can be

CONSERVATION ON THE QUIRIMBAS

The first survey work of the Quirimbas was carried out between 1996 and 1998 by Frontier-Mozambique, a project based on Ilha Quirimba and run by the Society for Environmental Exploration in conjunction with the Tropical Marine Department of the University of York in the UK, the Mozambican Department of the Environment (MICOA), the Mozambican Department of Fisheries (IDPPE) and the University of Eduardo Mondlane.

The project of a national park in the Quirimbas had – because of the region's very high biodiversity, great scenic beauty and important history – been under intermittent discussion since the 1970s. However, it was only in 2000 that the first protected marine area was established in the Quirimbas in the form of the Quilálea Marine Sanctuary, which was set up around the islands of Quilálea and Sencar (55km and 75km north of Pemba respectively) by a private company and endorsed by the government. In June 2002, at the request of 40 local community leaders, the 7,506km² Quirimbas National Park was created to encompass both the southern half of the archipelago and a 5,984km² tract of the facing mainland. The park's marine sector extends over 1,522km² and stretches 100km along the coast, from just north of Pemba to just south of Medjumbe Island. The park's headquarters are on Ibo Island.

The Worldwide Fund for Nature or WWF (w *wwf.org*) is heavily involved in the Quirimbas Park, and its website is a good source of information. The overall goal of the park, in this beautiful but ecologically fragile area, is 'to conserve the diversity, abundance and ecological integrity of all physical and biological resources in the park area, so that they may be enjoyed and used productively by present and future generations'. Nor is nature the only beneficiary. One of the park's six associated aims

made through the airline direct (m *84 490 9734;* e *reservations@craviation.co.mz;* w *craviation.co.mz*) or through Kaskazini (page 43). Depending on your exact route, fares are mostly between US$208 and US$283 one-way, plus a US$13 departure tax. The flights take up to 20 minutes and are a delight in clear weather.

By boat A cheaper direct possibility between Pemba and Ibo is the cargo boat operated by Rainer Gessner (m *86 144 3964*) on Ilha Quirimba (page 348), which typically does a weekly supply run in either direction. It is rare that he takes passengers but, given a bit of potential extra space, it would be worth asking if you are willing to pitch in for fuel. The trip takes about 12 hours. Cinco Portas on Ibo (page 339) can also arrange combined car and boat transfers from Pemba via Tandanhangue for US$250 one-way and US$400 round-trip per trip (not per person).

By car and dhow In the dry season, the most direct route to Quissanga and Tandanhangue, the departure point for dhows to Ibo, involves following the **EN106** (EN1) east out of Pemba for a few kilometres then turning right on to the coastal **EN247** (R762) running north through Metugé and Mahate. This route covers a distance of 125km and takes 3–4 hours in a private vehicle. The better but longer (250km) inland route, which you'd be forced to use in the rainy season, involves following the surfaced **EN106** (EN1) and **EN243** (N380) via Sunate (also known as Silva Macua) to Muaguide, then turning right on to the all-weather dirt **EN245** (R767) through Bilibiza to connect with the coastal road at Mahate, where you need to turn left for Quissanga. Like so many coastal towns in Mozambique, Quissanga involves contributing to 'the economic and social well-being of the park's ancestral inhabitants by promoting sustainable resource use strategies, by developing ecologically sensitive livelihood options and by prioritising their interests in the economic opportunities deriving from the establishment of the park'.

Park management currently runs largely on NGO funding, but the long-term goal is for park fees and other tourist revenue – of which 70% goes towards park management, another 20% to local communities and only 10% to state coffers – to make it financially self-sufficient. This goal, it has to be said, is a long way from being realised, as annual tourist arrivals stand at around 3,500 people, most them staying on Ibo or Matemo. However, ambitious plans for further development of community-based tourism on the oft-neglected mainland sector of the park have led to projections of 20,000 visitors annually by 2017.

Another player in the conservation of the island's natural and cultural assets is Ibo Island Lodge, which has aimed to provide clear community benefits since its inception. To this end it has established a series of projects run from the Ibo Island Conservation Centre. These include a long-term programme teaching English language to the communities on Ibo, and the creation of alternative-enterprise projects such as a market garden scheme, whereby locals can produce sellable crops in their own gardens, the development of Ibo Island Coffee as a premium brand, and the development of the island's ancient silversmithing industry. It has also helped to form a network of island guides to lead culture and heritage experiences. Another project is to record from oral and other sources the fascinating history of the island. More can be found out about these projects by checking Ibo Island Lodge's website (w *iboisland.com*).

splits into two halves – the administrative block up on the hill and the main fishing village down in the mangroves. If you are heading to Tandanhangue, you need to take the turning north at the administrative block. Either way, a 4x4 is a must, and there is safe parking at Tandanhangue (expect to pay around US$4/20 per day/week to the guard). Dhows for Ibo can only leave at high tide so, depending on arrival time, you could be in for a wait.

By chapa and dhow The more convoluted but cheaper option entails a combination of road transport and dhow, and you'd best resign yourself to a long bumpy ride. **Dhows** to Ibo leave from the fishing village of Tandanhangue, which lies on the coast north of Pemba a short distance past Quissanga. **Chapas** run from Pemba to Quissanga and Tandanhangue and, while there will be at least one a day, it is possible that there will only be the one on the day you are travelling, so be at the chapa point in Pemba before 05.00. Be prepared for a long, hot, dusty and rough journey. The trip costs US$8 and takes a good 5–6 hours, longer in the rains.

Once at Tandanhangue, there should be a dhow waiting on the shore where the chapa drops you though, if the tides work against you, you may be in for a wait of a few hours. All the dhows making the crossing are now motorised, and the journey is breathtakingly beautiful, even if the thrum of an outboard motor is considerably less charming an aural backdrop than the wind in the sails once was. It costs about US$2 and takes just over an hour. If you missed the public boat, it's possible to hire a private dhow for around US$30–40 one-way through one of the captains, whose numbers are posted on the baobab tree at the harbour. Note, however, that

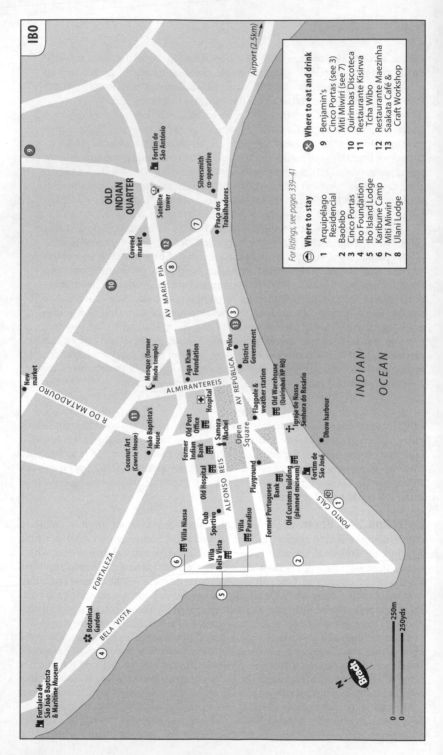

IBO

Airport (2.5km)

OLD INDIAN QUARTER

Fortim de São António

Silversmith co-operative

Satellite tower

Praça dos Trabalhadores

New market

Covered market

Mosque (former Hindu temple)

Aga Khan Foundation

ALMIRANTE REIS

Coconut Art (Cowrie House)

João Baptista's House

Old Post Office

Former Indian Bank

Hospital

Samora Machel

Open Square

Police

District Government

Old Warehouse (Quirimbas NP HQ)

AV REPÚBLICA

Igreja de Nossa Senhora do Rosário

Dhow harbour

INDIAN OCEAN

AV MARIA PIA

R DO MATADOURO

Villa Niassa

Club Sportivo

Villa Bella Vista

Old Hospital

Villa Paradiso

ALFONSO REIS

Playground

Former Portuguese Bank

Old Customs Building (planned museum)

Fortim de São José

PONTO CAIS

FORTALEZA

BELA VISTA

Fortaleza de São João Baptista & Maritime Museum

Botanical Garden

N

Brandt

0   250m
0   250yds

For listings, see pages 339–41

Where to stay
1 Arquipélago Residencial
2 Baobibo
3 Cinco Portas
4 Ibo Foundation
5 Ibo Island Lodge
6 Karibune Camp
7 Miti Miwiri
8 Ulani Lodge

Where to eat and drink
9   Benjamin's
    Cinco Portas (see 3)
    Miti Miwiri (see 7)
10 Quirimbas Discoteca
11 Restaurante Kisirwa
    Tcha Wibo
12 Restaurante Maezinha
13 Saakata Café & Craft Workshop

attempting to cross after dark isn't the safest option, and departure is still subject to the tide. The dhow will drop you on the beach in front of the Fortim de São José. Note that Miti Miwiri (page 340) also offers boat transfers from Tandanhangue by prior arrangement, costing US$60 for up to six people.

Coming from Mocímboa da Praia and points north, you'll need to catch a Pemba-bound chapa along the **EN243** (N380) and be dropped off about halfway through, at the junction with the dirt **EN245** (R767), where there is occasional transport towards Bilibiza and Mahate. You'll meet the coastal road at Mahate, where you can find onward transport for the remaining 20km to Tandanhangue.

It is possible to walk from Tandanhangue to Ibo at certain times of tide. It should only be attempted on low spring tides and you *must* take a local guide – if you stray off the path then you will very quickly find yourself trapped in knee-deep mud, with a very real risk of being stuck there until either someone comes along who can help you out or the tide comes in.

WHERE TO STAY *Map, opposite*
Exclusive/luxury

🏠 **Ibo Island Lodge** (14 rooms) ☎ +27 21 785 5498/2657 (South Africa), 269 60549 (lodge); m 82 605 7866; e enquiries@iboisland.com; w iboisland.com. The western waterfront was the most exclusive address in town during Ibo's glory days, dominated by a trio of 19th-century mansions that fell into ruin & decay as the town faded. 2 of these mansions, Villa Niassa & Villa Bella Vista, both of which served as governors' palaces at some point in their history, have been sensitively rehabilitated & restored as Ibo Island Lodge, & the 3rd mansion, Villa Paradiso, has also been restored to become a private, 12-sleeper villa with its own pool & garden. The rooms have lofty ceilings & are spacious, cool & filled with restored colonial-era or locally made hardwood furniture. The rooftop restaurant-bar has Wi-Fi & is a perfect place to watch the sun go down over the bay & the mangrove forest beyond. There is a lovely large garden, planted with frangipani, bougainvillea & palms, with 2 swimming pools & a garden restaurant-bar. Activities inc beach visits, snorkelling, fishing, massage, traditional safaris on a 14m custom-built dhow, kayaking, diving & experiences enabling interaction with islanders. The lodge also offers specials for residents & longer stays. The lodge can also arrange tailored mobile island-hopping dhow or kayak safaris through the entire archipelago (see w mozambiquedhowsafaris.com). Ibo Island Lodge is a highly commendable lodge with a well-thought-out programme that provides a measurable benefit to the local islanders. It should, however, be stressed that, while it will appeal to those seeking accommodation with a firm sense of place & historic character, & it offers daily excursions to a lovely sandbank beach, those looking for a conventional beach holiday might prefer some of the places listed later in the chapter. *US$555/810 sea-view sgl/dbl; US$525/750 historical or garden sgl/dbl. Rooms inc all meals & non-motorised activities, inc a daily transfer to a private beach with snorkelling, & informative guided historical & cultural tours. Rates increase by about 10% in the short high season.* **$$$$$**

Mid range

🏠 **Baobibo** (3 rooms) m 82 815 2892 or 86 175 8205; e baobibo.ibo@gmail.com; w baobibo. com. Opened in 2012 & set in a sandy compound on the western waterfront, this French-run lodge is a charming addition to Ibo's accommodation scene. The whitewashed bungalows are made from all local materials, & have individual verandas facing the water. Inside, rooms are bright & airy with wooden features, tea/coffee facilities, reading lamps, & traditional stone basin showers in recognition of the paucity of fresh water on Ibo. They've got a covered outdoor lounge area with book exchange, bikes & kayaks, & they also do excursions on their own dhow. *US$65 dbl; US$96 family room (sleeps 5); all rooms B&B. Rates increase by about 15% in the short high season.* **$$$**

🏠 **Cinco Portas** (7 rooms) m 86 926 2399 or 82 326 6771; e info@cincoportas.com; w cincoportas. com. Situated on the southern waterfront, this attractive pensão consists of a restored warehouse set in a small garden with an agreeable bar-restaurant, swimming pool, & lovely views over the old harbour. Accommodation is in a variety of en-suite rooms, most with AC, but ranging from a spacious apartment with 2 dbl beds & locally made furnishings to a small traditional Swahili-style room in a separate building. Activities on offer inc snorkelling & dhow trips to nearby beaches. *US$50–160 dbl; rates go up US$30–40 during high season. All rooms inc generous b/fast.* **$$$$**

🏠 **Ibo Foundation Hotel** (9 rooms) Set to open during the lifespan of this edition, this new establishment will have 8 dbl bungalows & at least 1 family room lining the mangrove shore on Av Bela Vista. An activity centre, swimming pool & restaurant are also planned.

🏠 **Miti Miwiri** (8 rooms) m 86 623 7785 or 82 543 8564; e mail@mitimiwiri.com; w mitimiwiri.com/n. Situated at the east end of the old town centre, this is another beautifully restored homestead, spanning 2 storeys & set in a large shady garden with a popular bar & restaurant with satellite TV. The restored rooms have an uncluttered appearance in keeping with the high-ceilinged ambience, attractive furnishings & a fan. Facilities inc swimming pool, free kayak use for guests, & internet access at around US$1/30mins. The management can arrange boat transfers to/from Tandanhangue or the other islands, as well as snorkelling trips (*all at around US$100 for up to 6 people*). *US$65/80/90/110 sgl/dbl/trpl/quad; all rooms B&B.* **$$$**

🏠 **Ulani Lodge** (8 rooms) m 82 343 8428 or 86 048 6485; e booking@ulanilodge.com;

w ulanilodge.com. The island's newest boutique hotel comprises a converted historical villa set in a lush garden complete with swimming pool & terrace offering fantastic views of Ibo & the sea. The individually decorated en-suite rooms have queen-size bed, hot water & fan. A restaurant is planned. *US$80–120 dbl depending on season; all rooms B&B.* **$$$**

Budget

🏠 **Arquipélago Residencial** (6 rooms) m 82 461 9830/802 0612; e arquipelagoresidencial@ yahoo.com.br. This block of rooms near the Fortim de São José is by no means unpleasant, but it does suffer from a distinct lack of character. Rooms are all tiled & en suite, pricier ones come with AC, & Rooms 1–3 overlook the sea. There's an on-site restaurant & bar & a small army of concrete chaises longues one could attempt to relax in. More importantly, Ibo's only internet café is attached. *US$30/50 dbl/exec.* **$$**

Shoestring and camping

🏠 **Karibune Camp** (4 rooms) m 82 703 2200 or 86 910 6597. Situated between Ibo Island Lodge & the Fortaleza de São João Baptista, this locally run lodge offers the choice of sleeping in a simple thatched hut or camping in a green compound literally a stone's throw from the sea. Simple meals can be prepared by advance order, & they organise dhow trips as well. *US$8–14 dbl/twin; US$3 pp camping.* **$**

✗ **WHERE TO EAT AND DRINK** *Map, page 338*

The best options are generally the exclusive and moderate lodges, all of which accept walk-in diners, but there are a few inexpensive bespoke restaurants dotted around town – it definitely pays to order ahead.

✗ **Benjamin's** m 86 175 8007; ⏰ b/fast, lunch & dinner daily. This new eatery serves hearty portions of local food for US$5–6 per plate. **$**

✗ **Cinco Portas** (page 339) A new chef now manages the lodge & restaurant & has subsequently enhanced the already quality dining experience, particularly the seafood. The bar-restaurant here can be a fun place to hang out in the evenings. *US$8–16.* **$$$$**

✗ **Miti Miwiri** (above) This lodge has a long-standing reputation for its popular bar & restaurant with satellite TV in the garden.

Sandwiches are around US$6 & the 3-course meal of the day is usually around US$13–16. **$$$$**

✗ **Restaurante Kisirwa Tcha Wibo** m 82 546 5818. In a reed building painted bright red, they've got a chalkboard out front with local meals of the day, although it seems like their business is winding down & not always open. *US$4–7.* **$**

✗ **Restaurante Maezinha** m 86 267 8354; ⏰ 06.30–22.00 daily. Located across from Ulani Lodge, this establishment serves up local food for around US$6 per plate. **$**

✗ Saakata Café & Craft Workshop m 86 144 6408; ⓕ saakataibo. Serving up coffee, snacks, cake & ice cream along with a colourful selection of locally made crafts & kapulana clothing. *US$1–2* $

☆ Quirimbas Discoteca m 82 859 4281. Behind the old Indian Quarter, this is what passes as Ibo's nightclub, & it's well attended at w/ends.

BANKS AND ATMS Ibo is scheduled to get its first ATM, through BCI, during the lifespan of this edition, but don't count on it unless you've called your accommodation ahead to check that it is functioning.

WHAT TO SEE AND DO Ibo's magic lies in the feeling of history that radiates from the walls of the old town, particularly around dusk, when you can almost feel the ghosts brushing past you as you walk the streets and alleys. Laid out in a rough triangle with the Fortaleza de São João Baptista forming the northwestern apex and the Fortim de São José and Fortim de São António at the base, the old town is so small that there is little need to follow a prescribed route around it but, for convenience's sake, the information below is organised along a circuit that starts at the western waterfront, near Ibo Island Lodge, then runs east along Avenida República to Fortim de São António, before returning west along Avenida Maria Pia to the Fortaleza de São João Baptista. If you prefer a guided tour, these are offered free to people staying at Ibo Island Lodge, and can also be arranged for a small fee through the island's other lodges and camps.

As is the case in several other old Mozambican towns, it is hard to establish the age of many of Ibo's buildings. While the dates on tiles and a few buildings seem to place much of the town centre in the early 19th century, a few buildings are older still, and it seems unlikely that many post-date the relocation of the Niassa Company's headquarters to Porto Amélia (Pemba) in 1904. Relics of pre-Portuguese times reputedly exist, including two ancient mosques and an Arab fortress, but if so they are difficult to locate, though excavations at the Fortaleza de São João Baptista have revealed the ruins of a Swahili house that pre-dates the fort's construction. A more surprising relict of pre-Portuguese times is the wild coffee shrubs, descended from plants brought by Arab traders, which have been growing on both Ibo and Quirimba for centuries. (The coffee is available for purchase at **Coconut Art (Cowrie House)** or you can buy it directly from the staff at Ibo Island Lodge, who will even roast an individual batch for you.)

A trio of striking mansions, now incorporated into Ibo Island Lodge, line the western waterfront. All three date to the late 19th century or earlier: **Villa Niassa** was originally the governor's palace but later became the headquarters of the Niassa Company, **Villa Bella Vista** served as a governor's palace sometime after that, while **Villa Paradiso** was built as the home of a rich merchant and later became an Indian restaurant.

A block east of the waterfront, Avenida República opens out to become **Praça dos Heróis Moçambicanos**, a central square surrounded by several of the island's oldest buildings. These include the former **Portuguese Bank** on the southwest side, the former **Indian Bank, old hospital** and **old post office** on the north, and a **former warehouse** (now housing the Quirimbas National Park headquarters and a carpentry co-operative) on the southeast side – all dating from the 19th century.

On the south side of the praça, the large, whitewashed **Igreja de Nossa Senhora do Rosário** (also sometimes known as Igreja de São João) still holds monthly services for the few dozen Christians who remain on the island. The pedigree of this church is somewhat uncertain. According to one source, it was built in 1580, a date lent some credibility by Dominican missionary records claiming some 16,000 converts in the Quirimbas by 1593. Other sources suggest a construction date of 1760, while inscriptions recording the church's wealthy benefactors place it c1800. The architectural style recalls the 18th-century cathedrals at Inhambane and Quelimane, and it is very possible that the present church was built at around that time on the site of an older predecessor. Beside the church are about 15 children's graves.

Next to the church, the **old customs building**, constructed in 1879, retains the ornate filigree railings typical of Indian buildings of that period. After closing as a customs house, it served as the town archive for several decades, and many papers dating from the late 19th century through to World War II are reputedly still stored inside. There was talk about reopening the building as a museum, but this doesn't seem likely any time soon. Alongside the old customs building, overlooking the semi-fortified southern waterfront, the moderately proportioned and architecturally mundane **Fortim de São José** was the first Portuguese-built fort on Ibo, dating to 1760, three years before the town was granted municipal status. It was used as a slave prison following the construction of the Fortaleza de São João Baptista, and eventually fell into disuse. It was renovated, but the money seems to have run out before the job did, and today it stands slightly more than half-restored.

Following Avenida República east, you pass several interesting buildings to your right, many of them old waterfront administrative buildings and warehouses, while to the left are a few rather dilapidated old mansions. About 500m past the main praça, the undistinguished **Praça dos Trabalhadores** offers a view over the dhow harbour, and another 200m or so brings you to an excellent **silversmith co-operative**, where you can watch the artisans at work and, if you like, buy some of their products. Turn left here and after another 200m you'll reach the **Fortim de São António**, which lies at the back of the town near the market. Built in 1847, this neat little fort offers a good view over the town from the tower, and the site was reputedly chosen because it has access to a natural tunnel that runs underground for about 1.5km to emerge near the airstrip. It was fully renovated in 2011.

From here, Avenida Maria Pia runs west through the **old Indian Quarter**, site of a covered market and a small handful of shops, eateries and bars that generate the closest thing on Ibo to a feeling of commercial buzz. About 500m west of this, a short diversion north along Avenida Almirante Reis leads to the most interesting of the town's **mosques**, whose hybridised appearance is explained by the fact that it was converted from a Hindu temple in 1975. This building, like the almost disused church, serves to remind us that while much of the architecture on Ibo is Portuguese or Indian, the town today is inhabited almost entirely by indigenous Africans, 99% of whom are Muslim.

Following Avenida da Fortaleza, you will pass the home of **João Baptista**, Ibo's semi-official historian, a genial octogenarian and veritable trove of information. He's got stories for days, but you'll need a little Portuguese. **Coconut Art (Cowrie House)** is just a couple of doors further along. They've got a reasonable selection of crafts and it's a good place to try Ibo coffee, but the house, completely covered in cowrie shells, is the real attraction. Continuing about 750m northwest from here, you will emerge in front of Ibo's most interesting and best-preserved building, the restored and whitewashed **Fortaleza de São João Baptista,** a large, star-shaped fort, complete with a dozen or so cannons and ringed by a grove of tall palms. Built in 1791 to protect the island from a French invasion from the island of Réunion, this fort was used as a prison into the 1970s, which explains the broken soft-drink bottles that line the tops of the walls. During the liberation war of 1965–75, it seems that Ibo and its fort became the Mozambican equivalent to South Africa's Robben Island (where Nelson Mandela and other political prisoners were detained at the height of apartheid). Some deeply disturbing stories relate to this period: locals say that the ramparts are haunted by the ghosts of political prisoners who drowned or died of disease after being locked into crowded waterlogged cells where they had no choice but to drink the same water in which all the cell's occupants were forced to defecate and urinate. Today, the fort is busier than it has been in years and an intriguing place to do some shopping – the ground floor is home to a handful of artisans' studios and community projects, including a sewing co-operative, carving workshop and a small but worthwhile **Maritime Museum**. There are also some traditional silversmiths at the entrance who will happily allow you to watch them at work without expecting you to buy anything.

OTHER ACTIVITIES As with the rest of the Quirimbas, Ibo is a useful base for marine activities, though the island itself lacks a real swimming beach on account of the high density of mangroves. Ibo Island Lodge is the island's only dive centre, with single dives starting at around US$90 for certified divers. They can also arrange custom dive safaris to sites around the Quirimbas. Snorkelling and kayak excursions can be arranged through any of the moderate or upmarket lodges in Ibo, as can dhow trips to beaches on other islands. The fishing is also very good. In addition, Ibo Island Lodge operates fully guided and catered adventure and luxury tailor-made dhow and kayak safaris, hopping between the very best of the islands south and north of Ibo see page 339 for contact details.

Out of town, Ibo Island also has some good walking possibilities, and bicycles can be rented through the local expert tour guide Raul (m 86 208 6046) for around US$15 per day. It is also possible to hire Raul for a guided walking tour of Ibo town and/or the island. If you prefer to walk on your own, a short distance out of town is the cemetery, along the airport road, where you'll find graves with inscriptions in several languages. Further afield, the dilapidated Majuca Lighthouse was established in 1873 on a separate seaward islet called Majuca, which lies about 5km east of Ibo town and can be reached on foot at low tide. This walk takes up to 2 hours in either direction, leading out past the Fortaleza de São João Baptista, then following the mangrove- and palm-lined northern shore past tidal flats that often support large flocks of waders and marine birds.

The dominant cultural group on Ibo, as in the rest of the Quirimbas, is the Mwani ('People of the Sea'), whose Kimwani (or Kimuane) tongue shares about 60% of its vocabulary with KiSwahili and, like that language, shows many unambiguous Arabic influences. Mwani culture combines Islamic beliefs with a strong core of typically ebullient African traditions, and the night air is often filled with the sound of drumming associated with initiation, funereal, wedding and other ceremonies. Sometimes the drumming might signal the start of a traditional procession through the streets, but more often you will need to ask around to see traditional Mwani dances. For those interested in traditional and contemporary Mozambican arts and culture, a good time to visit is over 24–5 June, when the Festa do Ibo, known as Kueto Siriwala – 'to not forget your roots' in Kimwani – is held to coincide with Independence Day. Another big event locally is New Year's Day, when the entire village jumps into the sea in a ritual cleansing ceremony known as Tomar de Banho (literally 'Bath-taking').

OTHER ISLANDS OF THE QUIRIMBAS

Although Ibo is the most important of the Quirimbas historically, and the only one that caters to travellers of all budgets, the chain comprises another 31 islands, of which about half a dozen host idyllic upmarket resorts that cater both for sun-worshippers and for those pursuing more active marine adventures. The southernmost 11 islands in the chain, including Quipaco, Mefunvo, Quirimba,

Ibo, Quilálea, Situ and Matemo, are now protected within Quirimbas National Park, while more northerly islands such as Medjumbe, Tambuze, Metundo, Vamizi, Rongui and Tecomaji are not formally protected, though several function as something close to a private sanctuary. The market for these resorts is almost entirely fly-in, which makes the area quite difficult to explore independently or on a budget, with the exception being Matemo Island, where there is a community camp aimed at backpackers, and transport from Ibo can be arranged through Miti Miwiri (page 340), or Quirimba Island, where the Gessner family offers mid-range accommodation by arrangement. Running from south to north, the islands that are of greatest interest to visitors are as follows:

ILHA QUIPACO The most southerly of the archipelago's major islands, Quipaco lies about 40km north of Pemba as the crow flies. It has never boasted much in the way of a settlement due to the scarcity of fresh water. The shallow ocean between here and Ponta do Diablo is known for its good game fishing and a private camp is reputedly under construction, although development seems to have halted (Kaskazini in Pemba will know as and when it opens).

ILHA QUISIVA This 3km² island was settled by the Portuguese in the late 16th century, and later became the main outpost of the Moraes family, who owned five of the Quirimba islands and dominated local trade in the early 18th century. The significant fortified Portuguese ruins on the island are said locally to date to the time of Vasco da Gama, but it seems unlikely they are quite that old, and there are also the remains of some old plantation houses. The sandy spit that protrudes westward from the main island is great for swimming. Quisiva is slated for development by Seasons in Africa (w *quisiva.com*) as an ultra-exclusive beach retreat.

ILHAS QUILÁLEA AND SENCAR These two islands comprise the terrestrial portion of the Quilálea Marine Sanctuary, a pioneering private reserve that was established in 2000 as the archipelago's first protected marine area but now officially forms part of the national park. Since the sanctuary's inception, local fishing has been banned within it, leading to a great increase in marine life. Turtles nest on the beaches, dugongs are sometimes sighted, and humpback whales shelter in the channel from July to January before journeying south. More than 375 different species of fish have been identified in the sanctuary area, giving snorkellers a rare and colourful treat. The shores of Quilálea are particularly rich in seashells. You can stroll round the whole of tiny (35ha) uninhabited Quilálea in well under an hour. Since 2011 it has been home to the exclusive and recently redesigned Azura at Quilálea.

ILHA QUIRIMBA Situated immediately south of Ibo, Quirimba is one of the larger islands in the chain, and is mostly covered by coconut plantations. It was the site of the archipelago's most important trade outpost in the pre-Portuguese era, and it remains one of the more densely settled islands, with a population estimated at 4,000. Farmed by the same German family since the 1920s, they have private chalets for rent with prior arrangement.

ILHA MATEMO The second-largest island in the chain at 24km², Matemo lies to the north of Ibo just within the boundaries of the national park. It was almost certainly settled when the Portuguese first sailed into the Indian Ocean, and its population was boosted when the infamous Zimba raids of the late 16th century encouraged the mainland Muslim community associated with the making of

Maluane cloth to take refuge on the island. Today there are two large villages on the island, along with Portuguese ruins dating to the time when Matemo's plantations were major suppliers of food to Ilha de Moçambique. Characterised by sweeping sandy beaches, lush vegetation and palm groves, it was home to the upmarket Matemo Island Lodge until this closed indefinitely in 2013, leaving the community-run Dade's Place as Matemo's only official lodging.

ILHA DAS ROLAS Only 10 minutes' boat trip from Matemo in calm weather, this tiny island has no fresh water whatsoever, and the small encampment there is used only by itinerant fishermen and their families, who cross to the mainland for water when they're in residence. It has an almost bipolar feel – the southern end is a spit of sand, bereft of any form of vegetation, while the northern end has low, rough scrub. There is a fairly large intertidal area that makes for good beachcombing. It has been recolonised as a breeding site by hawksbill turtles, who are resident in the surrounding reefs. Rolas is regarded as perhaps the best snorkelling site in the Quirimbas, and it is also good for diving.

ILHA MEDJUMBE Site of the exclusive **Medjumbe Island Lodge** this tiny islet (1km by 350m) north of Matemo hosts bird species including the black heron, while the offshore waters contain marlin, sailfish, dogtooth tuna, mackerel, bonefish and various species of kingfish. The diving is spectacular.

ILHAS VAMIZI, MACALOE AND RONGUI Outside the Quirimbas National Park, the Maluane Project was initiated in 1998 to protect an ecologically diverse area of coast that comprises this trio of islands, the surrounding coastal waters, and a 330km^2 wildlife reserve on the facing mainland. The project is supported by the Zoological Society of London and the Mozambican government, and has strong environmental and community links. The objective is to conserve and develop a stretch of coast whose marine wildlife includes turtles, humpback whales, whale sharks, dugongs, dolphins, manta rays and giant clams. It is of particular significance for its pristine reefs, which comprise 30 different genera of coral and support 350 species of reef fish.

The mainland section of the reserve is essentially an extension of the terrestrial sector of the Quirimbas National Park, and it supports a similar selection of species, including elephant, lion, buffalo, hippo, leopard, African wild dog, various antelope and monkey species, and a huge variety of birds. The long-term goal is that the reserve will be sustained by tourist revenue, part of which will be dedicated to associated communities, and to which end the exclusive lodge at Vamizi has been constructed. It is likely that lodges will eventually be built on the other two islands, as well as on the mainland part of the reserve.

GETTING THERE AND AWAY
By air As with Ibo, the easiest way to visit those islands that have tourist facilities is by air. **CR Aviation** operates a daily service connecting all the islands' airstrips to each other and to Pemba, though times and schedules are very flexible depending on the bookings for that day. See page 232 for contact details.

By boat For charter boats between the islands, speak to Miti Miwiri in Ibo, which regularly takes travellers to Dade's Place on Matemo and could presumably head out to islands further afield if you are prepared to pay for it. The Gessner family on Quirimba also runs a supply boat from Ibo and Pemba that accepts passengers (page 348).

By dhow Quirimba Island can be reached with relative ease by dhow, since regular boats run there from Quissanga (again, see the *Ibo* section for details of getting there). As with everything in the archipelago, the boat's timetable will be dictated by the tides and winds, but the crossing usually takes up to 2 hours and it will cost around US$2 per person. There may also be boats travelling between Ibo and Quirimba, but you'll have to ask around on Ibo to find out. Somewhat incredibly, it's also possible to walk from Ibo to Quirimba. If you're mad enough to try this then you need to do it at low spring tides, you *must* take a guide, and you should be prepared for a 3–4-hour walk that starts in the mangroves and ends in a wade across the small channel that separates the bottom of Ibo and the top of Quirimba. Miti Miwiri is the place to go for full details.

WHERE TO STAY As with the island descriptions on pages 343–5, the listings below follow the chain of islands from south to north. It is worth noting that the status of several island lodges is unclear at the time of writing: Matemo Island Resort is closed indefinitely, the lodges on Quipaco and Quisiva are both under development, and there is also talk of new lodges opening on Macaloe and Rongui as part of the Maluane Project. If you want to keep tabs on developments, visit our update website (w *bradtupdates.com/mozambique*) or get in touch with Kaskazini (w *kaskazini.com*).

The choice of budget accommodation other than on Ibo is extremely limited. The only formal possibility is Dade's Place (page 348), but travellers could quite easily find a place to stay in a local house on any of the inhabited islands, especially were they to carry a tent as a fall-back.

Exclusive/luxury

Quisiva Island Sanctuary (14 units)
Ilha Quisiva; +27 31 764 0600 (South Africa);
e info@seasonsinafrica.com; w quisiva.com.
Under development at the time of writing, this new luxury lodge with accommodation in 14 large villas set above a low coral cliff overlooking the sea will offer the full range of marine activities. Rates are likely to be at the very top end of the scale. **$$$$$**

Azura at Quilálea (9 units) +27 11 467 0907 (South Africa); e reservations@azura-retreats.com; w azura-retreats.com/quilalea. Reopened in Nov 2011 as part of Azura Retreats, this fully redesigned lodge on Ilha Quilálea has been highly rated by both tour operators & guests, who called it 'a jewel in Africa' & 'an instant classic'. The house reef is just a few flipper-strokes from the beach & activities inc big-game fishing, PADI dive courses, kayaking, birding, stargazing & excursions to other islands. The beachfront villas have all the expected luxuries, & guests can enjoy the cliffside swimming pool, fully stocked wine cellar & world-class spa treatments as well. Access is via helicopter from Pemba. *From US$750–1,050 pp sharing depending on villa, inc all meals, house wines & non-motorised activities.* **$$$$$**

Medjumbe Private Island (13 units)
Ilha Medjumbe; +27 10 003 8979 (South Africa) or 213 01618; e medjumbe@anatara. com; w medjumbe.anatara.com. Lying on a stretch of sand almost chimeric in its beauty, Ilha Medjumbe is hardly 1km long & 500m wide, tapering into an impossibly fine spit of sand at its western edge. There's an oceanside swimming pool, lounge & wandering opportunities aplenty around the island, while the spa treatments are world-class. Medjumbe is rightfully popular with honeymooners, as accommodation consists of a widely spaced row of beachfront chalets, each with a private jacuzzi/plunge pool set in an open-air deck, as well as a private outdoor shower. The seafood-dominated meals are superb & a full range of marine activities is offered, with plentiful sites for diving & snorkelling. *US$595/1,190 sgl/dbl, inc all meals, house wines & non-motorised activities. Rates slightly higher in peak season.* **$$$$$**

&Beyond Vamizi Island Lodge (10 rooms) Ilha Vamizi; +27 11 809 4300 (South Africa); e contactus@andbeyond. com; w andbeyond.com/vamizi-island. This ultra-exclusive lodge, the only one currently operating in the community-based sanctuary

Maluane Project, now owned & managed by &Beyond, has more of a bush aesthetic. The spacious chalets, strung out along a wide sandy beach, have a floor plan of 170m², king-size 4-poster beds with walk-in nets & paddle fans, a safe, complimentary minibar, & stylish marble bathrooms built with local materials. The beach here is one of the most important turtle-breeding sites in Mozambique, & the island is also home to an endemic dwarf python & the bizarre giant coconut crab. Snorkelling & diving on the pristine offshore reefs are spectacular, & other activities inc fishing, kayaking, dhow trips & forest walks. The food has been praised as among the best anywhere in Mozambique. *Rates vary throughout the year from US$1,970 to US$2,840 per dbl occupancy villa, all-inclusive.* **$$$$$**

GIANT COCONUT CRAB

Looking for all the world like a refugee from an improbable science fiction B-movie, the giant coconut crab is the world's largest terrestrial crustacean, attaining a mass of 5kg, a length of up to 50cm and a leg span of 1m. The foremost of its five leg-pairs terminates in deadly pincers capable of scything straight through a wooden broomstick, or of lifting an object six times its body weight. Pairs two to four, meanwhile, are tipped by smaller pincers that enable the crab to clasp tightly on to the trunks of the vertical palm trees it habitually ascends.

The first recorded description of this massive decapod was penned by the 17th-century Dutch naturalist Georgius Rumphius, who noted that it was 'always on land, without ever getting into the water' and that 'it climbs Coconut Trees, and pinches off the nuts, and then searches under the tree for the ones that were thrown down'. More than a century later, the 'monstrous' terrestrial crab and 'wonderful strength' of its pincers so captured the imagination of Charles Darwin that he devoted a full page of his landmark *Voyage of the Beagle* to describing how an associate 'confined one in a strong tin box… the lid being secured with wire; but the crab turned down the edges and escaped [and] actually punched many small holes through the tin!'

Darwin was the first to document the crab's ability to break open a coconut using its mighty pincers: 'The crab begins by tearing the husk, fibre by fibre, always from that end under which the three eye-holes are situated; when this is completed, the crab commences hammering with its heavy claws on one of the eye-holes till an opening is made. Then turning round its body, by the aid of its posterior and narrow pair of pincers it extracts the white albuminous substance.'

Unusually for a crustacean, the coconut crab only reaches sexual maturity at the venerable age of five years, and some individuals live to be at least 30. The young are amphibious but the adult is a confirmed landlubber that would drown were it to be submerged for any time. Several idiosyncrasies are associated with this terrestrial lifestyle. It has an acute sense of smell thanks to a 'nose' that most closely resembles those of terrestrial insects, a textbook example of convergent evolution.

Its remarkable capacity to climb smooth palm trunks to a height of 6m is encapsulated by Dr Karen Burns' evocative recollection of a 'big adult coconut crab dining on a dead rat that he had hauled high up onto a tree limb leopard-style'. Then there is its magpie-like propensity for wandering back to its daytime lair with a booty of shiny household objects, as alluded to in its German name *palmendieb* (palm thief) as well as in the Latin binomial *Birgus latro* (robber crab).

Mid range

🏠 **Situ Island Lodge** (8 rooms) Situ Island; ☏+27 43 704 4900 (South Africa); e bookings@ situisland.com; w situisland.com. Opened in 2011, this lodge aims to offer guests a peaceful island experience with a 'Robinson Crusoe' feel. Accommodation is in reed & thatch en-suite chalets with king-size or ¾ bed with net. Activities inc fishing, scuba diving, kayaking, hiking, birding & boating. Most guests arrive by boat transfer from Pemba. *US$400 dbl, FB.* **$$$$**

🏠 **Quirimba Lodge** m 86 144 3964; e quirimba.island@gmail.com. Owned by the Gessner family (Rainer), the stand-alone chalets here have a lovely site amid the coconut palms – peaceful & shaded with a stunning view of the sunrises over the Indian Ocean. Lodges on Ibo can arrange transfers here, or you can co-ordinate with Rainer to hop on board the supply boat (page 336). It's likely you'll be the only visitors. *US$50 dbl.* **$$**

Budget and camping

🏠 **Dade's Place** (4 units) Matemo Island; m 82 662 1704, 86 276 9426 or 87 250 0870, or contact through Miti Miwiri on Ibo. Set in the village of Palusansa (aka First Village), this community-run lodge comes highly recommended, offering accommodation in basic A-frames, camping & simple meals. You can also hire a bicycle or moto to explore the island with. Miti Miwiri can arrange transfers. *Rooms US$20 dbl B&B.* **$**

THE QUIRIMBAS MAINLAND

The mainland sector of the Quirimbas National Park, though often neglected in tourist literature, is a truly vast entity, protecting some 5,984km² of predominantly miombo woodland stretching 150km inland from the Indian Ocean to the east bank of the Messala River. Our ecological knowledge of the park is still limited, but it is known to support significant numbers of lion, leopard, spotted hyena, buffalo, plains zebra, sable antelope, eland, greater kudu, waterbuck, bushbuck, reedbuck, red duiker, suni, bushpig, warthog, samango monkey, vervet monkey and yellow baboon. The elephant population, estimated at 2,000, is thought to be partially migratory, with some seasonal movement to the more westerly Niassa Reserve, but a WWF study of eight collared individuals undertaken in 2009 was unable to establish this for certain. The park is also home to a substantial population of the endangered African wild dog, with a minimum of six packs and 60 individuals thought to be present, though once again it is unclear whether this should be considered as an eastern extension of the Niassa-Selous population.

An estimated 90,000 people live within the park, mostly along the road corridors and coastline, and another 30,000 inhabit the 10km-wide buffer zone that surrounds it. Although there is some conflict between the Quirimbas's human and animal inhabitants (elephants in particular often raid local subsistence farms), the park was established largely at the request of these local communities. And while tourist development of the park's mainland is still in its infancy, the few options that exist are all to some extent community-driven, a trend that will almost certainly continue as further lodges and camps are added.

 WHERE TO STAY *Map, page 332, unless otherwise stated*

🏠 **Guludo Beach Camp** (9 units) ☏269 60536; m 87 595 0590; e enquiries@guludo.com; w guludo.com. Founded on 'fair trade tourism' principles & operated in conjunction with a UK-registered charity, this small honeymoon-friendly lodge overlooks what was voted the world's 14th-best deserted beach by UK newspaper the *Observer* & the 13th-best location in the world by *Sábado* magazine in Lisbon – a long unspoilt stretch of white sand fringed with palm trees. Accommodation is in spacious beachfront tented or adobe bandas with macuti roofs & a barefoot luxury ambience. The restaurant serves food bought daily from local fishermen, & activities inc diving, snorkelling, village visits, seasonal whale watching, sunset cruises & visits to Ibo. An important & impressive aspect of the lodge is its support of local community projects, & it is also actively involved in marine research. The lodge is situated at the northern end of the park more or less opposite Matemo Island & about 15km south of Mucojo. Most people fly here from Pemba (landing at Matemo's airstrip for a boat transfer) but the road here is in good condition & a land transfer from Pemba is a lot cheaper than flying. *US$370–750 dbl depending on season & type of room, inc meals & most non-motorised activities.* **$$$$$**

⌂ **Mareja Lodge** (5 rooms) ☏ 272 20684; m 84 808 9522 or 87 569 2298; e mareja@live. co.uk or sofa.scott@outlook.com; w mareja.com. This lodge is set on the eponymous community-based Mareja Reserve, which protects a varied habitat of riverine, palm & upland forests, as well as coastal savannah & inselbergs, set within the mainland portion of Quirimbas National Park. Elephant, kudu, bushbuck, sable antelope, lion & leopard are resident, & African wild dog pass through from time to time. The project aims to train locals as rangers & has had success in limiting illegal hunting & logging in the area, thus providing a safe zone for local wildlife to thrive. Accommodation is in a restored colonial farmhouse abandoned after independence & sleeps up to 10, & camping is permitted. Meals can be provided if ordered in advance, while activities inc guided walks, game drives, birdwatching & community dances. The drive from Pemba to Mareja Lodge takes up to 3hrs, using 1 of 2 routes. The shorter (70km) coastal route along the Quissanga road via Metugé requires a 4x4

throughout & can be impassable during the rainy season. The longer route through the interior entails following the surfaced EN243 (N380) towards Mocímboa da Praia as far as Nanduli (about 100km from Pemba), then turning right on to a dirt road & following it for another 40km to the lodge. Transfers can be arranged through Kaskazini in Pemba. *US$20 pp bed, US$10 pp camping.* **$**

⌂ **Taratibu Bush Camp** [not mapped] (3 units) Contact Koos von Lansberg m 86 388 9959/509 3227 or 82 663 3570 for details. The only other place to stay in the mainland part of Quirimbas National Park, this fantastically remote camp comprises 3 self-catering chalets alongside a river & below a trio of dramatic inselbergs, 1 of which has an impressive baobab forest on its crown. Unfortunately, the chalets are currently in a state of disrepair & the camp is catering only to researchers, as severe poaching has drastically affected the elephant population. It is likely the camp will see a facelift during the lifespan of this edition, so don't completely count it out if you're not affiliated with a university. When the camp is back in full swing, guided walks are the main activity, with elephant & greater kudu common in the dry season, & the surrounding woodland & rivers host an immense variety of birds. Access is by 4x4 only & bookings are essential. It lies about 3hrs' drive from Pemba, following the EN242 (N14) west to within about 30km of Montepuez, then heading north along a dirt track (full directions can be obtained upon booking), so could be visited *en route* to the Niassa Reserve (page 366), though a stopover of at least 2 nights is recommended.

NUARRO LODGE

Set on Memba Bay about 100km south of Pemba and 50km north of Nacala, this isolated upmarket lodge is not actually situated within the Quirimbas, but it is similarly geared towards honeymooners, divers and marine enthusiasts seeking an exclusive beachfront retreat. Accommodation is in 12 vast beachfront chalets with king-size bed, walk-in nets, indoor and outdoor showers, a lounge area, and a large wooden veranda and sun deck. The lodge has a private dive centre that also offers snorkelling, sea kayaking, dhow trips to Ilha de Moçambique and Lúrio Falls, walking and cycling eco-trails, birdwatching and cultural village tours. Rates are US$525/700 single/double inclusive of meals and non-motorised activities (**$$$$$**).

For further details, contact ☏ *+27 21 813 6594 (South Africa);* m *82 305 3027/8;* e *reservations@nuarro.com;* w *nuarro.com.*

PANGANE

Situated about 50km east of the EN243 (N380), this remote Mwani fishing village – *sans* electricity, internet and, until recently, mobile-phone reception – boasts an extremely pleasant white beach, set on a spit of land that points out towards Ilha Macaloe, and a long-standing reputation as a good place to get away from it all. It lies less than 10km north of the Quirimbas National Park boundary, and the area still supports significant (but elusive) populations of large mammals such as buffalo, elephant and lion. But the focus of attention here is the beach, which offers a range of seaside activities – it's easy to hire a boat to explore the surrounding reefs or to any of the Quirimba islands – and offers stunning sunsets over the fishing boats moored off the sprawling village. Pangane is one of the few places in this part of the country that caters to backpackers, and it is relatively accessible on public transport, particularly for people who are already heading north from Pemba towards the Tanzanian border.

GETTING THERE AND AWAY

By car Coming from Pemba, you first need to follow the surfaced **EN106/243** (EN1/N380) towards Mueda as far as Macomia. Here, you must turn right on to the **EN528** (R766), the first 40km of which, as far as Mucojo, is hard dirt, variable in quality but overall quite easy to drive. The shorter 12km section between Mucojo and Pangane is more challenging, veering from rutted dirt road to sand track, and trying to do it in anything other than a 4x4 is foolish.

By chapa A few chapas run along the EN528 (R766), leaving from the same junction as buses north and south; some only go as far as Mucojo, while others continue to Pangane. The cost is the same, around US$5, and the journey time to Mucojo is around 4 hours. Pangane itself is another hour or so's drive. While you could walk it, it entails around 10km over rough road that turns into a sand track around halfway.

⌂ WHERE TO STAY

⌂ **Casa Suki** In the centre of the village, with small but pleasant enough rooms, though they can get very hot during the summer nights. *Rooms US$10.* **$**

UPDATES WEBSITE

You can post your comments and recommendations, and read the latest feedback and updates from other readers online at **w** bradtupdates.com/mozambique.

20

Niassa Province

Niassa is Mozambique's driest, most remote, poorest and least densely populated province. It's also one of the most beautiful, with scenery ranging from the mountains of the Rift Valley to the shores of Lago Niassa (Lake Malawi). Samora Machel used to treat the province as a dumping ground for people who weren't entirely behind Frelimo after independence, and it is still known as 'Ponte Final' among officials, for whom a posting here is regarded as a career dead end. This partly explains why Niassa was the birthplace of Renamo (albeit with Rhodesian midwifery) and why the opposition party still enjoys strong support here.

Niassa has the smallest population (1,722,100) in the largest area (129,056km²) of any Mozambican province, and the villages tend to be based along the roads and around the lake. Most travellers only see a small part of the province, skirting through Cuamba *en route* between Nampula and Malawi, but its real highlights lie further north. The shores of Lago Niassa provide a peaceful counterpoint to the busier Malawian side of the same lake, and the provincial capital Lichinga is a breezy montane town where you might finally find a use for the sweater that your mum made you bring along 'just in case it gets cold at night'. For wildlife enthusiasts, there is also the vast and remote Niassa Reserve, which extends over 42,000km² along the border with Tanzania.

CUAMBA

The most important route focus in northwest Mozambique, Cuamba was historically the western terminus of the railway line (and road) to Nampula (for Pemba and Ilha de Moçambique), the main roads north to Lichinga and Lago Niassa, a quieter route southeast via Gurué to Quelimane, and several crossing points west into Malawi. As of late 2016, the completion of the restoration of the Cuamba–Lichinga railway means that the seaport of Nacala is once again connected to Entre Lagos on the Malawi border, creating an important trade and passenger corridor for the movement of reasonably priced goods throughout Niassa. Formerly called Nova Freixo ('New Ash'), it has a population of around 108,000, making it one of the largest towns in the Mozambican interior. Set along the Muanda River at an altitude of 575m below a horseshoe of attractive mountains, it is not the most inspiring of places, being relatively dry, dusty and chilly, and rather quiet despite its status as a university town (the Catholic University's Department of Agriculture is based here).

Situated about 10km northeast of the town centre, Serra Mitucué rises to 1,803m above the surrounding plains and is the source of several streams, including a tributary of the Muanda that has been dammed at Chefe Namacôma to form a kilometre-long serpentine lake that provides hydro-electric power to the town. The dam is quite high up on the eastern side of the massif, and the hike from the base takes 2 hours. Guides and directions can be obtained from the Hotel Castel or Pensão São Miguel.

GETTING THERE AND AWAY

By car Roads to and from Cuamba are mostly unsurfaced and in quite poor condition, though this is rapidly changing with the resurfacing of 200km of the staggeringly beautiful 350km EN8 to Nampula, and the scheduled resurfacing of the 300km route to Lichinga. At Mutuali, about 65km east of Cuamba, a 100km unsurfaced road runs south to Gurué. Northwest of Cuamba, a 140km stretch of the EN8 runs to the Malawian border town of Mandimba, from where the **EN249** runs for about 145km north to the provincial capital Lichinga. Though it was unsurfaced at the time of writing, this road is in pretty good nick and can be covered in about 5 hours in a private vehicle.

By chapa and train Most **chapas** leave from around the railway station at the southern end of town. Chapas to Mandimba cost US$8 and take about 3 hours, while chapas to Lichinga cost US$12 and take about 6 hours. Direct pick-ups to Gurué leave at 05.00 and cost US$6, but it is also possible to take the **train** as far as Mutuali and catch road transport from there. There is a daily **Maning Nice** bus from Nampula to Cuamba for US$8 along with local, daily chapas in both directions. Coming from Nampula by train, you can be sure there will be chapas to the border towns of Mandimba and Entrélagos waiting for your arrival.

For details of the passenger train, operated by Corredor de Desenvolvimento do Norte or CDN, between Cuamba and Nampula, see page 280. The train from Cuamba to Lichinga takes 6–8 hours and costs around US$3, departing on Saturday at 06.00. The return train, from Lichinga to Cuamba, departs on Sunday, also leaving at 06.00. For updates on the train schedule visit w cdn.co.mz/en/passengers-transport or call the Nampula office (\ *213 44800*) for the latest on train transport in the north.

WHERE TO STAY *Map, opposite*

Mid range

Hotel Castel (20 rooms) Av 3 de Fevereiro; m 86 128 4706; e hotelcastel@yahoo.com. The closest thing to an international hotel in Cuamba, this long-serving, recently renovated central institution has clean, comfortable en-suite rooms with AC, hot water & TV. The terrace bar & restaurant (closed when we popped in, but planning to reopen) serves a predictable selection of chicken, fish & curry dishes. Wi-Fi available. *US$56 dbl B&B.* **$$$**

Pensão São Miguel Av 3 de Fevereiro; m 86 128 4706/353 5345. A couple of doors down from Hotel Castel, the São Miguel has quiet but slightly frayed rooms, some with en-suite bathroom, TV & fridge. It also has secure parking & an adequate restaurant. Overpriced. *US$36 en-suite dbl.* **$$**

Quinto Timbwa (25 rooms) 2km out of town off the Mandimba Rd; m 82 305 4938 or 86 605 5932. This unexpected gem, set in a patch of indigenous bush overlooking a small artificial lake, is the best place to stay for those with private transport & a possibility for those without, as it is only a 25min walk from the railway/chapa station, & well signposted. Accommodation ranges from small twin rooms with fan & shared bathroom to cottages with sitting room, TV, AC, fridge & en-suite bathroom with hot shower & tub. The restaurant, reached via a wooden bridge over the lake, serves very acceptable meals for around US$5–8, & an unusually hearty b/fast is included in all room rates. *US$24–50 en-suite dbl.* **$$**

Budget

Pensão Cariacó (22 rooms) Av 5 Novembro; \271 62595/685; m 86 135 1365/725 7807. An acceptable budget hotel set around a green courtyard about 5mins' walk from the railway station. The rooms are nothing to shout about but seem good value (at least unless you have just crossed from Malawi) & the pricier rooms come with private bathrooms &/or TV. Secure parking. *US$10/14 sgl/dbl; US$15–40 en-suite dbl.* **$$**

WHERE TO EAT AND DRINK *Map, opposite*

There isn't a huge range of places aside from the hotels, of which the **Hotel Castel** (🕓 *06.00–22.00 daily, but temporarily closed*) and the superior but less central

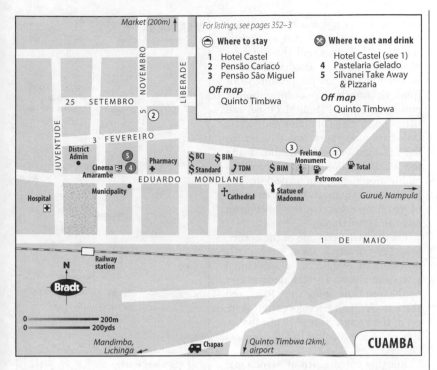

For listings, see pages 352–3

Where to stay
1 Hotel Castel
2 Pensão Cariacó
3 Pensão São Miguel

Off map
Quinto Timbwa

Where to eat and drink
Hotel Castel (see 1)
4 Pastelaria Gelado
5 Silvanei Take Away & Pizzaria

Off map
Quinto Timbwa

CUAMBA

Quinto Timbwa stand out. Alternatively the **Silvanei Take Away & Pizzaria** (⏲ *06.00–late daily*) is a local favourite among Peace Corps volunteers. Next door to the cinema, the **Pastelaria Gelado** serves a good range of pastries, drinks and sandwiches, and has a small supermarket. You'll also find snack kiosks in the parks and the Total gas station has a small café with a limited menu. The market is very small and has a limited range of fresh fruit and vegetables.

OTHER PRACTICALITIES
Banks and ATMs BIM Millennium has two branches, while BCI and Standard Bank each have one.

Hospital To the left-hand side of the square, in front of the railway station, and there's a pharmacy on Avenue Eduardo Mondlane.

Internet TDM used to have one PC with an internet connection in the same building as the post office, but it appeared to be closed on last inspection.

Post office In the centre of town, just over from the statue of the Madonna.

Security The disused airstrip south of the town centre is an army barracks, and best avoided or you risk a protracted run-in with the police.

MANDIMBA AND MASSANGULO

Situated at the west of the EN8 about 140km from Cuamba, Mandimba is the most popular and probably the best road crossing between northern Mozambique and

Malawi. There's not much to the town itself; just a block or two of slightly run-down buildings and the usual set of official buildings associated with a border town. If you are heading to or from Malawi, the Mozambican border post is 4km from Mandimba itself, and there's no shortage of motos and bicycle taxis to shuttle you across. The fee for the full 6km between Mandimba and the Malawian border at Chiponde is highly negotiable, but expect to pay US$1–3. Alternatively you can walk, or just hang around at the junction in town and try to hitch.

On the Malawian side of the border, a hugely attractive 35km road winds downhill to Mangochi, a substantial town with plenty of accommodation set on the west bank of the Shire River, and there is plenty of transport from there on to the evergreen resorts of Monkey Bay and Cape Maclear in Lake Malawi National Park.

Roughly 65km north of Mandimba, Massangulo is a characterful small town about 2km east of the main Cuamba–Lichinga road. It is situated at the base of a pretty mountain, and centred on the oldest Catholic mission in the region, whose extraordinary church was evidently built without cement. Massangulo could be an attractive place to spend a couple of nights, particularly if you like walking, though there is no formal accommodation as far as we can ascertain. Most vehicles heading between Cuamba and Lichinga don't divert to Massangulo, but you can ask to be dropped at the signposted turn-off and walk from there.

MANDIMBA

(SKETCH MAP)

Bradt

Not to scale

↑ Lichinga

Pensão João

Chapas

$ BIM

Supermarket

Police

Petromoc

Cell phone tower

Market

Governor's Residence

Malawi

Frelimo Monument

Cuamba ↓   ♪ TDM

Where to stay
1   Complexo Massinga *see below*

WHERE TO STAY, EAT AND DRINK *Map, above*

Complexo Massinga (11 rooms)
m 82 300 0778. The largest & nicest of a few adequate lodgings in Mandimba, a block or 2 north of the border junction along the road to Lichinga. Accommodation is a series of clean,

well-appointed rondavels. There's also a restaurant serving meals for around US$7–9, an open-air disco & secure parking. *US$24 en-suite dbl; US$30 with TV & AC.* **$**

LICHINGA

Founded in 1931 with the name of Vila Cabral, Lichinga is the capital of Niassa Province, the main domestic gateway to the Mozambican shore of Lago Niassa, and the country's eighth-largest city, with a rapidly growing population currently estimated at 224,000. It is the main population centre for the Yao people, who also live in bordering parts of Malawi, and whose long Muslim tradition dates back to their involvement in the 19th-century slave trade.

Set on a plateau that forms part of the eastern Rift Valley escarpment above Lago Niassa, Lichinga lies at an altitude of around 1,350m and has a refreshingly breezy climate. The well-watered and fertile soils around town support the unusual combination of exotic pine plantations and more characteristic tropical vegetation such as mango trees and leafy plantains.

Lichinga has a markedly different atmosphere from any other large town in Mozambique and, without being in any way spectacular, has a relaxed, temperate mood that might end up enticing you to stay slightly longer than you had planned.

GETTING THERE AND AWAY

By air There is an **airport** about 7km north of the city centre, off the road to Metangula, and **LAM** (*Av FPLM;* ↘ *271 20434*) flies here from Nampula, Beira, Quelimane, Tete and Maputo several times a week.

By road The main routes in and out of Lichinga are the 145km intermittently surfaced and pot-holed **EN249** south to Mandimba, the adequately surfaced 110km EN249 north to the lakeshore port of Metangula, and the magnificently nippy **EN242**, which is surfaced for 310km east to Marrupa. There are plenty of **chapas** in both directions along the EN249, leaving from the station next to the market, and it's not uncommon for **lorries** looking for passengers to swing by there as well. Chapas to Metangula or Mandimba cost around US$4 each, but getting to Marrupa will cost you about US$12. Several buses make the trek from Lichinga to Pemba for around US$25. For northbound travellers with a taste for roughing it, there's supposed to be a daily truck that heads to the Unity II Bridge over the Rovuma at Matchedje (also known as Segundo Congresso). Recent travellers report Tanzanian visas are now being issued here as well. There's another chapa station south of town, **Chiuaula**, which has buses to Cuamba, Marrupa and Pemba.

By train Train service has recently begun once again from Cuamba (page 352); the station is about 3km south of the town centre.

⌅ WHERE TO STAY *Map, page 356*
Upmarket
⌂ **Montebelo Lichinga Hotel** (72 rooms) Av Filipe Samuel Magaia; ↘271 21280; m 82 300 3676; e girassollichingahotel@ visabeira.co.mz; w montebelohotels.com. This 4-star hotel in the centre of the city caters mainly to business travellers, but is also the most comfortable option for tourists. The tiled en-suite rooms are very spacious if perhaps a little under-furnished, but they all come with DSTV, combination hot tub/shower & Wi-Fi. There is a good ground-floor restaurant. *US$97/109 sgl/dbl; from US$141 suites; all rates B&B.* **$$$$**

Mid range
⌂ **Pousada Lichinga** (12 rooms) Av Filipe Samuel Magaia; m 87 817 0522. Clean & simple rooms with fan & TV in a central location. There's an on-site bar, lounge & restaurant with the local fare for US$4–10. *US$40/60 twin using shared facilities/en-suite dbl.* **$$**

⌂ **Residencial 2+1** (25 rooms) Av Primeira; ↘271 21632; m 82 713 1210; e residential.rest. catering.2.1@gmail.com. Recognisable from afar thanks to the bright orange exterior, this pleasant & popular hotel has clean en-suite rooms with TV, fan, AC & hot shower. There's a restaurant as well serving mains for US$12–18. *US$36/40 sgl/dbl.* **$$**

⌂ **Residencial Bendiak** (13 rooms) Av do Trabalho; ↘271 20797; m 82 706 4790/857 6540; e residencialbendiak@hotmail.com. Set in an orderly green compound directly opposite the hospital, the tiled rooms here are all en suite with TV, fridge, kettle, nets & fan, & some with AC. Executive rooms have kitchen facilities. There's secure parking & a prim little garden with outdoor seating as well. Excellent value. *US$36/40 dbl/exec; all rooms B&B.* **$$**

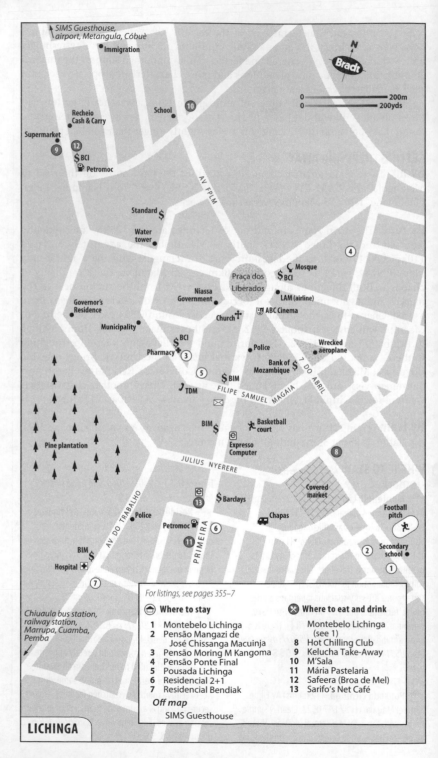

SIMS Guesthouse,
airport, Metangula, Cóbuè

• Immigration

N

Bradt

0 ————————— 200m
0 ————————— 200yds

• School ⑩

Recheio
Cash & Carry •

Supermarket
⑨ ⑫
$ BCI
🖳 Petromoc

AV FPLM

Standard $

Water
tower

④

Praça dos
Liberados

Ç Mosque
$ BCI

Niassa
Government

LAM (airline)

Governor's
Residence •

Church † 🎦 ABC Cinema

Municipality •

$ BCI
✚
Pharmacy ♪ ③

• Police

Wrecked
• aeroplane

⑤ $ BIM

Bank of
Mozambique $

7 DO ABRIL

♪ TDM

FILIPE SAMUEL MAGAIA

✉

BIM $

🏃 Basketball
court

Ⓔ
Expresso
Computer

⑧

Pine plantation

JULIUS NYERERE

Covered
market

Ⓔ
⑬ $ Barclays

🚐 Chapas

Football
pitch

AV DO TRABALHO

• Police

Petromoc 🖳 ⑥

PRIMEIRA

🏃
② Secondary
school •

BIM $
⑪

Hospital ✚

①

⑦

Chiuaula bus station,
railway station,
Marrupa, Cuamba,
Pemba

For listings, see pages 355–7

🛏 **Where to stay**

1 Montebelo Lichinga
2 Pensão Mangazi de
   José Chissanga Macuinja
3 Pensão Moring M Kangoma
4 Pensão Ponte Final
5 Pousada Lichinga
6 Residencial 2+1
7 Residencial Bendiak

Off map
SIMS Guesthouse

❌ **Where to eat and drink**

   Montebelo Lichinga
   (see 1)
8 Hot Chilling Club
9 Kelucha Take-Away
10 M'Sala
11 Mária Pastelaria
12 Safeera (Broa de Mel)
13 Sarifo's Net Café

LICHINGA

🏠 **SIMS Guesthouse** (10 rooms) Av Julius Nyerere; m 86 870 0869; e tim.george@sim. org. Operated by American Christian missionaries working for SIM (w sim.org), this guesthouse is primarily set up for local missionaries, who are given priority when booking. Non-missionary guests are welcome to claim a bed in the communal house with bed nets, hot water, kitchen & Wi-Fi. No smoking or alcohol. Excellent value. *US$20pp.* **$**

Budget

🏠 **Pensão Mangazi de José Chissanga Macuinja** (16 rooms) m 82 707 9480 or 84 271 5632. Magnificently named & tucked away on a street off the market, this place is only a 1min walk from the chapas, & pretty good value, the

higher-priced rooms having firm beds & en-suite bathrooms. *US$12 sgl using shared ablutions; US$20 en-suite sgl.* **$**

🏠 **Pensão Ponte Final** (14 rooms) Av Filipe Samuel Magaia; ☎ 271 20912; m 82 304 3632/567 6689. This comfortable lodge on the verge of the city centre has clean en-suite motel-style rooms with TV, hot water & fridge. Facilities inc restaurant & secure parking. *US$26/40 sgl/dbl inc cursory b/fast.* **$$**

Shoestring

🏠 **Pensão Moring M Kangoma** (25 rooms) m 82 551 2659. Also just around the corner from the chapa station, this rabbit warren of a place is as basic as it gets, but the dingy cell-like rooms seem clean & have nets. *US$6/8 sgl/dbl.* **$**

🍴 WHERE TO EAT AND DRINK *Map, opposite*

🍴 **Kelucha Take-Away** Av Julius Nyerere; m 86 654 5744; ◷ 08.00–22.00 daily. Looking every bit the hole in the wall, this Lichinga stalwart has a rotating daily menu of the usual chicken, fish & curry dishes, with some welcome additions such as chouriço & South African boerewors sausage. It's all done with a touch of class, & the laid-back bar stays open late. *Mains US$3–5.* **$**

🍴 **Mária Pastelara** Av Primeira; m 84 819 1366; ◷ 07.00–21.00 daily. A favourite among local Peace Corps volunteers, this café offers a range of snacks & meals, inc sandwiches & pizza alongside baked goods & espresso. *US$2–8.* **$$**

🍴 **Montebelo Lichinga** (page 355) ◷ 07.00–19.00 daily. This hotel restaurant is the smartest in town, & arguably the best. The food is a bit overpriced, but servings are generous & few other central options stay open in the evening. *Mains US$10–16.* **$$$$**

🍴 **M'Sala** Av FPLM; m 86 689 5295 or 84 487 4712; ◷ 10.00–22.00 Tue–Sun. In an unmissable yellow building just northwest of the central plaza, this casual eatery serves up Portuguese & Mozambican favourites with something of an Italian twist. There's a full bar, espresso, a choice of wine, & big family-style picnic tables to eat at. *Mains US$8–14.* **$$$$**

🍴 **Safeera Restaurant (Broa de Mel)** Av Julius Nyerere; ◷ 07.00–21.00 daily; m 86 777 8677. Prior to new management, this place normally boasts a lengthy menu, inc pizzas, pastries, sandwiches & shawarma. It is rumoured the owner will head back to town, in which event the full menu will return. If not, expect a limited menu with pizza, sandwiches & coffee. A new restaurant may open during the lifespan of this edition a bit more central in town, next to the ABC Cinema. *Pastries & sandwiches go for about US$3, while pizzas & mains start at US$5.* **$**

🍴 **Sarifo's Net Café** Av Primeira; ◷ 06.30–21.30 daily; m 82 739 8408. Situated diagonally opposite the Residencial 2+1, this place could reasonably bill itself as the 3-in-1: internet café, bakery serving fresh pastries & sandwiches, and restaurant serving a standard range of Mozambican fish, meat & chicken dishes. It's a friendly set-up, but the buffet starts to look a bit tired by the afternoon. *US$5–9.* **$$**

🍷 **Hot Chilling Club** Av Julius Nyerere; m 82 598 5513. One of a cluster of bars in the Feira Popular next to the market, this distinguishes itself from the pack by having satellite TV & pool tables.

OTHER PRACTICALITIES

Banks and ATMs All the main banks are represented in Lichinga, including Barclays, Standard, BIM Millennium and BCI, and most branches have ATMs within a block of the central Praça dos Liberados.

Hospital On Avenida Trabalho (✆ 271 20065).

Internet Your best option is the air-conditioned **TDM** office (🕐 07.00–19.00 Mon–Fri, 06.00–13.00 Sat), which has several computers and a good connection. Barring that, both **Expresso Computer** and **Sarifo's Net Café** on Avenida Primeira have some machines and are slightly cheaper than TDM, at 40Mt/hour (as opposed to 1Mt/min).

Police There is a police station on Avenida Trabalho opposite the hospital and another one on Avenida Primeira just down from Praça dos Liberados (✆ 271 20751).

Post office Opposite the BIM Millennium on the corner of avenidas Filipe Samuel Magaia and Primeira.

CICHLIDS OF LAGO NIASSA

The staggering diversity of Africa's terrestrial fauna is old news, but few people are aware that it also harbours the greatest freshwater fish diversity of any continent. And nowhere does this diversity reach such heights as in Lago Niassa, whose 850 described fish species – with more awaiting formal discovery – exceed the number of known freshwater species in Europe and North America combined.

Lago Niassa's fish diversity is the product of the most dramatic incidence of explosive speciation known to evolutionists. The majority of these fish species are cichlids – pronounced 'sicklids' – a perch-like family of freshwater fishes called Cichlidae that ranges through the Middle East, Madagascar, Asia and South and Central America. It is in Africa's three largest lakes, however, that this widespread family has undergone an unprecedented explosion of evolutionarily recent speciation that has resulted in it constituting an estimated 5% of the world's vertebrate species.

The cichlids of Africa's great lakes are generally divided into a few major groupings, often referred to by scientists by names used locally in Malawi and/ or Mozambique. These include the small plankton-eating *utaka*, the large, pike-like and generally predatory *ncheni*, the bottom-feeding *chisawasawa* and the algae-eating *mbuna*. People who have travelled in any part of Africa close to a lake will almost certainly have dined on one or other of the tilapia (or closely related *oreochromis*) cichlids, large ncheni that make excellent eating and are known locally as *chambo*. To aquarium keepers, snorkellers and scuba divers, however, the most noteworthy African cichlids are the mbuna, a spectacularly colourful group of small fish of which some 300 species are known from Lake Malawi alone.

The mbuna of Lago Niassa first attracted scientific interest in the 1950s, when they formed the subject of Dr Geoffrey Fryer's classic study of adaptive radiation. This term is used to describe the explosion of a single stock species into a variety of closely related forms, each of which evolves specialised modifications that allow it to exploit an ecological niche quite different from that occupied by the common ancestral stock. This phenomenon is most likely to occur when an adaptable species colonises an environment where several food sources are going unused, for instance on a newly formed volcanic island or lake. The most celebrated incidence of adaptive radiation – the one that led Charles Darwin to propose the theory of evolution through natural selection – occurred on the Galapagos Islands, where a variety of finch species evolved from one common seed-eating ancestor to fill several very different ecological niches.

Shopping If you are self-catering, there are several supermarkets to choose from. The best is probably the Recheio Cash & Carry on Julius Nyerere, but there are a few others along avenidas Primeira and Filipe Samuel Magaia. The central market has a better than average selection of vegetables, fruit and meat on offer.

LAGO NIASSA (LAKE MALAWI)

Better known to outsiders as Lake Malawi, Lago Niassa is the third-largest lake in Africa (and ninth largest in the world), running for 585km from north to south, and up to 75km wide from east to west. By any name, it is a remarkable body of water, lying at the southern end of the Rift Valley system, the immense geological scar that cuts through Africa all the way from the Red Sea to the Zambezi Valley. Up to 700m deep, it is hemmed in by the dramatic mountains of the Rift Valley escarpment, which

The explosive speciation that has occurred among Africa's cichlids is like Darwin's finches amplified a hundredfold. The many hundreds of cichlid species in Lake Tanganyika and Lago Niassa evolved from a handful of river cichlids that entered the lakes when they formed about two to three million years ago. (No less remarkable is the probability that the 200 or so cichlids in Lake Victoria all evolved from a few common ancestors over the 10,000–15,000 years since the lake last dried up.) In all three lakes, specialised cichlid species have evolved to exploit practically every conceivable food source: algae, plankton, insects, fish, molluscs and other fishes. Somewhat macabrely, the so-called kiss-of-death cichlids feed by sucking eggs and hatchlings from the mouths of mouth-brooding cichlids. No less striking is the diverse array in size, coloration and mating behaviour displayed across different species. In addition to being a case study in adaptive radiation, the cichlids of the great lakes are routinely cited as a classic example of parallel evolution – in other words, many similar adaptations appear to have occurred independently in all three lakes.

Why this should have occurred with the cichlids rather than any of several other fish families is a question that is likely to keep ichthyologists occupied for decades. One factor is that cichlids are exceptionally quick to mature, and thus have a rapid turnover of generations. Their anatomy also appears to be unusually genetically malleable, with skull, body, tooth and gut structures readily modifying over relatively few generations.

This capacity to colonise new freshwater habitats is boosted by a degree of parental care rare in other fish – the mouth-brooders, which include all but one of the cichlid species of Lago Niassa, hold their eggs and fry in their mouth until they are large enough to fend for themselves. Bearing in mind that the separation of breeding populations lies at the core of speciation, there is also mounting evidence to suggest that cichlids have a unique capacity to erect non-physical barriers between emergent species – possibly linked to a correlation between colour morphs and food preferences in diverging populations.

Africa's lake cichlids are never likely to rival its terrestrial wildlife as a tourist attraction. All the same, snorkelling and diving in Lago Niassa is both thrilling in itself, and a humbling introduction to what has justifiably been described as a 'unique evolutionary showcase'.

20

tower more than a kilometre above its surface in places. Known for its thrillingly clear water and relatively low pollution levels, it probably harbours a greater variety of fish than any other lake in the world, including hundreds of endemic cichlid species.

The bulk of Lago Niassa lies within Malawi, but the northeastern waters are territorially part of Tanzania, while some 200km of the eastern shore falls within the Mozambican province that shares its name. The Mozambican part of the lake is poorly developed for tourism compared with Malawian resorts such as Nkhata Bay and Cape Maclear, but it is no less beautiful, and its westward orientation is ideal for catching the sunsets for which the region is famed. Furthermore, there is a genuine sense of adventure attached to exploring this off-the-beaten-track corner of Mozambique, though the lakeshore does now host a couple of superb eco-friendly upmarket destinations in the form of the award-winning Manda Wilderness Community Conservation Area and the newer and less well-known Mbuna Bay Lodge (page 363). The Mozambican portion of the lake was officially gazetted as a reserve and designated as a Ramsar Wetland of International Importance in 2011.

There are three main points of access to the Mozambican shore of Lago Niassa. Starting in the south, Meponda lies almost directly east of Lichinga along a good 65km road, so is the easiest place to reach from the provincial capital. Metangula has better facilities than Meponda but is roughly 110km from Lichinga, albeit along a road that is now surfaced in its entirety. The more remote village of Cóbuè lies another 100km north of Metangula, along a road that can be tricky in parts, but its proximity to Malawi's popular Likoma Island makes it a good point to cross between Malawi and Mozambique.

The more adventurous traveller might be interested to know that there are walking paths between Meponda, Metangula and Cóbuè (though the sandy paths are not particularly suitable for cycling). The stretch from Meponda to Metangula, for instance, will take about three days for a good walker, who should carry

NIASSA OR MALAWI?

The original local name for Lago Niassa is something of a mystery. The name Niassa (or Nyasa) probably dates to 1859, when the explorer David Livingstone reached the lakeshore and mistakenly applied the generic local term for lake (Nyasa or Nyanza) to his discovery. Throughout the colonial era, the lake was officially known as Nyasa or Niassa, and the country we now know as Malawi was called Nyasaland. In 1964, however, Nyasaland gained independence from Britain under the leadership of Dr Hastings Banda, who retitled both the country and the lake Malawi.

Several explanations have been put forward for this. Banda himself once claimed that Malawi is an adaptation of 'Maravi', the name of a (possibly unrelated) lake depicted on J B B d'Anville's famous 18th-century map of southern Africa. Maravi is also the name of an iron-smelting empire that flourished in the region in the 15th century, and is widely seen as the precursor to the modern-day Chewa people of south-central Malawi. Another story is that Maravi is a local word meaning 'flaming water', a reference to the dazzling sunrises and sunsets that frequently illuminate the lake's surface.

Whatever the truth, while Malawians and most outsiders now know the lake as Malawi, this name has never been favoured in the other two countries that share its waters, so it is still officially and colloquially known as Lake Nyasa in Tanzania and Lago Niassa in Mozambique.

enough food and water to last the whole trip. If you're looking for inspiration, the admirable English doctor Peg Cumberland has walked the entire length of the coast innumerable times since 2004, with nothing but a backpack of medicine to treat locals who have no access to proper medical facilities. Known locally as Dr Peg, she has also trained about 400 locals as volunteer health carers, and was awarded an MBE in the New Year Honours List for 2010.

MEPONDA The closest lakeshore settlement to Lichinga, Meponda is little more than a glorified village whose few concrete buildings are mostly derelict. It lies on an attractive sandy beach that arcs for a kilometre or more below low wooded hills, and is host to the new **N'tendele Lodge** (m *87 407 4732;* e *info@ntendele. com;* w *ntendele.com*), complete with bar and restaurant. The lodge is eco-friendly and has private rooms, small cottages, a dorm and camping facilities (*US$40/80 small cottage/private dbl room, US$20 dorm, US$4 pp camping;* **$$$**). Chapas from Lichinga to Meponda cost around US$1.50 and take up to 2 hours. Meponda is also the southernmost port of call for the MV *Chambo* (page 365).

METANGULA The largest settlement on the Mozambican shore of Lago Niassa (which truly isn't saying a great deal), Metangula is of ignominious historical significance as the most important port on the eastern lakeshore when the slave trade was at its height in the mid 19th century. Back then, it effectively served as the eastern counterpart to Nkhotakota (Malawi), the base of the notorious Jumbe dynasty, founded in 1845 by coastal Arabs who shipped many thousands of coast-bound slaves across the lake to Metangula annually over the next five decades. So far as can be ascertained, few relics of those times survive in Metangula today, though the area remains predominantly Muslim while the more northerly part of the Mozambican lakeshore is mainly Christian.

Although it's the administrative centre for Lago district and the site of the country's only inland naval base, Metangula has a very out-of-the-way feel about it, and it comes across more like an amorphous sprawling village than a proper town. In the main administrative area, centred on a long oval of roads atop a hilly peninsula, a few ambitious but rather run-down government buildings rub shoulders with boarded-up shops and open green patches that could by no stretch of the imagination be called gardens. Between this and the main Lichinga–Cóbuè road is the low-rise commercial and residential centre, where a good market, a couple of pensões and a museum are set amid mud-and-thatch houses. On the plus side, this small peninsula town is enclosed by the lake on three sides and seems very relaxed and friendly, and plenty of English is spoken here.

Rumours that an upmarket lodge would be built at the tip of the village have yet to translate into reality. However, motorised visitors seeking good quality accommodation near Metangula are now catered for by the superb Mbuna Bay Lodge, which lies on an isolated bay about 15km out of town. For more budget-conscious travellers, the place to head for is the smaller village of Chiwanga (also spelt Chuanga), which has a lovely lakeshore location about 8km along the road to Cóbuè, and a couple of decent accommodation options. Note that Metangula now has a BCI ATM, but travellers coming from Malawi will have no problem changing excess kwacha here.

Getting there and away
By car Lichinga is connected to Metangula by a good surfaced 110km road, about 2 hours' drive and very doable in a saloon car, though there are a couple of moderately pot-holed stretches.

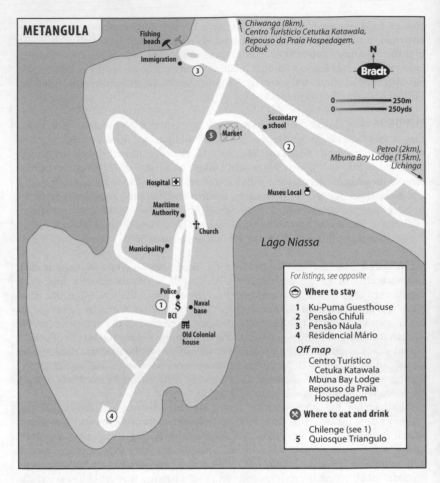

METANGULA

Fishing beach

Chiwanga (8km),
Centro Turísticio Cetutka Katawala,
Repouso da Praia Hospedagem,
Cóbuè

N

Bradt

Immigration

③

0 ——— 250m
0 ——— 250yds

Secondary
school

⑤ Market

② Petrol (2km),
Mbuna Bay Lodge (15km),
Lichinga

Hospital ✚

Maritime
Authority

Museu Local

✝ Church

Lago Niassa

Municipality

Police

① $ Naval
BCI base

Old Colonial
house

For listings, see opposite

🏠 **Where to stay**
1 Ku-Puma Guesthouse
2 Pensão Chifuli
3 Pensão Náula
4 Residencial Mário
Off map
Centro Turístico
Cetuka Katawala
Mbuna Bay Lodge
Repouso da Praia
Hospedagem

✖ **Where to eat and drink**
Chilenge (see 1)
5 Quiosque Triangulo

④

By chapa Regular chapas between Lichinga and Metangula cost around US$4 and take up to 3 hours. Heading for Cóbuè, there's a daily chapa that leaves mid morning and charges around US$5.

By boat Metangula used to be on the route for the MV *Ilala*, a comfortable and affordable Malawian boat that has been plying the lake waters between Monkey Bay and Chilumba since 1952 – but that is no longer the case. The MV *Chambo* (page 365) also calls at Metangula, and provides a scenic way of getting to Cóbuè if you're lucky enough to catch it – the schedule is rather undefined, but the MV *Chambo* usually makes the trip about twice a week. Ask at the Maritime Authority (m *82 791 5520*) or the MV *Chambo* captain (m *82 432 2222* or *86 610 3319*) for details.

If you are entering Mozambique this way, note that the immigration office at Metangula does not currently issue Mozambican visas and, if you arrive without one, expect to be given a rough time before being planted on the next chapa to Lichinga to get one there. Unless this changes, or you have bought a visa in advance, better to disembark the MV *Ilala* or *Chambo* at Likoma and cross from there to Cóbuè, where visas can be issued.

Where to stay *Map, opposite*
Upmarket
⌂ **Mbuna Bay Lodge** (13 rooms) m 82 536 7781 or 86 614 1986; e info@mbunabay.ch; w mbunabay.ch. Situated at Nkholongue village 15km south of Metangula, this Swiss-built lodge stands on a long sandy beach lined with baobabs & mango trees below the brachystegia-covered slopes of the Rift Valley wall. A very eco-friendly set-up, it operates on solar electricity only, employs almost all its staff from the nearby village, serves imaginative vegetarian meals made mainly with organic ingredients grown on-site, & allocates a significant portion of proceeds to community development projects inc construction of a clinic & primary school. In addition to a swimming beach, the rocky area offshore is good for snorkelling (plenty of colourful mbuna fish & the occasional otter); other activities inc kayaking, canoeing in modern or local boats, windsurfing, community visits to the local chief & a traditional doctor, yoga, a 2hr hike to the top of Mount Chifuli, or a guided lakeshore ramble to Metangula. The en-suite bamboo-&-thatch beach houses are spacious, characterful & very comfortable, with king-size beds under a walk-in net, as well as verandas with hammocks. There are also some more functional brick houses & private cob-built bungalows using outdoor hot showers. Coming from Lichinga, the turn-off is signposted to the left about 2km before you arrive in Metangula; from there is it another 12km on rocky sloping roads to the lodge itself (if in doubt, ask anybody to point you towards Nkholongue). *US$210/340 sgl/dbl cob house; US$190/300 sgl/dbl beach chalet; US$150/240 sgl/dbl brick bush bungalow; all rates FB inc some activities.* **$$$$**

Budget
⌂ **Centro Turístico Cetuka Katawala** (8 rooms) m 86 867 1981. Situated on the beach in Chiwanga, 8km north of Metangula, this good-value, slightly tired complex has adequate en-suite rooms, camping space & a decent restaurant serving fish-based meals for around

US$9. It is poorly signposted: coming along the Cóbuè road from the direction of Metangula, turn left about 10m past the first sign for 'Praia do Chuanga', follow this road for about 600m, turn left immediately after crossing a small concrete bridge, from where it is another 50m or so to the entrance. If you don't have a vehicle, you could walk here from Metangula – but it's a feat of endurance in the lakeshore heat, so you might prefer to try for a rare chapa or ask around town for a moto. The A-frame is the brightest & cleanest option. *US$20/30 sgl/dbl; US$5 per tent.* **$**

⌂ **Ku-Puma Guesthouse** (3 rooms) m 82 757 5740. Situated near the police station, this local favourite has a good restaurant & 3 clean rooms with AC using shared ablutions. May be noisy at night with the restaurant & bar next door. *US$24/30 twin/dbl.* **$**

⌂ **Repouso da Praia Hospedagem** (12 rooms) 271 20431; m 82 629 9780. Situated in Chiwanga directly behind Cetuka Katawala, this is not quite so nice as its neighbour & lacks a beachfront location, but the basic rooms are clean & en suite. A bar & restaurant are attached. *US$6/12 shared ablutions/en-suite dbl.* **$**

⌂ **Residencial Mário** m 82 388 2616. Offering a row of clean, good-value rooms & a local restaurant. *US$10/20 sgl/dbl twin room with shared ablutions; US$20 en-suite dbl; US$30 en-suite dbl with AC & sitting room.* **$**

Shoestring
⌂ **Pensão Chifuli** (10 rooms) Set in a quiet compound near the market, this has rather stuffy rooms with shared ablutions, dbl or ¾ bed, net & standing fan. *Rooms US$6–8 depending on size of room.* **$**

⌂ **Pensão Náula** (26 rooms) m 86 686 6692. Situated next to the beachfront immigration office at the northern end of Metangula town, this place has very basic rooms with ¾ beds. Ask for a room away from the bar if you are looking for shut-eye. *Rooms US$5/10 old/newer room with TV, dbl.* **$**

✕ Where to eat and drink *Map, opposite*
If you stay at Mbuna Bay or Chiwanga, you'll most likely want to eat at your hotel. Unsurprisingly, there are no tourist-orientated restaurants in Metangula itself, but you will find some local restaurants in the market. For a cold beer, try the **Quiosque Triangulo** near the market. You could also try to track down the

Chilenge Restaurant (m 82 757 5740), which has been recommended by a local, serving meals between US$6–12 ($$$) and is part of Ku-Puma Guesthouse in the administrative area near the police station.

What to see and do Metangula and Chiwanga are agreeable enough places to while away a day or two but, aside from the museum described below and the beach at Chiwanga, neither boasts much in the way of formal attractions. If you're looking for a guide to take you on hikes to Mount Chifuli or to a nearby waterfall, or want to go fishing in a local dugout canoe, ask near the market for a guide called Lourenço Thawe.

Museu Local (⊕ 07.00–noon Tue–Sun, 13.30–17.00 Tue–Sat; entrance free) Opened in 2008, this small but well-organised local history museum is housed in the former Escola Primaria João de Deus, a historic red-and-white building in the heart of Metangula. Exhibitions cover the history and cultures of Lago district from the Stone Age to the present. Archaeological artefacts from recent excavations include stone tools from Micuio, 5km south of Metangula, Iron Age pots found on nearby Mount Chifuli, and material containing the oldest evidence of sorghum cultivation in Africa. Other displays explore the region's role in the 19th-century slave trade and the associated arrival of Islam, as well as the spread of Christianity from the UMCA mission on Likoma Island, established in 1886 as part of a drive to end the slave trade. A separate exhibition looks at the exotic origins of crops such as maize, cassava, sweet potato and tomato, and at indigenous edible plants. There's also an oral history archive, where you can read or listen to 95 recordings of individual biographies, folk tales and songs, and a photo wall of locals who contributed to this collection. When we visited, it was closed – but ask around and someone will send for the caretaker to open it up.

CÓBUÈ The village of Cóbuè lies on the mainland opposite Likoma Island, and is heavily influenced by its proximity to this Malawian territory. Kwacha are more useful here than meticais, English is quite widely spoken, many mobile phones are on the Malawian network as the Mozambican network is limited to a patchy Mcel and Movitel service, and until a few years ago it was one of the ports serviced by the MV *Ilala*. Cóbuè is a lovely part of the world – very remote and quiet, but the main reason you'd visit is *en route* between Malawi and Mozambique (the crossing is very straightforward, and this is the one place on the lake where Mozambican visas are issued).

Besides the scenery, which is gorgeous, the only thing to see in Cóbuè is the surprisingly big Catholic church, which is looking as attractive as ever these days with a new roof and coat of paint, after standing derelict for many years after the war. About 9km south of the village is the small fishing village of Mala, site of House of Chambo Backpackers and a great place to experience traditional lakeshore living. Cóbuè is also the springboard for visits to Nkwichi Lodge in the Manda Wilderness Area (page 366).

Getting there and away
By car The 100km dirt road from Metangula clings to the lakeshore north for about 10km, just past Chiwanga, before it ascends the brachystegia-strewn slopes of the Rift Valley escarpment inland, then descends back to the lakeshore as it enters Cóbuè. It's an overall tougher drive than the preceding section of road to Metangula. Although parts have been graded, the road to Cóbuè has several tougher sections that are alternately rutted and sandy in parts, and there are some steep slopes to

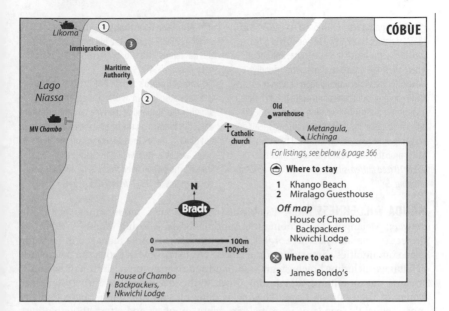

CÓBÙE

Likoma

Immigration ●

Lago Niassa

MV *Chambo*

Maritime Authority

Old warehouse

Metangula, Lichinga

† Catholic church

N

Bradt

0 ————— 100m
0 ————— 100yds

House of Chambo Backpackers, Nkwichi Lodge

For listings, see below & page 366

🏠 **Where to stay**

1 Khango Beach
2 Miralago Guesthouse

Off map
   House of Chambo
      Backpackers
   Nkwichi Lodge

❌ **Where to eat**

3 James Bondo's

contend with, but a 4x4 or strong pick-up should get through in 2–3 hours. The wild scenery serves as compensation for the bumpy ride, and you can expect to see some wildlife – most likely baboons and a variety of birds – along the roadside.

By chapa Chapas along this road amount mostly to pick-up trucks that cram as many people in the back as possible, then a few more. There's one daily truck for Metangula that leaves around 07.00 and charges US$5.

By boat The *Ilala* no longer stops at Cóbùe, but you can disembark at Likoma and catch a local boat across from there. These usually leave Cóbùe once daily, at around 07.00, and the fare is nominal, but they may not leave if there are insufficient passengers and you are unwilling to pay enough to make it worth the captain's while to make a special crossing.

The MV *Chambo* is a local boat service that runs between Meponda in the south and Aldeia Chiuindi at the Tanzanian border, stopping by request at all villages in-between, including Chiwanga, Mbueca and Cóbùe. The schedule is something of a work in progress, but it typically makes the trip twice weekly. You can get details at the Maritime Authority in Cóbùe, call the office in Metangula (m 82 791 5520) or speak with the captain directly (m 82 432 2222 or 86 610 3319).

Where to stay, eat and drink *Map, above*

🏠 **House of Chambo Backpackers**
(3 rooms) m +265 88 524 5836/871 3745 (Malawi); e reservations@houseofchambo.com or houseofchambo@gmail.com; w houseofchambo. com. Proudly set up & run by two employees of Nkwichi Lodge, House of Chambo is a very relaxed lakeshore lodge set in the tiny fishing village of Mala about 9km south of Cóbùe market. Just getting off the ground when we popped in, the lodge now has 3 rustic dbl beach bungalows crafted from bamboo with thatch roofing & beach sand floors, as well as a bar & basic restaurant. There's solar electricity, so a cold beverage won't be a problem, but otherwise limited facilities with a communal kitchen, & showers are taken under fig trees. It's a 3–4hr walk from Cóbùe or a boat can be hired for US$25 each way from Cóbùe. *US$25 pp, B&B.* **$**

Khango Beach (30 rooms) m +265 88 856 7885 (Malawi); m 82 997 3321 or 86 614 5121. Situated on the beach facing Likoma, in front of where the boats drop passengers, this friendly place offers basic accommodation in twin reed huts using common ablutions or en-suite brick chalets. It's a simple but very welcoming set-up, & they're fully clued-up on local transport options. Meals are available on request, & the attached bar-cum-TV hall is probably the liveliest hangout in Cóbuè. *US$6/10 reed hut/en-suite brick chalet dbl; US$2 pp camping.* **$**

Miralago Guesthouse (6 rooms) m 87 429 0997. Just up the hill from immigration, this has rooms with ¾ bed, electricity & mosquito nets. *Rooms US$10.* **$**

James Bondo's m 86 741 7807; ⊕ 07.00– late daily. Also known as Gloria's (depending on whether the husband or the wife is running it that day), this is down on the beach. The food is basic but good, & there's the usual range of soft drinks & beers available. He's willing to change meticais for kwacha should you need them, & he also has very cheap rooms for US$2. *Mains US$2–5.* **$**

MANDA WILDERNESS AREA Established in 1999 on a mountainous peninsula between Metangula and Cóbuè, the multiple-award-winning Manda Wilderness Project (w *mandawilderness.org*) is a 1,200km² game reserve managed in trust for local communities comprising some 20,000 Nyanja people. It protects a patchwork of habitats, including brachystegia woodland and riverine forest, savannah, swamps, streams and mountains, all running down to the lovely beaches and crystal-clear waters of Lago Niassa. Game viewing is done on foot or from a canoe, and the most frequently seen large mammals are zebra, monkeys and otters, though others present include lions and wild dogs. Though it falls within Mozambique, Manda operates mostly as an extension to the safari circuits in Malawi and Zambia, and can be reached by boat from Likoma or Cóbuè, or by charter flight from anywhere in the region.

Where to stay *Map, pages 254–5*

Nkwichi Lodge (6 chalets) m 82 709 7920; e info@nkwichi.com; w nkwichi.com; see ad, page 373. Sited about 10km south of Cóbuè, this is the only lodge in the reserve itself, & can cater for only 14 guests in 6 individual chalets. The site itself is stunning – the chalets are widely spread on a rocky peninsula flanked by a lovely white beach & dense brachystegia woodland, & are built from locally available materials & designed to blend into their surroundings, incorporating granite outcrops as part of the structure. Each has its own private bathroom with outdoor shower & bath, & there is a central double-floored restaurant, bar & library. There's plenty to keep you busy, from tracking animals to activities on the lake such as canoeing, snorkelling or sailing, & you also have the option of visiting some of the local communities to see how the project has benefited them. Then again, you can just sit in a hammock. The whole set-up is hugely impressive, & serves as a perfect example of how a lodge could & should be developed. *US$487/750 sgl/dbl, US$535/820 premiere sgl/dbl; rates inc all meals & non-motorised activities, with discounts for residents.* **$$$$$**

NIASSA RESERVE

Situated in the remote north of Mozambique bordering Tanzania, Niassa Reserve is Africa's third-largest wildlife sanctuary, extending over 42,000km² – that's twice as large as the Kruger Park, almost three times the size of the Serengeti, or (to place it in a non-African context) comparable in area to Denmark or the state of Massachusetts. Niassa is also one of Africa's most under-publicised and unvisited safari destinations, as well as one of the most important protected areas in Mozambique, and is considered a critical wildlife area for Africa. While the reserve's isolation has held back development, it has also allowed it to retain an untrammelled feel that is increasingly rare in modern Africa. Scenically, Niassa is hugely impressive, dominated by the Lugenda River, whose shallow perennial flow is hemmed in by wide sandbanks and a ribbon of lush riparian forest. Away from the river, there are vast tracts of miombo woodland studded with bulbous fleshy grey baobabs, and immense granite inselbergs that rise majestically into the deep blue African sky, hundreds of metres above the surrounding plains.

It should be stated clearly that Niassa is not a suitable safari destination for those seeking a quick 'Big Five' fix. True, all but one of this much-hyped quintet is present here in significant numbers (the exception being rhinos, who were poached to extinction in the 1980s) but the only near-certainty in the course of a standard three-to-four-day visit would be elephant. What Niassa offers is an altogether more holistic wilderness experience, one in which the reserve's mesmerising scenic qualities and wonderfully rich birdlife figure as prominently as its mammalian wildlife. This is also one of those rare reserves where activities need not be dominated by motorised game drives: guided game walks offer the opportunity to experience the African bush as its inhabitants do, on foot, without the constant roar of an engine providing an unwanted aural backdrop; while canoeing on the river – past spluttering hippos, drinking elephants and a splendid array of birds – is utterly entrancing. In short, Niassa offers as untrammelled an African bush experience as still exists in the 21st century.

HISTORY AND CONSERVATION The Niassa Reserve was established in 1954 to protect the dry and thinly inhabited territory that lies between the Ruvuma and Lugenda rivers, but it was effectively abandoned between 1975 and 1988 as a result of the civil war. The reserve's modern boundaries were established in 1998 and include the original 22,000km² core zone between the rivers, along with some 20,000km² of buffer zones. It was also in 1998 that the Mozambican government entered into an innovative partnership with the Sociedade para a Gestão e Desenvolvimento da Reserva do Niassa (SRN), a private organisation that retained exclusive rights to manage and develop the reserve until handing control back to the state in 2012. The SRN divided the reserve into 17 management zones, of which nine currently operate as hunting and/or photographic safari concessions (the most important being Block L7, aka Luwire Concession, which is the site of the former Lugenda Wilderness Camp), while another four are currently leased for ecotourism developments. The reserve is presently co-managed by the Ministry of Tourism and the Wildlife Conservation Society (w *wcs.org*).

The Niassa Reserve is one of two core components in the Selous-Niassa Transfrontier Conservation Area (SNTCA), the other being the Selous Game Reserve, which extends over 47,000km² of southern Tanzania. The SNTCA also incorporates Tanzania's Mikumi National Park, Udzungwa National Park and Kilombero Game Protected Area, all of which border the Selous, and its ecological integrity was greatly boosted in 1999 with the creation of the 17,030km² Selous-Niassa Corridor Reserve, which extends southward from the Selous border to share 175km of international Ruvuma frontage with the Niassa Reserve. All told, the SNTCA can now lay claim to being Africa's largest contiguously protected chunk of untrammelled bush, extending over a total area exceeding 150,000km², larger than Malawi. And it harbours some of Africa's most prodigious wildlife, including at least 5% of the global population of African elephant, around 20% of the world's free-ranging African wild dogs, and what are quite probably the largest existing populations of lion, buffalo, hippo and sable antelope.

Some 40,000 people living in 42 villages inhabit the Niassa Reserve and its immediate boundaries, a third of them in the district capital Mecula, which lies

The Manda Wilderness Trust (w *mandawilderness.org*) is a UK-registered charity that raises funds towards a mixture of conservation and community projects in the area surrounding Cóbuè. The fundraising activities are based around Nkwichi Lodge, a proportion of the revenue from the lodge going straight into the trust. The development of the lodge was dovetailed in with the development of the trust and many of the facets of the trust's work started before the lodge was open.

The trust is very much driven from the ground up. There are 15 local communities involved in the various projects, and each community has its own committee (known as an 'Umoji Association') to decide which facets of the trust's work they wish to be involved with.

The conservation projects are all focused on the reserve, which is made up of land donated by each of the communities. The nearly 48,000ha reserve was both officially gazetted and designated as Mozambique's second Ramsar Wetland of International Importance in 2011. In addition to this, there are plans to set up a similarly sized aquatic reserve in association with US Aid. An educational programme has been established to help the local communities develop methods of exploiting the reserve in a sustainable manner.

The trust runs a series of community projects aimed at improving facilities in each village, with each Umoji Association deciding what is most needed in its village. Thus far the trust has contributed to the construction of six schools with a further four or five planned, a maize mill to enable villagers to grind their own produce, and a clinic based in Cóbuè with equipment supplied from the UK and training carried out by a local NGO. To help bring the communities together, the trust organises regular events including canoe races, a local choir festival and a football league, supplying kit, goalposts, fees for referees and the possibility of arranging training schemes in the future.

A third strand, slightly smaller at the moment, is the agricultural project. The aim of this is to introduce local farmers to permaculture and find methods by which the local diet can be improved. Each Umoji Association selects up to five villagers who attend a training course at the lodge's farm. The training courses cover the importance of proper nutrition, soil conservation, planting and care of seeds and plants, pest control and the importance of healthy soil to the potential for selling excess produce in local markets.

The success of the trust can be gauged by the interest being shown by the Mozambican national government – in August 2005, 11 directors of the provincial governments visited the reserve and the trust, and in June 2006 President Guebuza visited Cóbuè, the first time in Mozambique's history that its president had visited Niassa Province.

within the eastern section of the core reserve below Serra Mecula. Despite this low density, the interests of the reserve's human and wildlife populations are often at odds. The greatest problem exists along the rivers, which are heavily fished, not only by local Mozambicans but also by people hopping over the border from Tanzania. A certain amount of snaring occurs along and away from the river, and occasional instances of commercial poaching have been reported, but the good news is that this appears to occur at sustainable levels and estimated numbers of most key species have remained stable or risen over the tenure of the SRN. While the reserve has created several hundred jobs in an area where they are otherwise scarce, the risks faced by people living in and around the reserve should also not be ignored: at least one to two people per year are killed in lion attacks, while elephants frequently raid smallholdings for crops, and crocodiles lurk in the rivers. In the long term, it is to be hoped that tourist revenue will alleviate these risks by generating further work opportunities and income for local communities.

GEOGRAPHY AND VEGETATION The Niassa Reserve accounts for about a third of Niassa Province's surface area, and also extends eastward into Cabo Delgado. It lies within the drainage basin of the Ruvuma River, which flows east for more than 300km along the reserve's northern border with Tanzania. The most important of several tributaries, and in many respects the lifeblood of Niassa, is the Lugenda River, which flows along the southeastern boundary between the core area and buffer reserve to its confluence with the Ruvuma. The Ruvuma and Lugenda are both large sand-bed rivers with a strong perennial flow, and their mutual watershed feeds numerous other seasonal rivers that flow only during the rainy season of late October to May. Although the eastern border of Niassa is a full 200km from the coast, the terrain is essentially low-lying, with a base altitude of 100m at the Lugenda–Ruvuma confluence, rising to around 600m in parts of the west. These flattish dry plains are interrupted – to thrillingly dramatic effect – by a liberal scattering of black granitic inselbergs that rise hundreds of metres above the canopy to give the reserve its unique scenic quality. The tallest mountain in the reserve is Serra Mecula, which rises to a prominent 1,441m peak above the town of the same name.

Some 95% of the Niassa Reserve consists of miombo woodland, which can be divided into two broad types. Dominant in the southwest is tall closed brachystegia-dominated woodland, while elsewhere there tends to be a more open cover of mixed broadleaved woodland including various brachystegia, julbernadia, combretum and terminalia species. The two main rivers support a ribbon of evergreen riparian woodland and riverine thickets, and patches of acacia woodland are often associated with the clayey soils close to the rivers. Niche habitats include roughly 1km² of montane forest in half a dozen scattered patches on the upper slopes of the Serra Mecula, the rocky cliffs and slopes associated with the reserve's trademark granite outcrops, and seasonally flooded grassy depressions called dambos, whose boundaries are often demarcated by a ring of waterberry trees.

WILDLIFE Wildlife in Niassa tends to be less visible than in some other more iconic African reserves, but there is plenty of it around. The most recent published figures, based on 2004 estimates, are 7,000 buffalo, 2,500 bushbuck, 3,500 Lichtenstein's hartebeest, 5,000 warthog, 3,500 plains zebra and around 1,000–1,500 of each of impala, greater kudu, waterbuck, wildebeest and reedbuck. Three of these animals are represented by subspecies endemic to this part of Africa: Niassa wildebeest (slightly larger than other subspecies), Crawshay's zebra (lacks the shadow stripes of other southern zebra subspecies) and Johnston's impala (slightly smaller than most subspecies). More recent estimates (2011) place the elephant population at around 11,000 (significant poaching has brought the number down from 20,000 with at least 2,500 elephants killed between 2010 and 2011), while yellow baboon, vervet monkey and blue monkey are all quite common, with the last mostly restricted to riverine woodland. The reserve evidently supports one of the world's largest populations of sable antelope, estimated at 13,500 in 2004.

In practical terms, impala, waterbuck and greater kudu are common around the former Lugenda Wilderness Camp (page 373) throughout the year, as are warthog and elephant. Hippos belch and wallow in the river near camp, while pairs of dainty klipspringer antelope bound around the boulder-strewn slopes. As the dry season takes its grip, larger concentrations of ungulates gather along the river, and sightings of zebra, wildebeest, buffalo, Lichtenstein's hartebeest and sable antelope become more frequent. Unusually, predators are most visible in the early part of the dry season, when the lush vegetation encourages them to follow game-viewing tracks as they patrol their territories or search for prey. Lion sightings are not quite an everyday occurrence, but the reserve harbours a healthy population of 1,000–1,200, one-third of Mozambique's lion population. It's one of the better places to look for African wild dog (box, above), and 20 other carnivore species have been recorded, of which leopard, genet and civet are all quite commonly observed on night drives.

BIRDLIFE The birding in Niassa is excellent. Some of the more interesting everyday species that enjoy high visibility are purple-crested turaco, green woodhoopoe, lilac-breasted roller, brown-hooded kingfisher, brown-headed parrot, African grey hornbill, black-collared barbet (the unusual streaky-breasted *zombae* race), white-fronted bee-eater, collared palm thrush, black-headed oriole and African paradise-flycatcher. It is a good place to see several miombo specials, including racquet-tailed roller, pale-billed hornbill, miombo pied barbet, Stierling's wren-warbler, Arnot's chat and Shelley's sunbird, while riverine forest and thicket support the likes of Pel's fishing owl, trumpeter hornbill, brown-throated barbet, Böhm's bee-eater, broad-billed roller, Livingstone's flycatcher and black-throated wattle-eye. Niassa is probably the best site in Mozambique for birds of prey: bateleur and African fish eagle are among the more conspicuous large raptors, while the inselbergs support cliff-nesting species such as Verreaux's (black) eagle, augur buzzard, lanner falcon and the very localised Taita falcon, and the massive crowned eagle and handsome Dickinson's kestrel are frequently seen in the riparian forest.

One disappointment is that the river supports so few waterbirds, possibly as a result of overfishing – you might well see saddle-billed and woolly-necked storks,

One of the longest and most remote roads in Mozambique, the EN242 (N14) is of interest to self-drive visitors, first as the most direct route between the coastal port of Pemba (page 355) in Cabo Delgado and the highland town of Lichinga in Niassa, and secondly as the main access road to the Niassa Reserve. The 725km journey from Pemba to Lichinga breaks up into three distinct phases, and while it could be covered in one long day with a very early start and a modicum of luck, it is probably more realistic to bank on overnighting somewhere en route, ideally the small town of Montepuez.

The first stretch is the 200km run from Pemba to Montepuez, which involves following the EN106 (N1) west for about 95km to the junction town of Metoro, which is where the westbound road becomes the EN242 (N14). This is a good tar road the whole way, passing through rather unmemorable scenery and a few equally undistinguished small towns, and you should easily get through within 3 hours. Montepuez, the largest town along this road, has a fair selection of places to sleep and eat, covered in greater detail on page 325.

The shortest stretch on paper – around 190–210km, depending on which map you believe, and how many unintended diversions you take – is the unsurfaced road between Montepuez and Marrupa. It is also the longest and most difficult stretch in practice, carrying perhaps half a dozen vehicles along a road that frequently amounts to little more than a pair of sandy tyre tracks running through the dense brachystegia woodland typical of this region (an experience reminiscent of how travel was in most of Mozambique shortly after the civil war). This area is fantastically remote, with only a few tiny villages as urban punctuation, and you might well see some wildlife on the way. You shouldn't require a 4x4 in the dry season, but it could come in handy, and you will definitely need good clearance and a powerful engine, and may want to deflate tyres in places. In the rainy season, a 4x4 will be absolutely essential.

After about 140km of laborious trundling west from Montepuez, you'll enter Niassa Province and find yourself, apropos of absolutely nothing, on what is arguably the finest road anywhere in Mozambique, a nippy 390km stretch of pristine surfaced bliss that can easily have you arrive in Marrupa within an hour and Lichinga within five – assuming you're not too distracted by the memorable mountain scenery.

Marrupa itself is a district capital and the junction town for the Niassa Reserve (Kiboko Gate lies 100km to the north along a fair dirt road (R731)). It's a more substantial place than you might expect, with a large market, a few adequate restaurants, and a handful of basic pensões – try **Restaurante Marrupa**, **Residencial Triangulo** or **Centro Social** if you wind up overnighting here.

With a bit of determination, this route is also doable on public transport, except for the stretch between Balama and Marrupa, where you'll have to hitch. Sleep in Montepuez and get the first chapa for Balama (US$3; 90 mins). Once in Balama you'll find others waiting for a lift westward as well. Most traffic this way consists of heavy trucks – make sure they're going all the way to Marrupa, as they will sometimes terminate at logging camps in the bush. From Marrupa, chapas go to both Lichinga and Cuamba, but they leave first thing in the morning, so arriving in the afternoon you'll either have to spend the night in town or try to hitch once again; the Petromoc 2km down the Lichinga road is a good place to wait. Chapas to Lichinga cost US$10 and can take up to 7 hours.

SERRA JECI (NJESI PLATEAU)

*With Keith Barnes & Josh Engel (*w *tropicalbirding.com)*

Like Mount Namuli (page 274), this remote area of northwest Niassa offers some incredible birding. The same warnings for Mount Namuli apply here – bring plenty of provisions, 4x4 vehicles, and learn some Portuguese to maximise your experience. The most enticing species of this area are long-billed forest warbler (formerly called long-tailed or Moreau's tailorbird) and red-capped forest warbler (formerly called African tailorbird), otherwise only spotted in very small areas of Tanzania. There are many other species that could turn up here, such as Chapin's apalis or Winifred's warbler… or perhaps something completely unknown.

The long-billed forest warbler is perhaps one of the rarest birds in all of Africa, once thought extinct until surveys in the 1980s rediscovered the species in the Amani area of the East Usambaras in Tanzania. Birds from the population on the Serra Jeci were only seen again in 2001, when a team from the University of Cape Town rediscovered them here. Continued surveys suggest the entire world population comprises a few hundred birds, and given the massive geographical distances between the two populations one may question whether they are best treated as the same species, and both may be extremely rare and critically endangered.

Besides the forest warblers, there is a long list of tempting birds found in and around Serra Jeci, including Stierling's and speckle-throated woodpeckers, cinnamon-breasted tit, spotted creeper, and olive-headed and Bertram's weavers. The Serra Jeci area remains extremely little known, and given the correct provisions it is worth spending several days exploring the region.

possibly African skimmer, but there are very few waterfowl, waders or lapwings. Get your timing right, however, and the most alluring avian attraction of Niassa has to be the Angola pitta, a spectacularly coloured but very seldom observed species that usually renders itself conspicuous by call during its brief mating season over two to three weeks in November.

GETTING THERE AND AWAY

By air Niassa is a very long way from anywhere by road, and it is possible to fly there on a charter from Pemba or the Quirimbas, although it must be noted that at the time of writing only camping facilities for self-sufficient tourists existed.

By car It is perfectly possible to drive to Niassa from Pemba or Lichinga, assuming that you have a 4x4 and some time at your disposal. The main urban springboard for self-drive visits is Marrupa, which lies about 100km south of the Kiboko entrance gate along a well-maintained unsurfaced road (R731) that can be covered in 2 hours. This road continues north to Mecula across what is the only bridge across the Lugenda into the core area of Niassa Reserve. The Kiboko entrance gate closes at 17.00 and you may be refused entry if you arrive later, so try to set off from Marrupa before 14.30.

There are three main approaches to Marrupa. The best is the surfaced **EN242** (N14) running 310km east from Lichinga, but travellers coming from the coast will more likely use the EN242 (N14) west, a somewhat more challenging dirt road that may require a 4x4 and leads to Pemba after 400km. Both roads are covered in the boxed text on page 371. Another option, coming from the south, is the **EN248** (N360), an adequate but unsurfaced 250km road running northeast from Cuamba. If you use this route, the mission at Maúa and the even more remote mission at Nipepe both have beautiful churches decorated in traditional style.

WHERE TO STAY Tourism development in Niassa is still very much in its infancy. There are several hunting camps in some concessions, but at present there is no formal option for less bloodthirsty visitors, though hopefully a new tourist concession will eventually replace the former Lugenda Wilderness Camp following its recent closure. For the time being, self-sufficient self-drivers could head to the **Mussomo Community Campsite**, which is located on the Lugenda River and open during the dry season only. It is also possible to camp at the staff headquarters at **Maputo Camp**, which has a reasonable toilet block but few other facilities.

Appendix 1

LANGUAGE

Mozambicans speak Portuguese in a more sing-songy way than the Portuguese themselves, and their speech is much easier to understand than the guttural string of consonants Europeans use. There are two renderings of the verb 'to be'. *Ser* (*sou, és, é, somos, são*) is more or less for characteristics or permanent states, and *estar* (*estou, estás, está, estamos, estão*) for temporary states. Many words can be guessed from English or Spanish, and some Spanish speakers get along quite well with a mixture of *português* and *espanhol*, popularly known as *portanhol*. Examples include many words ending with -ion in English and -on in Spanish which are similar in Portuguese but end in -ão (plural usually -ões) – *televisão, razão* (reason), *verão* (summer).

Take care, though, for some similar Spanish and Portuguese words have completely different meanings: *niño* (Spanish = child) versus *ninho* (Portuguese = nest); *pretender* means 'intend' rather than 'pretend' (*fingir*); and it is best not to describe an ordinary man as *ordinário* as this implies he is common or vulgar.

Asterisks (*) denote words derived in or specific to Mozambique or Africa.

I would strongly recommend that, in addition to a phrasebook, you get a good pocket Portuguese dictionary. While phrasebooks have a place in the early stages of learning a language, their limitations very soon become a hindrance to both the learning process and simple communication. A good pocket dictionary is a useful tool – we use the *Oxford Portuguese Mini-Dictionary*, although there are other equally good ones out there.

PRONUNCIATION

ã + a followed by m	nasal (similar to 'ang')
c	ss before i or e; k elsewhere
ç	ss
cc	ks
ch	sh
g	soft j before i or e; hard g elsewhere
j	soft j (as in French)
lh	ly (as in Spanish ll)
nh	ny (as Spanish ñ)
o or ô	oo when unstressed
o or ó	o when stressed (as in hot)
ou	o sound (as in both or window)
õ + o followed by m	nasal (similar to 'ong').
qu	k before i or e; kw elsewhere
s	z or sh (at end of syllable)
x	sh or s
z	soft j

Double vowels are pronounced separately:

compreendo	*compree-endo*
cooperação	*coo-operassaoo*

VOCABULARY
Greetings

Good morning	*Bom dia*
Good afternoon	*Boa tarde*
Good evening	*Boa noite* (meeting at night as well as taking leave)
Hello	*Hola*
Goodbye	*Até logo* (until later)
What is your name?	*Como se chama?*
My name is	*Chamo-me* [*shamow mu*]
How are you?	*Como está* [*komo shta*]?
I am well	*Estou bem* [*shtow be(ng)*]) (or a reply to *como está* might be *bom, obrigado*/*boa, obrigada* = I am good, thank you)

Basic phrases

please	*se faz favor* (or *por favor*)
thank you	*obrigado/a* (I'm obliged)
you're welcome	*de nada* (ie: 'it's nothing' – reply to thank you)
There is no…	*Não há* (or *falta*)…
Excuse me	*Desculpe* (or *Perdone me*)
Give me	*De me*
I like to…	*eu gosto de…*
I would like…	*(eu) queria…*
How?	*Como?*
How much?	*Quanto?*
How much (cost)?	*Quanto custa/é isso?*
What?	*(O) Quê?*
What's this (called)?	*Como se chama isso?*
Who?	*Quem?*
When?	*Quando?*
Where?	*Onde?*
From where?	*Donde?* (contraction of *de onde*)
Where is…?	*Onde fica/é/está…?*
Do you know?	*Você sabe?*
I don't know	*Não sei*
I don't understand	*Não compreendo* (also *não percebo*)
yes	*sim*
no	*não*
perhaps	*talvez* [*talvej*]
good	*bom/boa* (m/f)

Food and drink

bean	*feijão* (*feijoada* = a dish of rice, beans and pork)
beef	*carne de vaca*
beer	*cerveja*
bon appétit	*bom apetite*
bread	*pão*

breakfast	*matabicho* (* lit. 'kill beast')
cake	*bolo*
cassava, manioc	*mandioca*
chicken	*frango* (as food)
chips, French fries	*batatas fritas*
coffee	*café*
dinner	*jantar*
drink (noun)	*uma bebida*
drink (verb)	*beber*
eat	*comer*
eggs	*ovos*
fish	*peixe* [*payshy*] or *pescado* (as food)
fizzy soft drink	*refresco*
juice, squash	*sumo*
lunch	*almoço*
maize beer	*byalwa* (*)
maize, mealies	*milho*
maize porridge	*vuswa* (*) or *nsima* (* in the north, *nsheema*)
meat	*carne*
milk	*leite*
pasta	*massa* (NB *pasta* = file or briefcase)
pork	*carne de porco*
potato	*batata*
restaurant	*restaurante*
rice	*arroz*
rum (local)	*cachaça*
snack	*merenda* or *lanche* (elevenses)
spirits	*aguardente*
sweet potato	*batata doce*
tea	*chá*
water	*água*

Other useful words

a little (not much)	*pouco/a*	child	*criança*
a lot (very, much)	*muito/a*	church	*igreja*
aeroplane	*avião*	city, town	*cidade*
after	*depois (de)*	cold/hot water	*água fria/quente*
bank	*banco*	(hard) currency	*devisas*
bathroom, toilet	*casa de banho*	day	*dia*
battery (dry)	*pilha*	diarrhoea	*diarréia*
bed	*cama*	doctor	*médico*
before	*antes (de)*	dry season	*estação seca*
block (of buildings)	*quarteirão*	enough	*bastante*
boarding house	*pensão*	fever	*febre*
book	*livro*	film (roll of)	*película*
bus	*machimbombo* (*)	hill	*colina*
	autocarro	hospital	*hospital*
	(Portuguese)	hotel	*hotel*
car	*carro*	house	*casa*
casualty department	*banco de socorros*	hut	*palhota*
change	*câmbio*	ill	*doente*

lake	*lago*	road	*estrada* [*shtrada*]
large	*grande*	sea	*mar*
lorry, truck	*camião*	shop	*loja*
malaria	*malária, paludismo*	small	*pequeno/a*
market	*mercado*	street, road, highway	*rua*
money	*dinheiro*	swamp, marsh	*pântano*
mosque	*mesquita*	today	*hoje*
mosquito net	*mosquiteiro*	tomorrow	*amanhã*
mountain	*montanha*	to hurt (or ache)	*doer*
never	*nunca*	to swim	*nadar*
night	*noite* [*noyty*]	toilet paper	*papel higiênico*
nightclub	*boite* [*booat(y)*]	too much	*demais/demasiado/a*
nothing	*nada*	train	*comboio*
now	*agora*	travellers' cheques	*cheques de viagem*
on the beach	*na praia*	village	*aldeia*
railway	*caminho de ferro* (n)	yesterday	*ontem*
	ferroviário/a (adj)	you	*você* (polite, formal),
rain	*chuva*		*tu* (familiar)
river	*rio*		

NUMBERS Each part of a cardinal number is changed to ordinal when referring to a place in a sequence (eg: 2,112th = two thousandth hundredth tenth second), so it is simpler to call the 11th floor of a building *andar número onze* than *o décimo primeiro andar*, for instance. For days of the month only the first is an ordinal number (first of May but two of May, etc). Therefore, one can get by with only the cardinal numbers and *primeiro/a* (= first).

1	*um/uma*	21	*vinte e um/uma*
2	*dois/duas*	30	*trinta*
3	*três*	40	*quarenta*
4	*quatro*	50	*cinquenta*
5	*cinco*	60	*sessenta*
6	*seis*	70	*setenta*
7	*sete*	80	*oitenta*
8	*oito*	90	*noventa*
9	*nove*	100	*cem*
10	*dez*	1,000	*mil*
11	*onze*	1,000,000	*milhão*
20	*vinte*		

Appendix 2

FURTHER INFORMATION

Note that many of the books below are difficult to locate through mainstream bookshops; but most can be ordered new or secondhand through online booksellers such as Amazon.

HISTORY AND BACKGROUND

Newitt, Malyn *A History of Mozambique* C Hurst & Co Publishers, 1994. Probably the best single-volume history of an African country that I've ever come across. At more than 600 pages, it is authoritative, stimulating and highly readable, though coverage ends in the mid 1990s. Nobody with an interest in Mozambique's history should visit without reading it.

For those requiring greater detail on a particular period, books that I found to be both useful and readable include the following:

Axelson, Eric *Portugal and the Scramble for Africa 1875–1891* Wits University Press, 1967
Axelson, Eric *Portuguese in East Africa 1488–1600* Wits University Press, 1973
Axelson, Eric *Portuguese in East Africa 1600–1700* Wits University Press, 1960
Beach, David *The Shona and Zimbabwe 900–1850* Heinemann, 1980. A recommended read for its wider coverage of the Karonga Kingdoms and Manomotapa.
Isaacman, Allen and Barbara *Mozambique: From Colonialism to Revolution 1900–1982* Westview Press, 1983

Some of the better books covering more recent events in Mozambique are:

Emerson, Stephen A. *The Battle for Mozambique: The Frelimo–Renamo Struggle, 1977–1992* Helion & Co Ltd, 2014
Finnegan, William *A Complicated War: The Harrowing of Mozambique* University of California Press, 1992
Hanlon, Joseph *Mozambique: Who Calls the Shots?* James Currey, 1991
Main, Michael *Zambezi: Journey of a River* Southern Book Publishers, 1990. An eminently readable introduction to almost every aspect of southern Africa's largest watercourse, with solidly researched material on the region's history and a wealth of obscure anecdotal detail about some of the more eccentric characters who have been associated with the Zambezi.
Minter, William *Apartheid's Contras: An Inquiry into the Roots of War in Angola and Mozambique* Booksurge, 2008
Vine, Alex *Renamo: From Terrorism to Democracy in Mozambique* James Currey, revised and updated edition, 1996
World Biographical Series No 78: Mozambique (edited by Colin Darch and Calisto Pacheleke) Clio Press, 1987. The definitive annotated bibliography of books about Mozambique.

TRAVELOGUES

Crook, Sally *Viva Mozambique* Starling Books, 1997. A personal account of the author's six years of living and working in the country.

Gillespie, Amy *Six Years in Mozambique, Things I Haven't Told Mom* CreateSpace Independent Publishing, 2014. Explores one woman's experience of the gritty reality of aid work, sexuality and spirituality in sub-Saharan Africa.

Green, Lawrence *Harbours of Delight* Howard Timmins, 1969. A lively and anecdotal travelogue covering most of Africa's main harbours.

Kirkman, James *Men and Monuments on the East African Coast* Willmer Brothers, 1964. An excellent survey of the important old buildings of the Swahili coast.

Middleton, Nick *Kalashnikovs and Zombie Cucumbers: Travels in Mozambique* Phoenix, 1994. Something of a companion piece to Swift's book – though infinitely better – this book offers a snapshot of Mozambique 20 years on, during the closing stages of the civil war and shortly after the signing of the 1992 Peace Accord. Hanging out with NGO workers rather than generals, Middleton punctuates his languid and often very funny travelogue with pithy insights into the detrimental effects of the Western aid industry, a clear background to the war, and some fascinating stuff on the occultism that lies close to the surface of rural life.

St Aubin de Terán, Lisa *Mozambique Mysteries* Virago, 2007. This autobiographical account of the establishment of a tourism college at Mossuril (on the mainland opposite Ilha de Moçambique), though a little self-absorbed, contains plenty of interesting material.

Swift, Kerry *Mozambique and the Future* Don Nelson Publishers, 1974. According to the blurb, Swift was the last journalist to conduct a comprehensive tour of Mozambique before the 1974 coup in Portugal. Notwithstanding a few reservations about assertions such as 'South Africa appears to be sincere in her promises of sovereign independence for the Homelands' and the author's admiration for the gung-ho antics of the Portuguese officers he encounters, this offers an interesting snapshot during the closing stages of the liberation war.

FIELD GUIDES Any of several field guides to the mammals of southern Africa will be close to comprehensive for Mozambique. For birders, several field guides to southern African birds are available, and these include all species recorded in Mozambique south of the Zambezi.

Hemstra, Phil and Elaine *Coastal Fishes of Southern Africa* National Inquiry Services Centre, 2007. Probably the best one-volume guide to the region's marine fish, although it is a bit hard to source a print copy nowadays. A secondhand copy is your best bet.

King, Dennis, and Fraser, Valda *The Reef Guide* Penguin Random House South Africa, 2014. Documenting over 800 reef fishes and invertebrates of east and south coastal Africa, each species with colour photo and description.

Newman, Kenneth *Birds of Southern Africa* (2010 edition) Struik, South Africa. Recently revised, this classic bird guide remains arguably the most useful book of its type in the field.

Richmond, Matthew *Field Guide to the Seashores of Eastern Africa* (2011 edition) SIDA, 2002. Distinctly rucksack-sized.

Sinclair, Ian, Hockey, Phil, Warwick, Tarboton, and Ryan, Peter *Sasol Birds of Southern Africa* (2011 edition) Struik, South Africa. Many South African birders now prefer this to Newman's.

Sinclair, Ian, and Ryan, Peter *Birds of Africa: South of the Sahara* (2011 edition) Struik, South Africa. Worth carrying for serious birders heading north of the Zambezi, an area for which coverage in the two guides listed above is incomplete.

Stuart, Chris and Tilde *Field Guide to the Larger Mammals of Africa* (2014 edition) Penguin Random House, South Africa, 1988. Good all-round guide for a country still starting out as a safari destination.

OTHER AFRICA GUIDES AND TRAVEL LITERATURE For a full list of Bradt's Africa guides, see w bradtguides.com/shop.

Travel guides

Briggs, Philip *Malawi* (7th edition) Bradt Travel Guides, 2016
Briggs, Philip *South Africa Highlights* Bradt Travel Guides, 2011
Briggs, Philip, and McIntyre, Chris *Northern Tanzania* (4th edition) Bradt Travel Guides, 2017
McIntyre, Chris *Zambia* (6th edition) Bradt Travel Guides, 2016
Murray, Paul *Zimbabwe* (3rd edition) Bradt Travel Guides, 2016
Unwin, Mike *Swaziland* (1st edition) Bradt Travel Guides, 2012

Travel literature

HRH Princess Michael of Kent *A Cheetah's Tale* Bradt Travel Guides, 2017
Jackman, Brian *Savannah Diaries* Bradt Travel Guides, 2014
Scott, Jonathan *The Big Cat Man* Bradt Travel Guides, 2016
Scott, Jonathan, and Scott, Angela *The Leopard's Tale*, Bradt Travel Guides 2013

Wildlife guides

Briggs, Philip, and McIntyre, Chris *Tanzania Safari Guide* (8th edition) Bradt Travel Guides, 2017
Unwin, Mike *Southern African Wildlife* (2nd edition) Bradt Travel Guides, 2011

HEALTH

Wilson-Howarth, Dr Jane *The Essential Guide To Travel Health: Don't Let Bugs, Bites and Bowels Spoil Your Trip* Cadogan, 2009
Wilson-Howarth, Dr Jane, and Ellis, Dr Matthew *Your Child Abroad: A Travel Health Guide* Bradt Travel Guides, 2014

WEBSITES Particularly recommended to independent travellers is the website w mozguide.com maintained by travel guru Mike Slater. For self-drive tourists, the Facebook group 🅕 DriveMoz is a great platform for relatively immediate travel updates on road conditions and the like. The following websites contain Mozambique-related news stories in English, plus links to other sites relevant to Mozambique:

w allafrica.com/mozambique
w mozambiquenews.com
w clubofmozambique.com

 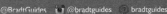

Index

Page numbers in **bold** indicate major entries; those in *italics* indicate maps.

accommodation **59–61**
Beira 202–6
Maputo 94–101
African hunting (wild) dog
30, **370**
AIDS/HIV 72
air travel
deep-vein thrombosis
(DVT) 70
Maputo 92, 110
in Mozambique 55, 92,
178, 200, 218, 243, 260,
280, 294
to Mozambique 2, 45–6, 92
Alto Molócuè 267–9, *268*
Angoche 285–8, *286*
antelope 31–3
art 25–6
at a glance 2
ATMs 54
Azgo Festival 108

background information
3–27
Baixa (Maputo) *98–9*,
115–17
banditry 49
Banhine National Park 144
bargaining 64
Barra Beach 171
Barraco dos Assassinatos
168
Barreto, Francisco 9
Bazaruto National Park 39,
177, 189–93, *190*
beaches 41
beer 63
Beira **199–212**, *201*, *204–5*
accommodation 202–6
banking 207–8
by boat 211
Cultural Centre 208

getting there and away
200–2
golf 208
history 199–200
internet 208
orientation 202
population 200
restaurants 206–7
shopping 208–9
sightseeing 209–212
swimming pools 209
Beira Corridor 58, **213**
Bela Vista 126–7
Benguerra Island *see*
Bazaruto National Park
Bilene 138–40, *139*
bilharzia 73
binoculars 52–3
birds **34–6**, 42, 124–5, 129,
229, 234, 235, 239, 274,
275, 370, 372
boat travel **55**
central Mozambique 211
northern Mozambique 211,
299, 325, 328, 345–6, 362
southern Mozambique 123,
125–6, 156
Bobole 138
bookshops 110, 284
border crossings **46–8**
Malawi 48, 276–7, 353–4,
362, 364
South Africa 47, 92–3, 142
Tanzania 48, 325–31
Zimbabwe 47–8, 92
Boroma Mission 251–2
breakdown triangles 57
bribery 50, 108
budgeting 54–5
bureaucracy 50
buses **58–9**, 93, 178, 200–2,
216, 243, 260, 294

Cabaceira Grande 309
Cabaceira Pequena 309
Cahora Bassa Dam 248–50
Caia 238–40, 257
Calómuè 48
camping 52, 61
canoeing 143
car hire 57–8, 94, 178
car importation 46
carbon emissions 66
Casa dos Noivos 275
Cascata de Namuli 275
cashew apples 317
Cassacatiza 48
Catapu Forestry Concession
238
Catembe 125–6
central Mozambique **195–
252**, *196–7*
Centre Cultural Franco-
Mozambicain 25, 107,
116
Chai 326–7
chapas 58–9, 94
charities 67–8
Chicualacuala 48
Chidenguele 149–50
children, travel with 51
Chiloane Island 211
Chimanimani National
Reserve 226–7
Chimoio 2, 198, **215–20**,
217
Chimoio and the Manica
Highlands **213–28**, *214*
Chinhamapere Rock Art
Site 224–5
Chinizuia Forest 239
Chissano, Alberto 25, 118
cichlids 358, 359
civil war 16–17
climate 2, 3, 41

clothing 52
Cóbuè 48, 364–6, *365*
coelacanth 40
Colonial period 12–15
communications 65–6
conservation 141, 336–7
consulates 45
contact lenses 53
coral reefs 40, 78, 80
crab, giant coconut 40
crafts 63, 64, 110, 183
  see also Makonde carvings
credit cards 54, 112
crime 49–5
crocodile 32, 36
Cuamba 351–3, *353*
Cuchamano 47
culture 25–7, 107–8
currency 2, 52, **54**, 55, 112,
  134
currency controls 45
customs 44–5
Cyclone Dineo 153

dapple-throat 274
Das Rolas Island 345
decompression illness 79–80
dehydration 70–1, 73
diarrhoea 71–2
disabled travellers 51
diving 42, 75–81, 134,
  170–1, 184, 192, 299
document requirements **44**,
  46–7, **53**, 56, 57–8, 108
dog, African wild 30, **370**
dolphins 38–9
drinking water 72
drinks 63
driving *see* car hire; car
  importation; road travel
drugs 107
dugong 39
DVT (deep-vein
  thrombosis) 70

early history 5–7
East African Coast 1530–
  1600 8–9
East African Coast 1600–
  1800, 9–10
eating 61–2
economy 2, 15, 20–1
electricity 53
electricity exports 21, 22
elephants 32, 33
email 66
embassies 45, 111

Entre Lagos 48
Espungabera 47
exchange rates 2, 55, 112
eye problems 72

FACIM Trade Fair 23
Fernandes, António 8
ferries *see* boat travel
field guides 379–80
fines 50, 57
first-aid kit 70
fish 39–40, 358, *359*
flag 2
flights *see* air travel
floods (2000) 17, 20
food 55, 61–2
food hygiene 70–1
foreign exchange 22
foreign investment 21–2
Fortaleza de São Sebastião
  300–2
Fortalezada Nossa Senhora
  da Conceição 114
Frelimo 14–15, 16–17,
  18–19, 20, 215, 216, 327
further reading 378–80

game fishing 184
gay travellers 51
geography 2, 58
getting around 55–9
getting involved 1, 67–8
getting there and away 45–8
giant coconut crab 347
Gilé National Reserve
  269–70
Giriyondo 47, 142
Goba 47
Gorongosa and the Caia
  Road **229–40**
Gorongosa National Park
  30, 31, **229–37**, *230*
government 20
Great Limpopo
  Transfrontier Park *see*
  Limpopo National Park
Gurué 270–3, *271*

handicrafts *see* crafts
health **69–75**
high commissions 45
highlights 41–2
hippo 32, 33
historic towns 42
history **5–20**
  19th century 10–12
  20th century 13–17

21st century 17–20
Beira 199–200
early history 5–7
East African coast 8–10
Ilha de Moçambique
  291–4
Inhambane 154–6
Maputo 87, 88–9
northern Mozambique
  258–60, 286–7, 300, 302,
  317–18, 334–5
hitching 59
HIV/AIDS 72
holidays, public 2, 41, 63
homosexuality 51
hospitals **69**, 112, 159, 183,
  208, 284, 299
hurricanes 153

Ibo Island 42, 334–43, *338*
Ilha de Moçambique **291–**
  313, *296–7*
  accommodation 294–7
  banking 299
  boat trips 299
  cultural tours 300
  Fortaleza de São Sebastião
    300–2
  getting there and away 294
  history 291–4
  hospital 299
  internet 299
  Maritime Museum 303
  Palace Museum 305
  restaurants 298
  Sacred Art Museum 303–4
  São Paulo Palace 302–3
  shopping 299
  sightseeing 300–5
  slave trade 293, 304
  snorkelling 299
Ilha da Xefina 117
Ilha Portuguesa 125
immunisations 69–70
Inchope 237
Independent Mozambique
  15–17
Inhaca Island 88, 121–5,
  122
Inhamba 10
Inhambane 42, **153–60**, *157*
Inhambane and surrounds
  153–75, *154–5*
Inhassoro 177, 185–9, *187*
insect bites 71, 73–4
insurance
  car 46, 57

medical 69, 79
internet **66**, 110, 183, 208, 284, 299

jackals 30
jellyfish 80

kitesurfing 107, 171, 185
Kruger National Park
  (South Africa) 118, 142

Lago Niassa 351, 358, 359–61
Lake Chicamba 220–1
Lake Malawi *see* Lago Niassa
Lake Nikwita 324
Lake Poelela 150
landmines 50
languages 2, 24–5, 374–7
leopard 30
liberation war 14–15
Lichinga 354–9, *356*
Limpopo National Park 137, **140–4**
Limpopo Valley and Coast South of Inhambane **137–51**
lion 30, 33
literacy 15
literature 26, 110
Livingstone, Mary 240
lizards 37
luggage 51–2
Lumbo 308

Macaloe Island 345
Macaneta 138
Machel, Samora 16, 116
machimbombos 58, 59
Machipanda 47
Macomia 326
Macua face masks 316
Magaruque *see* Bazaruto National Park
Magoé National Park 242
Makonde carvings 64, 109, 285, **323**
Malangatana Ngwenya 25–6
malaria 69, 70–1
Malawi, border crossing 48, 276–7, 353–4, 362, 364
Maluane Project 345, 347
mammals 30–4, 38–9
Manda Wilderness 68, 366, 368
Mandimba 48, 353–4

Manica 213, 215, **221–5**, *222*
Manyikeni Ruins 184
Mapiko dances 329
maps 53, 111
Maputaland *120*, **120–35**
Maputo **87–118**, *90–1*
  accommodation 94–101
  airlines 92, 110
  airport 92
  ATMs 92
  Baixa *98–9*, 115–17
  banks 112
  bookshops 110
  Casa de Ferro 116
  Centre Cultural Franco-Mozambicain 25, 107, 116
  chapas 94
  Costa do Sol 117
  day trips from 117–18
  embassies 111
  entertainment 107–8
  football 107
  Fortaleza da Nossa Senhora da Conceição 114, 116
  Geological Museum 113
  getting around 93–4
  getting there and away 92–3
  handicrafts 110
  harbour 115
  history 87, 88–9
  hospitals 112
  Ilha de Xefina 117
  internet 110
  Jardim Tunduru 116
  Louis Trichardt Memorial Garden 116, 117
  maps 111
  markets 109
  Matola 117–18
  medical 112
  money 112
  Mucapana Park 117
  museums and galleries 113–14
  Natural History Museum 113, 115
  nightlife 105–6
  Núcleo de Arte 25, 114
  Old Town 115
  passports 108
  Polana *95*, 114
  police 108, 112–13
  population 87
  post 111
  Praça dos Trabalhadores 115

railway station 115
restaurants 101–5
safety 106–7
shopping 109–110
sightseeing 113–17
supermarkets 109
taxis 92, 93–4
telephone 111
tours 94
Vila Algarve 115
walks 114–17
Maputo Special Reserve *120*, 121, **127–9**
marine life 38–40
Marine Megafauna Foundation 165
marrabenta 27
Marracuene 137–8
Marromeu Buffalo Reserve 240
Marrupa 371, 372–3
Mary Livingstone's grave 240
Massangulo 354
Massinga 174
Matchedje 48
Matemo Island 344–5, 348
Matola 117–18
Maxixe 153, 160–2, *161*
MDM (Mozambique Democratic Movement) 18, 20
media 65–6
medical facilities 69–70
Medjumbe Island 345, 346
Meponda 361
Metangula 361–4, *362*
Milange 48, 276–8, *277*
mining 21, 22
mobile phones 52, 65–6, 111
Moçimboa da Praia 329–30
Mocuba 265–7, *266*
Mondlane, Eduardo 14
money 2, **54**, 55, 112, 134
money belts 52
monkeys 30, 33
Montepuez 324–5, *324*
Moribane Forest Reserve 227
Morrungulo 174
mosquitos 33, 70, 74
Mossuril 308–9
Mossuril Bay 305–9, *307*
motor vehicles *see* car hire; car importation; road travel
Mount Binga 227–8
Mount Chiperone 276–7

Mount Gorongosa 229,
235–7
Mount Mabu 276–7
Mount Namuli 273–5
Mount Tsetsera 228
Mozambique in the 19th
century 10–12
Mozambique in the 21st
century 17–20
Mozambique Island *see* Ilha
de Moçambique
Mucapana Safari Park 118
Mucumbura 48
Mueda 327–9, *327*
music 27–8

Nacala 309–13, *311*
Namaacha 47
Namialo 289, *289–90*
Nampula **279–90**, *282–3*
Namuiranga 48
national anthem 2
national parks and reserves
Banhine 144
Bazaruto 39, 177, 189–93,
190
Chimanimani 226–7
Gilé 269–70
Gorongosa 30, 31, **229–37**,
230
Limpopo 137, **140–4**
Magoé 242
Maputo Special Reserve
120, 121, **127–9**
Marromeu 240
Moribane 227
Niassa 30, 31, 366–73
Quirimbas 336–7, 344,
348–9
Zinave 144
natural history **29–40**
Negomane 48
newspapers 65
Niassa Province **351–72**
Niassa Reserve 30, 31,
366–73
nightlife 105–6
Nile crocodile 36
Njesi Plateau 372
northern Mozambique
253–72, *254–5*
Nuarro Lodge 349

opening hours, restaurants,
61
overland borders *see* border
crossings

Pafuri 47, 142
Palma 330–1
Pangane 250
Pansy Island 192–3
parking 57
parques nacionais *see*
national parks and
reserves
passports 44, 53, 108
Pebane 264
Pemba 315–23, *315*, *318*
Pemba and the northeast
314, 315–31
Penhalonga 225–6
people 23–4, 42
personal safety 49–50, 179
pharmacies 112
photography 64–5
police 56, 108, 112–13
politics 20
Pomene 174
Ponta da Linga Linga 174
Ponta do Ouro 47, 130–4,
131
Ponta Malongane 129–30
Ponta Mamoli 129–30
population 2, 24
Portuguese language 2,
24–5, 374–7
Portuguese occupation 7–9,
88–9
post 66, 111
practical information
41–68
Praia do Xai-Xai 148–9
prickly heat 72
Primeiras Archipelago
288–9
provinces 4
public holidays 2, 41, 63

Quelimane 257–63, *259*
Quilálea Marine Sanctuary
344
Quipaco Island 344
Quirimbas National Park *see*
Quirimbas
Quirimbas 31, *332*, 336–49
Quisiva Island 344, 346
Quissico 150

rabies 70, 73
radio 65
rail travel 55, 58, 92, 280
ray, manta 40, 165, 170
red tape 44–5
religion 2, 25

Renamo 16, 17, 18–19, 20,
216
reptiles 36–7
reserves *see* national parks
and reserves
responsible tourism 66–7
Ressano Garcia 47
restaurants **61–2**
Beira 206–7
Maputo 101–5
rhinos 33
Rio Elefantes Canoeing
Trail 143
road travel
buses **58–9**, 93, 178, 200–2,
216, 243, 260, 294
hitching 59
Inchope to Caia road
(EN1) 237
in Mozambique **56–9**
Pemba to Lichinga road
(EN242) **371**, *372–3*
safety 49, 74
taxis 93–4
useful items 53
see also border crossings
rock art 224–5
Rongui Island 345
Ruvuma ferry 326, 328

safety
dangerous animals 32–3
food hygiene 70–1
Maputo 106–7
personal safety 49–50, 179
road travel 49, 74
Salamanga 126–7
Santa Carolina Island *see*
Bazaruto National Park
Segundas Archipelago
288–9
Sena Railway Bridge 240
Sencar Island 344
Serra Jeci 372
sharks 40, 80–1
Shingwedzi 4x4 Eco-trail
142
shopping **63–4**, 109–10,
134–5, 183, 208–9, 299
SIM cards 52
skin infections 72
slave trade 11, **293**, 304
snake bites 74
snakes 33, 36–7
snorkelling 81–2, 134, 184,
192, 299
Sofala 6–7, **210**

soft drinks 63
Songo 249–50
South Africa, border
    crossings 47, 92–3, 142
southern Mozambique
    83–193, *84–5*
speed limits 56
sport 107
sun, protection from 72–3, 82
Swaziland, border crossing 47

Tanzania, border crossings
    48, 325–31
taxis 93–4
telephone codes 65
telephones 52, 65–6, 111
television 65
terrapins 37
Tete (province) 198, 241–2,
    248–52
Tete (town) 242–8, *244*
tickbite fever 1, 73–4
Tofinho 162, 163, 168
Tofo 162–71, *163–4*
tortoises 37
tour operators 42–4, 94, 117
tourism industry 23
tourist information 42–4
traffic police 56
travel information

central region convoys 216
costs 55
getting there and away
    45–8
Maputo 93–4
in Mozambique 55–9, 93
transport corridors 58
see also air travel; boat
    travel; rail travel; road
    travel
travellers' cheques 54, 112
travellers' diarrhoea 71–2
tribes 23–4
Trichardt, Louis 116, 117
turtles 39

Unity Bridge (Ruvuma
    River) 48, 326, 328
Unity II Bridge (Ruvuma
    River) 48

vaccinations 69–70
Vamizi Island 345, 346–7
vegetation 29–30
Vila Gorongosa 237–8
Vilankulo *176*, 177–85
Vilankulo, Inhassoro and
    Bazaruto National Park
    176–93
visas 44, 219

water sterilisation 72
websites 42, 380
Western Highlands 270–8
whale shark 165, 170
whales 38, 42
what to take 51–4
when to visit 51
Wi-Fi 66
wild dog 30, **370**
wildlife 29, 30–4
    see also national parks and
    reserves
Wimbe Beach *see* Pemba
women travellers 50–1

Xai-Xai **144–8**, *146*

Zalala Beach 264
Zambezi River 249
Zambézia **257–78**
Závora 150–1
Zimbabwe, border crossings
    47–8, 92
Zinave National Park 144
Zóbuè 48
Zongoene 149
Zumbo 48, 252

INDEX OF ADVERTISERS

The Africa Image Library   28
Dana Tours   86
Dunes de Dovela
    Eco-Lodge   2nd colour section
Fátima's Backpackers   119

Nkwichi Lodge   373
Turtle Cove   152
Wanderlust travel magazine   136
White Pearl Resorts   2nd colour section